"TMS Motor Group driving forward into the millennium."

A family company that has been established for over 50 years, with a reputation for quality, value and excellent service, ensures continued commitment and satisfaction into the millennium.

Across the group is a common link of class leading products at the forefront of innovation and quality. Volvo, Land Rover and TVR are all well renowned for their exceptional vehicles in terms of style, performance and safety.

Combining the forces of these top marques, together with a Corporate Sales Division and our own Accident Repair Centre, TMS offer a friendly and professional service for all your motoring requirements.

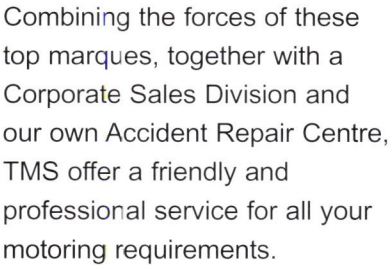

Land Rover, Melton Mowbray
01664 480033

Land Rover, Lincoln
01522 877200

Volvo, Melton Mowbray
01664 410595

Volvo, Grantham
01476 564114

TVR, Melton Mowbray
01664 481065

Corporate Sales
01664 482800

Accident Repair Centre
01664 410404

Visit our website at:
www.tmsgroup.co.uk

ARRIVA
serving the Fox County

Leicestershire Busline:
0116 2511 411

Season Tickets:
0116 253 9534

Daytrips & Holidays:
0116 251 1416

www.arriva.co.uk

Speedi-Cut Services Ltd.
Fully Computerised Fabric Cutting Service

For Lingerie, Leisurewear & Babywear

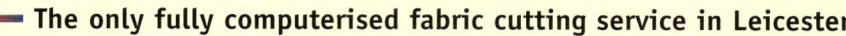

A Cut above the Rest!

- The only fully computerised fabric cutting service in Leicester
- Skilled staff ensuring top quality work
- Full audit paper work
- Rapid turnaround - our reputation for speed is legendary
- Competitive prices
- All fully automated laying-up machines
- Tremendous capacity
- Flexibility - we can handle orders of any size
- Central location in Leicester
- Huge fabric storage area
- Excellent loading / unloading facilities
- Ample on-site car parking

STATE-OF-THE-ART MACHINERY

Why not pay us a visit to see our excellent facilities.

For an appointment please contact our production manager, Mr Tony Cox on
Tel: 0116 276 1626 • Fax: 0116 276 1518 • www.speedi-cut.co.uk
SPEEDI-CUT SERVICES LTD, 10 FAIRFAX ROAD, LEICESTER LE4 9EH

CONTENTS

Introduction to Leicestershire and Rutland 5-11

How to use this Street Guide 13

Index to Districts 14

Grid Map 15

Key to Map Symbols 15

Section One - Countywide Street Maps

    Rural Leicestershire (1:32,000) 17-55, 72-107

    City of Leicester (1:16,000) 56-71

Section Two - Enhanced Town and Village Maps

Individual Towns and Villages at 1:16,000 109-177

Street Index

    Section One 178-192

    Section Two 193-208

ACKNOWLEDGEMENTS

Arrow Publishing would like to thank the following organisations for their assistance in producing this publication;

Leicester City Promotions and Rutland County Council for supplying editorial material and photographs for the introduction.

Leicestershire County Council for advice regarding cartographic layout.

This street guide has been published by :

Arrow Publishing
Lytham Assembly Rooms
Dicconson Terrace
Lytham St Annes
Lancs FY8 5JY
Tel: 01253 731824
Fax: 01253 731823

ISBN: 1-900722-11-9

Disclaimer
Whilst Arrow Publishing and Overview Mapping have taken every effort to ensure accuracy throughout this publication, no liability can be accepted for any errors and/or omissions.

HARVEY MIDDLETON
SHOPFITTING & CONSTRUCTION

Construction and Harvey Middleton are the perfect match! Anything from Extensions to Veterinary Centres and Houses, to complete building projects, from concept, to the finished product.

PROJECTS OF ALL KINDS ARE CARRIED OUT BY OUR TRAINED STAFF, MAJOR REFURBISHMENTS, FAST EFFICIENT REFITS, AND ALL TYPES OF SHOPFITTING.

Harvey Middleton are registered with the National Inspection Council for Electrical Installation Contracting.

This guarantees a very high standard of electrical work at all times whether it is complete new installations, additions and alterations or maintenance of existing installations.

Harvey Middleton also carry out all types of testing and inspection, including Fixed Installation, Periodic Inspection and Certification and Portable Appliance Testing.

National Inspection Council for Electrical Installation Contracting

NICEIC

APPROVED CONTRACTOR

COALVILLE
LEICESTERSHIRE

For further information on all aspects of their work, please contact by Telephone or Fax at:

HARVEY MIDDLETON SHOPFITTING & CONSTRUCTION

Unit 1, Stephenson Court, Brindley Road, Stephenson Industrial Estate, Coalville, Leicestershire LE67 3HG

TELEPHONE: 01530 838006 ~ 838333

or Fax your enquiry to: 01530 836636 for immediate attention

A Beautiful County ...
... A Vibrant City

Leicestershire is beautiful - it's traditional rolling landscape of hawthorn-edged fields is dotted with small woods and copses, ancient earthworks, picturesque villages - and some of the finest church architecture in England. Our County towns of Ashby de la Zouch, Coalville, Loughborough, Melton Mowbray, Market Harborough and Hinckley are all proud of their heritage, and provide visitors with a combination of traditional charm and a modern outlook. Equally rich in character, history and architecture is the cosmopolitan city of Leicester - also a marvellous centre for culture, shopping and night life.

There's so much to see and do that a visit is an experience to be enjoyed and treasured. You can walk through ancient woodlands, or along quiet riverbanks. You can explore historic ruins and re-live exciting moments from the past, or you can wander around the city and county's many art galleries and museums, take in a concert, or sample the pulsating night life.

Everywhere you go, you will find surprising contrasts, the latest trends and technologies in partnership with traditions and character; innovation and creativity alongside conservation and environmental initiatives. A rich multicultural community brings life to the city streets, exotic spices to foods, and exuberant colours to shops and markets.

If you haven't visited Leicestershire before, then you're in for a real surprise! Whatever you may have been expecting, it will both excite and delight you with a huge variety of attractions.

And when you're looking for somewhere to stay, you'll be spoilt for choice. We've everything you could wish for: from the freedom of a self-catering apartment, to the pampered luxury of a historic country house hotel.

A True Commitment

Britain's first 'Environment City' - that was the accolade given to Leicester in recognition of its commitment to green issues and its environmental achievements. Leicester's Environment City project was also recognised as one of the best in the world at the Rio Earth Summit - and when you visit the city, it's easy to see why...

Although you're in the middle of a city, there are so many parks and open spaces that you never have to go far to find a peaceful green oasis. You can explore these natural wonders by strolling or cycling along Leicester's Green Ringway, or one of the many cycleways around the city. And when you visit the Eco House in Western Park or the Ark in St. Martins Square, you'll find all kinds of advice on making your home and lifestyle greener.

The city also has a surprisingly rich architectural heritage, with over 350 listed buildings. Many of them, such as the City Rooms and the strikingly ornate Clock Tower are prime examples of Victorian architecture, while others, including the beautiful Guildhall, date back to mediaeval times.

The River Soar, Grand Union Canal and the Ashby Canal were once the commercial lifeblood of Leicestershire. Now, restored and conserved, they provide ribbons of tranquillity, where you can take a peaceful waterside stroll - or hire a boat and spend a day or two taking in the charm of life in the slow lane. Meander across the county from the Soar Valley through Watermead Country Park. Continue on into the city where you can discover Leicester's industrial and commercial heritage at the Bede Island development, from its best vantage point on the canal. Cruise onto the famous staircase of locks at Foxton, where the grand canal rises 75 feet - and while you're there, take a look at the remains of the Inclined Plane, an extraordinary Victorian steam-powered boat life.

Alternatively, follow the route of the Ashby Canal through the beautiful countryside of west Leicestershire, linking the towns of Hinckley, Market Bosworth, Measham and Moira with the chance to explore Bosworth Battlefield, the steam railway, Measham museums and Moira Furnace along the way. Whilst at Moira, call into the new Heart of the Forest Visitors Centre. The forest is creating a new landscape for the area with many woodlands, picnic areas, trails and cycleways ready to be explored.

Leicestershire's rural character is reflected in the number and variety of farm parks and attractions where the whole family can learn about the countryside and its wildlife. Each with its own individual character, the many

farm parks offer tractor and trailer rides, nature trails, pond dipping, great tea shops and a whole host of animals, many of which are rare breeds.

There's so much to discover and explore. You could even choose your own theme for a weekend break - how about waterways and wildlife? ... farming and forests? ... ecology and architecture? And you can choose to stay in the depths of the country or the heart of the city - it's all there in our accommodation guide.

A Surprising County

Call into the Heart of the National Forest Visitor Centre at Moira, stroll along the woodland trails and find out about the first planned new British Forest for a Millennium. Opening in 2001 will be the Millennium Forest Discovery Centre, the national centre for woods and woodland.

Close by, the historic town of Ashby de la Zouch offers fine shopping, the town museum and the imposing ruins of Ashby Castle. Just a couple of miles away is the splendid Staunton Harold Estate comprising of the Hall, National Trust Church, Reservoir and Visitor Centre, the renowned Ferrers Centre for Arts and Crafts plus, to round off a perfect visit, tea rooms and gift shop. For something completely different, head south and enjoy a visit to Twycross Zoo, known throughout the world for its conservation work with apes and monkeys.

At the southern edge of Leicestershire, Market Harborough sits on an arm of the Grand Union Canal. The Old Grammar School in the centre of town is one of the county's more unusual buildings, timber framed it stands on massive wooden stilts. Next, we head north to explore High Leicestershire's broad landscapes of rolling hills, meadows and charming villages. At Burrough on the Hill, an Iron Age Hill fort stands almost 700 feet above sea level, overlooking the Wreake Valley and Borrough House - where the Duke and Duchess of Windsor met in the 1930's.

The north east corner of Leicestershire is characterised by the sweeping Vale of Belvoir, culminating in the gothic splendour of Belvoir Castle, home of the Duke and Duchess of Rutland.

Melton Mowbray is associated with Stilton 'the King of Cheeses', pork pies and Melton Hunt Cake - all can be bought and sampled here. Visit on a Tuesday and experience the hustle and bustle of Melton's street and cattle markets. At the Carnegie Museum you can delve into the town's history and come face to face with Melton's famous two-headed calf!

Completing our tour around the County, we return to Charnwood and the town of Loughborough where, appropriately enough, Thomas Cook pioneered modern tourism. Whilst here, call in to John Taylor's Bell Foundry Museum. Don't miss the charm and nostalgia of the Great Central Railway, before completing the steps at Britain's first grand Carillon. You will be rewarded with magnificent views of the Charnwood Forest - where our tour began.

Discover Leicester....diverse & cultural city

Travel through the ages and around the world in this exciting, vibrant and cosmopolitan city. Leicester is one of the few cities in England that can trace its growth from

the Iron Age. Thomas Cook organised his first package tour from Leicester to Loughborough by train in 1841; this was the beginning of tourism as we know it.

The Old Town Heritage Quarter of the city encompasses the Cathedral, historic Castle Mound, dramatic Jain Temple and gives access to peaceful riverside walks. It is also home to many of the City's excellent Museums.

These are just some of the examples of Leicester's fascinating past...and where better to create a most exciting future. The National Space Science Centre, a multi-million pound landmark project, supported by the Millennium Commission opens to visitors in the Spring of 2001. The centre will house a planetarium,

a research centre, artefacts from space and the only Challenger Learning Centre outside North America.

But Leicester is more than this...for shoppers it is an oasis of different experiences from glitzy high street malls, speciality shops, atmospheric lanes and Victorian Arcades. You'll quickly get absorbed in Leicester's cosmopolitan atmosphere. From the remarkable range of fish from around the world in Europe's largest covered market, to fashion, food and gifts from the Caribbean, Orient, Asia and beyond. Take time out to explore Leicester's Golden Mile. This unique Asian Quarter excites the senses with an unrivalled display of foods, fashion, jewellery, cooking ingredients and utensils.

Leicester guarantees excitement, from the traditional lights of Christmas to a flavour of the Caribbean and Asia. The city is not only made up of various cultures, it celebrates them with a passion and thousands of visitors flock to experience it first hand. Be here when the streets come alive with festivals and events. Barely a month goes by when the City is not ablaze with the colour and light of a festival procession.

Explore the night time experience of pubs, clubs and eating out in a City that can truly boast cuisine from across the world. Why not take in a major concert at De Montfort Hall or a new production at the nationally respected Heymarket Theatre and you'll see why Leicester has it all. Add in the quality mix of accommodation and you really wonder why you've not shared the excitement of the city before. ∎

... Around the County

BLABY

Blaby District epitomises the diversity that can be found in Leicestershire. Modern shopping facilities rub shoulders with ruined castles and derelict mediaeval villages. Country parks adjoin modern sports and leisure centres. The area has been at the heart of Britain's transport routes since Roman times: High Cross was the meeting place of Watling Street and Fosse Way. Now Fosse Park, where the M1 and M69 motorways meet, provides a similar focus for a comprehensive range of leisure and business facilities.

Commerce and industry rapidly give way to rural charm as you ascend the valley of the River Soar. Fosse Meadows, with 140 acres of woodland and hay meadows is just one of the ten country parks in the district - and don't miss Kirby Muxloe Castle, built of brick, never completed, but still impressive.

If you prefer something a little more active, there are six golf courses in the area and for the adventurous, there's both Stiney Cove, the UK's largest inland scuba diving centre, and jet-ski lake at Stoney Stanton.

CHARNWOOD

Charnwood is an area of jagged crags, secluded valleys, attractive woodland and picturesque reservoirs. Most of the villages and towns of Charnwood can be found listed in the Doomsday Book of 1086. Large areas of land which were used as hunting parks were gifted to the City and the County of Leicestershire. One such area was Bradgate Park and other gifts of hills and woods have ensured Charnwood retains its heritage.

Charnwood is a walking and cycling paradise with an abundance of routes through Beacon Hill, Swithland Wood, Bradgate Park, Jubilee Wood, The Outwoods & Bluebell Woods and Watermead Country Park.

Bradgate

Snibston Discovery Park

The ancient market town of Loughborough is Charnwood's largest town offering first class entertainment and shopping. Some of the county's top tourist attractions can be found here which will include the Great Central Railway, the Bell Foundry Museum, Charnwood Museum and the Grand Carillon.

The River Soar and Grand Union Canal runs through the Borough enabling the more leisurely tourist to take a boat trip to attractions like the award winning Stonehurst Farm and Motor Museum.

HINCKLEY & BOSWORTH

Hinckley and Bosworth Borough neatly balances thriving industry and commerce with rural character and a wealth of tourist attractions. There are many popular places to visit, including Bosworth Battlefield and its fascinating visitor centre; the Battlefield Railway; Twycross Zoo, home of the famous TV chimps, and renowned breeding centre for endangered species; Desford Tropical Bird Gardens and Mallory Park motor racing circuit. For nature lovers, Burbage Common and Woods has spectacular ground flora, while the tranquillity of Thornton Reservoir is the ideal place for a waterside stroll.

Hinckley has a strong industrial heritage - traditional industries included frame knitting, boot and shoe making, and mining: all served by an extensive canal network, much of which has been restored and preserved.

Threading through the area from Hinckley to Snarestone without a single lock is the Ashby Canal. Along the way it passes the fine old town of Market Bosworth famous for its success in the Britain in Bloom competition.

NORTH WEST LEICESTERSHIRE

Arts and crafts... the Civil War... our industrial heritage.... natural history... and the wonders of technology - you can explore them all in a single voyage of discovery around North West Leicestershire.

One of the major attractions is Snibston Discovery Park. Built around an old colliery, it combines exhibits and information about coal mining and life in the 19th Century, with exciting experiments and displays that bring technology to life. You can travel back even further in time at Ashby Castle, a Royalist stronghold in the Civil War - the nearby Ashby de la Zouch Museum tells you all about it, and more.

The fourteen craft work shops at the Ferrers Centre at Staunton Harold produce contemporary items ranging from furniture to jewellery - and there are more at Moira Furnace, as well as one of the best preserved blast furnaces in Europe.

The district is at the centre of the new National Forest. You can find out all about it and everything to do with trees and woodlands at the Heart of National Forest Visitors Centre. ■

Mick & Den

THE HOUSE CLEARANCE MEN

Will purchase all old & modern furniture & effects
Houses cleared ~ Top prices paid

Visit our showroom at:
107 Lothair Road, Leicester

(0116) 233 8828 or 287 8500 eves.

Regional Office:

Dawson House,
63 Forest Road, Loughborough,
Leicestershire LE11 3NW

Tel: 01509 262282
Fax: 01509 238808
Mobile: 07957 404404

Members of the Platinum
Priviledge Card Scheme

Your home is at risk if you do not keep up repayments on a mortgage or other loan secured upon it.

Independent Mortgage Advice throughout Leicestershire

Independent Advice on:

- All aspects of mortgage lending
- First time buyer guidance
- Mortgages arranged with any Building Society, Bank, Specialist Lender.
- Re-mortgages
- Residential/Commercial

12 YEARS EXPERIENCE ~ HOME VISITS ARRANGED

Call (01509) 262282

Representing only (for Introductions only) the J. Rothschild Assurance Marketing Group (members of which are regulated by the Personal Investment Authority and/or IMRO), which takes responsibility for its representatives only in respect of advice given on, and the sale of, life assurance, pensions and unit trust products of members of the Marketing Group.

... So much in so little

Rutland Water

'Multum in Parvo' says the Latin motto of Rutland - 'so much in so little'. This tiny County is packed with character and beauty, blending charming townscapes and simple country cottages for quintessentially English appeal.

Rutland lies at the heart of the Shire Counties, surrounded by Leicestershire, Lincolnshire and Northamptonshire with Nottinghamshire just to the North. Rolling countryside, historic sites and modern cities offer a huge variety of interest to visitors. The natural and man-made charms of the area encourage film-makers to use the scenery and buildings in their productions time and again.

Historic Towns and Villages

Rutland has two towns, Oakham and Uppingham, and around fifty villages.

At the heart of Oakham lies the great hall of an ancient Norman Castle, filled with symbolic horseshoes donated by royalty and peers of the realm over the centuries. Today, it is open to the public and is becoming a popular location for weddings. Close by, in the Market Place, you can find an old Butter Cross and Town Pump. Rutland County Museum is full of historic artefacts and exhibits, as well as temporary shows.

Uppingham is known far and wide for its art galleries, antique and antiquarian book shops.
A network of fascinating historic alleyways winds between beautiful stone buildings, creating the unique character of Uppingham.

Both towns are successful entrants in Britain in Bloom competitions in the summer and both celebrate Christmas with marvellous street and shopping events.

Among the prettiest villages in the County are Exton, which clusters around a tree-edged village green, and Barrowden, which centres on a duck pond. Naturally, both villages have traditional pubs.

ALLBRITE VALETING

Pure quality in car valeting, be it once a week or for that special occasion

c/o Leicester City Bus
Abbey Park Road
Leicester LE4 5AH
Tel/Fax: 0116 251 0506
Mob: 07970 024 525

Earthwise™ Publications from the British Geological Survey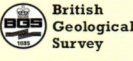

Presents five easy to read titles, primarily aimed at the leisure market and at students of Earth Science key stage 2 to 4. Priced at £6.50 each.

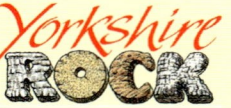
a journey through time
64pp (ISBN 0 85272 2699)

EARTHQUAKES
our trembling planet
72pp (ISBN 0 85272 287 7)

GROUNDWATER
our hidden asset
60pp (ISBN 0 85272 304 0)

Fossils
the story of life
64pp (ISBN 0 85272 284 2)

origins of the *'water of life'*
72pp (ISBN 0 85272 290 7)

For orders or more information contact:
Sales Desk, British Geological Survey, Keyworth,
Nottingham NG12 5GG

Tel: 0115 936 3241   Fax: 0115 936 3488   e-mail: sales@bgs.ac.uk

---

COUNTY ROOFING

SLATING - TILING - FELTING
SINGLE PLY - OVER ROOFS
CLADDING - SHEETING - COATINGS
ASPHALT ROOFS & FLOORS

INDUSTRIAL - DOMESTIC
MAINTENANCE - CONSULTANTS

10 Rose Tree Avenue, Birstall, Leicester LE4 4LR
Telephone: (0116) 267 5546
Fax: (0116) 267 7575

D. Calver

General Haulage and Commercial Vehicle Repairs

Breakdown Call Outs
Fabrication Work
All Types of Welding
Aluminium Specialist
(Steel, Cast, Stainless Steel)

Tel: 0116 2640854
Fax: 0116 2604272 • Mobile: 0780 1924014

Round Rutland Water

At the heart of Rutland is Rutland Water, a horseshoe-shaped lake created as a reservoir over twenty years ago. Today it is a nature reserve and a centre for outdoor sports. Visitors come from all over the world for;

- Birdwatching
- Cycling
- Walking around the lake
- Fishing
- Windsurfing
- Sailing
- Taking trips on the Rutland Belle cruiser
- The Drought Garden, designed for Anglian Water by Geoff Hamilton
- The Butterfly House
- The Rockblock climbing centre
- Cafes and shops
- Rutland Water Tourist Information Centre

History abounds in Rutland villages. You can find:

- A Bishop's Palace at Lyddington, later converted into a Bede House and open to the public through English Heritage.
- An ancient turf maze at Wing, its origins lost in history
- The room where Guy Fawkes hatched the Gunpowder Plot at Stoke Dry church
- A Thankful Village at Teigh
- Poet Laureate John Betjeman's favourite little church at Brooke
- Ancient stocks and connections with Sir Isaac Newton at Market Overton
- A huge Norman arch in a tiny village church at Tickencote

Great houses and historic castles surrounding Rutland are open to the public at various times of the year.

North of Rutland, the Vale of Belvoir is dominated by Belvoir Castle, ancestral homes of the Duke of Rutland. This historic house is open to the public and often hosts events including outdoor concerts.

Close to Grantham are great houses including Belton (National Trust) and Grimsthorpe Castle. Woolsthorpe Manor (also National Trust) was the family home to Sir Isaac Newton and the scene of his discovery of the force of gravity.

On the outskirts of Stamford, Elizabeth Burghley House was created for the Cecil family as one of the grandest homes in England.

Heading into Northamptonshire, there are still more great houses. Lamport Hall is famous for antique events. Deene Park has wonderful parkland. Beautiful Kirby Hall (English Heritage) is open to the public. Rockingham Castle has connections with Dickens and often hosts craft fairs and historic re-enactments. ■

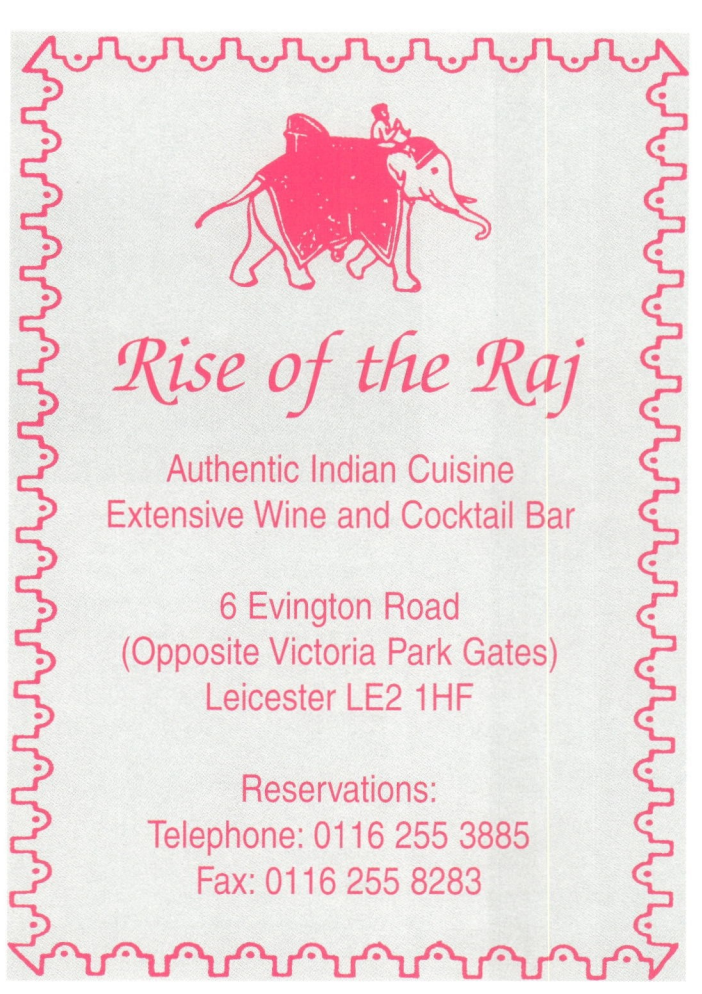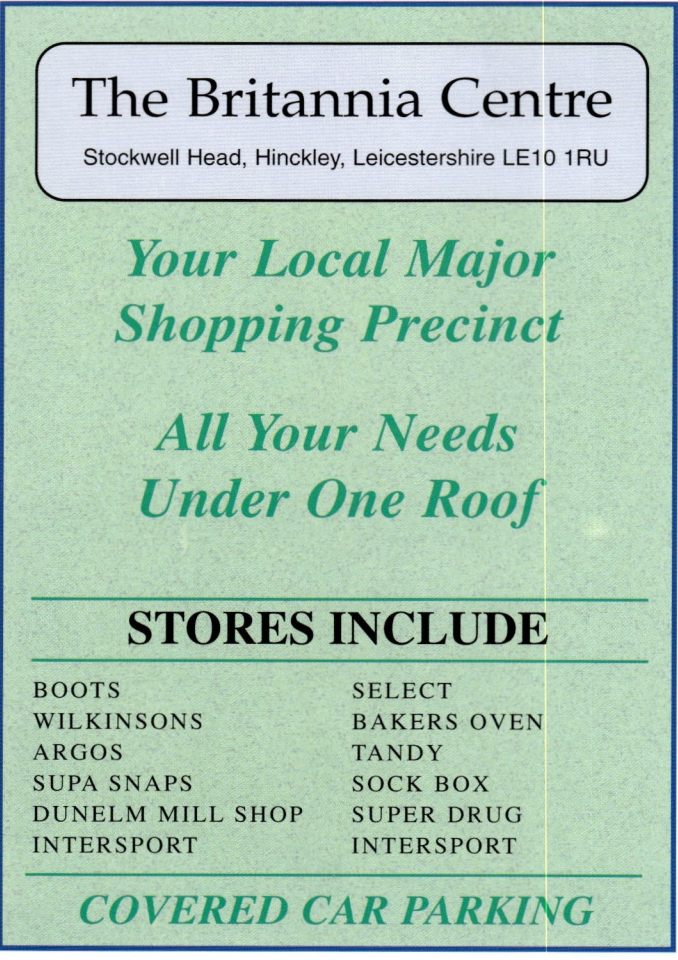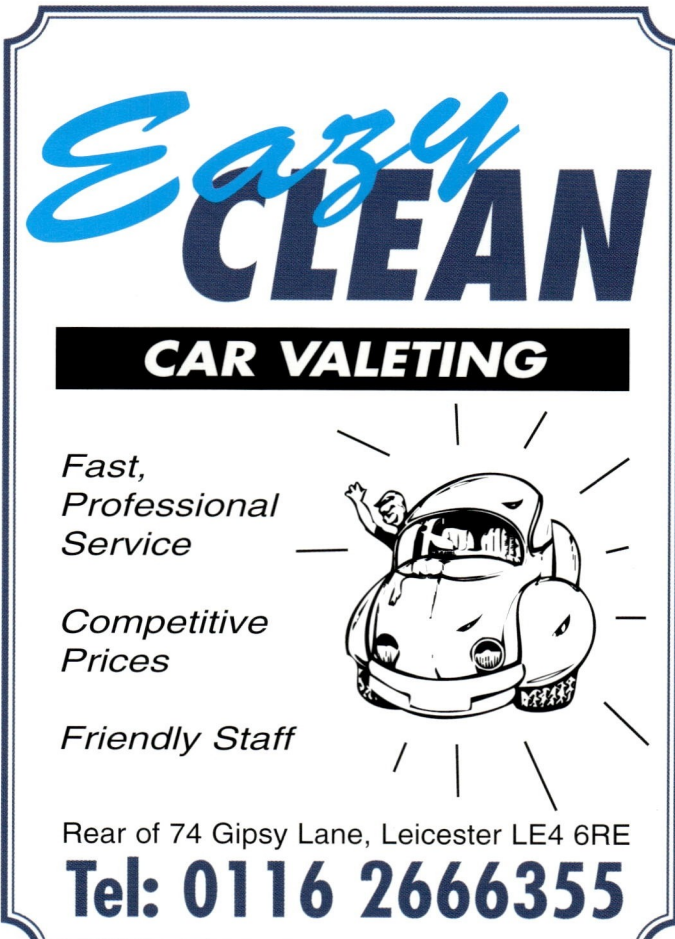

HOW TO USE THIS STREET GUIDE

The maps within this Street Guide fall into two sections;

In Section One, the rural areas of Leicestershire and Rutland are covered at a scale of 1:32,000. These areas are featured on Maps 1-36 and 53-85.

At this scale, it is not possible to give detailed coverage of all streets within built-up areas, so, for the most part, only motorways, A roads, B roads and minor roads are covered in detail. The emphasis on these pages is on cross-navigation between towns/villages throughout the region.

The City of Leicester is covered in Section One, but at a scale of 1:16,000 to enable complete street coverage.

In Section Two, all major urban population centres outlined in Section One are covered in detail on an individual town/village basis at a scale of 1:16,000.

A complete list of districts covered is given on page 14 and the overall layout of maps appears on the Grid Map on page 15.

IMPORTANT - *All maps are referenced by the Map Number, shown in bold type in the page margin. Similarly, all streets in both sections of the Street Index refer to the Map Number. The Map Number is not to be confused with the page number shown at the foot of each page.*

For example

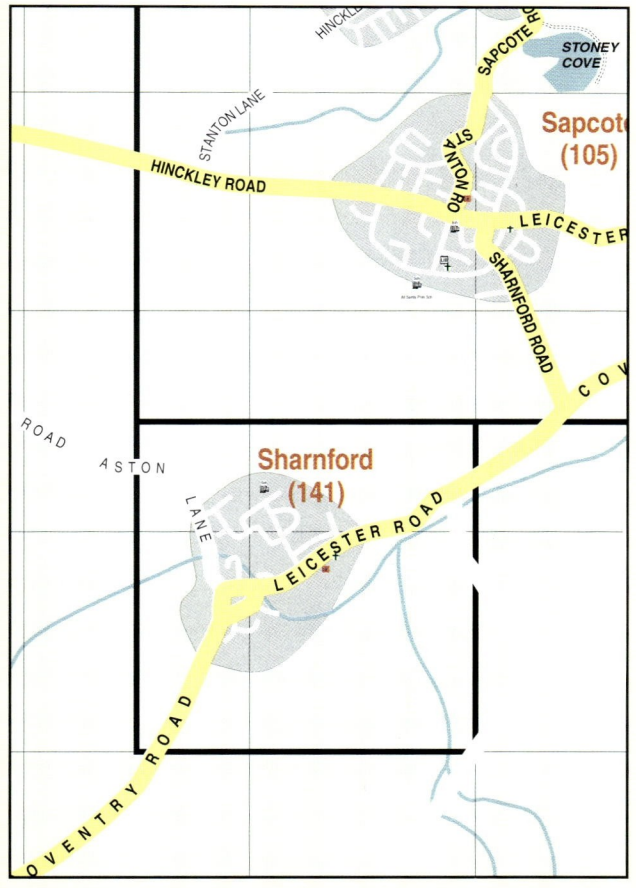

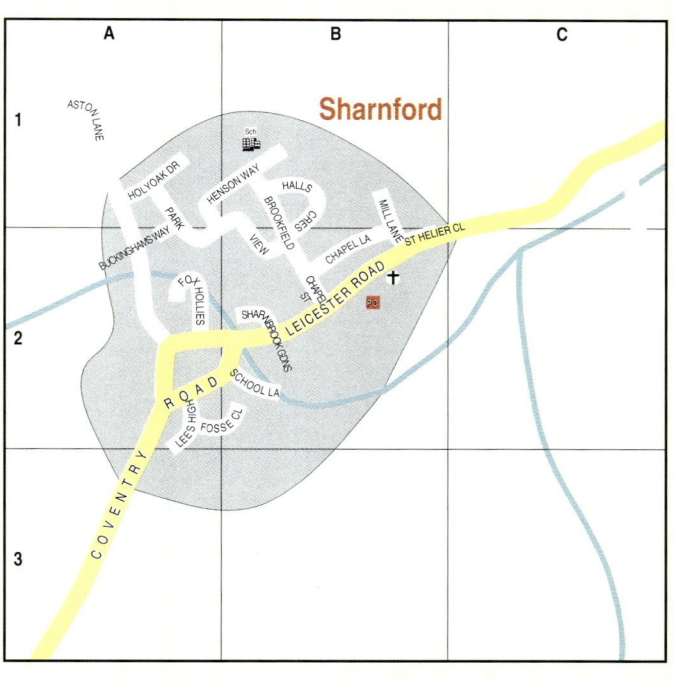

Map 141 (Section Two)

Map 72 (Section One)

INDEX TO DISTRICTS

① = Page Location in Section One ② = Page Location in Section Two n/c = Not Covered in Section

District	①	②
Ab Kettleby	16	n/c
Acresford	20	n/c
Agar Nook	22	111
Albert Village	9	n/c
Allexton	66	124
Alverton	1	n/c
Anstey	38	n/c
Appleby Magna	20	117
Appleby Parva	33	n/c
Arnesby	74	117
Asfordby	16	123
Asfordby Hill	16	120
Ashby Folville	27	n/c
Ashby Magna	73	n/c
Ashby Parva	80	n/c
Ashby-de-la-Zouch	10	86
Ashley	77	n/c
Ashwell	29	123
Aston-on-Trent	4	n/c
Atherstone	60	n/c
Atterton	61	n/c
Austrey	33	n/c
Aylestone	45	n/c
Ayston	67	n/c
Bagworth	35	n/c
Bardon	22	111
Barkby	25	n/c
Barkestone le Vale	2	127
Barlestone	35	87
Barleythorpe	29	102
Barrow upon Soar	14	116
Barrowden	69	125
Barsby	26	n/c
Barton in the Beans	34	n/c
Barwell	62	112
Beeby	53	n/c
Belmesthorpe	32	149
Belton	11	127
Belton in Rutland	67	124
Belvoir	2	n/c
Billesdon	65	114
Bilstone	34	n/c
Birstall	39	n/c
Bisbrooke	68	125
Bittesswell	80	98
Blaby	50	n/c
Blackfordby	9	n/c
Botcheston	36	n/c
Bottesford	1	123
Branston	7	n/c
Braunston in Rutland	56	126
Braunstone	45	n/c
Braunstone Frith	41	n/c
Breedon on the Hill	11	128
Bretby	9	n/c
Brooke	56	n/c
Broughton Astley	73	88
Bruntingthorpe	74	n/c
Buckminster	18	n/c
Burley	30	n/c
Burrough on the Hill	27	n/c
Burton Lazars	28	126
Burton on the Wolds	14	129
Burton Ovary	64	130
Bushby	53	153
Cadeby	62	n/c
Caldecott	78	129
Calke	10	n/c
Careby	32	n/c
Carlby	32	n/c
Carlton	34	n/c
Castle Donington	4	89
Chadwell	7	n/c
Chilcote	20	n/c
Church Gresley	9	n/c
Church Langton	76	n/c
Claybrooke Magna	72	139
Claybrooke Parva	79	139
Clipsham	31	n/c
Clipston	83	n/c
Coalville	22	110-111
Cold Newton	54	n/c
Cold Overton	28	n/c
Coleorton	11	n/c
Collyweston	69	n/c
Colsterworth	19	n/c
Congerstone	34	n/c
Copt Oak	23	n/c
Corby	78	n/c
Cosby	73	90
Cossington	25	n/c
Coston	18	n/c
Cotes	13	n/c
Cotesbach	80	n/c
Cottesmore	30	126
Cottingham	78	n/c
Countesthorpe	74	125
Cranoe	77	n/c
Croft	72	139
Cropston	24	n/c
Croxton Kerrial	8	130
Dadlington	62	n/c
Denton	3	129
Desford	36	n/c
Diseworth	4	146

District	①	②
Donisthorpe	20	118
Drayton	78	n/c
Duddington	69	n/c
Dunton Bassett	73	135
Earl Shilton	63	113
East Farndon	83	n/c
East Goscote	26	119
East Langton	76	n/c
East Norton	66	n/c
Easton on the Hill	59	n/c
Eastwell	7	n/c
Eaton & Branston	7	124
Edith Weston	57	127
Edmondthorpe	18	n/c
Egleton	56	96
Ellistown	22	n/c
Elmesthorpe	63	113
Empingham	58	135
Enderby	49	n/c
Essendine	32	n/c
Evington	44	n/c
Exton	30	140
Fenny Drayton	61	131
Field Head	36	100
Flawborough	1	n/c
Fleckney	75	93
Foxton	76	140
Freeby	17	n/c
Frisby on the Wreake	15	131
Frolesworth	72	n/c
Gaddesby	26	132
Garthorpe	18	n/c
Gaulby	64	n/c
Gilmorton	80	141
Glaston	68	n/c
Glenfield	42	n/c
Glooston	76	n/c
Goadby	65	n/c
Goadby Marwood	7	n/c
Great Bowden	83	99
Great Casterton	59	n/c
Great Dalby	27	n/c
Great Easton	78	141
Great Glen	64	130
Great Oxendon	83	n/c
Greetham	30	132
Grimston	15	n/c
Groby	37	n/c
Gumley	75	n/c
Gunby	19	n/c
Hallaton	66	133
Halstead	54	n/c
Harby	6	n/c
Harston	3	n/c
Hartshorne	9	n/c
Hathern	12	106
Heather	21	135
Higham on the Hill	70	n/c
Hinckley	71	94-96
Hoby	15	n/c
Holwell	16	n/c
Hose	6	134
Hoton	13	n/c
Houghton on the Hill	53	142
Huncote	63	130
Hungarton	53	134
Husbands Bosworth	82	142
Ibstock	22	131
Illston	65	136
Isley Walton	4	n/c
Kegworth	5	132
Ketton	58	133
Keyham	53	n/c
Kibworth	75	97
Kilby	74	n/c
Kilvington	1	n/c
Kimcote	81	n/c
King's Norton	64	n/c
Kingston on Soar	5	n/c
Kirby Bellars	16	n/c
Kirby Mallory	62	128
Kirby Muxloe	36	91
Knighton	47	n/c
Knipton	3	136
Knossington	55	152
Langham	29	122
Laughton	75	n/c
Leicester	37-52	n/c
Leicester Forest East	45	n/c
Leire	73	135
Lilbourne	84	n/c
Little Bowden	83	99
Little Casterton	59	n/c
Little Dalby	28	n/c
Little Stretton	64	n/c
Littlethorpe	49	n/c
Lockington	5	n/c
Loddington	66	n/c
Long Bennington	1	n/c
Long Clawson	6	134
Long Whatton	12	106-109
Loughborough	12-13	106-109
Lount	10	n/c
Lowesby	54	n/c
Lubenham	83	122

District	①	②
Lutterworth	80	98
Lyddington	67	143
Lyndon	57	n/c
Magna Park	79	143
Manton	57	137
Marefield	54	n/c
Market Bosworth	35	136
Market Harborough	83	99
Market Overton	30	137
Markfield	23	100
Measham	20	144
Medbourne	77	144
Melton Mowbray	16	120-122
Middleton	78	n/c
Moira	20	118
Morcott	68	138
Mountsorrel	24	101
Mowsley	75	n/c
Muston	3	n/c
Nailstone	35	87
Nanpantan	12	108
Narborough	49	n/c
Nether Broughton	n/c	145
Netherseal	20	n/c
Nevill Holt	77	n/c
New Swannington	22	114
Newbold	11	n/c
Newbold Verdon	35	145
Newhall	9	n/c
Newton	84	n/c
Newton Burgoland	34	146
Newton Harcourt	52	n/c
Newton Linford	37	n/c
Newton Regis	33	n/c
Newton Unthank	36	n/c
Newtown Linford	23	n/c
No Mans Heath	33	n/c
Normanton on Soar	12	n/c
Normanton	1	n/c
Normanton le Heath	21	n/c
Norris Hill	20	138
North Kilworth	81	146
North Luffenham	57	139
North Witham	19	n/c
Norton Juxta Twycross	33	139
Nuneaton	70	n/c
Oadby	48	102
Oakham	56	102
Oakthorpe	20	118
Odstone	34	n/c
Old Dalby	15	147
Orton-on-the-Hill	33	n/c
Osbaston	35	n/c
Osgathorpe	11	n/c
Overseal	20	n/c
Owston	55	n/c
Packington	21	147
Peatling Magna	74	n/c
Peatling Parva	74	n/c
Peckleton	63	128
Pickwell	28	n/c
Pickworth	31	n/c
Pilton	68	n/c
Pinwall	60	n/c
Plungar	2	140
Preston	67	n/c
Queniborough	26	148
Quorn	24	116
Ragdale	15	n/c
Ratby	36	91
Ratcliffe Culey	60	n/c
Ratcliffe on Soar	5	n/c
Ratcliffe on the Wreake	25	n/c
Ravenstone	22	110
Rearsby	26	119
Redmile	2	n/c
Ridlington	67	148
Rockingham	78	n/c
Rolleston	65	n/c
Rotherby	26	n/c
Rothley	25	101
Ryhall	32	149
Saddington	75	93
Saltby	8	n/c
Sapcote	72	105
Saxby	18	n/c
Saxelby	16	n/c
Scalford	7	140
Scraptoft	53	153
Seagrave	14	149
Seaton	68	141
Sewstern	19	n/c
Shackerstone	34	n/c
Shangton	65	n/c
Shardlow	4	n/c
Sharnford	72	141
Shawell	84	142
Shearsby	74	142
Sheepy Magna	60	143
Sheepy Parva	60	143
Shenton	61	n/c
Shepshed	12	103
Short Heath	20	n/c
Sibbertoft	82	n/c
Sibson	61	n/c

District	①	②
Sileby	25	104
Skeffington	65	143
Slawston	77	n/c
Smeeton Westerby	75	97
Smisby	10	n/c
Snarestone	34	n/c
Somerby	28	151
South Croxton	26	n/c
South Kilworth	85	n/c
South Luffenham	69	150
South Witham	19	n/c
Sproxton	8	152
Stainby	19	n/c
Stamford	59	n/c
Stanford on Soar	13	n/c
Stanton under Bardon	23	n/c
Stapleford	17	n/c
Stapleton	62	112
Stathern	2	150
Staunton in the Vale	1	n/c
Stockerston	67	n/c
Stoke Golding	61	137
Stonesby	8	n/c
Stoney Stanton	72	105
Stoneygate	48	n/c
Stoughton	64	n/c
Stretton	31	145
Stretton en le Field	20	n/c
Sutton	2	n/c
Sutton Bassett	77	n/c
Sutton Bonington	5	n/c
Sutton Cheney	62	n/c
Swadlincote	9	n/c
Swannington	22	n/c
Swepstone	21	n/c
Swinford	84	145
Swithland	24	n/c
Syston	25	92
Teigh	29	n/c
Theddingworth	82	n/c
Thistleton	19	n/c
Thornborough	22	n/c
Thornton	36	152
Thorpe Acre	12	106
Thorpe Arnold	17	121
Thorpe Langton	76	n/c
Thorpe Satchville	27	n/c
Thringstone	11	114
Thrussington	26	119
Thurcaston	24	n/c
Thurlaston	63	146
Thurmaston	40	n/c
Thurnby	53	153
Tickencote	58	n/c
Ticknall	10	n/c
Tilton on the Hill	54	151
Tinwell	59	n/c
Tixover	69	n/c
Tonge	11	n/c
Tugby	66	147
Tur Langton	76	n/c
Twycross	33	147
Twyford	27	n/c
Uffington	59	n/c
Ullesthorpe	79	144
Upper Bruntingthorpe	81	148
Upper Hambleton	57	n/c
Uppingham	67	138
Upton	61	n/c
Wakerley	69	n/c
Walcote	80	148
Waltham on the Wolds	7	149
Walton	81	n/c
Walton on the Wolds	14	149
Wanlip	25	n/c
Wardley	67	n/c
Wartnaby	16	n/c
Warton	33	n/c
Welham	77	n/c
Wellsborough	61	n/c
West Langton	76	n/c
Weston by Welland	77	n/c
Weston-on-Trent	4	n/c
Whetstone	50	90
Whissendine	29	151
Whitwell	57	n/c
Whitwick	22	114-115
Wigston	51	n/c
Willey	79	n/c
Willoughby Waterleys	73	n/c
Wilson	4	n/c
Wing	57	150
Wistow	74	n/c
Witham on the Hill	32	n/c
Witherley	60	n/c
Woodhouse	24	n/c
Woodhouse Eaves	24	151
Woodthorpe	13	109
Woodville	9	n/c
Woolsthorpe by Belvoir	3	n/c
Worthington	11	150
Wykin	71	n/c
Wymeswold	14	152
Wymondham	18	96
Zouch	12	n/c

GRID MAP

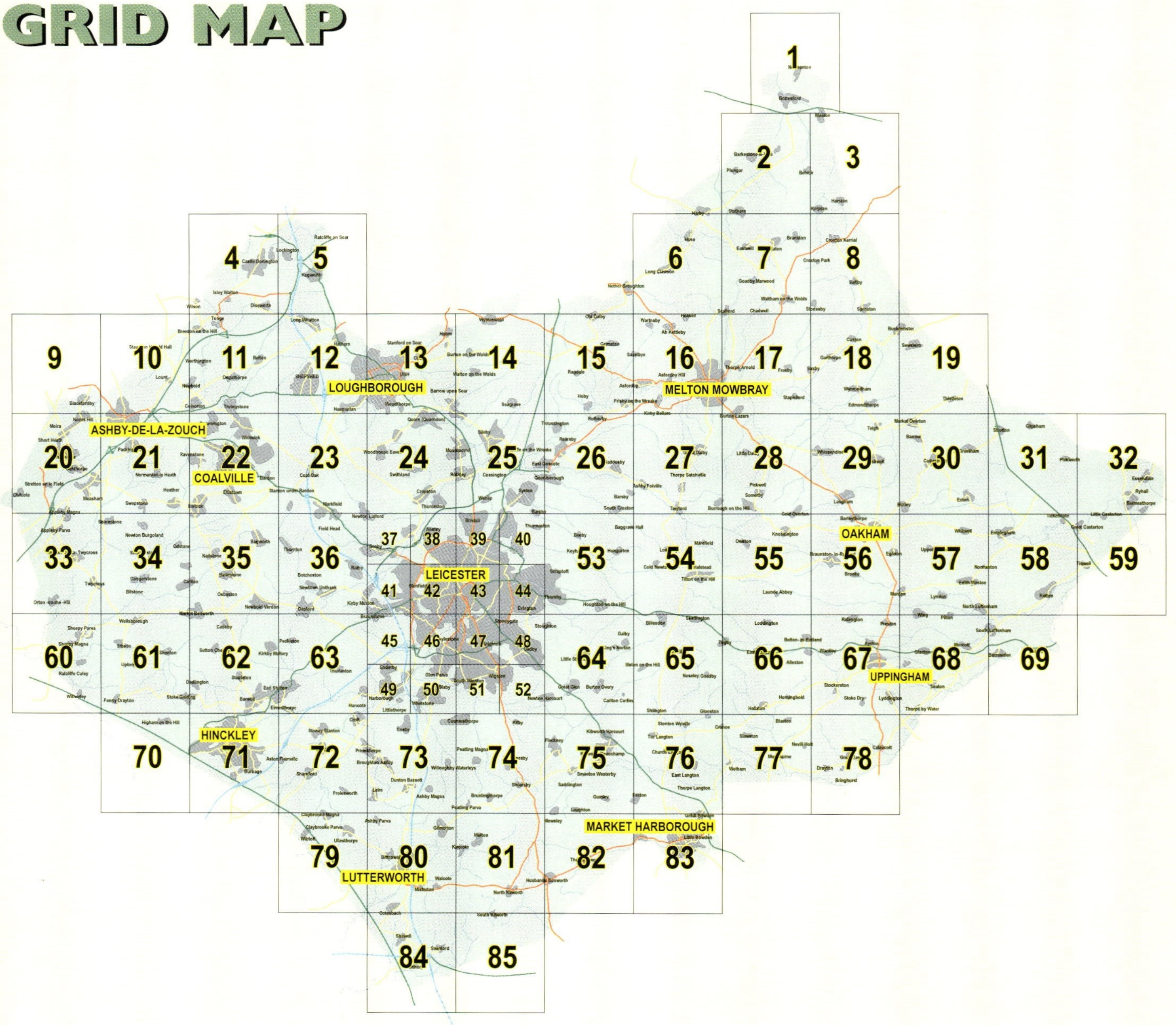

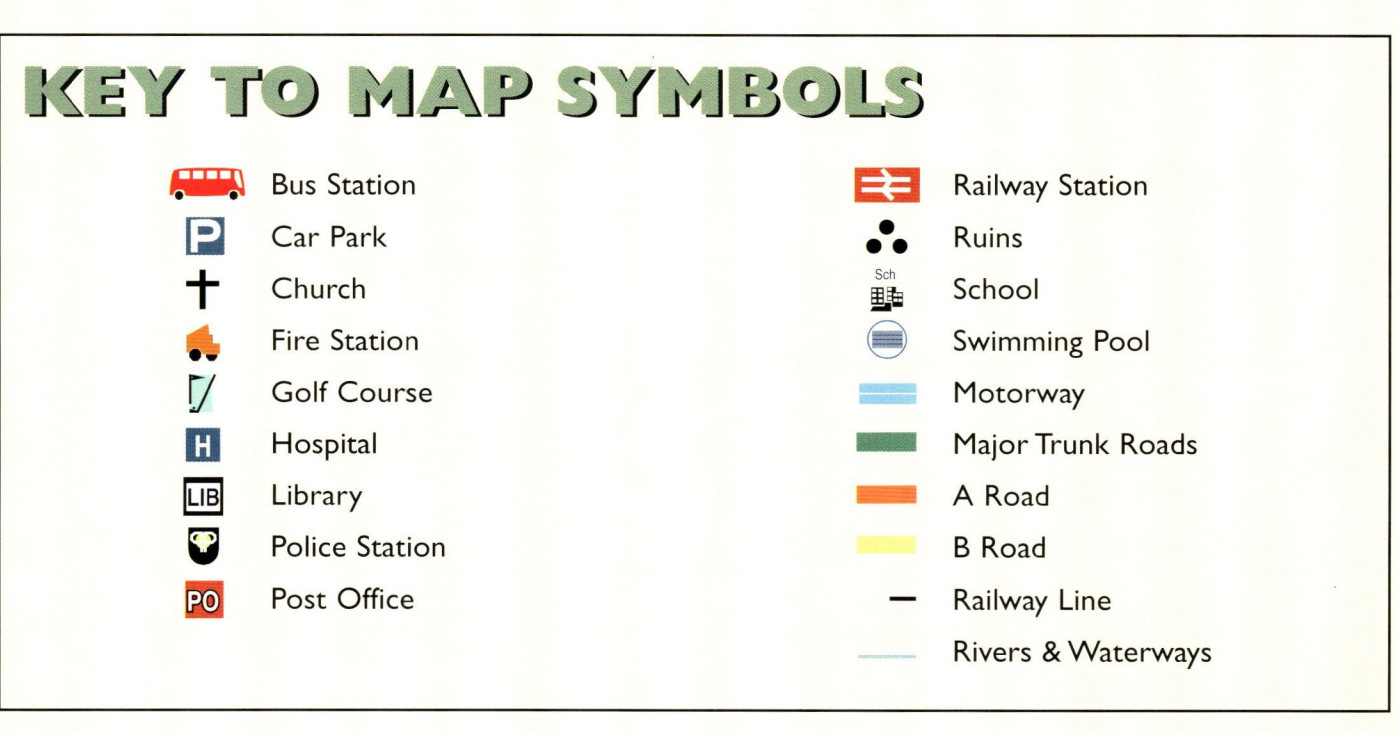

KEY TO MAP SYMBOLS

🚌 Bus Station		≠ Railway Station	
P Car Park		⋮ Ruins	
† Church		Sch School	
🚒 Fire Station		Swimming Pool	
Golf Course		Motorway	
H Hospital		Major Trunk Roads	
LIB Library		A Road	
Police Station		B Road	
PO Post Office		— Railway Line	
		Rivers & Waterways	

~15~

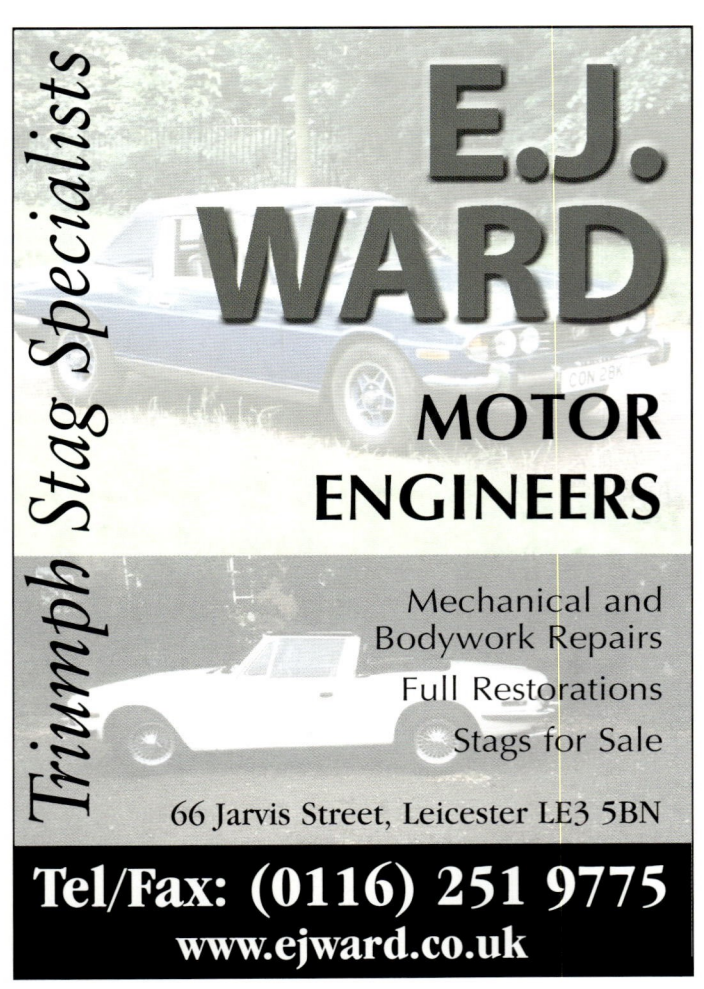

Leicester's finest Jewellers since 1881

Leah Marks House
10-12 Market Street
Leicester.
Telephone: 0116 255 1233

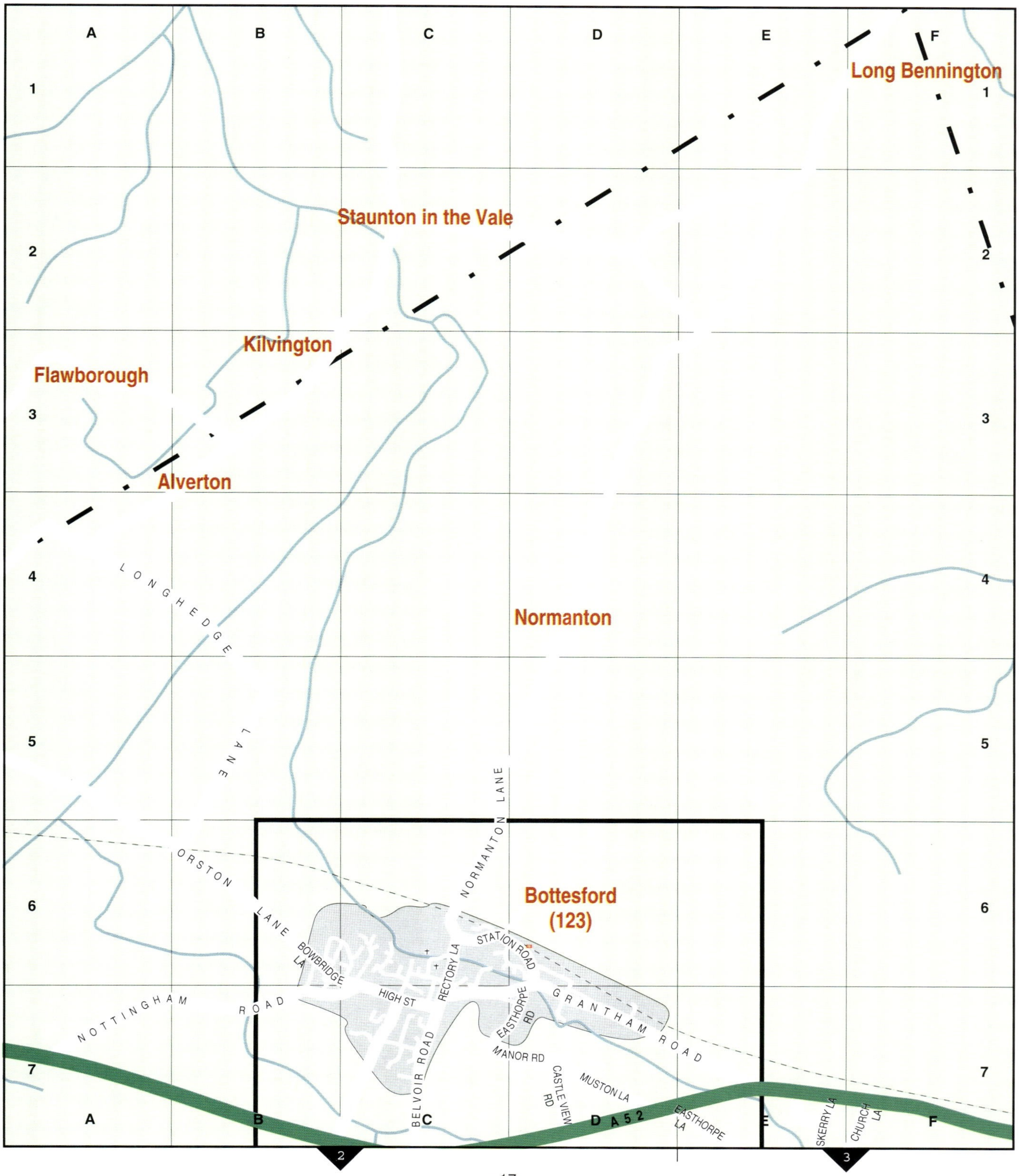

De Montfort Hotel
Prop: Rachel Catherine Howard

Offers our guests a home from home welcome

Bed & Breakfast - Evening Meal - Licensed Bar/Lounge - Quality En-Suite Rooms

The Hotel is a Victorian building conveniently situated within five minutes walk from the town centre and even closer to the Great Central Railway Steam Trust which is one of the Country's leading attractions. We are also only a few minutes from the University, Bell Foundry, Airport, the beautiful Charnwood countryside and Bradgate Park. We have nine bedrooms, nearly all of which have en-suite or private facilities with tea/coffee making facilities and TV.

A famous history...
Our Hotel is named after the Frenchman Simon De Montfort, who came to England in 1229. Favoured by Henry III, he was made Earl of Leicester. In later years, as King Henry strayed further from the Magna Carta, Simon and the King waged war upon each other...
On the 4th August 1265, Simon De Montfort was killed in battle at Evesham in Worcestershire. Simon was loved by the common people of England and, although dead, his cause triumphed and he is known as the father of the English Parliament.

88 Leicester Road, Loughborough, Leicestershire LE11 2AQ. Telephone: (01509) 216061 Fax: (01509) 233667

~18~

Protheroe's

The Protheroe Motor Group Limited
Northampton Road, Market Harborough, Leicestershire LE16 9HD
www.protheroes.co.uk

Tel: (01858) 465511 Fax: (01858) 432656

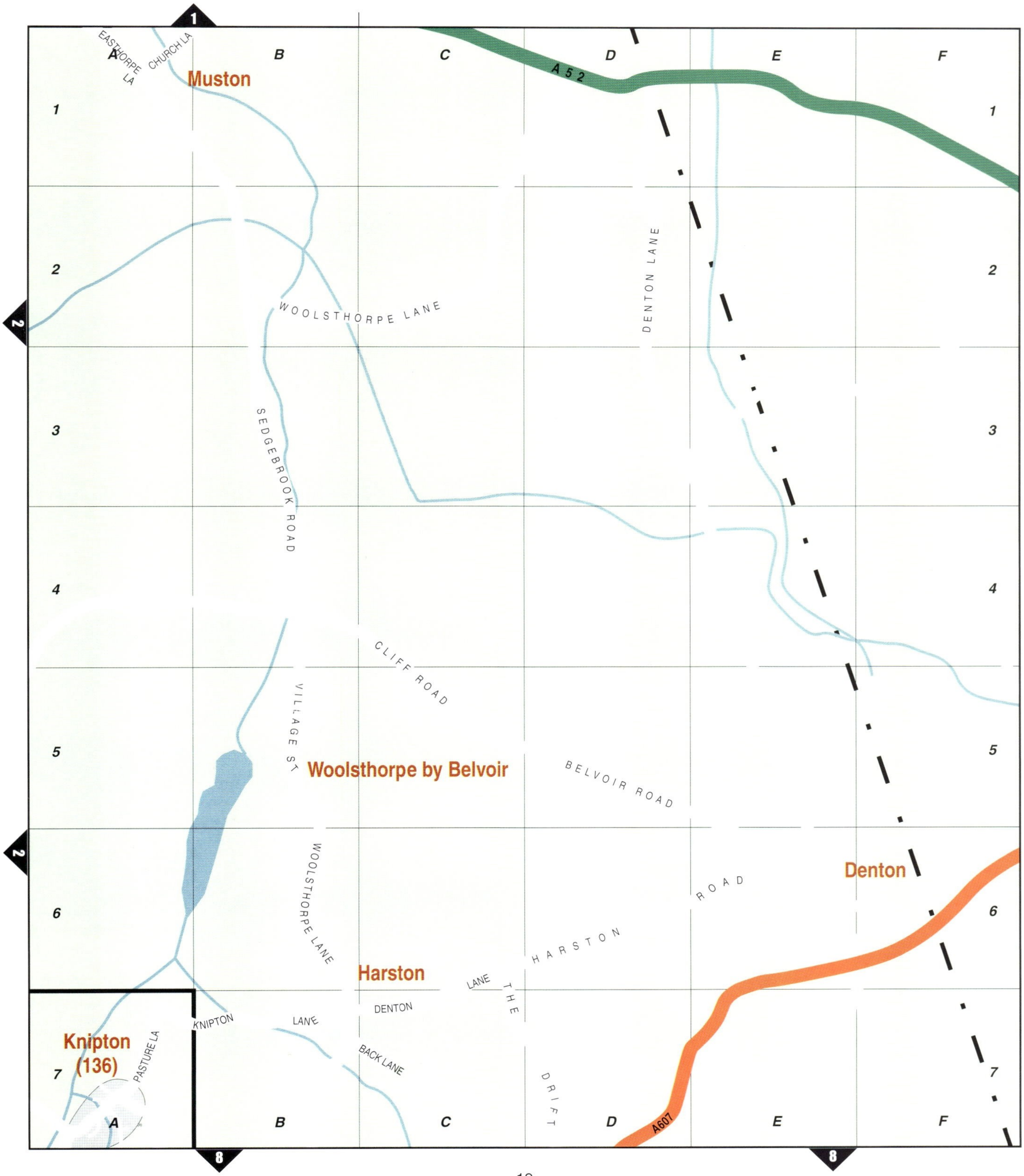

HILL TOP GARAGE (Thurcaston) Ltd

**Motor Engineers for any Make or Model
Service • Repairs and Complete Overhauls
Petrol, Oil, Tyres and Accessories**

LEICESTER ROAD • THURCASTON • LEICESTERSHIRE • LE7 7JH
Telephone: (0116) 2362773 (2 Lines) • Fax: (0116) 2362773

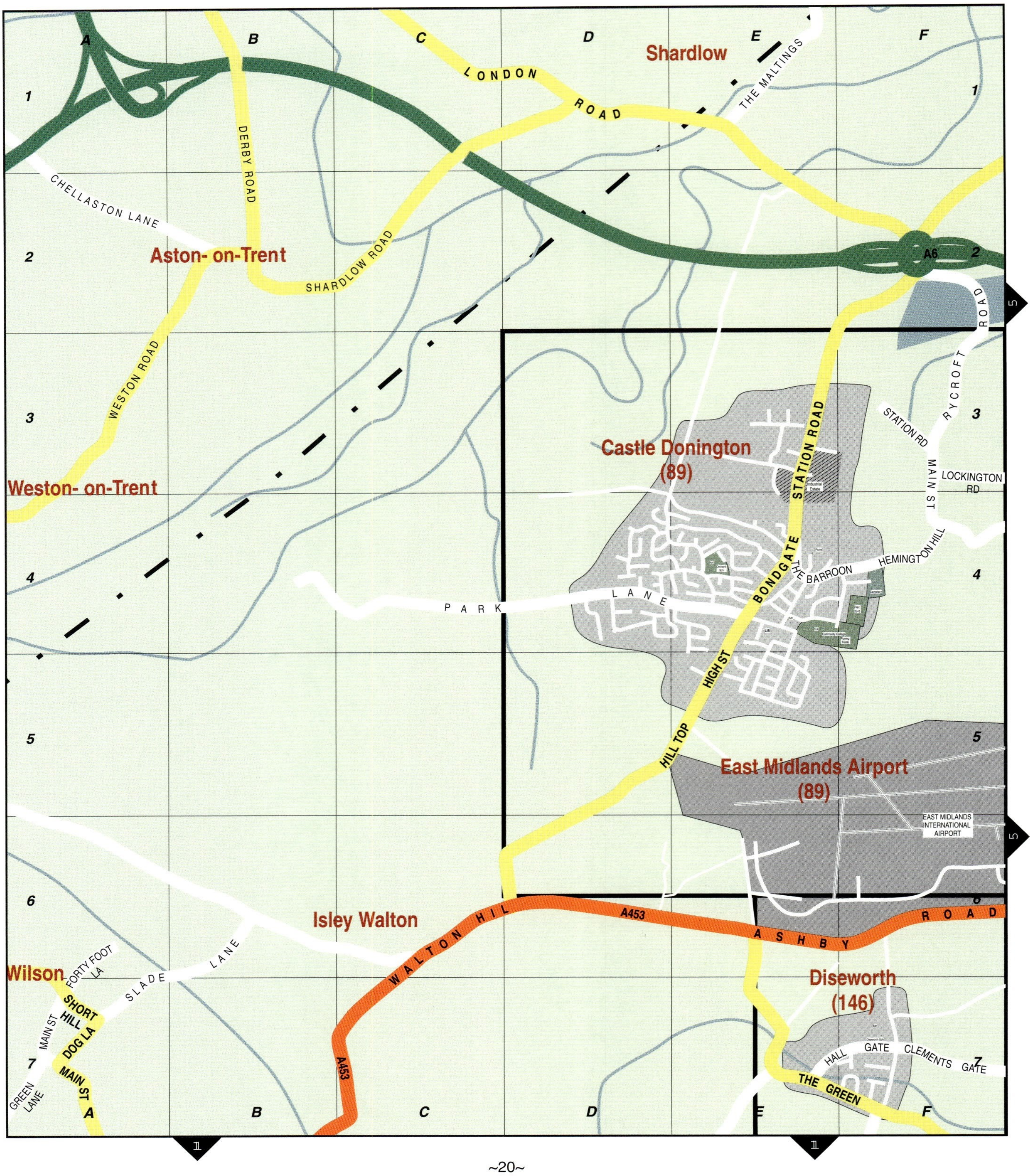

5

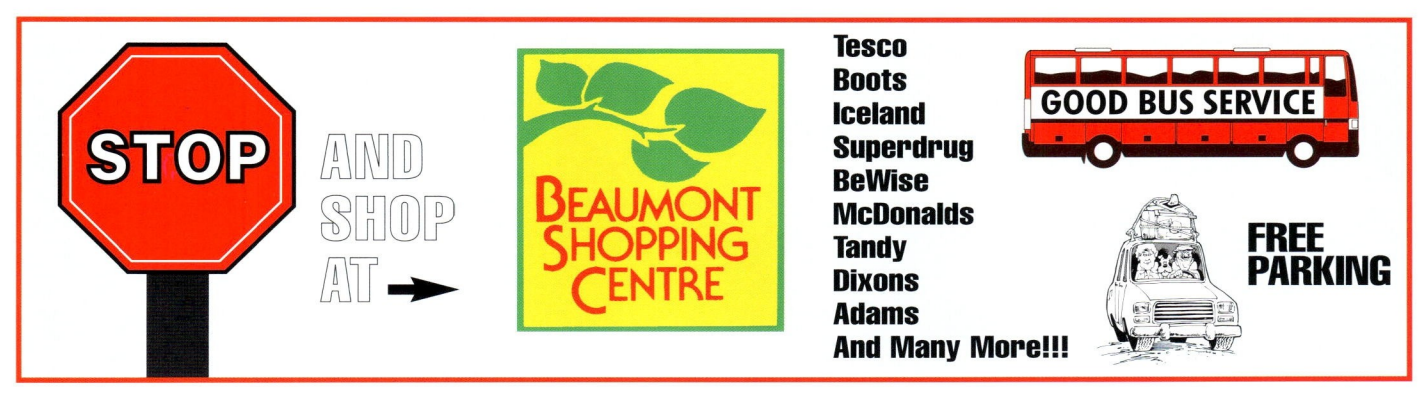

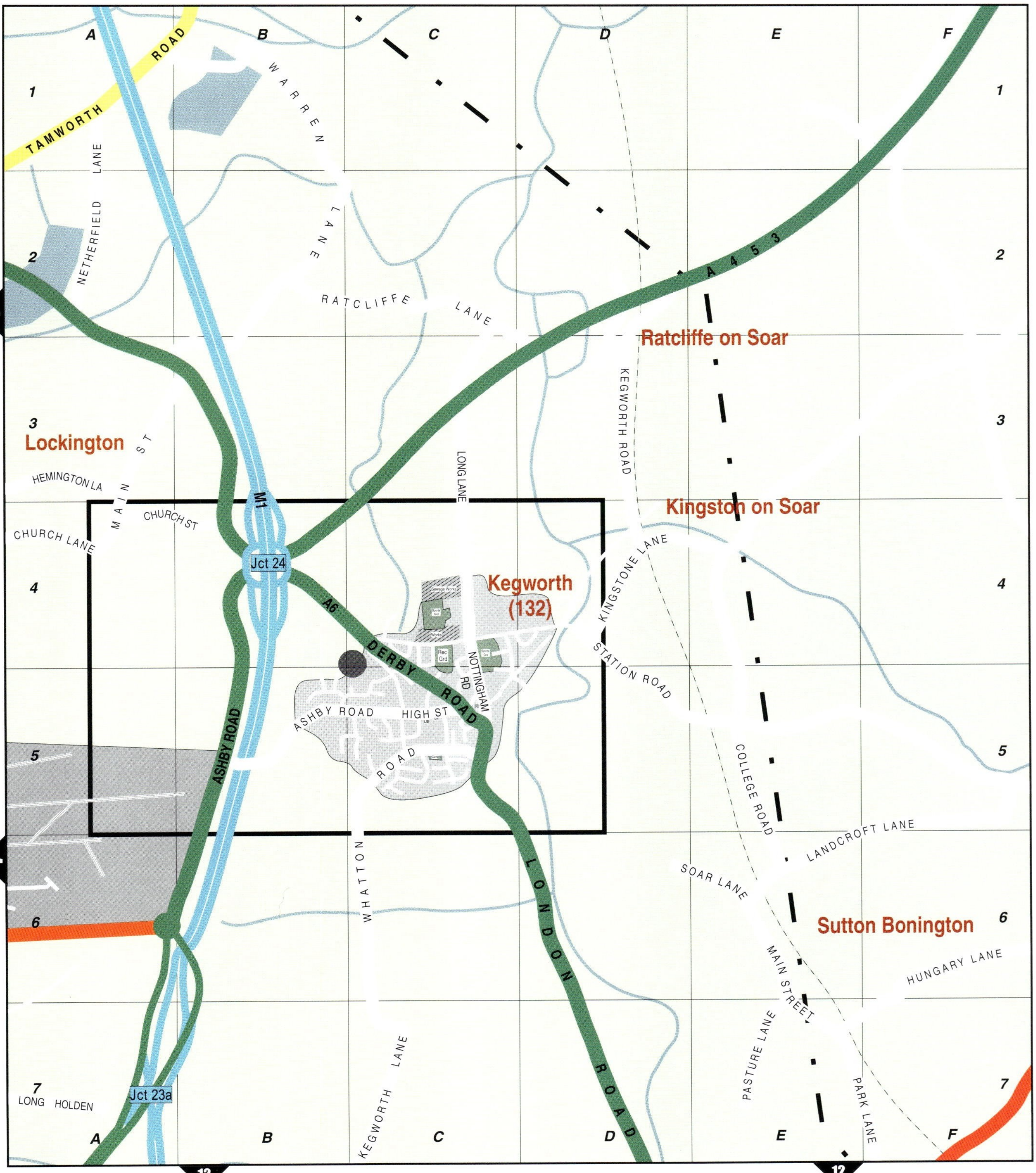
A
B
C
D
E
F
1
2
3
4
5
6
7
TAMWORTH ROAD
WARREN LANE
NETHERFIELD LANE
RATCLIFFE LANE
A453
Ratcliffe on Soar
Lockington
MAIN ST
HEMINGTON LA
CHURCH LANE
CHURCH ST
M1
Jct 24
LONG LANE
KEGWORTH ROAD
Kingston on Soar
KINGSTONE LANE
Kegworth
(132)
A6
DERBY ROAD
NOTTINGHAM RD
STATION ROAD
ASHBY ROAD
HIGH ST
ROAD
COLLEGE ROAD
LANDCROFT LANE
SOAR LANE
Sutton Bonington
HUNGARY LANE
MAIN STREET
WHATTON
LONDON ROAD
KEGWORTH LANE
PASTURE LANE
PARK LANE
Jct 23a
LONG HOLDEN
4
12

ASHFIELDS
RESTAURANT

Ashfields Restaurant is privately owned by Ashley and Paul Hadfield. It was bought in 1987 and has been transformed from a derelict public house known as the Old Bowling Green Inn into a popular eating establishment.

Ashfields is conveniently situated on the main A47 between Leicester and Hinckley in the village of Earl Shilton, with ample car parking opposite.

The Restaurant has recently been refurbished and now comprises two rooms, each holding between 40 and 50 guests, and a comfortable bar in which to have a pre-dinner drink or relax over coffee. There is also a Spanish Style terrace which is opened during the summer months.

Whether it is a business lunch, birthday celebration, anniversary dinner, small wedding or family Sunday lunch, we have a superb choice of menus to suit every occasion.

High Street Earl Shilton Leicestershire
Telephone 01455 841556 ~ Facsimile 01455 851167

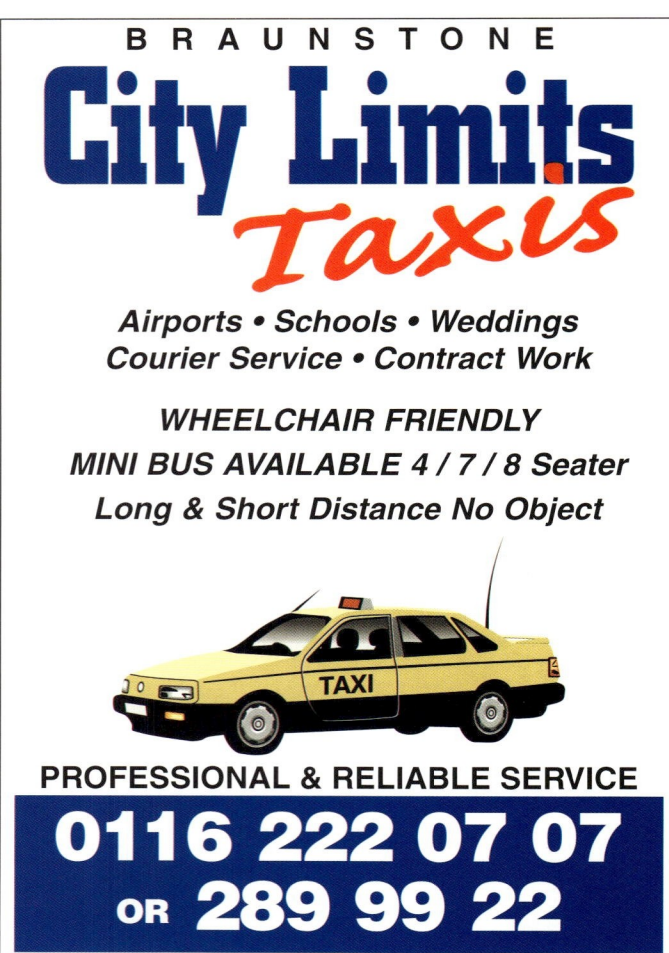

BRAUNSTONE
City Limits
Taxis

Airports • Schools • Weddings
Courier Service • Contract Work

WHEELCHAIR FRIENDLY
MINI BUS AVAILABLE 4 / 7 / 8 Seater
Long & Short Distance No Object

PROFESSIONAL & RELIABLE SERVICE
0116 222 07 07
OR 289 99 22

Kibworth Garden Centre
The Plantsman's Plant Centre

Growers of
Herbaceaous Perenials
Cottage Garden Plants
Shrubs

Seasonal stocks of
Bulbs
Bedding Plants
Seed Potatoes
Onion Sets

Hanging Baskets Filled
Finest Quality Compost
Sundry Gardening Supplies
Garden Gift Vouchers
Calor Gas Supplier

CALOR Gas
HTA

Open daily from 09:00am

Kibworth Garden Centre
FLECKNEY ROAD, KIBWORTH, LEICESTER LE8 0HJ
Tel: 0116 279 2754

STATUS SERVICES LIMITED

Bodyworks & Accident Repair Centre

Navigation Street, Off Belgrave Gate,
Leicester LE1 3UR

TEL: 0116 262 8800
FAX: 0116 251 9950

KIRBY GARAGE DOORS

Specialists in Installation, Remote Control, Repairs & Spares
Insurance Work Undertaken • All Work Guaranteed

FOR A FREE QUOTATION & EXPERT ADVICE CONTACT PAUL LAURENCE

0116 299 9145

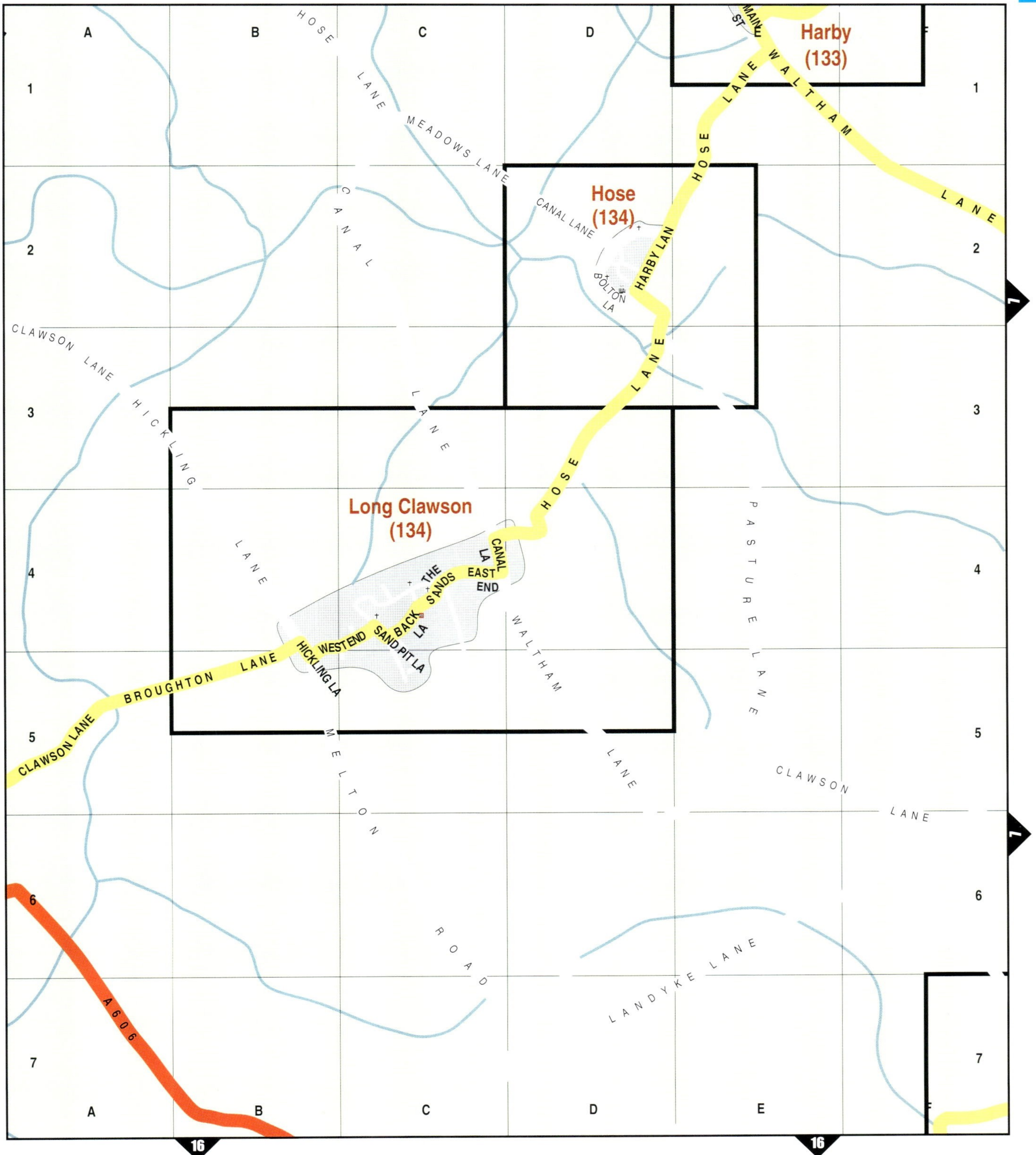

Premier Warehousing and Distribution Company Ltd.

Covered Storage • Open Storage • Fork Truck Facilities • Transport
Crane Facilities • Bulk Break and Distribution • Assembling Facilities

UNIT 9, THURMASTON INDUSTRIAL ESTATE, WREAKE ROAD, off MELTON ROAD, THURMASTON, LEICESTER LE4 8BX
TELEPHONE: 0116 269 8844 • FACSIMILE: 0116 269 8910 • Email: info@premierwarehousing.co.uk

Access Aerials and Satellites

Family Run Business • Established 10 Years • Member of the Confederation of Aerial Industries
AERIAL AND SATELLITE INSTALLATIONS REPAIRS AND REMOVALS • DIGITAL AGENT FOR SKY AND BRITISH BROADCASTING
Free Estimates • 2 Year Written Guarantee • Insurance Work Welcome • Excellent After Care Service
TEL: 0116 276 4665 • Mobile: 07790 415259 • Fax: 0116 210 1710
HEAD OFFICE, 98 WOODLAND ROAD, LEICESTER – ALL AREAS COVERED SAME PRICE IN ALL AREAS

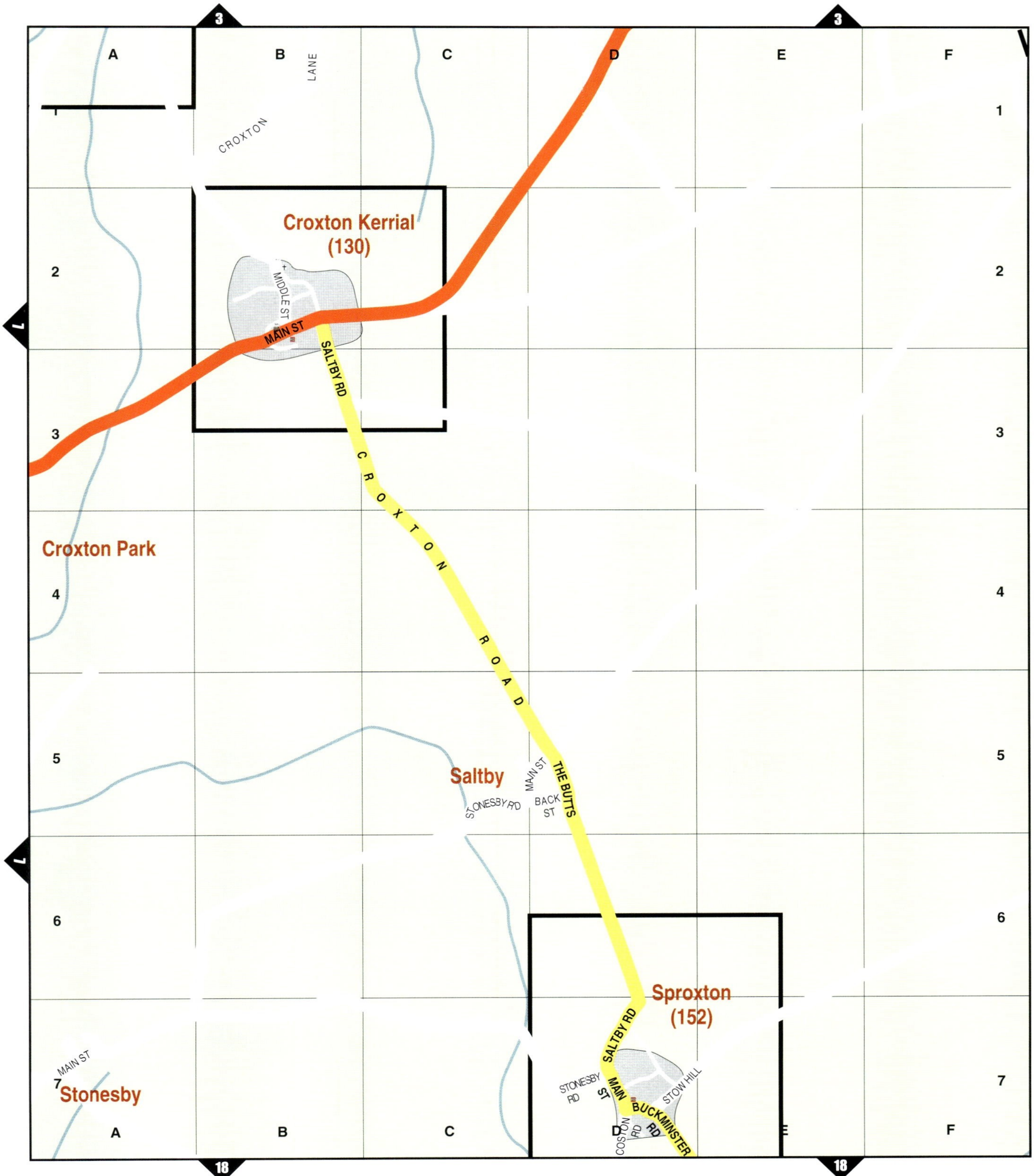

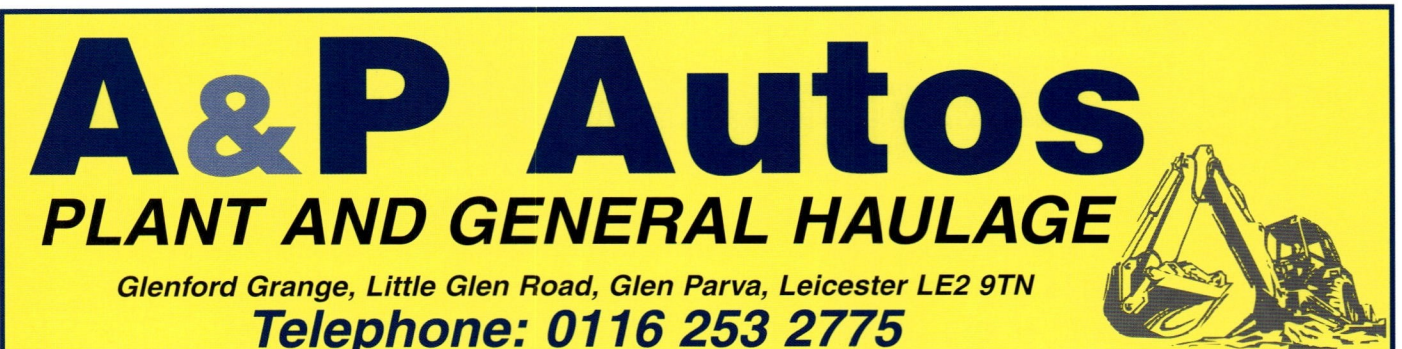

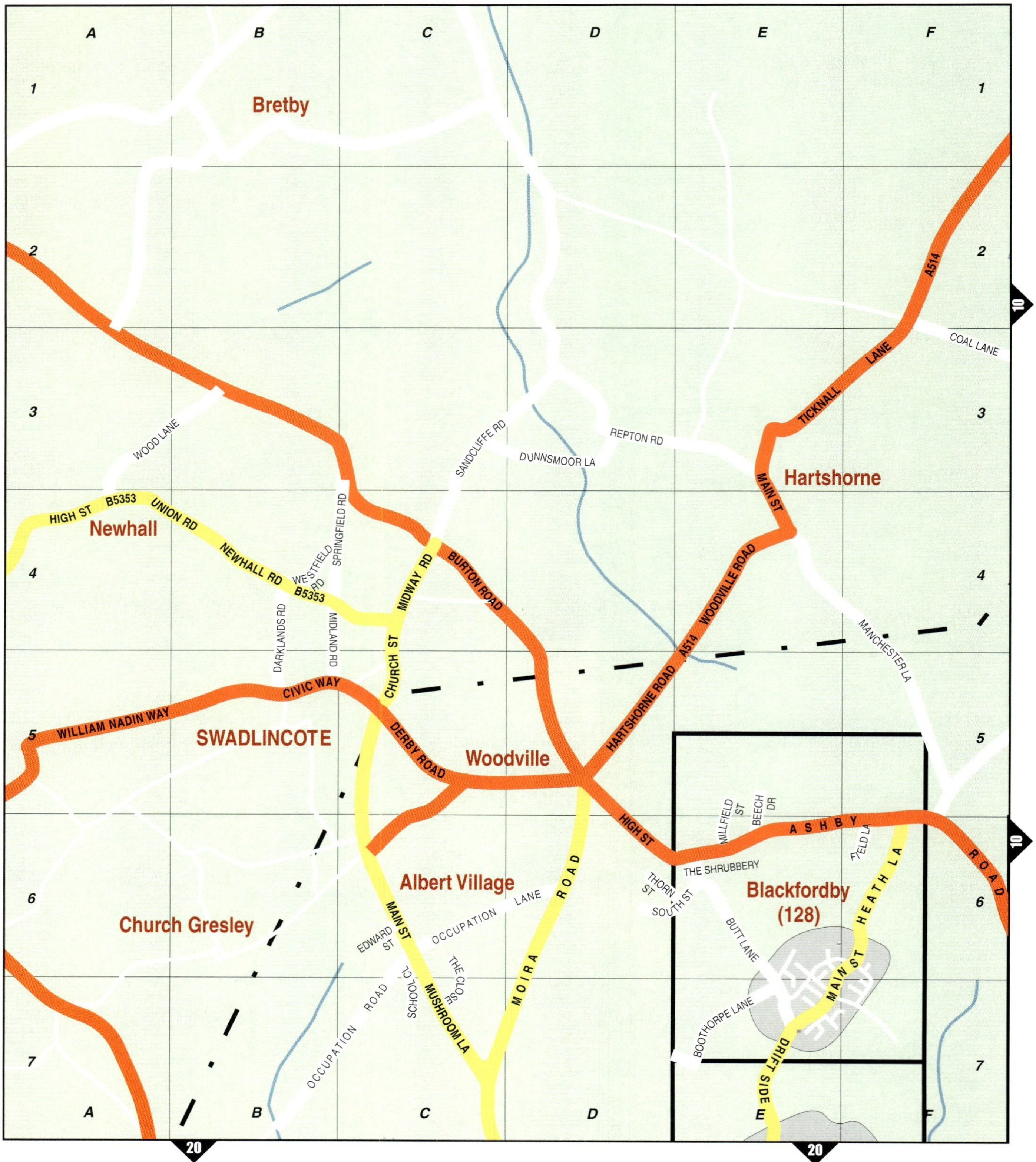

A
B
C
D
E
F
1
2
3
4
5
6
7
Bretby
10
A514
COAL LANE
TICKNALL LANE
WOOD LANE
SANDCLIFFE RD
DUNNSMOOR LA
REPTON RD
Hartshorne
MAIN ST
HIGH ST
B5353
UNION RD
Newhall
SPRINGFIELD RD
WESTFIELD RD
NEWHALL RD
B5353
MIDWAY RD
BURTON ROAD
WOODVILLE ROAD
DARKLANDS RD
MIDLAND RD
CHURCH ST
A514
MANCHESTER LA
HARTSHORNE ROAD
CIVIC WAY
WILLIAM NADIN WAY
SWADLINCOTE
DERBY ROAD
Woodville
HIGH ST
MILLFIELD ST
BEECH DR
ASHBY ROAD
FIELD LA
THE SHRUBBERY
Albert Village
MOIRA ROAD
LANE
OCCUPATION
THORN ST
SOUTH ST
Blackfordby
(128)
HEATH LA
Church Gresley
MAIN ST
EDWARD ST
BUTT LANE
SCHOOL CL
THE CLOSE
MUSHROOM LA
OCCUPATION ROAD
BOOTHORPE LANE
MAIN ST
DRIFT SIDE
20

**71 VAUGHAN WAY
LEICESTER LE1 4SG**

**Telephone: 0116 251 4343
Fax: 0116 251 8881**

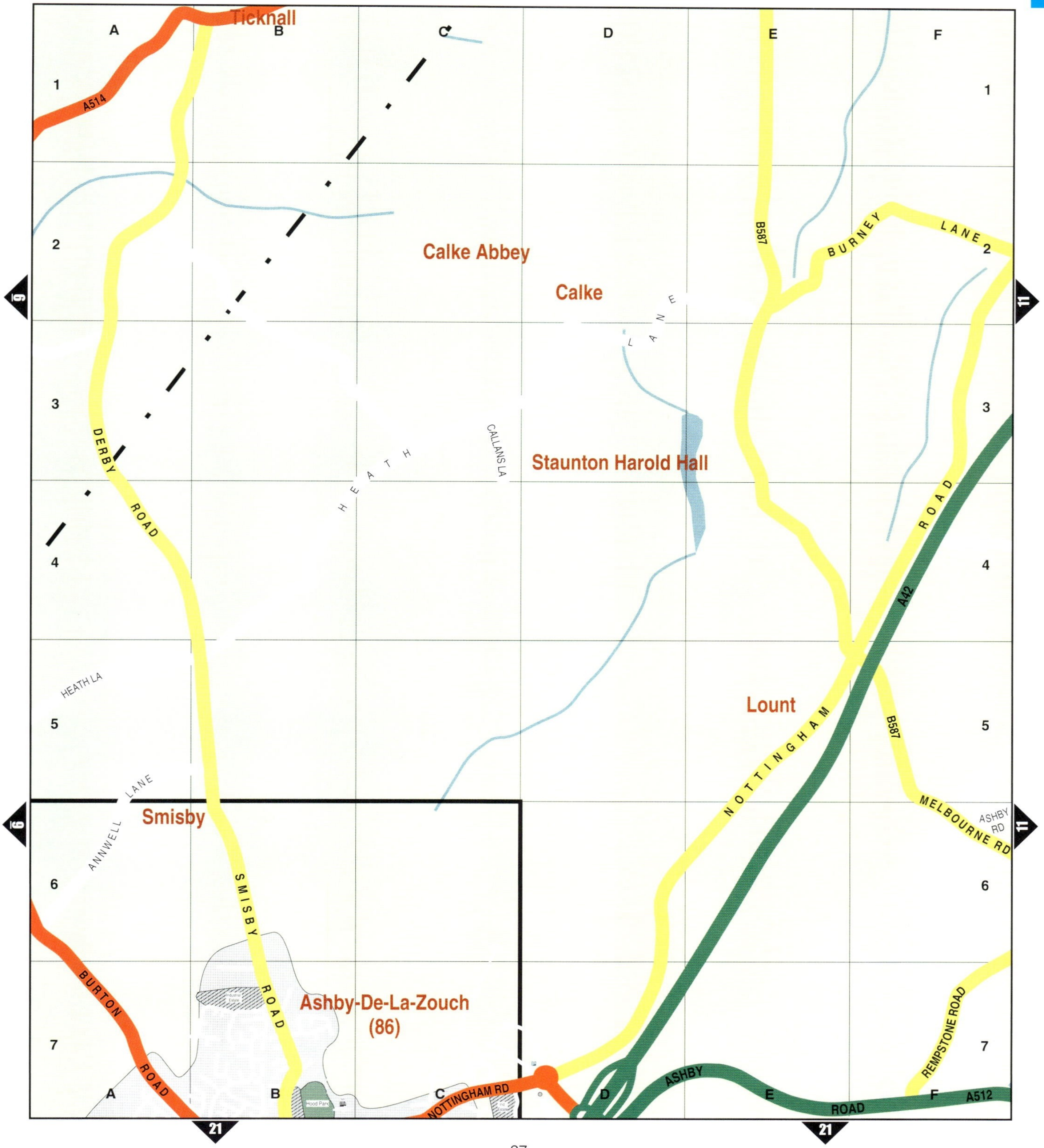

Ken Bailey at Wistow
HOUSE AND GARDEN PLANT CENTRE

Wistow Rural Centre
Kibworth Road
Wistow
Leicester
LE8 0QF

T. 0116 259 2009

- Garden Sundries • Compost • Garden Ornaments
- Shrubs • House Plants • Terracotta & Stone Pots
- Garden Sheds • Summer Houses • Mixed Aggregates

Visit our branch at:

Craighall Nurseries
Craighill Road
Knighton
Leicester
LE2 3WQ

T. 0116 270 7065

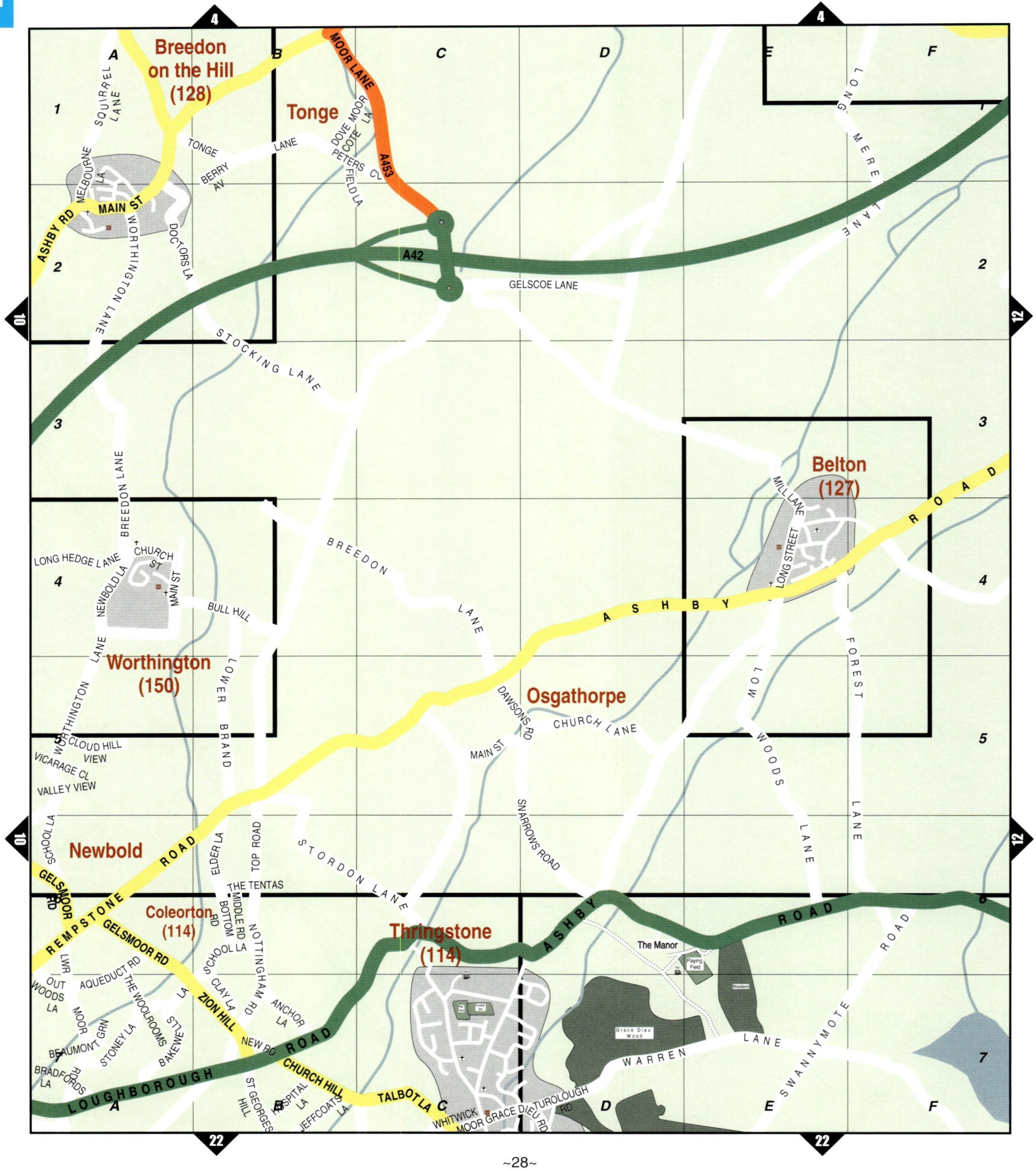

Simply Print

Telephone: (01509) 213821
Fax: (01509) 230277

Quality Printing Service at Competitive Prices

Simply Print Limited, Unit F,
Little Moor Lane, Loughborough,
Leicestershire LE11 1SF

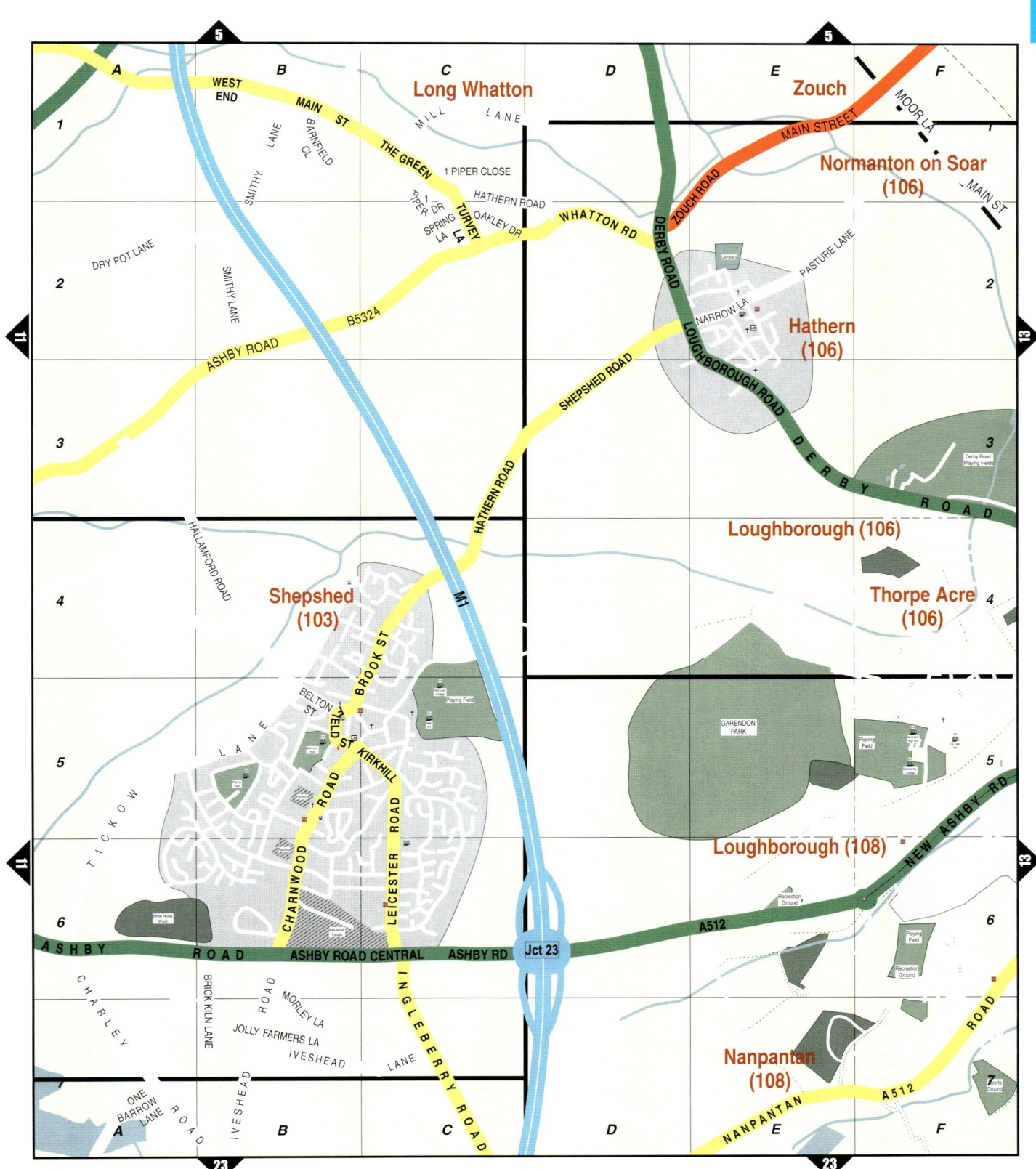

Forest Road
Dental Practice

Patrick Bottom BDS (Sheff) DGDP (UK)
Andrew Slevin BDS (U Manch)

16 Forest Road, Loughborough, Leics LE11 3NP
Telephone: (01509) 233323

Friendly family practice

Strong emphasis on education in preventative oral health care

State of the art dental treatment provided

Call to find out more or simply visit
We *are here to help.*

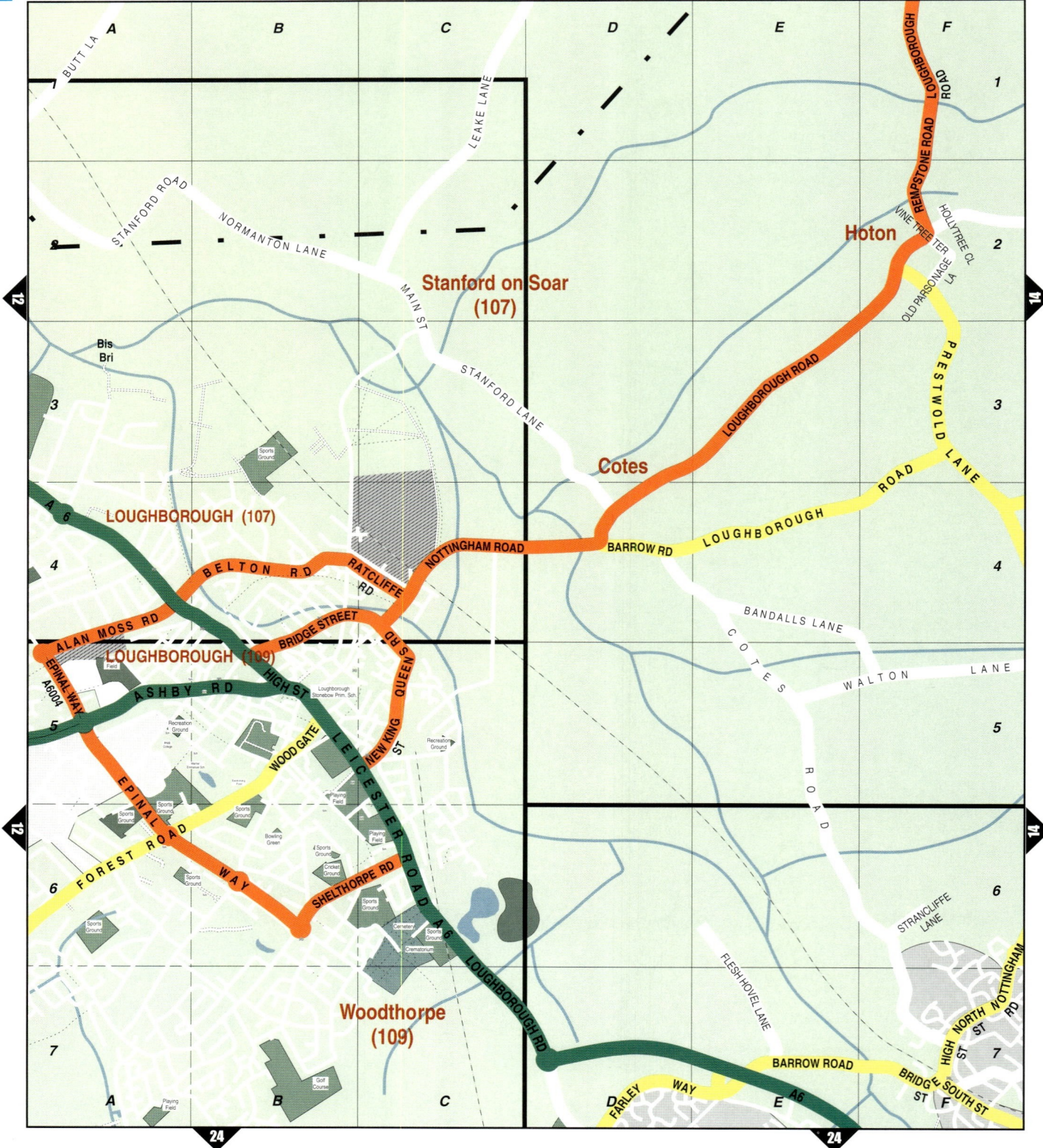

MEMBER OF THE BRITISH STANDARDS INSTITUTE & THE INSTITUTE OF ASPHALT TECHNOLOGY

49 Laburnum Road, Garden City Estate,
Humberstone, Leicester LE5 1FS
Telephone: 0116 276 5029   Fax: 0116 2201895
Mobile: 07785 953667   Email: jag.technical@ntlworld

Coating Plant & Site Technical Personnel
Catering for staff shortages, contractual requirements or lacking experience

Coated Pavement Consultancy
To advise and specify materials and construction for new works or remedials

Pavement Failure Investigations
Road or driveway in contention, mediation between client and supplier or contractor

Quality Consultancy
To oversee workmanship & material quality

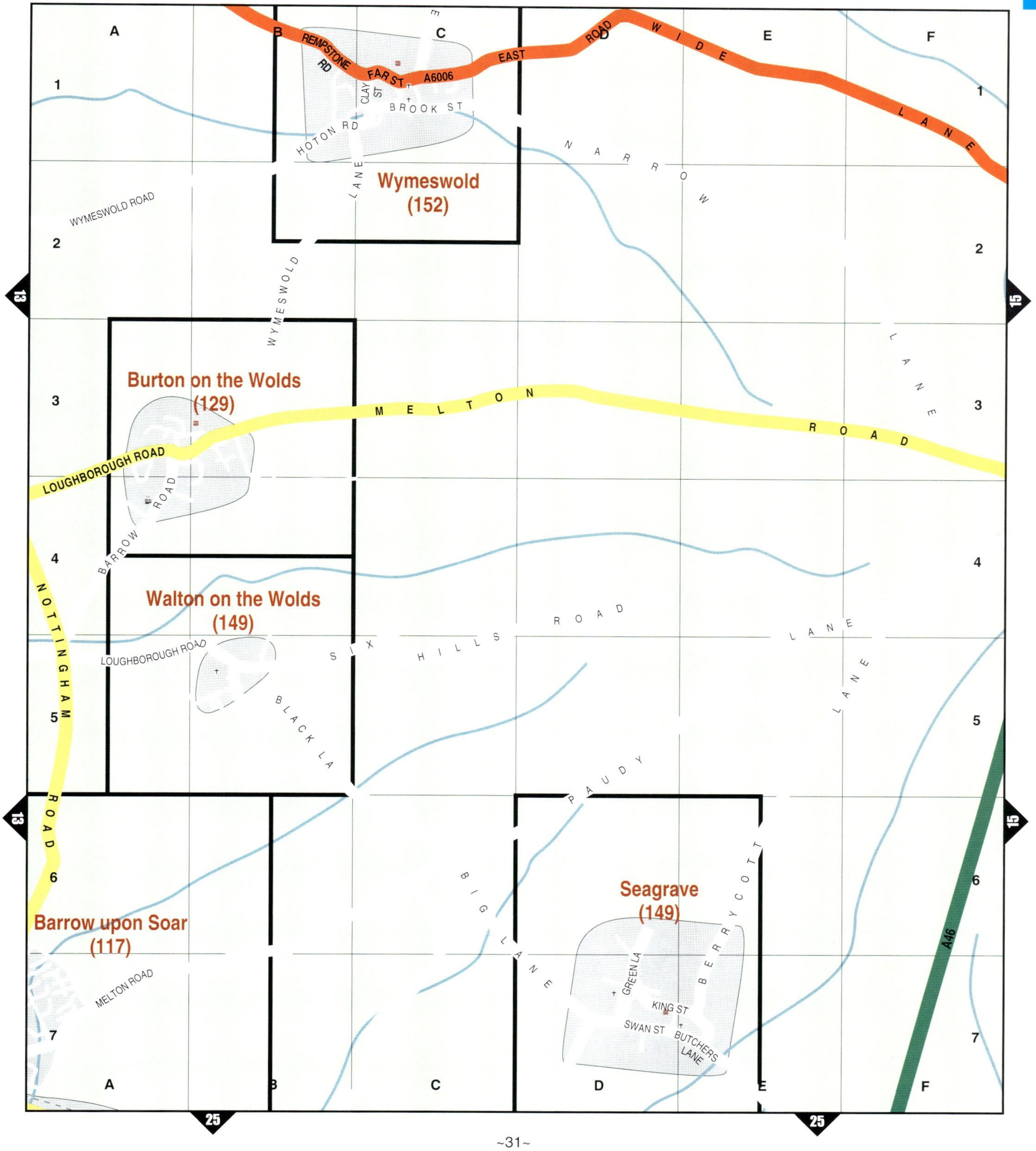

A
B
C
D
E
F
1
2
3
4
5
6
7
14
16
26
HADES LANE
A46
PADDYS LANE
GIBSONS LANE
MAIN RD
WOOD HILL
LAWN LANE
Old Dalby (147)
STATION LA
SIX HILLS LANE
PERKINS LANE
Grimston
MAIN ST
SAXELBYE LA
SHOBY LA
OSTLER LA
A6006
SIX HILLS ROAD
Ragdale
LOUGHBOROUGH ROAD
HOBY ROAD
Frisby on the Wreake (131)
RAGDALE ROAD
ASFORDBY ROAD
WASHSTONES LA
WATER LANE
GREAT LA
Hoby
CHAPEL LA
REGENT RD
CHURCH LA
LOWER LA
HOLMFIELD CL
ROTHERBY LANE
OLD GATE ROAD

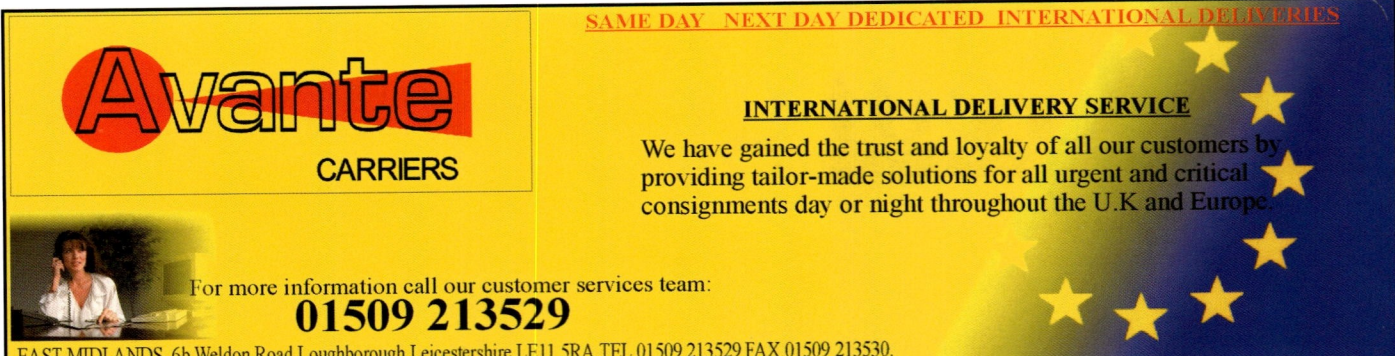

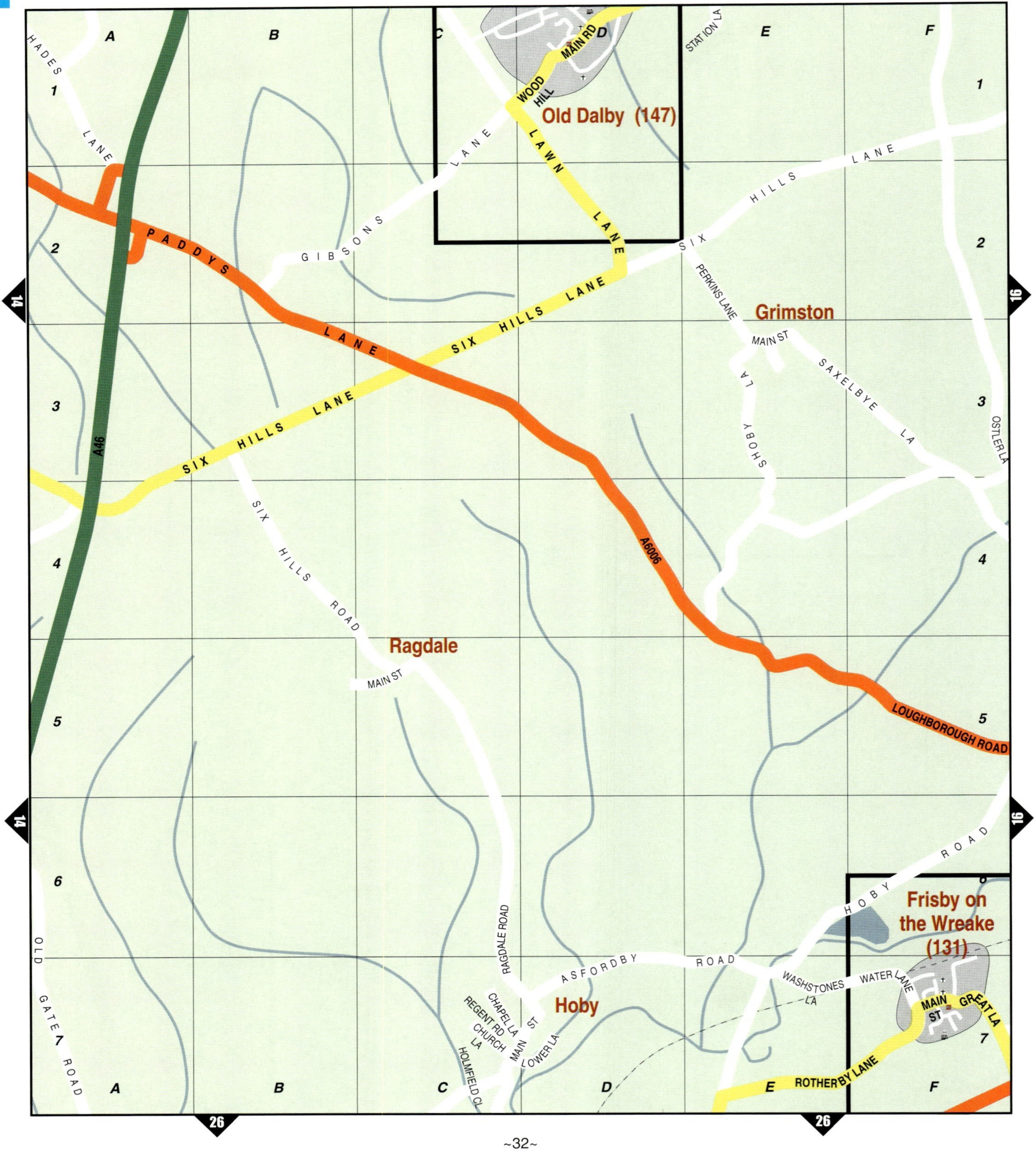

Freedom Vending Services
Excellence in Refurbishment
Telephone: 01664 410480

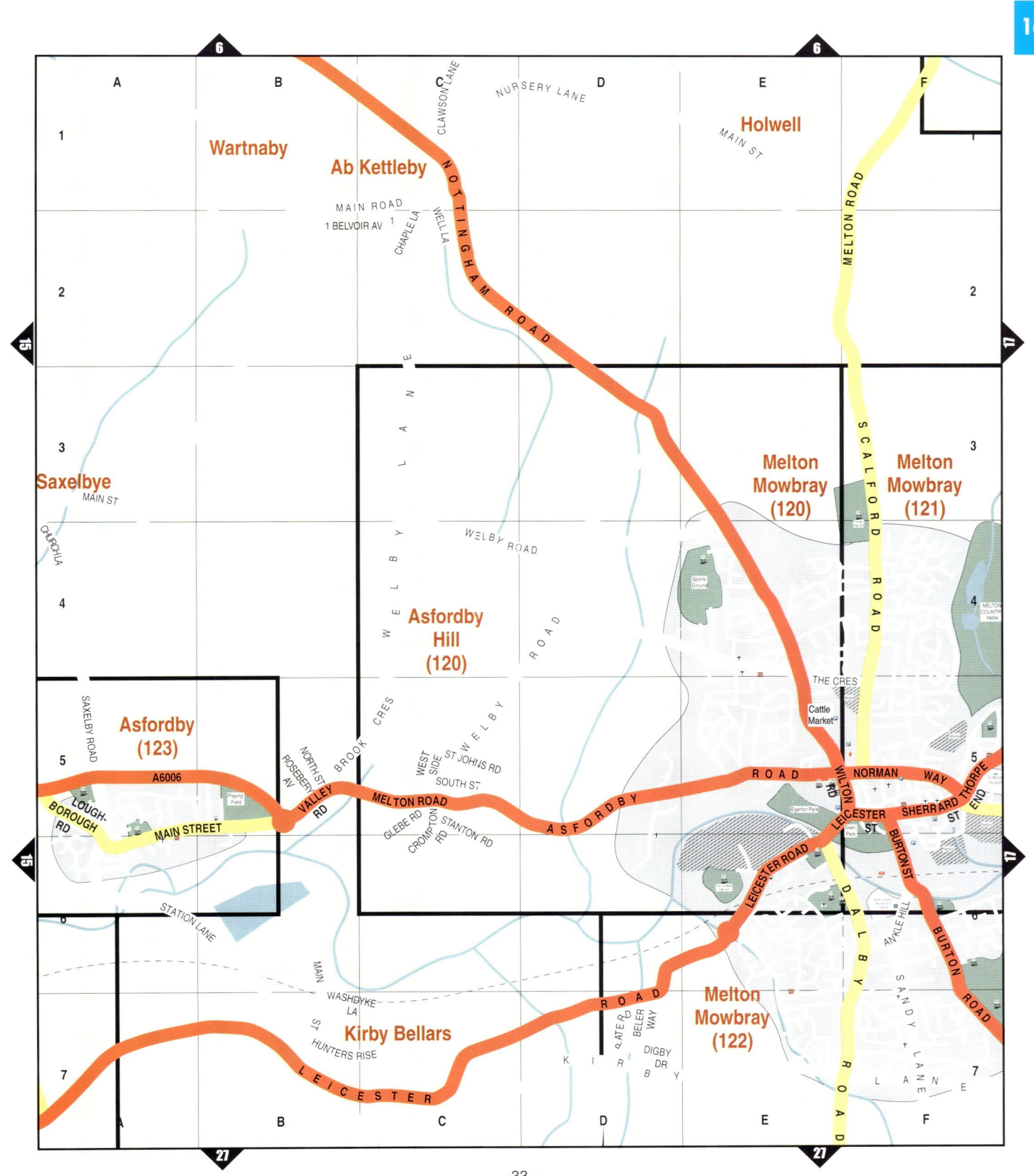

Snowflake Laundry

FAMILY FIRM ESTABLISHED IN 1918

For all your Laundry requirements
Domestic Household Laundry ~ Iron Only Service
Hotel & Restaurant Linen
Free Collection & Delivery in many areas

FOR FURTHER INFORMATION CONTACT 01664 562046

17-19 HUDSON ROAD, MELTON MOWBRAY, LEICESTERSHIRE LE13 1BS

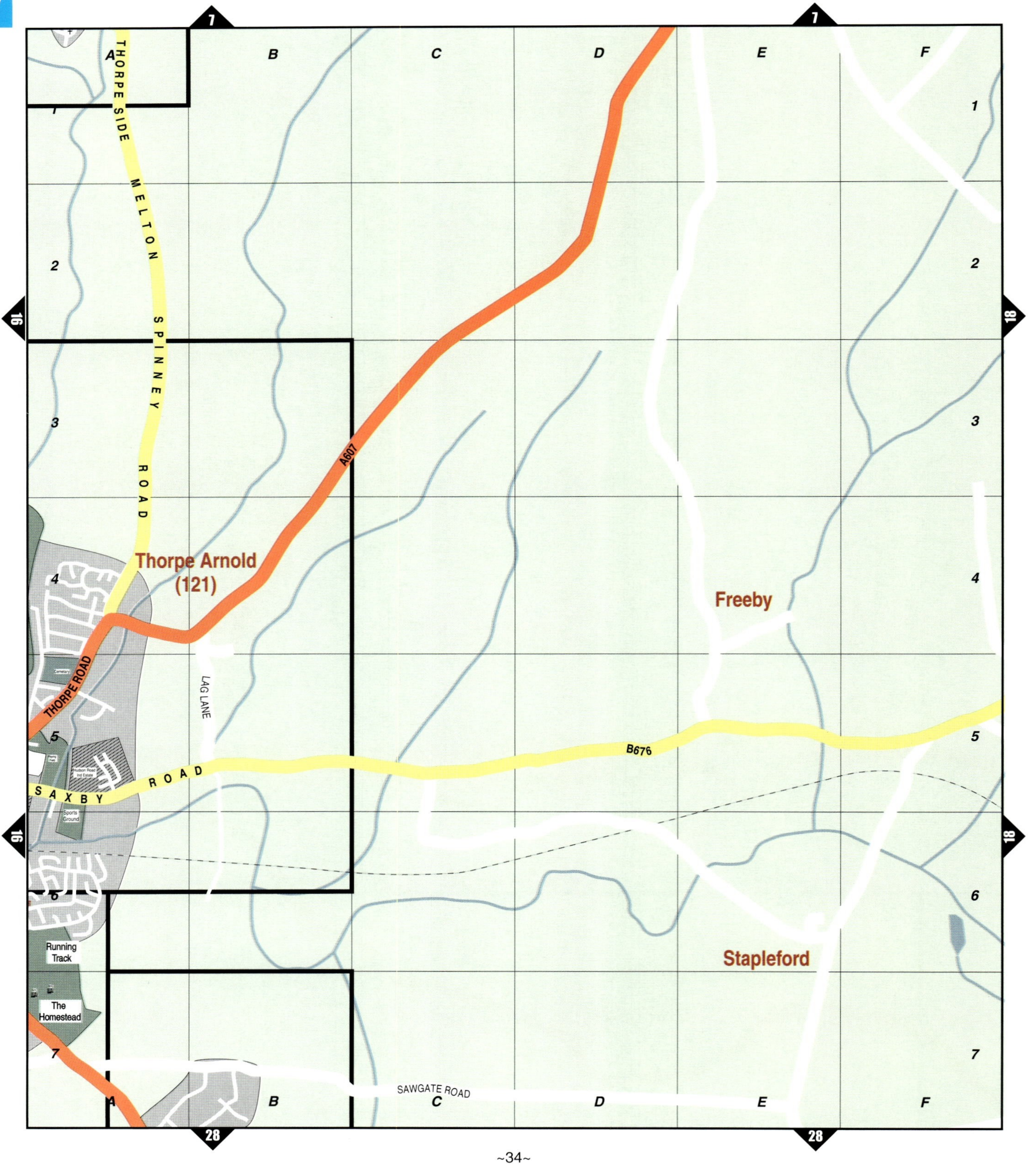

Thorpe Arnold (121)

Freeby

Stapleford

THORPE SIDE · MELTON SPINNEY ROAD · A607 · THORPE ROAD · LAG LANE · SAXBY ROAD · B676 · Running Track · The Homestead · Sawgate Road

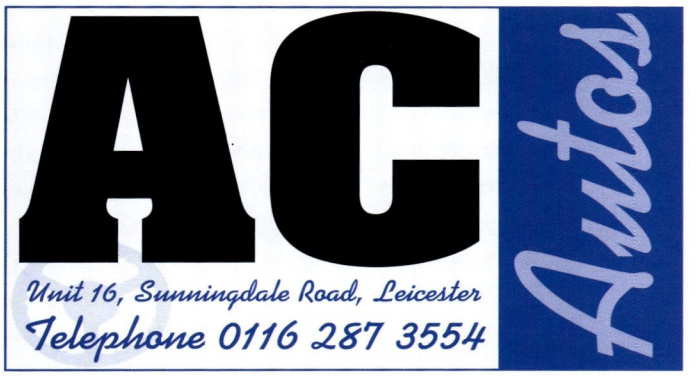

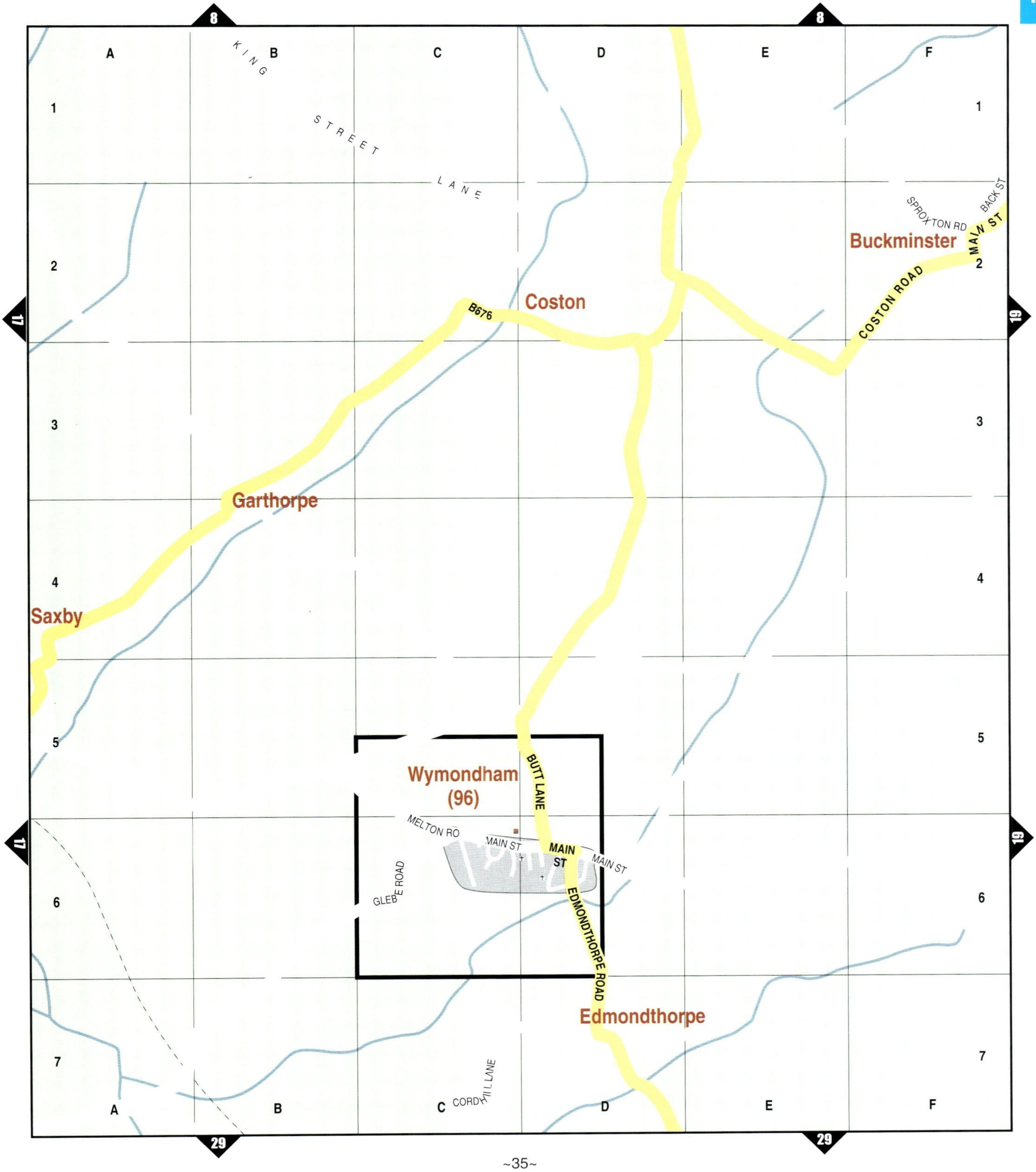
8
A
B
C
D
E
F
KING STREET LANE
1
2
3
4
5
6
7
SPROXTON RD
BACK ST
MAIN ST
Buckminster
COSTON ROAD
B676
Coston
Garthorpe
Saxby
Wymondham
(96)
BUTT LANE
MELTON RD
MAIN ST
MAIN
ST
MAIN ST
GLEBE ROAD
EDMONDTHORPE ROAD
Edmondthorpe
17
19
29

Stephen Howgill Design

Industrial Design
&
Software Development

123 Leicester Road, Thurcaston, Leicester LE7 7JL
Tel: 0116 2368120

Leicester Book Clearance

20 MARKET STREET • LEICESTER • LE1 6DN
TEL: 0116 285 6655

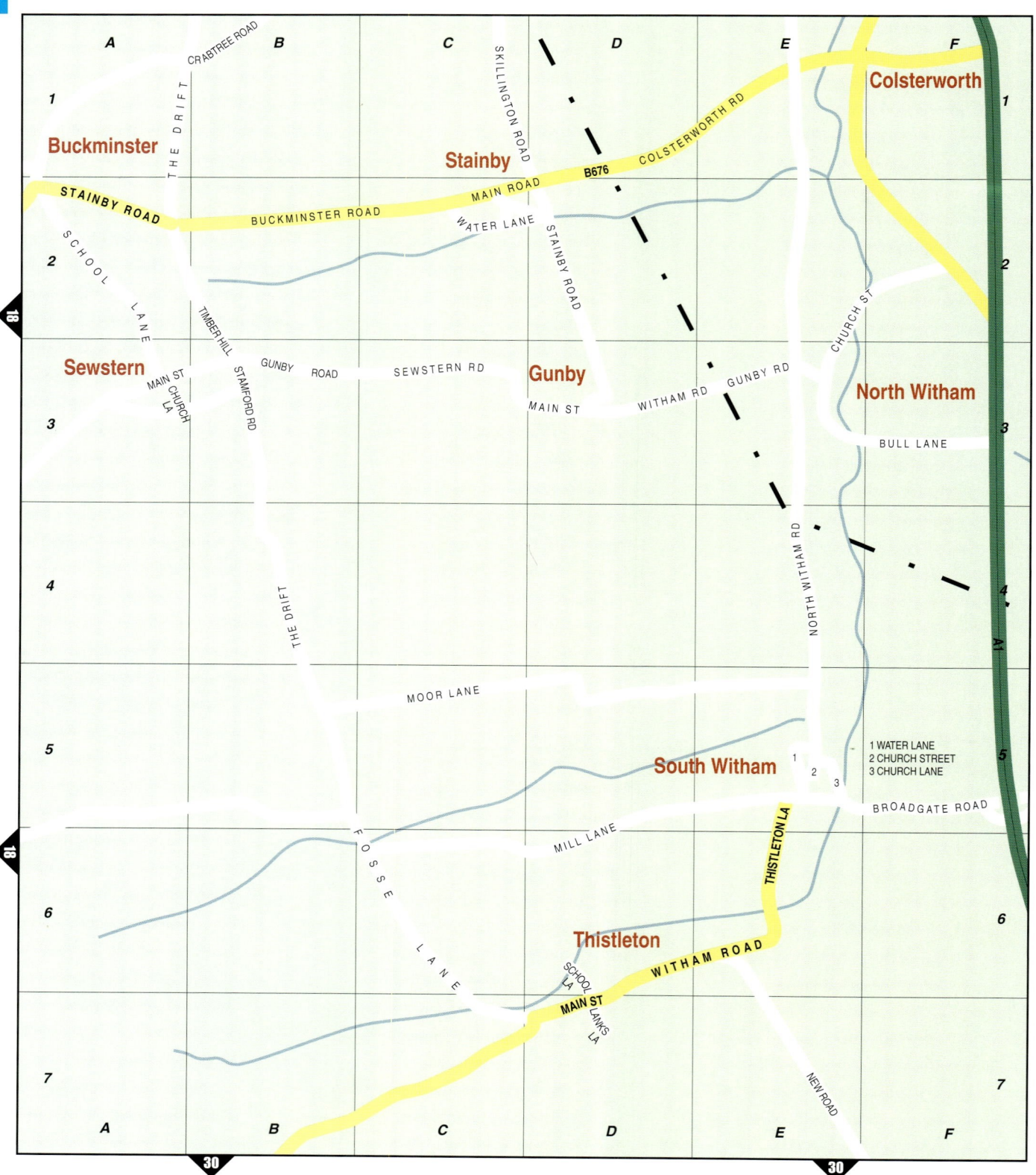

QUALITY MANAGEMENT & TECHNICAL SERVICES LTD

With over thirty years industrial experience offering Professional Consultancy and Contracting Services at competitive rates, including

Installation of QMS's for ISO 9001 / 2 registration
Writing of Quality Procedures
Project Quality Engineering
Internal Auditing and Training
Supplier Assessments and Surveillance
Control Systems Project Management
Quality Improvement Group Co-ordination
Writing and installation of H & S and
Product Safety procedures

TELEPHONE/FAX: 0116 271 5269

Mobile: 07885 375 986
Website: www.qmats.co.uk

JOE SHRIGLEY C.Eng MIEE MIQA AIMC Registered Lead Assessor
24 ASH TREE ROAD, OADBY, LEICESTER LE2 5YA

FOSSE BRIDGE MOTORS

- Supplier of Quality Used Cars
- Licensed Credit Brokers
- Service
- Bodywork
- Resprays
- Spares

Tel: (0116) 255 3174

143 Fosse Road South, Leicester LE3 0FW

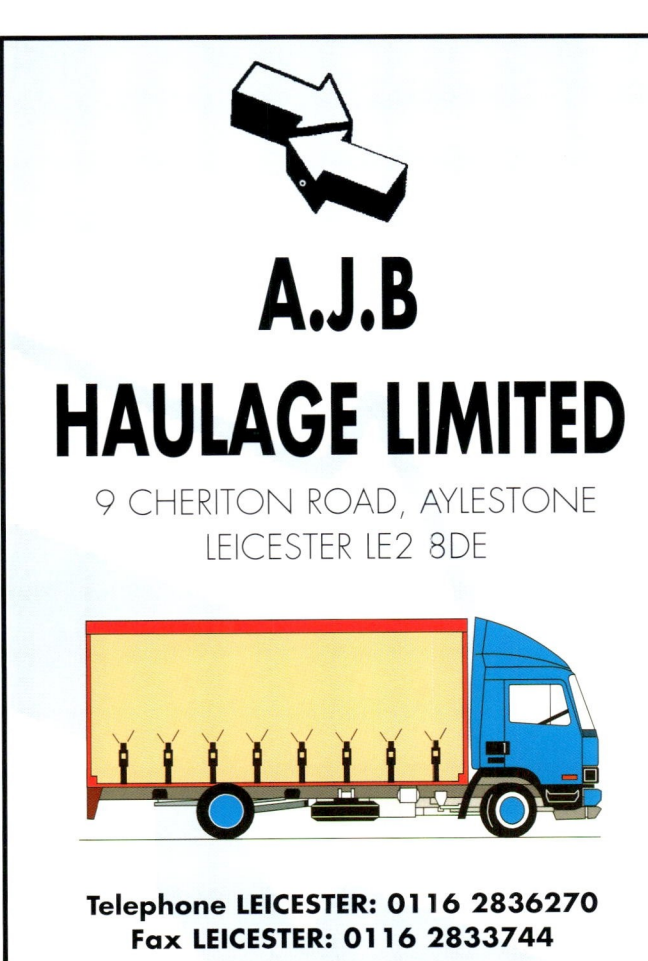

A.J.B HAULAGE LIMITED

9 CHERITON ROAD, AYLESTONE
LEICESTER LE2 8DE

Telephone LEICESTER: 0116 2836270
Fax LEICESTER: 0116 2833744

first images photography

- Specialists in Wedding photography Videography ~ Studio ~ Commercial
- Make Over photography
- Full range of framing services available
- Extensive range of Albums
- Instant Passport photographs
- Tape transfer Cine-Video
- American NTS - English PAL & vice versa
- Dubbing, titling and special effects on your home videos
- Mass copying of video tapes
- Computer manipulation i.e. black & white to colour, add photos to prints.
- Restore old photographs
- Tuitions also available

150 Harrison Road, Leicester LE4 6JT

Tel/Fax: 0116 224 0424
Mobile: 07973 663 393

Brookside
Service Station

Nottingham Road, Melton Mowbray
Leicester LE13 0NR

**Telephone:
01664 562527**

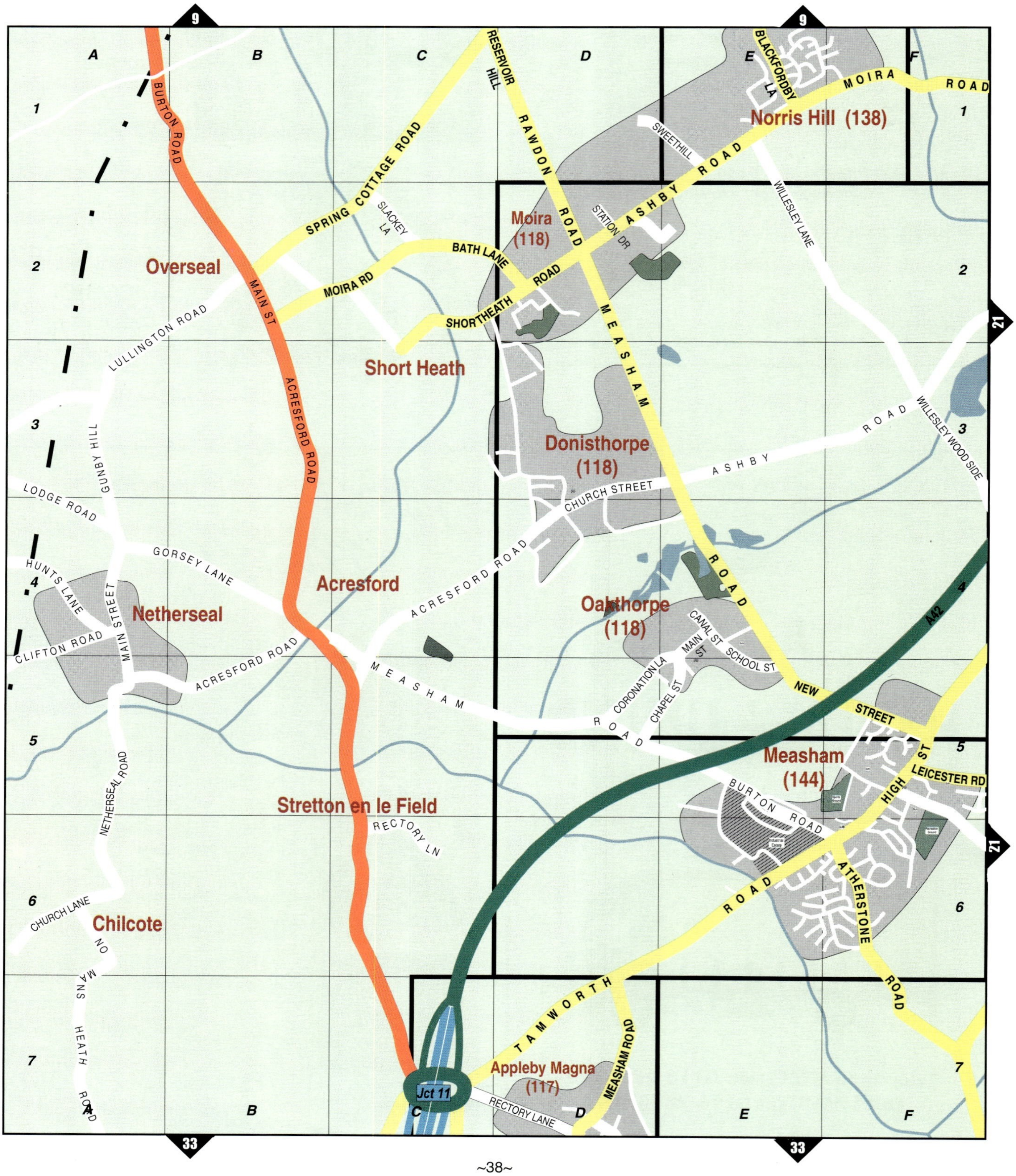

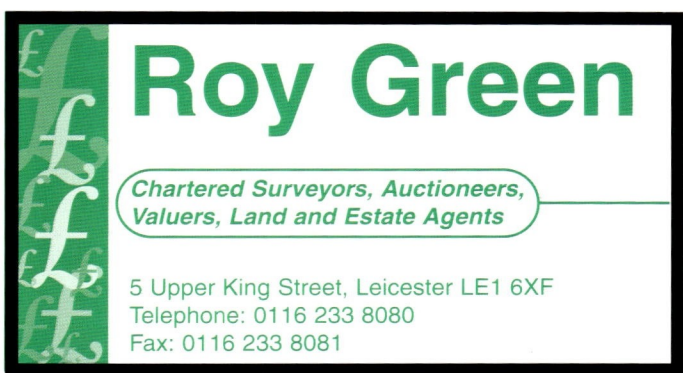

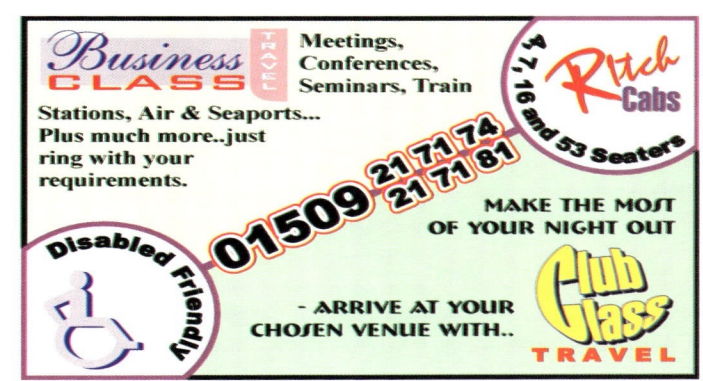

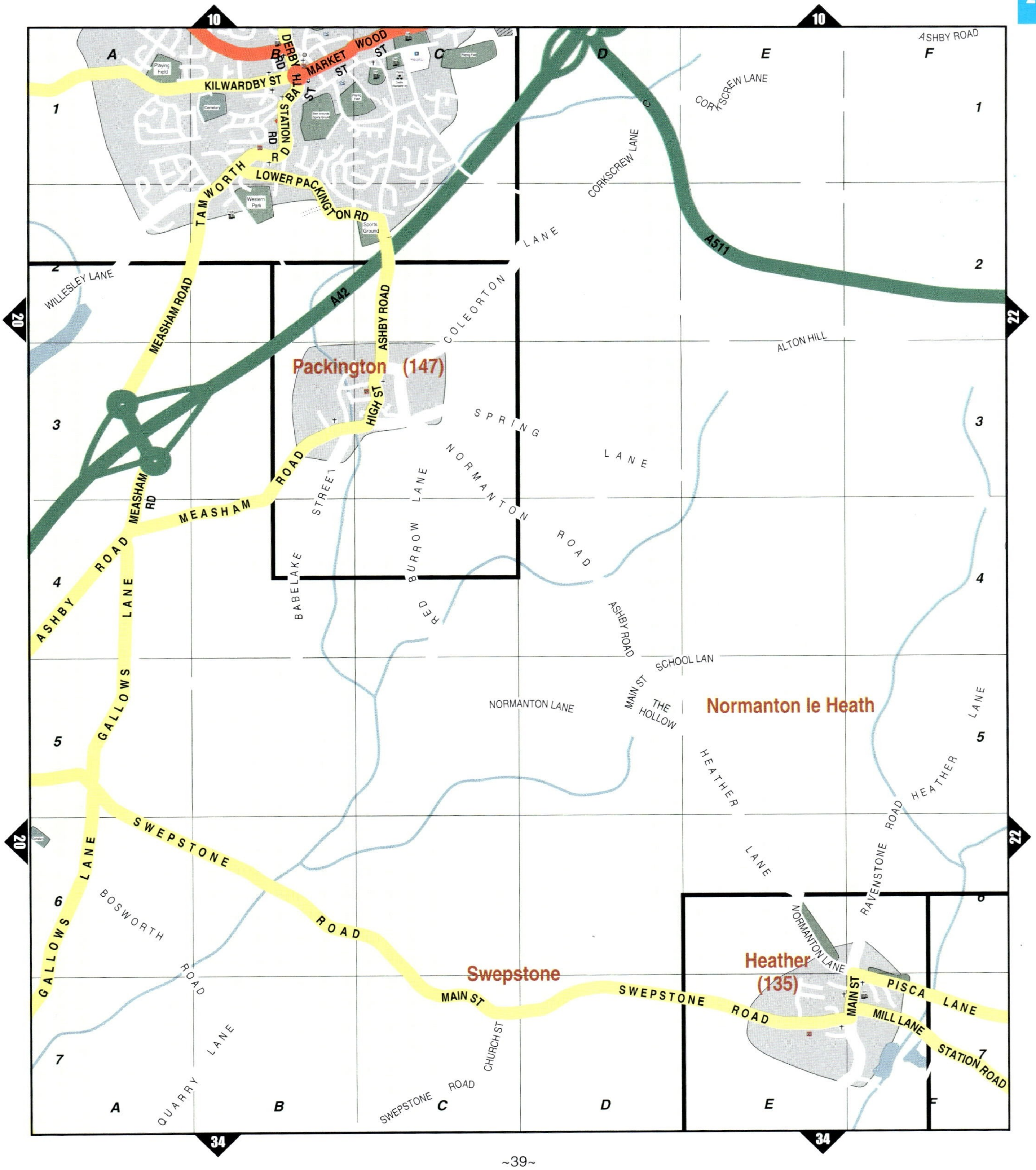

10
A
B
C
D
E
F
1
2
3
4
5
6
7
20
22
34
KILWARDBY ST
DERBY RD
MARKET ST
WOOD ST
BATH ST
STATION RD
LOWER PACKINGTON RD
TAMWORTH RD
WILLESLEY LANE
MEASHAM ROAD
A42
ASHBY ROAD
Packington (147)
HIGH ST
COLEORTON LANE
CORKSCREW LANE
ASHBY ROAD
A511
ALTON HILL
SPRING LANE
NORMANTON ROAD
MEASHAM RD
MEASHAM ROAD
ASHBY ROAD
STREET
BABELAKE
BURROW LANE
RED
ASHBY ROAD
SCHOOL LAN
MAIN ST
THE HOLLOW
NORMANTON LANE
Normanton le Heath
GALLOWS LANE
HEATHER LANE
HEATHER ROAD
RAVENSTONE
SWEPSTONE ROAD
BOSWORTH ROAD
Swepstone
MAIN ST
SWEPSTONE ROAD
CHURCH ST
QUARRY LANE
Heather (135)
NORMANTON LANE
MAIN ST
PISCA LANE
MILL LANE
STATION ROAD

DREW-EDWARDS KEENE
Chartered Architects and Conservation Consultants

Specialists in conservative repair to Listed and Historic Buildings, Drew-Edwards Keene have extensive experience of work on churches in the Diocese of Leicester, historic buildings, refurbishment and new build projects including Housing, Commercial, Education and Leisure facilities.

150 Upper New Walk
Leicester, LE1 7QA
Tel: 0116 254 5015
Fax: 0116 254 8019
E-mail: RJWoodDEK@aol.com

Contact: Richard J Wood, BSc(Hons), B Arch(Hons), RIBA
(Surveyor of the Fabric to Leicester Cathedral)

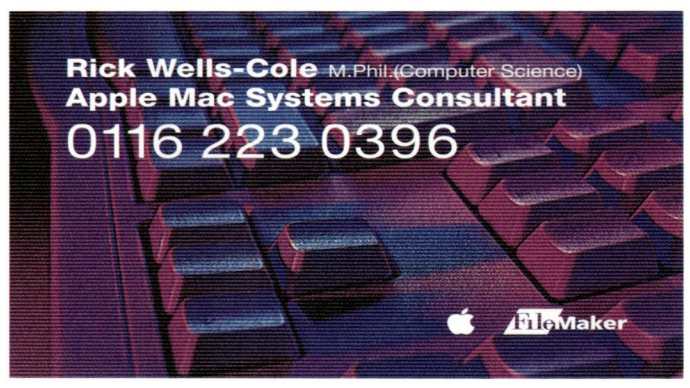

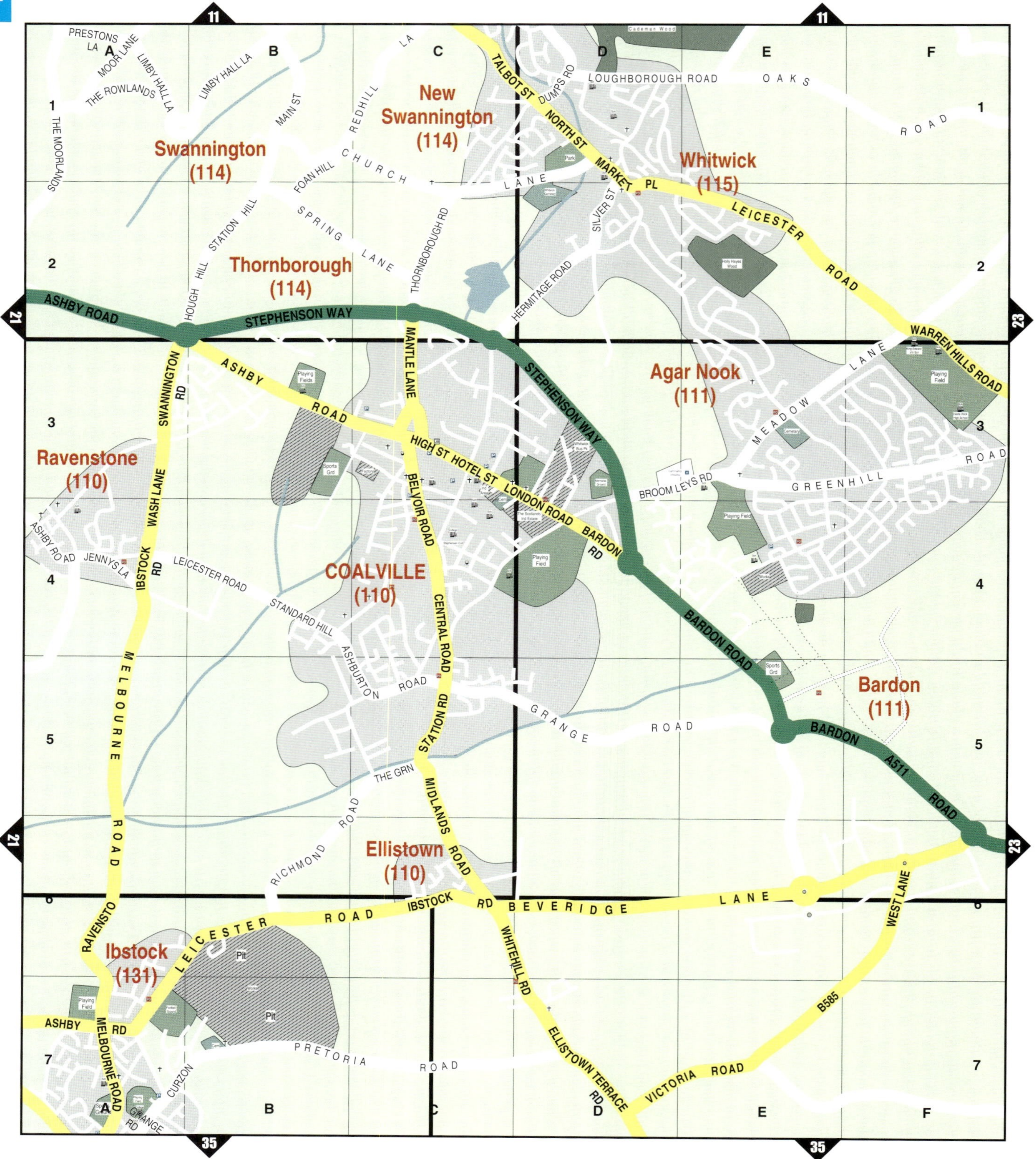

Rick Wells-Cole M.Phil.(Computer Science)
Apple Mac Systems Consultant
0116 223 0396

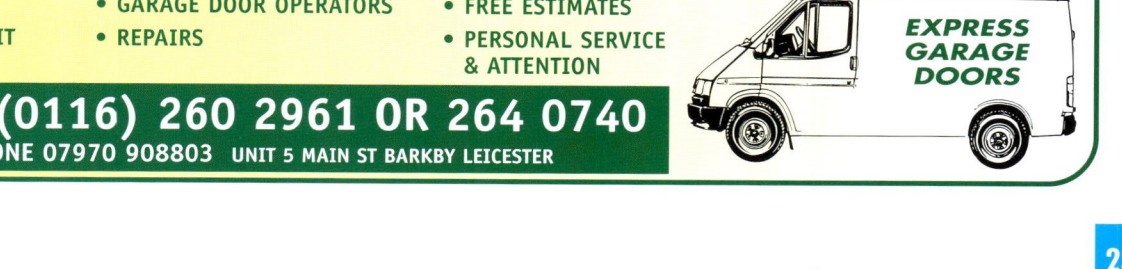

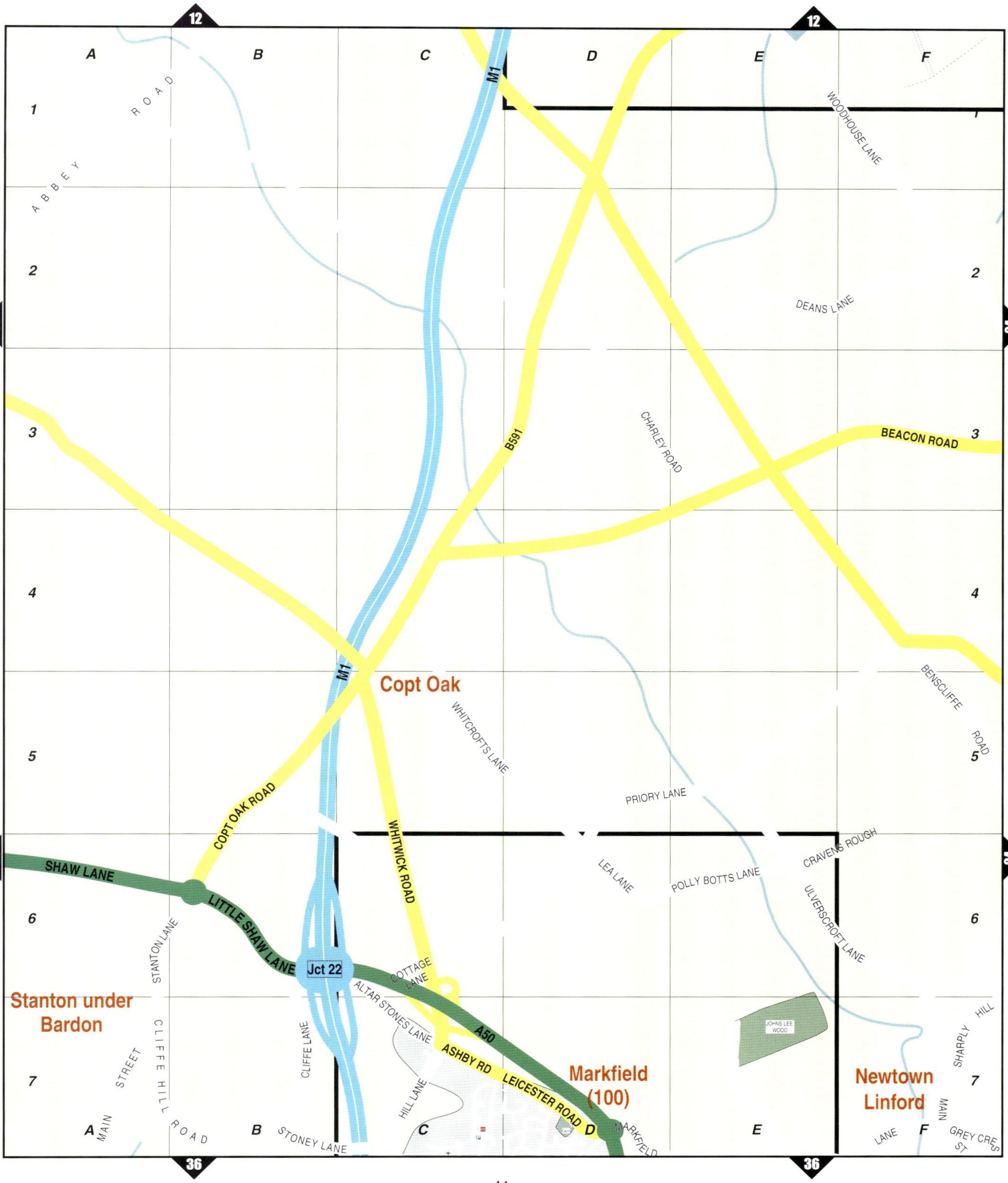
12
12
22
22
24
24
36
36
A
B
C
D
E
F
1
2
3
4
5
6
7
ABBEY ROAD
M1
WOODHOUSE LANE
DEANS LANE
CHARLEY ROAD
B591
BEACON ROAD
Copt Oak
WHITCROFTS LANE
BENSCLIFFE ROAD
PRIORY LANE
COPT OAK ROAD
WHITWICK ROAD
SHAW LANE
LITTLE SHAW LANE
Jct 22
COTTAGE LANE
ALTAR STONES LANE
A50
ASHBY RD
LEICESTER ROAD
LEA LANE
POLLY BOTTS LANE
CRAVENS ROUGH
ULVERSCROFT LANE
STANTON LANE
Stanton under Bardon
CLIFFE HILL ROAD
MAIN STREET
CLIFFE LANE
HILL LANE
STONEY LANE
Markfield (100)
MARKFIELD
JOHNS LEE WOOD
Newtown Linford
SHARPLY HILL
MAIN
LANE
GREY CRES
ST

Park Dental Surgery

10, The Green, Mountsorrel, Leicestershire LE12 7AF
Telephone: 0116 2375321

Surgery Hours:
Monday - Friday • 8.30am - 12.30pm • 1.30pm - 5.30pm
Saturday • 9.00am - 1.00pm

- FRIENDLY, MODERN SURGERY IN PLEASANT, WELL APPOINTED SURROUNDINGS
- <u>ALL</u> PATIENTS ACCEPTED ON THE N.H.S.
- A COMPREHENSIVE RANGE OF PRIVATE TREATMENT ALSO OFFERED
- HYGIENIST

PRINCIPAL DENTAL SURGEON: Mr R. D. Inkley B.D.S.

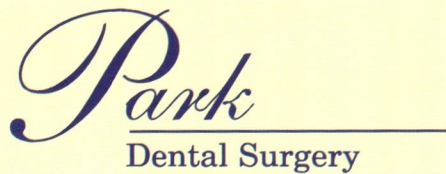

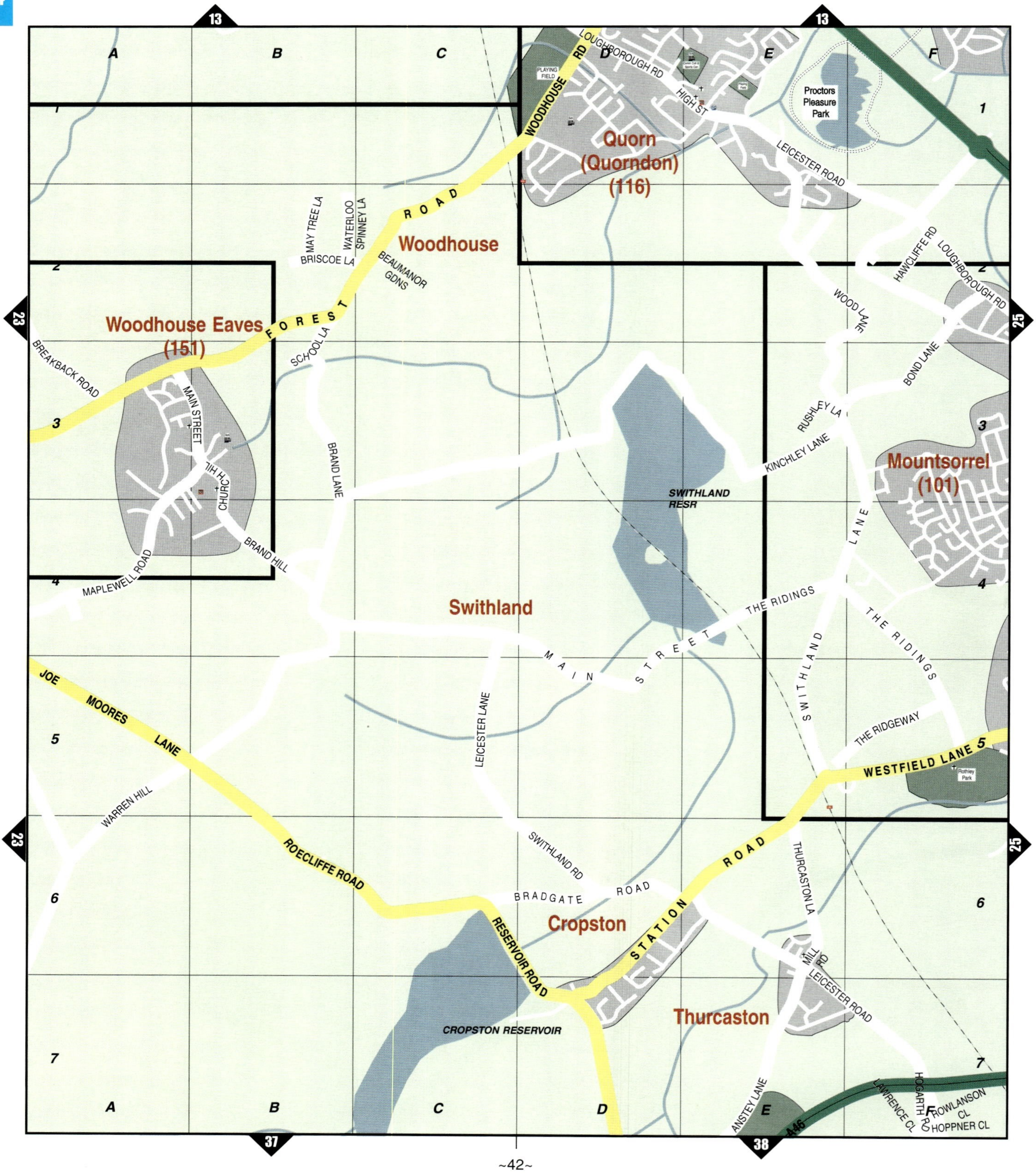

Ratcliffe College

Inspired by the spirit of the Gospel and informed by the traditions of the Catholic faith, we aim to provide an environment in which each individual student can learn, feel known and valued, and be happy.

Excellent facilities, elegant buildings and attractive grounds provide many opportunities for our boys and girls to develop their sporting, cultural and artistic talents, for which Scholarships are offered.

For our boarders, in addition to all the above, we provide total care in a homely atmosphere during their critical adolescent years.

Please come and see for yourselves, we would be delighted to meet you and show you around our school.

FOSSE WAY • RATCLIFFE ON THE WREAKE • LEICESTER • LE7 4SG • TEL: 01509 817000 • FAX: 01509 817004

Excellence

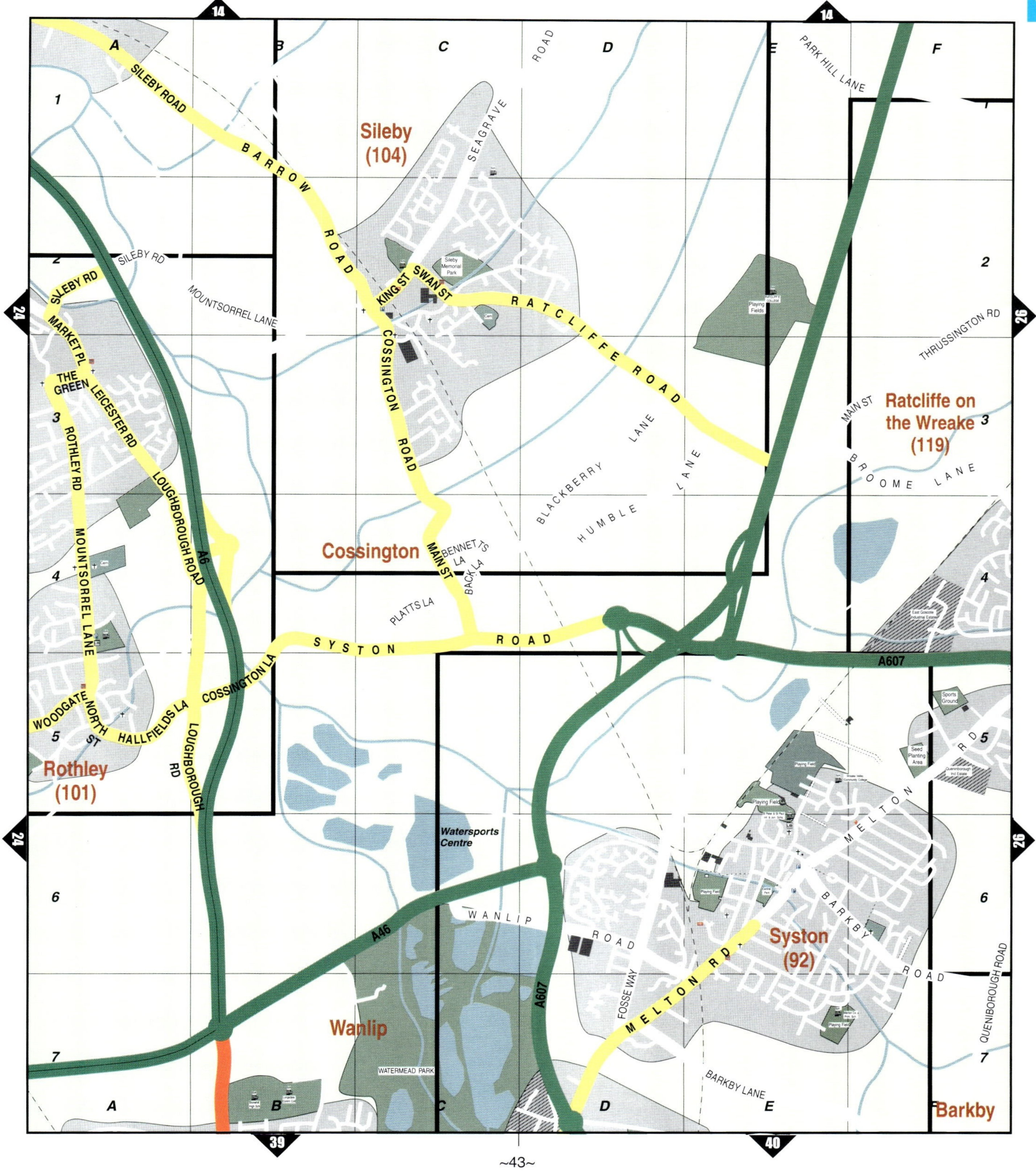

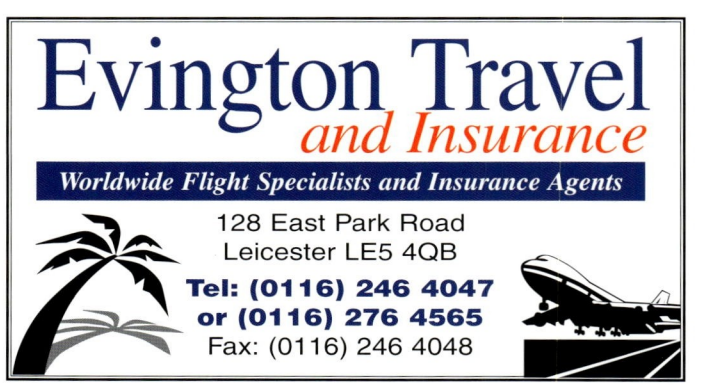

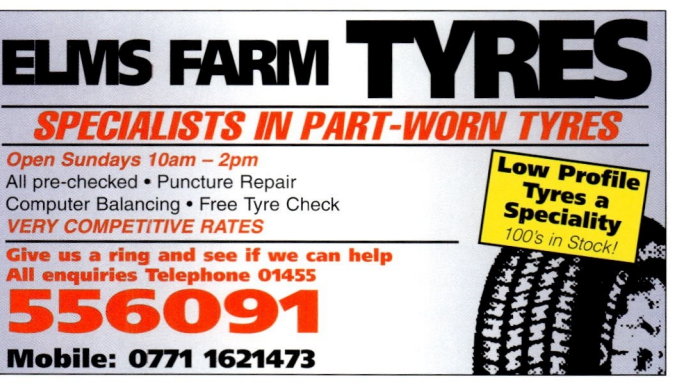

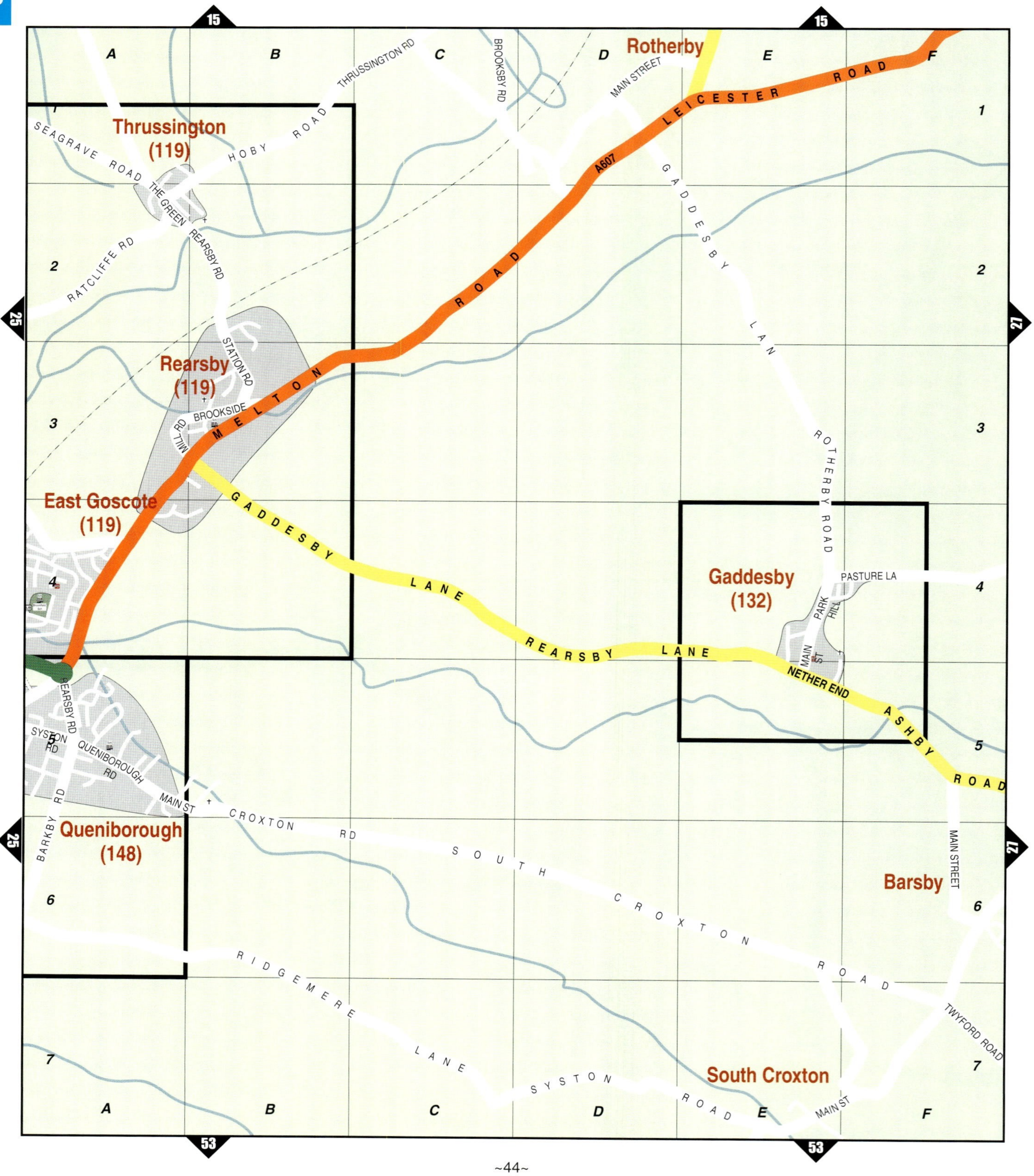

15
15
A
B
C
D
E
F
1
2
3
4
5
6
7
Thrussington
(119)
Rearsby
(119)
East Goscote
(119)
Queniborough
(148)
Rotherby
Gaddesby
(132)
Barsby
South Croxton
SEAGRAVE ROAD
HOBY ROAD
THRUSSINGTON RD
BROOKSBY RD
MAIN STREET
LEICESTER ROAD
A607
THE GREEN
RATCLIFFE RD
REARSBY RD
GADDESBY LAN
MELTON ROAD
STATION RD
BROOKSIDE
MILL RD
GADDESBY LANE
ROTHERBY ROAD
PASTURE LA
PARK HILL
MAIN ST
REARSBY LANE
NETHER END
ASHBY ROAD
SYSTON RD
QUENIBOROUGH RD
BARKBY RD
CROXTON RD
SOUTH CROXTON ROAD
MAIN STREET
RIDGEMERE LANE
SYSTON ROAD
TWYFORD ROAD
25
25
27
27
53
53

Stewart Morris Partnership Ltd

Consulting Civil & Structural Engineers

130 New Walk, Leicester LE1 7JA
Tel: (0116) 254 6922
Fax: (0116) 254 7257

CONTROL INSTALLATIONS Ltd.

5 TUCKETT ROAD,
WOODHOUSE EAVES,
LOUGHBOROUGH,
LEICESTERSHIRE LE12 8SE

Telephone:
(01509) 891 263
Mobile:
07803 115737
Fax:
(01509) 891 056

Co. Reg. No.: 3435420

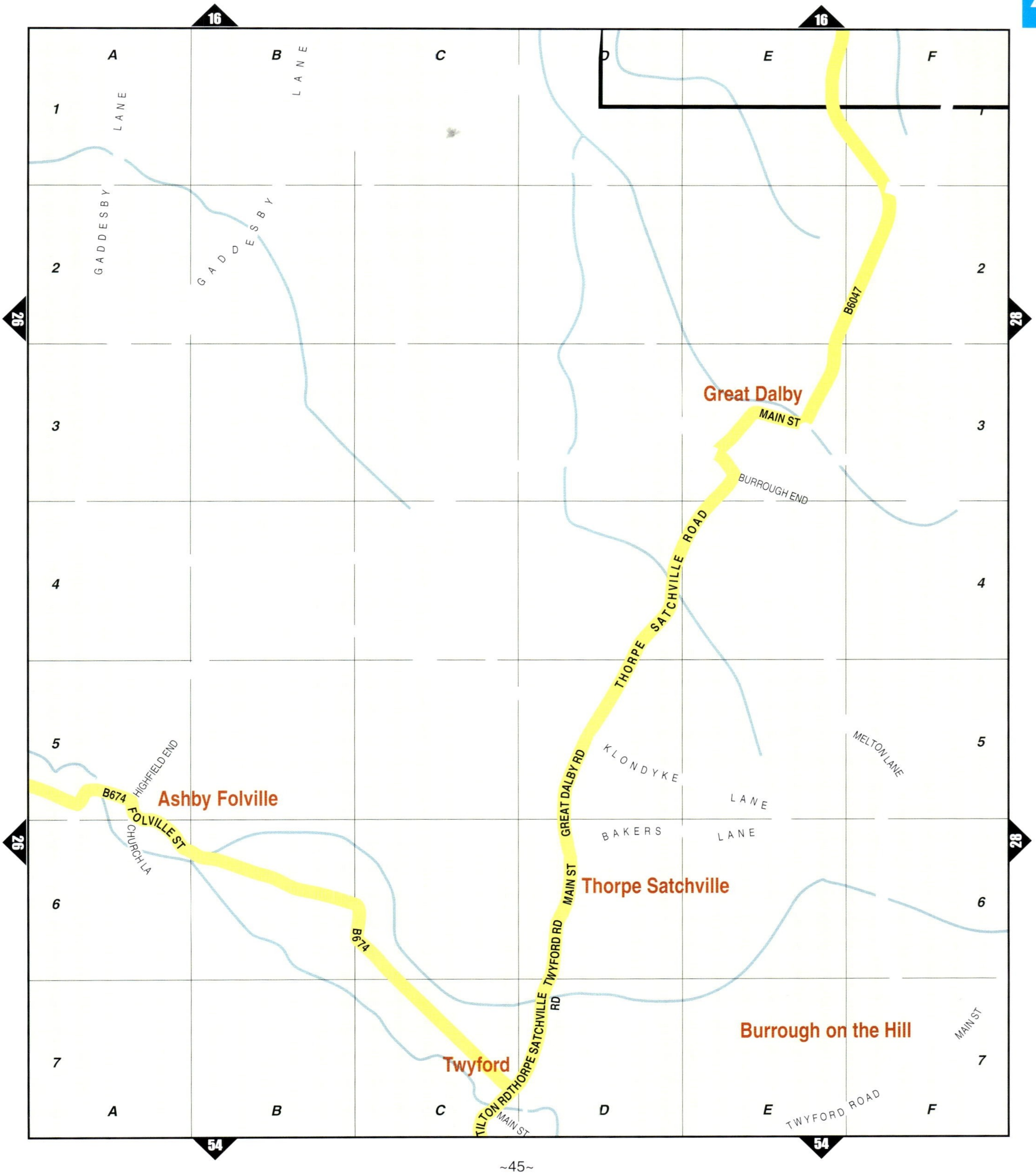

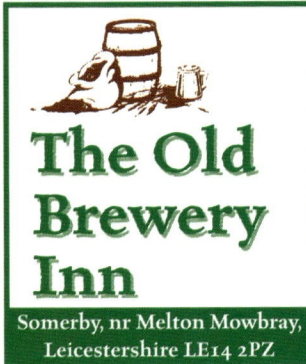

The Old Brewery Inn

Somerby, nr Melton Mowbray,
Leicestershire LE14 2PZ

Excellent Quality Real Ales Made in the Traditional Way on the Premises
PARISH & JOHN O'GAUNT ALES ON PERMANENTLY • REGULAR LIVE MUSIC

Warm Welcome from friendly staff and roaring fires in the winter, only 1 mile from Burrough Hill Car Park
Traditional Menu includes Somerby Sausages, Steak Pie, Lasagne, Hot Pot, Regular Specials
Large Function Room Free hire for Weddings, Parties etc. Excellent for Meetings & Conferences. Own Bar and Facilities
Brewery Visits by prior arrangement

We are open: Mon-Fri 11.30am-3pm, 6pm-11pm
Sat 11.30am-11pm
Sun 12pm-10.30pm
FOOD Tue-Sat 12pm-2pm, 7pm-10pm
Sun 12pm-2pm, 7pm-9pm

ANNUAL BEER FESTIVAL: Bank Holiday at the end of May
40+ Real Ales • Live Bands • BBQ • Hog Roast

FOR MORE DETAILS CONTACT THE JOHN O'GAUNT BREWING Co. **01664 454 777**

28

Burton Lazars (126), Little Dalby, Pickwell, Somerby (151), Cold Overton

ASHWELL ROAD • OAKHAM • RUTLAND • LE15 7QN
TELEPHONE 01572 723583

the RUTLAND Garden CENTRE

FOR ALL YOUR GARDENING REQUIREMENTS

HANGING BASKETS & SEASONAL BEDDING PLANTS A SPECIALITY

- TREES • SHRUBS • PLANTS • BULBS
- FENCING • PAVING & WALLING
- TEA & COFFEE SHOP

ROOFWISE

Roofing Contractors — Local Authority Approved

40 YEARS EXPERIENCE
24HR RESPONSE

20 YEARS BBA AND SOLVENCY GUARANTEES — DOMESTIC • INDUSTRIAL • COMMERCIAL
BUILT UP FLAT ROOFING SYSTEMS • TORCH APPLIED HIGH PERFORMANCE • METAL PROFILE
SHEETING AND CLADDING • SLATING AND TILING • DISCOUNTED RATES FOR SENIOR CITIZENS

FAMILY RUN BUSINESS
FREE ESTIMATES

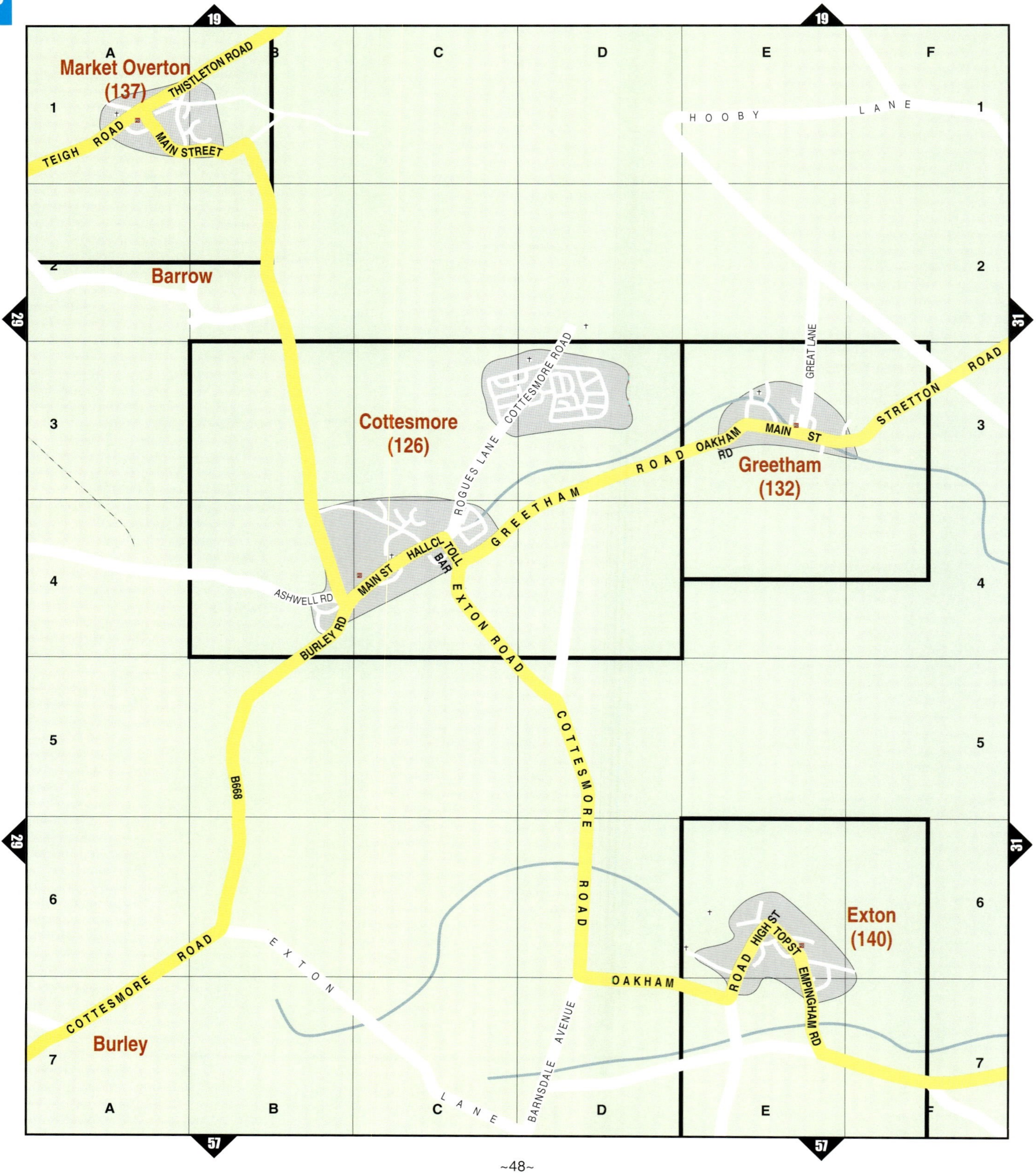

FREEPHONE: 0800 056 7859
MOBILE: 07850 245 465 • UNIT 2, ABBEY COURT, WALLINGFORD ROAD, LEICS

THE CURTAINSIDED SPECIALISTS

Rigid Trucks
Semi-Trailers
Insulated
Rolling Floor
Sliding Roof

Southfields

Tel: 01509 266461
Fax: 01509 610 718
E-mail: info@southfields.co.uk

14 Bakewell Road,
Loughborough,
Leicestershire
LE11 5TL

Parts Sourcing Service for all your Transport Requirements

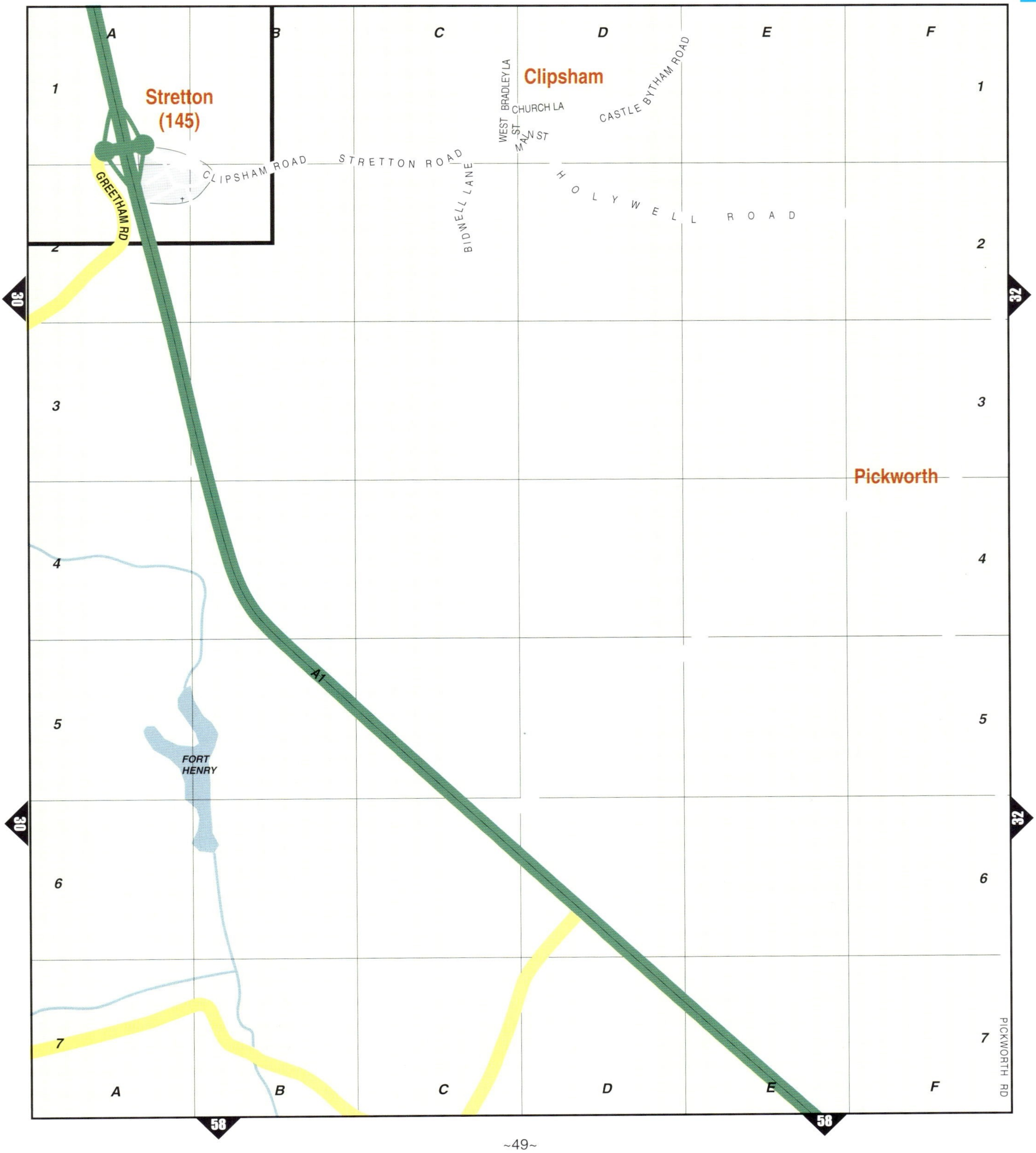

Forest East Catering Services

Supplier of all types of Catering Equipment New or Reconditioned

Telephone: 0116 223 7970
Mobile: 0771 1765522

~50~

BROOKSIDE
CONSTRUCTION (LEICESTER) LTD

Professional Surfacing and Paving Contractors

Roads, Car Parks, Footpaths, Playgrounds, Forecourts etc.

CONTRACTORS TO LOCAL AUTHORITIES

**19A Church Street
Oadby, Leicester LE2 5DB
Tel: 0116 271 0680
Fax: 0116 271 0991**

Jon Robinson Woodwork

39 IRIS AVENUE, BIRSTALL,
LEICESTER LE4 4HP

Telephone: (0116) 260 3139

"The Ultimate Name For Fine Videography"

SANGAM VIDEO PRODUCTIONS - LEICESTER

Tel: 0116 234 0062

*Commercials • Festivals
Live Shows • Promotionals
Trainings • Weddings*

PROFESSIONAL VIDEO SERVICES FOR ALL OCCASSIONS

Corporate interiors

OFFERING TOTAL SOLUTIONS TO CREATE A PERFECT IMAGE

- partitioning
- suspended ceilings
- lighting
- furniture
- mezzanine floors
- floor finishes
- computer floors
- turnkey projects
- electrics
- plumbing
- decoration
- blinds
- lockers
- room dividers

FREE ON-SITE SURVEY

Telephone: 0705 001 4518 • Facsimile: 0116 235 1082
114 RECTORY LANE, THURCASTON, LEICESTER LE7 7JQ

MDM *Services*

HIGH CLASS JAGUAR SERVICING, REPAIRS AND RESTORATIONS

Unit 3 ~ Glenmore Foundry ~ Thurmaston ~ Leicester ~ LE4 8AS
TELEPHONE: 0116 260 3344

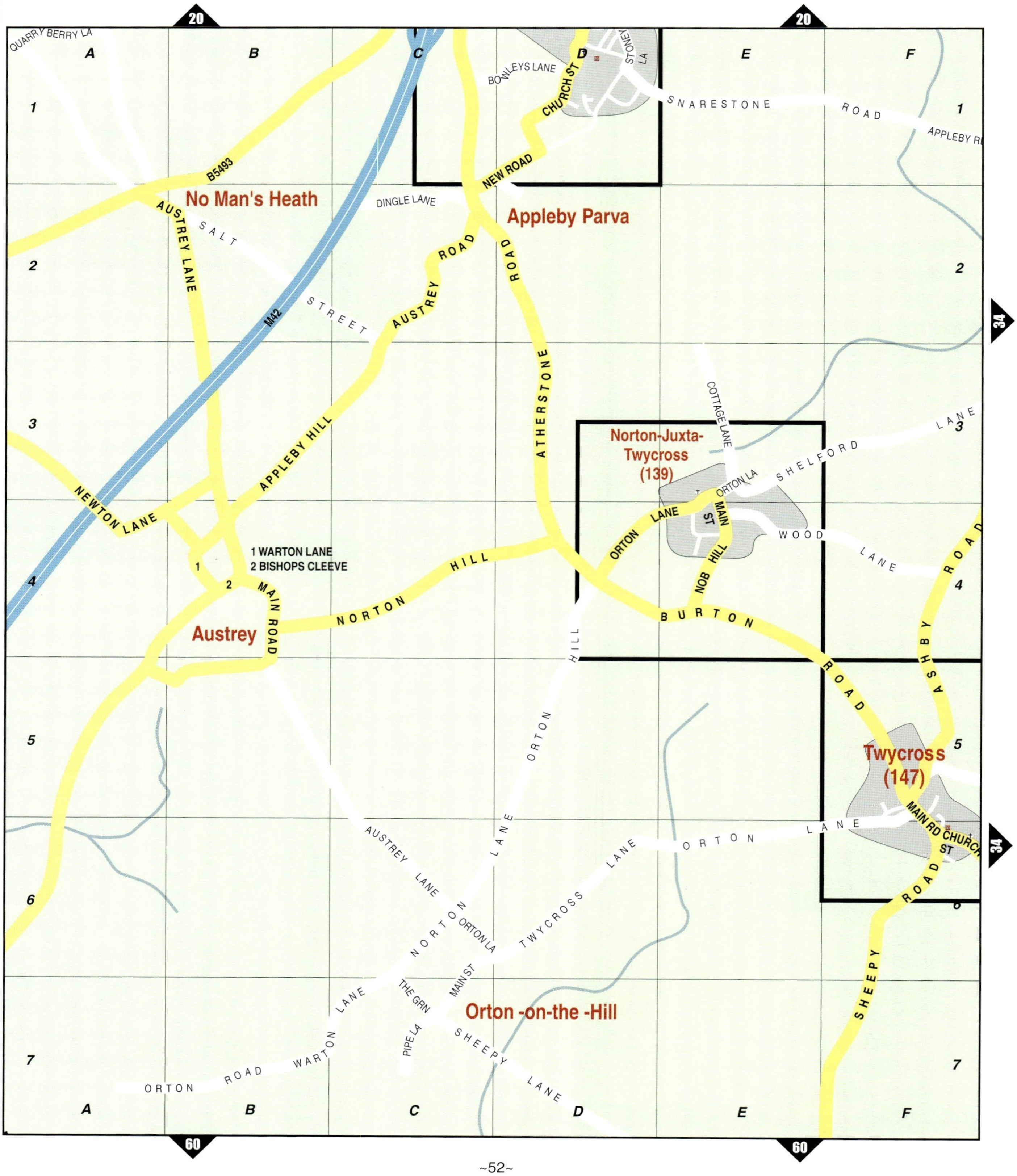

infinity

Private Fleet & Exhibition Work

Freephone: 0800 458 0777

Professional Vehicle Preparation

COVERING THIS WHOLE AREA

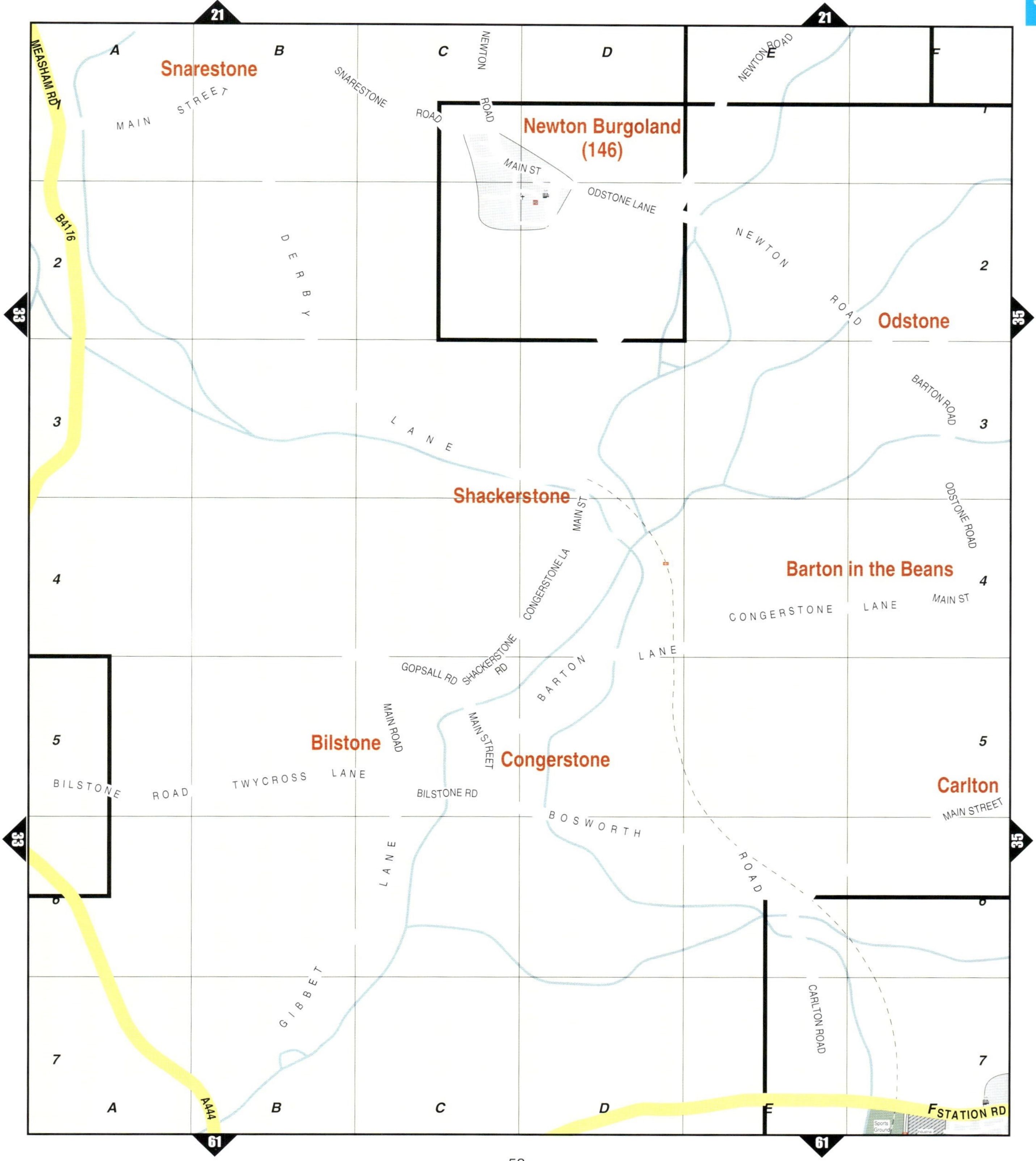

Map 34

Locations shown:
- Snarestone
- Newton Burgoland (146)
- Odstone
- Shackerstone
- Barton in the Beans
- Bilstone
- Congerstone
- Carlton

~53~

BROAD STREET GARAGE
Broad Street, Enderby, Leicester. LE9 5AA

Quality car & commercial sales
Services, repairs & MOT's for all makes
Air con service

Your local answer to motoring peace of mind!

Tel: 0116 2861416   Fax: 0116 2867136   Mobile: 07715 479281

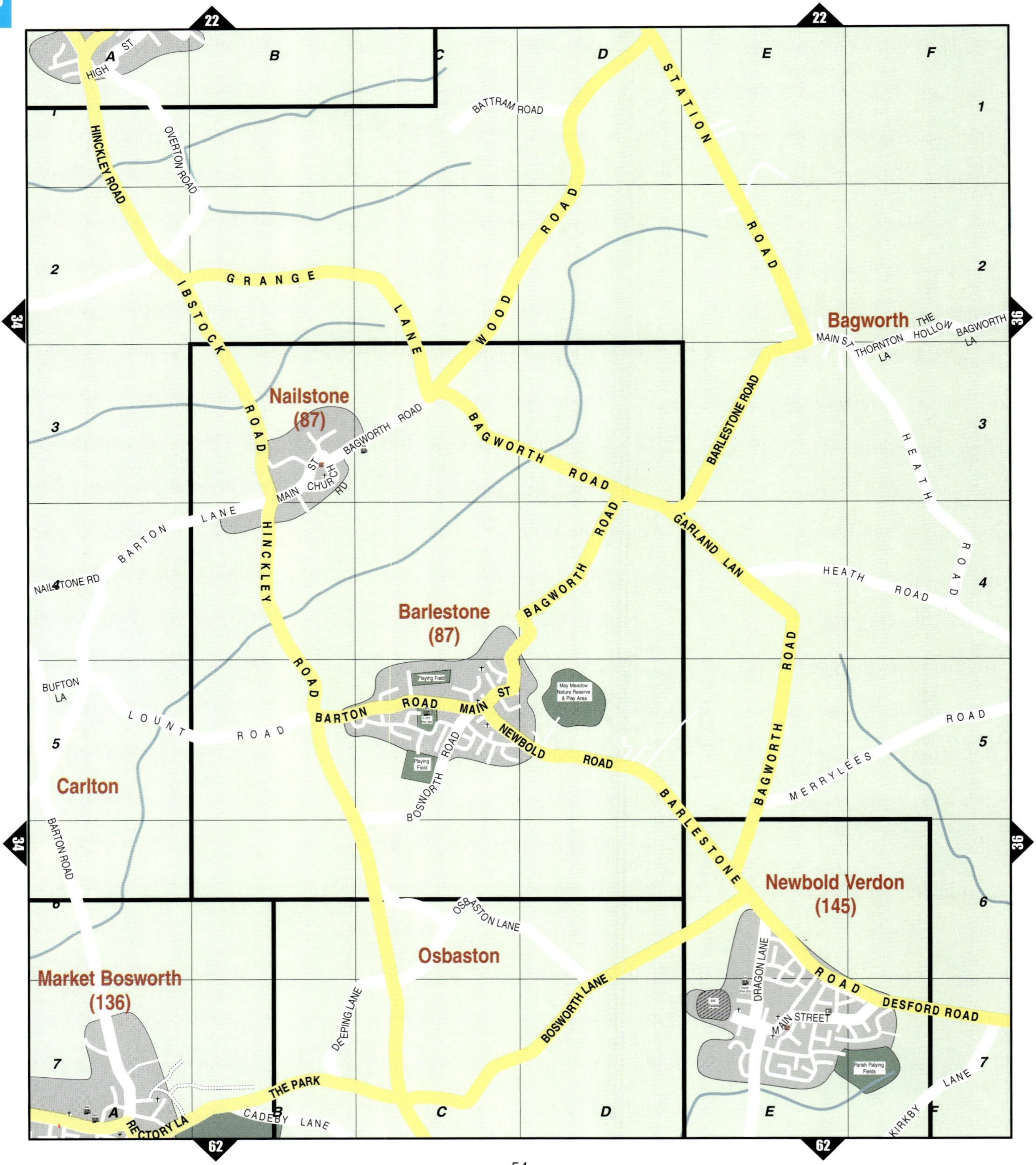

SISSONS & ALLEN LTD.

ESTABLISHED 1963

ELECTRICAL CONTRACTING ENGINEERS

Commercial & Industrial Installations

Registered Office:
Desford Road, Kirby Muxloe, Leicester LE9 9BF
Telephone: (01455) 824782 Fax: (01455) 823386

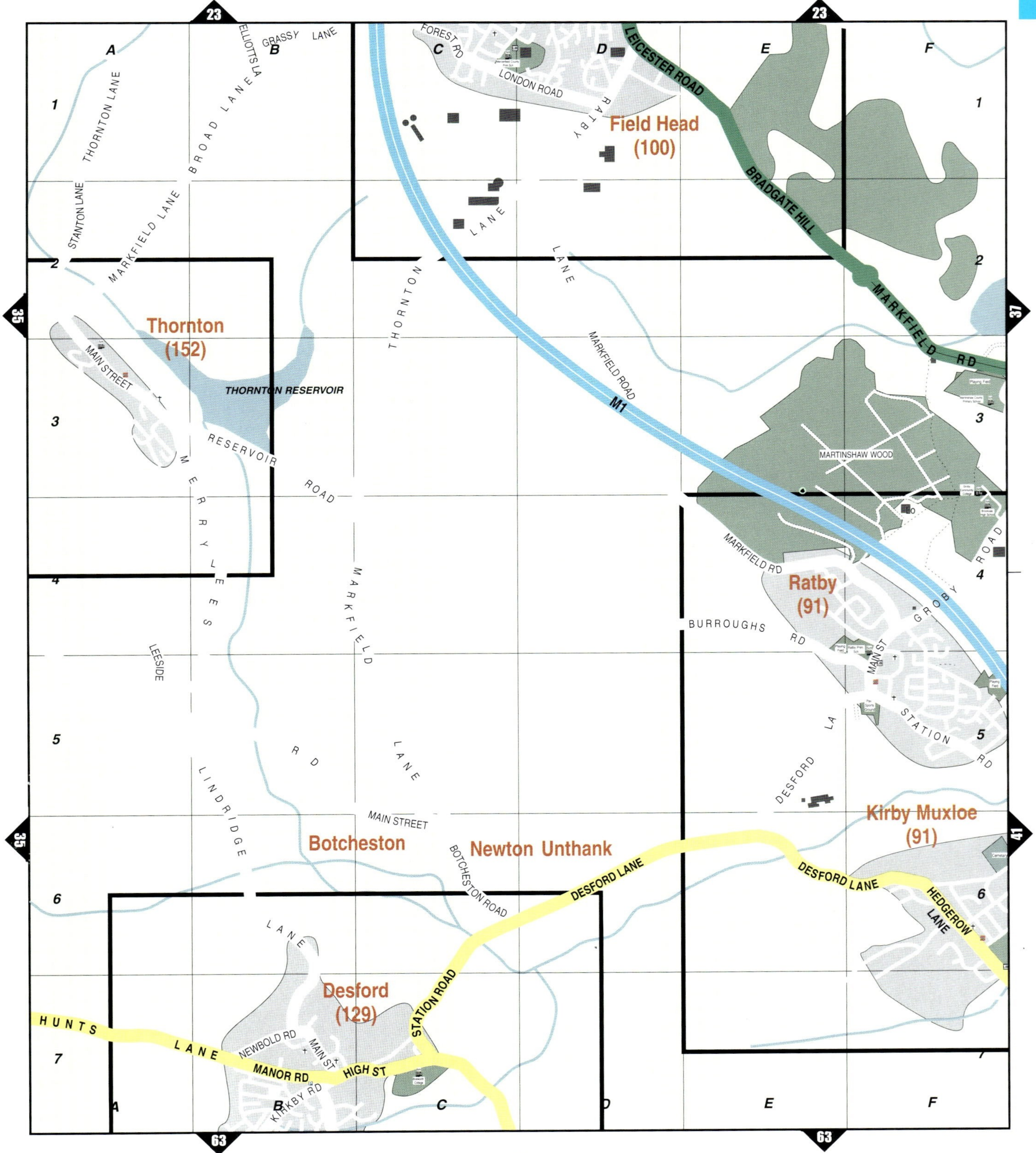

24
24
A
B
C
D
E
F
1
2
3
4
5
6
7
36
36
38
38
41
41
Newton Linford
BRACKEN HILL
BRADGATE ROAD
GROBY LANE
NEWTOWN LINFORD LANE
GROBY POOL
Rifle Range
Quarry (Dis)
Groby
GROBY PASS
MARKFIELD RD
LEICESTER RD
ANSTEY LA
GROBY RD
Castle Hill
Old Hall
PARKSIDE
Village Hall
Nursery
Stone Lodge
BRANTING HILL
ANSTEY LANE
A46
A50
Laurel Fm.
Marina Park
Public Open Space
Brant Farm
Gynsills Park
GYNSILL LANE
LEICESTER RD
Martin High Sch
LINK ROAD
BRADGATE RD
CHURCH LANE
SCHOOL HSE CL
PARK RD
Cowpen Spinney
Springfield
Elizabeth Woodville Sch.
Prim. Sch

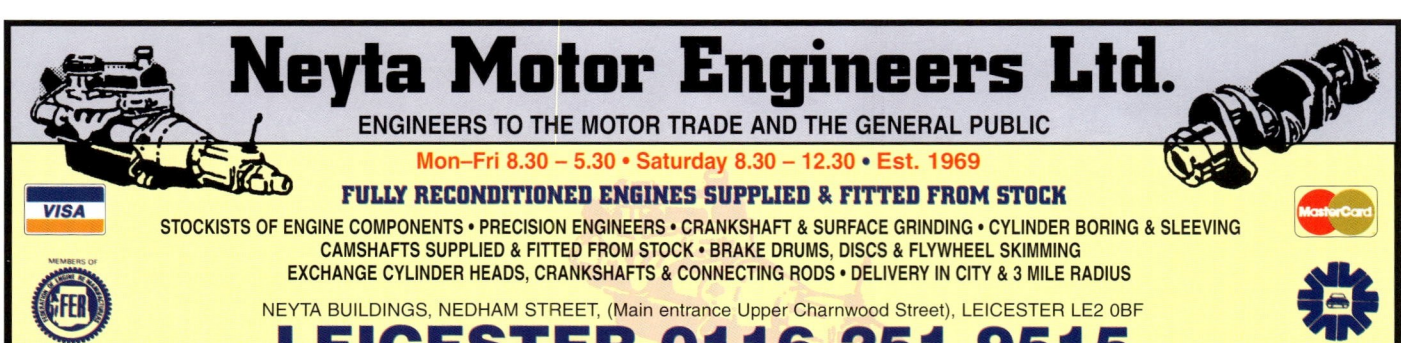

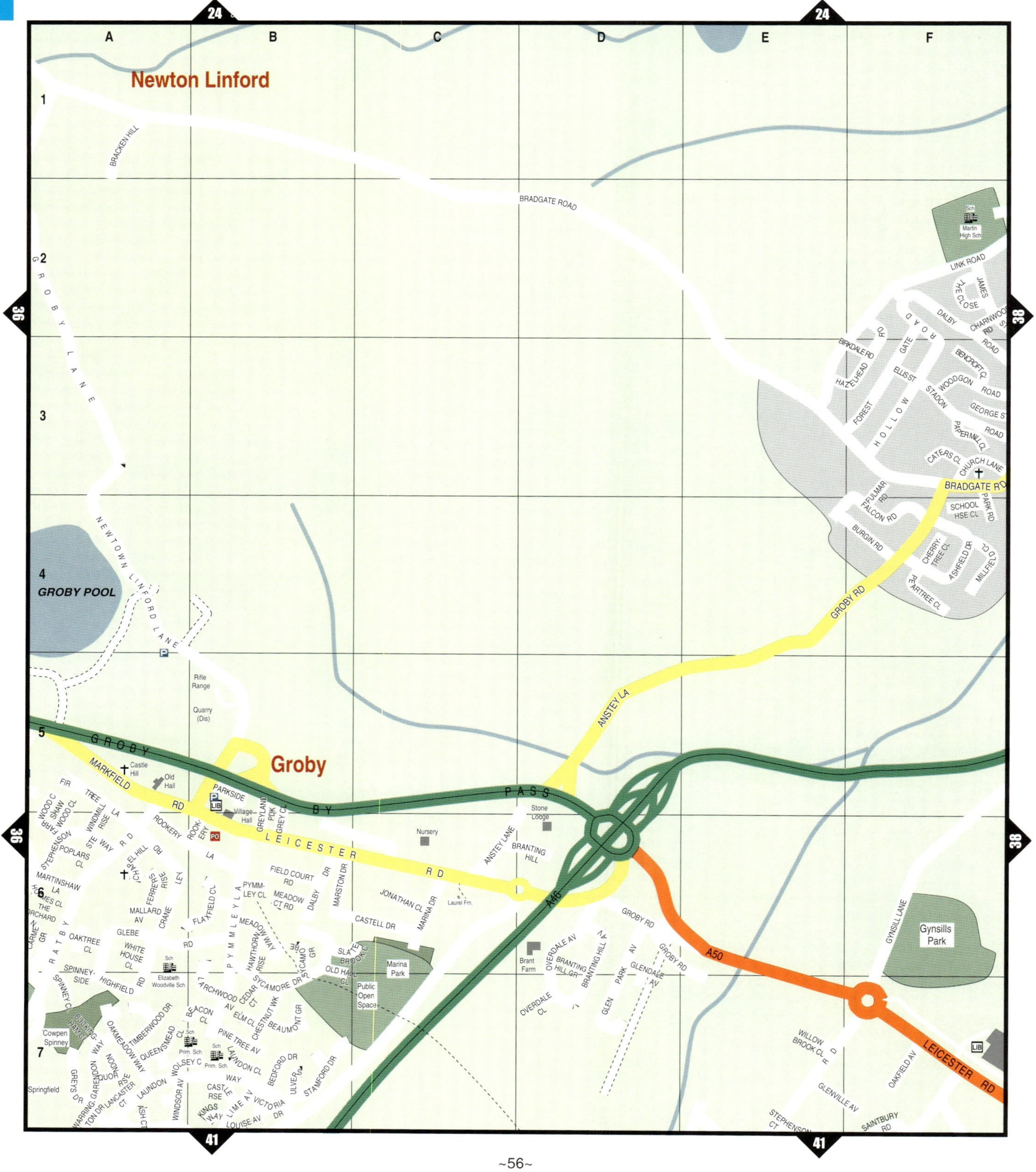

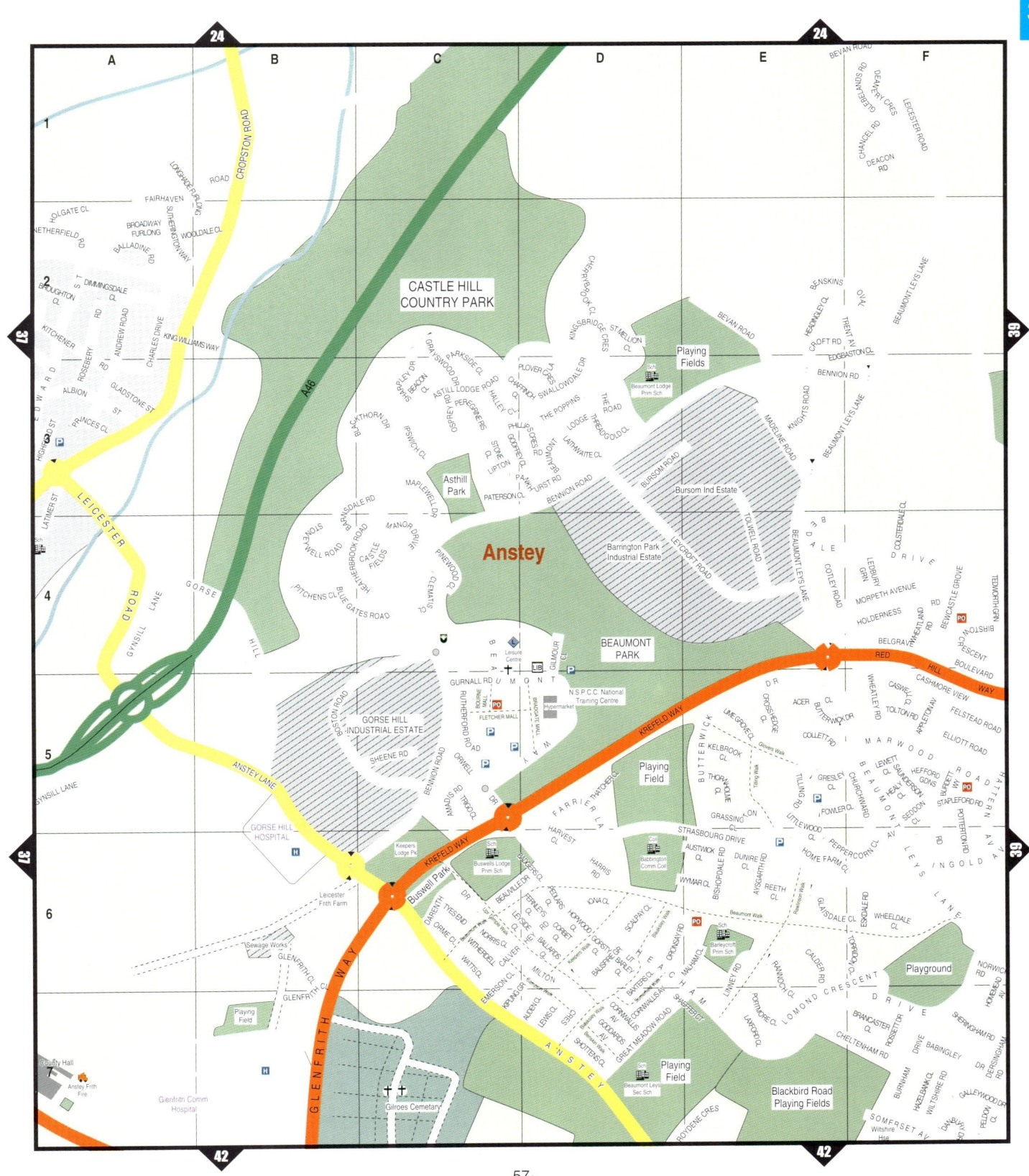

CENTAUR BIKE TRAINING

For Expert and Friendly Training for a complete range of courses
50cc, 125 and 500cc – ALL NEEDS CATERED FOR
A Complete Range of Hired Bikes Available
ONE TO ONE Training Available – Written Details on Request

298 GIPSY LANE • LEICESTER • LE4 9BX

FREEPHONE 0800 542 3050

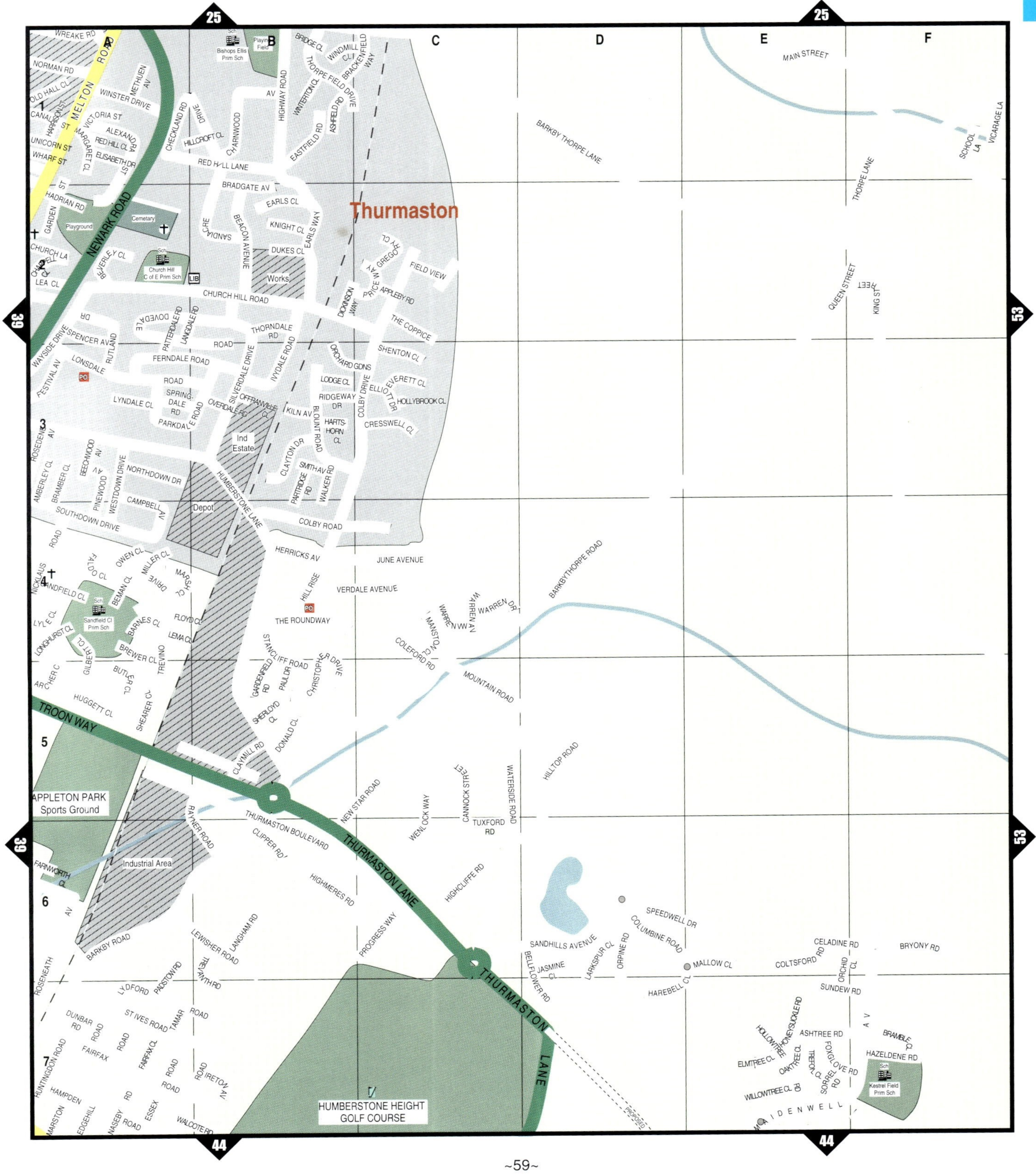

0116-2433294

For URGENT Sameday Deliveries 0990 888555

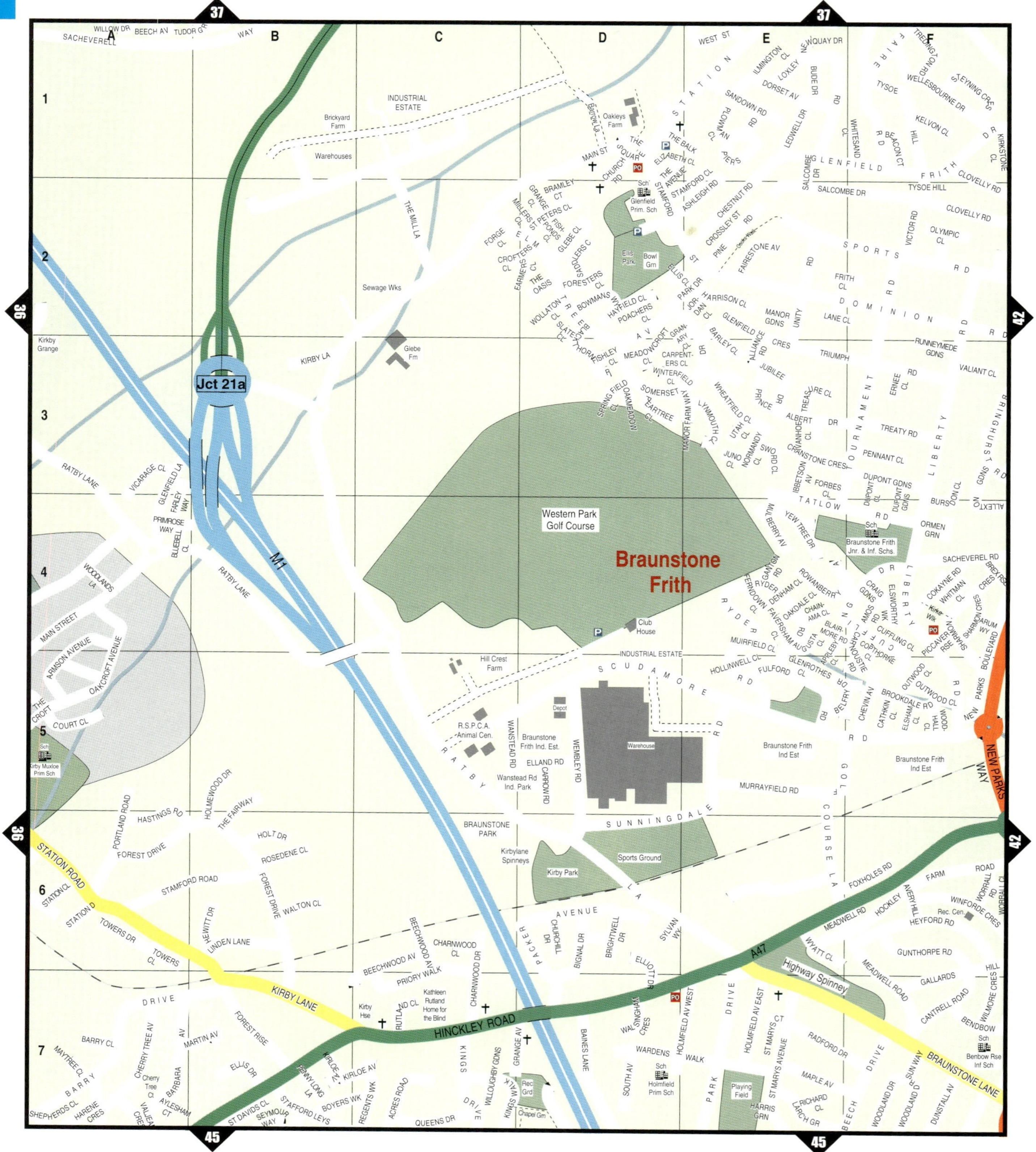

Sticky-Dickys
THE SIGNMAKERS
Metal fabricated - Powder coated - Acrylic - Illumination
Safety - Special projects - Fleet - Forecourt - And more!
Call 01455 220072 or www.sticky-dickys.com

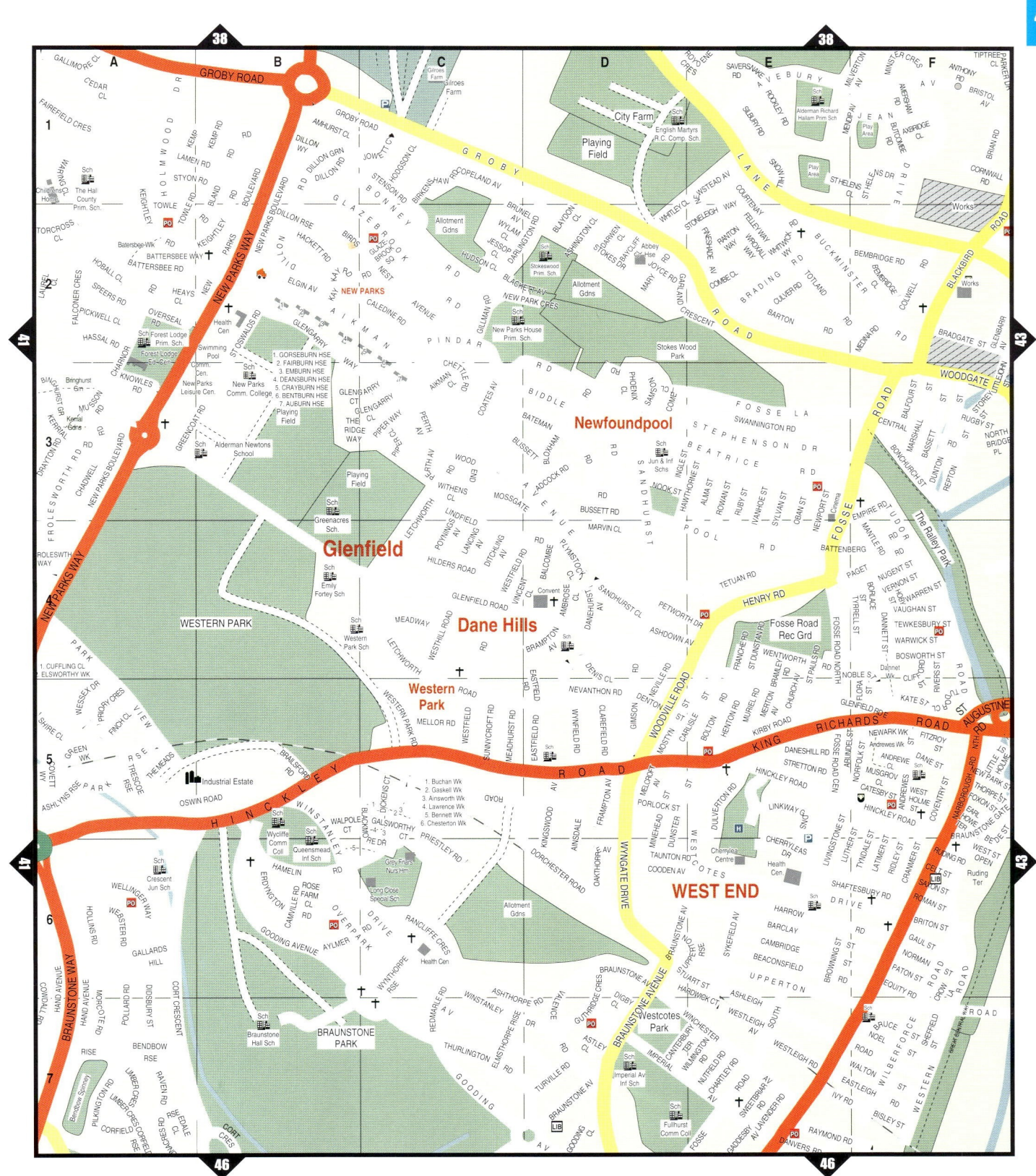

AC 2000

Air Conditioning for Leicestershire

- Sales – Never Knowingly Undersold
- Installation – Quality that Counts
- Service – Second to None
- Maintenance – Giving you Peace of Mind

For the best Deal in the County Phone, Fax or Email on

Telephone 0116 - 224 2425
Facsimile 0116 - 224 2426
E-mail: acleicester@ac2000.co.uk
www.ac2000.co.uk
224 Blackbird Rd, Leicester LE4 0AG

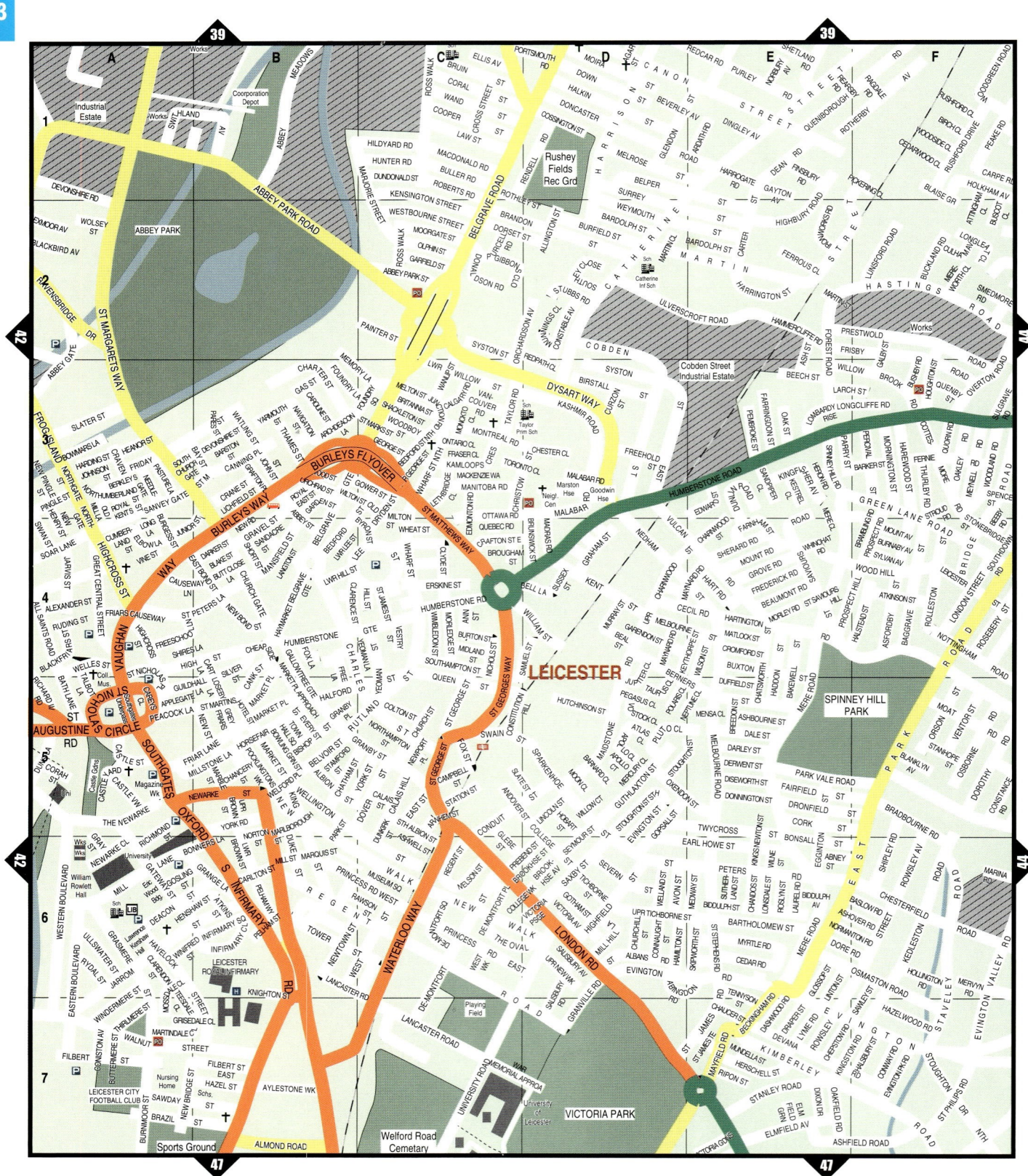

40
40
43
43
53
53
48
48
A
B
C
D
E
F
1
2
3
4
5
6
7
ANEFORD RD
DUNHOLME RD
NORTHFIELD ROAD
BRAYBROOKE ROAD
VICTORIA ROAD
IRETON
TOMLIN
CORDELIA CL
LEVERIC RD
MALLORY PL
BECKETT RD
PORTISHEAD RD
BRIGHTON RD
TAILBY AV
CLAYDON RD
THE PORTWEY
WYCOMBE ROAD
Mundella Comm College
HALLATON RD
TURNER RD
HUMBERSTONE DRIVE
GIPSY LANE
The Towers Hospital
Humberstone Manor
GIMSON CL
HUMBERSTONE DR
GREENLAND AV
GREENLAND DR
TENNIS CT DR
HAYLING CRES
WEST DR
NORTH DR
SOUTH DR
PINE TREE AVENUE
STANLEY DRIVE
Manor Farm
Church Farm House
COLIN GRUNDY DR
KEYHAM LANE
MAIN STREET
LIDSTER CL
LOBBS WOOD CL
VICARAGE LANE
Monks Rest Gardens
Hospital
ABBOTS COURT
HOTOFT RD
STEINS LA
HUMBER CL
KEYHAM CL
HUNGARTON BOULEVARD
Humberstone Inf & Jnr Sch
SCRAPTOFT LANE
CARDINALS WALK
ARNCLIFFE RD
WANSBECK GDNS
ST MARYS AV
WIGLEY ROAD
ARMADALE
CARDINALS
HARTFIELD RD
NETHER HALL ROAD
TOLCARNE ROAD
LABURNUM ROAD
KEYHAM
PRESTON RISE
CRANESBILL ROAD
MEADOWSWEET RD
High Leas Special Sch
CHESTNUT AV
FERN RISE
SELBY AVENUE
BARRY ROAD
LIMEHURST RD
GREENBANK RD
Recreation Ground
Scraptoft Valley Prim Sch
St Josephs Prim Sch
MOORFIELDS
PARKSTONE ROAD
LYMINGTON RD
LYMOUTH RD
UPPINGHAM ROAD
DUXBURY RD
ST BARNABAS ROAD
FRENCH RD
BEATTY AV
SMITH DORRIEN RD
ROBINSON ROAD
GOUGH ROAD
HAYNES ROAD
COLEMAN ROAD
SALTERSFORD RD
COLEMAN CL
THE BRIANWAY
FREEMAN RD
HUMBERSTONE PARK
SCRAPTOFT MEWS
THE CROFT
TREETOPS CL
PETERS
BARBARA
HAVENCREST
THE PARKWAY
BRYNGARTH CRES
ELMCROFT AV
OCEAN CL
GLENDOWER CL
SEXTANT
RADIANT RD
THURNCOURT CL
VALE CL
COMPASS
THURNCOURT
GERVAS ROAD
SOMERS
DUDLEY AVENUE
AMYSON RD
JENNETT CL
MERTHULL RD
BROOK
TUSKAR RD
BRIAR RD
CHATER CL
Comm Centre
NURSERY
Works
Factory
GREEN LANE
DEEPDALE
THE WAYNE WAY
THE LANGHILL
BROAD AVENUE
KITCHENER
CLUMBER
COPDALE ROAD
CROWN HILLS AV
ELIZABETH ST
TEMPLE RD
WICKLOW DRIVE
HILL
AMBASSADOR ROAD
HARROWDEN RISE
DAVISON CL
ALLINSON CL
ROWLATTS
SANDFORD CL
BALDERSTONE CL
AVONSIDE DR
CROPTHORNE AV
BARNES HEATH ROAD
HIGGS CL
ROCKINGHAM CL
THOMASSON ROAD
DAVETT CL
AVOCA DRIVE
WESTMEATH AVENUE
WALSHE RD
WITHCOTE AVENUE
SILVERWOOD CL
GREYSTONE AV
PERKIN RD
OGWEN CL
GELERT AV
WINTERSDALE ROAD
VALENTINE RD
LODGE FARM RD
SUMMERLEA RD
UPPINGHAM RD
UPPINGHAM CL
Sports Grd
DAVENPORT ROAD
BEECHWOOD CL
GAMEL ROAD
SKAMPTON RD
NELOT WY
GREENACRE
GOODWOOD ROAD
GOODWOOD CRES
HARRINGWORTH
OAKSIDE
SUNNYFIELD CL
OAKSIDE CL
SPENCEFIELD LANE
ENGLEFIELD ROAD
FERMAIN CL
WELLAND VALE ROAD
ROGERSTONE RD
DURSTON CL
ALCESTER DRIVE
FALLOWFIELD RD
WOODNEWTON DRIVE
Playing Fields
DOWNING DRIVE
HAMBURY RD
EARLSWOOD RD
SWINSTEAD RD
CHATTERIS AV
BALLATER CL
KILVERSTONE AV
BIDEFORD RD
PEVENSEY AV
CRANTOCK CL
BARNSTAPLE RD
NEWHAVEN
MARYDENE DRIVE
GEDDING RD
DRINKSTONE RD
BRADFIELD CL
GWENDOLEN ROAD
HILLCROFT RD
CROWN HILLS RISE
THE CIRCLE
THE RETREAT
THE APPROACH
WORKS
NANSEN
Playing Fields
WAKERLEY ROAD
GWENDOLINE RD
HOSPITAL CLOSE
CROYDE CL
FALMOUTH ROAD
CLOVELLY RD
LULWORTH CL
ETHEL ROAD
EVINGTON DRIVE
BADEN RD
NORWOOD RD
MAYFLOWER RD
OKEHAMPTON AV
HATHERLEIGH RD
PLYMOUTH DR
BODNANT AV
HOMEWAY ROAD
LINDEN DRIVE
SIDMOUTH AV
HEXTALL ROAD
BLUNDELL ROAD
HEADLAND ROAD
EVINGTON PARK
HARWIN RD
ALDGATE AV
CORDERY ROAD
ST DENYS ROAD
GIFFORD CL
WHITEHALL ROAD
ANGELA DR
JUDITH DR
SUSAN AV
MICKLETON DR
SPENCEFIELD DR
THURNVIEW ROAD
INGARSBY DRIVE
YELVERTON AV
HAWTHORNE DR
THE COMMON
Evington
MAIN ST
FAIRFORD AV
BIGGIN HILL RD
WOODBOROUGH RD
HAYWOOD CL
HAZELNUT CL
ELLWOOD CL
WATERFIELD ROAD

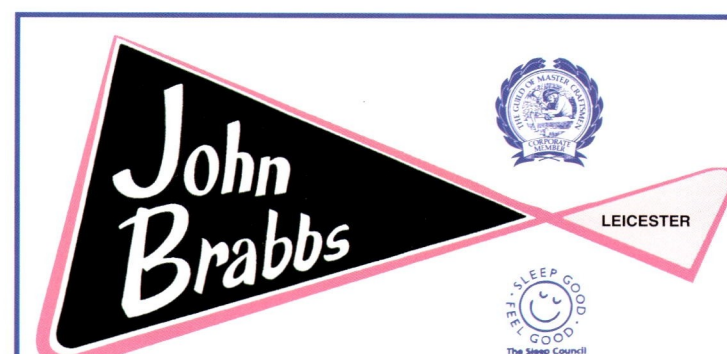

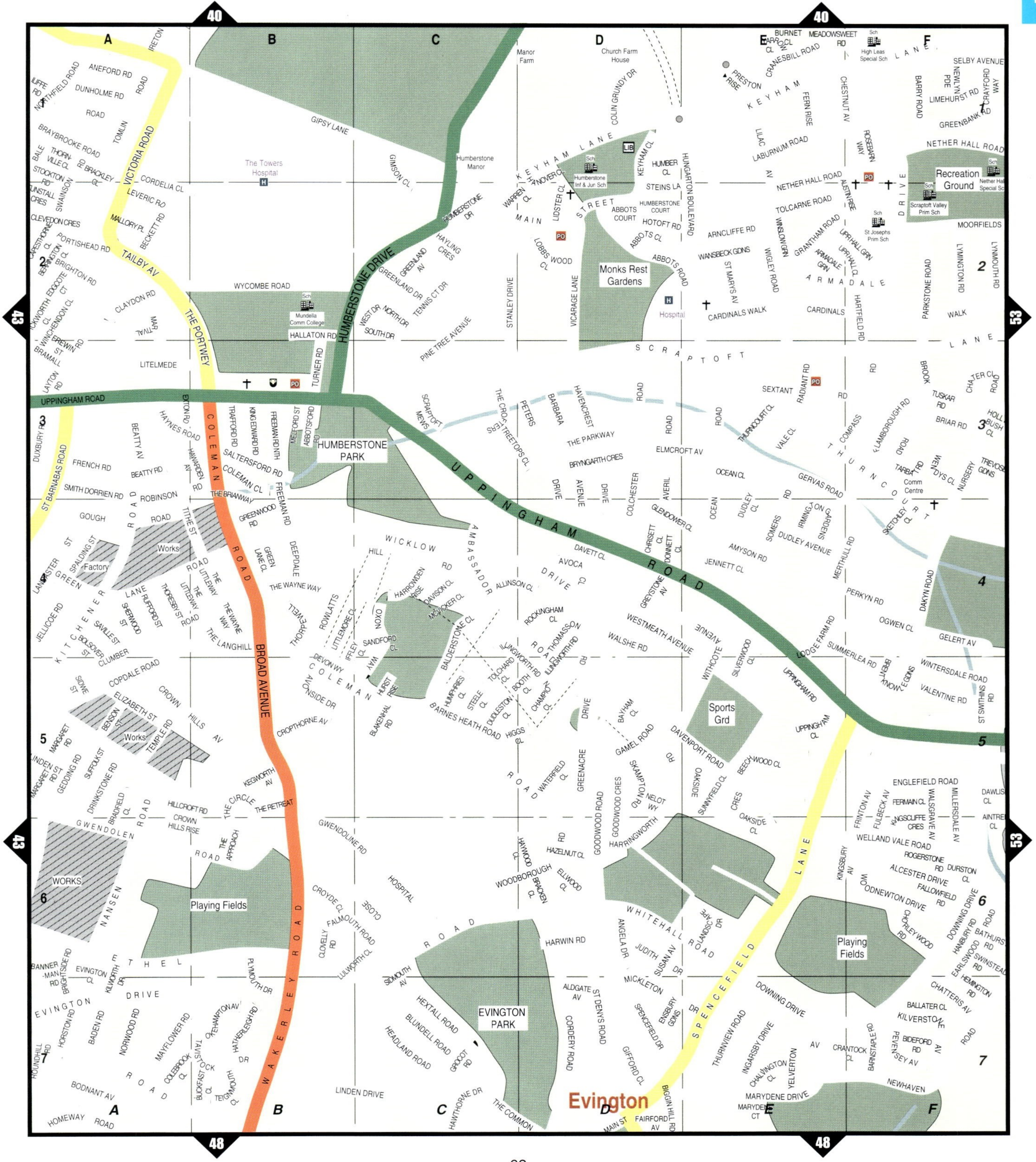

SUPERFINISH ELASTICS LTD

TRIMMERS FOR LEISUREWEAR, HOSIERY AND FASHION WEAR

A family owned business since 1983, we can offer you many years of trading, experience and knowledge in the garment industry. Welcoming any size of enquiries from the UK and abroad.

ELASTICS • KNITTED • BONADEX • S/POLY THREADS • 120 • S/POLY 75/80 • THREAD OVERLOCKING YARNS • SILK BOWS • OL YARNS • LACES FROM 1" TO 8" WITH ELASTANE
LACES FROM 1" TO 5" RIGID LACE • CORDED LACE • FABRICS • COTTON LACE 1" TO 5" • FISH NET FABRICS • SHIFFON FABRICS • SHOULDER TAPE • TENSION TAPE • DAISY CHAIN
BRAIDED CORD • KNITTED CORD • FRINGES NYLON • FRINGES ACRYLIC • BOW TIE • RIBBON • KNITTED WEBBING • WOVEN WEBBING • VELCRO TAPES • ACRYLIC & WOOLLY HATS

42 London Street, Leicester LE5 3RU England • Tel: (0116) 276 1007 Fax: (0116) 276 1005
Email: mustak@superfinish.freeserve.co.uk

P. F. HASTIK

GENERAL REPAIRS • SERVICING • BODYWORK
TYRES • BATTERIES • EXHAUSTS

Motor Engineers • Insurance and Accident Work • MOT Repairs and Breakdown
British, American and Foreign Cars Undertaken • Member of the R.M.I.F.

ACCESS AND VISA WELCOME

TELEPHONE 0116 262 7358

DEVONSHIRE ROAD • LEICESTERSHIRE • LE4 0BF

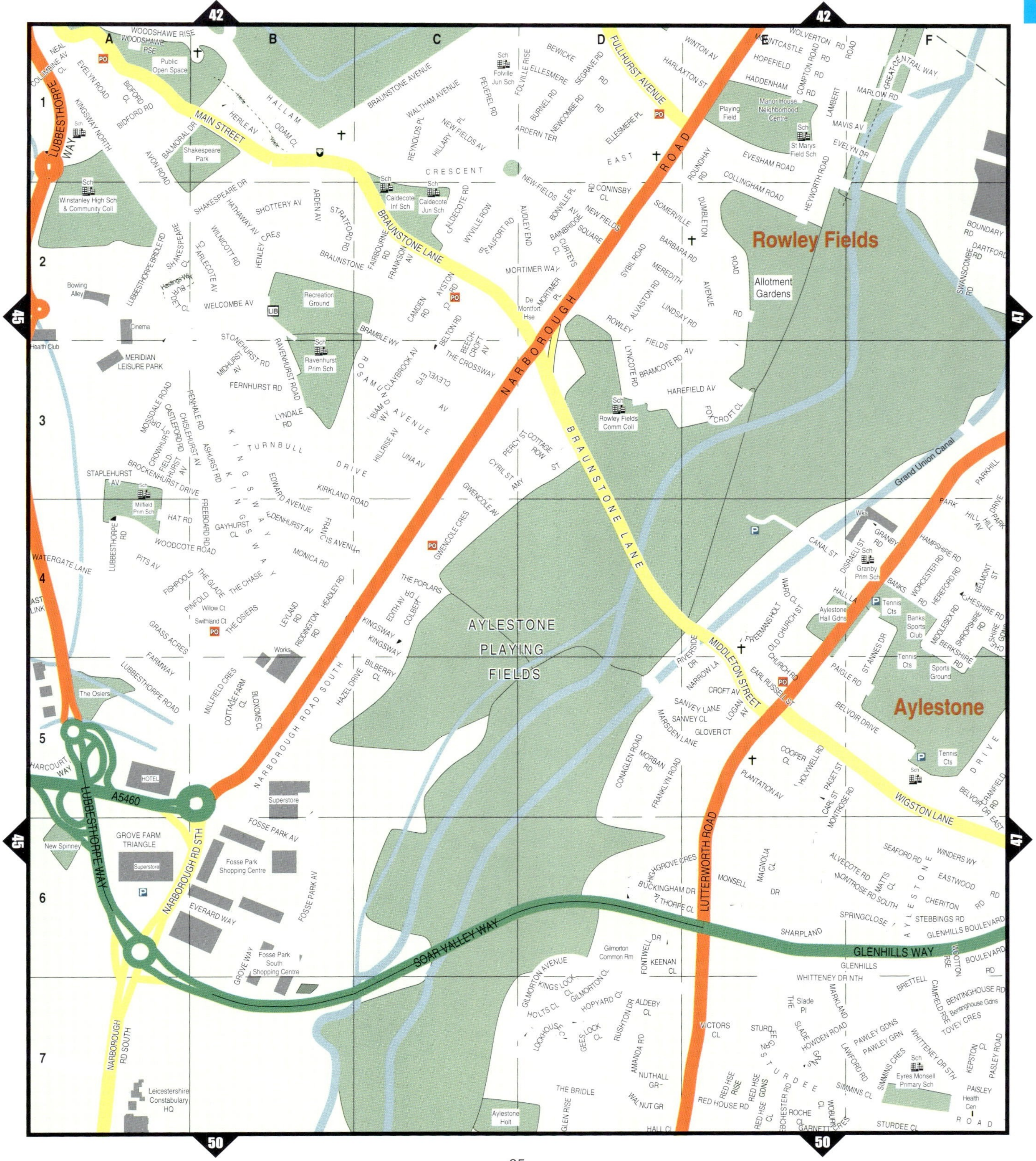

46

K.B AUTOMOTIVE
Mobile Mechanic
Tel Keith on: Leics (0116) 208 2880   Mobile: 07802 853015

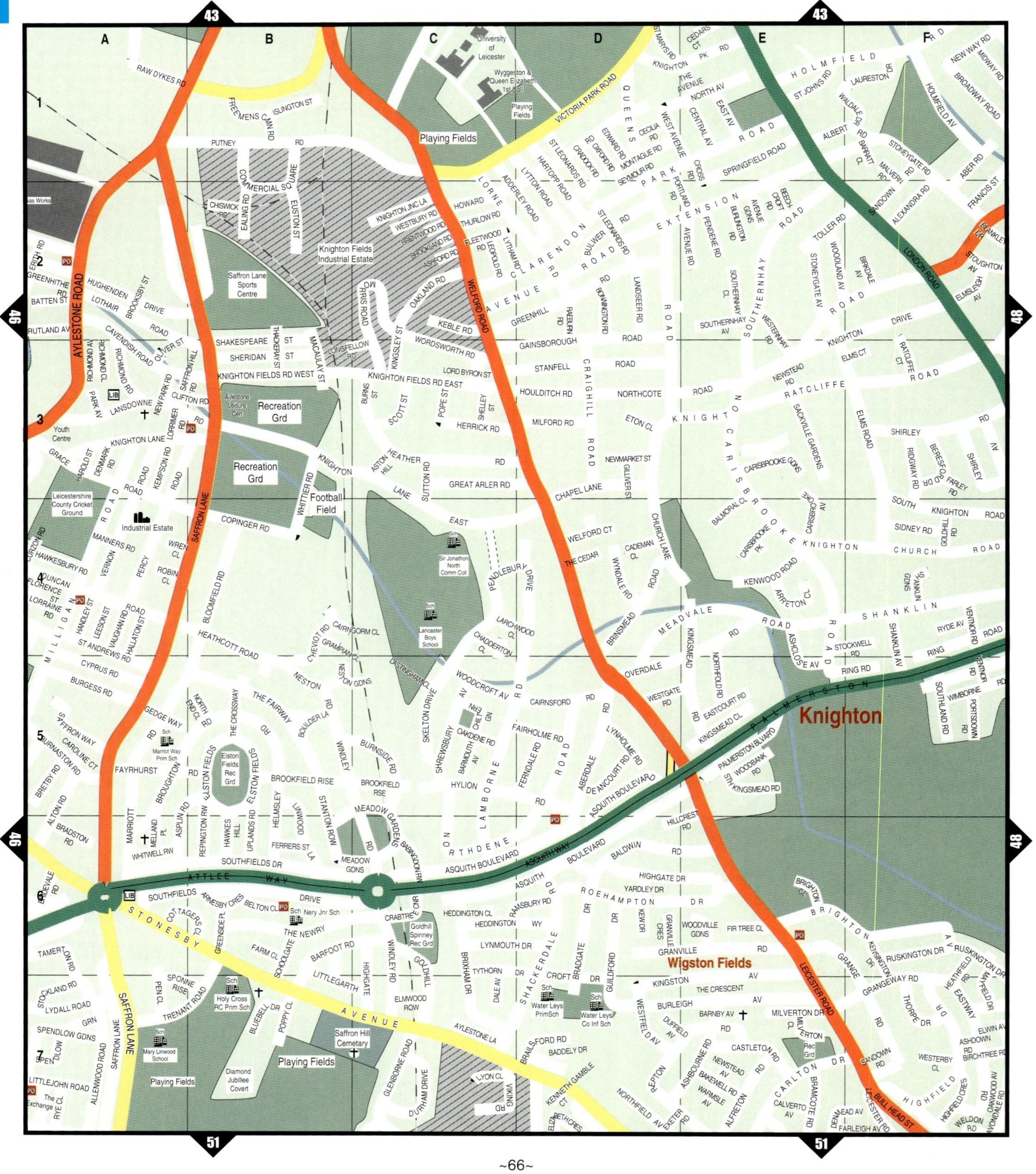

Nuha Restaurant

13 The Parade
Oadby
Leicester
LE2 5BB

Tel: 0116 2710482

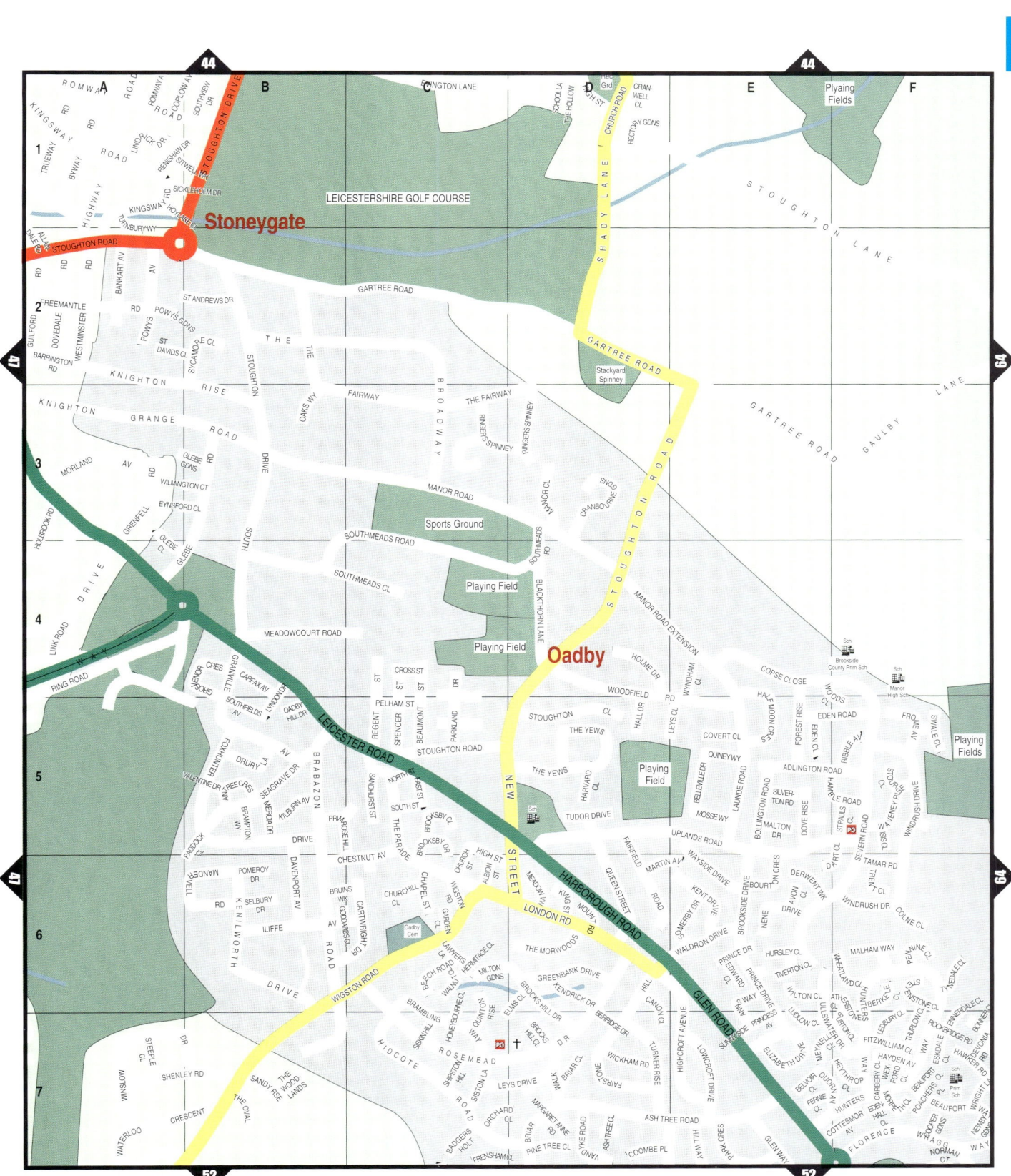

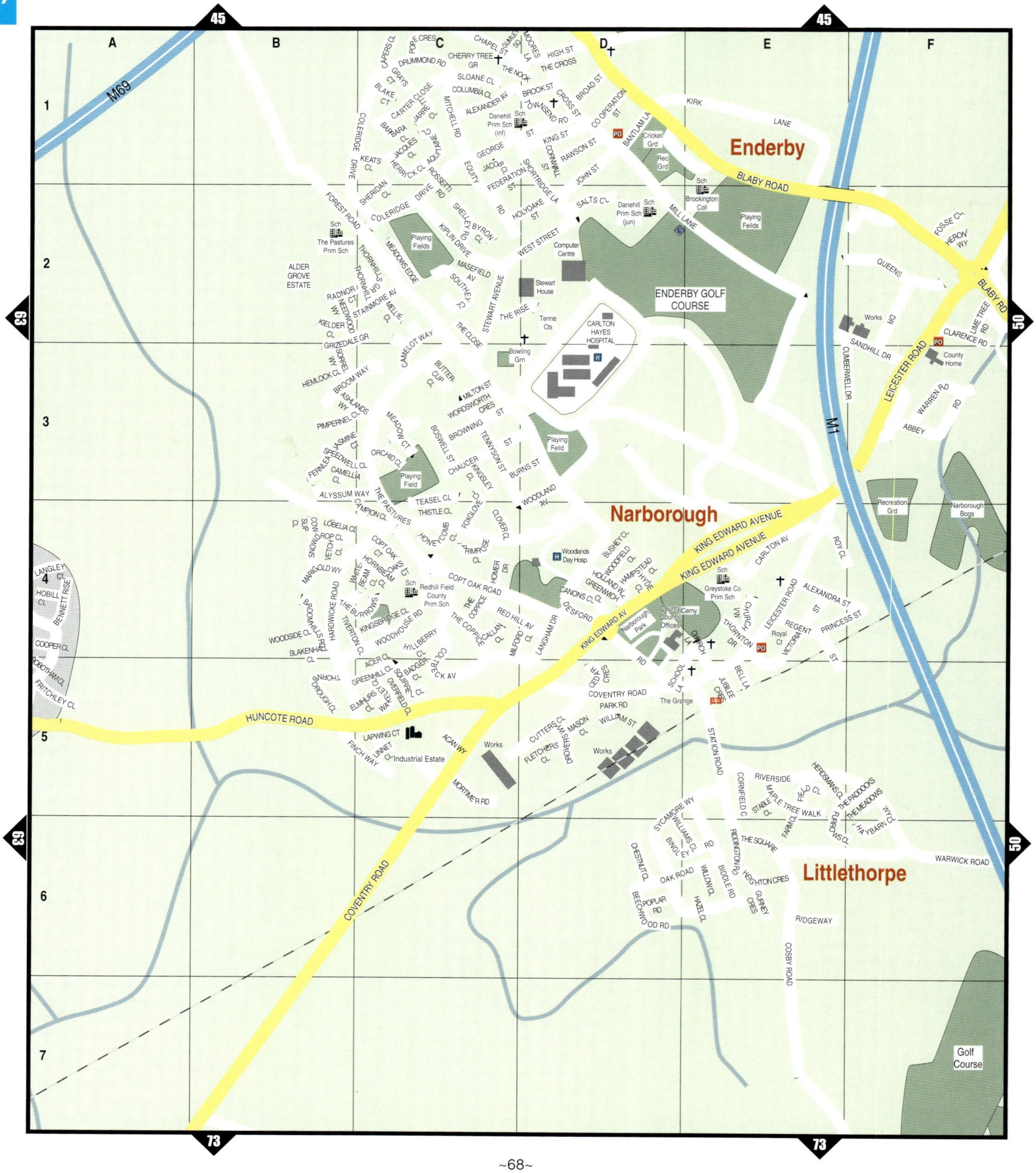

Paul Francis Joinery

- *Staircases and Replacement Balastrades*
- *Made to Measure Furniture*
- *All Joinery Work*

Telephone 0116 277 5930 ~ 0780 1789074

BIG ENOUGH TO COPE, SMALL ENOUGH TO CARE

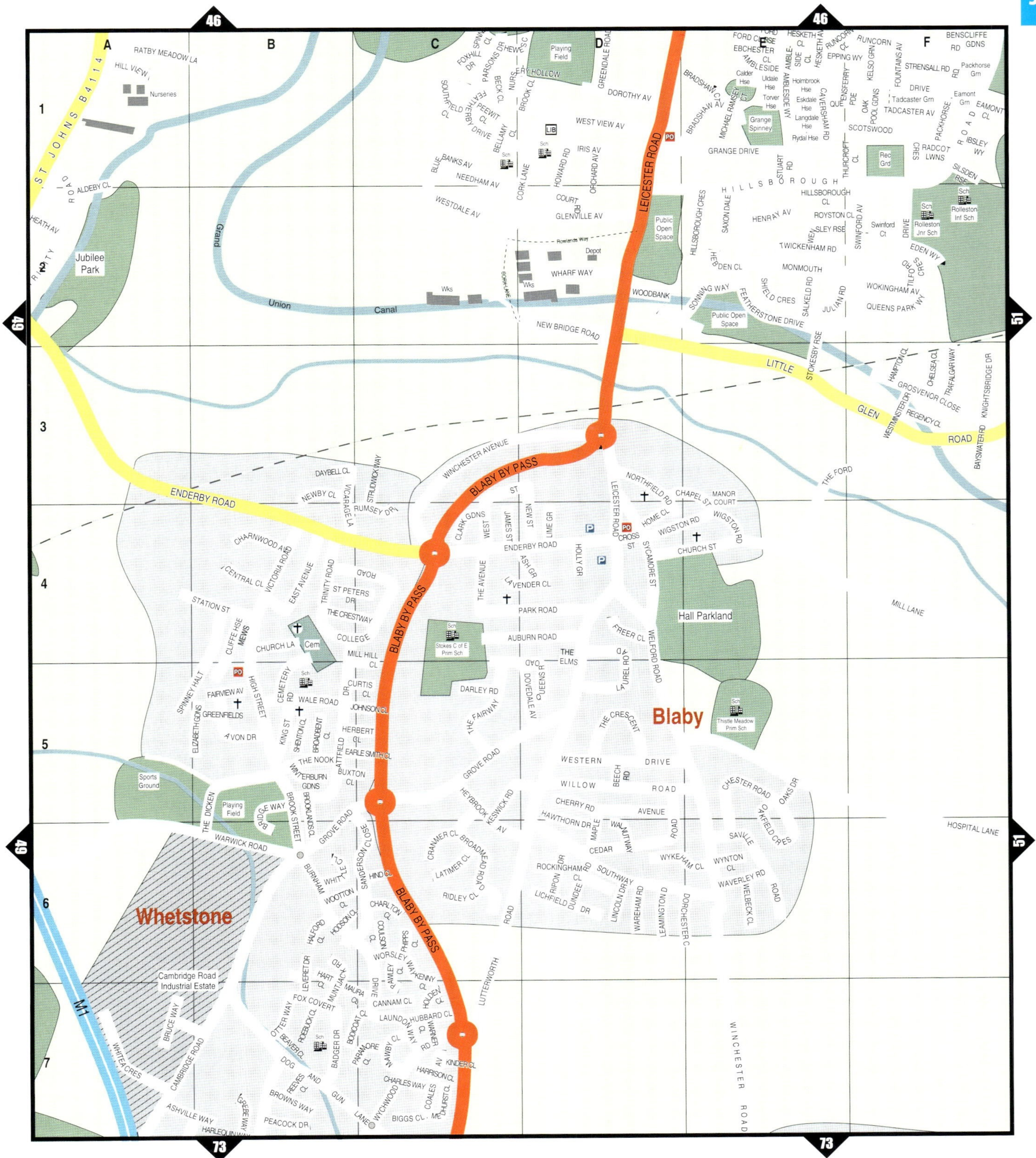

Thompson's Windows

U.P.V.C. Windows, Doors and Conservatories
Replacement windows and patio doors

**Unit 8, Premier Works, Canal Street, South Wigston,
Leicester LE18 4PL • Telephone: 0116 247 7428**

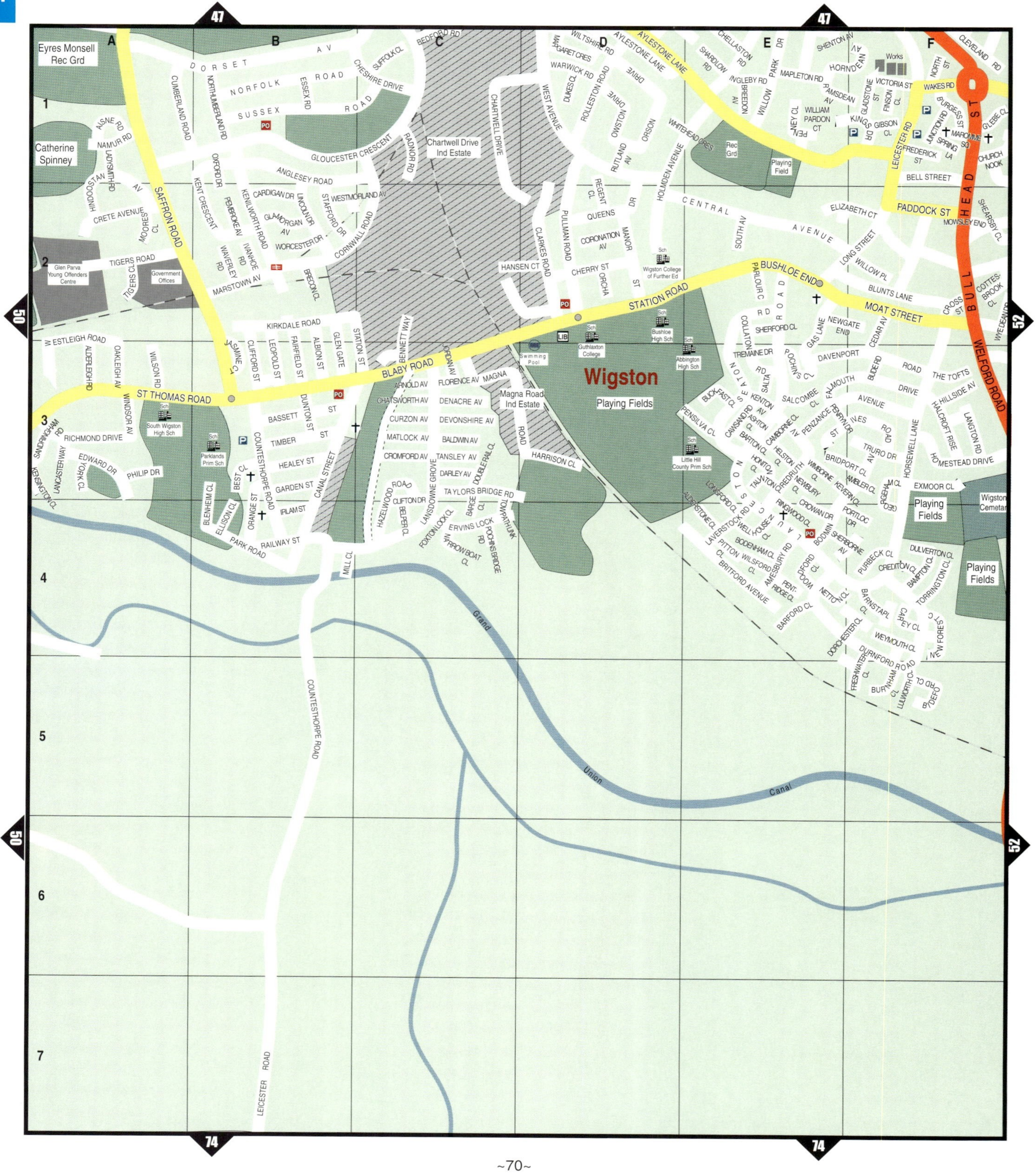

Introducing Autotecnic, the BMW Approved Specialist

Anyone can call themselves a BMW specialist, but Autotecnic can claim to be something much better: we're Britain's only BMW Approved Specialists.

Which means that, whether you already own a BMW or are thinking of buying one, your local Autotecnic centre is the only place outside a BMW dealership that officially meets BMW's exacting standards.

AUTOTECNIC 33 PARKER DRIVE, **LEICESTER** LE4 0JP
0116 2999090

BMW Approved Specialist

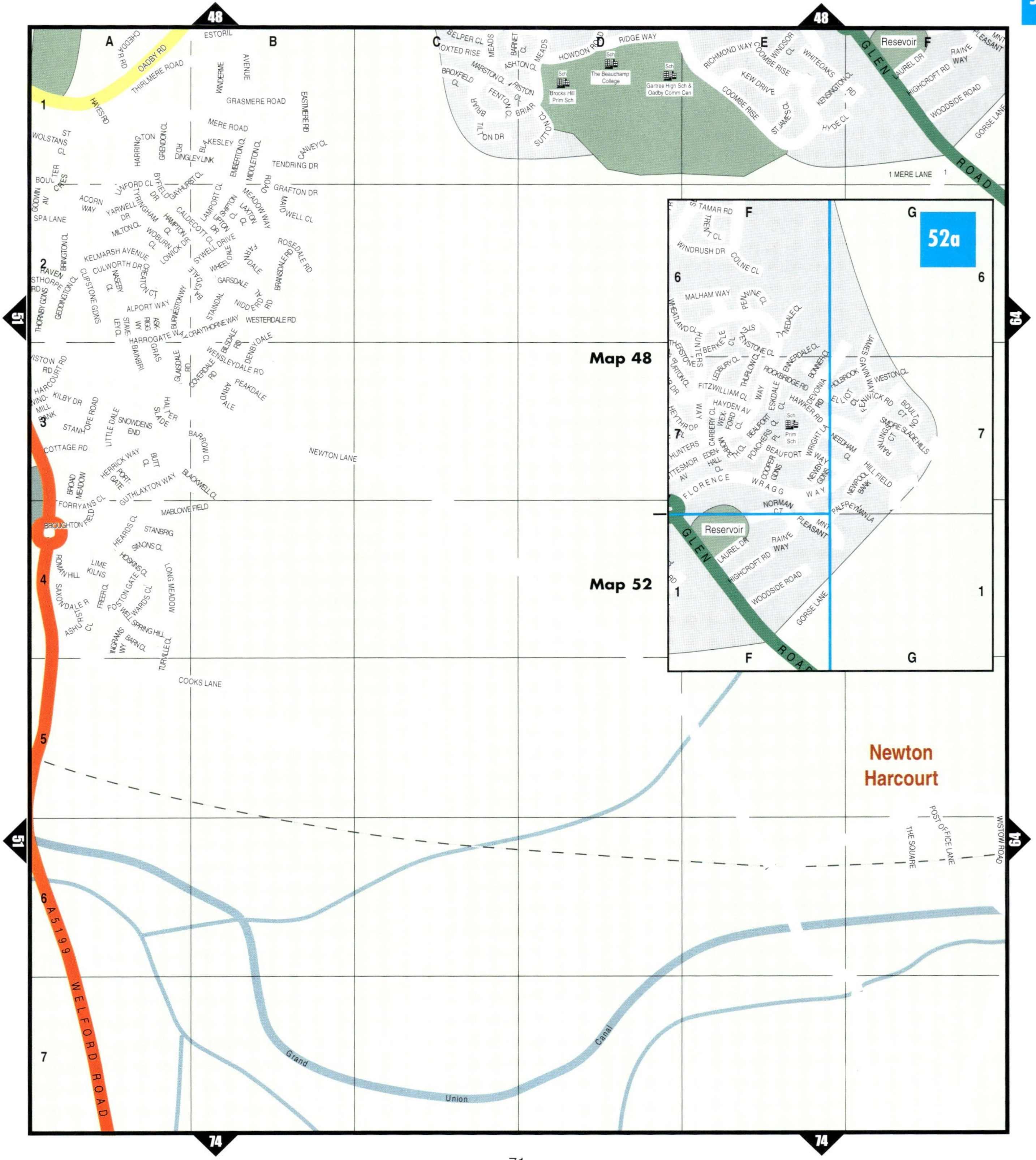

HiLiffe Travel
EXECUTIVE COACH AND CAR SERVICES

PRIVATE HIRE, BRITISH & CONTINENTAL
SHORT BREAKS & HOLIDAYS
CORPORATE HIRE & ORIENTATION TOURS

Coaches equipped with Reclining Seats, all with Seat Belts, Video, PA System, Toilet/Washroom, Fridge, Hot and Cold Drink Facilities, Digital Telephone, Optional Extra of Air Conditioning
24hr Emergency Telephone
Full International Licence

Jet House, Station Road, Ratby, Leicester LE6 0JN Tel: 0116 2387783 • Fax: 0116 2387128 Email: hiliffe@hiliffe.co.uk • Web: www.hiliffe.co.uk

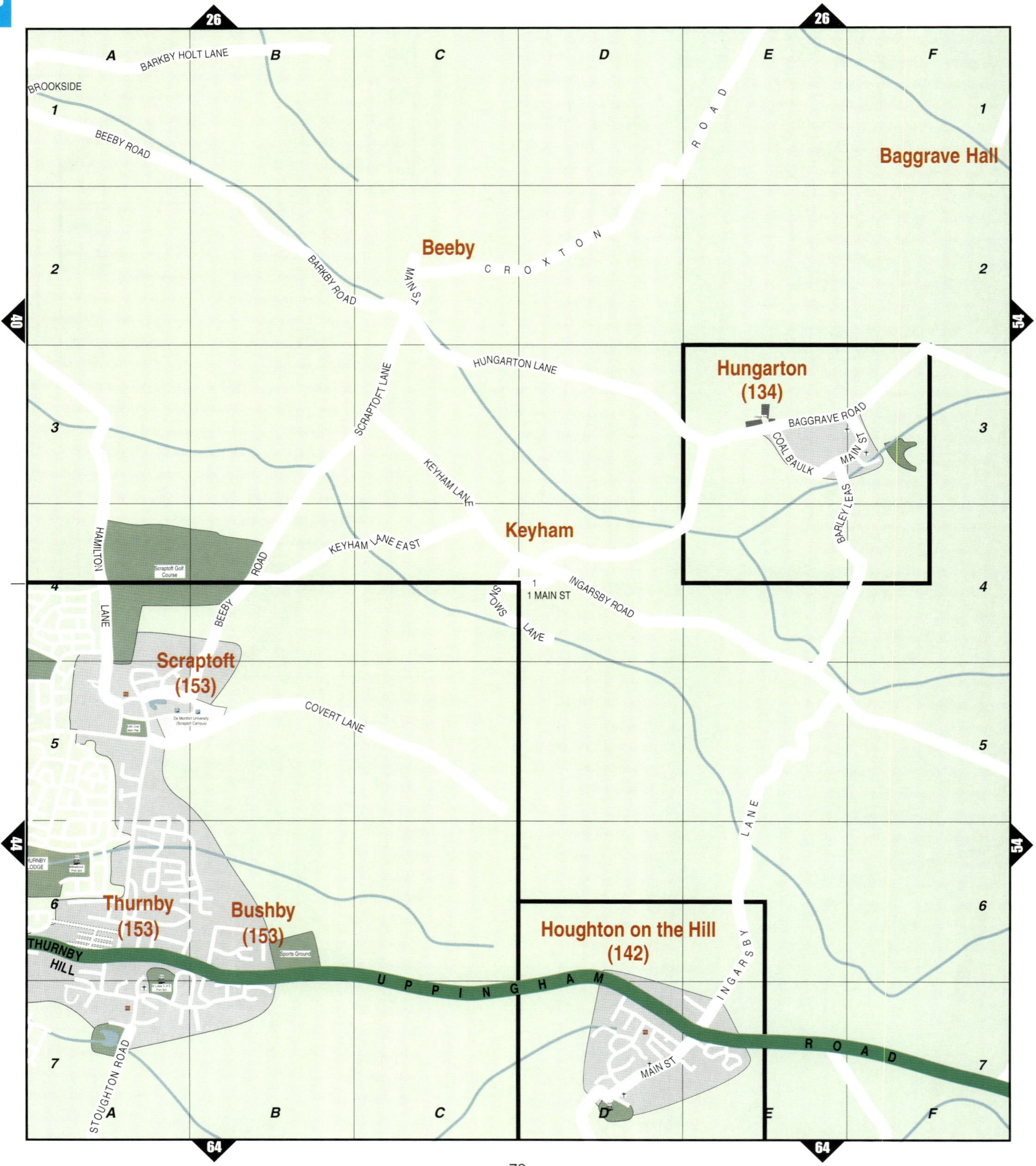

~72~

Tilton Garage Filling Station

Leicester Road, Tilton-On-The-Hill, Leicester LE7 9DB
Tel: (0116) 2597614 Mob: 07769 505635

Gas Oil *(Red Diesel)* supplied
On the pump and in
5 gallon drums
Not to be used as a road fuel
Quality Used Cars For Sale

OPEN
Mon-Fri 7am–7pm
Sat 8am–4pm
Sun 10am–2pm

ALL MAJOR CREDIT CARDS ARE ACCEPTED

Hong Kong Chinese & Cantonese Cuisine

219-219A UPPINGHAM ROAD, LEICESTER
TEL 0116 276 8652

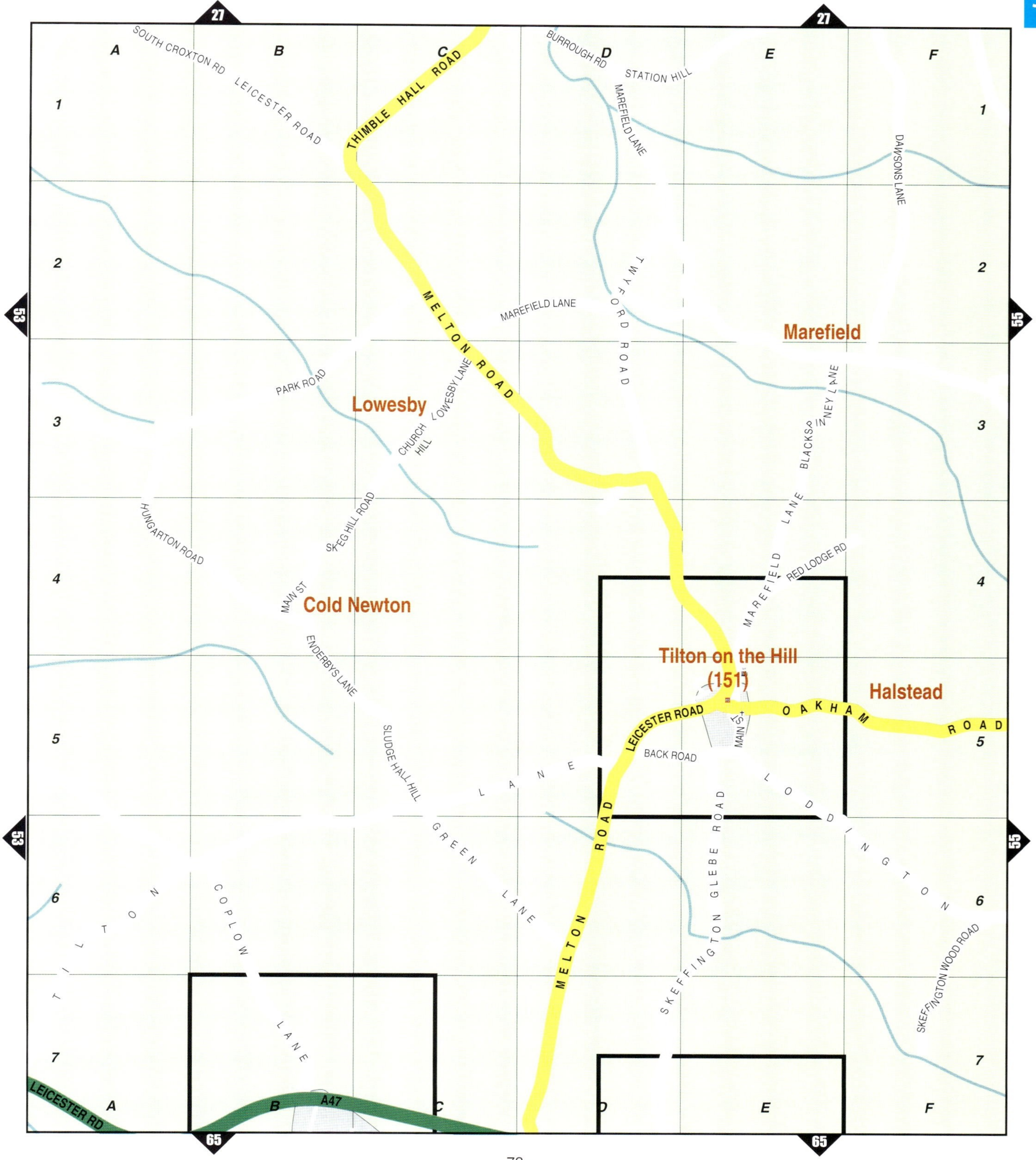

DELIVERY AVAILABLE — ESTABLISHED 1970

HOURS OF BUSINESS
Sun-Thurs 5.00pm-12midnight
Fri-Sat   12noon-2.00pm
            5.00pm-12midnight
Delivery   5.30pm-11.30pm
Open all Bank Holidays

NEW TAKEAWAY SHOP AT 260 NARBOROUGH ROAD

No.1 Commercial Surveyors & Valuers

0116 255 2694

9 DE MONTFORT STREET LEICESTER LE1 7GE
FAX 0116 255 5460 E-Mail leicester@lsh.co.uk

f & c.d. wells ltd

DECORATING CONTRACTORS

Professional Decorators for over 80 Years

Rowlands Way, Glen Parva, Leicester LE2 9HS

Telephone: (0116) 2771771   Mobile: 07850 027378
Fax: (0116) 2477339

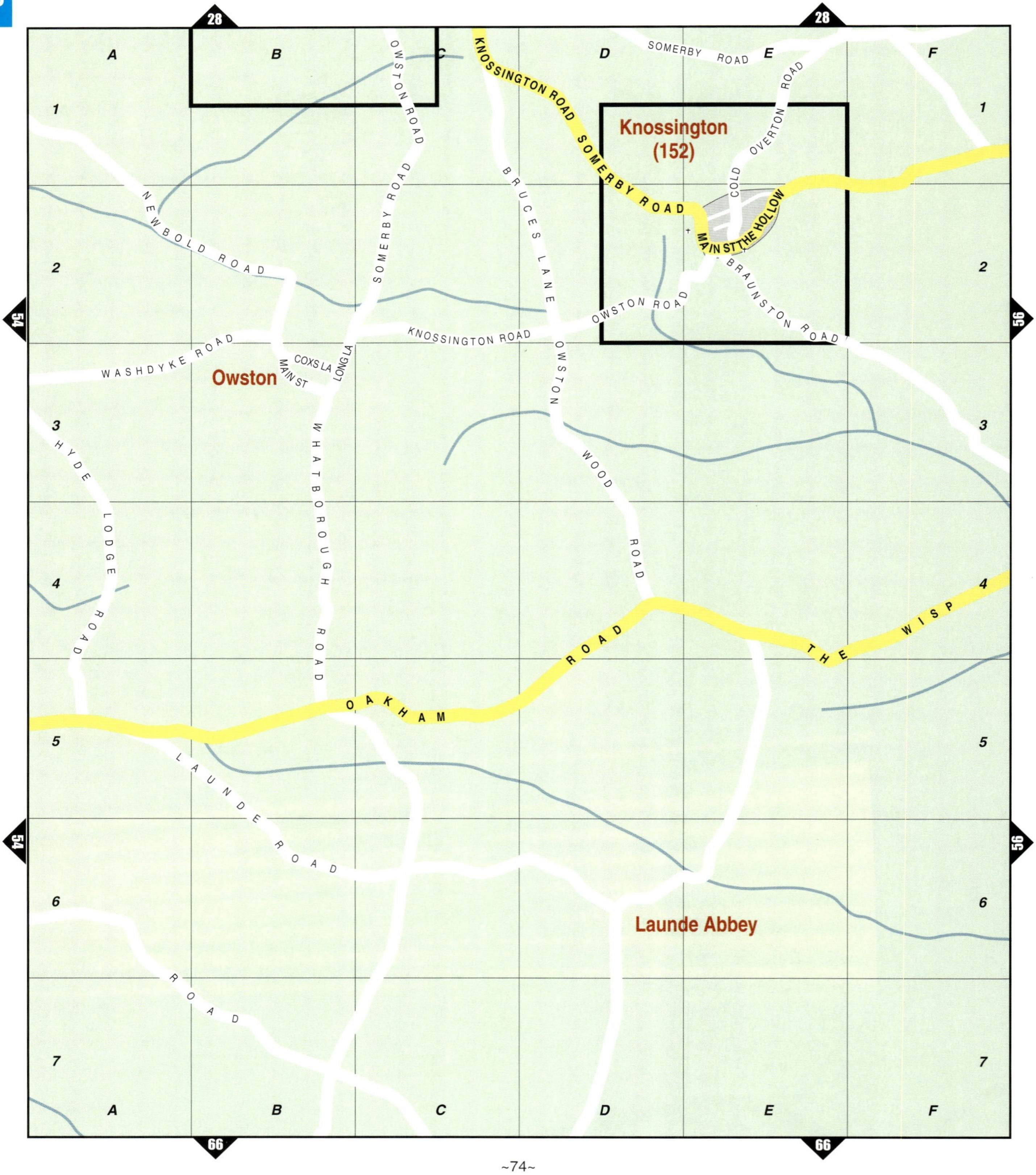

Rutland Outdoor Leisure

Outdoor Furniture
Full range of Charcoal and Gas Barbecues • Tents • Sleeping Bags
Outdoor Clothing • Cotton Parasols • Cool Boxes • Walking Boots
Hunter Wellingtons (all sizes) • etc.
Caravan Servicing • Witter Towbars   Autogas™

For All Your Outdoor Needs

STATION APPROACH, OAKHAM
TEL: 01572 724300

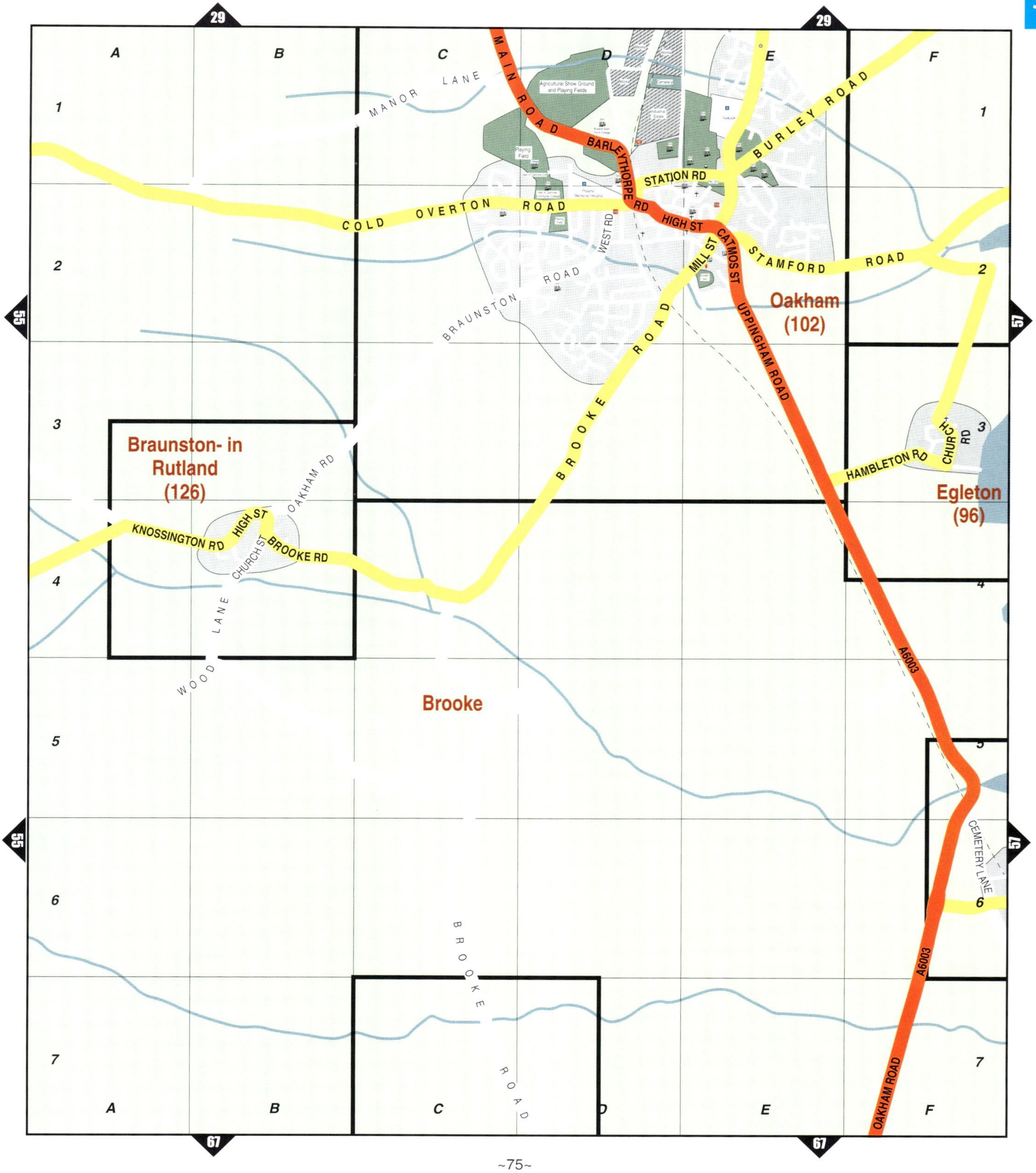

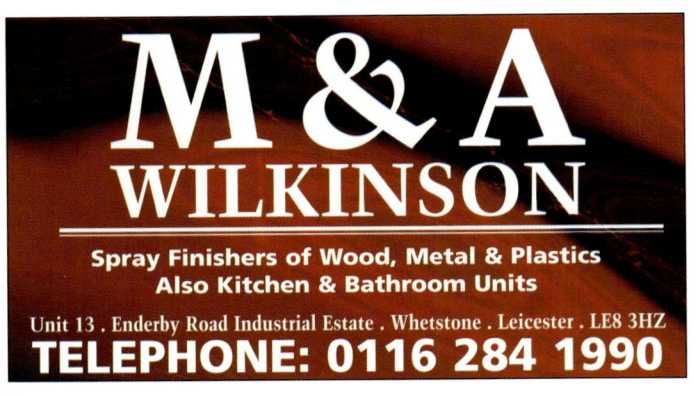

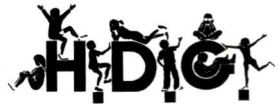

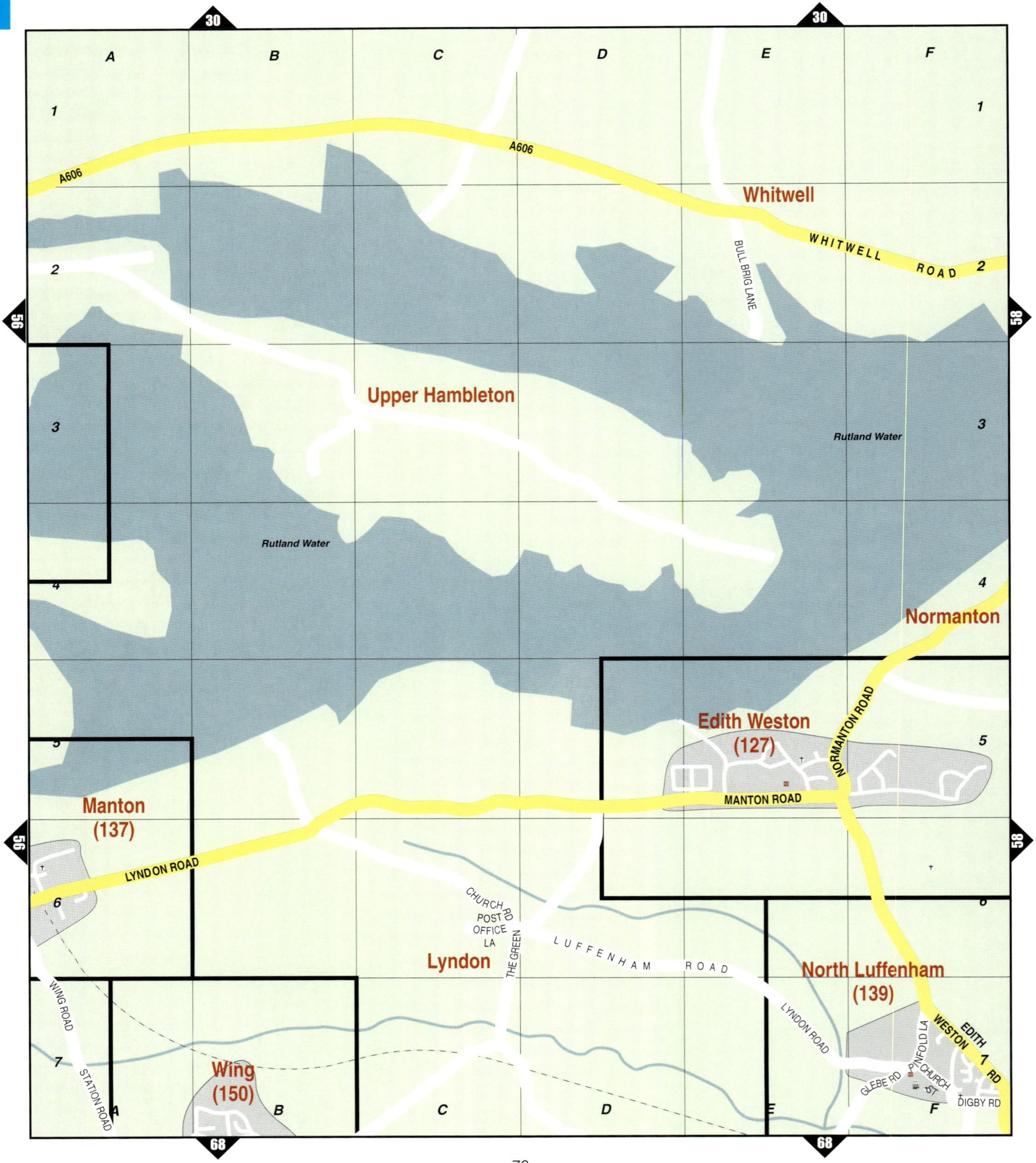
30
30
A
B
C
D
E
F
1
2
3
4
5
6
7
56
58
68
A606
Whitwell
WHITWELL ROAD
BULL BRIG LANE
Upper Hambleton
Rutland Water
Rutland Water
Normanton
NORMANTON ROAD
Edith Weston
(127)
MANTON ROAD
Manton
(137)
LYNDON ROAD
CHURCH RD
POST OFFICE LA
THE GREEN
LUFFENHAM ROAD
Lyndon
North Luffenham
(139)
LYNDON ROAD
WING ROAD
STATION ROAD
Wing
(150)
EDITH WESTON RD
PINFOLD LA
CHURCH ST
GLEBE RD
DIGBY RD

Uni-Coat

Spray Finishers for Displays and P.O.S.

Staining, Marble, Wood Effects, Metallics

74 Blackfriars Street, Leicester
Tel: 01162516188 ~ 07070714252

The B.M.G Consultancy

Arboricultural and Landscape Surveys, Planning and Design

46 Brookfield Street, Syston, Leicester LE7 2AD
Telephone/Fax: 0116 269 5388
E-Mail: BMG Group@AOL.Com

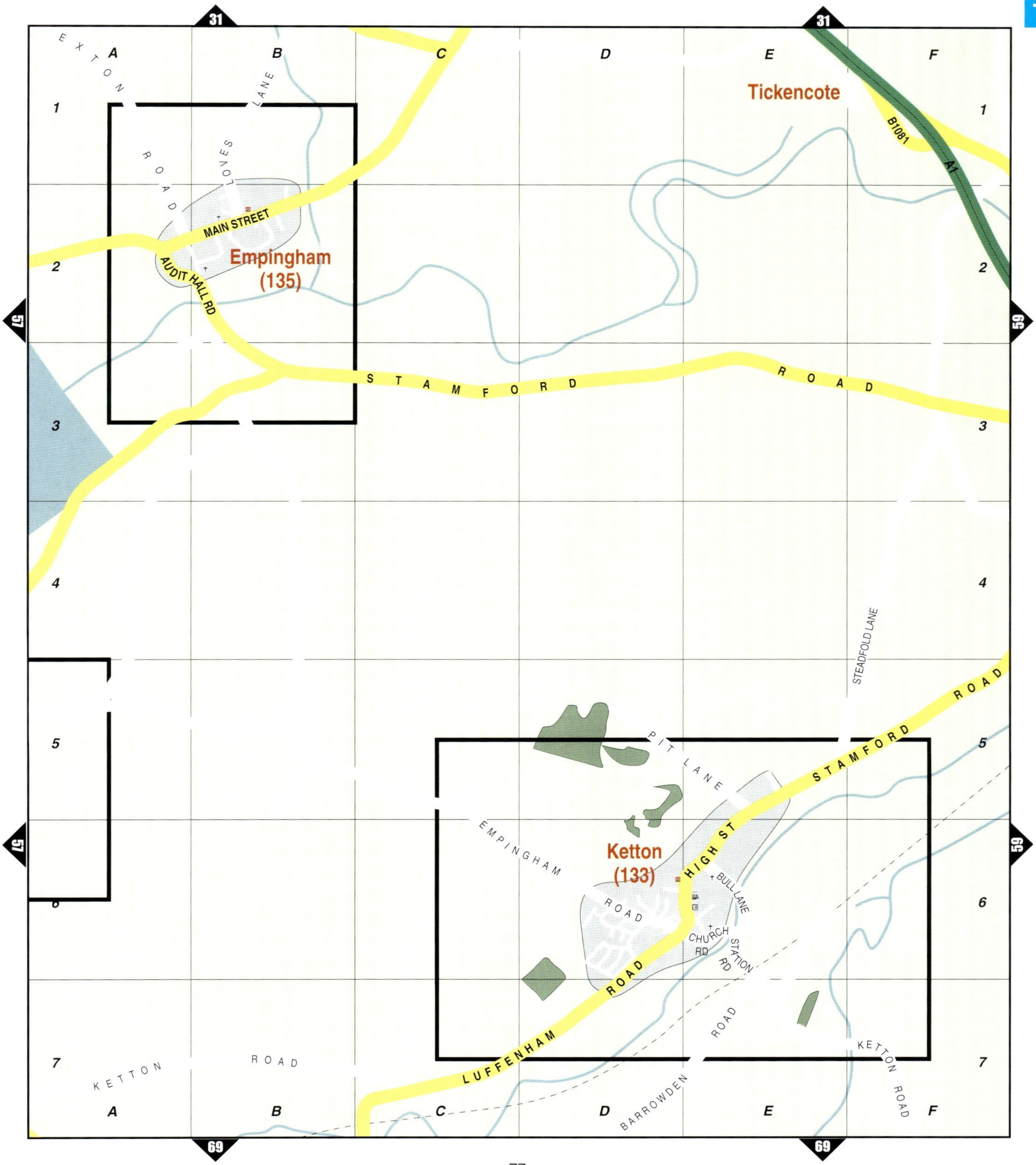

PYRAMID CARPETS & FLOOR COVERINGS FLOORING

FREE ESTIMATE
FREE DELIVERY
FREE FITTING

Suppliers of Quality Carpets, Vinyls, Rugs, Underlay, ETC.
Large Selection of Carpet Sample books also available for selection

1 Morley Road, Highfields, Leicester LE5 3HN
Tel: (0116) 2511 171 • Mobile: 07802 934292

DIAMOND
THE WORLD'S MOST VERSATILE SCROLL SAW

Will out-perform any other known make
(we stand by the Trade Descriptions Act with the above statement).
From a 4" max cut to the finest veneers. The fast change blade holders will take any blade from 4" to 12" long, pin end or plain end.
1/2 HP (375 watt motor).
3 Models with full variable speed.
Full range of accessories
BRITISH MADE with 5 year guarantee.
Phone or write for colour brochure.

J.D. WOODWARD. Power Tool Engineers, Dept SA, 6 The Narrows, Hinckley, Leics. LE10 1EH. **Tel: 01455 613432.** Export enquiries welcome.

ROBERT BAKEWELL

COUNTY PRIMARY SCHOOL AND COMMUNITY CENTRE

BARSBY DRIVE
LOUGHBOROUGH
LEICS
LE11 0UJ
Telephone: (01509) 231646 / 237811
Fax: (01509) 261230

Headteacher/Warden: TERRY MASON

K.G.B.
Grounds Maintenance

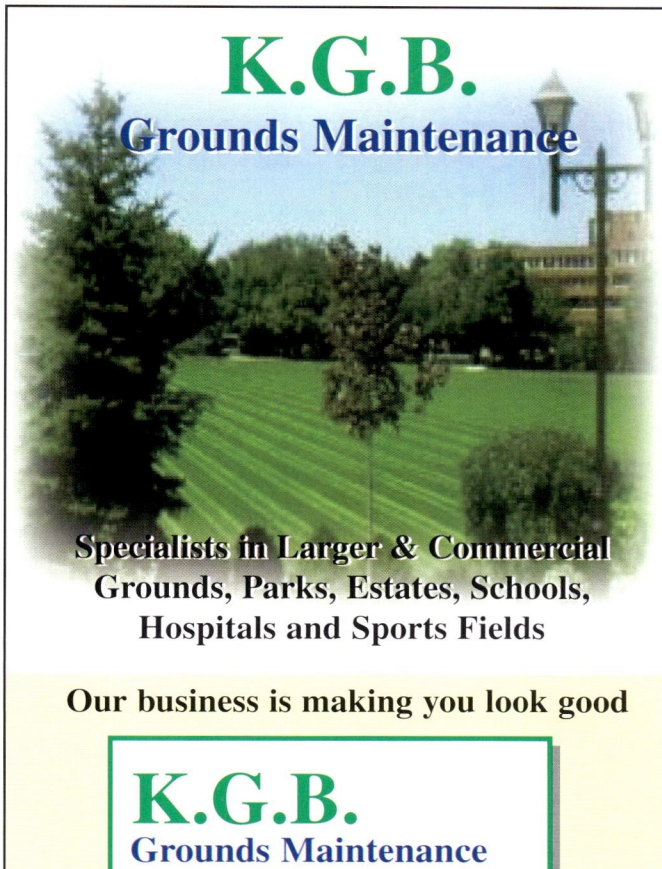

Specialists in Larger & Commercial Grounds, Parks, Estates, Schools, Hospitals and Sports Fields

Our business is making you look good

K.G.B.
Grounds Maintenance
Tel/Fax: 0116 2765388

BLACKFRIARS

"A Good Habit To Get Into"

Our specialities include:
- Real Fruit and Toffee Muffins
- Flapjacks
- Eccles Cakes
- NEW 94% Fat Free Fruit Cake

"We bake them the way You like to make them"

For further enquiries please call Karen or Jill

BLACKFRIARS BAKERY, 7-9 BLACKFRIARS STREET, LEICESTER. LE3 5DJ
TELEPHONE: 0116 2622836
FAX: 0116 2530023 • E-mail: mike@blackfriarsbakery.co.uk

The George at Great Oxendon

Relax and enjoy the peace and quiet of our country home with log fires, candelit dinners and beautiful country walks on the doorstep.

PRIVATE FUNCTIONS AND BUSINESS CONFERENCES
MEETING ROOM FOR UP TO 10 PEOPLE

Harborough Road, Great Oxendon,
Market Harborough, Leics.
Tel and Fax: (01858) 465205

THE ULTIMATE DETERRENT IN THE FIGHT AGAINST CRIME

Professional Protection for your Property

THE POLE provides a simple, secure and cost effective method of protecting your vehicles, your home and garage or simply controlling access.

THE POLE is simply lifted out of the ground and in seconds is locked in the upright position using its integral high security push button lock.

When not in use, the pole slides smoothly back beneath the ground and locks, leaving just the lid visible.

PROTEC POLES

19 Kirkhill, Shepshed, Loughborough,
Leicestershire LE12 9PA
Tel: 01509 505879 Fax: 01509 505943
http://www.protecuk.demon.co.uk
E-mail: sales@protecuk.demon.co.uk

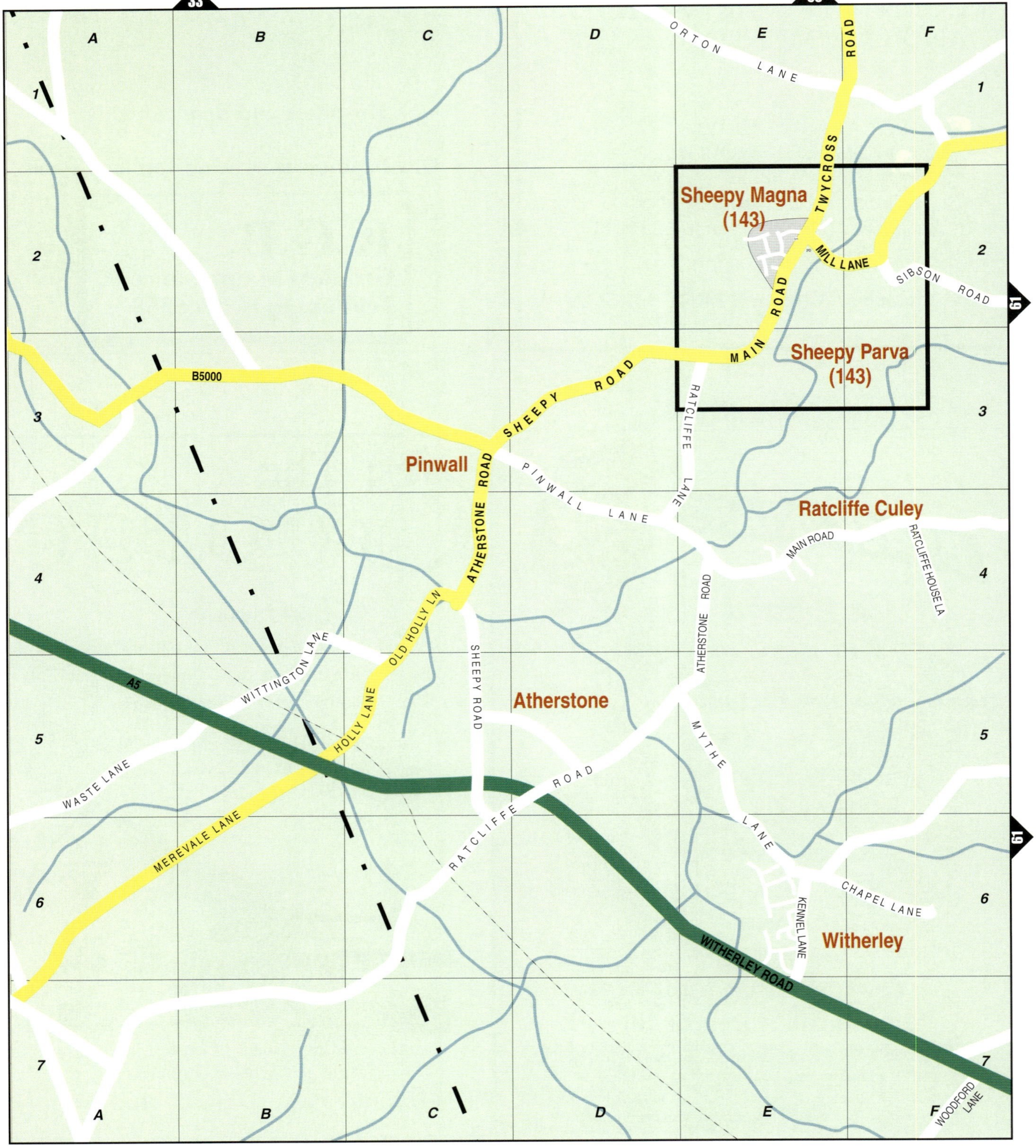

MK Autos
**Full Servicing & Mechanical,
Including Body Work and MOT Repairs
All Car Makes and Models Work Undertaken**
2/6 Bonsall Street, Leicester LE5 5AD
Tel: (0116) 2545439
Mobile: 07802 450605

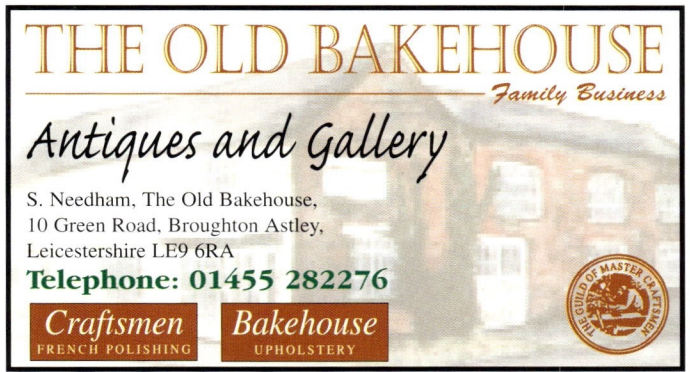

THE OLD BAKEHOUSE
Family Business

Antiques and Gallery

S. Needham, The Old Bakehouse,
10 Green Road, Broughton Astley,
Leicestershire LE9 6RA
Telephone: 01455 282276

Craftsmen FRENCH POLISHING | **Bakehouse** UPHOLSTERY

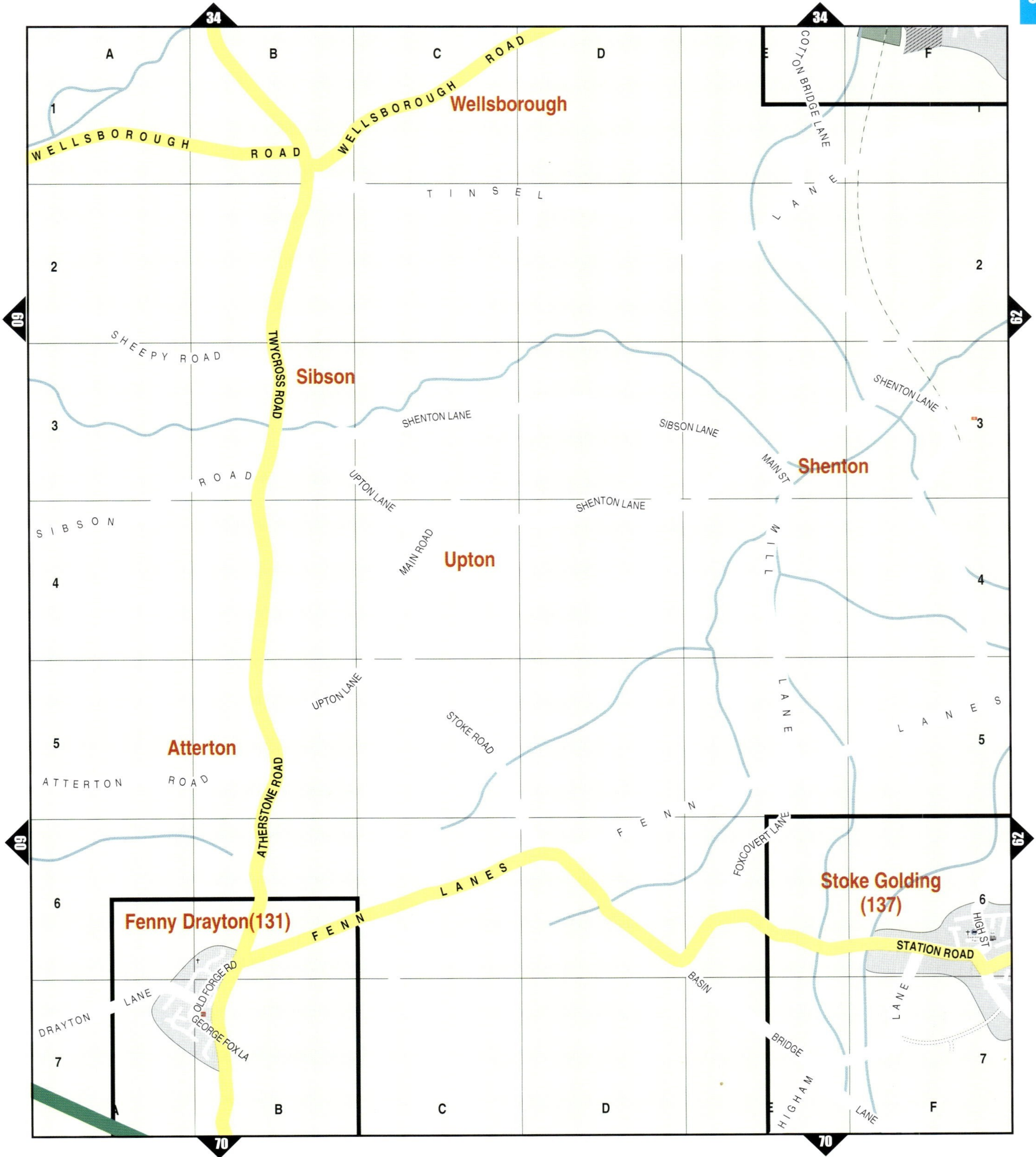

CHALOSS CO. LTD.
Tail Lifts and Hydraulic Engineers

Commercial Vehicle body repairs – Tail Lift repairs – Painting – Steam Cleaning.

Trailer Sales, from Camping to 3½ ton.
One **STOP** Facility for all your Transport needs.

Member

ISO9002 REGISTERED COMPANY
Certificate No. 6156

Tel: 01455 843303
Fax: 01455 847105

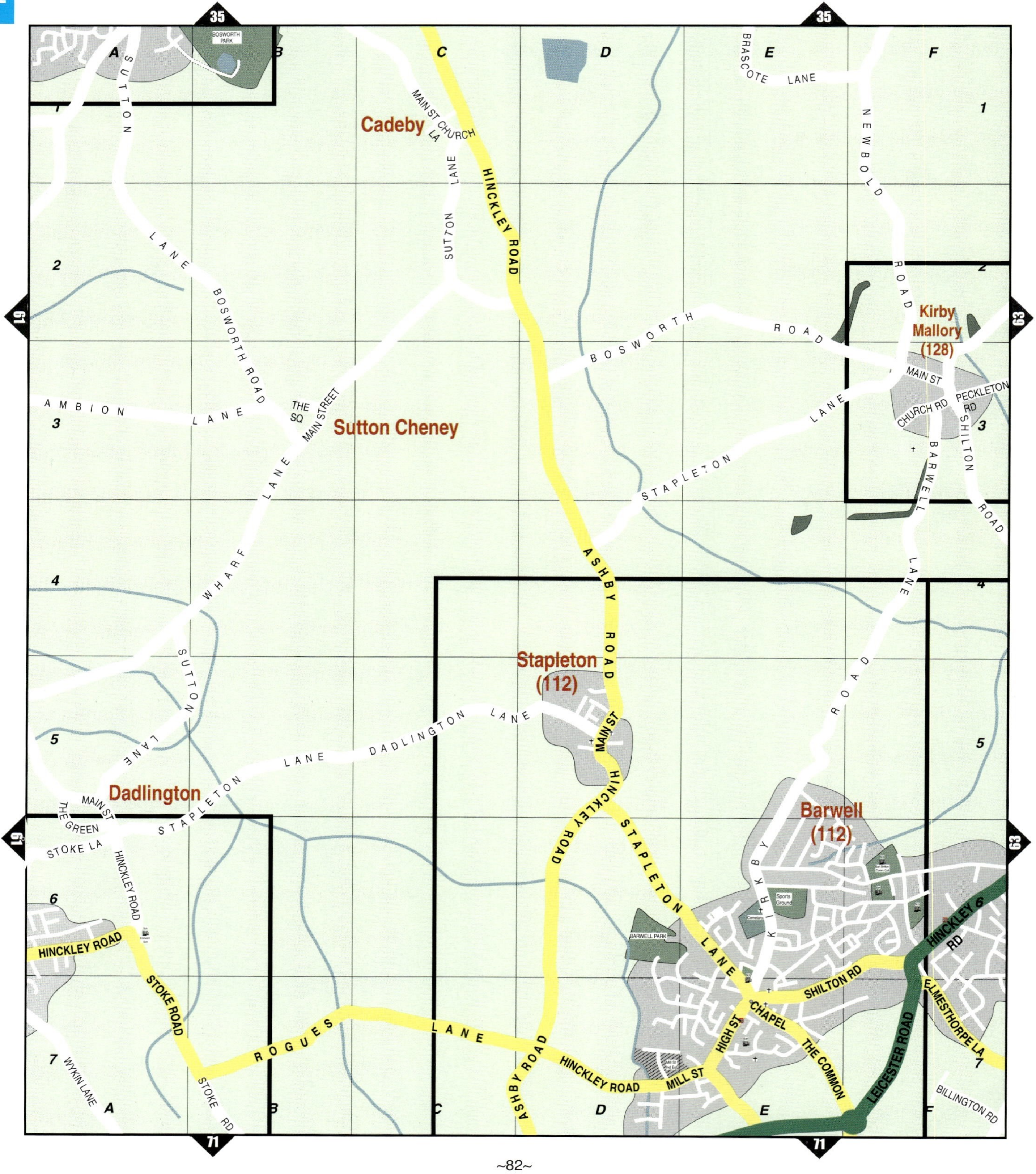

SHIRLEY SKIP HIRE
DO IT ALL PAY LESS

Skips Big or Small give us a call.
Household, Commercial and Builders • Waste Undertaken
Licensed Waste Carrier

01455 220672 • 0116 287 9758
CHURCH VIEW, LEICESTER ROAD, WOLVEY LE10 3LB

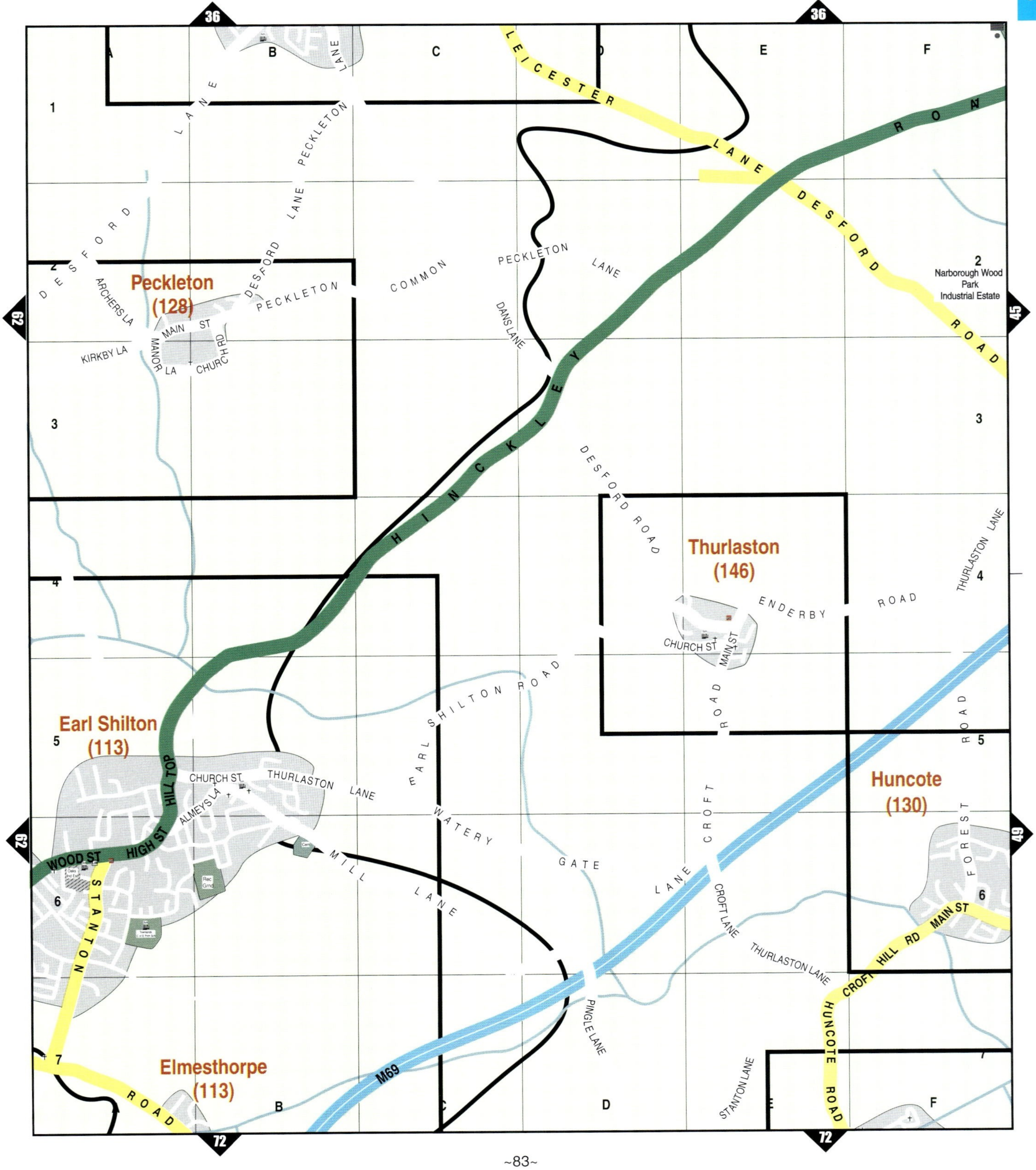

D.J. PLANT HIRE

TEL 07971061858
TEL/FAX 0116 2593125

AVAILABLE FOR HIRE WITH OR WITHOUT OPERATORS
360'S FROM 1 TON TO 15 TON
2CX'S & 3CX'S
ALL AVAILABLE WITH BREAKERS
3CX'S WITH PATCH PLANERS
TRACTORS FROM 35hp TO 145hp
• • • • • • • • • • • • • •
FREE ESTIMATES
ACCESS KERBS DROPPED
DRIVES TARMACED
SITES CLEARED

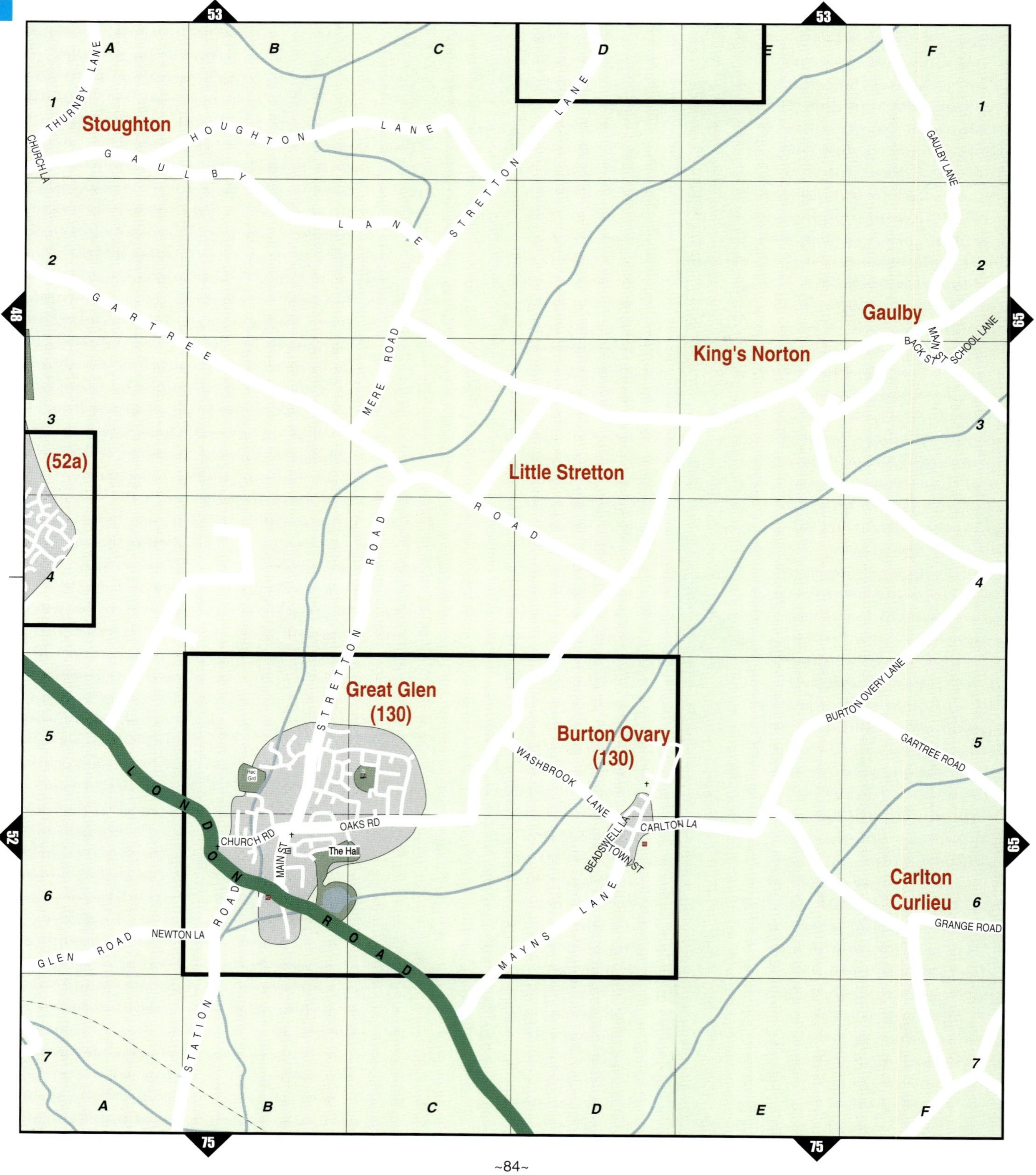

- Stoughton
- Gaulby
- King's Norton
- Little Stretton
- (52a)
- Great Glen (130)
- Burton Ovary (130)
- Carlton Curlieu

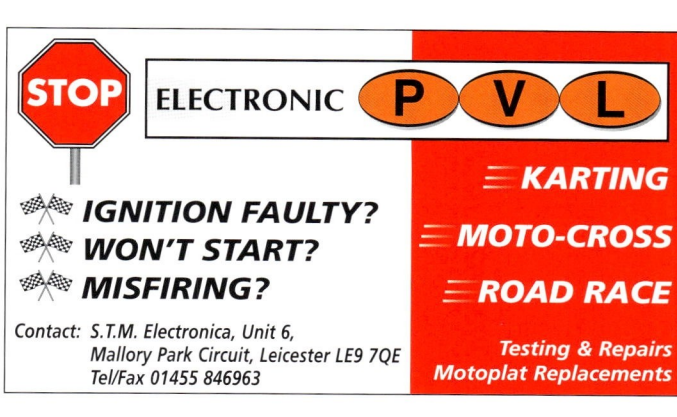

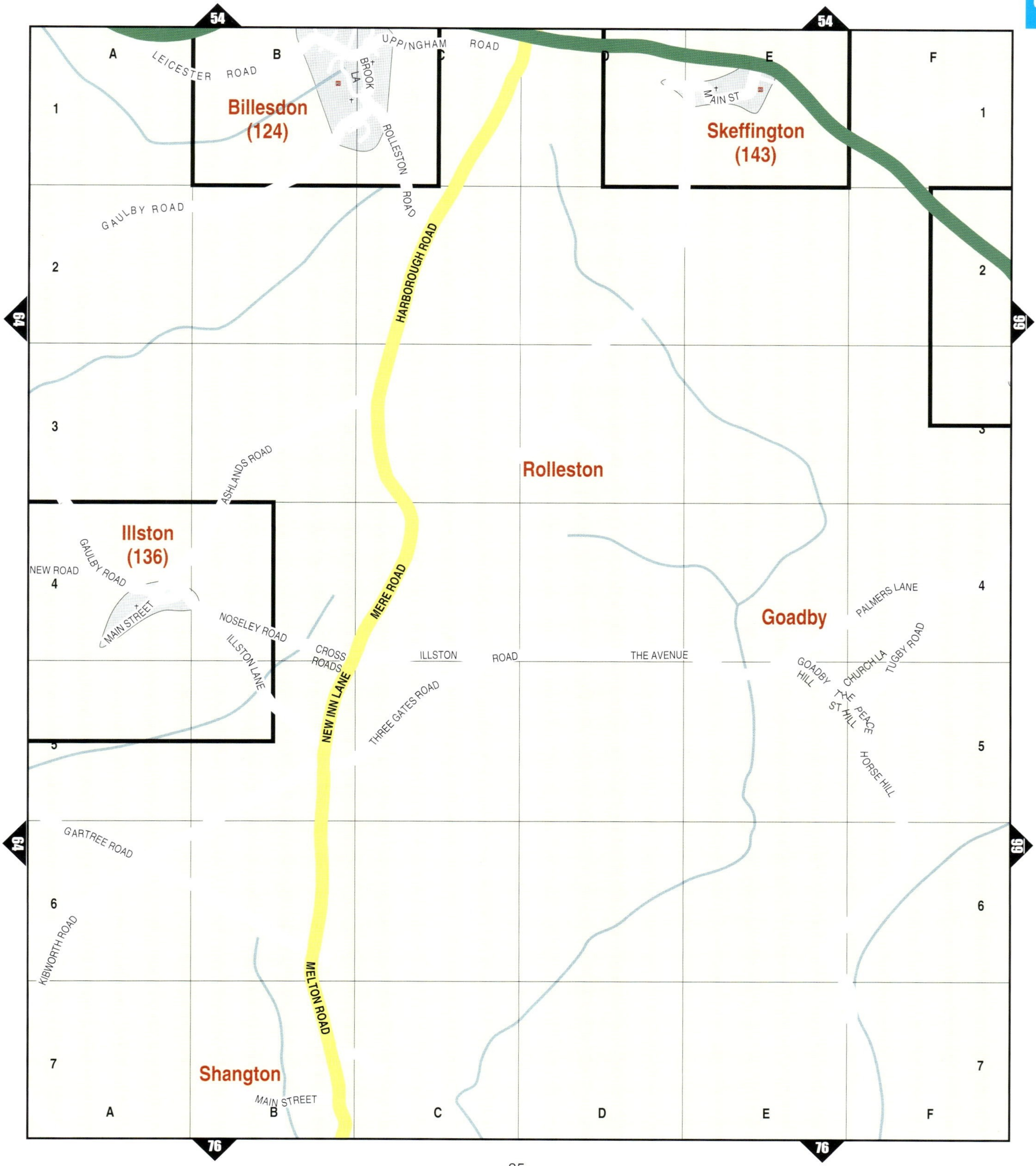
54
54
Billesdon
(124)
Skeffington
(143)
Rolleston
Illston
(136)
Goadby
Shangton
UPPINGHAM ROAD
LEICESTER ROAD
BROOK LA
ROLLESTON ROAD
MAIN ST
GAULBY ROAD
HARBOROUGH ROAD
ASHLANDS ROAD
GAULBY ROAD
NEW ROAD
MAIN STREET
NOSELEY ROAD
ILLSTON LANE
CROSS ROADS
MERE ROAD
NEW INN LANE
ILLSTON ROAD
THE AVENUE
THREE GATES ROAD
PALMERS LANE
TUGBY ROAD
CHURCH LA
GOADBY HILL
THE PEACE
ST HILL
HORSE HILL
GARTREE ROAD
KIBWORTH ROAD
MELTON ROAD
MAIN STREET
A
B
C
D
E
F
1
2
3
4
5
6
7
64
64
66
66
76
76

BROOK LANE GARAGE
Commercial Vehicles Sales and Service

Hunts Lane, Desford, Leicestershire LE9 9LJ
Telephone: 01455 822251 & 823639
Fax: 01455 822429

DPL Office Furniture

With products from the UK's leading manufacturers, DPL have all your office furniture answers, whatever your taste and budget.

- From one chair or filing cabinet, to a complete refit.
- All furniture delivered and installed with the minimum of downtime.
- Sales staff who will visit and discuss your requirements.
- Our Turn Key project approach leaves you free to carry on your business.
- Full design and build service.
- Part exchange allowance with all old furniture removed.
- Suppliers of Banqueting and Conference Furniture. Please call for details.

56 Snow Hill, Melton Mowbray, Leicestershire LE13 1PH
Phone: 01664 482585 • Fax: 01664 481376

66

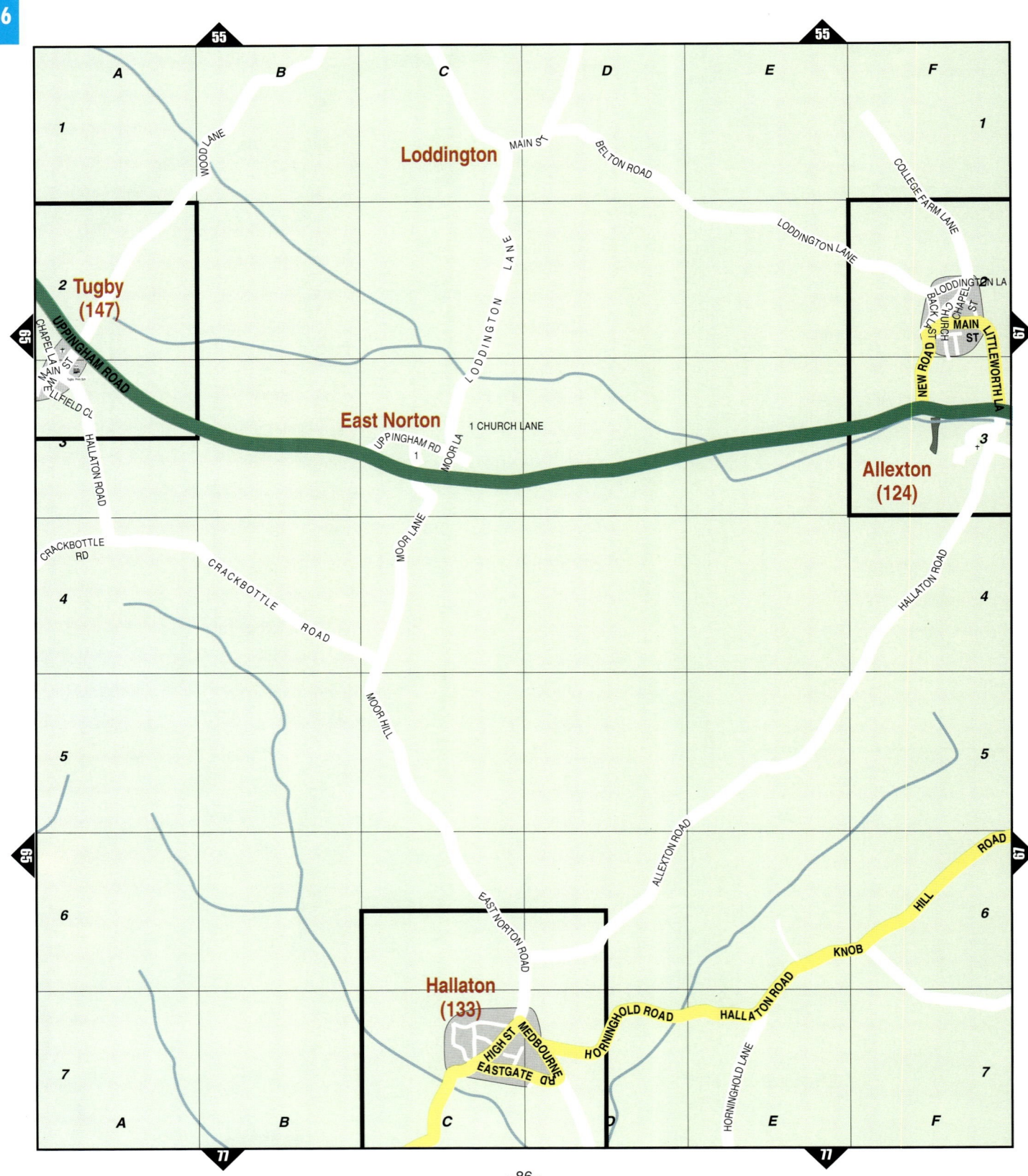

~86~

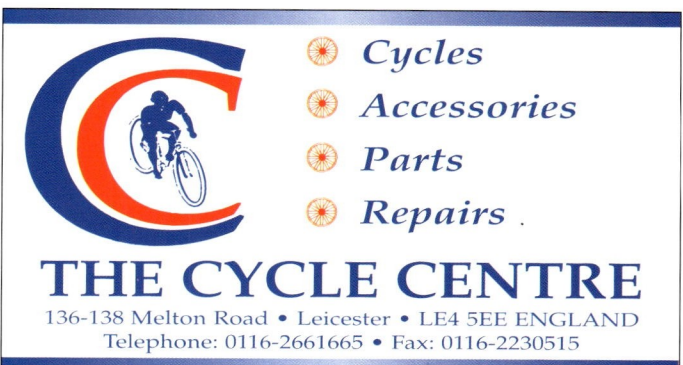

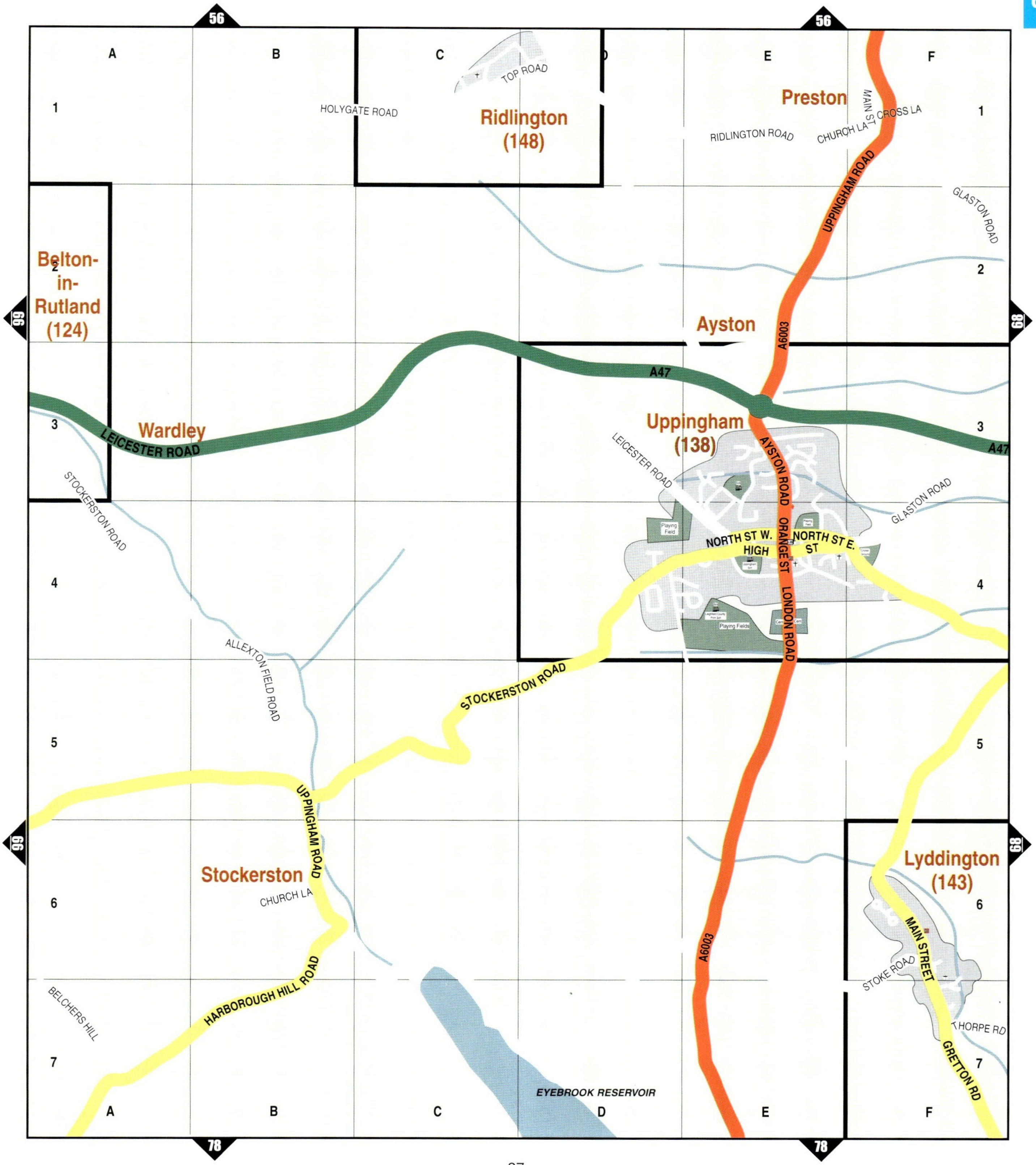
56
A
B
C
D
E
F
1
2
3
4
5
6
7
HOLYGATE ROAD
TOP ROAD
Ridlington
(148)
Preston
MAIN ST
CROSS LA
CHURCH LA
RIDLINGTON ROAD
UPPINGHAM ROAD
GLASTON ROAD
Belton-
in-
Rutland
(124)
66
68
Ayston
A6003
A47
Wardley
LEICESTER ROAD
Uppingham
(138)
LEICESTER ROAD
AYSTON ROAD
GLASTON ROAD
NORTH ST W.
NORTH ST E.
HIGH
ST
ORANGE ST
LONDON ROAD
Playing Fields
STOCKERSTON ROAD
ALLEXTON FIELD ROAD
STOCKERSTON ROAD
UPPINGHAM ROAD
Stockerston
CHURCH LA
Lyddington
(143)
MAIN STREET
STOKE ROAD
THORPE RD
GRETTON RD
BELCHERS HILL
HARBOROUGH HILL ROAD
A6003
EYEBROOK RESERVOIR
78

Lumbers

Leicester's finest Jewellers since 1881

Leah Marks House
10-12 Market Street
Leicester.
Telephone: 0116 255 1233

C.S. ELLIS (GROUP) LTD
Established 1933

INCORPORATING
palletine plc
Palletised distribution for the UK and Europe

- **STORAGE & DISTRIBUTION** — 100,000 sq.ft. covered and 2 hectares uncovered
- **DISTRIBUTION THROUGHOUT THE UK**
- **EUROPEAN GROUPAGE SERVICE**

Wireless Hill, South Luffenham, Oakham, Rutland LE15 8NF

STAMFORD (01780) 720133
FAX: (01780) 721801
EMAIL: mail@csellis.co.uk
www.csellis.co.uk

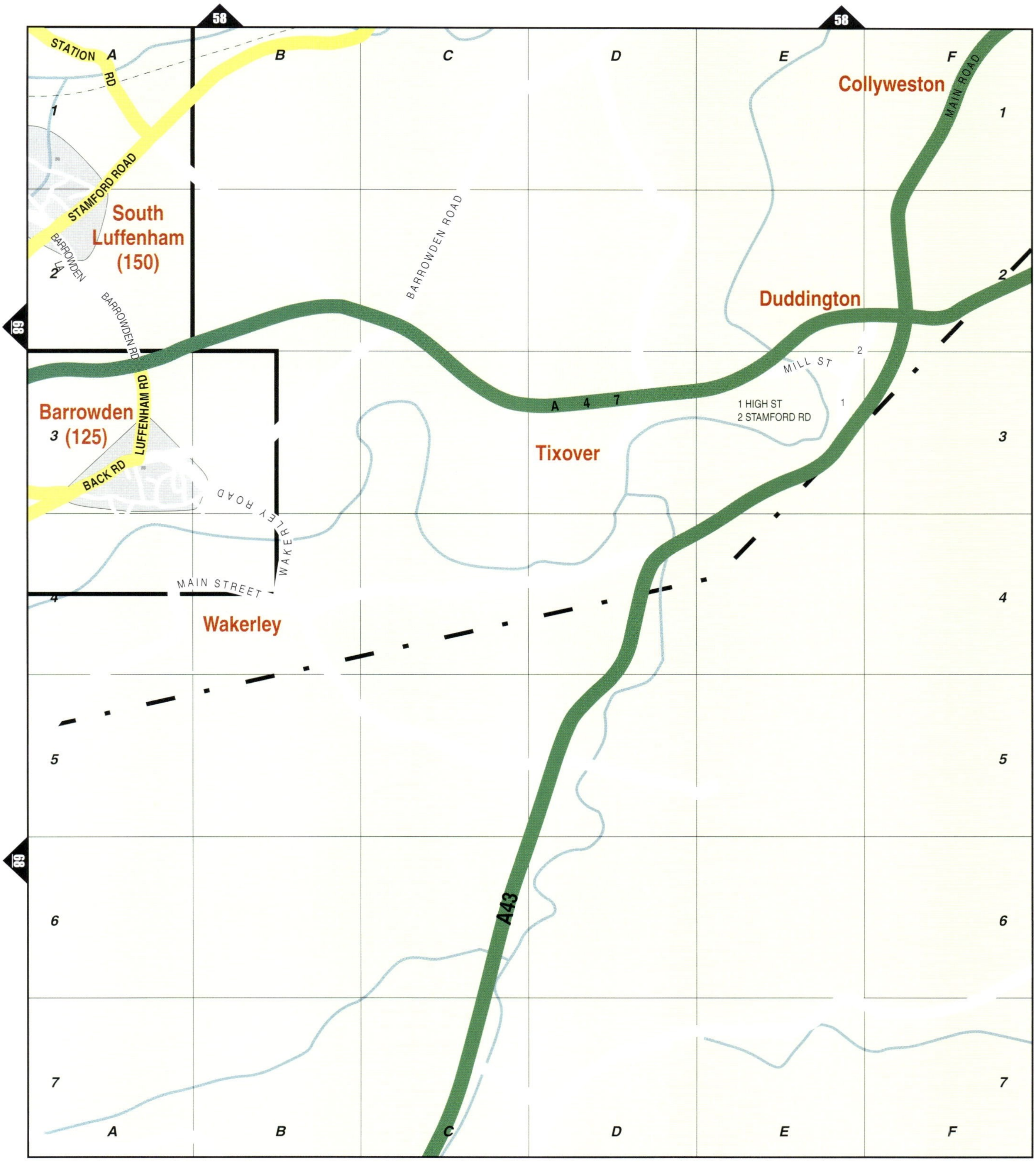

69

Map showing South Luffenham (150), Barrowden (125), Wakerley, Tixover, Duddington (1 High St, 2 Stamford Rd), Collyweston. Roads include Station Rd, Stamford Road, Barrowden Rd, Luffenham Rd, Back Rd, Main Street, Wakerley Road, Barrowden Road, Mill St, Main Road, A47, A43.

LOOKING FOR INDUSTRIAL PREMISES?

Telephone Leicester (0116) 265 7031 for a FREE copy of the

Leicestershire Industrial Property Bulletin.

Updated bi-monthly, this publication lists all known industrial factory, workshop and warehouse premises available in Leicester and Leicestershire.

LEICESTERSHIRE COUNTY COUNCIL
DEPARTMENT OF PLANNING AND TRANSPORTATION

When telephoning, please say where you saw this advert

CITROËN SERVICE CENTRE
SERVICE • CAR SALES MOT REPAIRS

21 Main Road
Nether Broughton
Melton Mowbray
Leicestershire LE14 3HB

Telephone
Workshop: 01664 822273
Mobile: 07971 190418

Map 145 B2

WRIGHT PLASTICS LTD

Plastic Injection Moulders

Product Design
Mould Making
Injection Moulding
Assembly
Hot Foil Printing
Transfer Printing

Fernie Road, Market Harborough,
Leicester LE16 7PH
Tel: 01858 4656651 Fax: 01858 431831
E-mail: wright@wplastic.demon.co.uk
Web: www.wplastic.co.uk

A warm welcome awaits you at the

T & K Balti House Restaurant

132 / 134 Green Lane Road,
Leicester LE5 3TL

For a Reservation
(0116) 274 3310

PARTIES CATERED FOR

HOLLYCROFT ENGINEERING LIMITED

Tel: 01455 635845
Fax: 01455 250273

7 Teal Business Park,
Dodwells Bridge Industrial Estate,
Hinckley, Leicestershire LE10 3BZ

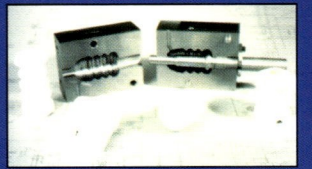

Precision Experimental and General Machining • Mould Making • Jigs • Fixtures • Tool Design

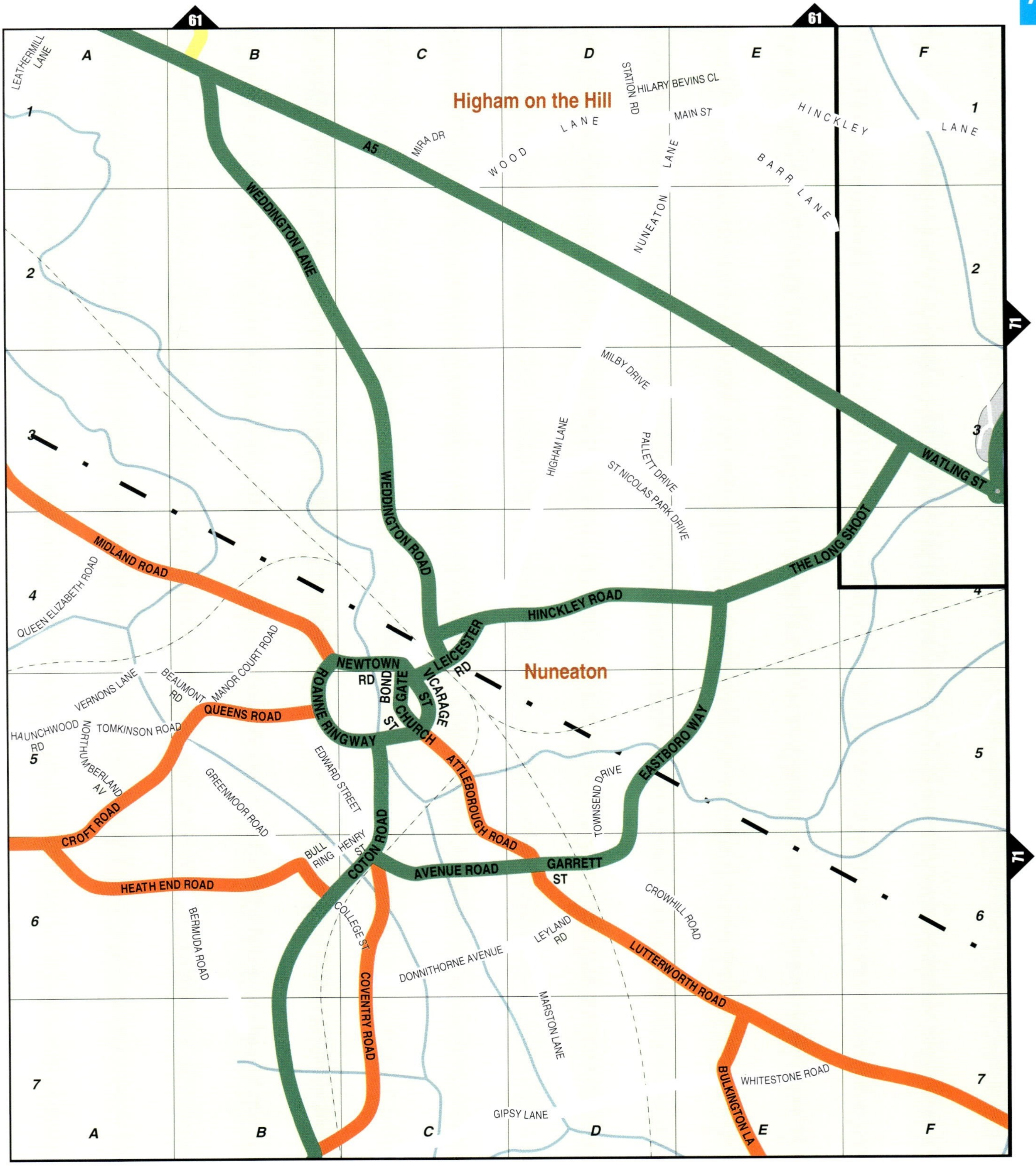

KAW beauty

78 Castle Street
Hinckley
Leicester
LE10 1DD

Tel: 01455 891785

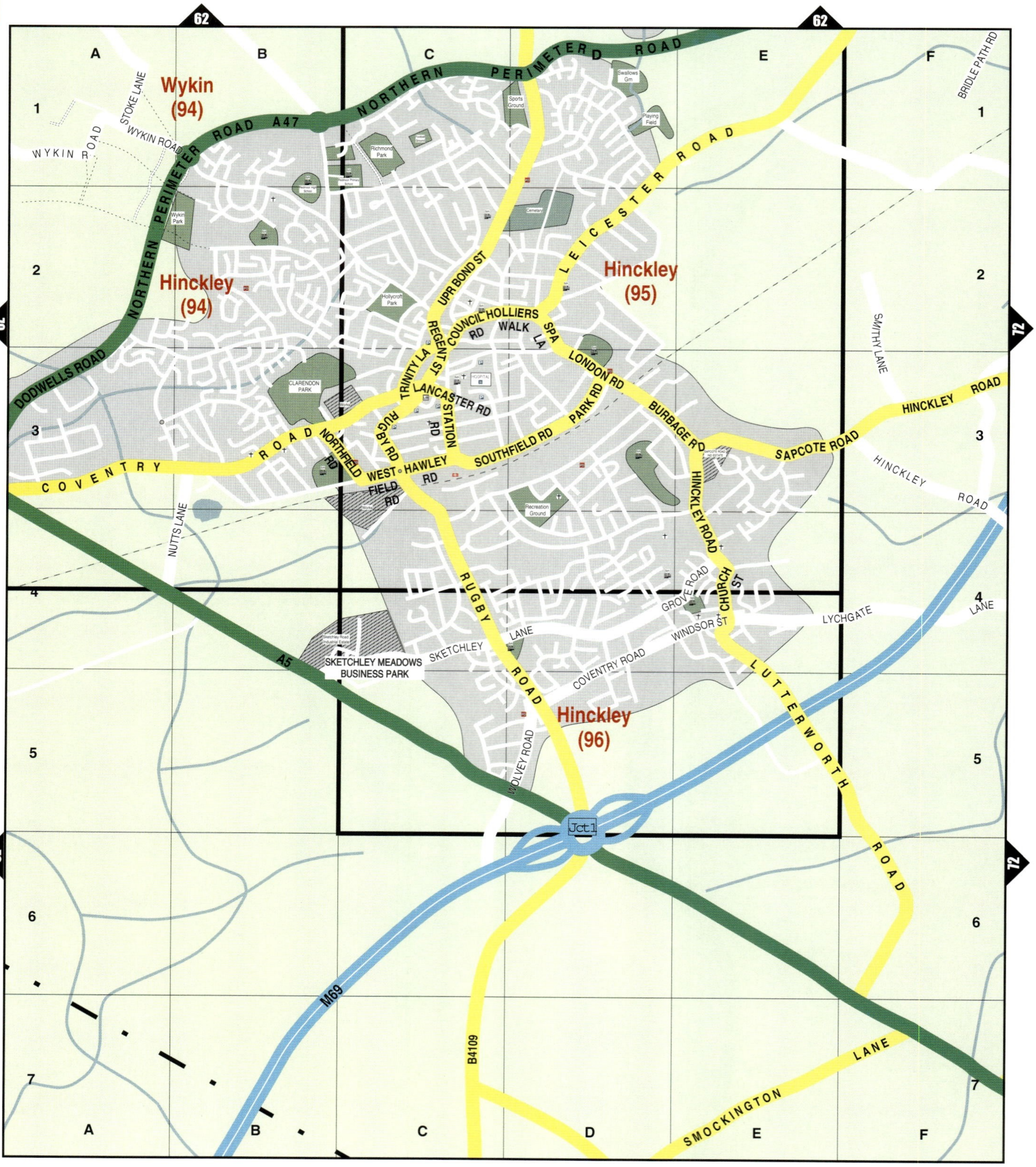

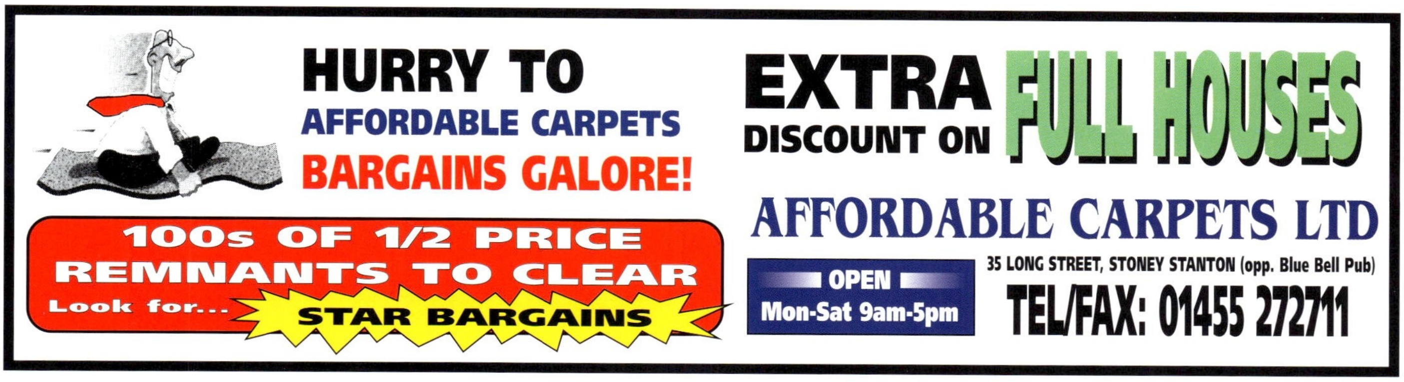

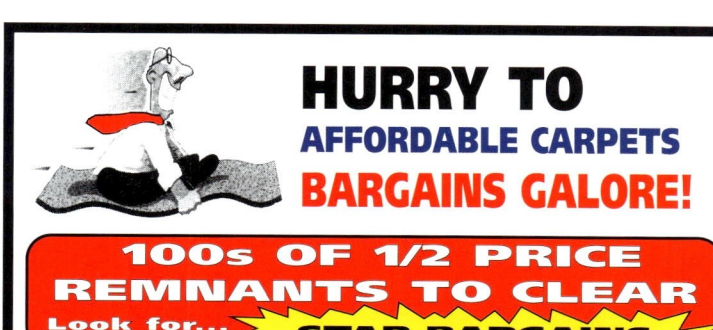

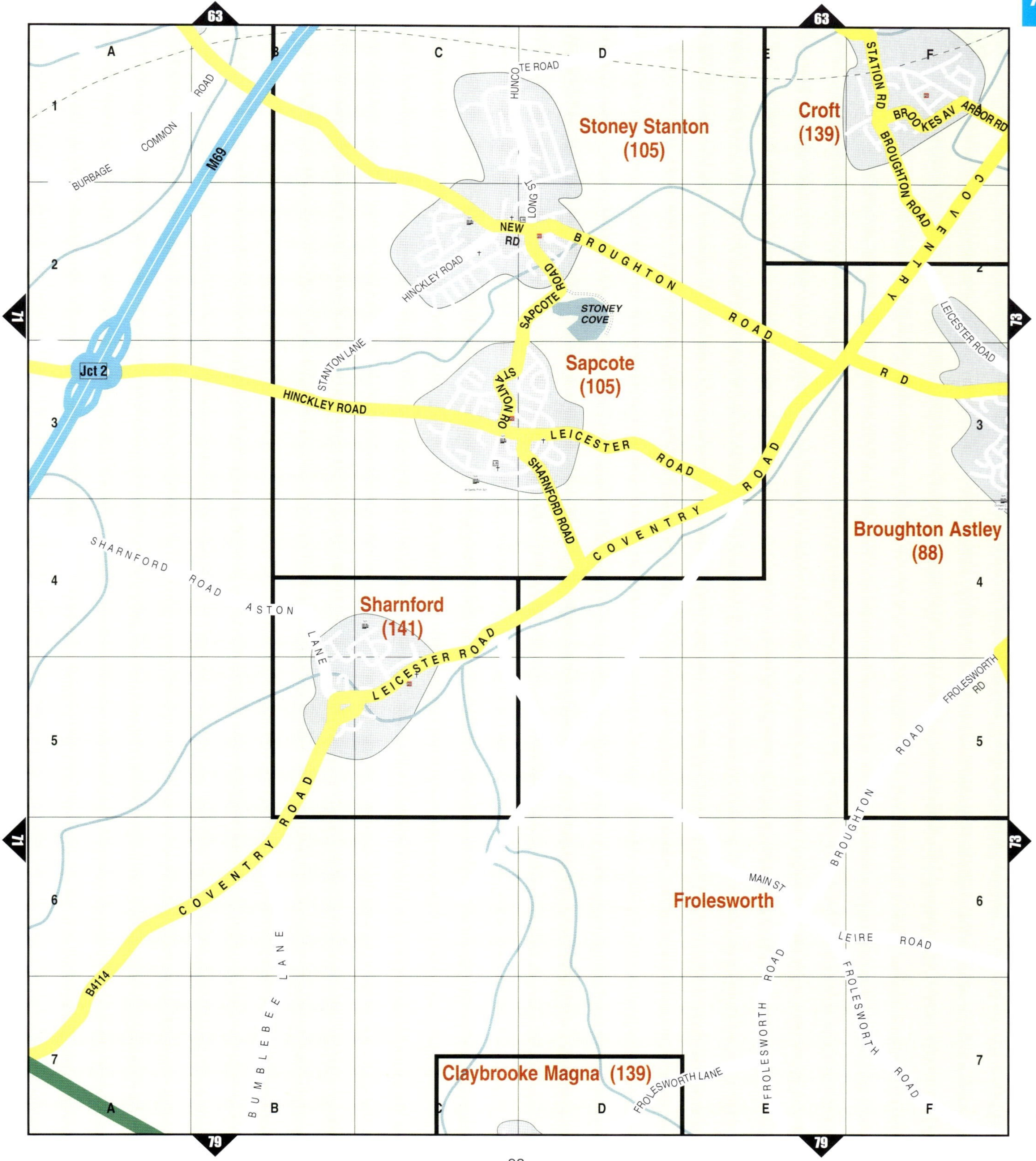
63
63
A
B
C
D
E
F
1
2
3
4
5
6
7
71
71
73
73
79
79
Stoney Stanton
(105)
Croft
(139)
Sapcote
(105)
Sharnford
(141)
Broughton Astley
(88)
Frolesworth
Claybrooke Magna (139)
M69
Jct 2
BURBAGE
COMMON
ROAD
HUNCOTE ROAD
LONG ST
NEW
RD
HINCKLEY ROAD
BROUGHTON
ROAD
SAPCOTE
ROAD
STONEY
COVE
STANTON LANE
STANTON RD
HINCKLEY ROAD
LEICESTER
ROAD
SHARNFORD ROAD
COVENTRY
ROAD
STATION RD
BROOKES AV
ARBOR RD
BROUGHTON ROAD
COVENTRY
RD
LEICESTER ROAD
SHARNFORD
ROAD
ASTON
LANE
LEICESTER ROAD
COVENTRY
ROAD
B4114
BUMBLEBEE
LANE
FROLESWORTH
RD
ROAD
BROUGHTON
MAIN ST
LEIRE
ROAD
ROAD
FROLESWORTH
FROLESWORTH
ROAD
FROLESWORTH LANE

COSBY GOLF CLUB

18 HOLE PARKLAND COURSE
PAR 71 • SSS 71 • 6410 YARDS

Chapel Lane, off Broughton Road, Cosby, Leicester LE9 1RG

Secretary: 0116 286 4759 ~ Fax: 0116 286 4484 ~ Pro Shop/Fax: 0116 284 8275

- Regular venue for county events
- Visitors (with handicap) welcome Mon-Fri before 4pm
  Advise telephone Pro Shop
- Societies welcome (min 12, max 80)
  Contact Secretary for details
- Qualified PGA Professional offering individual or group lessons 7 days a week.
- Full club repair service (24 hrs) and custom fit centre
- All leading brands at competitive prices including Callaway, Taylor-Made, Ping, Titleist, F.J., Adidas, Lynx, P.G.A. Collection

Email: secretary@cosby-golf-club.co.uk • www.cosby-golf-club.co.uk

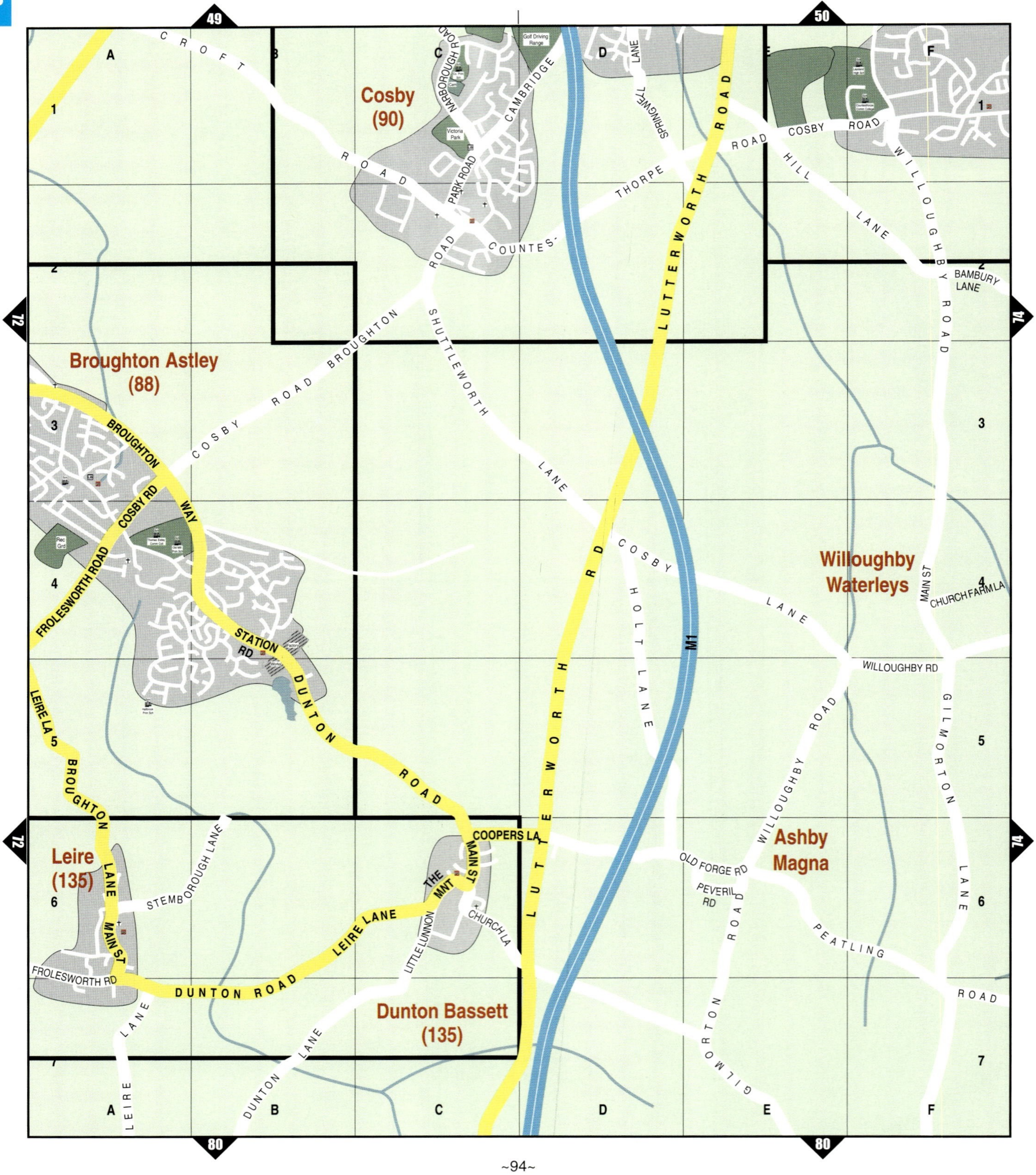

Beacon Cycles

FOR BIKES, BITS AND EVERYTHING TO GET YOU CYCLING ROUND THE COUNTY

CYCLE CORNER,
88 DERBY ROAD (A6)
LOUGHBOROUGH LE11 0AG

☎ 01509 - 215448

Thurmaston Garden and Floristry Centre

For all your Gardening and Floral Needs

all at competitive prices

Garden Plants, Shrubs, Conifers, Fencing, Trellis, Archway, Supply & Erect, Free Quotations, Garden Furniture, Stone Ornaments, Self Contained Water Features, Pool, Pumps, Liners, Full Range of Garden Sundries.

TELEFLORIST
Flowers for all Occasions, Fresh, Silk, Dried Flowers, Bouquets, Baskets, Arrangements. OPEN 7 DAYS.

600 Melton Road, Thurmaston, Leicester
Telephone: 0116 269 2541

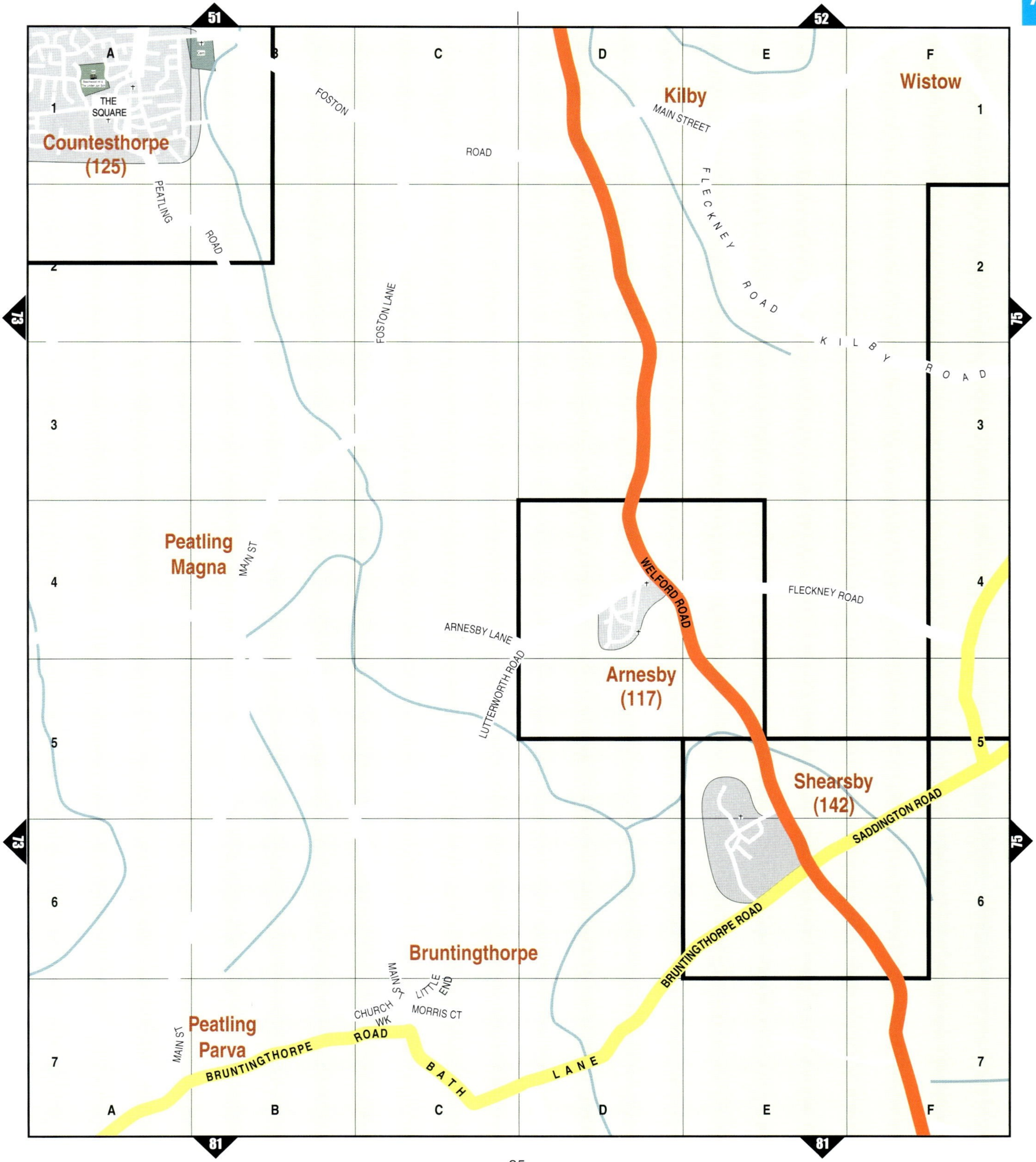

Established over 40 Years

74

Countesthorpe (125) — THE SQUARE — PEATLING ROAD — FOSTON ROAD — FOSTON LANE — Peatling Magna — MAIN ST — ARNESBY LANE — LUTTERWORTH ROAD — Arnesby (117) — WELFORD ROAD — Kilby — MAIN STREET — FLECKNEY ROAD — KILBY ROAD — Wistow — Shearsby (142) — SADDINGTON ROAD — BRUNTINGTHORPE ROAD — Bruntingthorpe — MAIN ST — CHURCH WK — LITTLE END — MORRIS CT — Peatling Parva — BRUNTINGTHORPE ROAD — BATH LANE

~95~

SIDDONS
FLOOR PREPARATION — SFP

**101 Leicester Road
Fleckney, Leics.
LE8 8BG**

**Telephone or Fax:
(0116) 2402709**
Mobile: 07778 684517

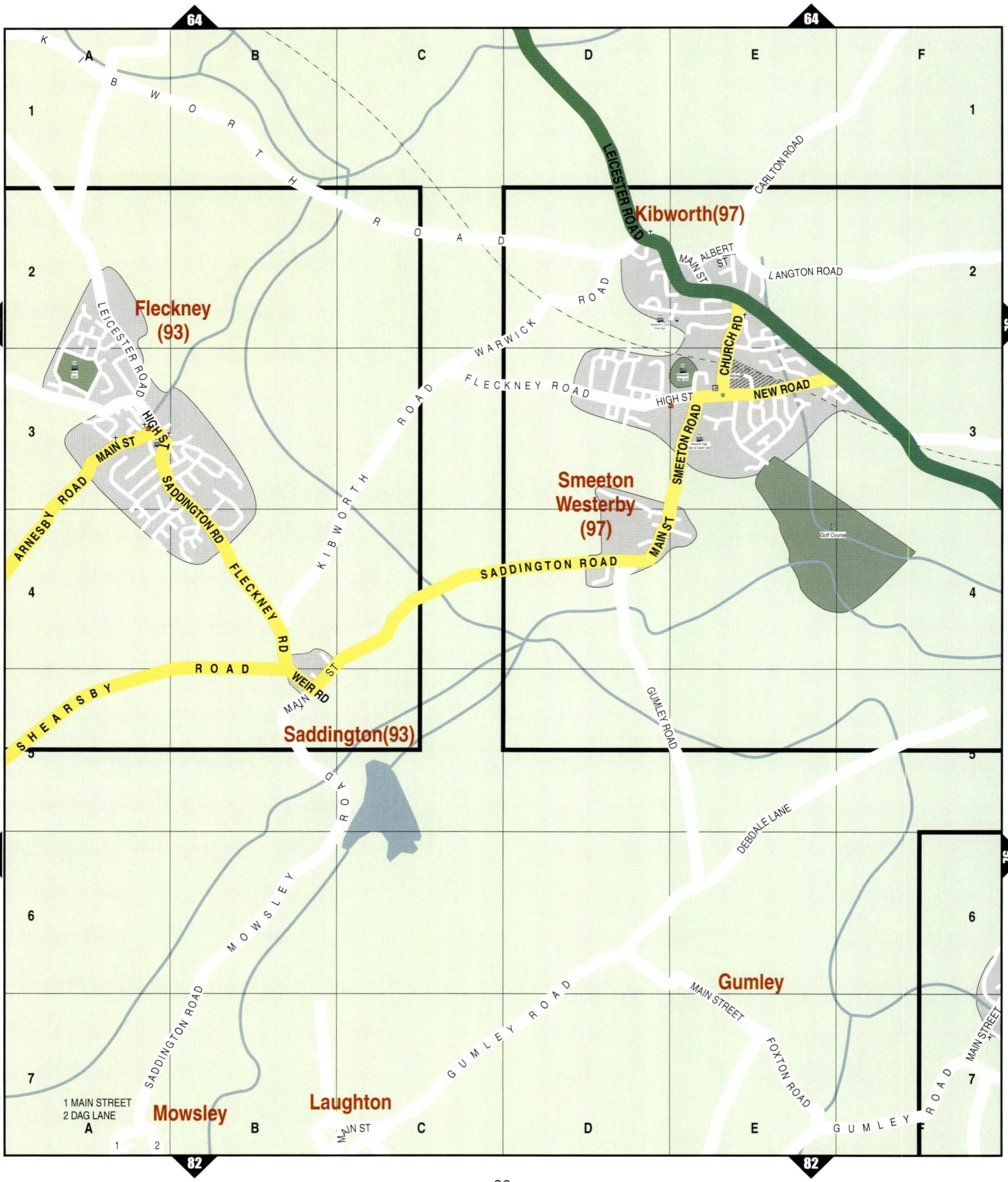

Industrial and Domestic:
Shot Blasting / Scabbling / Diamond Grinding
Barrel Sanding for Factories / Garages
Shops and Houses

The Porcupine Company

Manufacturers & Finishers
of Quality New & Reclaimed Pine Furniture
Crafts & Gifts

Wistow Garden Center, Kibworth Road, Wistow, Leics. LE8 0QF
Tel/Fax: 0116 259 3000   www.theporcupinecompany.co.uk

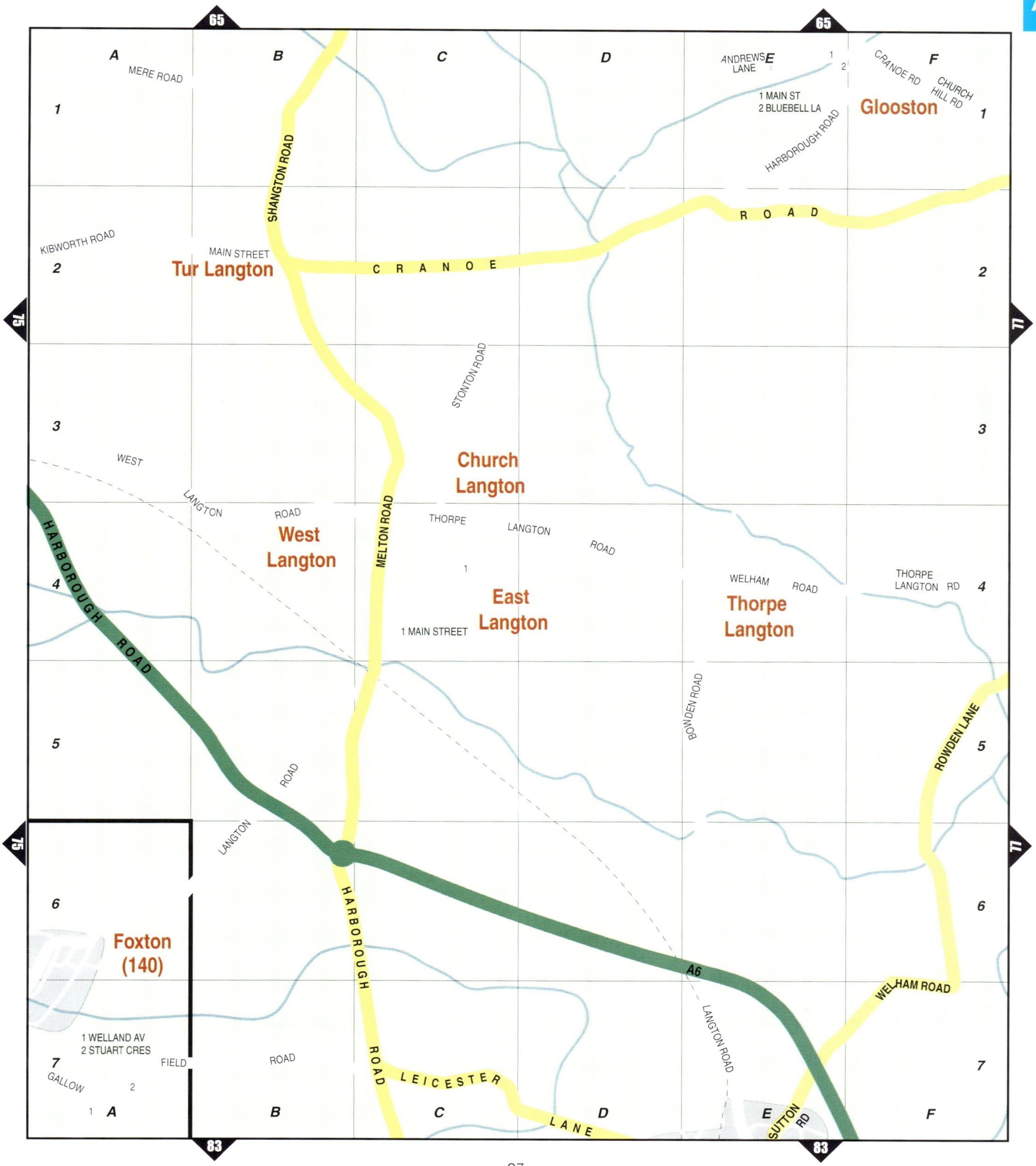

76

Map grid references A–F, 1–7

- MERE ROAD
- KIBWORTH ROAD
- SHANGTON ROAD
- MAIN STREET — **Tur Langton**
- CRANOE ROAD
- ANDREWS LANE
- 1 MAIN ST
- 2 BLUEBELL LA
- CRANOE RD
- CHURCH HILL RD
- **Glooston**
- HARBOROUGH ROAD
- STONTON ROAD
- WEST LANGTON ROAD
- **West Langton**
- MELTON ROAD
- THORPE LANGTON ROAD
- **Church Langton**
- 1 MAIN STREET — **East Langton**
- WELHAM ROAD
- THORPE LANGTON RD
- **Thorpe Langton**
- HARBOROUGH ROAD
- BOWDEN ROAD
- ROWDEN LANE
- LANGTON ROAD
- **Foxton (140)**
- 1 WELLAND AV
- 2 STUART CRES
- GALLOW FIELD ROAD
- HARBOROUGH ROAD
- LEICESTER LANE
- A6
- LANGTON ROAD
- SUTTON RD
- WELHAM ROAD

C. V. Lane & Son
PLUMBING & HEATING CONTRACTORS

We are specialists in:
- Plumbing & Heating Installations and Alterations
- Plumbing Maintenance
- Gas Appliance Service and Repair

39a OWEN STREET, COALVILLE, LEIC LE67 3DA

TEL : (01530) 832700
FAX : (01530) 830701

Flagstones
Pine & Interiors

Hand Finished • Antique, Old & Reproduction
Stripped Pine Specialists
Decorative Accessories & Lighting

Old Pine Stains • Colourwash Paints • Waxes & Glazes
Dipping & Stripping Service

24 Burton Street • Melton Mowbray • Leics
Telephone: 01664-566438   www.flagstonespine.co.uk

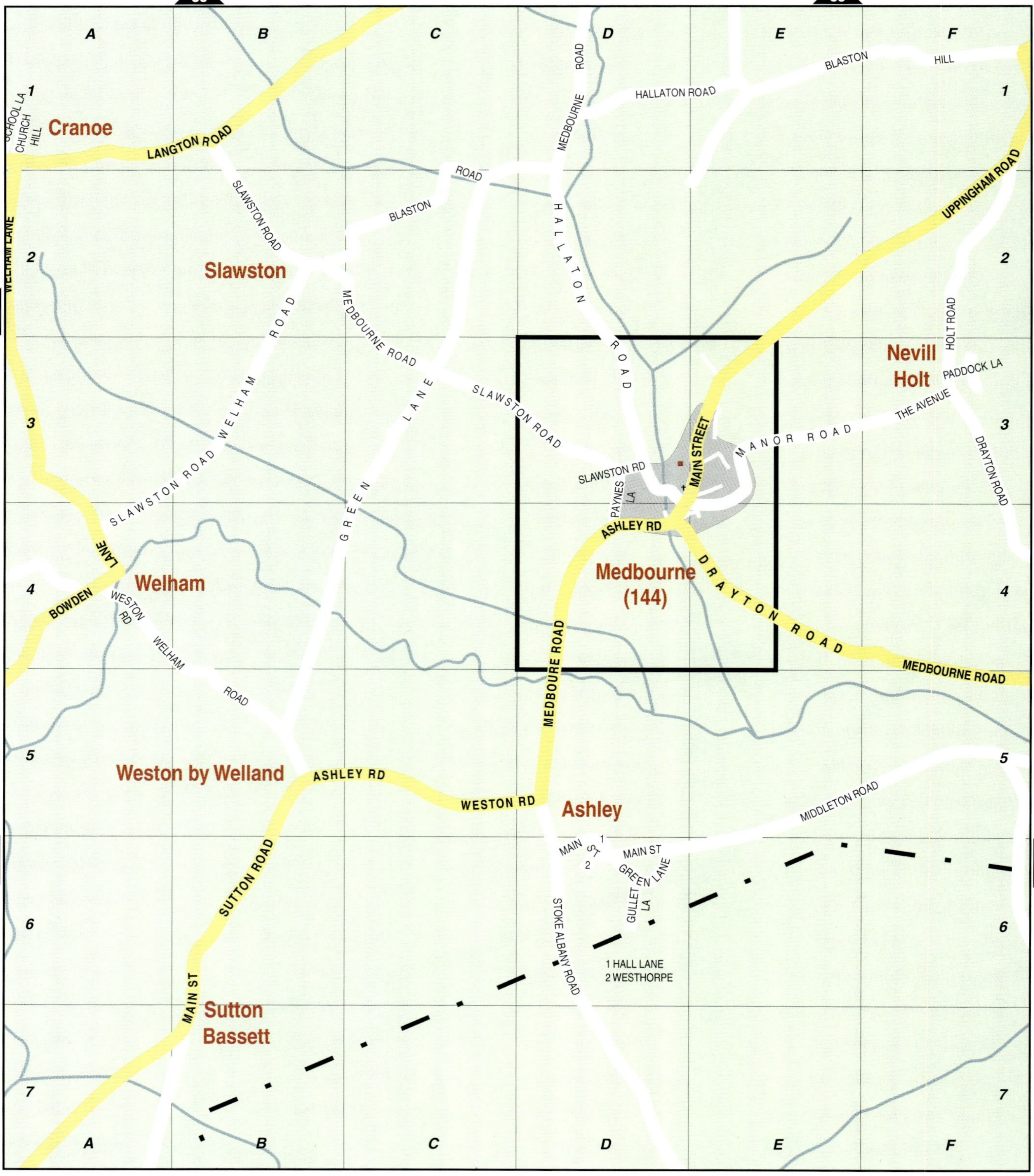

77

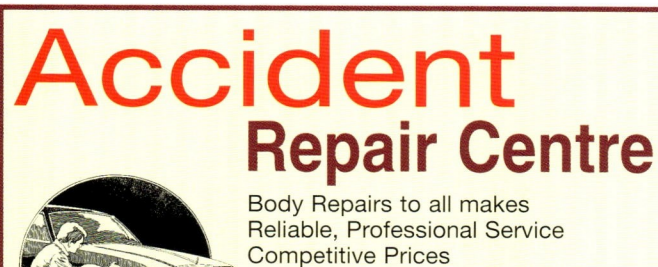

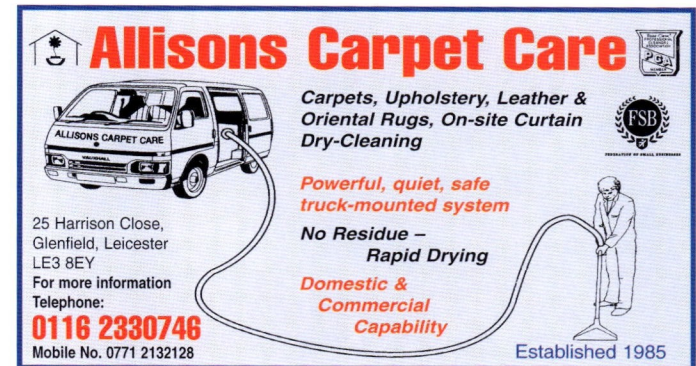

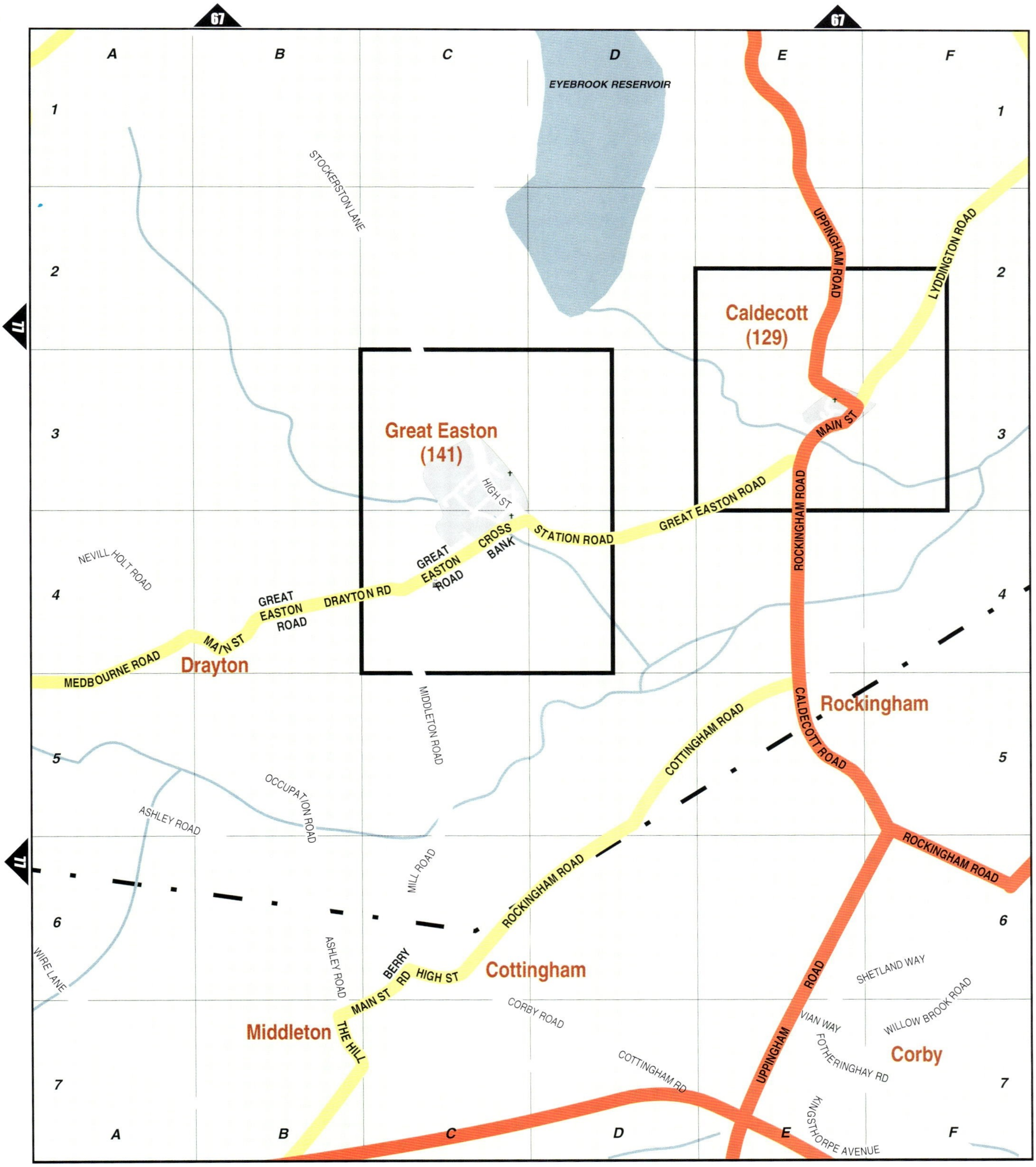
67
67
77
77
A
B
C
D
E
F
1
2
3
4
5
6
7
EYEBROOK RESERVOIR
STOCKERSTON LANE
UPPINGHAM ROAD
LYDDINGTON ROAD
Caldecott
(129)
MAIN ST
Great Easton
(141)
HIGH ST
CROSS BANK
STATION ROAD
GREAT EASTON ROAD
ROCKINGHAM ROAD
NEVILL HOLT ROAD
GREAT EASTON ROAD
DRAYTON RD
GREAT EASTON ROAD
MAIN ST
MEDBOURNE ROAD
Drayton
MIDDLETON ROAD
Rockingham
CALDECOTT ROAD
COTTINGHAM ROAD
OCCUPATION ROAD
ASHLEY ROAD
MILL ROAD
ROCKINGHAM ROAD
ROCKINGHAM ROAD
WIRE LANE
ASHLEY ROAD
BERRY RD
HIGH ST
MAIN ST
Cottingham
CORBY ROAD
SHETLAND WAY
ROAD
Middleton
THE HILL
VIAN WAY
WILLOW BROOK ROAD
FOTHERINGHAY RD
Corby
COTTINGHAM RD
UPPINGHAM
KINGSTHORPE AVENUE

WILTON STREET GARAGE

19 Wilton Street
Leicester LE1 3NP
Tel/Fax: 0116 2620936

Repairs • Servicing • Tuning to all makes

Find us on Map 43 B3

THE PRICE IS RIGHT!

£££

90a Narborough Road
Leicester LE3 0BS

Tel: 0116 255 2516

Need a Part? Any Part?

THE BMW USED PARTS CENTRE

7-8 Buckland Road, Leicester LE5 0NT
Telephone: 0116 276 6799 Mobile: 07710 129773

FREEPHONE 08080 269772

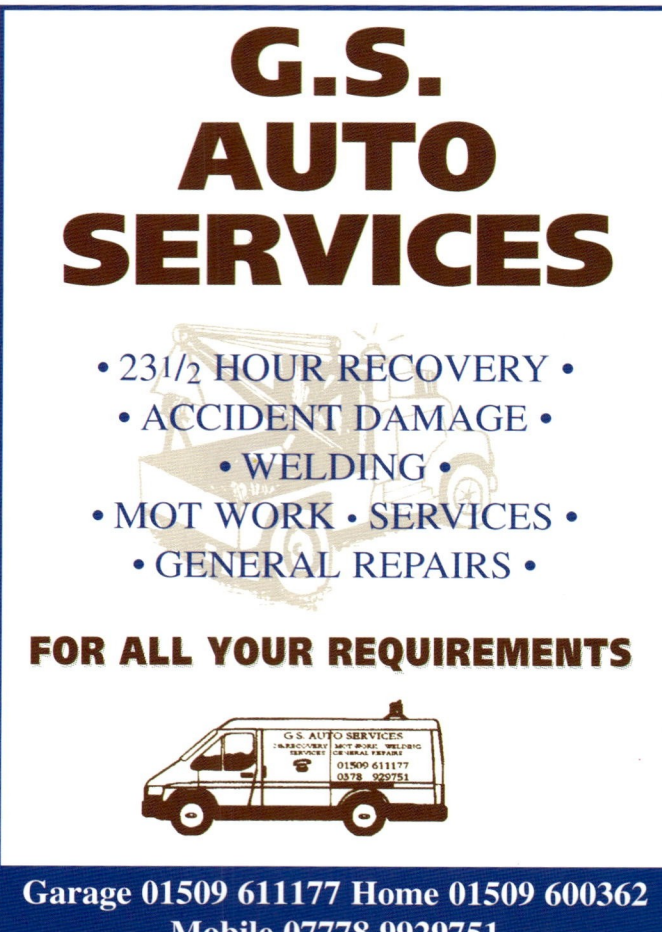

G.S. AUTO SERVICES

- 23½ HOUR RECOVERY •
- ACCIDENT DAMAGE •
- WELDING •
- MOT WORK • SERVICES •
- GENERAL REPAIRS •

FOR ALL YOUR REQUIREMENTS

Garage 01509 611177 Home 01509 600362
Mobile 07778 9929751

ULLESTHORPE COURT
HOTEL, GOLF & LEISURE CLUB

Frolesworth Road, Ullesthorpe, Leicestershire LE17 5BZ
Tel: 01455 209023 Fax: 01455 202537
Website: www.ullesthorpecourt.co.uk

17th Century Manor House Setting
38 En-suite Bedrooms, Traditional A la Carte Restaurant, Lincoln's Inn Bar Snacks
Six Conference Suites

Leisure Facilities Include:
*Indoor Swimming Pool, Jacuzzi, Sauna, Steam Room, Solarium,
Tennis Courts, Large Gymnasium, Aerobics, Beauty Room, Snooker Room with 2 Tables*

18 Hole Championship Length Course
Free Car Parking for 500 Vehicles

M1 JUNCTION 20 ONLY 4 MILES • M69 JUNCTION 1 ONLY 4 MILES
Leicester only 10 miles, Coventry only 12 Miles   ★★★

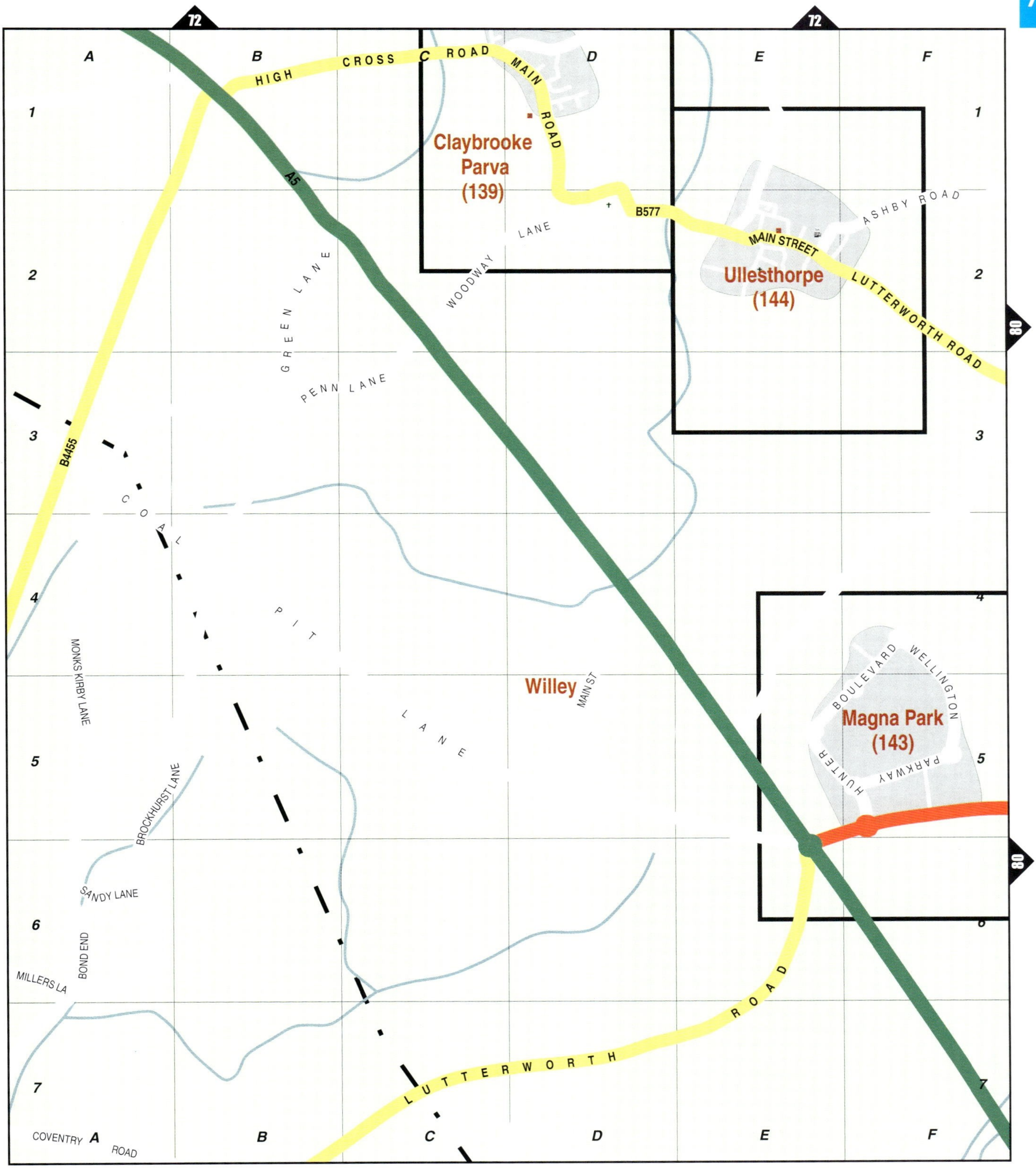

Howells
Real Estate Agents

Hours of Business
Weekdays 9am – 7pm
Saturday 9am – 5pm
Sunday 10am – 4pm

2 BELL STREET,
LUTTERWORTH,
LEICS
LE17 4DW

Tel: 01455 559007
Fax: 01455 559020
E-mail: info@howells-estates.co.uk

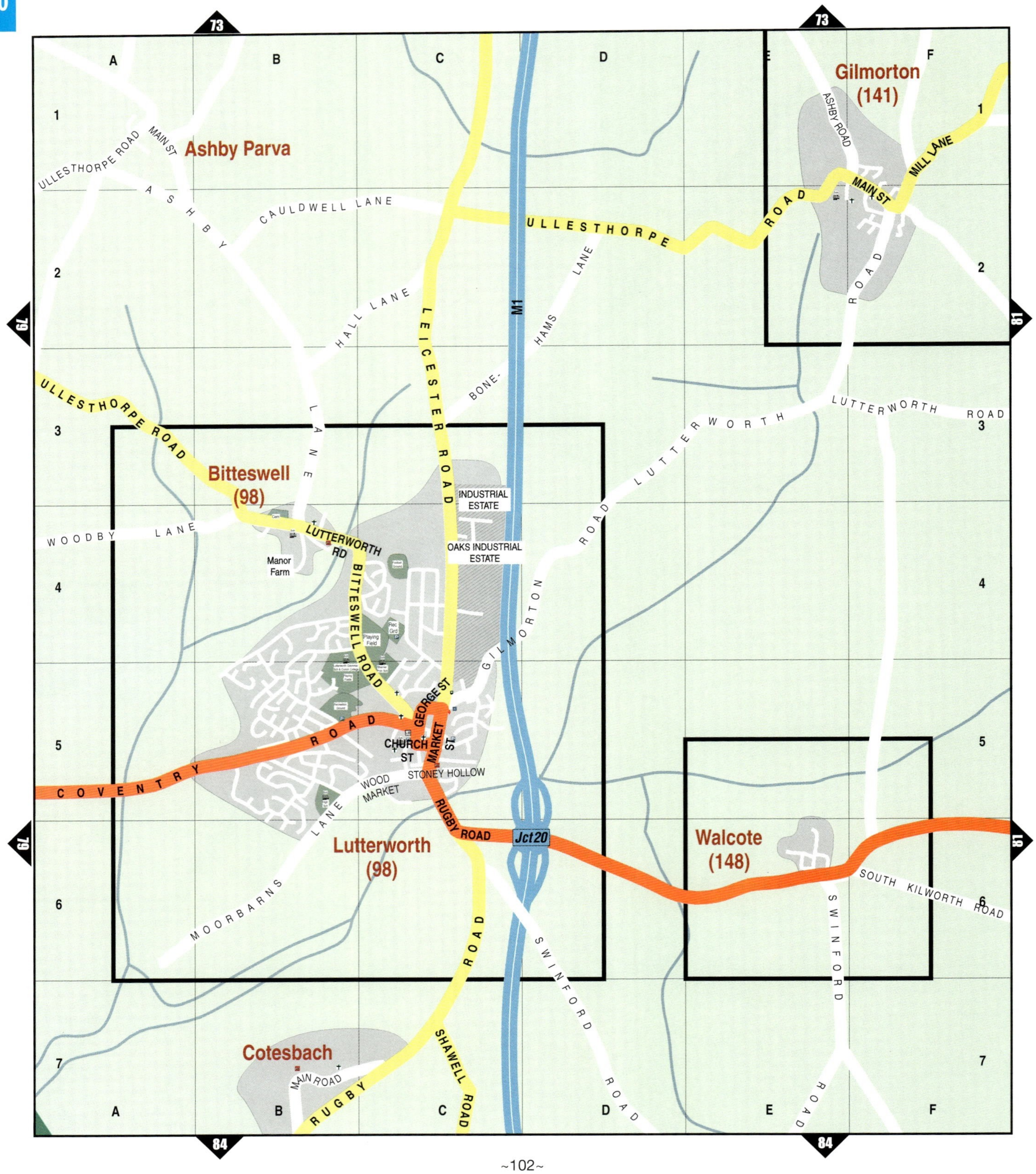

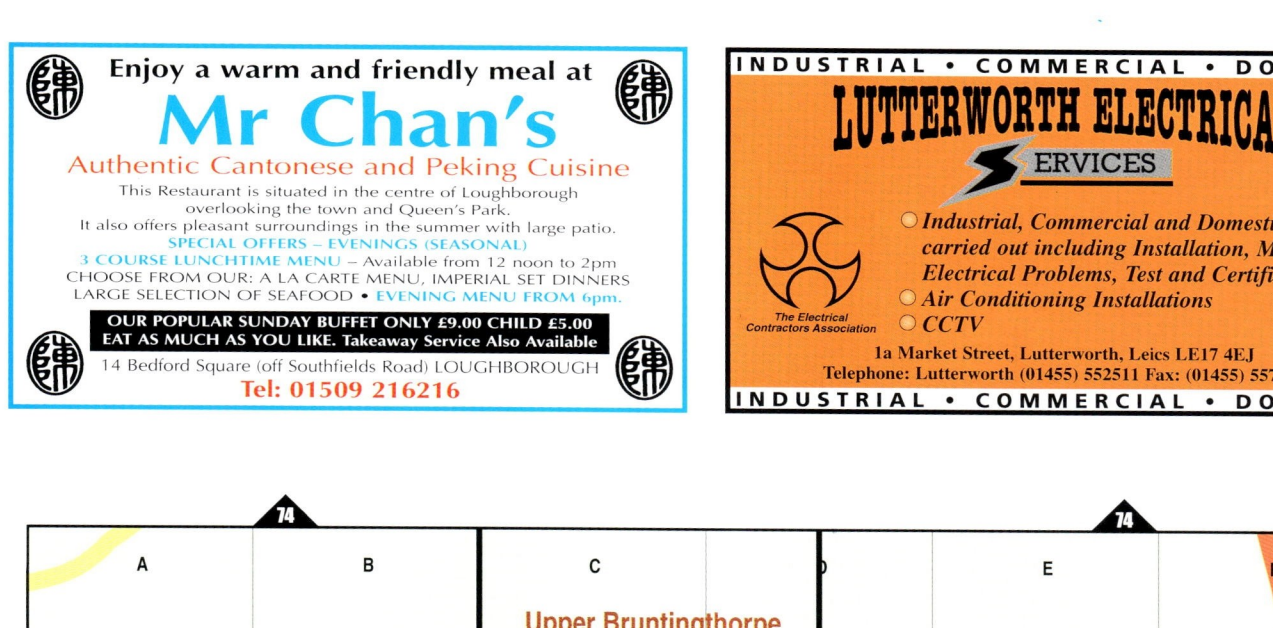

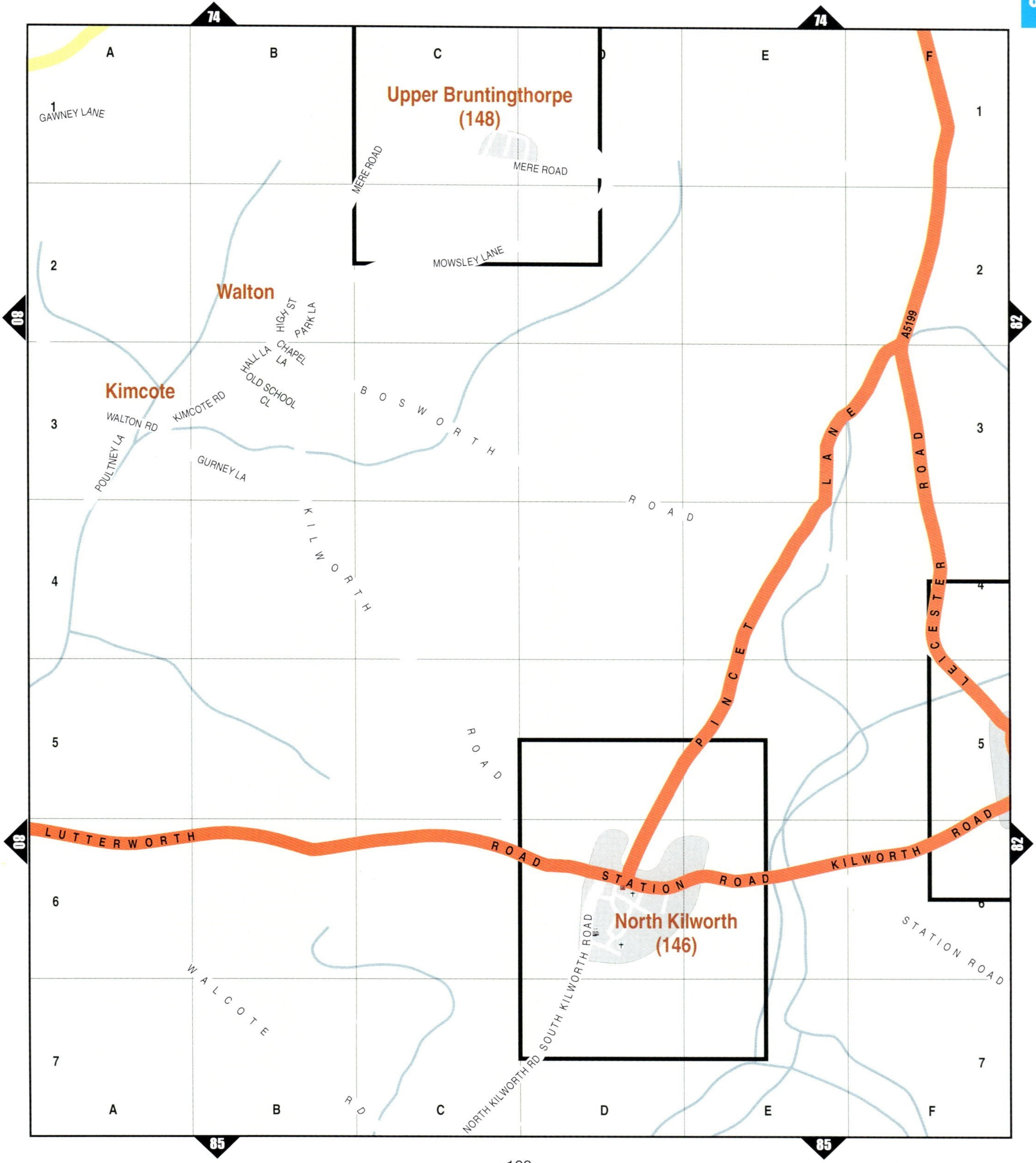
74
A
B
C
D
E
F
1
2
3
4
5
6
7
Upper Bruntingthorpe
(148)
MERE ROAD
MERE ROAD
MOWSLEY LANE
GAWNEY LANE
Walton
HIGH ST
PARK LA
CHAPEL LA
HALL LA
OLD SCHOOL CL
Kimcote
KIMCOTE RD
WALTON RD
POULTNEY LA
GURNEY LA
BOSWORTH ROAD
KILWORTH ROAD
LANE
PINCET
A5199
LEICESTER ROAD
LUTTERWORTH ROAD
STATION ROAD
KILWORTH ROAD
North Kilworth
(146)
SOUTH KILWORTH ROAD
NORTH KILWORTH RD
WALCOTE RD
STATION ROAD
80
82
85

CAFÉ ELIOT'S RESTAURANT

Don't miss this exceptional dining experience - visit us soon!

This famous Mediterranean restaurant is under the personal management of international top chef Camilla Snow, whose creative cuisine is complemented by her beautifully remodelled air-conditioned dining room and friendly and attentive staff.

35 HIGH STREET • MARKET HARBOROUGH • LEICESTERSHIRE • LE16 7NL • TEL: 01858 446966

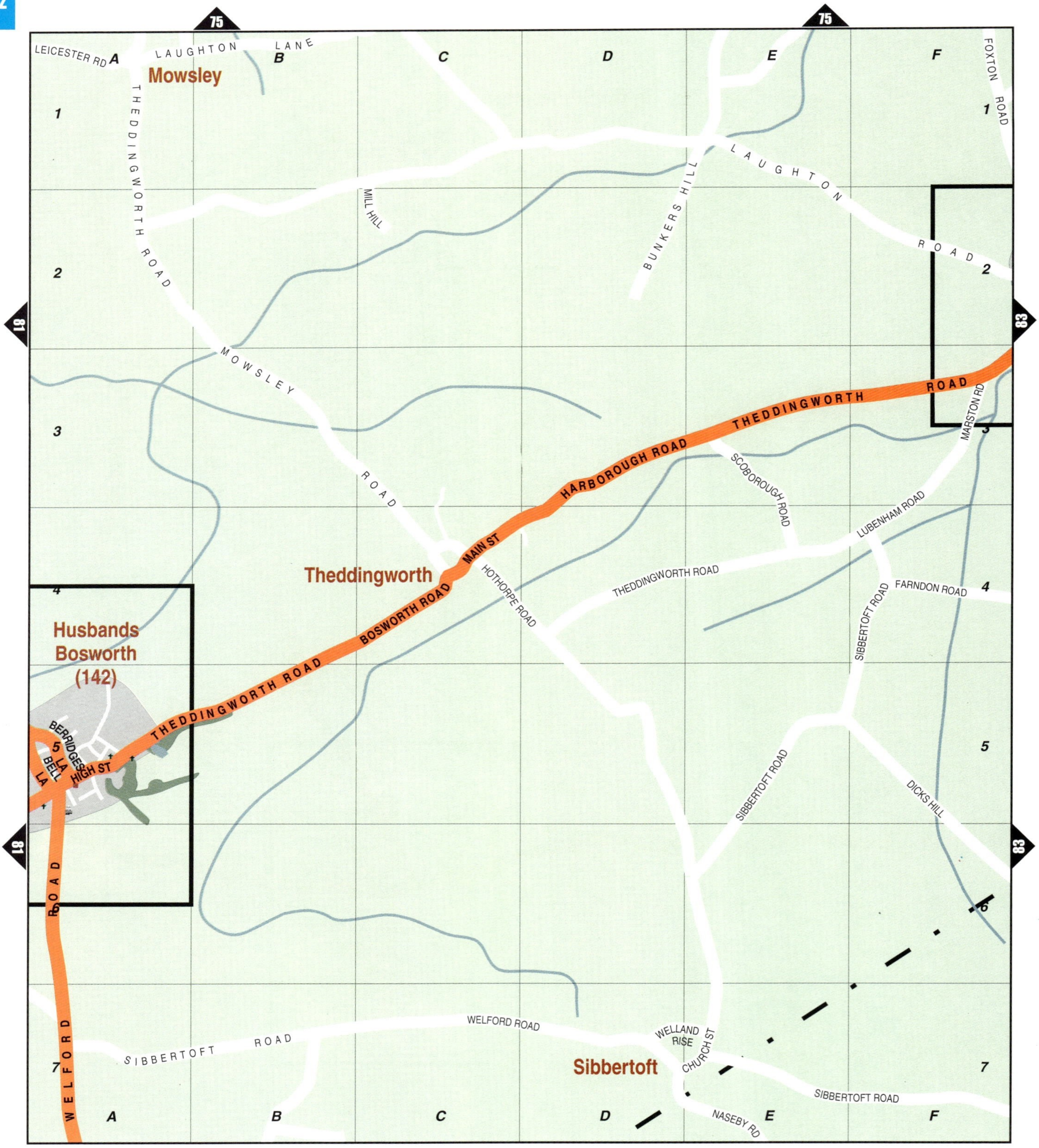

~104~

BRAY & BRAY
SOLICITORS

51 High Street, Market Harborough, Leicestershire LE16 7AF. Telephone (01858) 467181

ALL TYPES OF LEGAL WORK UNDERTAKEN

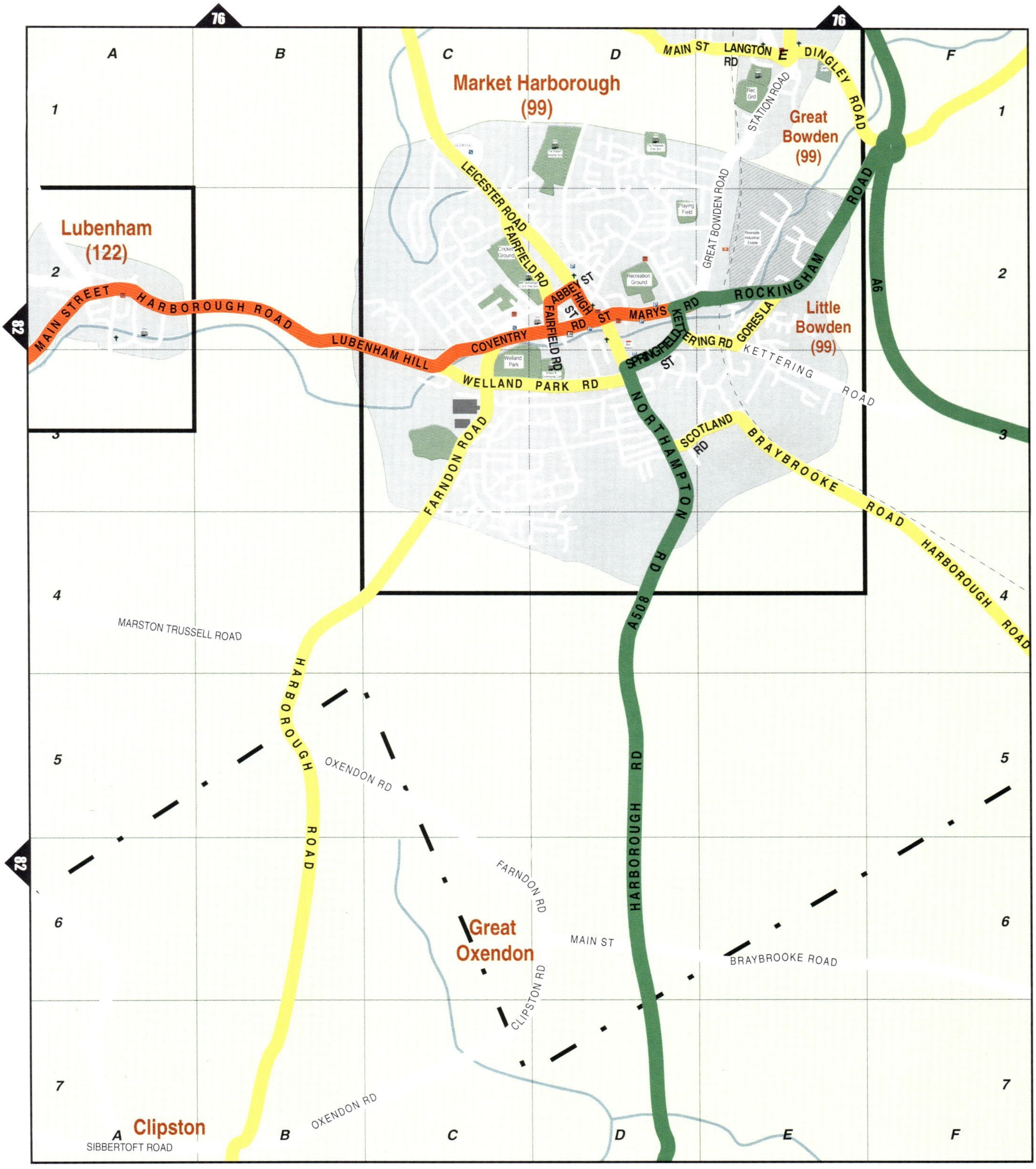

Courtesy Cars (subject to availability) — **Ashby Garage** — **Free Collection and Delivery**

AIR CONDITIONING SERVICING

SAAB Specialists • Any make of new or used car supplied
Servicing and Repairs (all makes) • Bodywork Repairs
Valeting • MOT Tests • FREE Estimates

 Main Street • Ashby Parva • Lutterworth • Leicestershire • LE17 5HS
Telephone: (01455) 209191 • Facsimile: (01455) 202300

 Members of the Retail Motor Industry Federation

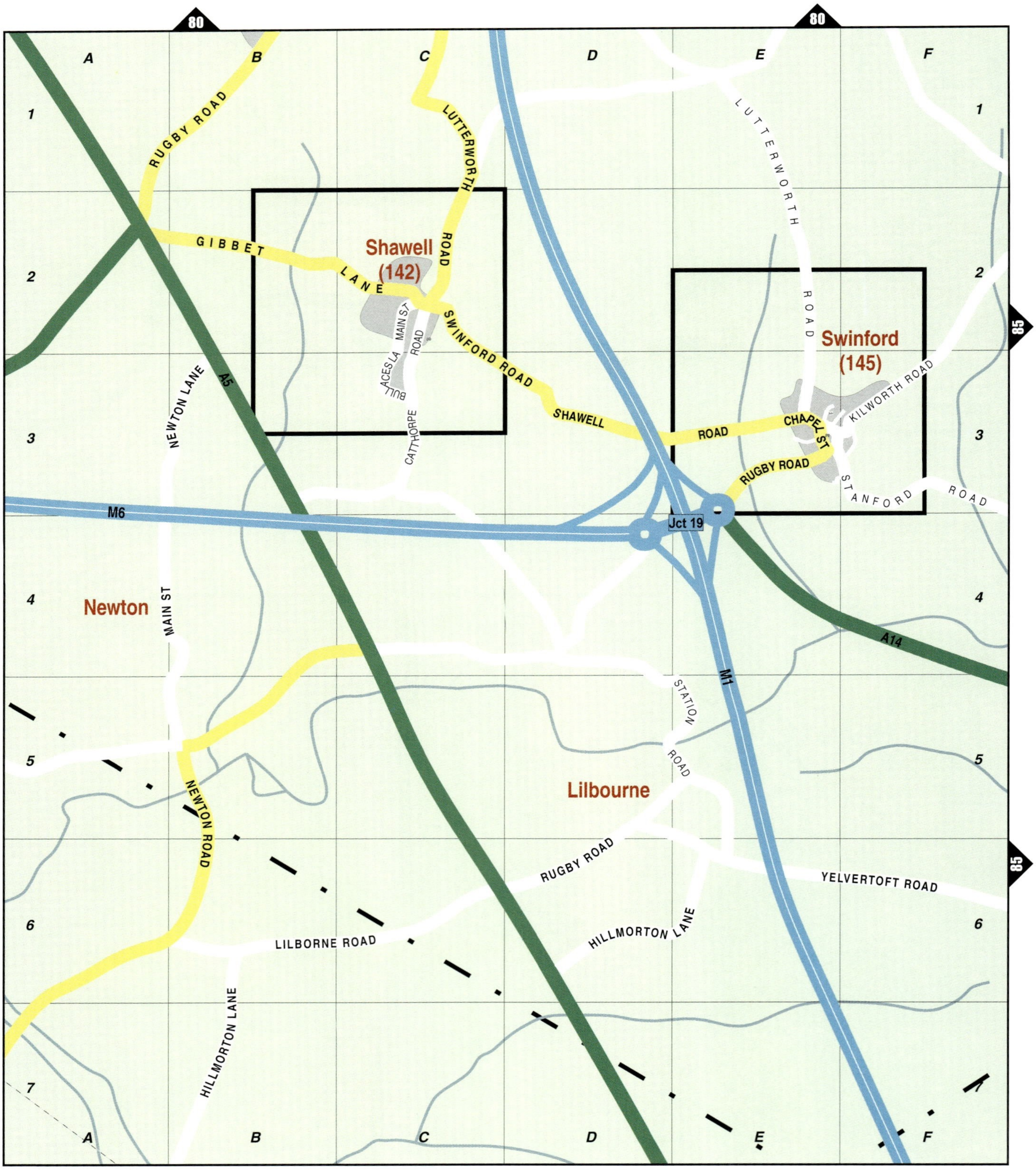

FOX CABS YOUR LOCAL TAXI COMPANY

5-seat London style taxis
All cabs are wheelchair accessible
We never close

24 hour radio control
Airports, couriers, long distance
Senior Citizen tokens accepted

Fox Cabs (0116) 262 5262

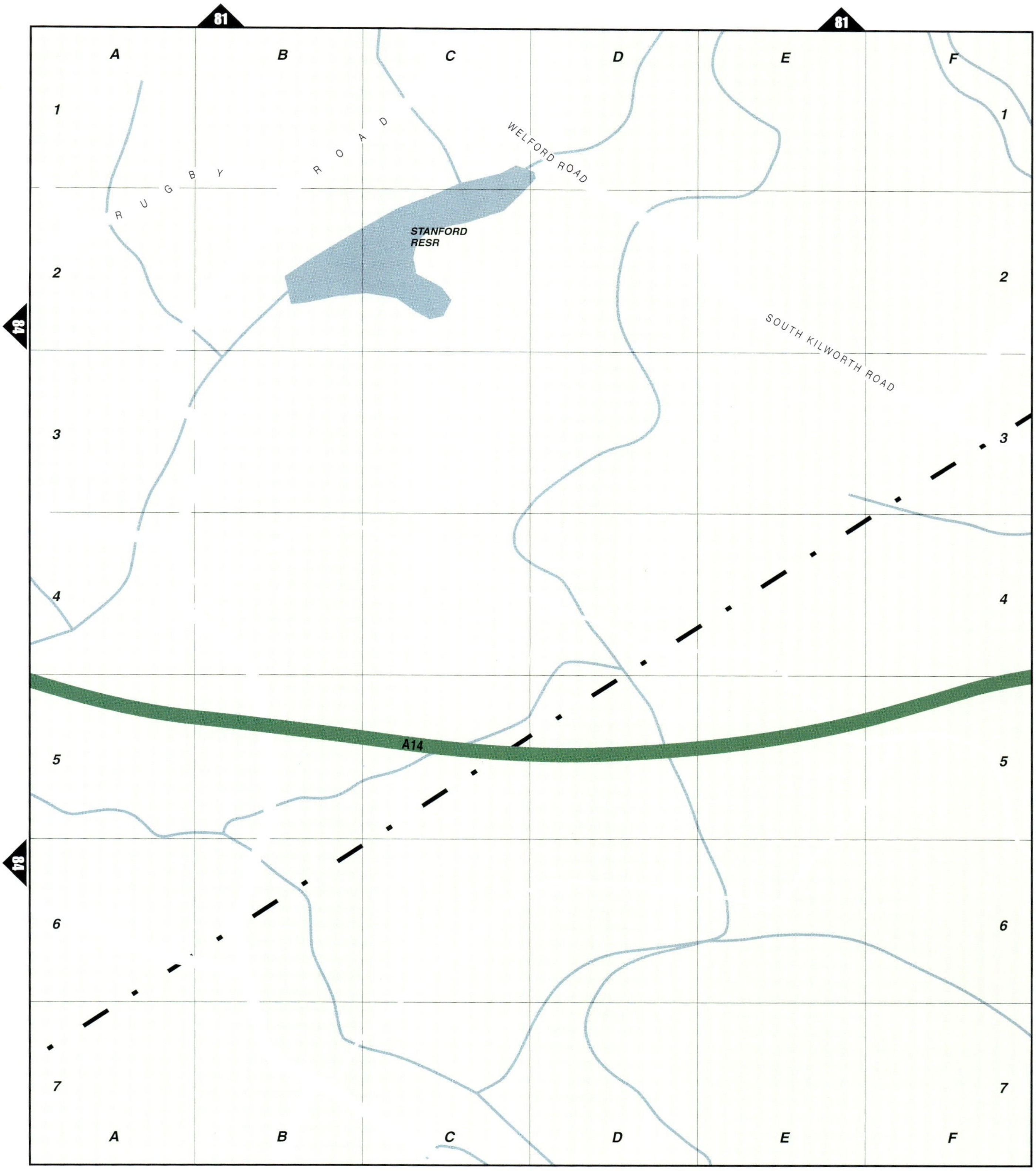

The Landing

Tel: 0116 2519022

Imaginative vegetarian food with an international flavour, freshly prepared on the premises. Licensed to sell organic wines & beers.

OPENING HOURS

10.00AM - 5.00PM, MONDAY - SATURDAY

7.30PM - LATE, SATURDAY EVENING FOR CANDLELIT DINNERS

The Landing Restaurant: above The Ark environment centre, St. Martins Walk, Leicester. LE1 5DG

The Ark

Green Shop - Restaurant - Information Centre

EXPRESS®
BURTON-UPON-TRENT

For the business and leisure traveller, the hotel is situated within close proximity to fast trunk roads that lead quickly to many major cities, our central location makes it easily accessible to Derby, Birmingham, Nottingham, Leicester and Sheffield.

The hotel offers outstanding value for money on a 'price per room basis' that includes the following facilities:

- 82 tastefully decorated bedrooms all with en-suite facilities
- 5 bedrooms specifically designed for the physically challenged
- Remote control Colour Television with 'in room movies' and Sky Television available
- Direct Dial Telephone and Voice Mail
- Computer Points
- Tea and Coffee Making Facilities
- Hairdryer – Trouser Press available on request
- Free Overnight Parking
- Bar/Lounge Area
- Pub/Restaurant adjacent

Along with excellent accommodation, Holiday Inn Express offers fully equipped conference facilities, designed both for comfort and concentration.

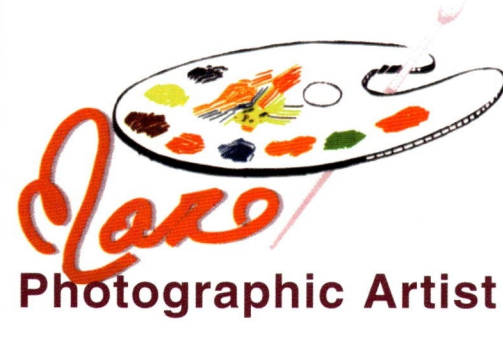

Photographic Artist

Photo Centre

Maz Mashru
M.Photog (USA) • FMPA • HON. FBPA • ABIPP • ARPS • ASP

Award Winning Photographer

The Portrait House
111a – 113a Belgrave Road,
Leicester LE4 6AS (UK)
Tel: 0116 268 0822
Fax: 0116 261 1167

Friendly and helpful expert advice

Working displays and show gardens

Much, much more besides...

waterworks
aquatic centre

**Waterworks, Staunton Harold Nurseries
Staunton Harold, Leicestershire
Telephone 01322 865665**

Specialist in water features, ponds, filtration, fish and aquatic plants

Ashby-De-La-Zouch

Malcolm Miles
MOTOR ENGINEER

SAAB SPECIALISTS

15 Erith Road, Aylestone Road, Leicester LE2 7QA
TELEPHONE: (0116) 283 9044

Forte Posthouse — Leicester

Forte Posthouse
Braunstone Lane East
Leicester
Leicestershire LE3 2FW
Telephone: 0116 263 0500
Facsimile: 0116 282 3623

- 172 fully refurbished bedrooms
- All en-suite facilities, interactive TV
- Free Car Parking
- Group Rates Accepted
- Large comfortable restaurant/bar/lounge
- Meeting and Conference Suites (will accommodate 2–80 persons)
- We specialise in all special events from Weddings to private Parties
- Professional, friendly team
- Please ring to discuss your requirements on **0116 263 0500**

87

Nailstone (B2) — Ibstock Road, Hinckley Road, Barton Lane, Occupation Rd, Rectory La, Veros Lane, Main Street, Malthouse, Church Road, Bagworth Road, PO, Sch

Barlestone (C5/D5) — Bagworth Road, Newbold Road, Bosworth Road, Barton Road, Gregory Rd, Gregory Cl, Bus Depot, Playing Field, Curtis Way, Copedale Cl, Deacon Av, Manor Road, Cunnery Cl, The Glebe, Avondale Rd, Spinney Drive, Orchard Cl, Meadow Cl, Ferrers Croft, Rushey Cl, Brookside, Chapel St, West Fields, The Pingle, Church Rd, Washpit La, St Giles Cl, Crofters Vale, Main St, New St, Smit Road, C of E Prim Sch, Church Farm, Garden Farm, May Meadow Nature Reserve & Play Area, Mill Farm, Sefton House Farm

~110~

Let Us Take The Worry Out Of Your
BOOK-KEEPING & PAYROLL
VAT Returns • Management Accounts
Computerised Payroll Bureau

Professional ★ Personal ★ Cost Effective

  **B.B.S** — BUSINESS BOOK-KEEPING SERVICES

e-mail: bbs@dial.pipex.com
37 Thorpe Street • Leicester LE3 5NQ
Tel: (0116) 255 5688 • Fax: (0116) 254 0926

The Old Tudor Rectory Hotel

The Old Tudor Rectory Hotel is a Grade II Listed Building with a wealth of old timbers and original staircases.

All Bedrooms are ensuite with telephone, television, hospitality trays and hairdryers.

We also cater for conferences, buffets and wedding parties.

Please contact us for further information on:

Main Street, Glenfield, Leicester LE3 8DG
Tel. 0116 2915678
Fax: 0116 2911416

E.M.T.B. — English Tourist Board — AA★★ — RAC

88

Broughton Astley

~111~

Forest Lodge Hotel

We are a privately run 17 bedroom Hotel with a Bar Lounge, Television Room and Licensed Dining Room. We also have three Function Rooms, enabling us to cater for parties of between 20 and 120 people.

All our bedrooms are en-suite, with telephone, radio alarms and televisions, and tea making facilities.

CATERING FACILITIES • CONFERENCE ROOMS
PRIVATE DINNER DANCES • WEDDINGS
PRIVATE PARTIES • CHRISTMAS FUNCTIONS

TELEPHONE 0116 239 3125

FAX 0116 239 2733

DESFORD ROAD
KIRBY MUXLOE
LEICESTER LE9 2BB

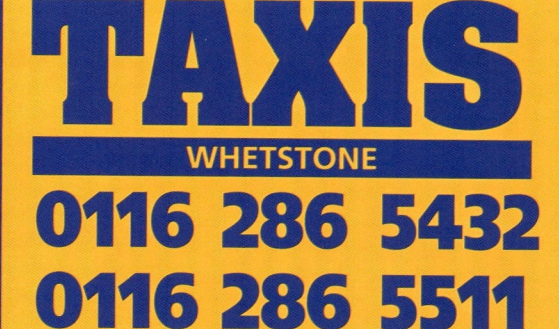

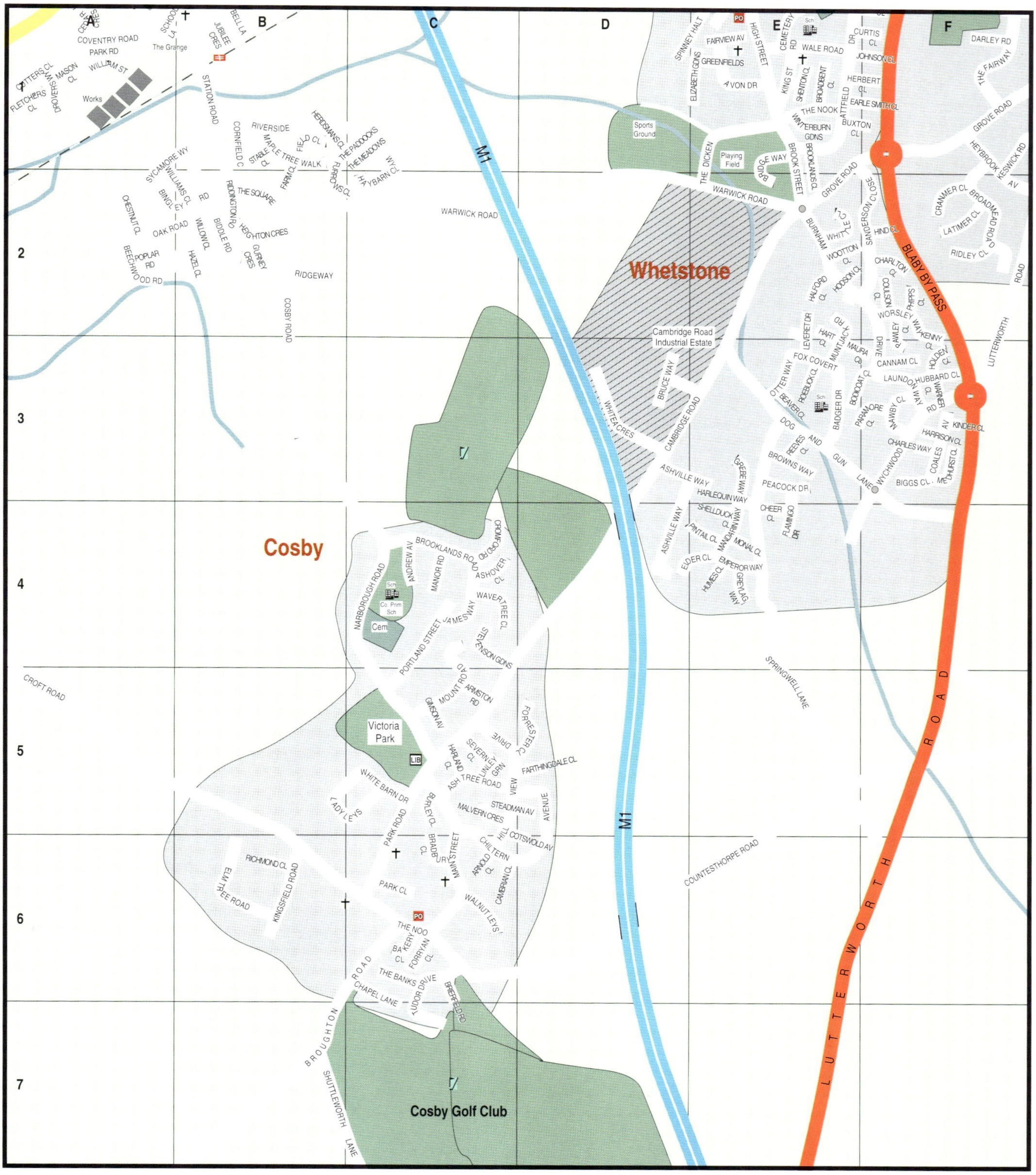
A
B
C
D
E
F
2
3
4
5
6
7
Whetstone
Cosby
Cosby Golf Club
Victoria Park
Cambridge Road Industrial Estate
Sports Ground
Playing Field
M1
BLABY BY PASS
LUTTERWORTH ROAD
COVENTRY ROAD
PARK RD
WILLIAM ST
STATION ROAD
The Grange
Works
WARWICK ROAD
RIDGEWAY
COSBY ROAD
CROFT ROAD
SPRINGWELL LANE
COUNTESTHORPE ROAD
BROUGHTON ROAD
SHUTTLEWORTH LANE
NARBOROUGH ROAD
BROOKLANDS ROAD
PORTLAND STREET
MAIN STREET
CHAPEL LANE
THE BANKS
PARK CL
PARK ROAD
WHITE BARN DR
KINGSFIELD ROAD
ELM TREE ROAD
RICHMOND CL
ASHVILLE WAY
PEACOCK DR
BROWNS WAY
HIGH STREET
WALE ROAD
AVON DR
GREENFIELDS
FAIRVIEW AV
GROVE ROAD
DARLEY RD
THE FAIRWAY
HEYBROOK AV
KESWICK RD
BROADMEAD ROAD
LATIMER CL
RIDLEY CL
CRANMER CL
CAMBRIDGE ROAD
BRUCE WAY
WHITEACRES
THE DICKEN
BROOK STREET
FOX COVERT
CANNAM CL
LAUNDON WAY
HUBBARD CL
HARRISON CL
CHARLES WAY
BIGGS CL
KINDER CL
RIVERSIDE
OAK ROAD
POPLAR RD
BEECHWOOD RD
CHESTNUT CL
HAZEL CL
WILLOW CL
BIDDLE RD
THE SQUARE
SYCAMORE WY
FARTHINGDALE CL
STEADMAN AV
MALVERN CRES
COTSWOLD AV
ASH TREE ROAD
CAMBRIAN CL
WALNUT LEYS
TUDOR DRIVE
BRIERFIELD RD
AVENUE
PO
Sch
LIB
Cem
Co Prim Sch

Kirby Vale — Ratby

Visit our Kirby Vale development in Ratby & you will discover a superb choice of houses & bungalow's to suit all requirements and budgets

ALL PROPERTIES FEATURE

- Low maintenance PVCu windows, facia's & soffits
- High standards of insulation *(all meet S.A.P 80+)*
- Landscaped front gardens
- NHBC buildmark warranty

For Further Information Contact
CAWREY LIMITED
Kirby Grange Farm, Taverner Drive,
Ratby, Leicester. Tel: 0116 239 0600

First Leicester

PICK UP A TIMETABLE BOOKLET FOR YOUR AREA AT OUR

TRAVEL SHOP
5 CHARLES STREET
LEICESTER LE1 3FF

or write to us and we will send you one

Bus Service Enquiries 0116 - 2538000

First Citycoach *of* Leicester

Great Days Out • Extended Tours
Musicals/Shows • Concerts • International Hire

Seat Belted Coaches
Day Trips 0116 - 2514155
Coach Hire 0116 - 2514030

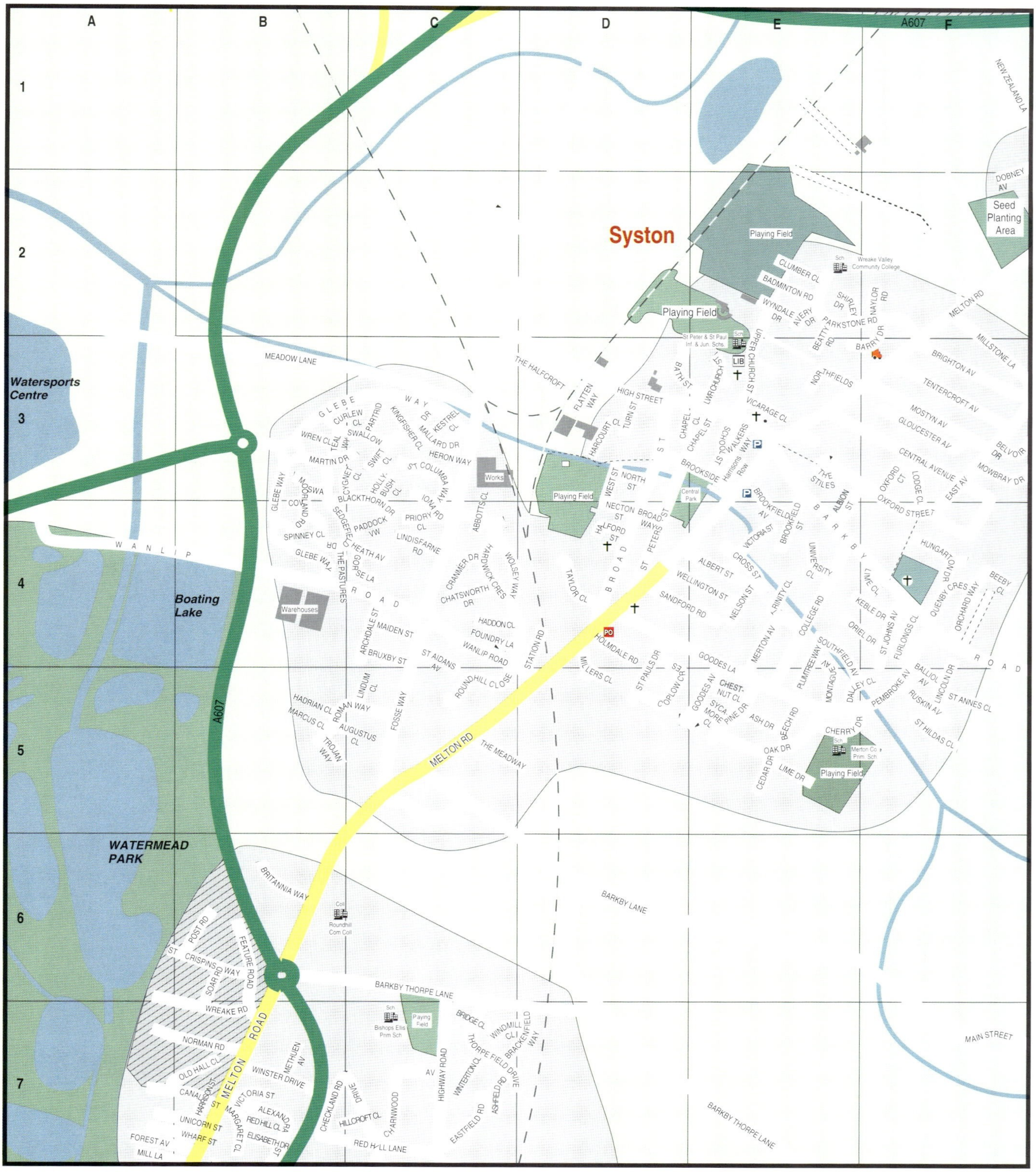

Hollis Packaging Services
6a Hawley Road
Hinckley
Leicestershire
LE10 0PR
Tel: 01455 234235
Fax: 01455 251607

Specialised Finishing Services to the Printing and Allied Trade

Cutting and Creasing
Window Patching
Carton & Folder Gluing (Board & PVC)
Technical Consultancy Services

Call or Fax Details for a Prompt Quote

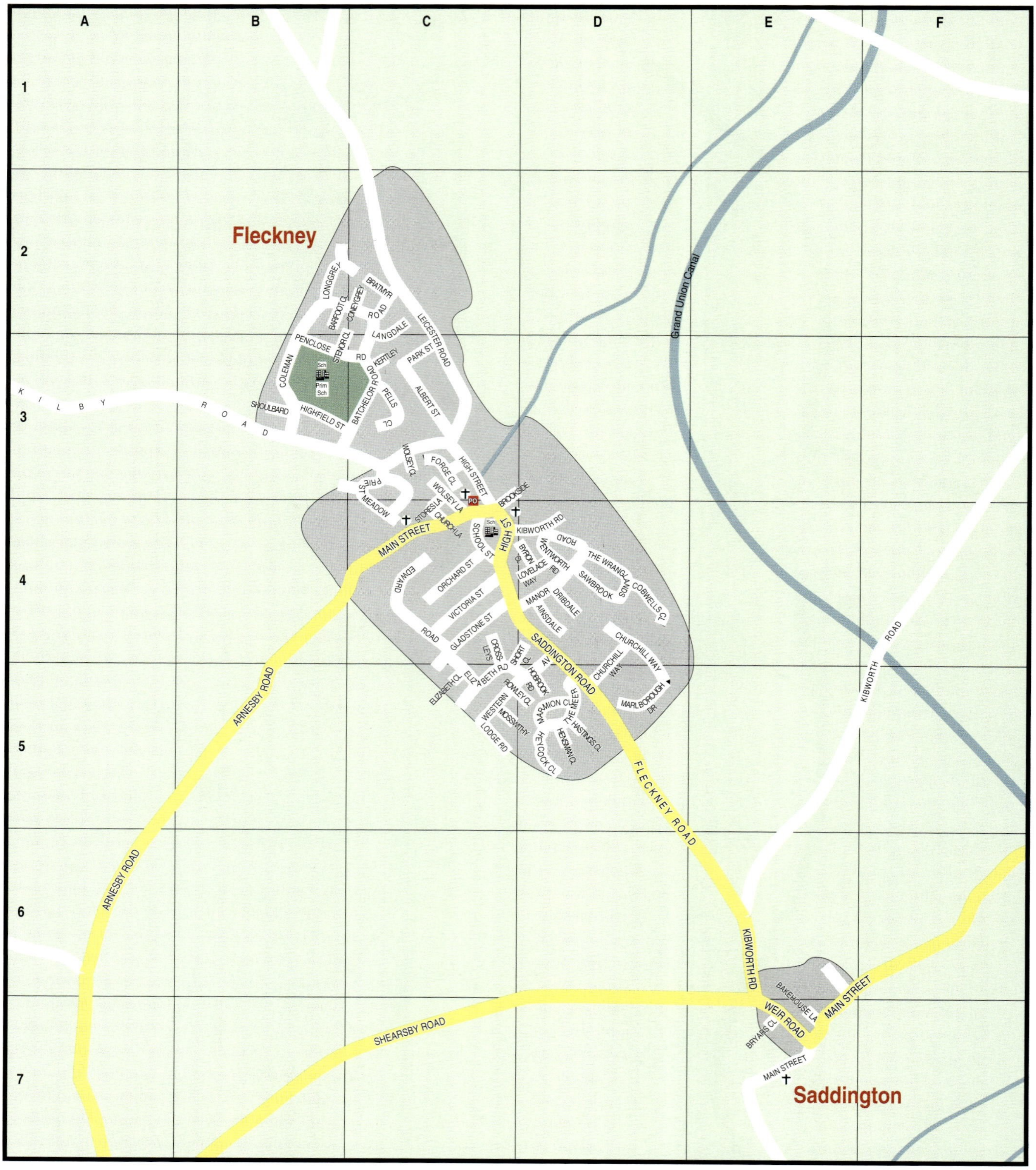

93

Clean 'A' Car

CONTRACT CLEANING • OFFICE CLEANING • MOBILE CAR VALETING

162 STRATHMORE ROAD, HINCKLEY,
LEICESTERSHIRE, LE10 0LS

TELEPHONE: Office 01455 440805
Mobile 07970 817417

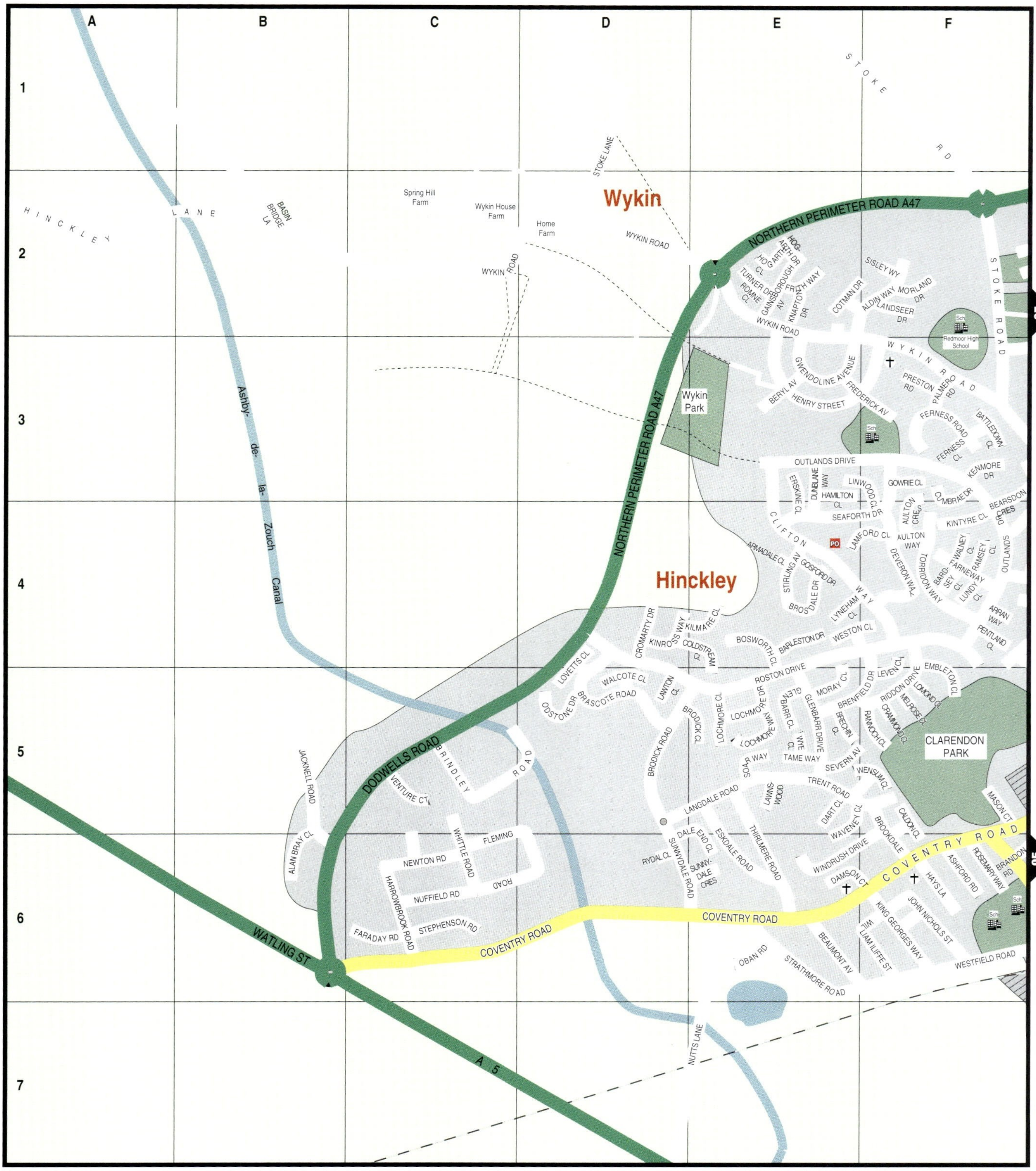

BRAY & BRAY
SOLICITORS

33, Station Road, Hinckley, Leicestershire LE10 1AP. Telephone (01455) 238993

ALL TYPES OF LEGAL WORK UNDERTAKEN

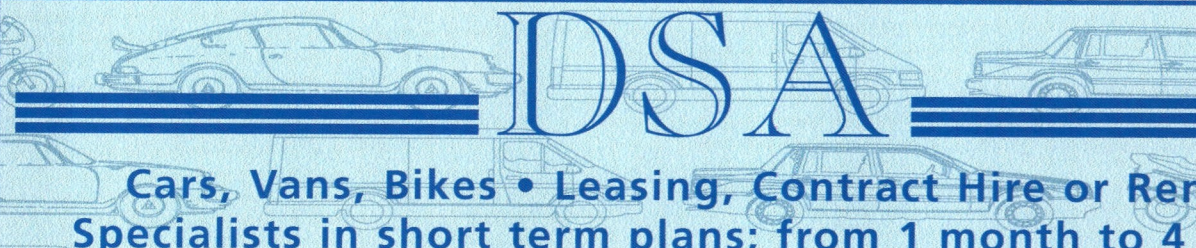

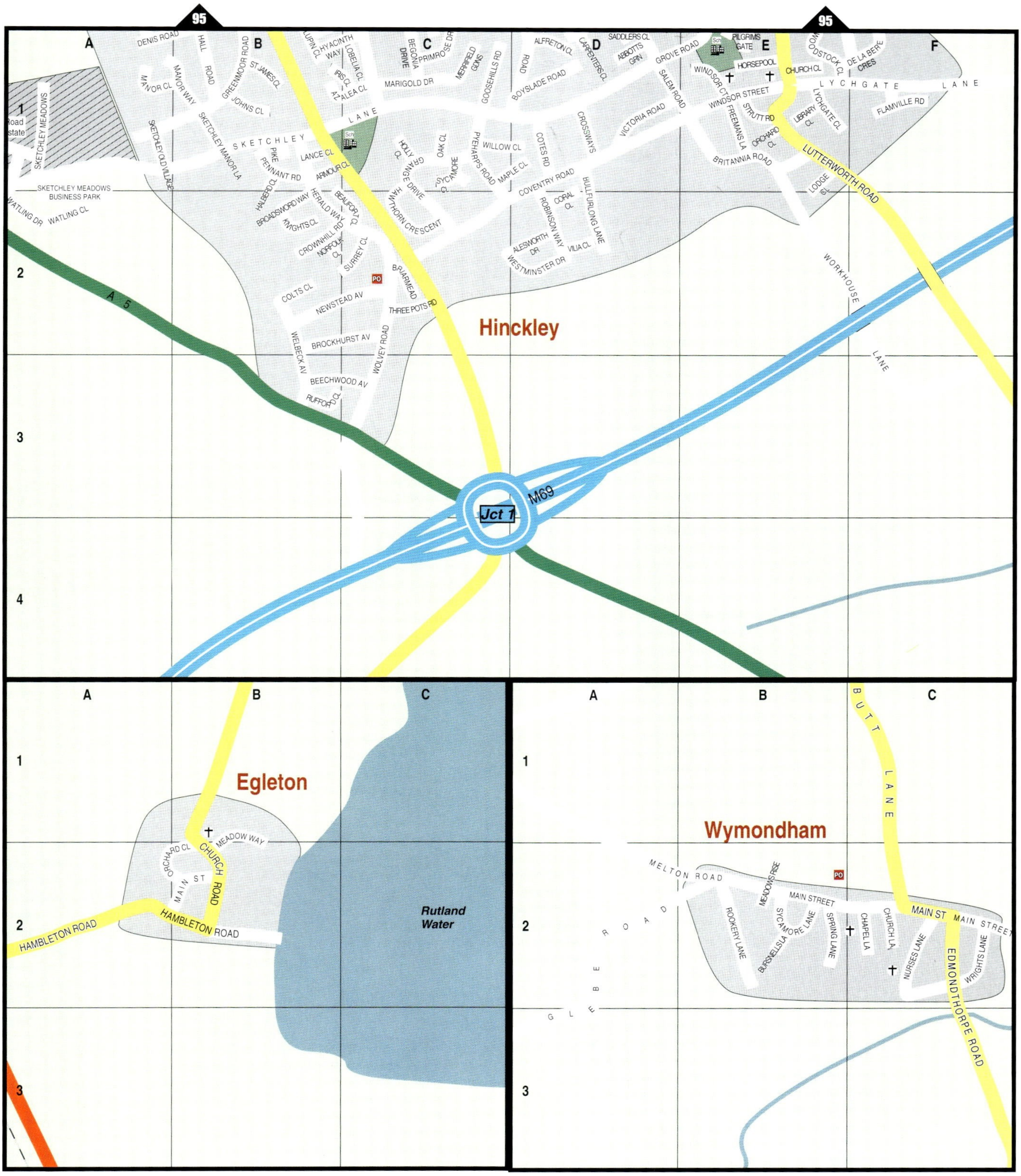

95
95
Hinckley
SKETCHLEY MEADOWS
SKETCHLEY MEADOWS BUSINESS PARK
WATLING DR
WATLING CL
DENIS ROAD
MANOR CL
MANOR WAY
HALL ROAD
GREENMOOR ROAD
ST JAMES CL
JOHNS CL
SKETCHLEY OLD VILLAGE
SKETCHLEY MANOR LA
SKETCHLEY LANE
PIKE
PENNANT RD
LANCE CL
ARMOUR CL
BROADSWORD WAY
HERALD WAY
KNIGHTS CL
CROWNHILL RD
NORFOLK
SURREY CL
BEAUFORT CL
COLTS CL
NEWSTEAD AV
BROCKHURST AV
WELBECK AV
BEECHWOOD AV
RUFFORD CL
WOLVEY ROAD
THREE POTS RD
BRIARMEAD
HAWTHORN CRESCENT
GRANGE DRIVE
HOLLY CL
OAK CL
SYCAMORE CL
HYACINTH WAY
LUPIN CL
LOBELIA CL
IRIS CL
AZALEA CL
BEGONIA DRIVE
PRIMROSE DR
MARIGOLD DR
MERRIFIELD GDNS
GOOSEHILLS RD
PYEHARPS ROAD
WILLOW CL
MAPLE CL
COTES RD
COVENTRY ROAD
CORAL CL
ROBINSON WAY
ALESWORTH DR
WESTMINSTER DR
VILIA CL
BULLFURLONG LANE
CROSSWAYS
BOYSLADE ROAD
ALFRETON CL
CARPENTERS CL
SADDLERS CL
ABBOTTS GRN
GROVE ROAD
SALEM ROAD
VICTORIA ROAD
WINDSOR CT
WINDSOR STREET
PILGRIMS GATE
HORSEPOOL
CHURCH CL
FREEMANS LA
STRUTT RD
ORCHARD CL
BRITANNIA ROAD
LIBRARY CL
LYCHGATE CL
LYCHGATE LANE
DE LA BERE CRES
FLAMVILLE RD
LUTTERWORTH ROAD
LODGE CL
WORKHOUSE LANE
A5
M69
Jct 1
Egleton
CHURCH ROAD
MEADOW WAY
ORCHARD CL
MAIN ST
HAMBLETON ROAD
Rutland Water
Wymondham
BUTT LANE
MELTON ROAD
GLEBE ROAD
ROOKERY LANE
MEADOWS RISE
MAIN STREET
SYCAMORE LANE
BURSNELLS LA
SPRING LANE
CHAPEL LA
CHURCH LA
NURSES LANE
MAIN ST
EDMONDTHORPE ROAD
WRIGHTS LANE

Shagorika

AUTHENTIC INDIAN FOOD

16 St. Mary's Road, Market Harborough, Leicestershire, LE16 7DU
For Reservations Telephone: (01858) 464644 or 468700

We are proud of our restaurant's quality home style cooked food
• Service with a smile •

Established since March 1980 under the same family
We recently celebrated 21 years of successful business in the town
TAKE AWAY AVAILABLE
OPENING HOURS:
Sunday - Thursday • 12 noon - 2.30 pm • 6.00 pm - 11.30 pm
Friday & Saturday • 12 noon - 2.30 pm • 6.00 pm - 12.30 am
(Bank Holidays as Sunday - Thursday hours)

SHAGORIKA - Bengali for "the seashore"

CONNECTIONS

Consultancy and Training Services

Organisational Change and Development
Employee Resource Development
Management Competencies
Positive Action
Equality and Service Values

24 AVOCA Close, Leicester LE5 4RA
Tel: (0116) 246 0953

CONSULTANCY AND TRAINING SERVICES

THUNDER ENGINEERING

Map 43 C2

prototype precision production

conventional & CNC machining

motorsport specialist

1 Garfield Street • Leicester • LE4 5GF
Tel/Fax: 0116 253 1105
www.thunderengineering.co.uk

MICHAEL JOHN
CARPETS

Established 1946

Suppliers of Fine Quality Carpets and Rugs
~ Largest Selection in the Midlands ~

Natural Wood, Laminate & Amtico Floorings
Lowest Prices Guaranteed

188 - 190 NARBOROUGH ROAD
LEICESTER LE3 0BU
Telephone: 0116 254 1853 or 0116 254 5013
Fax: 0116 254 3924

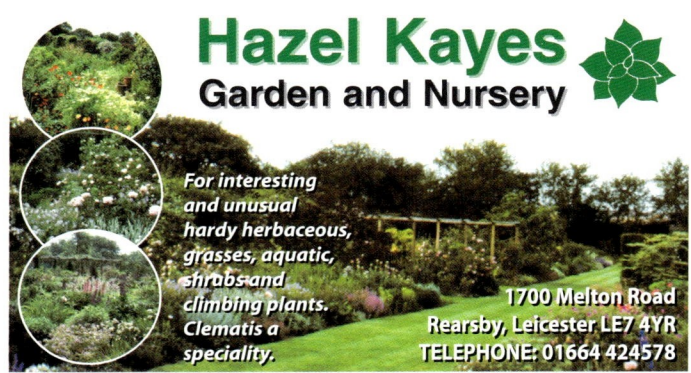

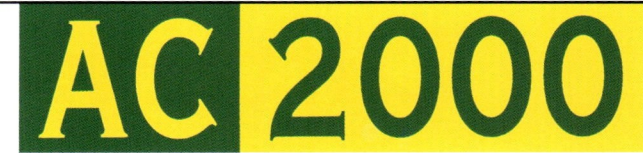

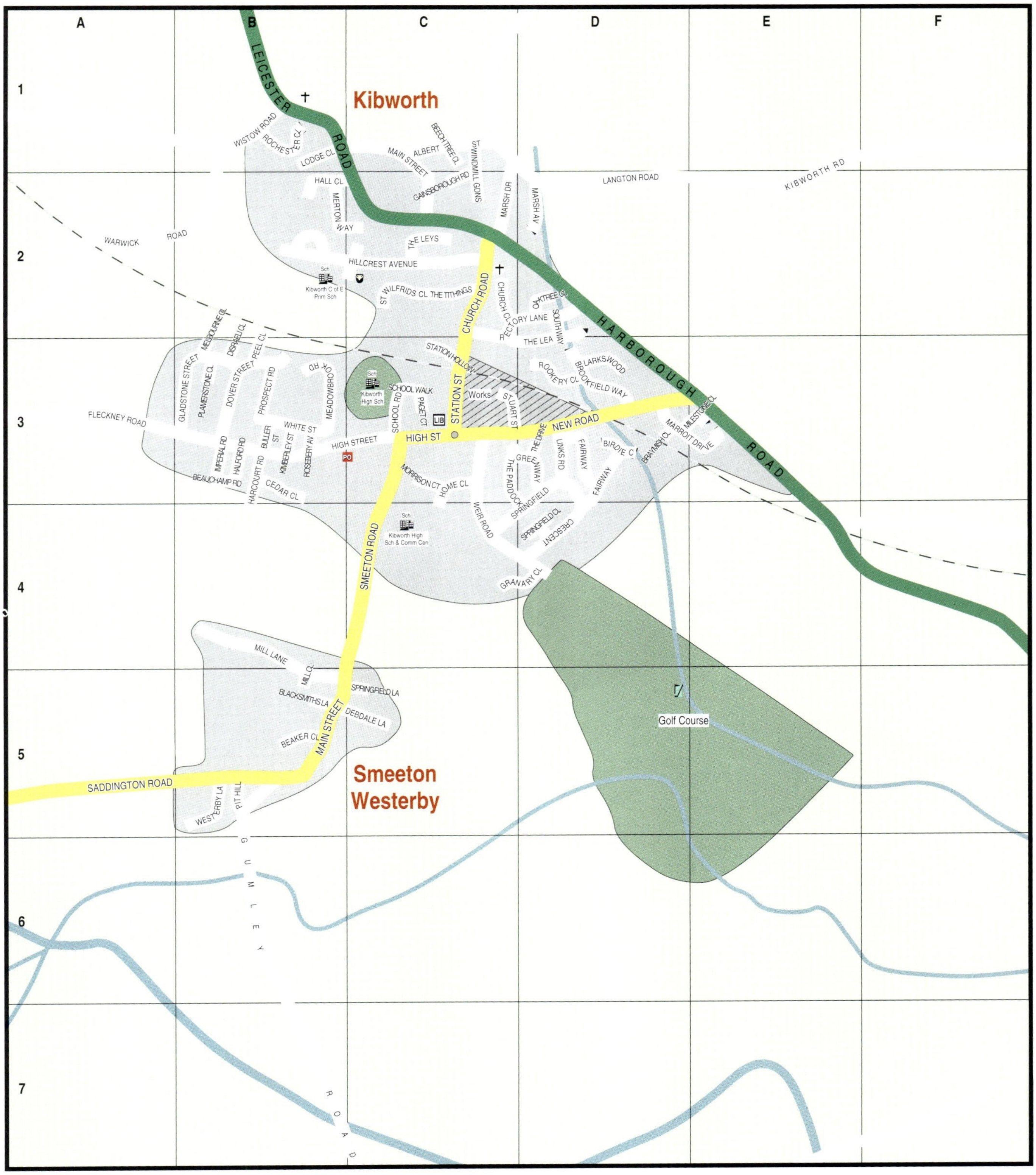

A
B
C
D
E
F
1
2
3
4
5
6
7
Kibworth
Smeeton Westerby
LEICESTER ROAD
HARBOROUGH ROAD
WISTOW ROAD
ROCHESTER CL
LODGE CL
HALL CL
MERTON WAY
MAIN STREET
ALBERT
BEECH TREE CL
WINDMILL GDNS
GAINSBOROUGH RD
MARSH DR
MARSH AV
LANGTON ROAD
KIBWORTH RD
WARWICK ROAD
THE LEYS
HILLCREST AVENUE
Sch
Kibworth C of E Prim Sch
ST WILFRIDS CL
THE TITHINGS
CHURCH ROAD
CHURCH CL
RECTORY LANE
OAKTREE CL
SOUTHWAY
THE LEA
LARKSWOOD
BROOKFIELD WAY
ROOKERY CL
STATION HOLLOW
MELBOURNE CL
DISRAELI CL
PEEL CL
GLADSTONE STREET
PLAMERSTONE CL
DOVER STREET
PROSPECT RD
MEADOWBROOK RD
Sch
Kibworth High Sch
SCHOOL WALK
SCHOOL RD
PAGET CT
STATION ST
Works
STUART ST
LIB
FLECKNEY ROAD
WHITE ST
HIGH STREET
HIGH ST
NEW ROAD
PO
IMPERIAL RD
HALFORD RD
BULLER ST
KIMBERLEY ST
ROSEBERRY AV
BEAUCHAMP RD
HARCOURT RD
CEDAR CL
MORRISON CT
HOME CL
WEIR ROAD
THE PADDOCK
GREENWAY
THE DRIVE
LINKS RD
FAIRWAY
BIRDIE CL
MILESTONE CL
MARRIOT DRIVE
BRAYMISH CL
SPRINGFIELD
SPRINGFIELD CL
CRESCENT
Sch
Kibworth High Sch & Comm Cen
SMEETON ROAD
GRANARY CL
Golf Course
MILL LANE
MILL CL
SPRINGFIELD LA
BLACKSMITHS LA
DEBDALE LA
BEAKER CL
MAIN STREET
SADDINGTON ROAD
WESTERBY LA
PIT HILL
GUMLEY ROAD

Lutterworth Coaches

- Special Interest Day Excursions, UK and Continental Holidays
- Private Coach Hire
- As well as Packaging Holidays and Mini-tours, we can *'tailor'* your Day Trip to include Meals, Shows, Boat Trips etc - **Just leave it to us**

For friendly, professional service contact Lutterworth Coaches Ltd:
Leicester Road, Lutterworth, Leicestershire LE17 4NJ
Telephone: 01455 553353 ~ Facsimile: 01455 559596

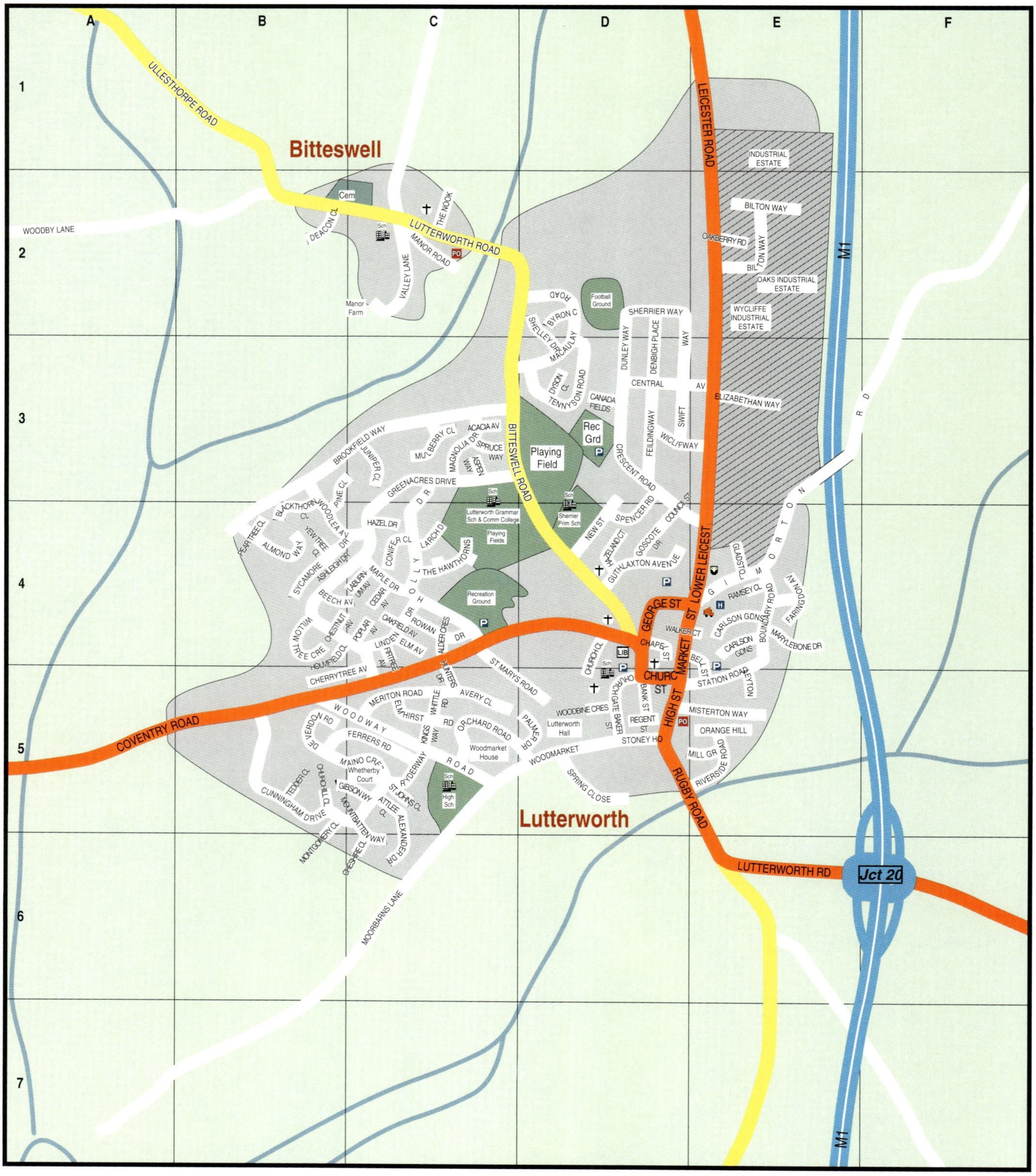

Protheroe's

The Protheroe Motor Group Limited
Northampton Road, Market Harborough, Leicestershire LE16 9HD
www.protheroes.co.uk

Tel: (01858) 465511   Fax: (01858) 432656

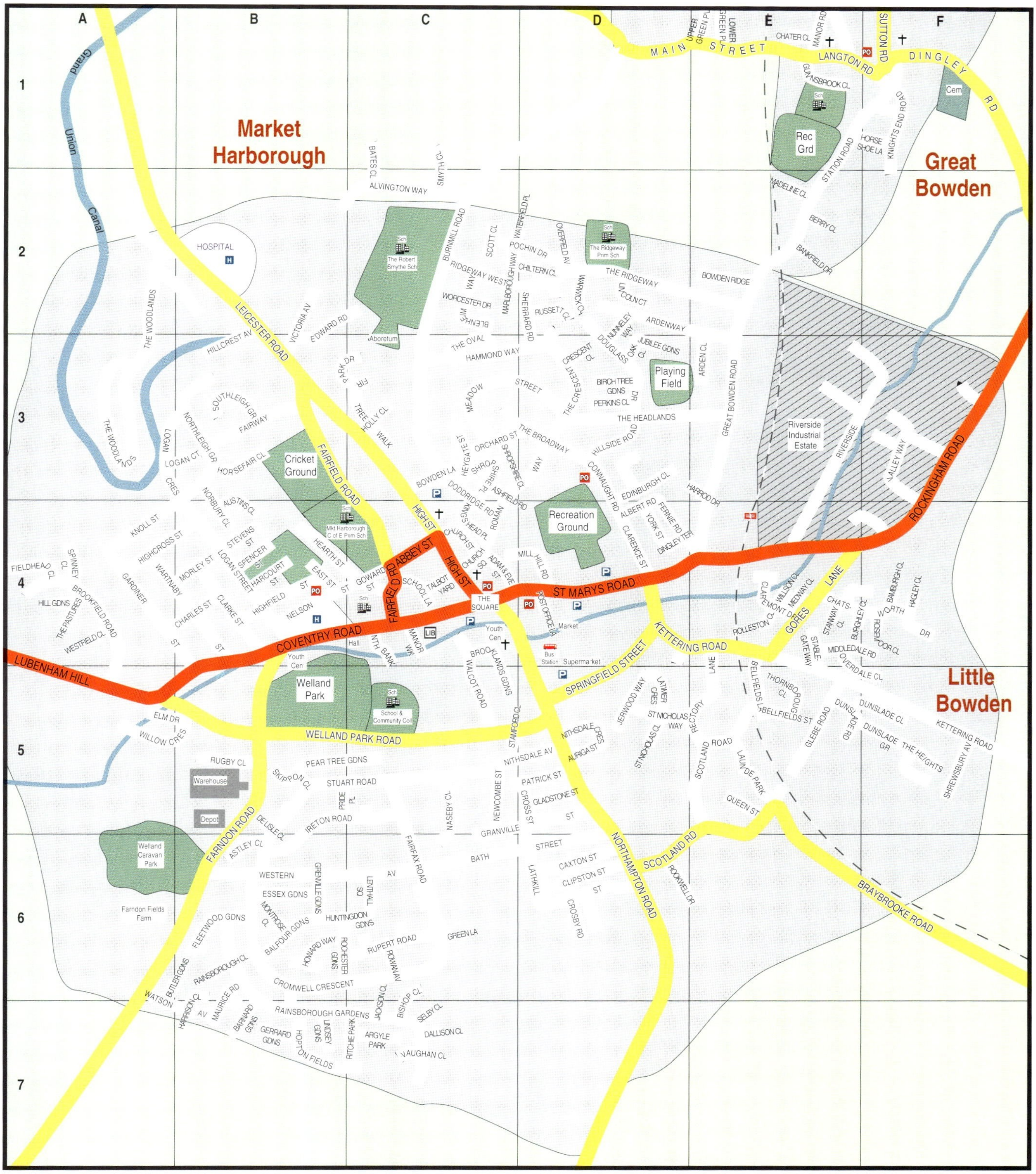

BRIDGE PERSONNEL

BRIDGE HOUSE . 68 MAIN STREET . BROUGHTON ASTLEY . LEICESTER . LE9 6RD
TELEPHONE: 01455 286 666 FACSIMILE: 01455 286 888

Driving:	*01455 286 666*
SkillTech:	*01455 286 555*
OfficeSelect:	*01455 283 333*

*Wide range of Quality Temporary & Permanent Job Opportunities
Excellent Rates of Pay & Working Patterns to Suit all Circumstances
For a reliable and honest service, call the agency that works...For You!*

LEICESTER...
Machine Movers Ltd.

40 Great Central Street
Leicester
LE1 4JT

Tel: (0116) 253 6662
Fax: (0116) 2510631
Mobile: 07850 365262

100

~124~

SILVER STAR GARAGES

Specialising In The Service And Repair Of Mercedes-Benz Vehicles

★ All Other Makes of Vehicles Undertaken ★

Lazarus Court   Woodgate   Rothley   Leicester   LE7 7LL
Telephone 0116 230 3801

EST 1978

PARTNERS
NICK ALDRIDGE
CHRIS PARKINSON

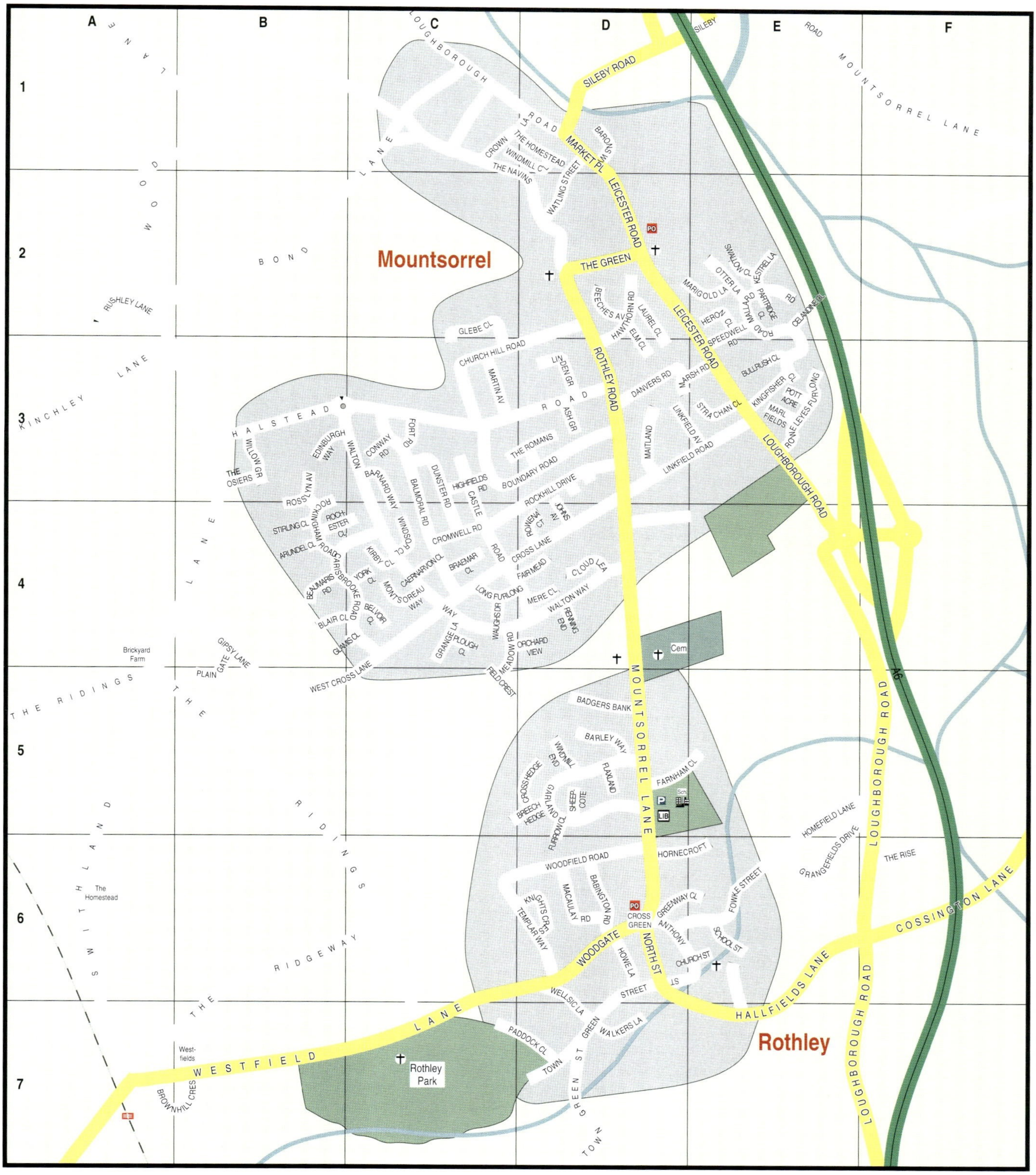

Swans Antiques & Interiors

*Specialists in French Antique Beds
Handpainted Furniture & Interior Decor Items*

17 Mill Street, Oakham, Rutland LE15 6EA • Telephone 01572 755094 • Open 7 days

Situated on the banks of Rutland Water, Whitwell is one of the country's premier training venues. With a comprehensive portfolio of training programmes and a track record in bespoke training services for some of the UK's most prestigious companies, whatever your organisation's training needs, we will offer you a service second to none. Our programmes make full use of our superb location, with indoor and outdoor exercises simulating today's business environment of rapid change and uncertainty. From skills training to team building, choose your training well - choose Whitwell.

Call now for more details.

Whitwell Training & Development Centre,
Whitwell, Oakham, Rutland LE15 8BW
Tel: 01780 686555 Fax: 01780 686549

Whitwell
The Ultimate Training Location

Looking for the ultimate **Training Location?**

You've just found it!!!

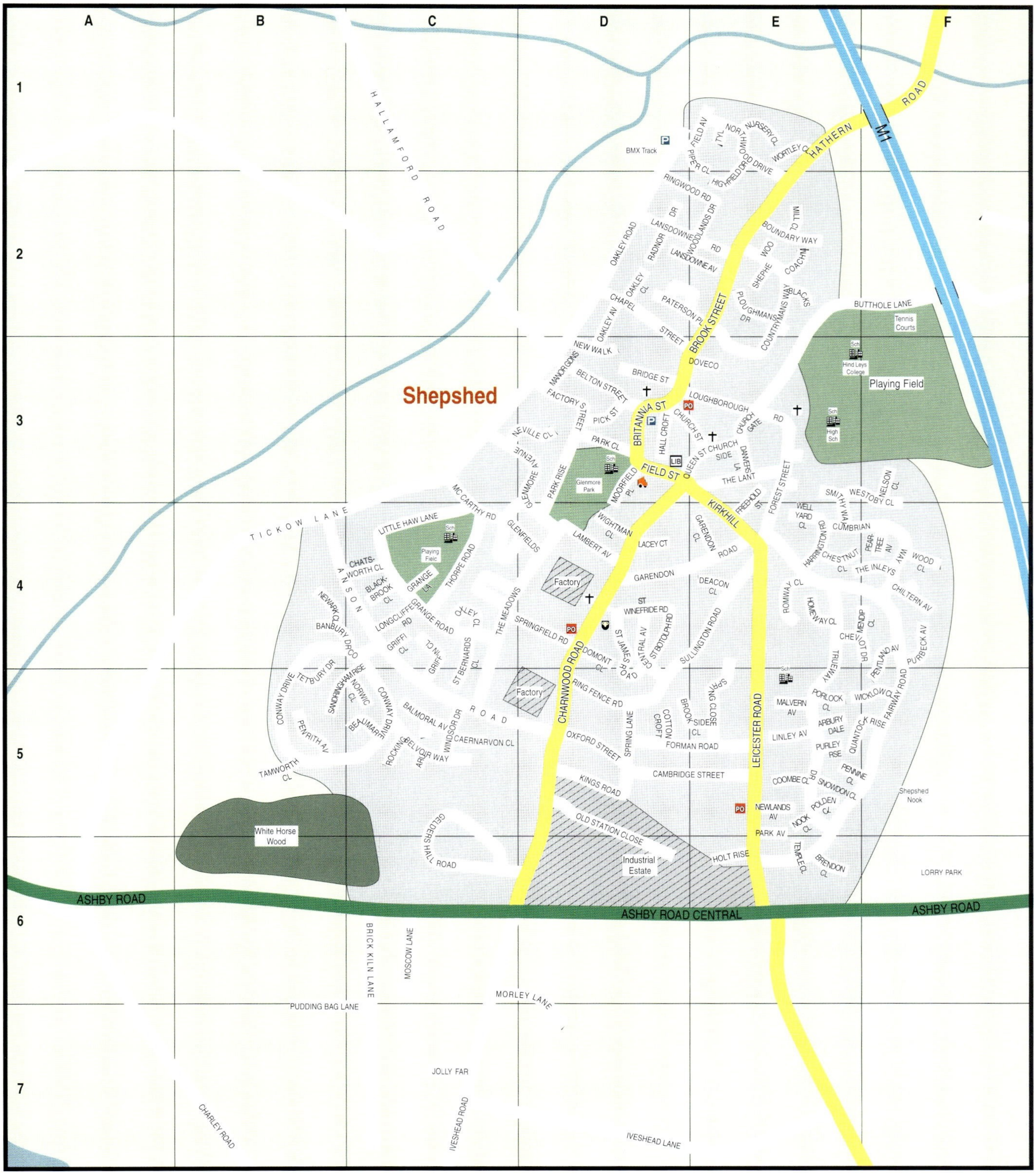

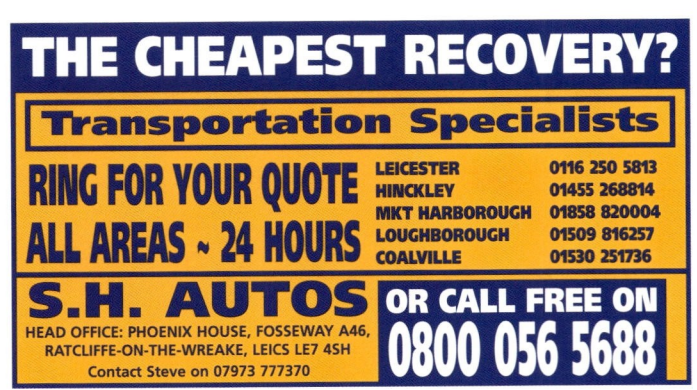

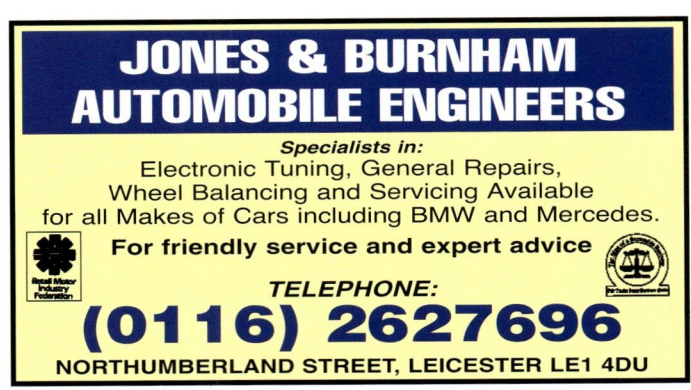

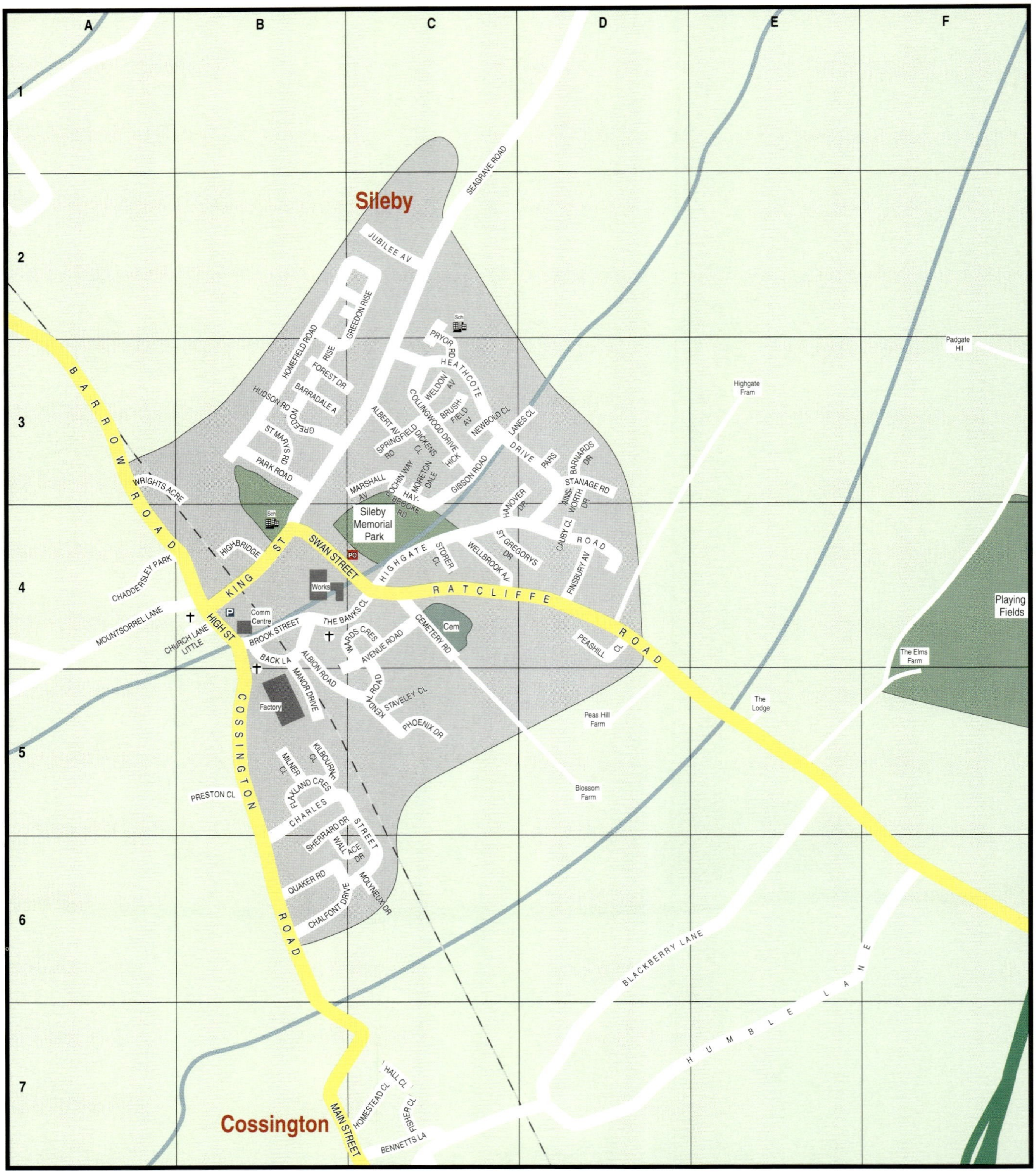

A
B
C
D
E
F
1
2
3
4
5
6
7
Sileby
Cossington
SEAGRAVE ROAD
JUBILEE AV
GREEDON RISE
HOMEFIELD ROAD
RISE
FOREST DR
HUDSON RD
BARRADALE A
GREEDON
ST MARYS RD
PARK ROAD
PRYOR RD
HEATHCOTE
WELDON AV
COLLINGWOOD DRIVE
BRUSHFIELD AV
ALBERT AV
SPRINGFIELD RD
DICKENS CL
HICK
NEWBOLD CL
LANES CL
DRIVE
PARS
BARNARDS DR
STANAGE RD
GIBSON ROAD
MARSHALL AV
COCHIN WAY
MORETON DALE
HAYBROOKE RD
HANOVER DR
WINSWORTH DR
CAUBY CL
ROAD
FINSBURY AV
ST GREGORYS DR
WELLBROOK AV
STORER CL
HIGHGATE
Sileby Memorial Park
PO
Sch
BARROW ROAD
WRIGHTS ACRE
HIGHBRIDGE
KING ST
SWAN STREET
RATCLIFFE ROAD
CHADDERSLEY PARK
MOUNTSORREL LANE
CHURCH LANE LITTLE
HIGH ST
P
Comm Centre
Works
BROOK STREET
THE BANKS CL
WARDS CRES
AVENUE ROAD
CEMETERY RD
Cem
PEASHILL CL
BACK LA
ALBION ROAD
MANOR DRIVE
Factory
KENDAL ROAD
STAVELEY CL
PHOENIX DR
COSSINGTON ROAD
MILNER CL
KILBOURNE CL
FLAXLAND CRES
PRESTON CL
CHARLES STREET
SHERRARD DR
WALLACE DR
QUAKER RD
CHALFONT DRIVE
MOLYNEUX DR
Padgate Hll
Highgate Fram
Playing Fields
The Elms Farm
The Lodge
Peas Hill Farm
Blossom Farm
BLACKBERRY LANE
HUMBLE LANE
HALL CL
HOMESTEAD CL
FISHER CL
BENNETTS LA
MAIN STREET

Phone 01455 271222

- Accounting Systems
- Bespoke Software
- Visual Basic
- SQL
- Internet/Intranet/ASP

Complete Business Systems
a simple solution to complex problems

Phone 01455 271222 Fax: 01455 271071
Email: complete@completebs.com
Website: http://www.completebs.com

Complete Business Systems
Studio 2, Highfields Farm Enterprise Centre, Huncote Road,
Stoney Stanton, Leics LE9 4DJ

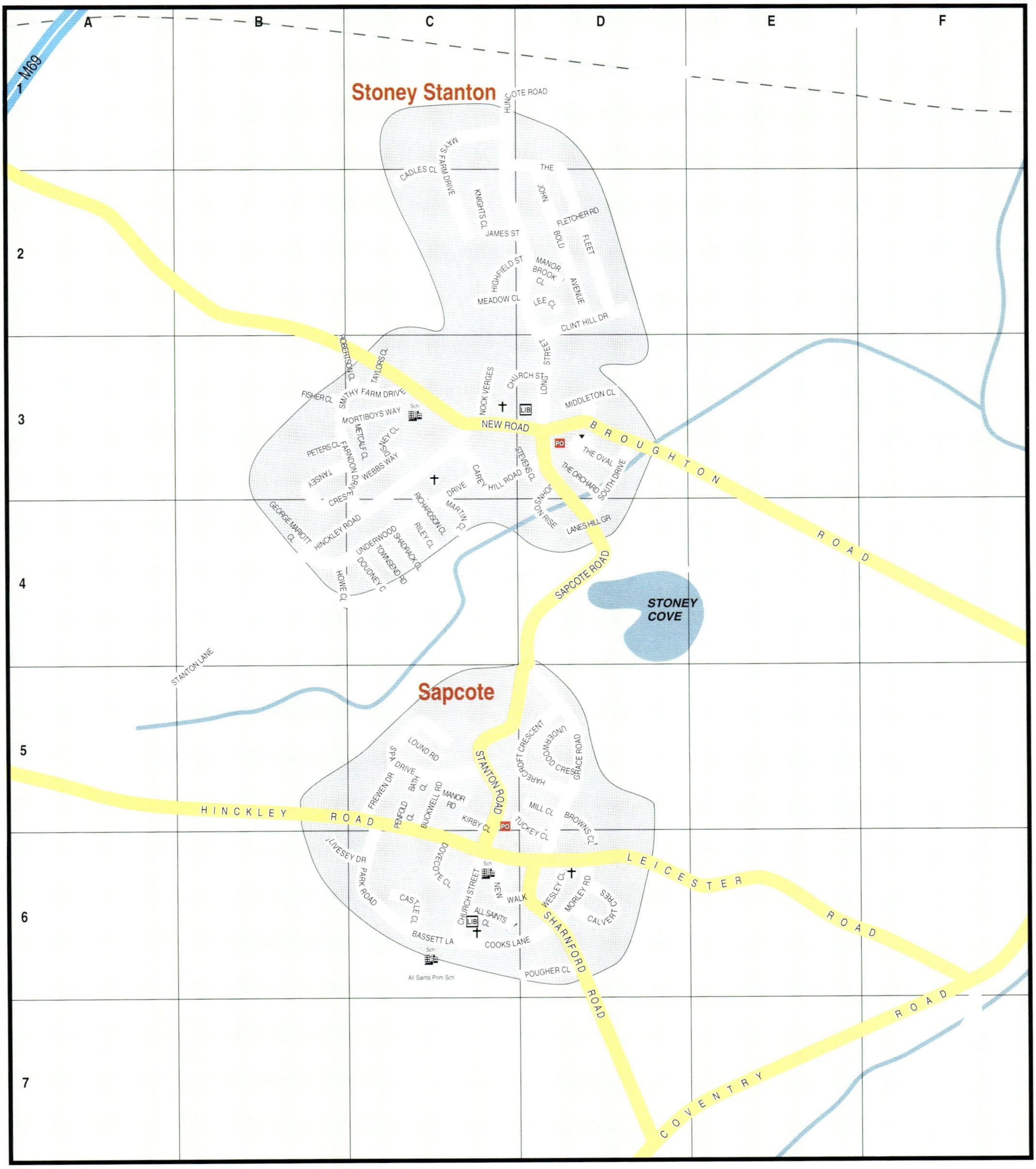

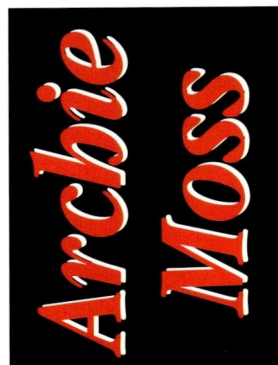

Your Local Approved Vauxhall Dealer
NEW & USED CARS & COMMERCIAL VEHICLES

APPROVED ACCIDENT REPAIRS • SERVICING • PARTS
CAR HIRE • M.O.T. WHILE YOU WAIT • SALES OPEN 7 DAYS
SERVICE OPEN 6 DAYS

Motability
BELTON ROAD, LOUGHBOROUGH

LOUGHBOROUGH (01509) 213030

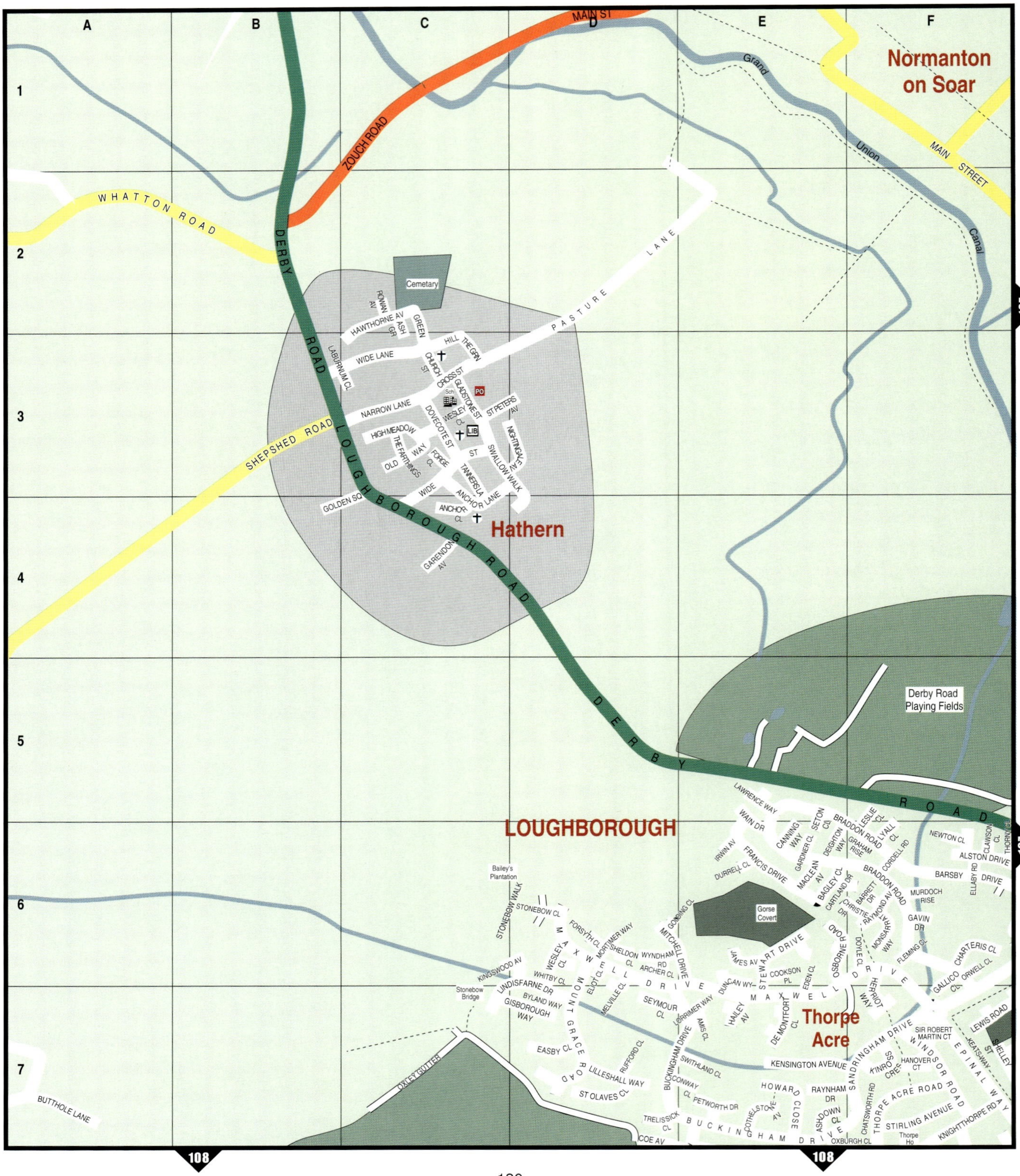

Servicing & Repairs to all makes of Vehicles
MOT Testing Station

Hanford Way, Loughborough,
Leicestershire LE11 1LS
☎ 01509-235726
Fax 01509-236000

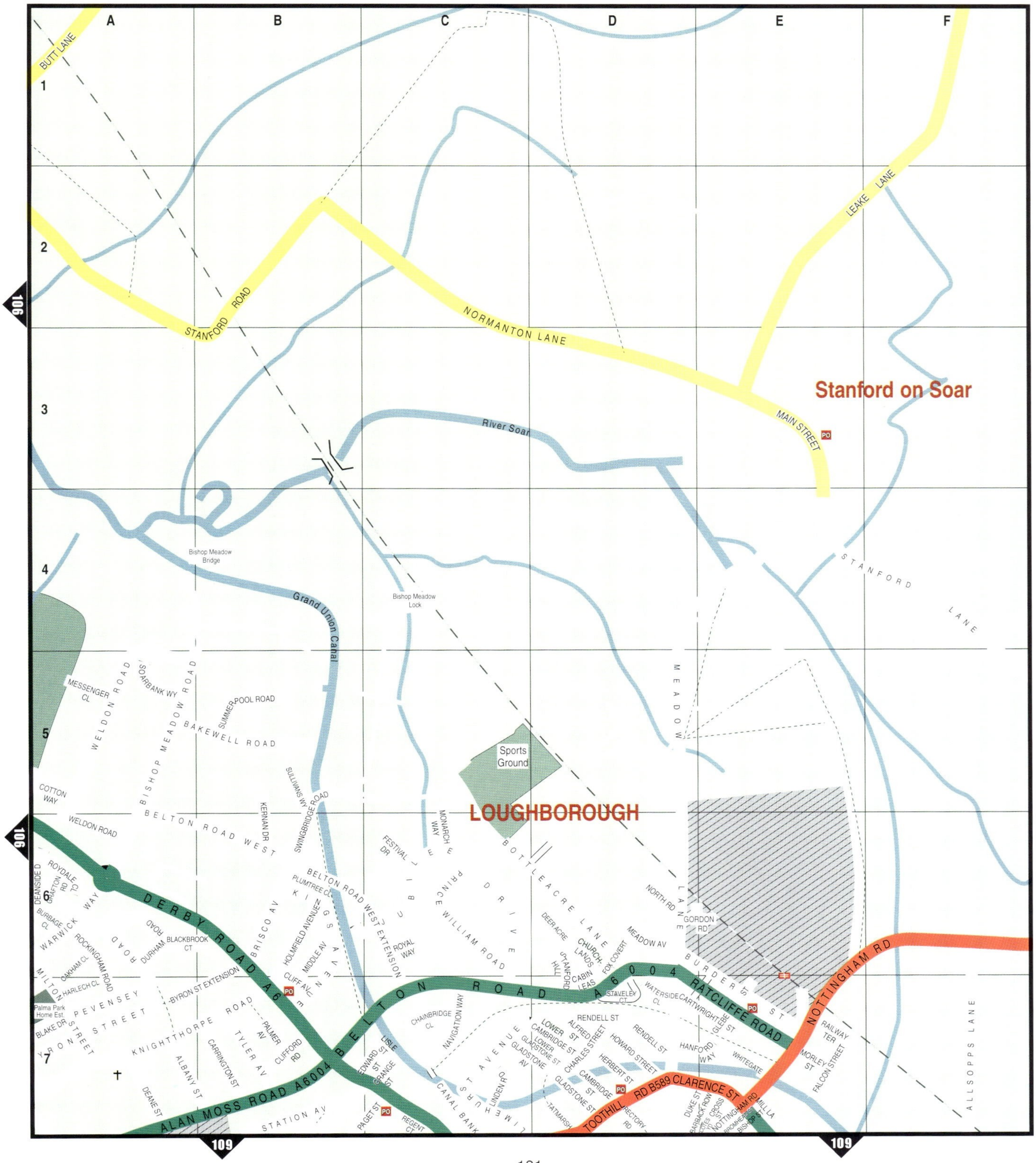

Essex, Abel, Hodgkinson & Co.

CHARTERED CERTIFIED ACCOUNTANTS
CHARTERED TAX ADVISORS AND REGISTERED AUDITORS
~ Established for over 60 years ~

FREE INITIAL CONSULTATION

LOUGHBOROUGH
01509 267827

35 GRANBY ST., LOUGHBOROUGH

EXISTING BUSINESS OR JUST STARTING OUT? YOU NEED THE RIGHT ADVICE!

SELF ASSESSMENT ...WE KNOW THE FORM

We offer a full range of services which include:

Cash Flow & Profit Forecasts
Personal & Corporate Tax Advice
Book-keeping, Payroll and VAT

Auditing & Accounts Preparation
Affordable Computerisation
Financial Advice

Looking for a School for your Daughter?

We offer...
~ High Academic Achievement
~ Individual Attention in Small Classes
~ A Happy and Caring Environment
~ Christian Values
~ On-site Dyslexia Tuition
in the following departments...

Montessori, Infants, Juniors, Seniors and Sixth Form

Our Lady's Convent School, Burton Street, Loughborough, Leics LE11 2DT
Telephone: 01509 263901 ~ Facsimile: 01509 236193

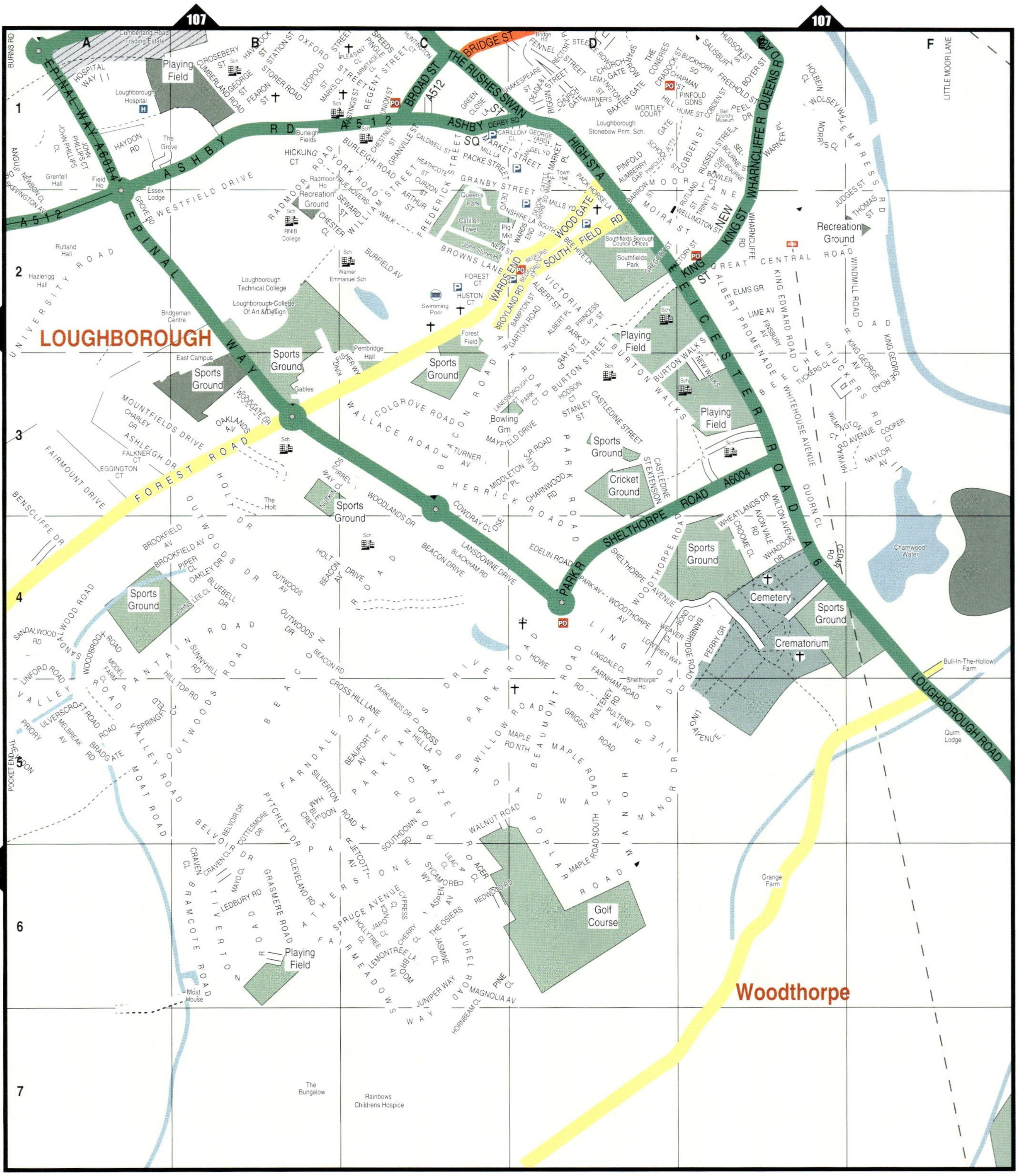

Our Lady's Convent School
For girls aged 3 to 18
Established in 1850

KENT BROS. AUTO SALVAGE

Quality Guaranteed Used Spares • Off The Shelf Service
Cash Buyers Of Insurance Write-Offs and Accident Damaged Vehicles

"RECYCLING THE PAST TO SAVE THE FUTURE"

Hector Rd, Hermitage Ind Est, Coalville, Leics LE67 3FR Tel: 01530 810363

FIND-A-PART MEMBERS

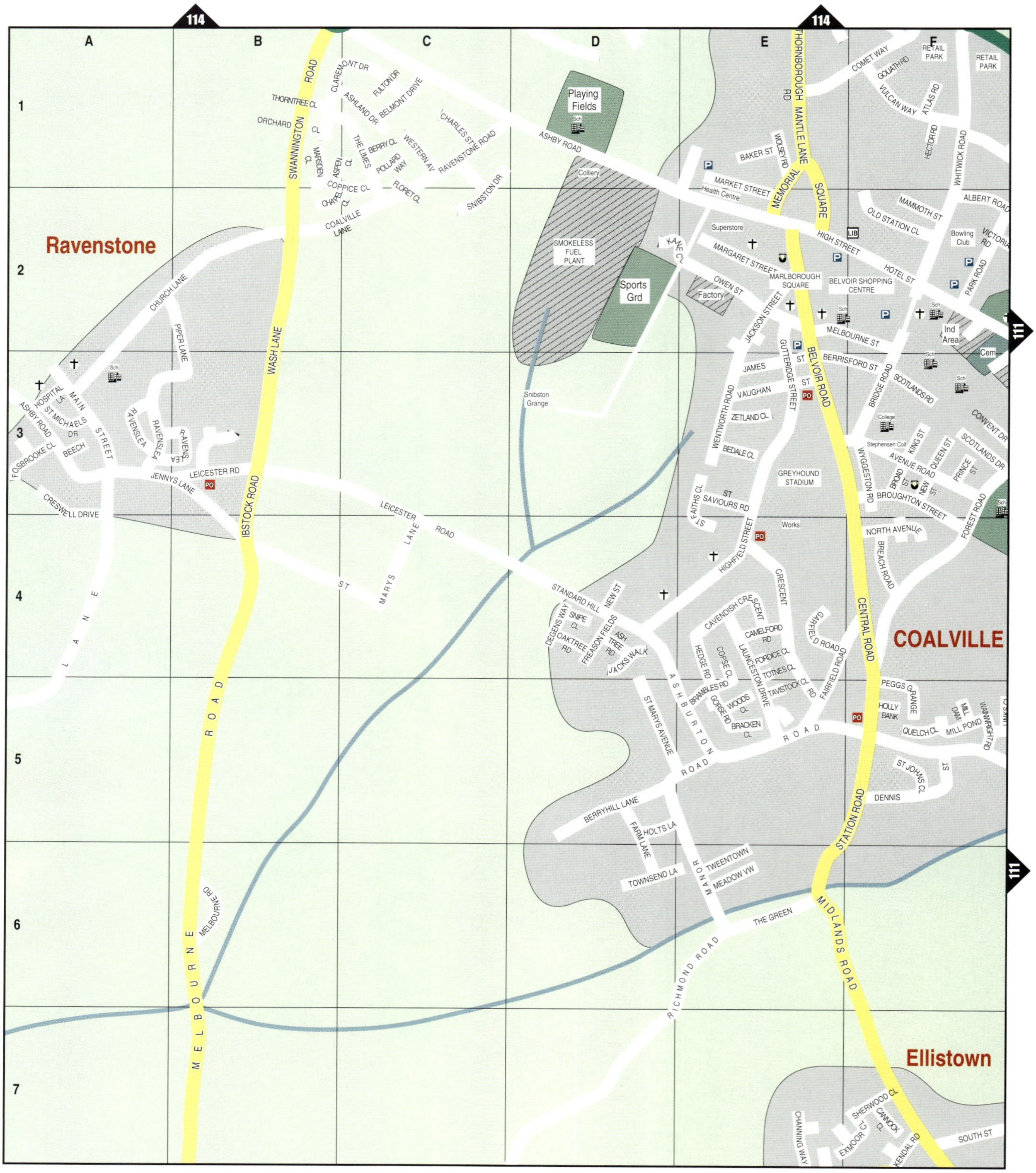

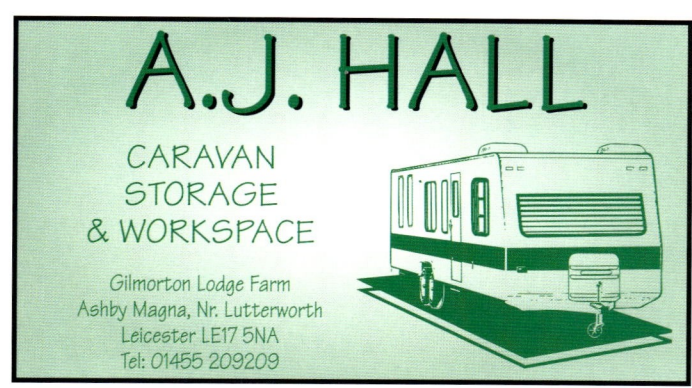

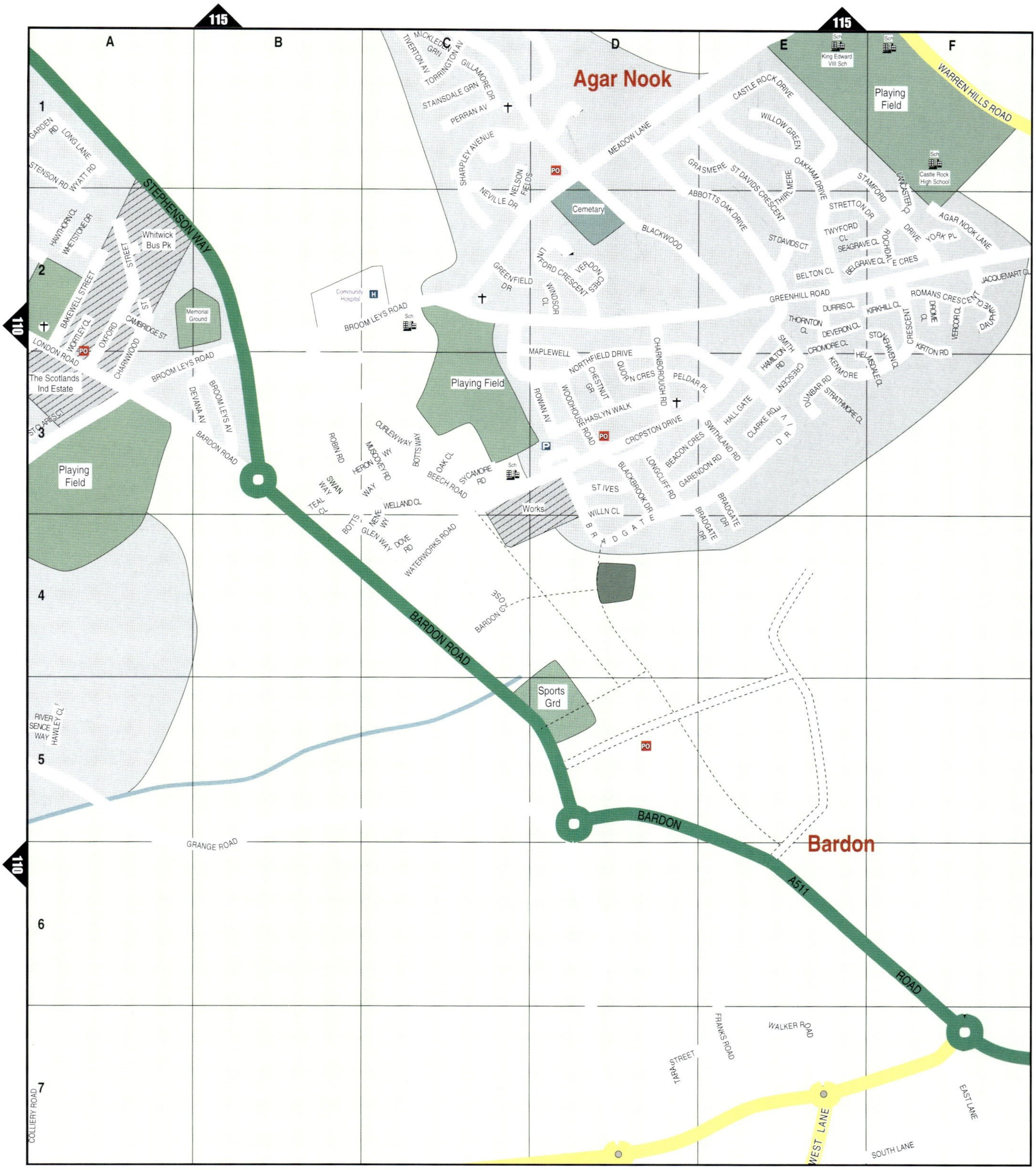

115
A
B
C
D
E
F
1
2
3
4
5
6
7
110
Agar Nook
Bardon
Playing Field
Cemetary
Community Hospital
Memorial Ground
Whitwick Bus Pk
The Scotlands Ind Estate
Works
Sports Grd
King Edward VIII Sch
Castle Rock High School
STEPHENSON WAY
BARDON ROAD
BARDON
A511
ROAD
GRANGE ROAD
BROOM LEYS ROAD
GREENHILL ROAD
MEADOW LANE
CASTLE ROCK DRIVE
WARREN HILLS ROAD
AGAR NOOK LANE
ROMANS CRESCENT
CHARNBOROUGH RD
CROPSTON DRIVE
NORTHFIELD DRIVE
MAPLEWELL
BLACKWOOD
SHARPLEY AVENUE
WILLOW GREEN
OAKHAM DRIVE
ABBOTTS OAK DRIVE
ST DAVIDS CRESCENT
GRASMERE
STAMFORD
STRETTON DR
BELTON CL
LONDON ROAD
BAKEWELL STREET
CAMBRIDGE ST
OXFORD
CHARNWOOD
BROOM LEYS AV
DEVANA AV
BARDON ROAD
BEECH ROAD
WATERWORKS ROAD
BARDON CLOSE
WALKER ROAD
FRANKS ROAD
TARA STREET
WEST LANE
SOUTH LANE
EAST LANE
COLLIERY ROAD
RIVER SENCE WAY
HAWLEY CL
LONG LANE
STENSON RD
WYATT RD
PERRAN AV
STAINSDALE GRN
GILLAMORE DR
TORRINGTON AV
TIVERTON AV
MICKLEDEN GRN

CROWFOOTS CARRIERS LTD

THE MIDLANDS LEADING EXPRESS PARCELS SERVICE IS NOW IN LANCASHIRE AND YORKSHIRE

Established 1912

VOLUME CONTRACT AT _VERY_ COMPETITIVE RATES
- NO premium charge for express service • NO weight restrictions
- FULLY computerised distribution • IMMEDIATE communication with drivers

Mill Street Industrial Estate, Barwell, Leicester, LE9 8EY.
Tel: 01455 842911 Fax: 01455 841647 Email: phil@crowfoots.co.uk

A
B
C
D
E
F
1
2
3
4
5
6
7
112
112
Earl Shilton
Elmesthorpe
SHILTON ROAD
HILL TOP
HIGH STREET
THE HOLLOW
WOOD STREET
HINCKLEY ROAD
HEATH LANE
GARTREE CRES
HIGH TOR WEST
HIGH TOR EAST
GREEN LA
KEATS LANE
KEATS CL
WEST STREET
PROSPECT WAY
PARK ROAD
TOWER ROAD
CARRS ROAD
MOUNTFIELD RD
KINGS WALK
CLEARVIEW CRES
THE BEECHES
CHURCH STREET
CHAPEL ST
ROMAN CL
THE POPLARS
NOCK VERGES
BOSWORTH GRN
KING RICHARDS HILL
KNIGHTS LINK
THURLASTON LANE
MAUGHAN ST
ALMEYS LANE
AVENUE
AVENUE NTH
EARL STREET
WILFRED MDW
MONTGOMERY RD
AVENUE
FRANK BOOTH CL
Cem
VICARAGE ST
OXFORD ST
ALEXANDER
SOUTH
RONALD TOON RD
WEAVER RD
MONTGOMERY RD
Rec Grnd
ASTLEY ROAD
THE LEECROFTS
CANDLE LA
PEGGS CL
COTTAGE GDNS
LYNDENE CL
CONISTON CL
WINDERMERE CL
OAKS WAY
Oaks Ind Est
LAND SOCIETY LA
THE CLOISTERS
MELTON ST
BYRON ST
JAMES ST
METCALFE ST
LUCAS WAY
MONA ST
NEW STREET
ROSSENDALE RD
HOLLYDENE CRES
LABURNUM DR
HIGHFIELD ST
FIELD WAY
NURSERY GDNS
DOCTORS FIELDS
DERWENT CL
LYNDENE CL
EAST EQUITY ROAD
BORROWDALE CL
ULLSWATER CL
NORTHLEIGH WAY
MEADOW COURT RD
Townlands C of E Prim Sch
HURST RD
EQUITY RD
THE GRANGE
STATION RD
STONEYCROFT ROAD
BALMORAL ROAD
EDINBURGH RD
OAKDALE ROAD
ASH ROAD
LIME GR
MAPLE WAY
ROAD
ALMOND WAY
MAPLE WAY
WILEMANS CL
SANDRINGHAM AV
CORONATION
CEDAR
ELMDALE ROAD
BIRCH CL
ELMESTHORPE LANE
WILKINSON LANE
BREACH LANE
MILL LANE
Church Farm
THE CRESCENT
BILLINGTON ROAD
BRIDLE PATH ROAD
STANTON ROAD
LEIGHTON CRES
LOVELACE CRES
THE ROUNDHILLS
M69
PO
LIB
Sch

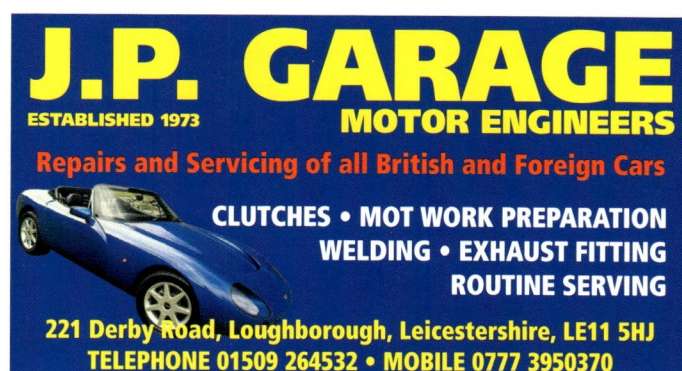

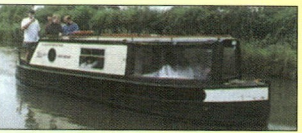

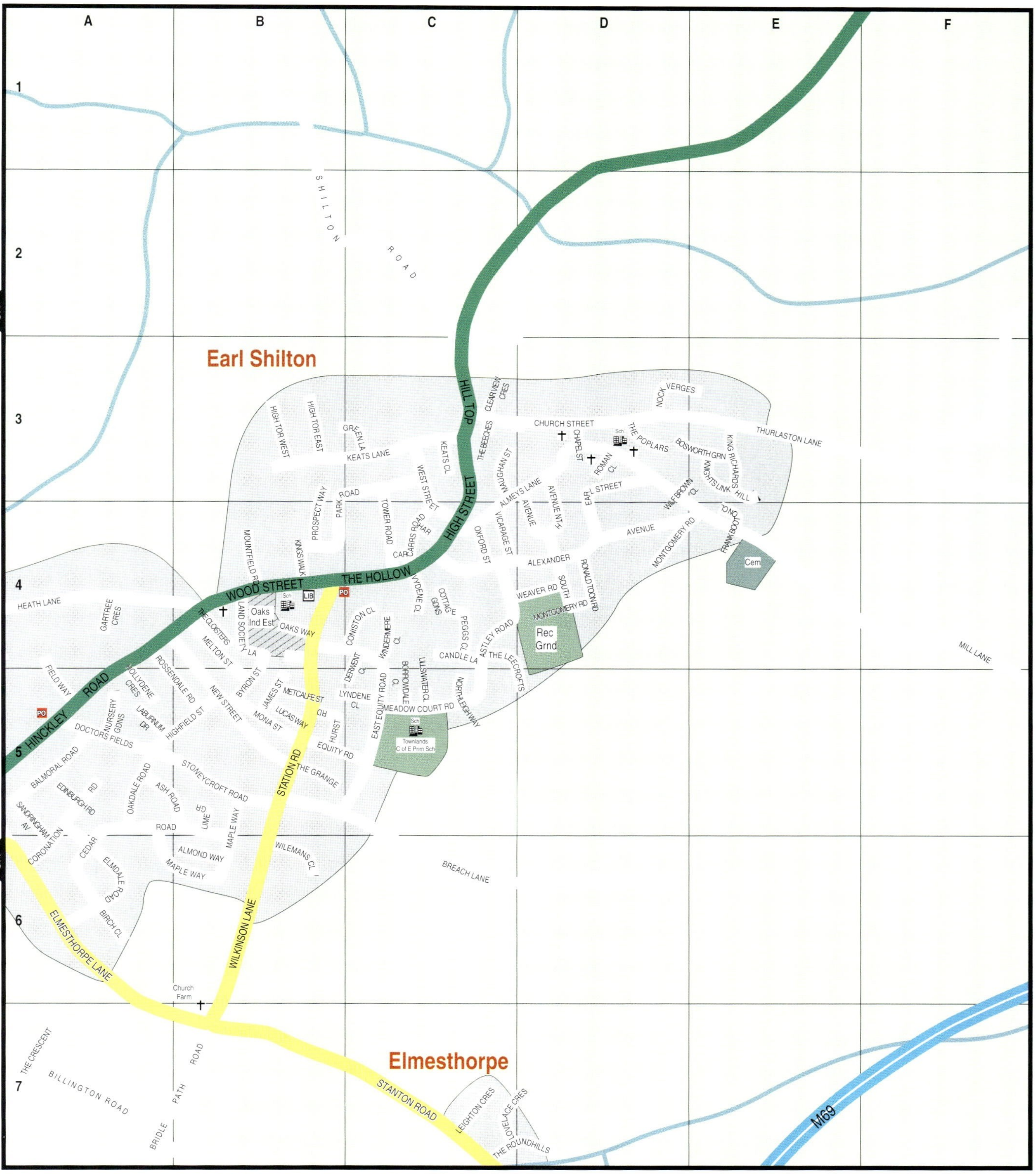

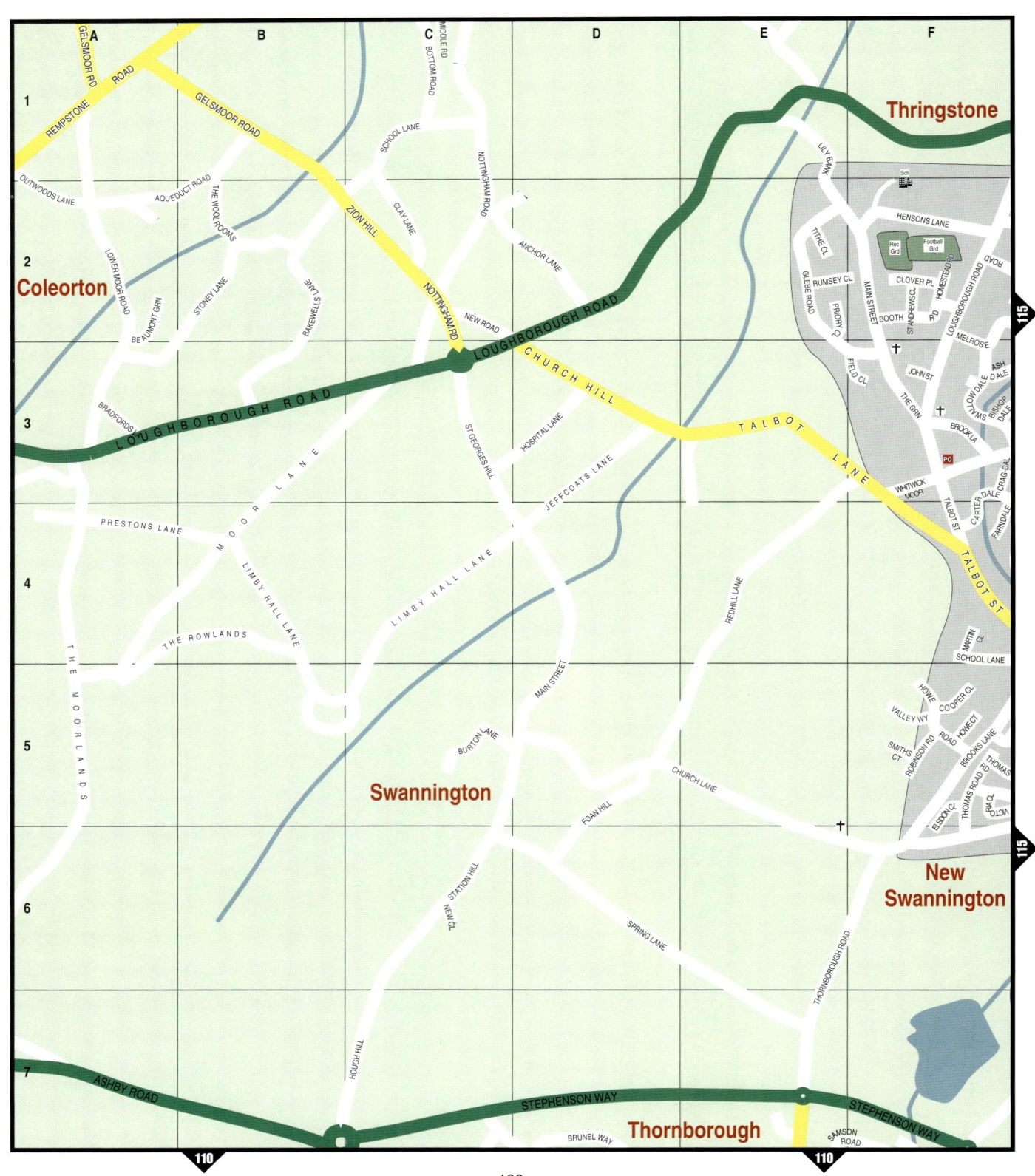

CRANE VEHICLE SPECIALISTS

J. A. RENTON & SONS

J.A. RENTON & SONS
Ashby Road, Thringstone, Coalville, Leicester LE67 4LS
TELEPHONE: 01530 222224

THE Machine Tool Movers

Crane Vehicle Specialists • Machine Tool Movers

Whitwick

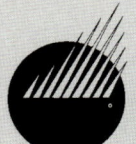
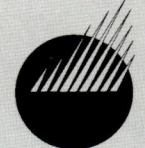

Stevensons Garage

AUSTIN HEALEY SPECIALISTS

**RESTORATIONS • SPORTS CARS
BOUGHT & SOLD • DIESELS & CATALYSTS
MOT • SERVICING • PETROL**

39 – 43 SOUTH STREET
BARROW-ON-SOAR
LEICS LE12 8LY

TEL: 01509 412469

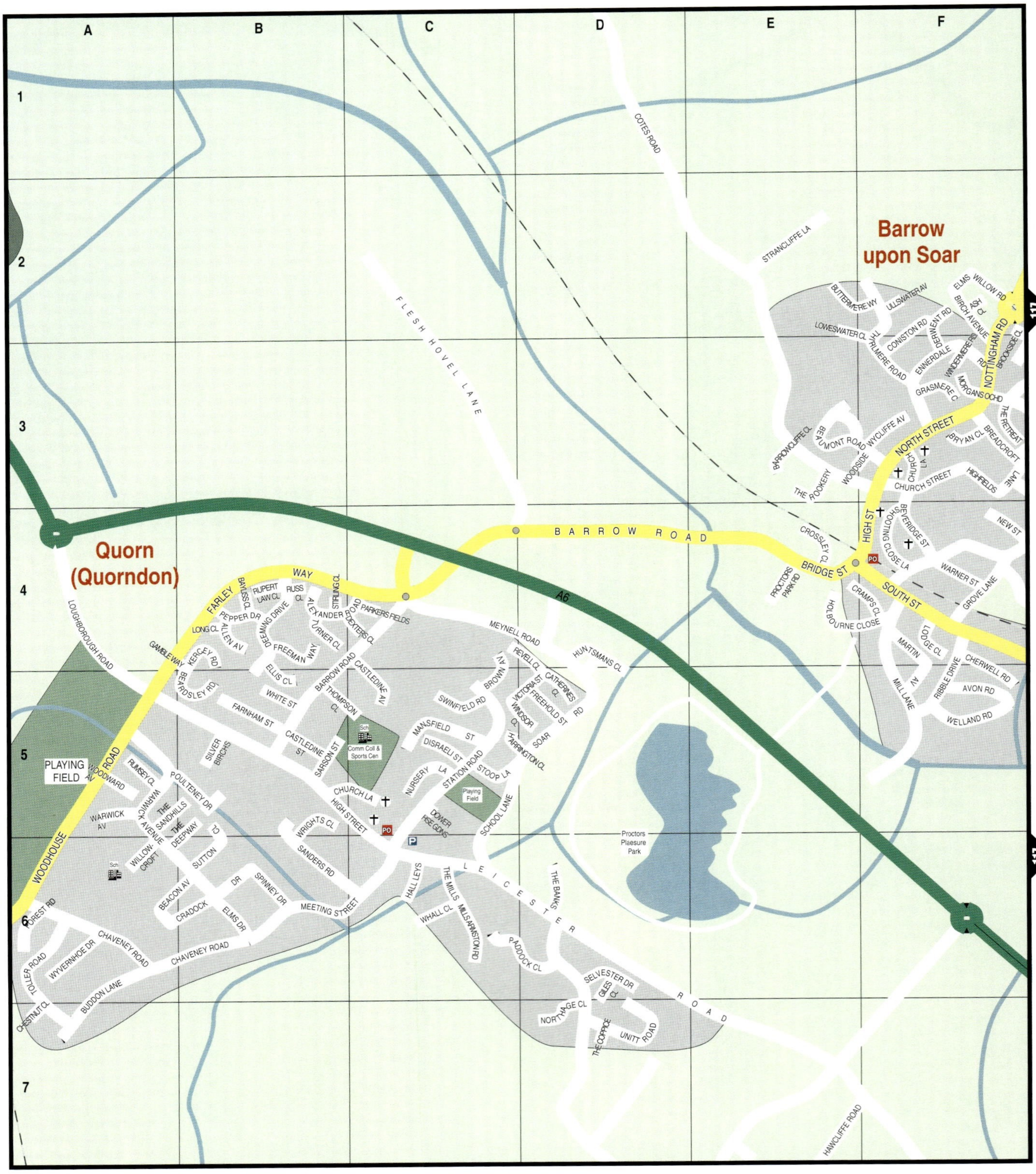

The Springboard Centre (Coalville) Limited

Mantle Lane, Coalville, Leics. LE67 3DW Phone: 01530 839531 Fax: 01530 810231

We offer a unique service!
Fully serviced offices and industrial units • Monthly Licence, no legal costs.
Reception, telephone answering, message taking, photocopying, fax, typing, hot & cold refreshments • 24 hour access
Call 01530 839531 for details and friendly service

CATERING & EVENT ORGANISATION

INDIVIDUALLY TAILORED CATERING & EVENTS
CATERING WITH IMAGINATION & FLAIR

Corporate Hospitality ~ Banquets ~ Buffets ~ Barbecues
Hog Roasts ~ Weddings ~ Cocktail & Dinner Parties
Any number of Guests catered for
Marquees, Flowers, Sound & Lighting available
for complete Event Management

108 Loughborough Road, Hathern, Nr Loughborough

LOCAL CALL 0345 413191

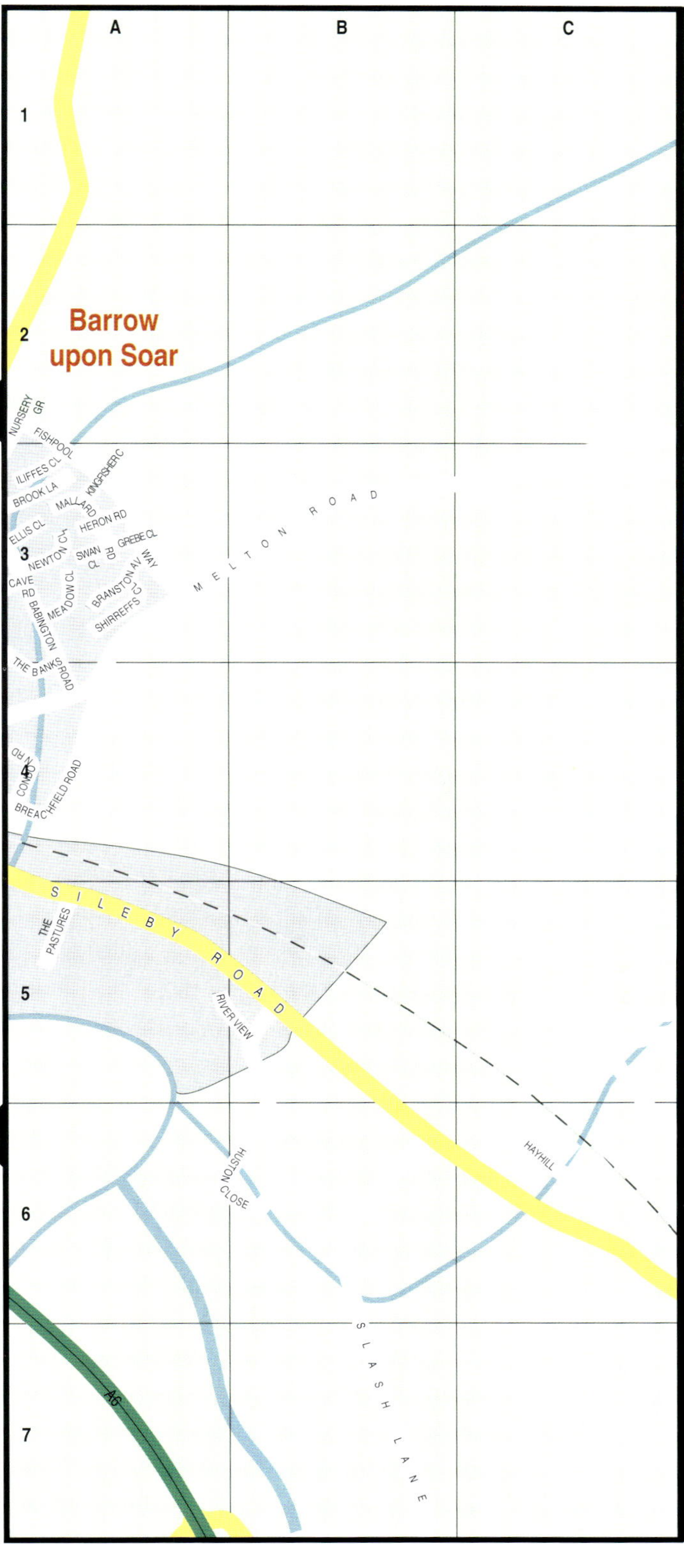

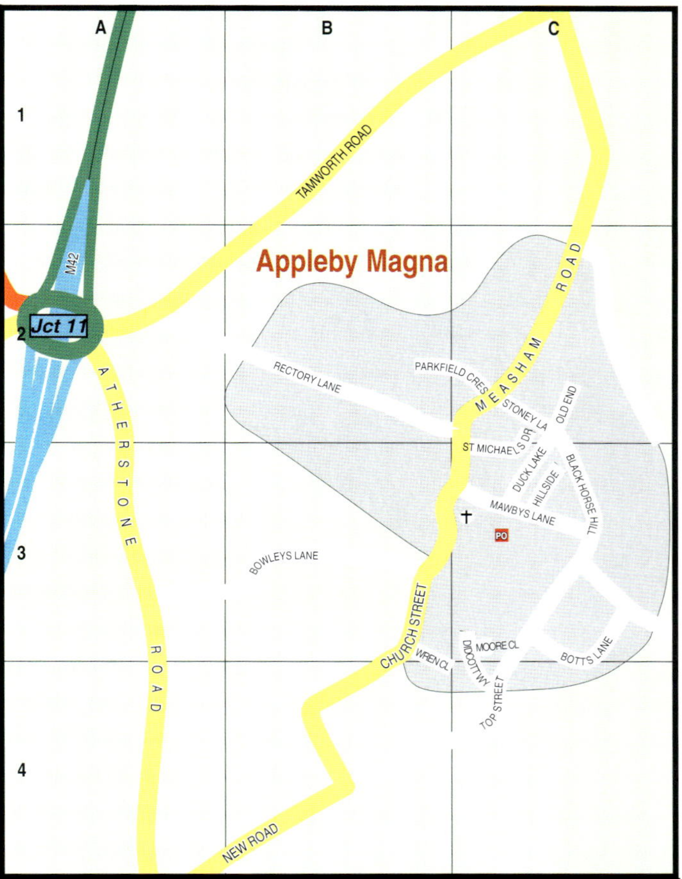

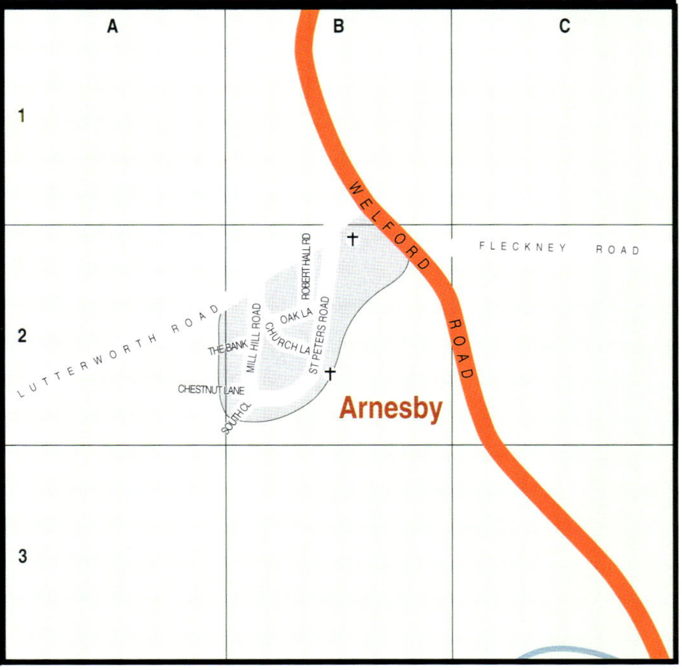

117

Barrow upon Soar

Appleby Magna

Arnesby

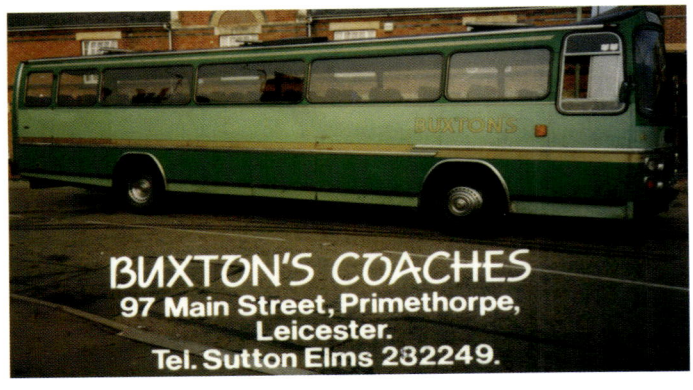

BUXTON'S COACHES
97 Main Street, Primethorpe,
Leicester.
Tel. Sutton Elms 232249.

400 year old thatched country inn situated on the village green in one of Leicestershire's most picturesque villages.
Serving a large range of home cooked bar meals every lunchtime and evening.
Accompanied by a good selection of real ales.
Across the courtyard, in the converted stables, is the Bewick's Tea Room and Gift Shop.

The Bewicke Arms, Hallaton, Leicestershire LE16 8UB **Telephone:** (01858) 555217

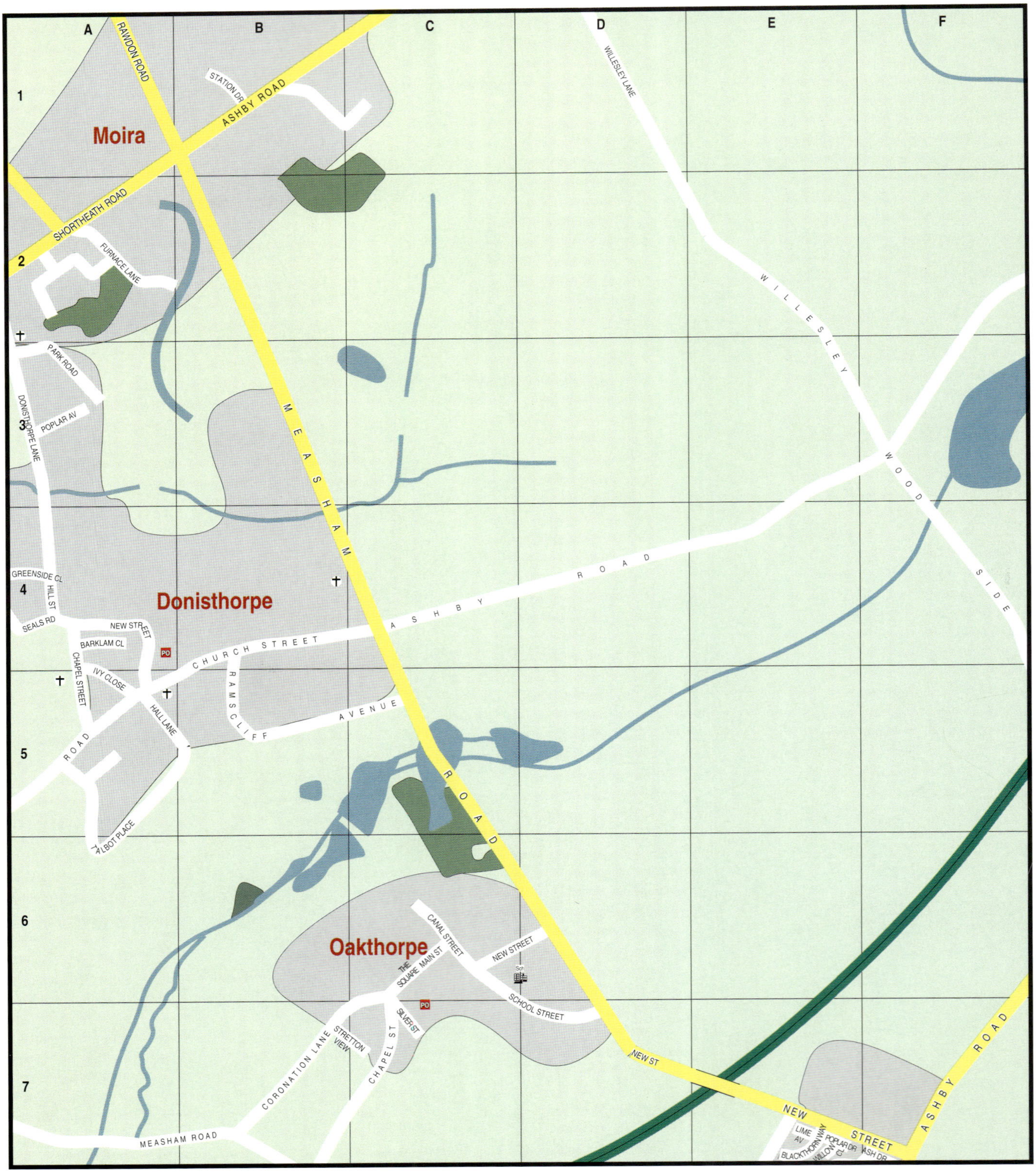

REARSBY Roses Ltd

Map 119 E5

Specialist Rose Growers and Suppliers in Leicestershire

- OPEN TO THE PUBLIC
- ROSES AVAILABLE ALL YEAR ROUND
- MAIL ORDER AND CONSULTANCY/PLANNING AVAILABLE
- FREE ROSE DIRECTORY AVAILABLE ON REQUEST
- CONTACT: MELTON ROAD, REARSBY, LEICESTERSHIRE LE7 4YP
- TELEPHONE 0116 260 1211 ~ FAX 0116 264 0013

Autoseat Technologies Limited
provides manufacturing facilities for interior trim components, as well as providing a full prototype and product development service.

19-20 Brindley Road, Dodwells Bridge Ind Est
Hinckley, Leicestershire LE10 3BY
TEL: 01455 613220
FAX: 01455 612701

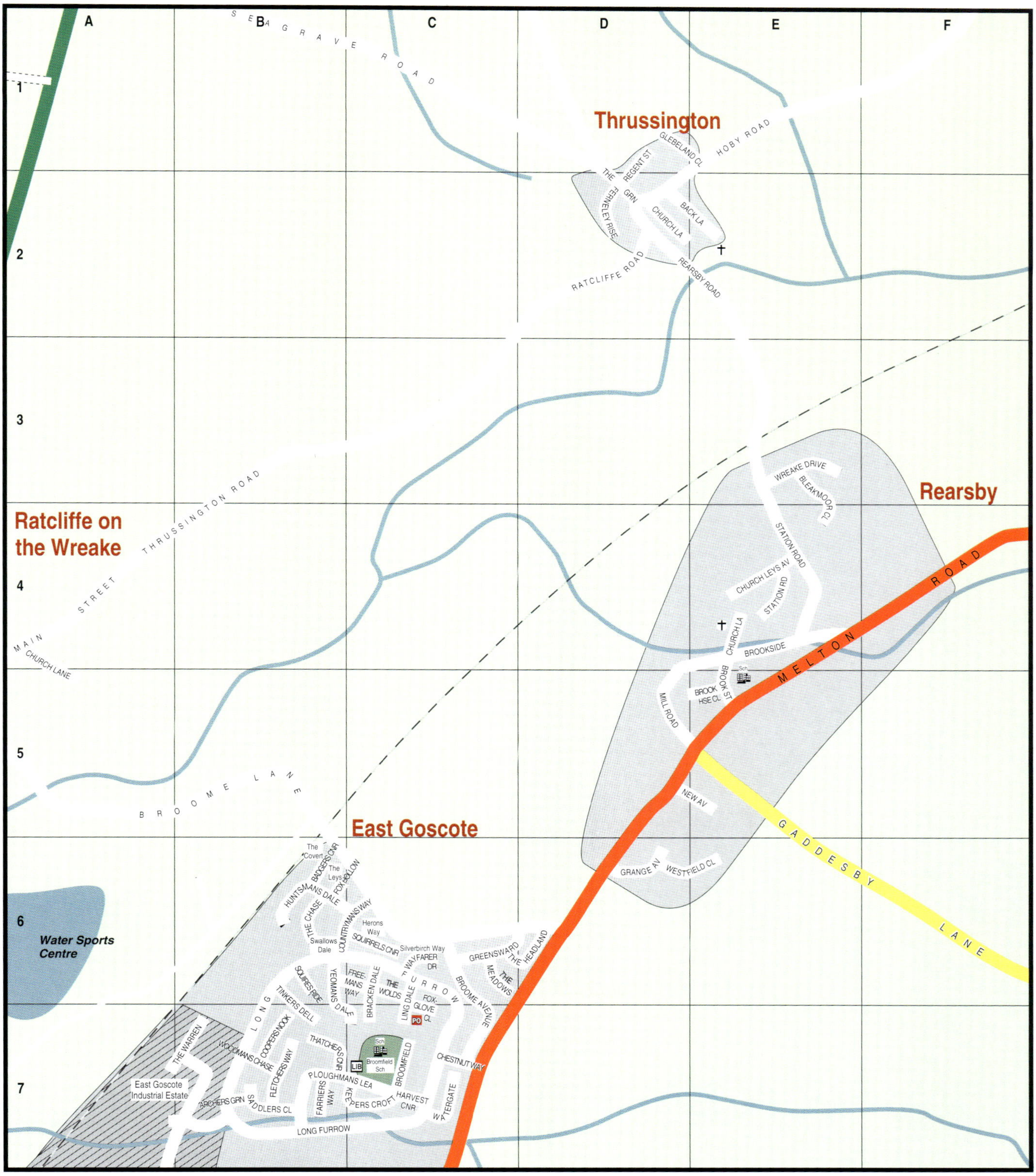

119

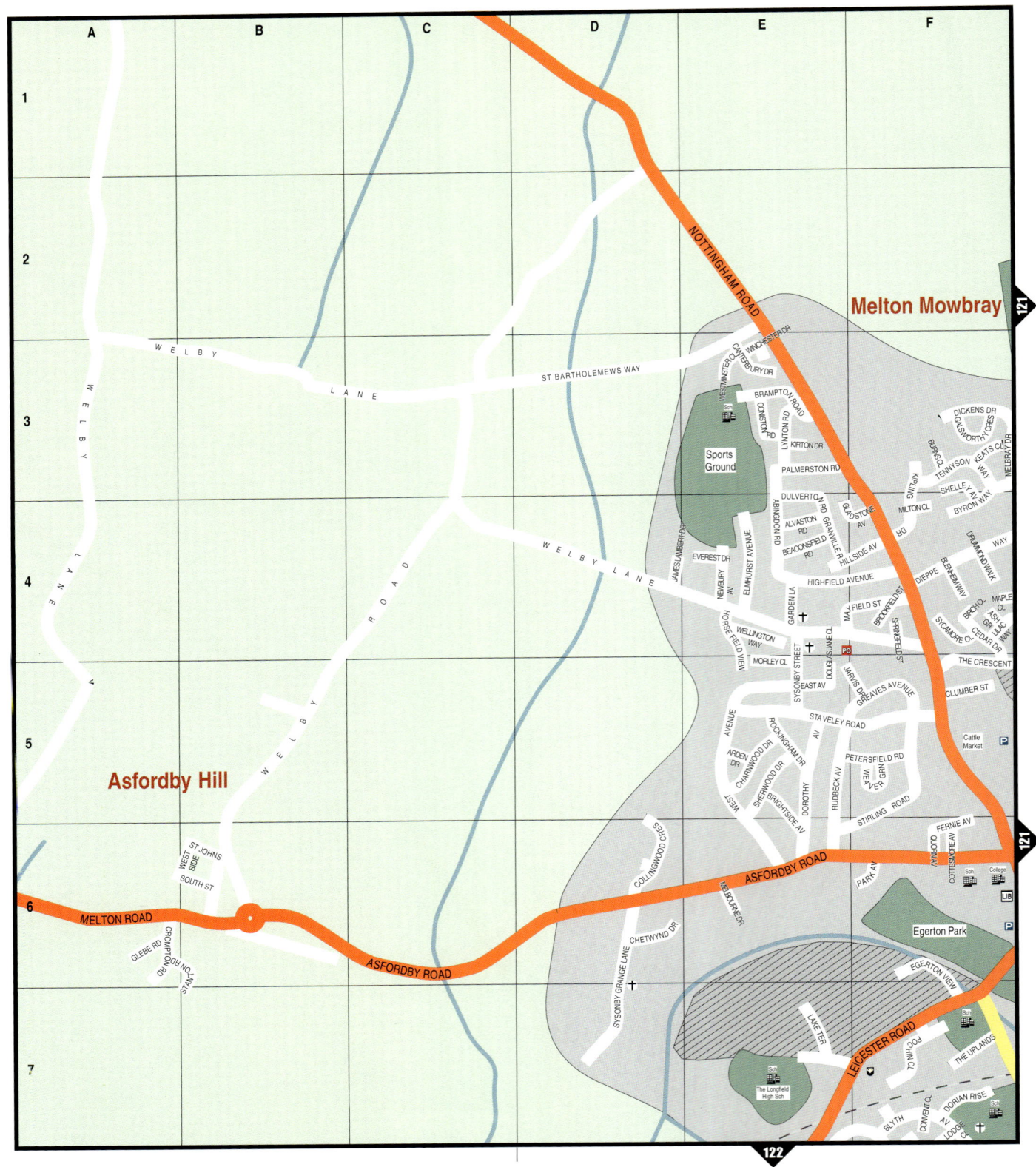

You're on the right road with the Melton......

Branches:
39 Nottingham Street, Melton Mowbray, Leics., LE13 1NR. Tel: 01664 480214

23 High Street, Oakham, Rutland, LE15 6AH. Tel: 01572 757911

Agencies in Bottesford, Leicester & Uppingham

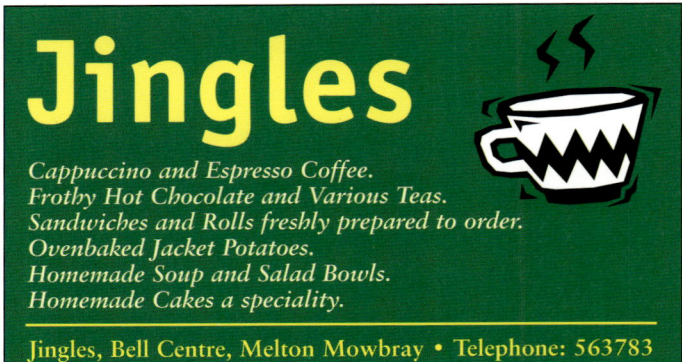

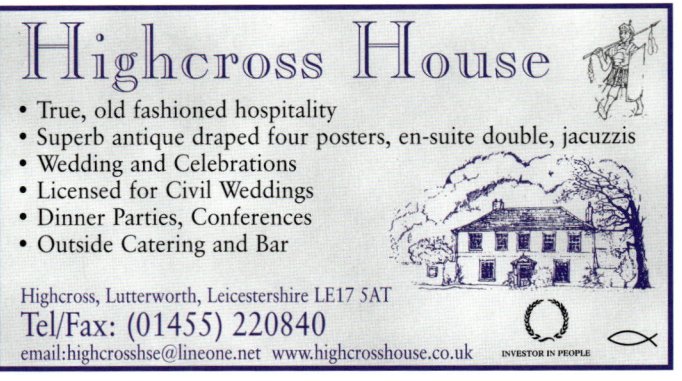

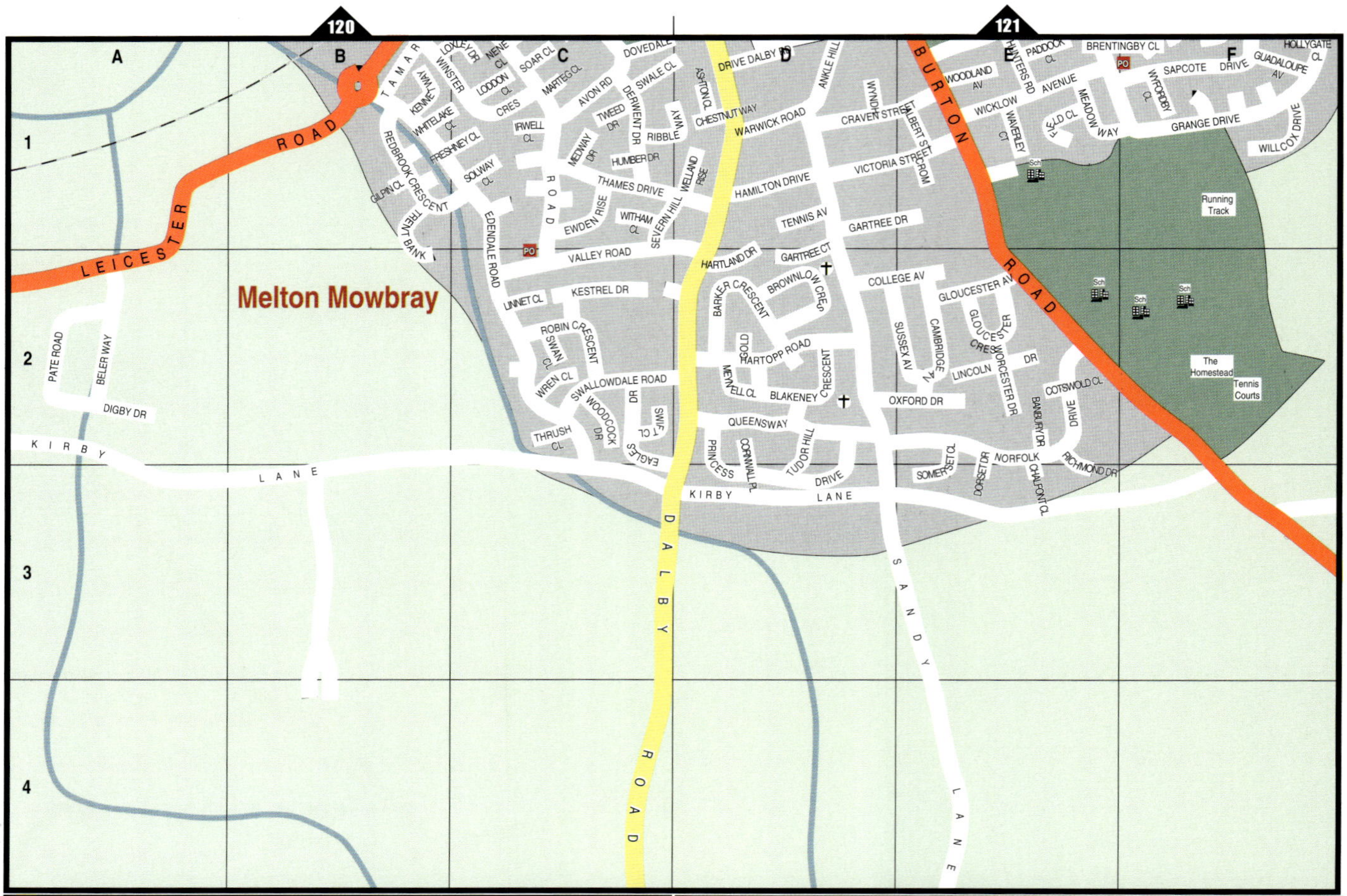

120
121
Melton Mowbray
LEICESTER ROAD
BURTON ROAD
DALBY ROAD
SANDY LANE
KIRBY LANE
VALLEY ROAD
HAMILTON DRIVE
VICTORIA STREET
WARWICK ROAD
COLLEGE AV
GRANGE DRIVE
DIGBY DR
PATE ROAD
BELER WAY
Running Track
The Homestead
Tennis Courts

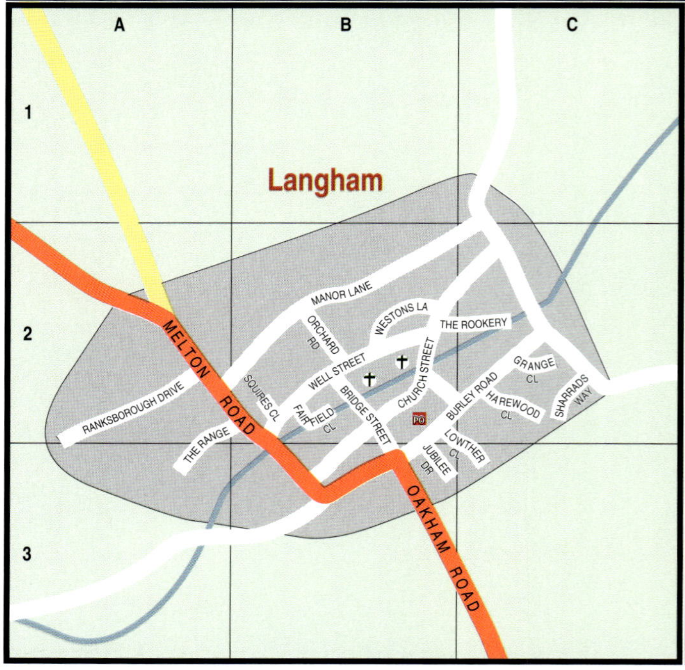

Langham
MELTON ROAD
OAKHAM ROAD
MANOR LANE
THE ROOKERY
CHURCH STREET
BRIDGE STREET
RANKSBOROUGH DRIVE
THE RANGE
BURLEY ROAD

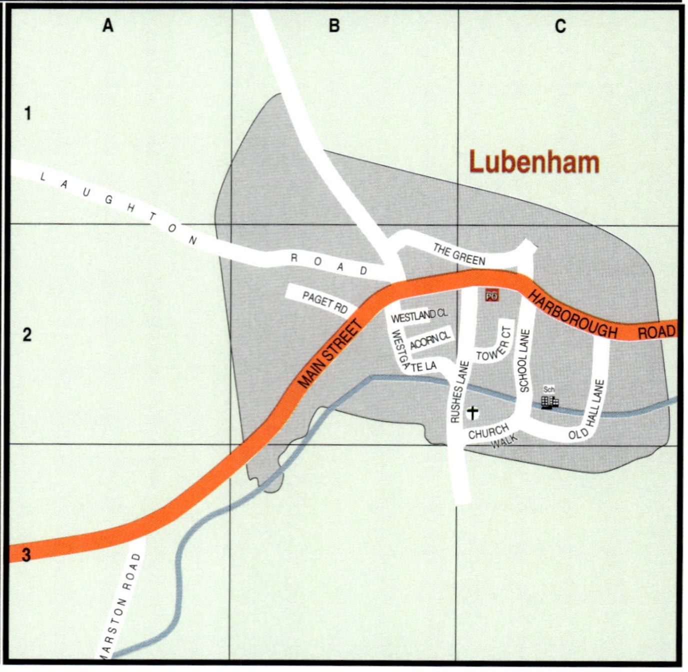

Lubenham
LAUGHTON ROAD
HARBOROUGH ROAD
MAIN STREET
THE GREEN
PAGET RD
RUSHES LANE
SCHOOL LANE
OLD HALL LANE
CHURCH WALK
MARSTON ROAD

Gardening at its best

The Grange Garden Centre Limited
Asfordby Hill, Melton Mowbray
LE14 3UQ

Telephone:
01664 812012
Fax: 01664 813636
Mobile: 07860 267179
Email: Houghty@garden-products.demon.co.uk

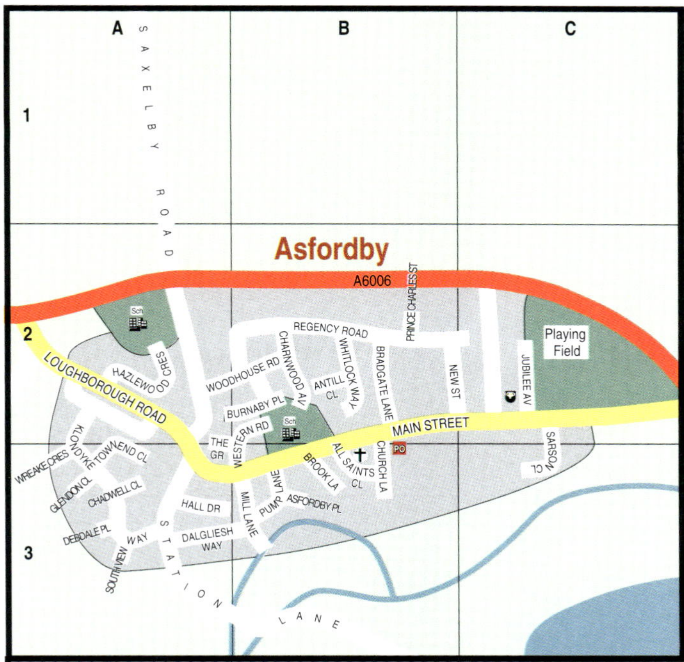

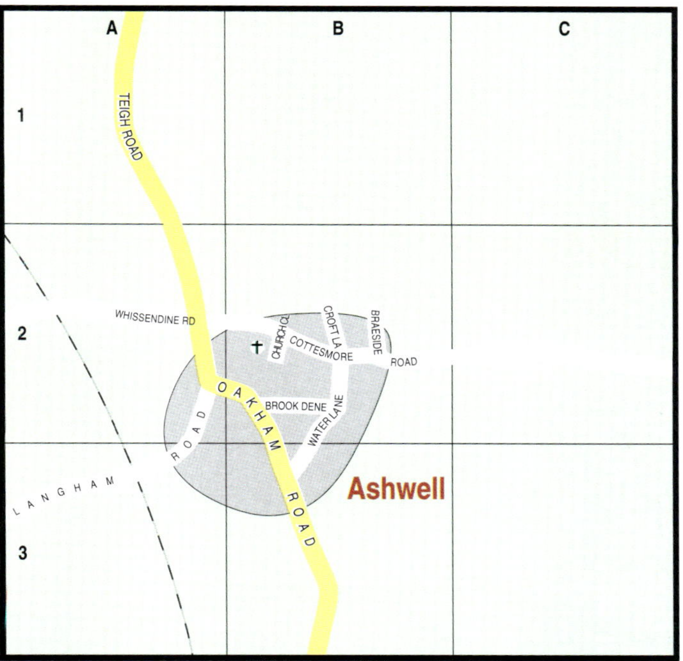

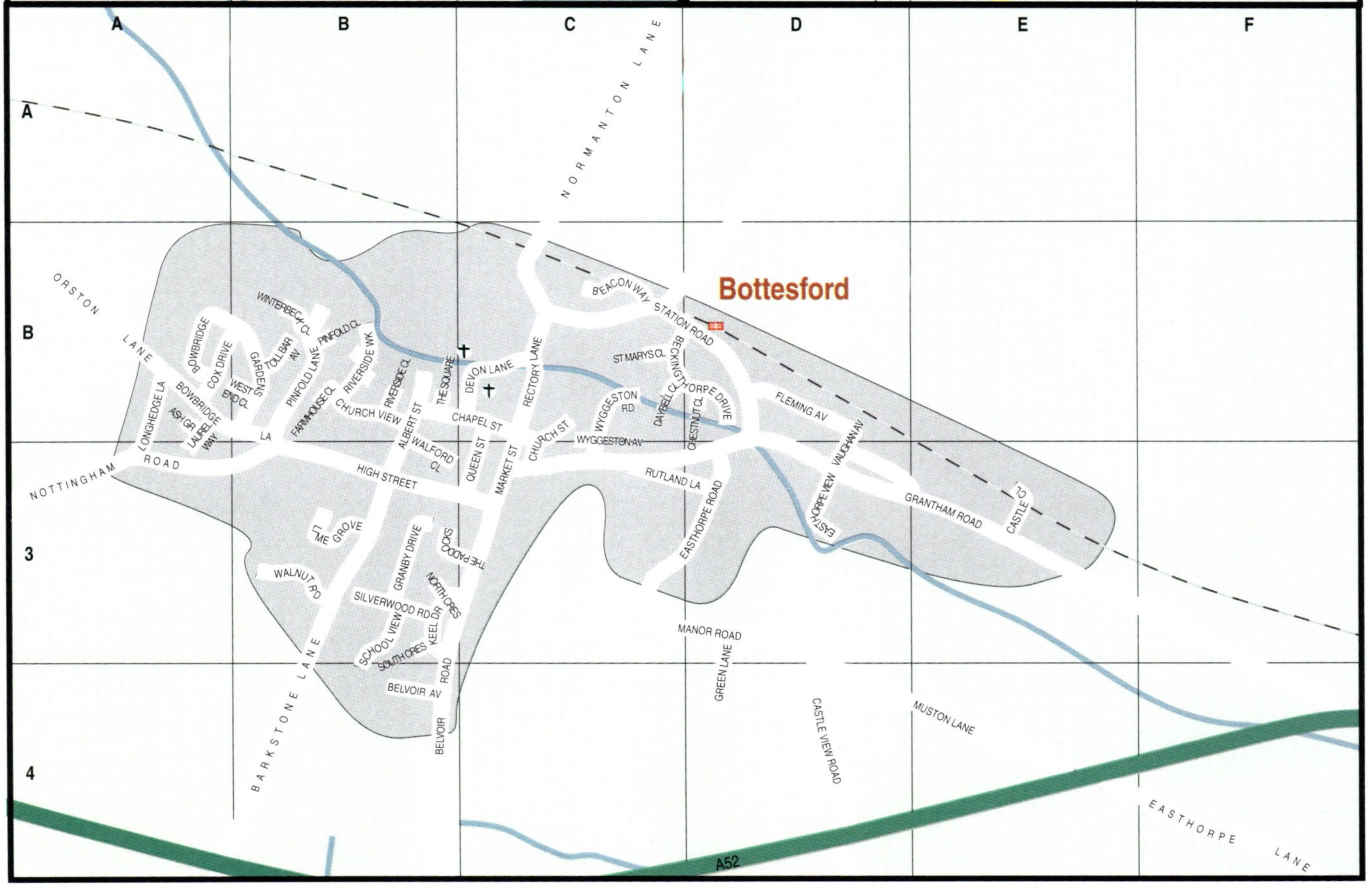

123

~147~

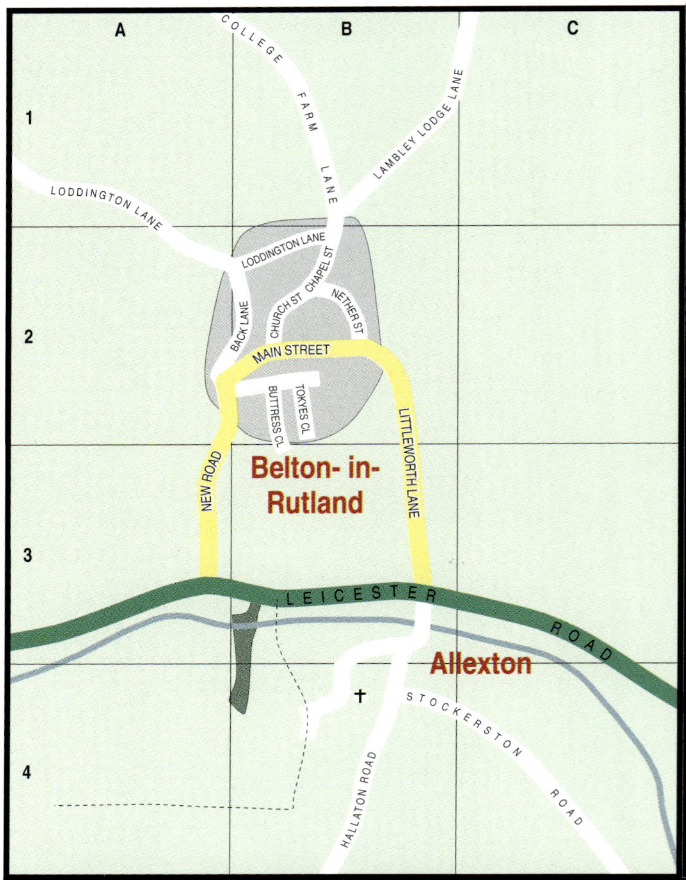

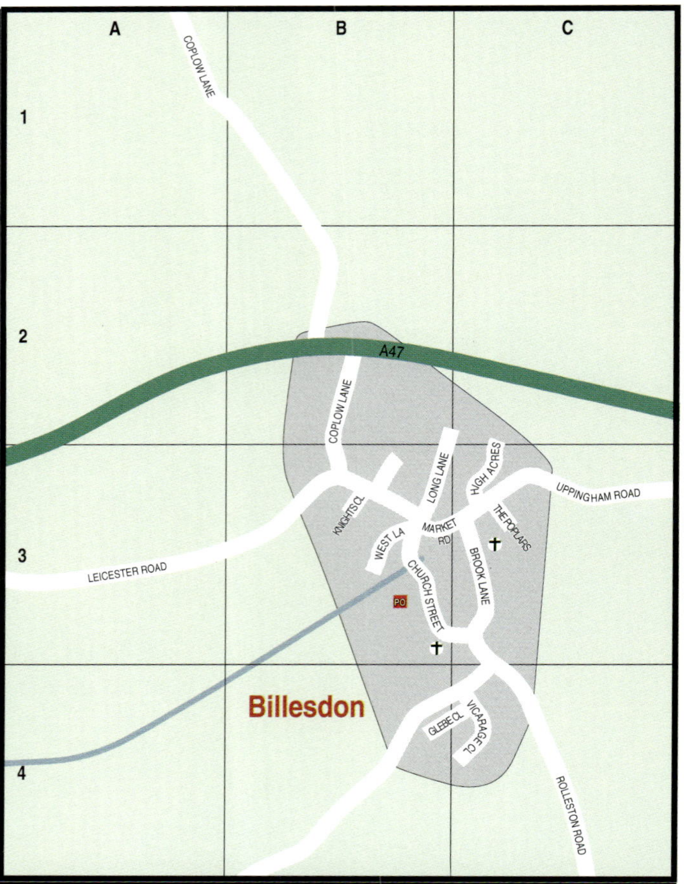

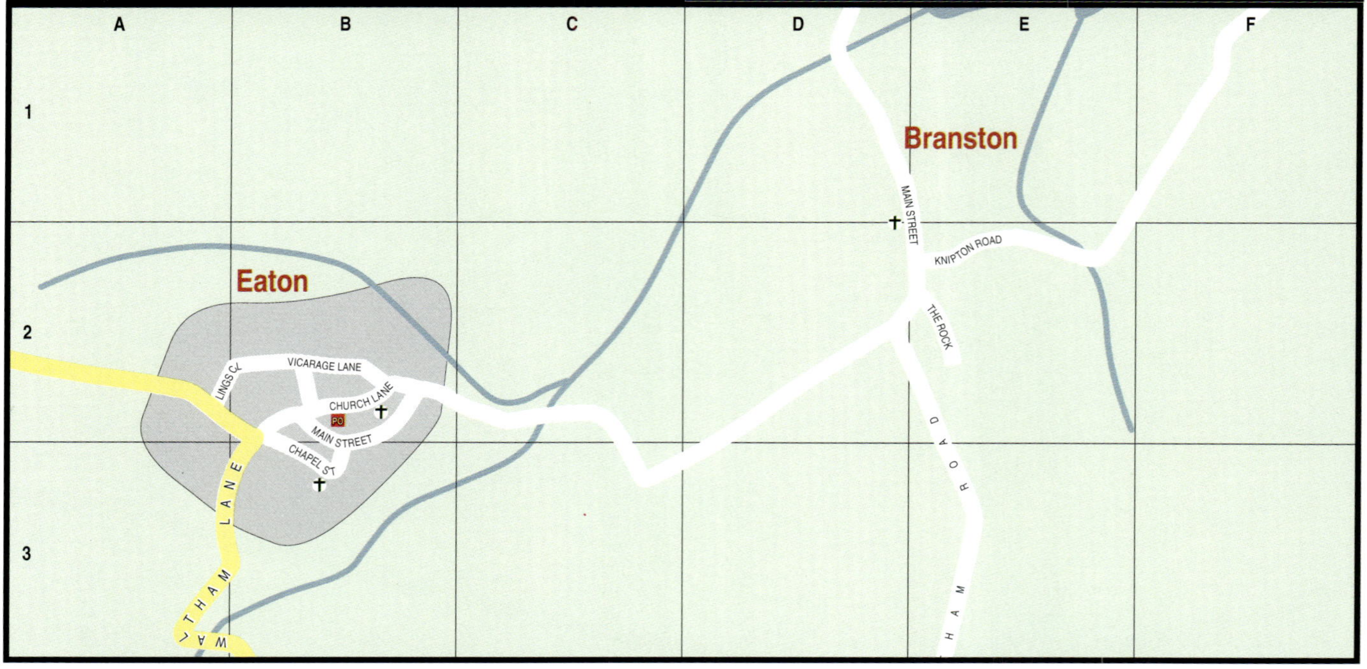

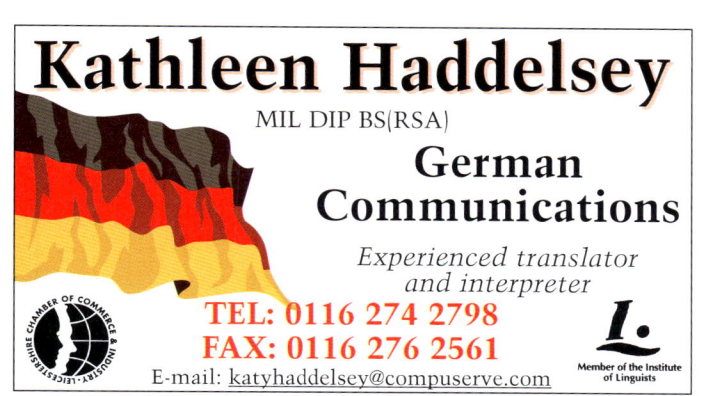

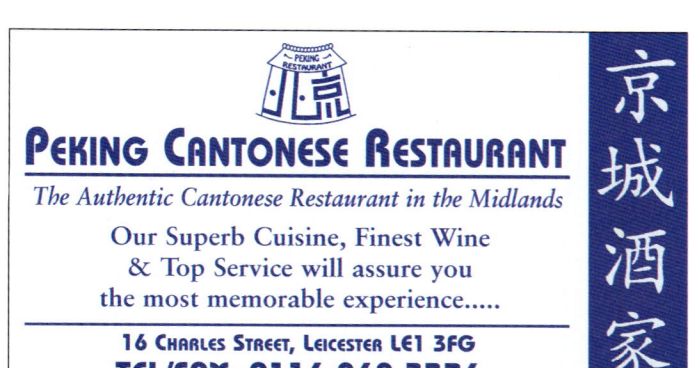

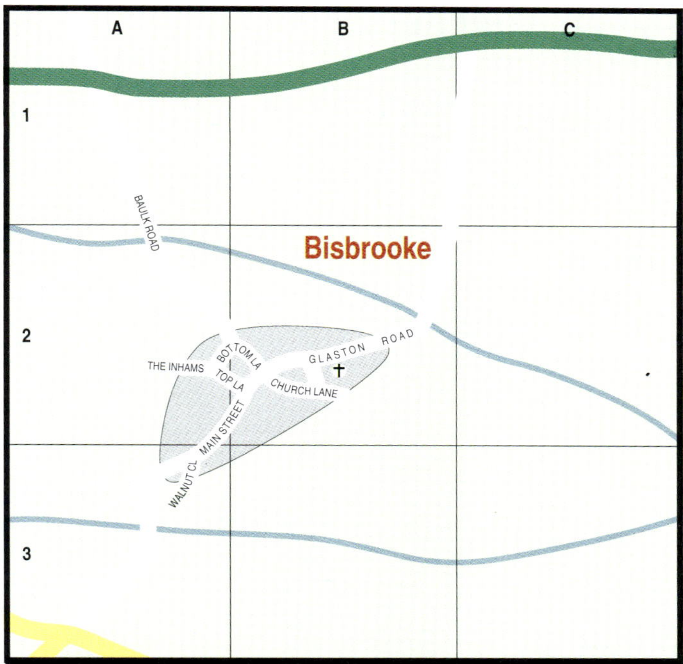

A
B
C
1
2
3
Bisbrooke
BAULK ROAD
GLASTON ROAD
THE INHAMS
BOTTOM LA
TOP LA
CHURCH LANE
MAIN STREET
WALNUT CL

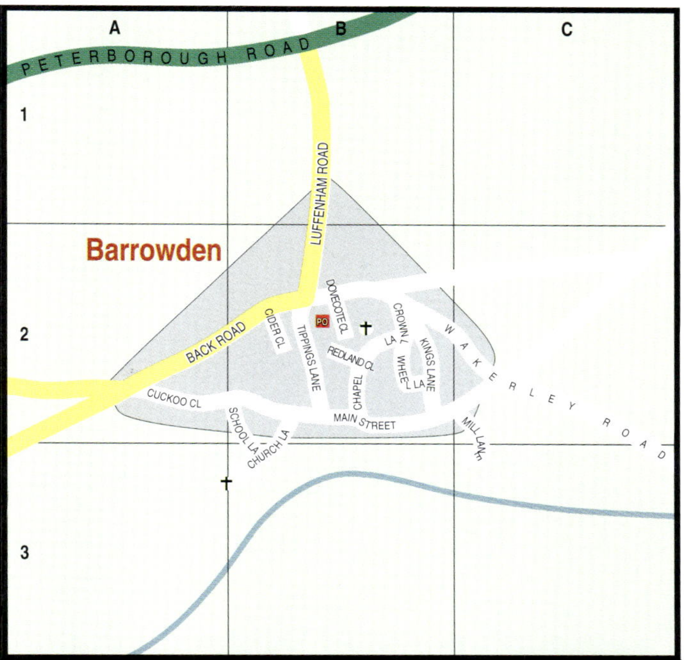

A
B
C
1
2
3
Barrowden
PETERBOROUGH ROAD
LUFFENHAM ROAD
BACK ROAD
CIDER CL
DOVECOTE CL
TIPPINGS LANE
REDLAND CL
CHAPEL
CROWN LA
WHEEL LA
KINGS LANE
WAKERLEY ROAD
CUCKOO CL
MAIN STREET
SCHOOL LA
CHURCH LA
MILL LANE
PO

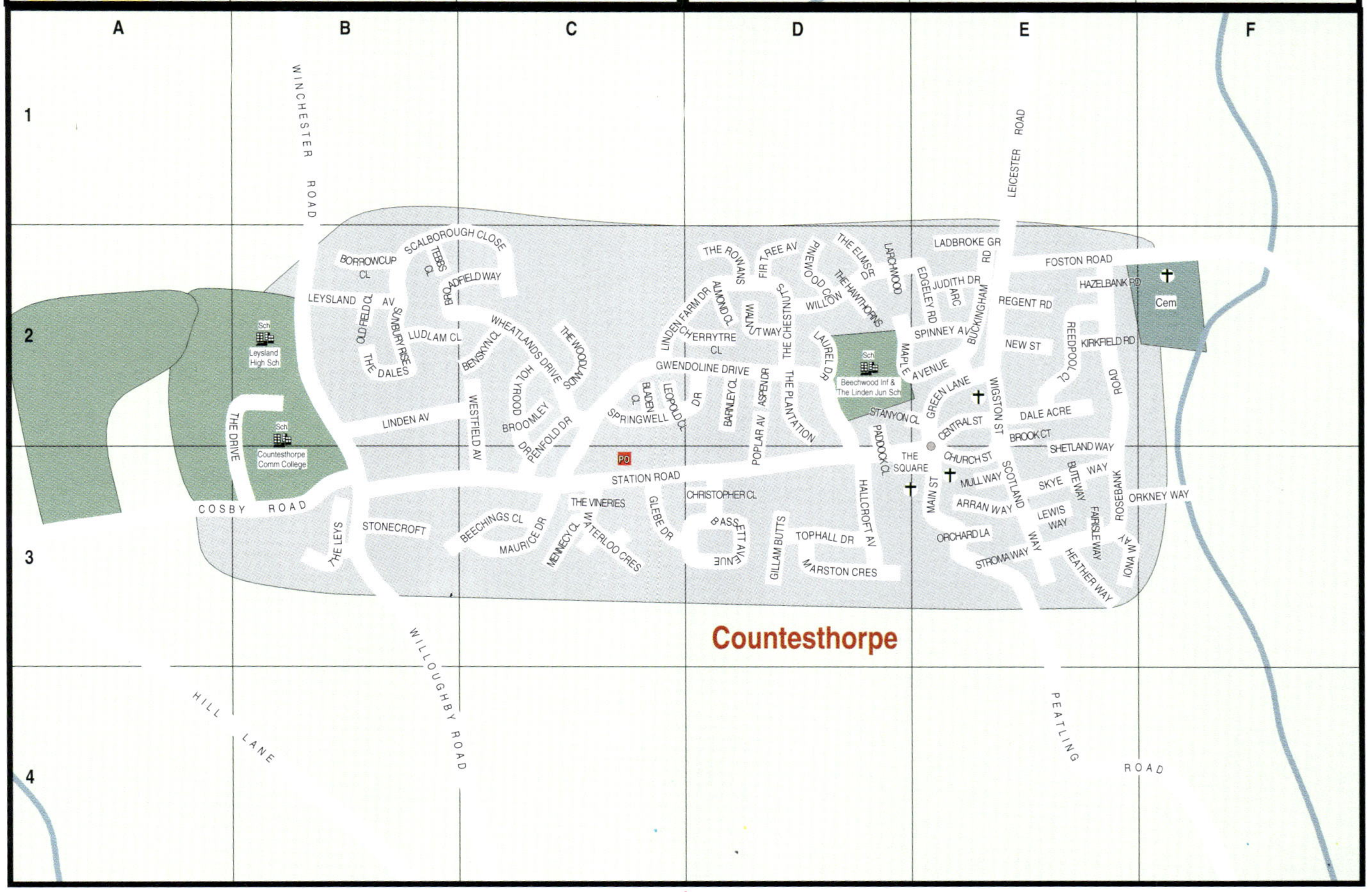

A
B
C
D
E
F
1
2
3
4
Countesthorpe
WINCHESTER ROAD
LEICESTER ROAD
SCALBOROUGH CLOSE
BORROWCUP CL
LEYSLAND AV
Leysland High Sch
Countesthorpe Comm College
THE DRIVE
COSBY ROAD
THE LEYS
STONECROFT
LINDEN AV
WESTFIELD AV
STATION ROAD
BEECHINGS CL
MAURICE DR
THE VINERIES
WATERLOO CRES
GLEBE DR
CHRISTOPHER CL
TOPHALL DR
MARSTON CRES
GILLAM BUTTS
GWENDOLINE DRIVE
SPRINGWELL
BROOMLEY
RENFOLD DR
WHEATLANDS DRIVE
THE WOODLANDS
THE ROWANS
FIR TREE AV
ALMOND CL
LINDEN FARM DR
CHERRYTREE CL
THE CHESTNUTS
WILLOW
THE ELMS DR
THE HAWTHORNS
LARCHWOOD
LAUREL DR
POPLAR AV
ASPEN DR
THE PLANTATION
Beechwood Inf & The Linden Jun Sch
LADBROKE GR
JUDITH DR
EDGELEY RD
BUCKINGHAM
MAPLE AVENUE
GREEN LANE
STANYON CL
PADDOCK CL
HALLCROFT AV
THE SQUARE
MAIN ST
CENTRAL ST
CHURCH ST
MULL WAY
ARRAN WAY
ORCHARD LA
STROMA WAY
WIGSTON ST
SCOTLAND
FOSTON ROAD
HAZELBANK RD
REGENT RD
NEW ST
REEDPOOL CL
KIRKFIELD RD
DALE ACRE
BROOK CT
SHETLAND WAY
SKYE WAY
LEWIS WAY
BUTE WAY
FAIRISLE WAY
HEATHER WAY
ROSEBANK ROAD
ORKNEY WAY
IONA WAY
Cem
PO
WILLOUGHBY ROAD
HILL LANE
PEATLING ROAD

This beautiful country house, set in a formal garden of two acres with sweeping lawns and outstanding views, surrounds you with elegance, comfort and friendly care. All bedrooms are en-suite and furnished to a high standard with telephone, television and tea/coffee making facilities. There is a ground floor suite suitable for disabled guests. The spacious drawing room has an open log burning fire and contains many family antiques. We are licensed to serve drinks to guests. Restricted smoking. Sorry, no pets.

Single Room: £29.50-£35 ~ **Double Room:** £44.50-£54.50

THE GRANGE

New Road, Burton Lazars,
Nr. Melton Mowbray,
Leicestershire LE14 2UU
Telephone & Fax 01644 560775

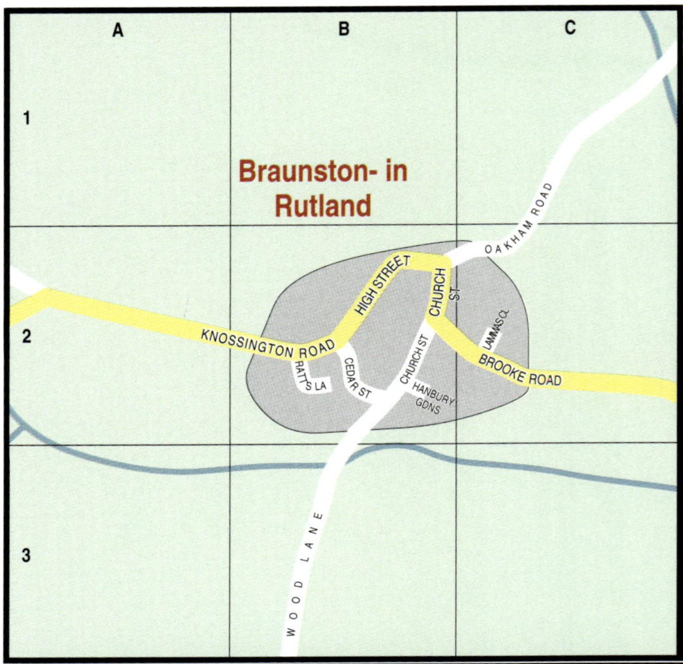

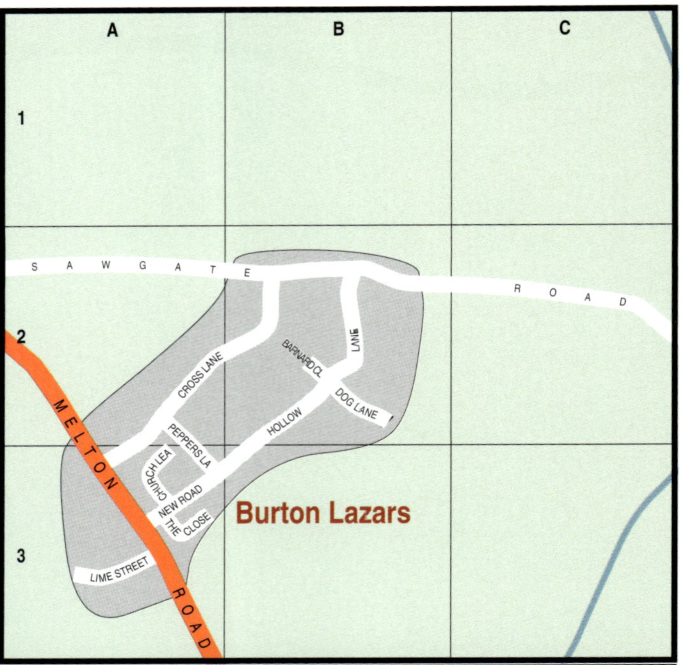

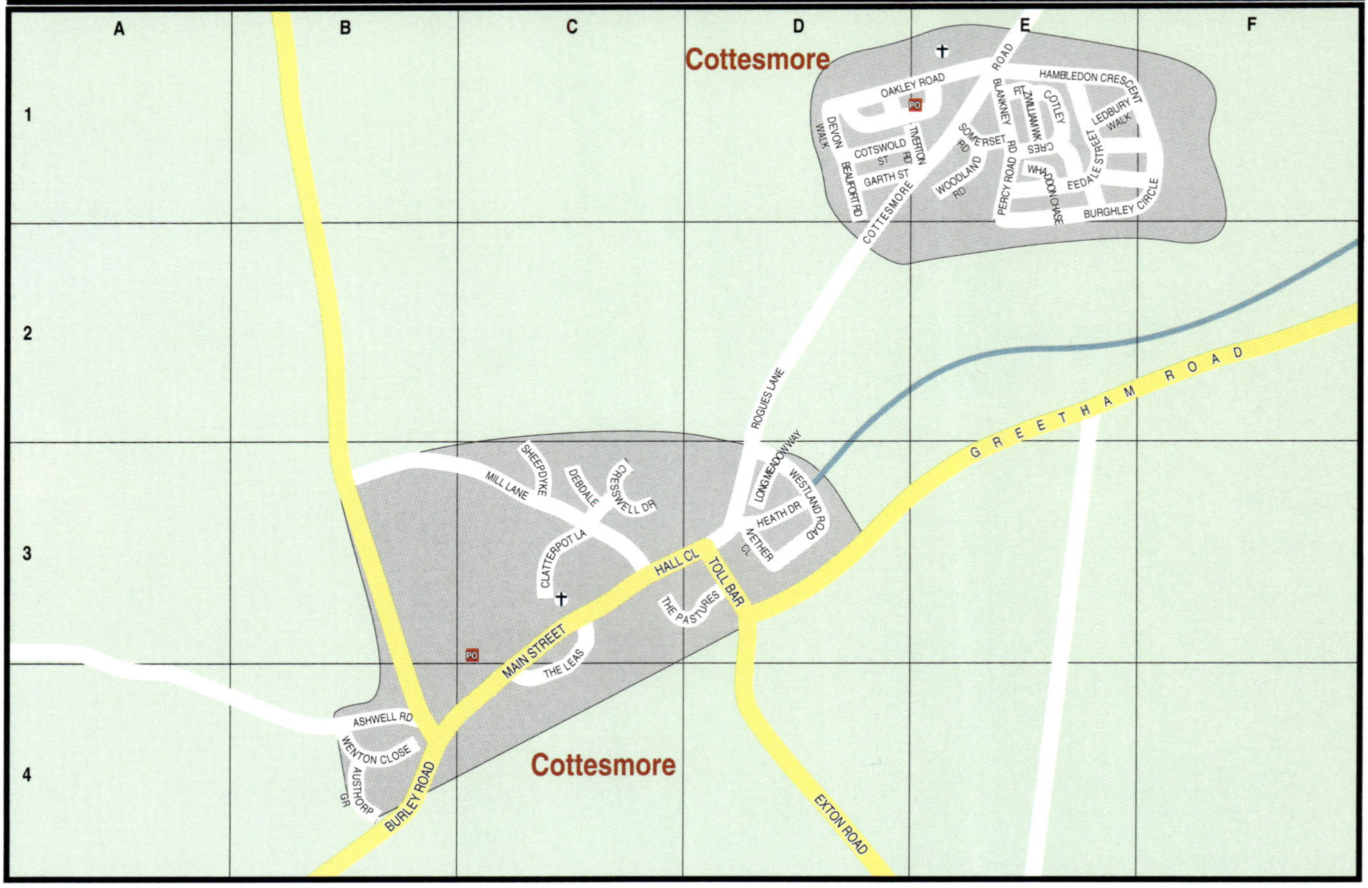

Milling, Drilling and Light Fabrications C.N.C. Turning

45A Highmeres Road
Leicester
LE4 9LZ

Tel: 0116 246 4100
Fax: 0116 246 4100

MINI-SCENE
1322 Melton Road, Syston, Leicester LE7 2EQ
Telephone: (0116) 269 2305

DOLLS HOUSE CENTRE
Everything you need for your Dolls House

Tuesday – Saturday 10.00am – 5.00pm

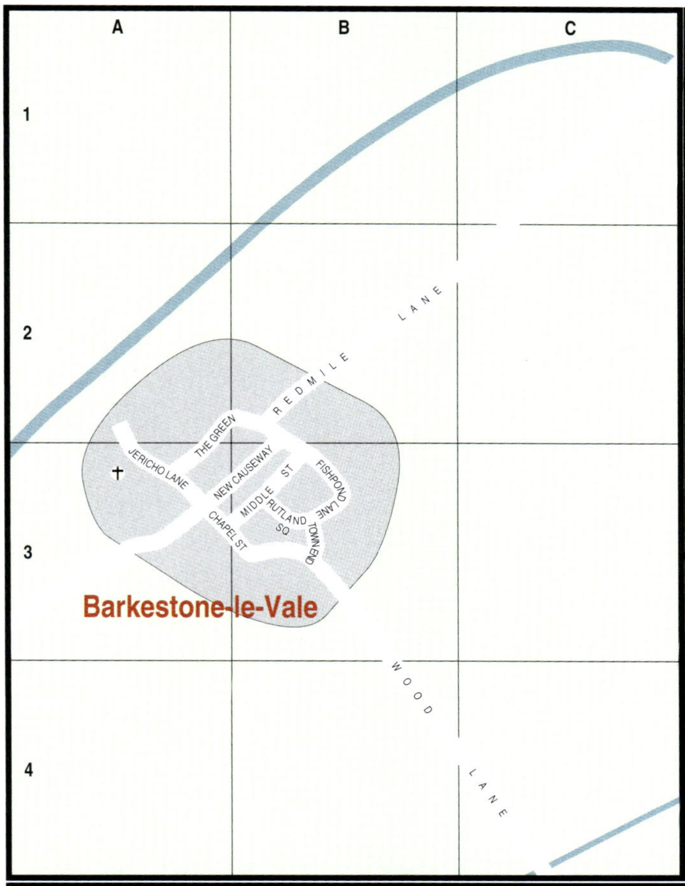

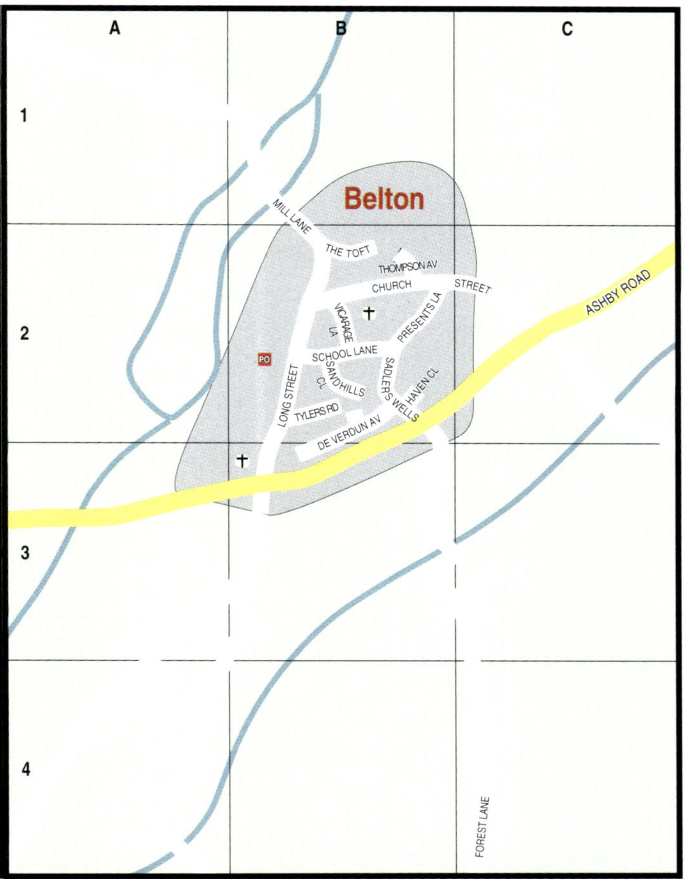

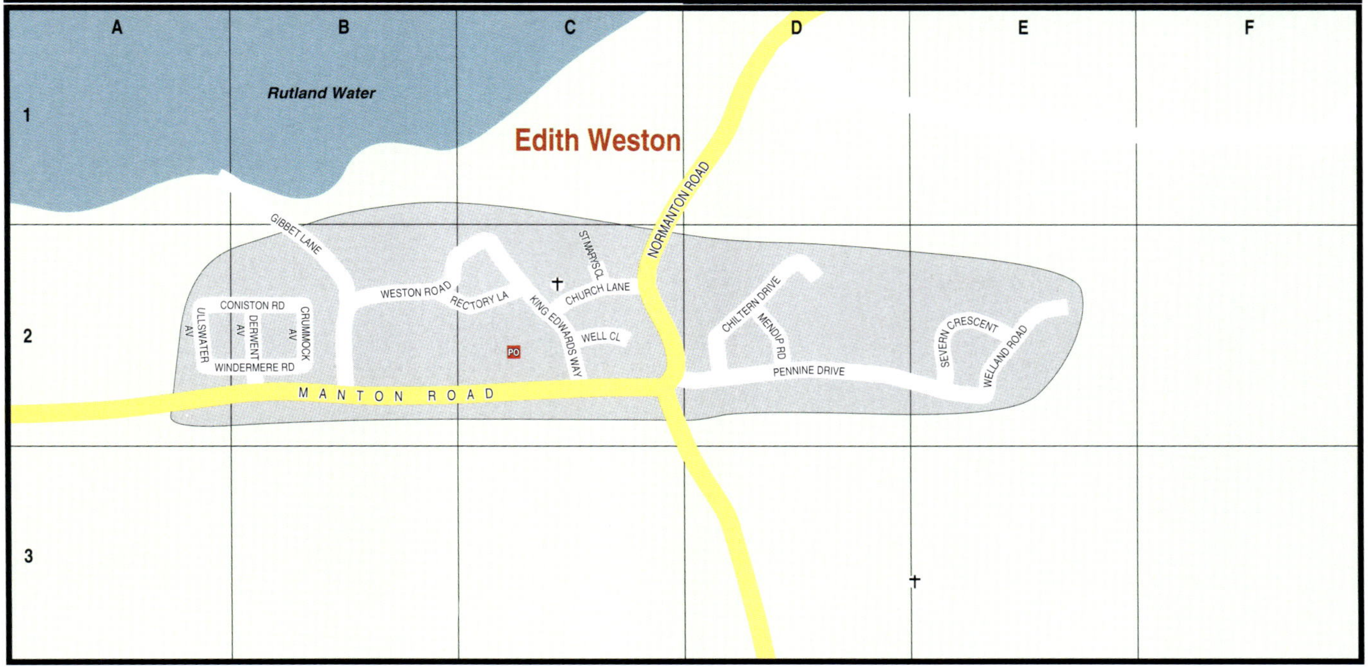

MALLORY PARK

Mallory Park offers you speed, colour and excitement, with great viewing, close racing, affordable entertainment and a range of opportunities for business

Mallory Park (Motorsport) Ltd, Mallory Park Circuit, Kirkby Mallory, Leicestershire, Le9 7QE
Tel: 01455 842931   Fax: 01455 848289   www.mallorypark.co.uk

Mallory Park Circuit, off the A47 between Leicester and Hinckley

EYEBROOK TROUT FISHERY

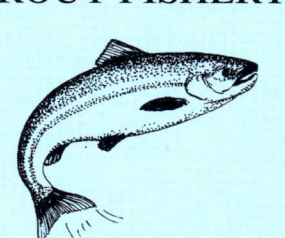

Mature 400 acre reservoir on Leics/Rutland/Northants border, renowned for top of the water sport
Open 30 March to 29 October 2000
Excellent value, generous stock levels, friendly atmosphere and idyllic surroundings.
3 Day Special - £99.00 (fly fishing for two anglers with motor boat)
Day permit - £13.50 (8 fish) or C&R

For further details, contact:-
The Fishing Lodge, Eyebrook Reservoir, Great Easton Road, Caldecott, Leics. LE16 8RP
Tel: 01536 - 770264 (Fax: 01536 - 404699)
Email: roger.marshall@corusgroup.com www.rutnet.co.uk/eyebrook

Fishing Permits	Price £	Bag Limit Day	Week
Day	13.50	8	
Evening	9.00	5	
Senior Citizen	9.00	8	
Junior	6.75	8	
Novice	4.00	2	
Full Season	375.00	8	30
Mid-Wk Season	299.00	8	20
Snr.Cit. Season	260.00	8	30
Junior Season	187.00	8	30
3 Day Special	99.00	8	

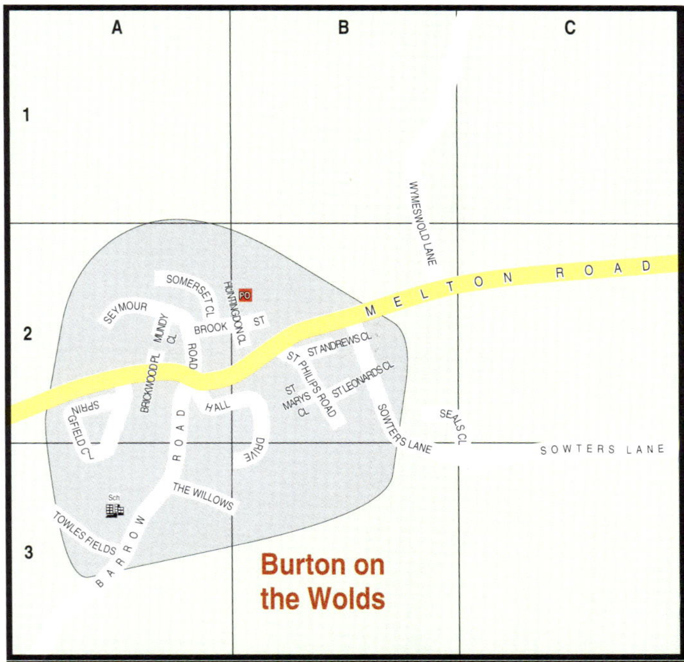

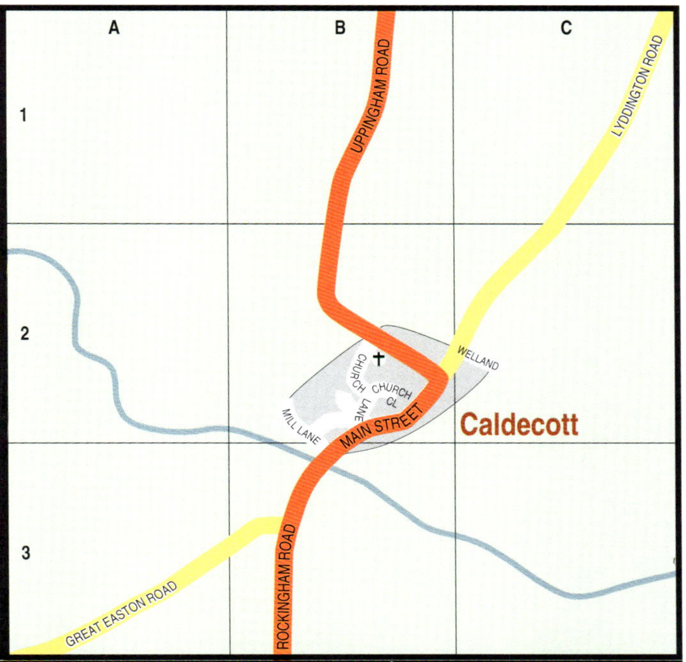

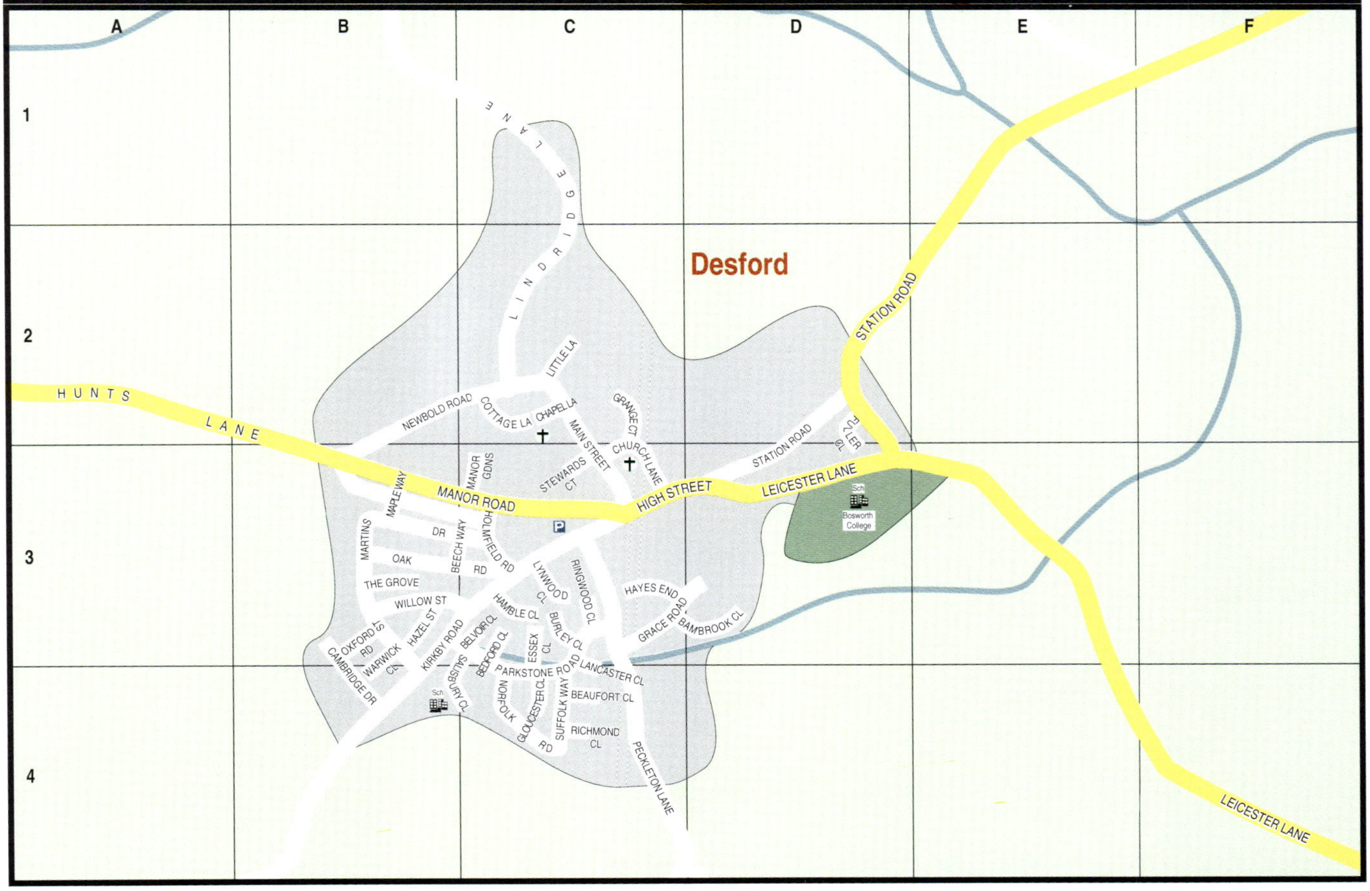

Burton on the Wolds

Caldecott

Desford

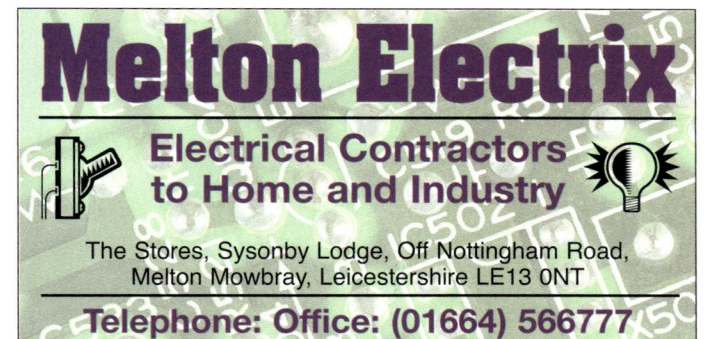

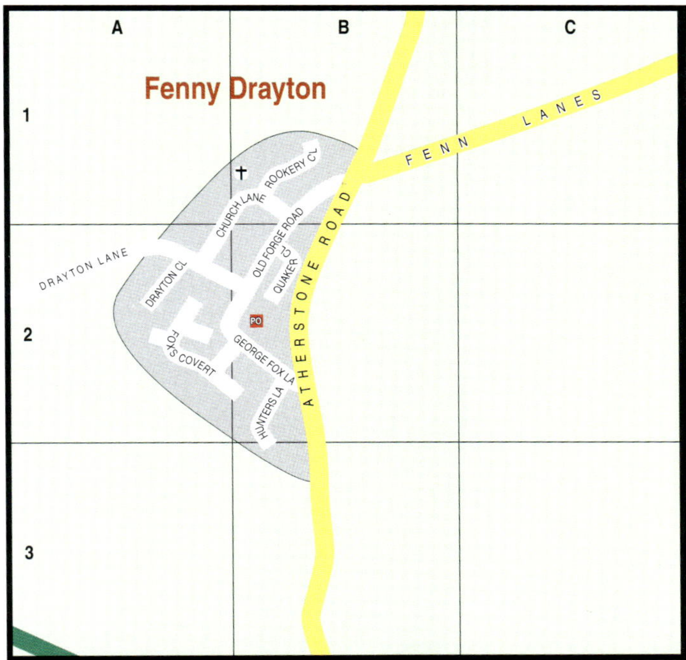

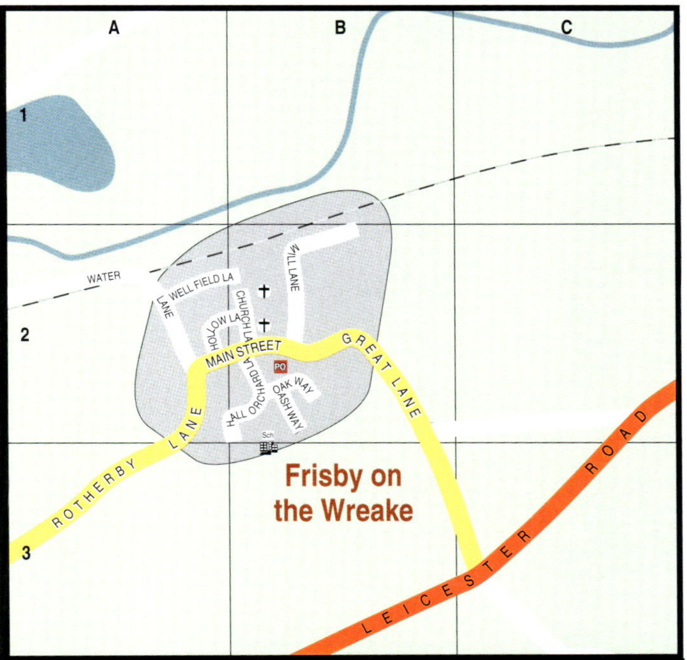

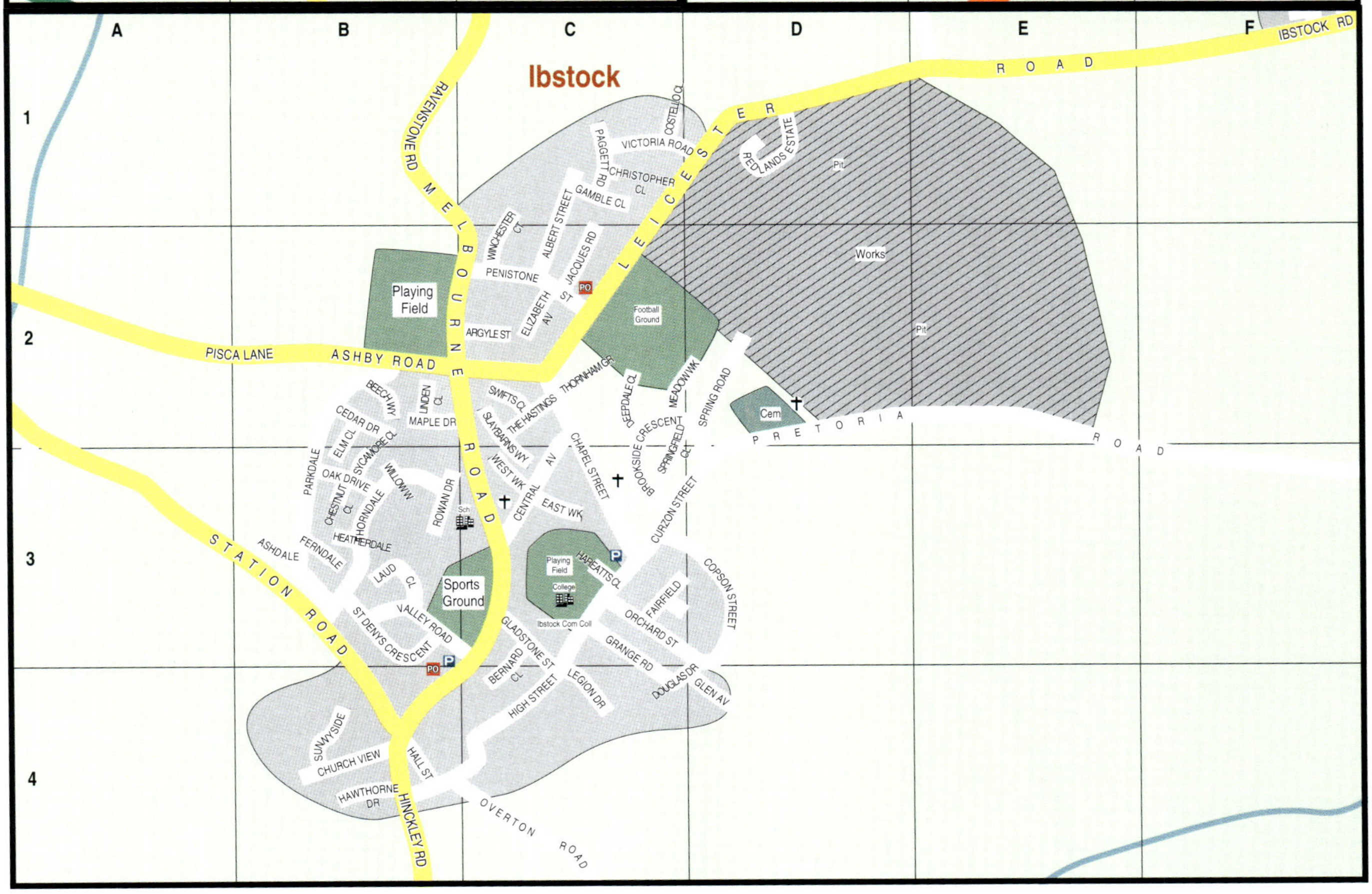

TURVY MOTORS

36 Sowters Lane
Burton-on-the-Wolds
Loughborough, Leics
LE12 5AL

Telephone: (01509) 881596

The Forest Rise HOTEL

Forest Rise Hotel Ltd
55-57 Forest Road
Loughborough
Leicestershire
LE11 3NW

Excellent accommodation for business guests or tourists with 23 various types of en-suite bedrooms. Colour TV, Tea & Coffee making facilities. Ample Car Parking. Walking distance from Town Centre and the University & Colleges. Easy access to M1. Our reputation for good food, excellent service and a friendly atmosphere is your guarantee.

Telephone: 01509 215928
Fax: 01509 210506

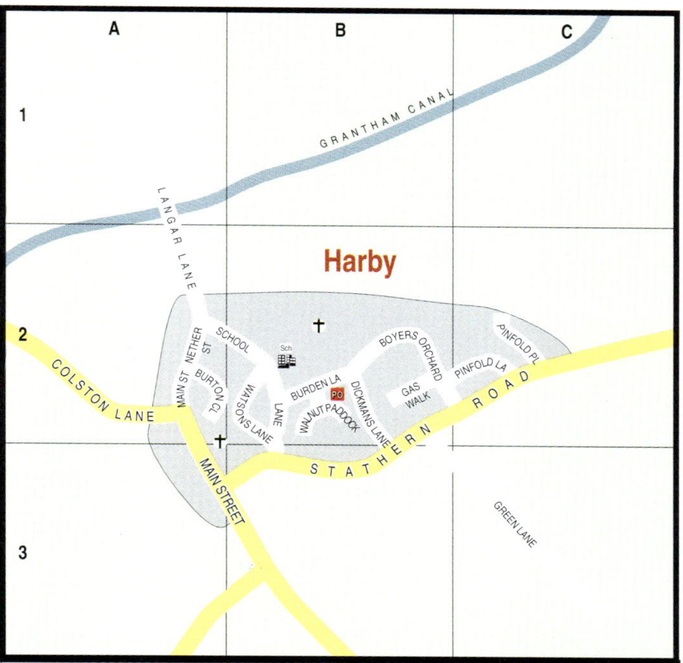

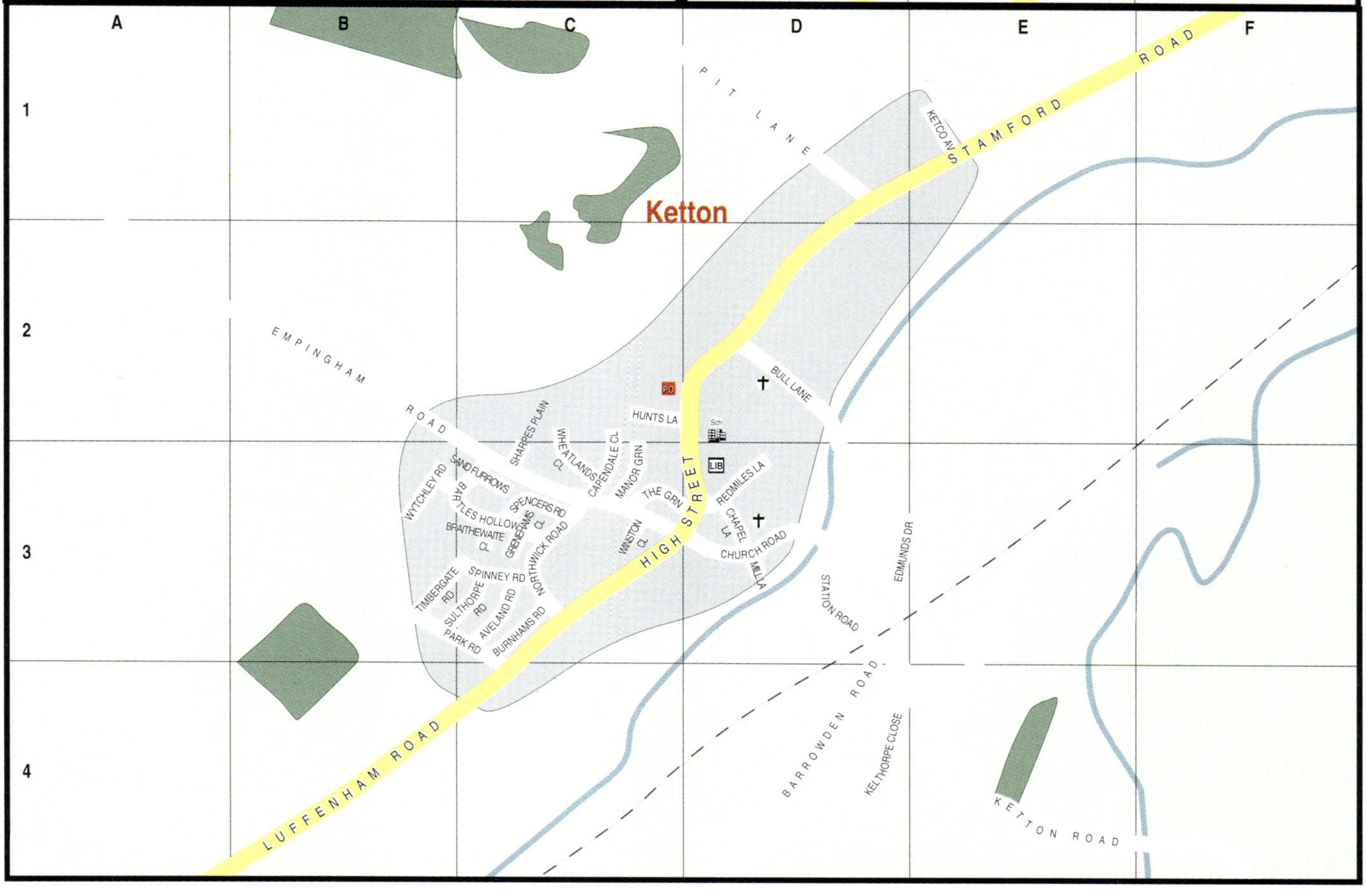

133

~157~

A
B
C
1
2
3
Hungarton
Village Fm
BAGGRAVE ROAD
STREET
COAL BAULK
TOWNEND
MAIN
CHURCH LA
BARLEY LEAS

A
B
C
1
2
3
Hose
CANAL LANE
STROUDS CL
CHAPEL LANE
COAL LA
HOME PASTURES
HARBY LANE
THE GRN
MIDDLE ST
DAIRY LA
CHURCH CL
BOLTON LANE
Sch
HOSE LANE
PASTURE LANE

A
B
C
D
E
F
1
2
3
4
Long Clawson
CANAL LANE
HOSE LANE
HICKLING LANE
WATER LA
CANAL LA
EAST END
WALTHAM LANE
THE SANDS
BARKERS FIELD
CHURCH LANE
SCHOOL LANE
MILL LANE
HOLLYTREE LA
SAND PIT LANE
BACK LANE
PO
WEST END
CLAXTON RISE
KINGS ROAD
SAND PIT LANE
BROUGHTON LANE
CORONATION AV
MELTON ROAD

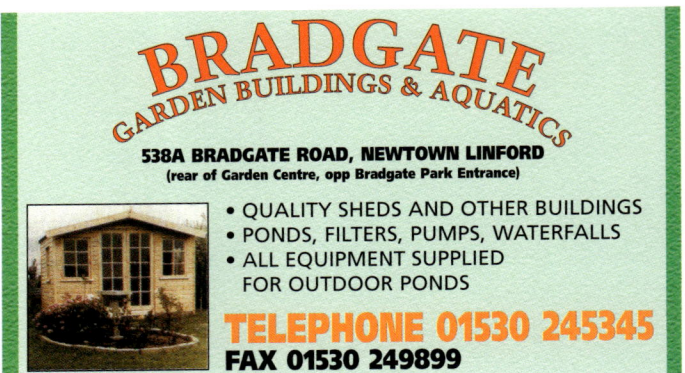

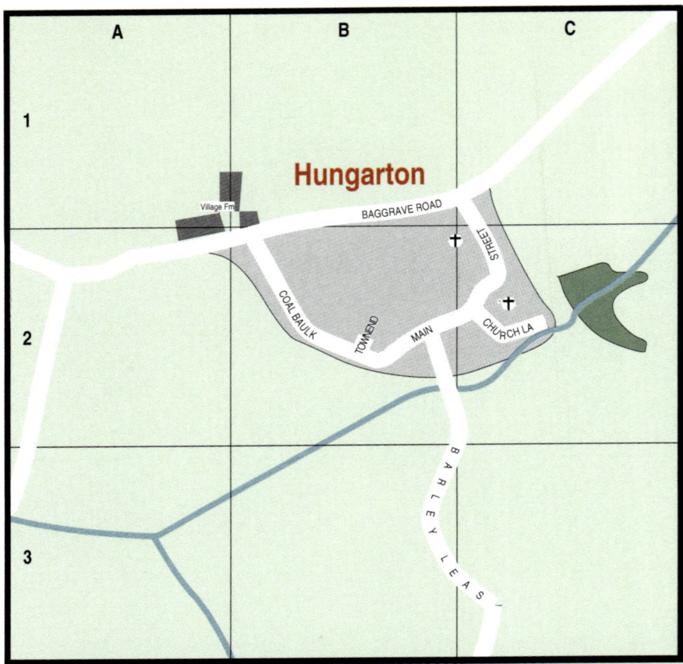

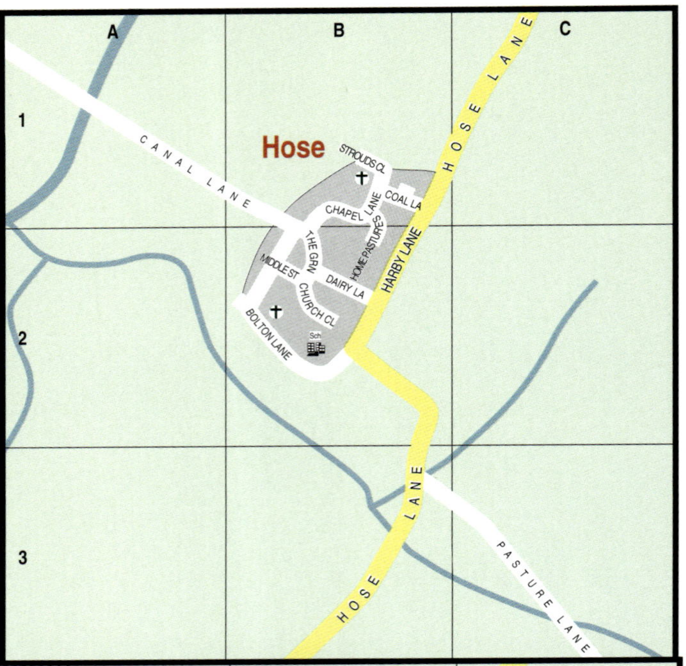

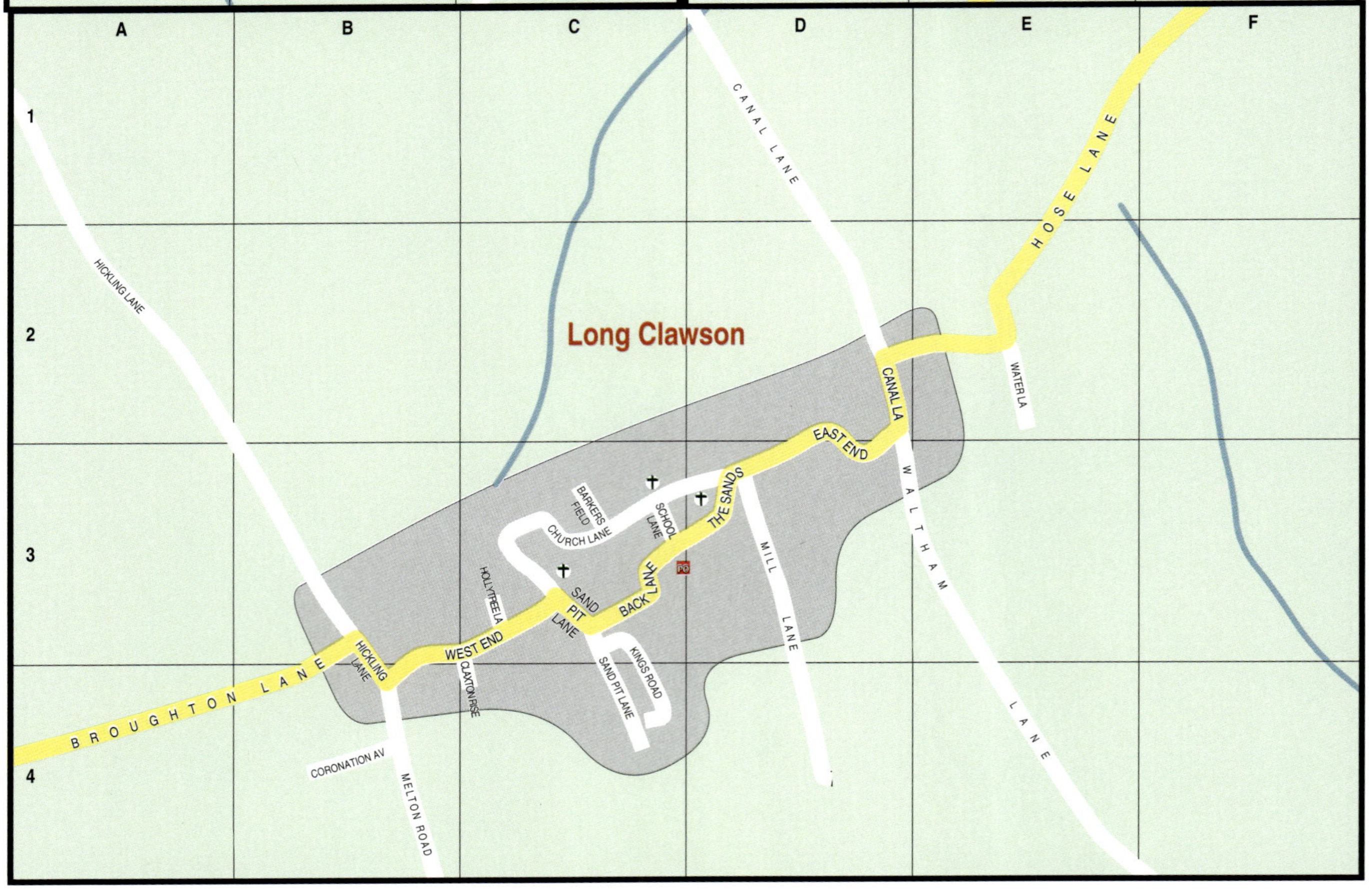

K.J.N PRECISION ENGINEERS

Milling • Turning • Grinding • Fabricating • Assembly • Polishing • Spark Eroding

Eaglesfield Farm, Main Street, Leire, Lutterworth, Leicester LE17 5HF

Tel/Fax: 01455 209915   Mobile: 07050 152005

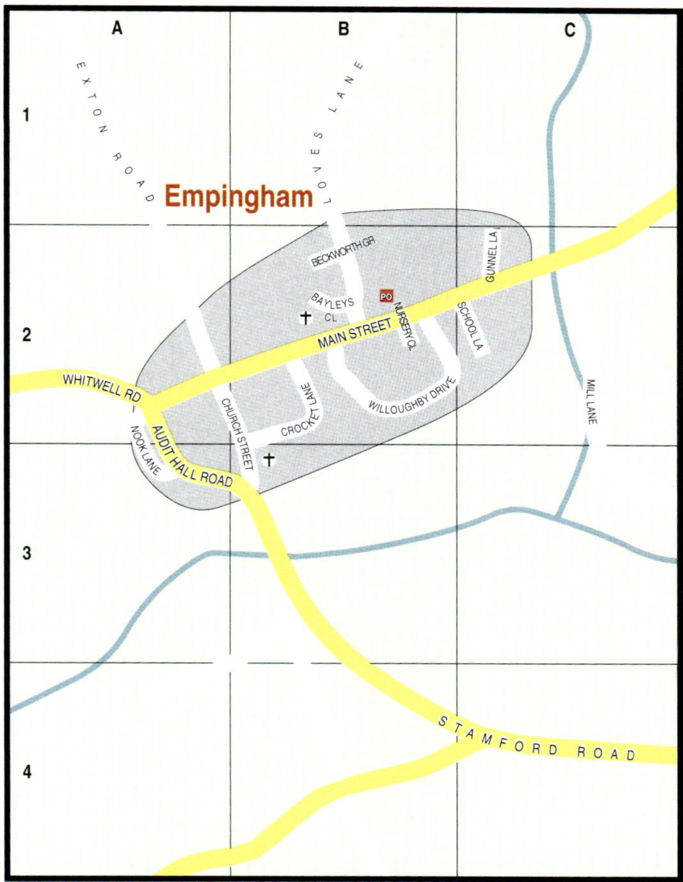

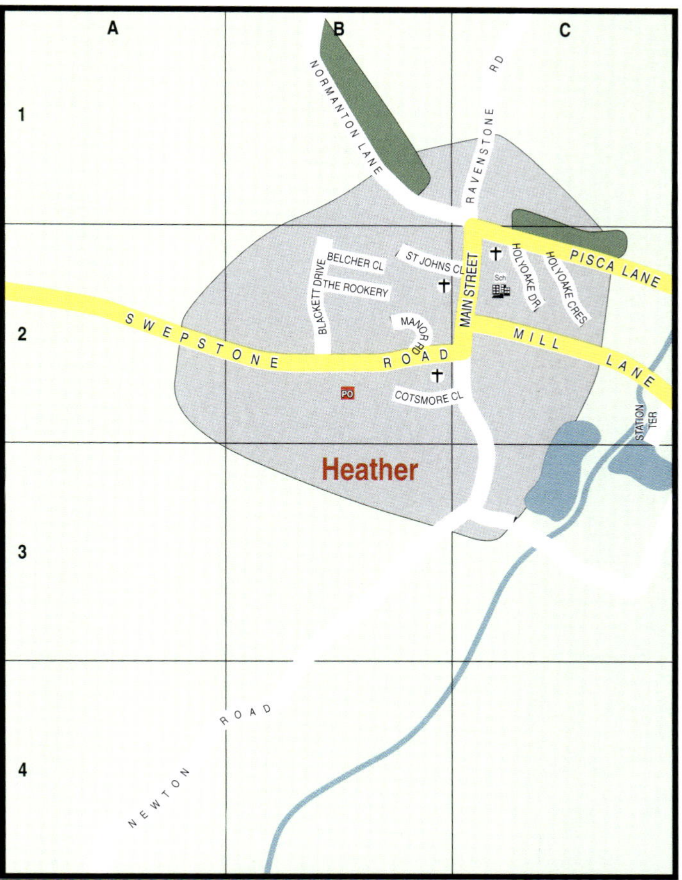

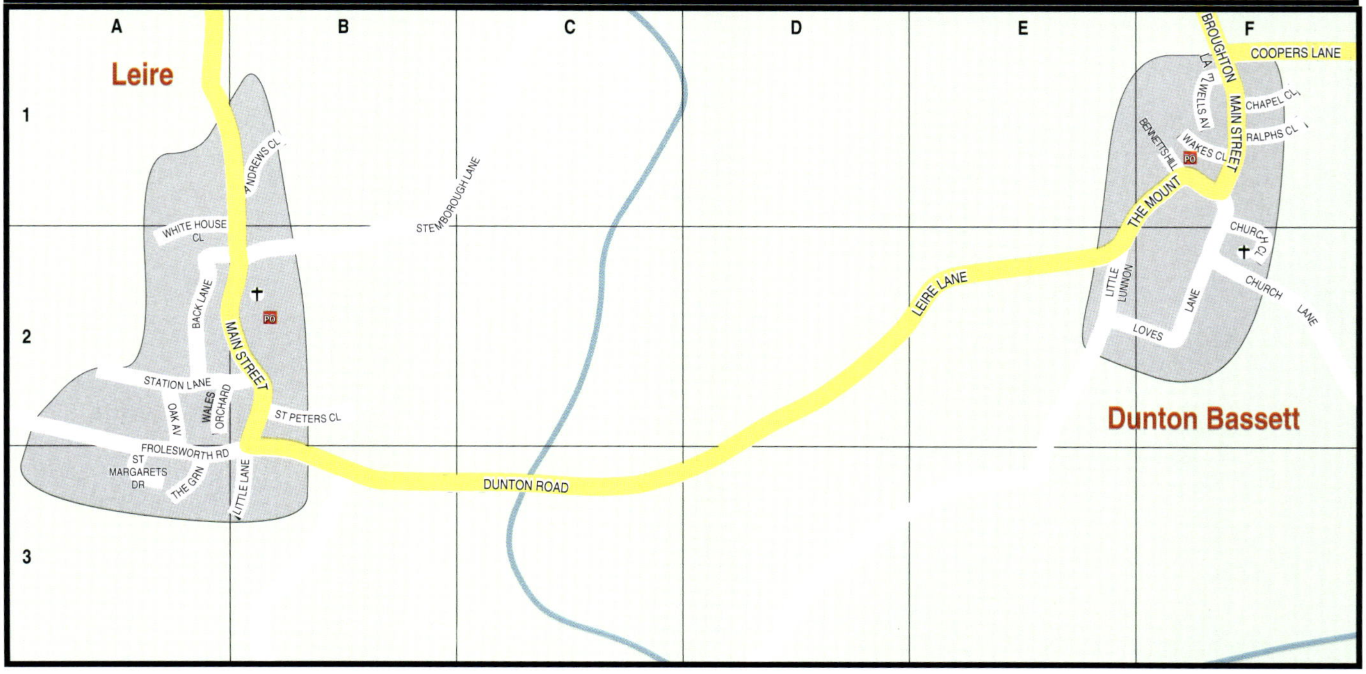

ASL

Motor Repairs to makes and models

Vehicle Alarms supplied and fitted

Expert Advice

60 Rolleston Street
Leicester LE5 3ST
Tel: 0116 276 2024

CARILLON IN CAR
01509 260403

CAR AUDIO IN CAR TV VIDEO NAVIGATION EXPERTS

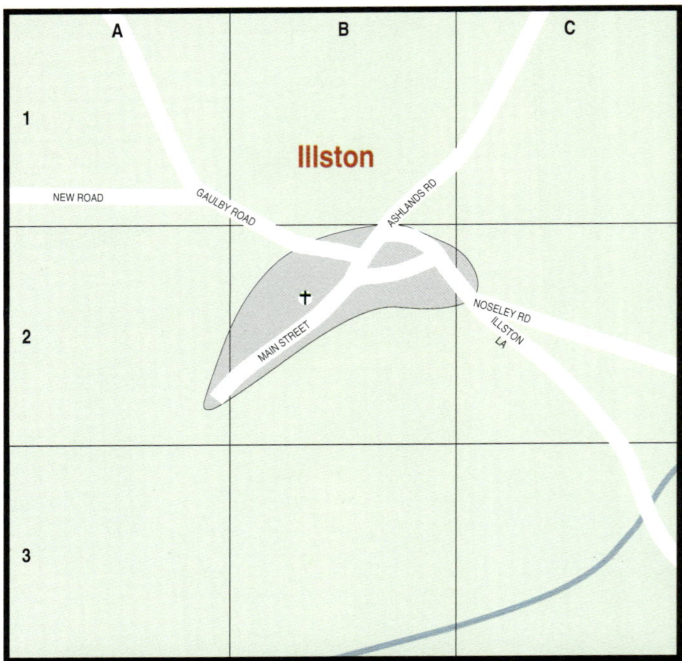

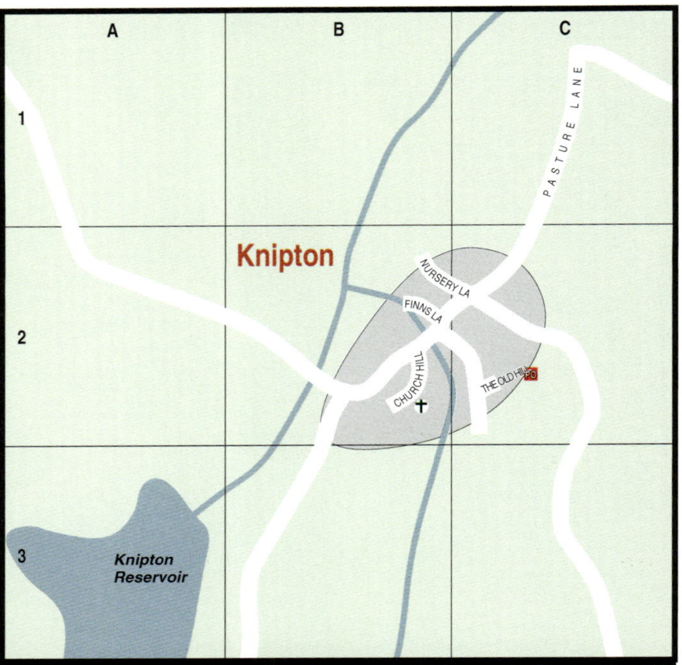

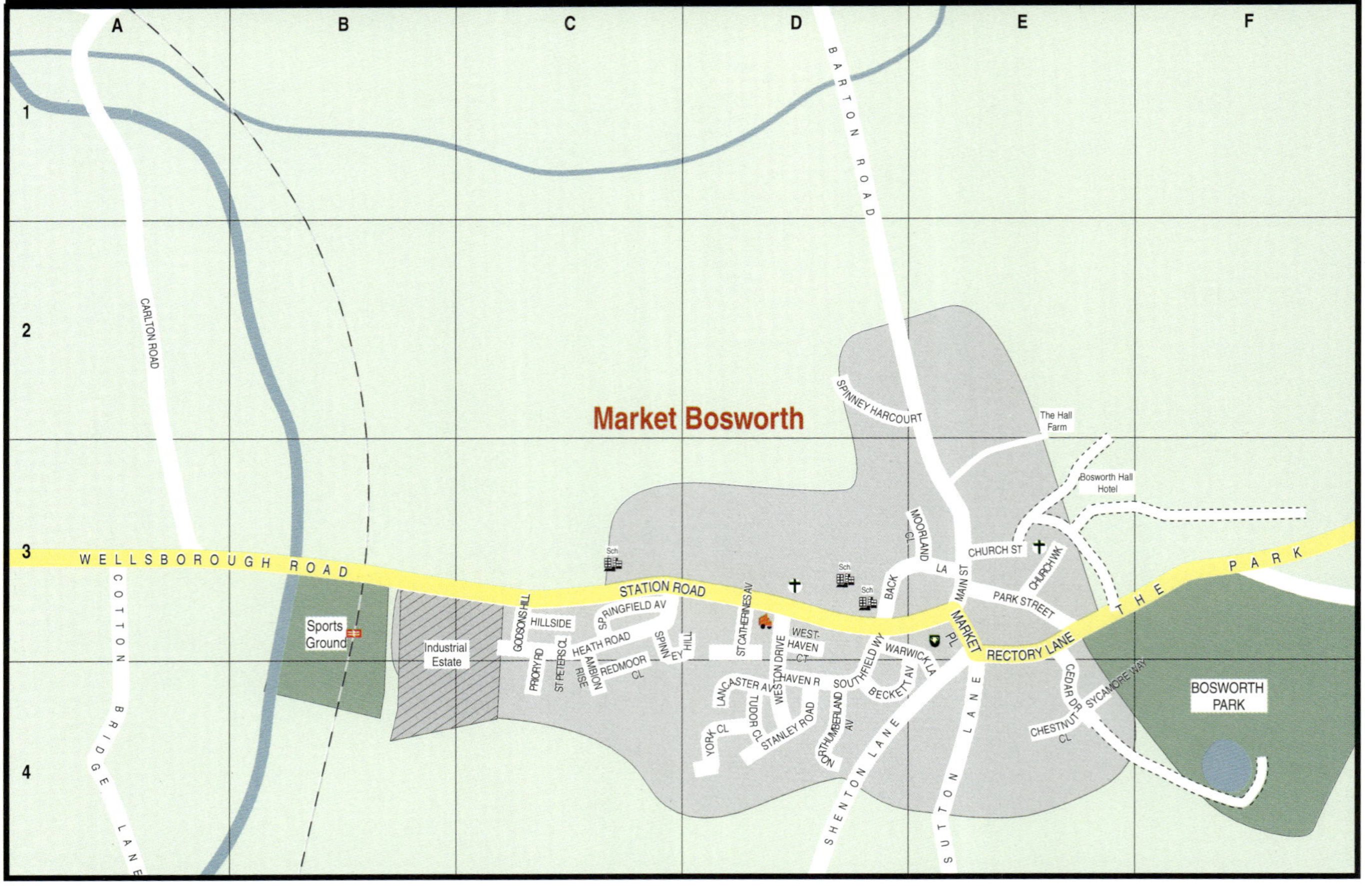

FULL FITTING AND FABRICATION SERVICE
R.T.A TESTING

Opening Hours: Monday – Friday 9am/6pm
Saturday 10am/5pm

25 Derby Road, Loughborough,
Leic's LE11 5AD
CAR PARK AT REAR

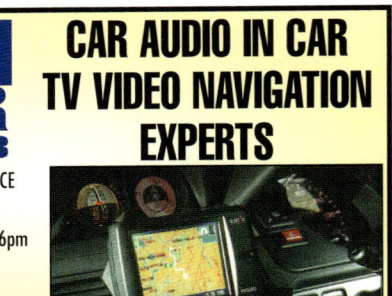

Illston

Knipton

Knipton Reservoir

Market Bosworth

Michael Dean

Motor Vehicle Repairs and Sales
Used Mini Spares
Body Repairs and Welding on all makes

MINI SPECIALIST

23 Beler Way, Leicester Road Ind Est,
Melton Mowbray, Leicestershire
TELEPHONE 01664 410287

Hillside House

PRICES FROM £18.00-£20.00

Hillside House is a charmingly converted 19th century old farm building with views over rolling countryside, conveniently situated on the outskirts of Burton Lazars. The restored accommodation is spacious and very comfortable. The old market town of Melton Mowbray, famous for pork pies, Stilton cheese and Hunt cake, has markets on Tuesdays and Saturdays. Within easy reach are Belvoir Castle (jousting), Barnsdale, Stamford (Middlemarch) and Rutland Water. Closed Christmas and New Year. 2 twin (1 en-suite), 1 double en-suite. Children welcome 10 years and over.

For further information please contact Sue Goodwin, Hillside House, 27 Melton Road, Burton Lazars, Melton Mowbray, Leicestershire LE14 2UR
Tel: 01664 566312 • Fax: 01664 501819 • Email: hillhs27@aol.co.uk

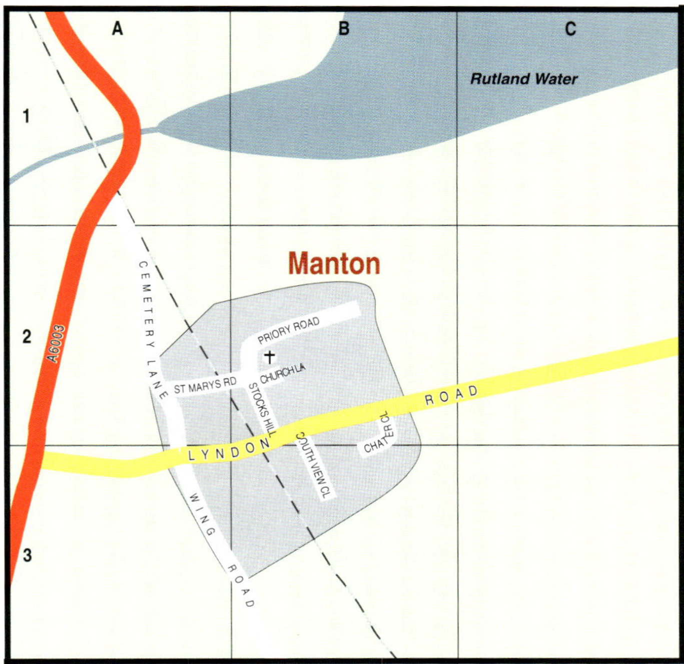

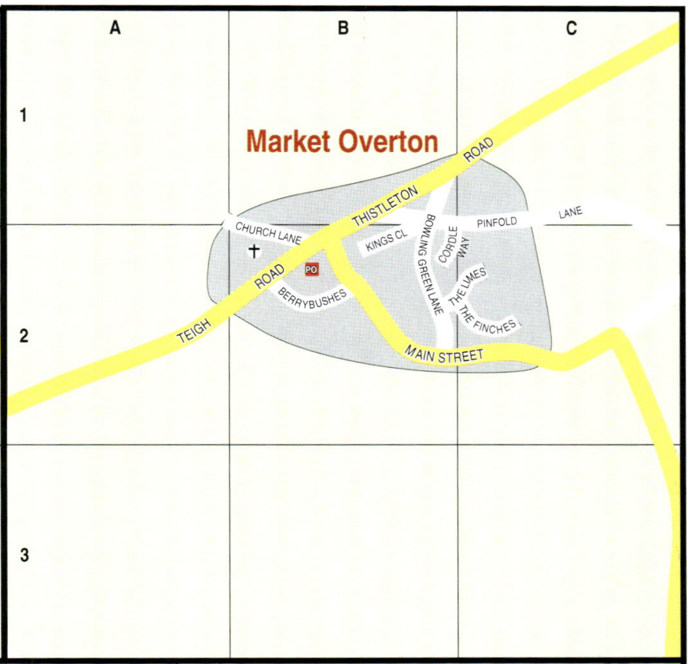

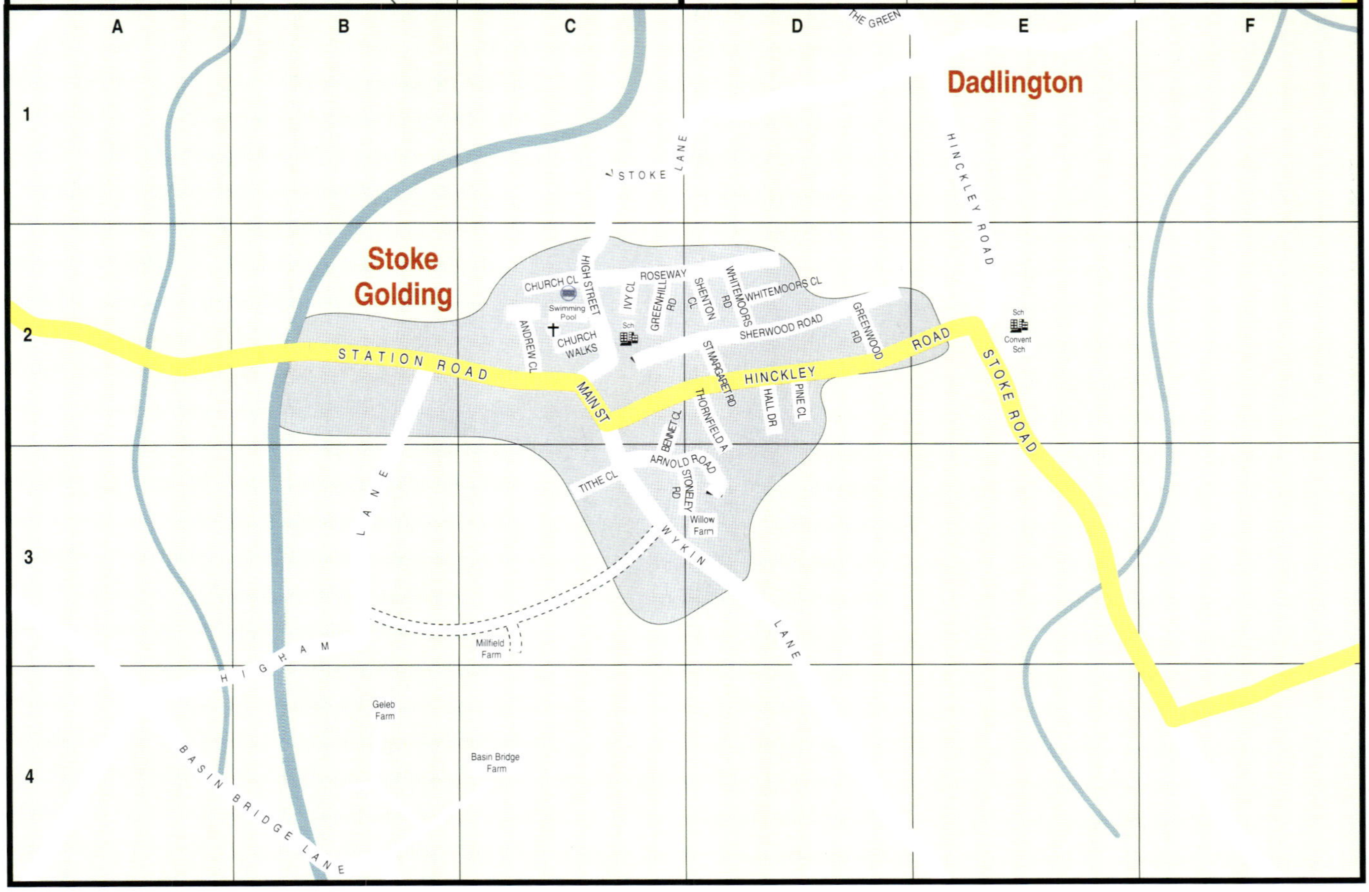

137

FourThinking Partnership

Accountancy (Sage)
Business Planning
Marketing (Strategy)
Project Management
Business Information Systems
Business Development and Change
Operations Management

The FourThinking Partnership offers a comprehensive range of consultancy services to provide a complete and personal service for each client, according to their individual business needs.

Tel: +44 (0)116 242 4031 Fax: +44 (0)116 262 6636
E-mail: thefour@fourthinking.co.uk

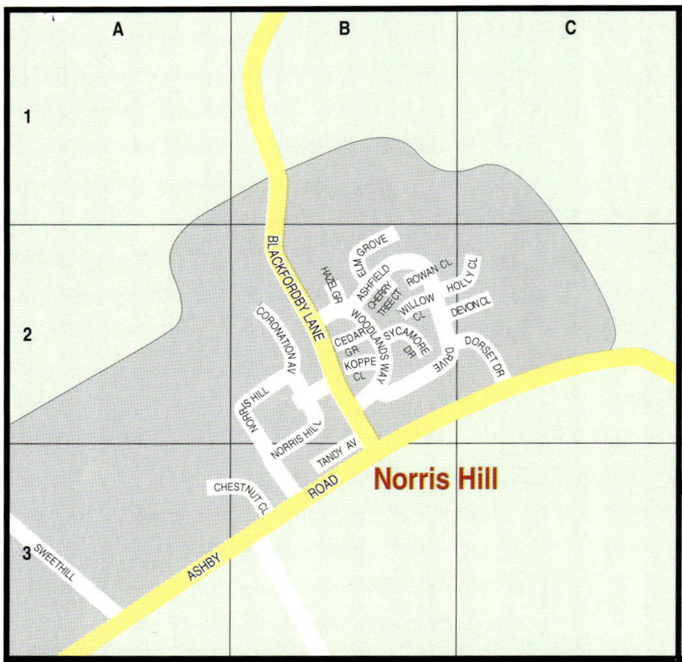

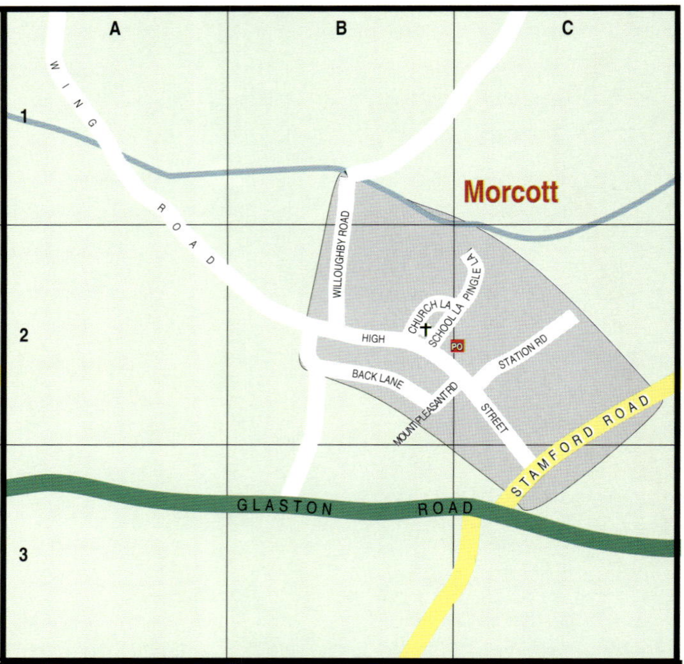

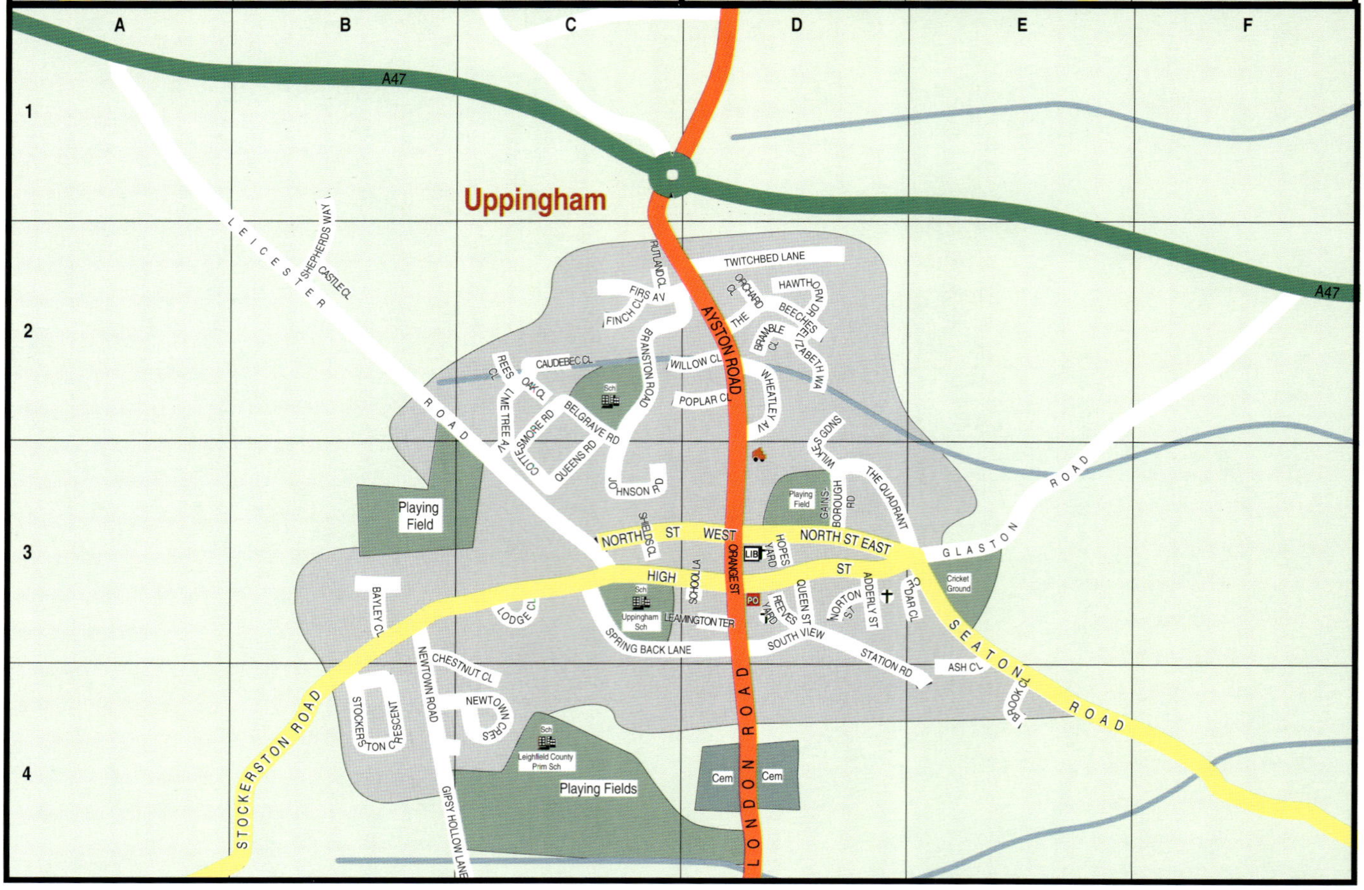

Shaftesbury Junior School and Community Centre

Latimer Street, Hinckley Road, Leicester LE3 0QE
Tel: 0116 254 9203   Fax: 0116 254 9939
email: Leic_Shaftesbury_Junior_School_EDU_@msn.com

Leicester City Council Education

Shaftesbury Junior School and Community School
Headteacher Mr NBP Gavin JP BA MEd

A to Z Transport Services
(01509) 416101 or 07850 383228
Full or part loads up to 6 1/2 tonnes. Curtainside, Flat & Crane Vehicles
Courier Vans and Flats Same Day Service
R.H.A. Members and Insurance Standards

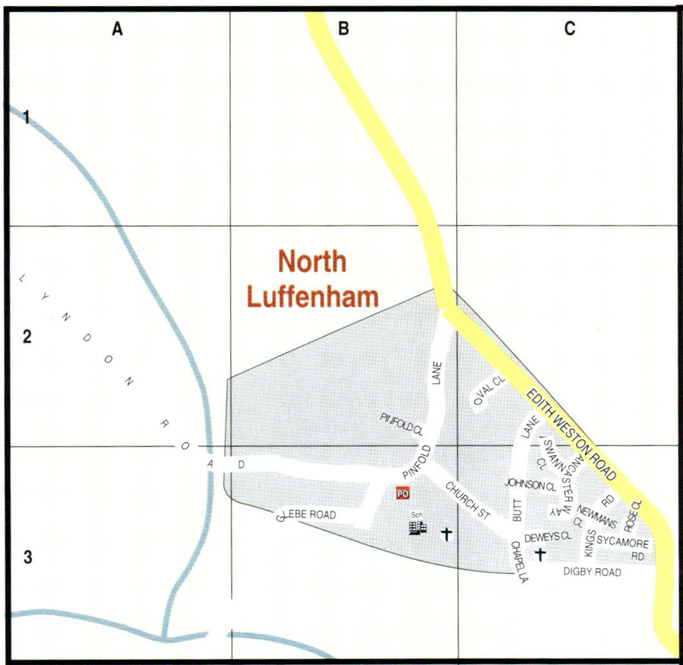

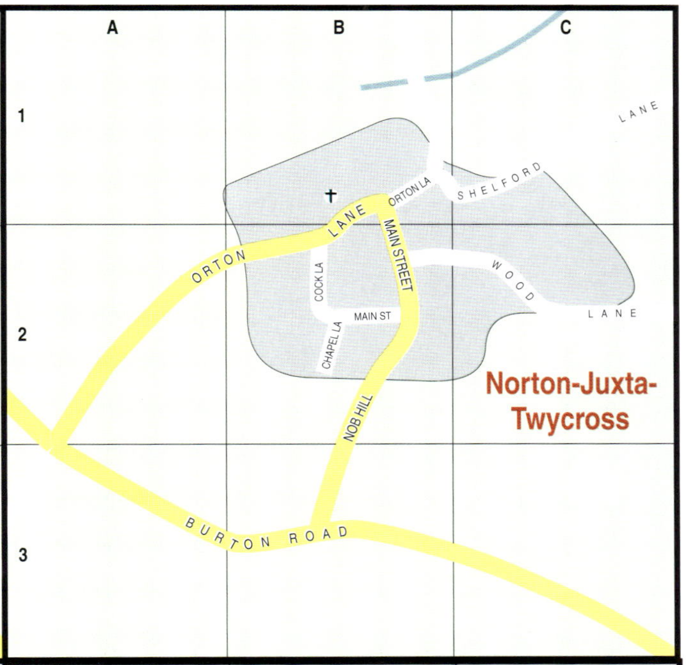

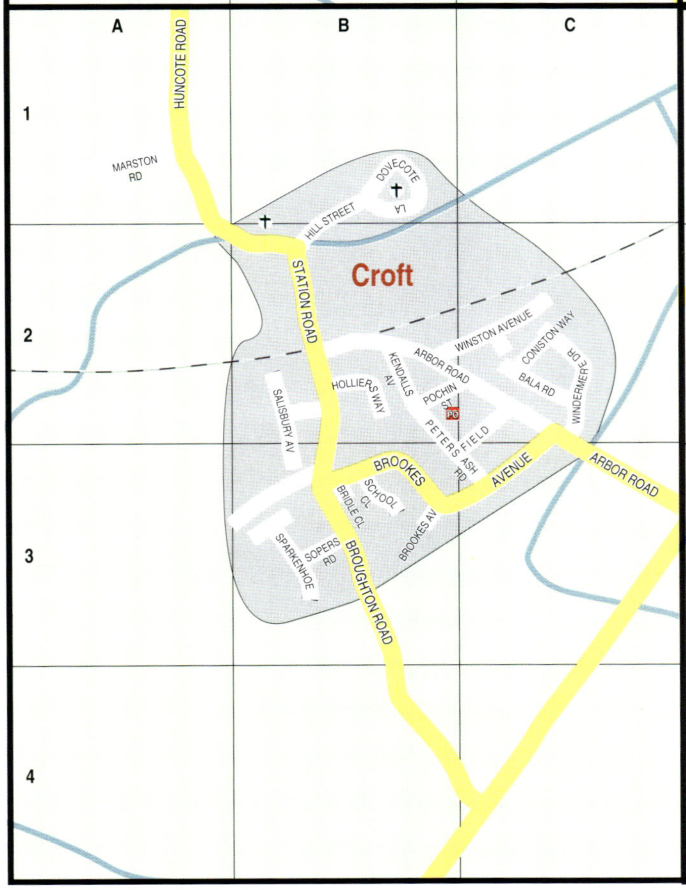

139

Maps: North Luffenham; Norton-Juxta-Twycross; Croft; Claybrooke Magna; Claybrooke Parva

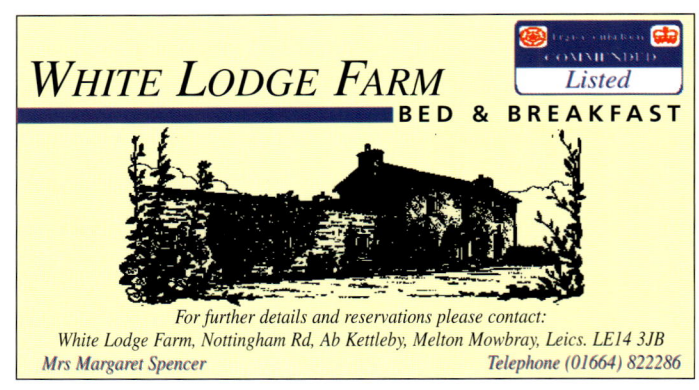

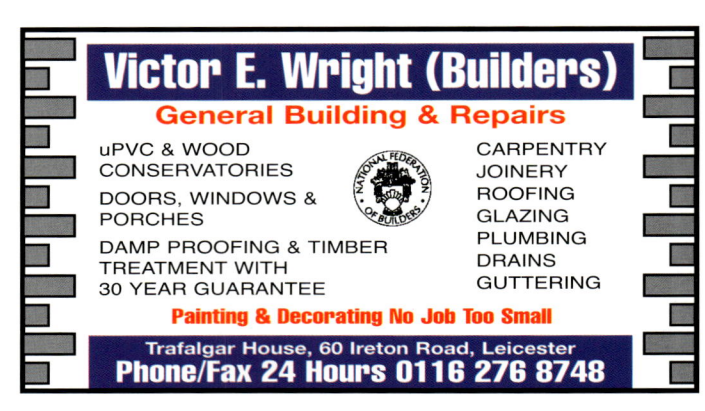

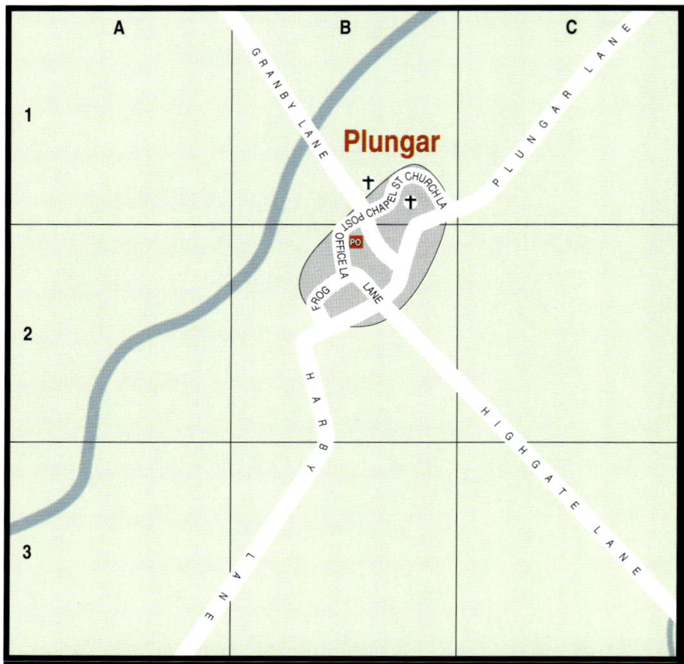

A
B
C
1
2
3
Plungar
GRANBY LANE
PLUNGAR LANE
CHAPEL ST
CHURCH LA
POST OFFICE LA
FROG LANE
PO
HARBY LANE
HIGHGATE LANE

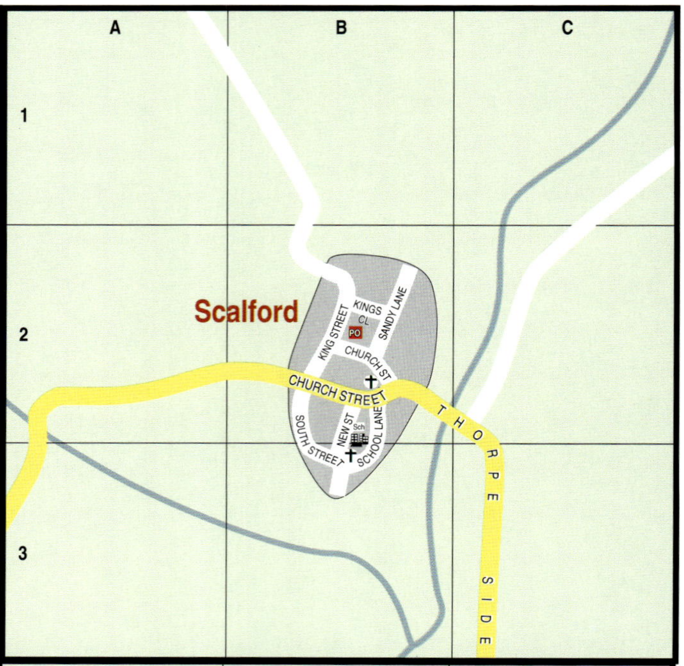

A
B
C
1
2
3
Scalford
KING STREET
KINGS CL
SANDY LANE
PO
CHURCH ST
CHURCH STREET
SOUTH STREET
NEW ST
Sch
SCHOOL LANE
THORPE SIDE

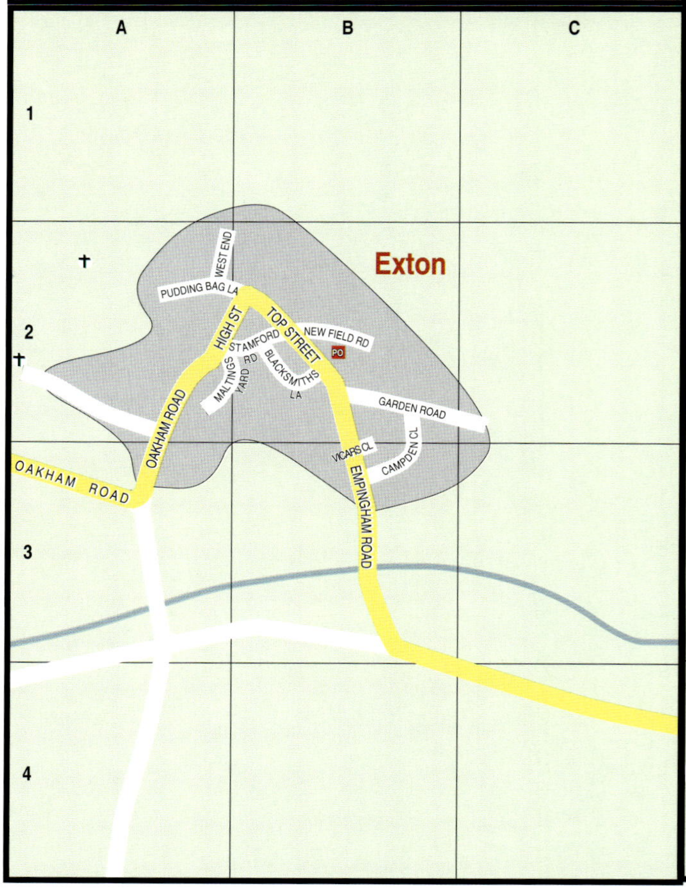

A
B
C
1
2
3
4
Exton
WEST END
PUDDING BAG LA
HIGH ST
TOP STREET
STAMFORD RD
NEW FIELD RD
PO
MALTINGS YARD
BLACKSMITHS LA
GARDEN ROAD
OAKHAM ROAD
VICARS CL
CAMPDEN CL
EMPINGHAM ROAD

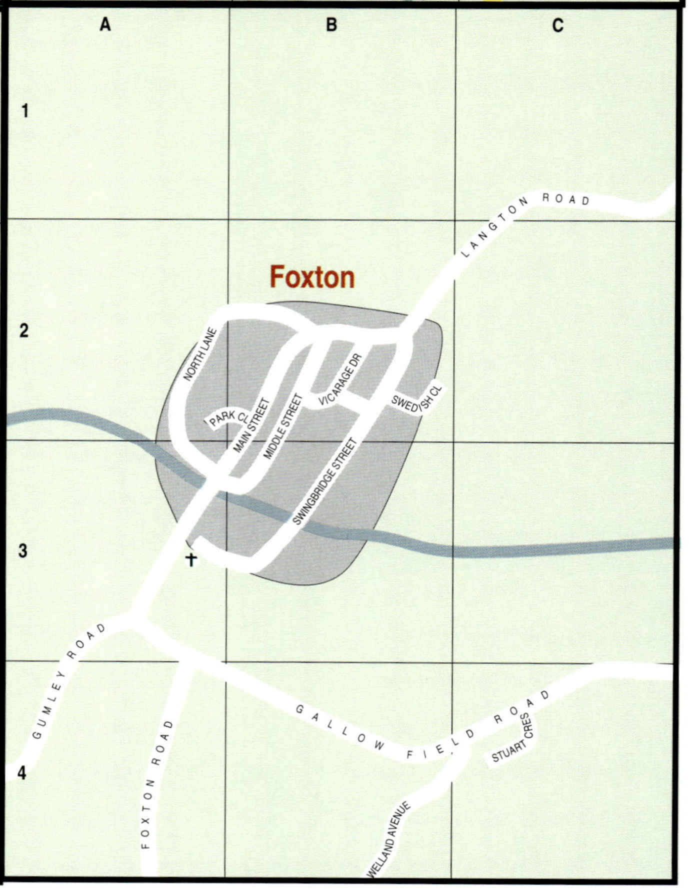

A
B
C
1
2
3
4
Foxton
LANGTON ROAD
NORTH LANE
VICARAGE DR
SWEDISH CL
PARK CL
MAIN STREET
MIDDLE STREET
SWINGBRIDGE STREET
GUMLEY ROAD
FOXTON ROAD
GALLOW FIELD ROAD
STUART CRES
WELLAND AVENUE

Rutland Garden Machines

Hire • Sales • Service

Studio Workshops,
41 South Street, Oakham, Rutland LE15 6BG
Telephone: 01572 756458

The Path to Weed Control...

When you need safe, effective weed treatment talk to the experts.

Languard Ltd

Call now for a brochure on:
01858 880898

or contact us at:
Church Lane Husbands Bosworth
Lutterworth Leicestershire LE17 6LS
Fax: 01858 880720

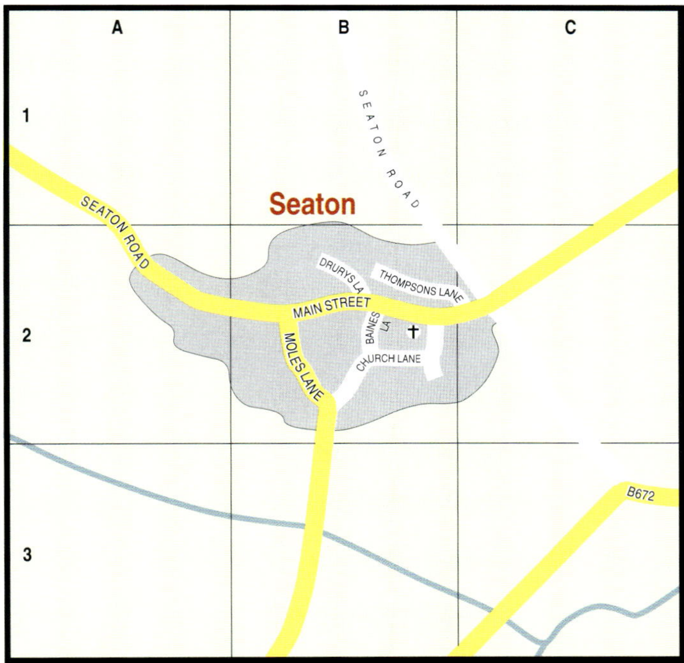

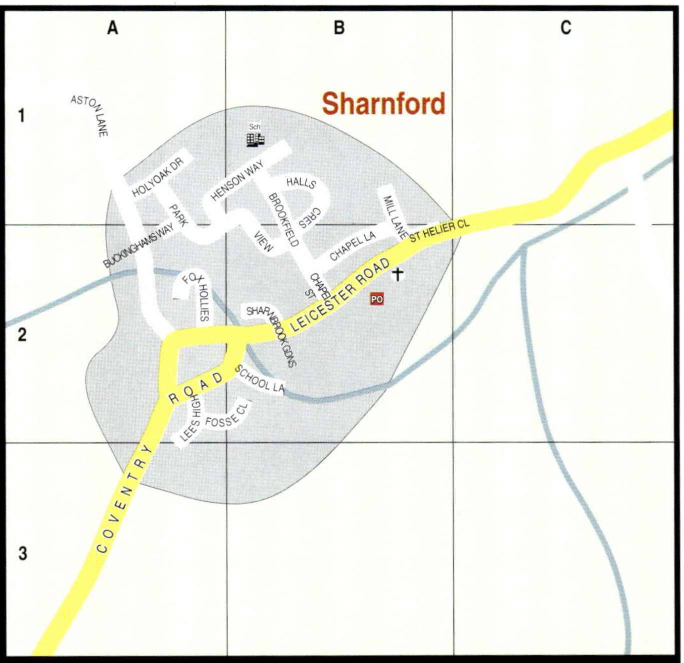

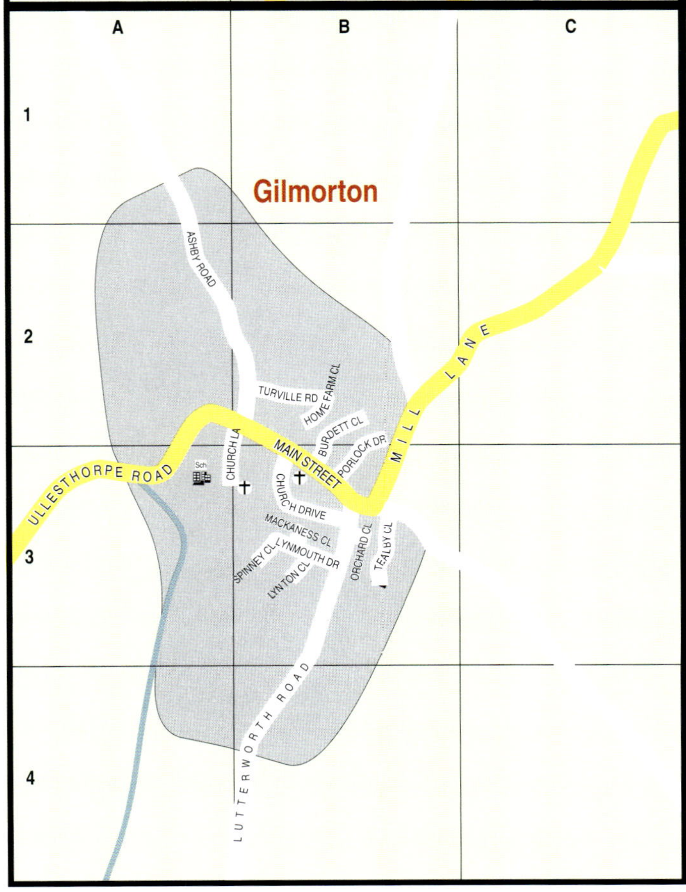

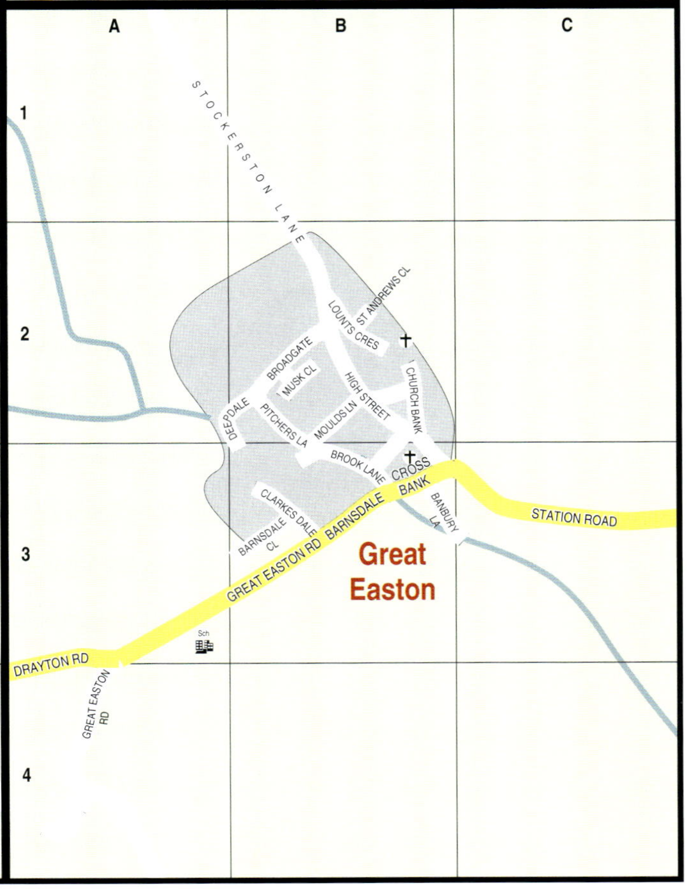

141

Seaton

Sharnford

Gilmorton

Great Easton

~165~

Shawell
A
B
C
1
2
3
GIBBET LANE
LUTTERWORTH ROAD
MAIN ST
SWINFORD ROAD
MAIN STREET
ROAD
CATTHORPE
BULL ACES LANE
PO

Shearsby
A
B
C
1
2
3
WELLFORD ROAD
SADDINGTON ROAD
BRUNTINGTHORPE ROAD
CHURCH LANE
BACK LANE
THE BANK
THE SQUARE
MAIN ST
FENNY LA
MILL LANE

Houghton on the Hill
A
B
C
1
2
3
4
UPPINGHAM ROAD
INGARSBY LANE
INGARSBY CL
DEANE GATE DR
LINWAL AV
THOMAS CL
WINCKLEY CL
WAY NORTH
SCOTLAND LA
SCOTLAND WAY
THE RISE
ST CATHARINES WAY
CHAPEL CL
ELIZABETH CL
END FORSELLS
MAIN STREET
WEIR LANE
FIRS ROAD
FREER CL
SCHOOL LA
Sch
PO
STRETTON LANE

Husbands Bosworth
A
B
C
1
2
3
4
LEICESTER ROAD
THEDDINGWORTH RD
MOWSLEY ROAD
HIGHCROFT
HUNTERS CL
BERRIDGES LANE
BELL LANE
GREEN LA
HILLCREST LA
WELLS CL
HONEYPOT LA
CHURCH ST
CHURCH LA
HIGH STREET
BUTT LA
LAMMAS CL
SCHOOL LA
Sch
PO
KILWORTH ROAD
WELFORD ROAD

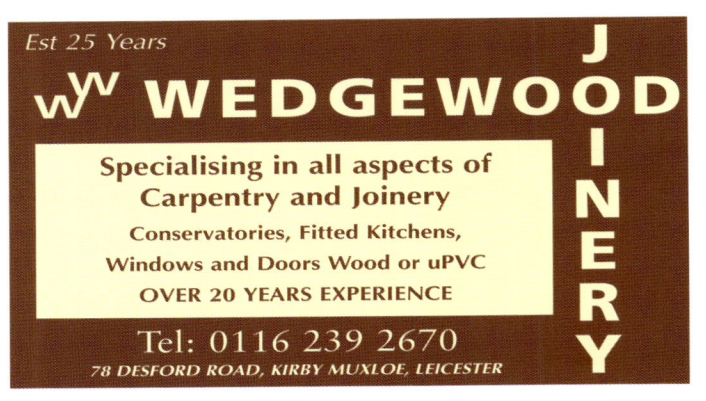

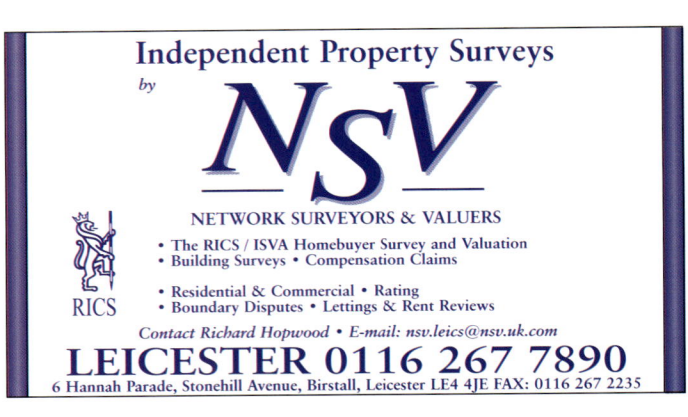

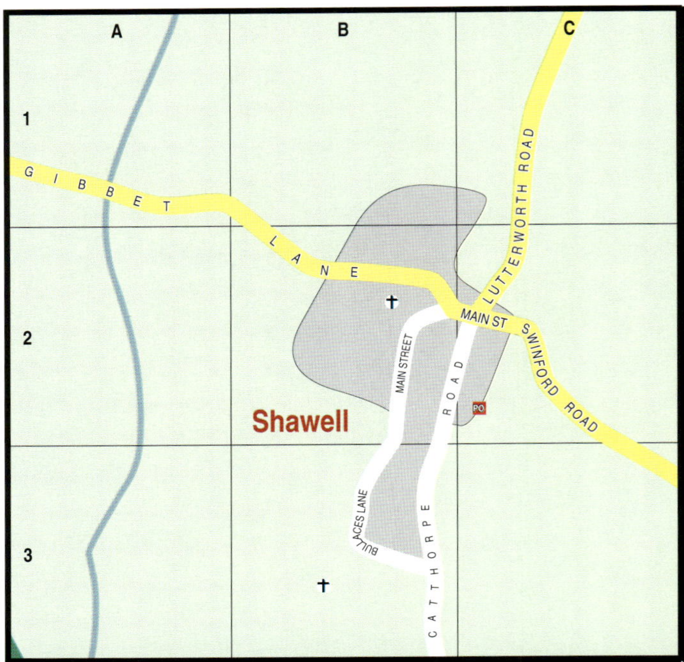

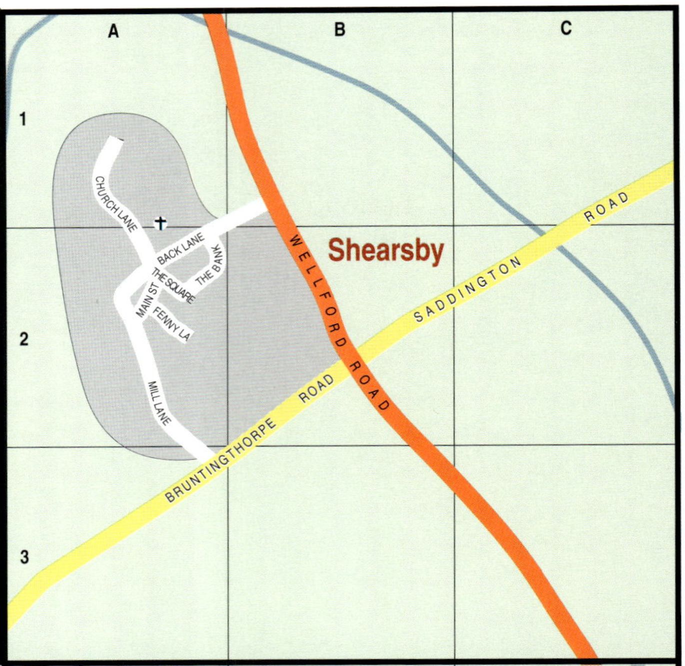

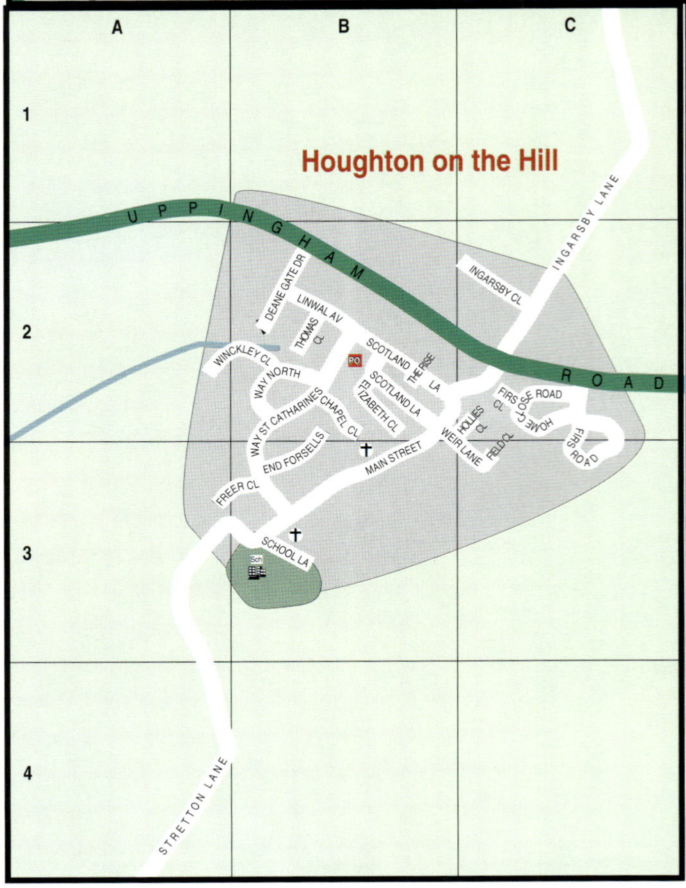

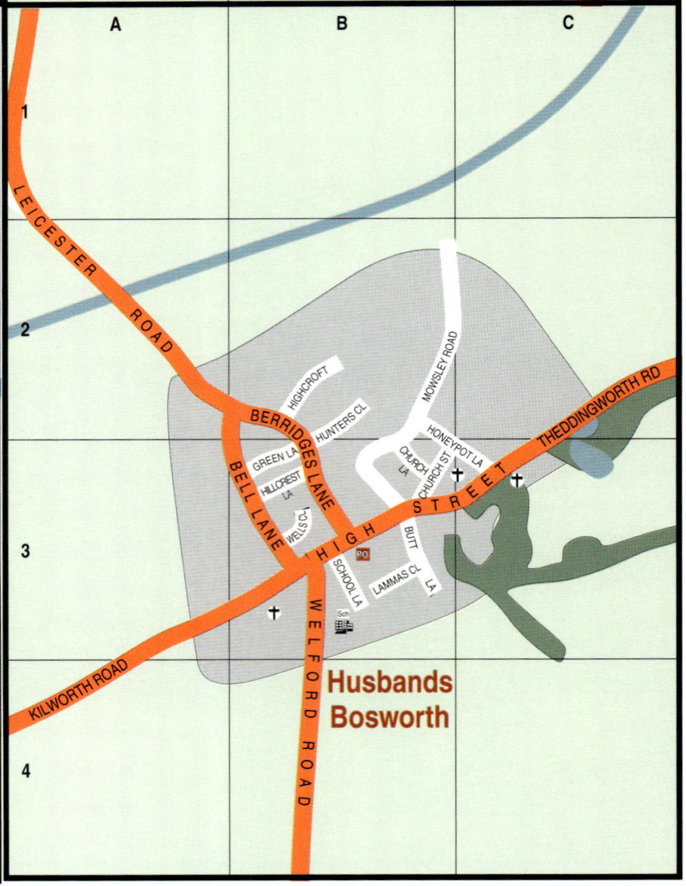

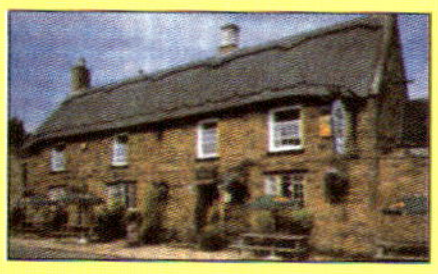

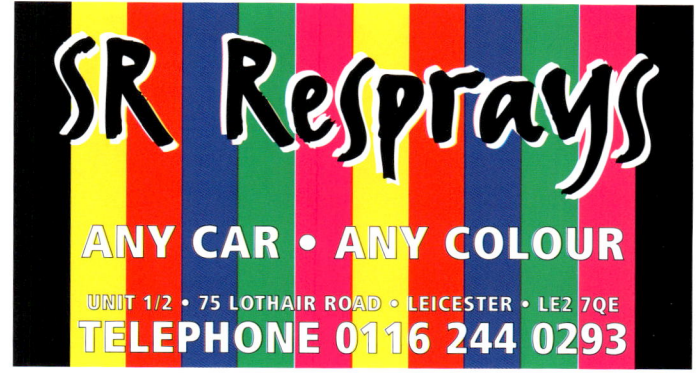

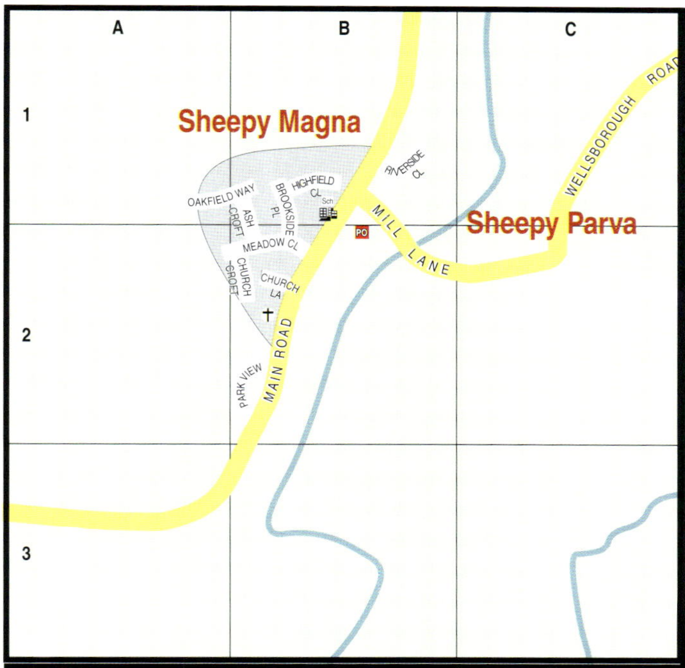

A
B
C
1
2
3
Sheepy Magna
Sheepy Parva
OAKFIELD WAY
ASH CROFT
BROOKSIDE PL
HIGHFIELD CL
Sch
RIVERSIDE CL
MILL LANE
WELLSBOROUGH ROAD
MEADOW CL
CHURCH CROET
CHURCH LA
PO
PARK VIEW
MAIN ROAD

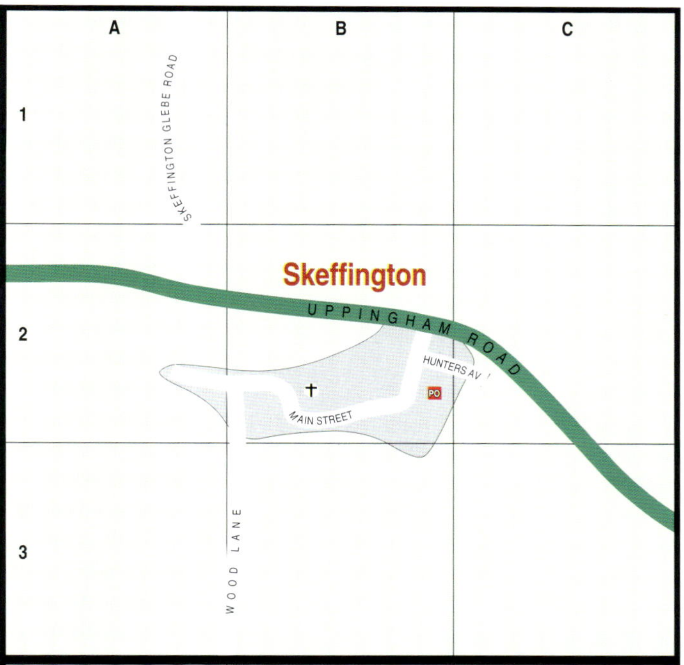

A
B
C
1
2
3
SKEFFINGTON GLEBE ROAD
Skeffington
UPPINGHAM ROAD
HUNTERS AV
PO
MAIN STREET
WOOD LANE

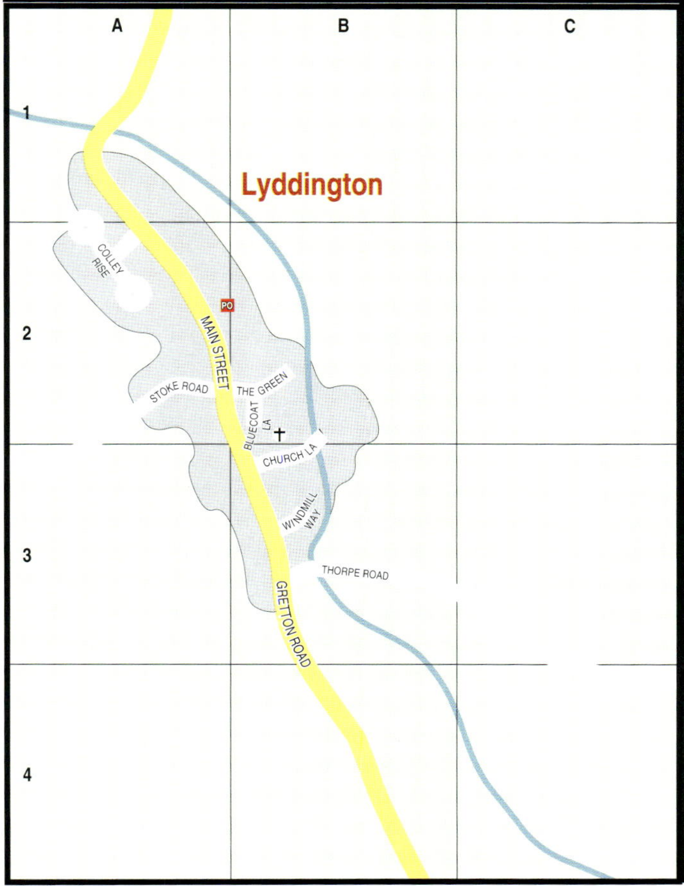

A
B
C
1
2
3
4
Lyddington
COLLEY RISE
PO
MAIN STREET
STOKE ROAD
THE GREEN
BLUECOAT LA
CHURCH LA
WINDMILL WAY
THORPE ROAD
GRETTON ROAD

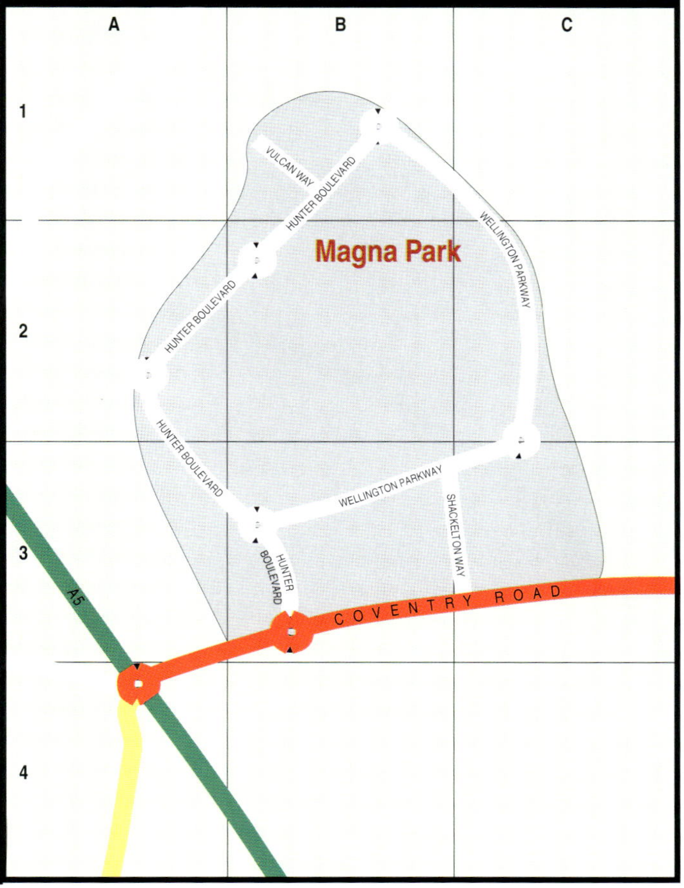

A
B
C
1
2
3
4
VULCAN WAY
HUNTER BOULEVARD
Magna Park
WELLINGTON PARKWAY
HUNTER BOULEVARD
HUNTER BOULEVARD
WELLINGTON PARKWAY
SHACKELTON WAY
HUNTER BOULEVARD
A5
COVENTRY ROAD

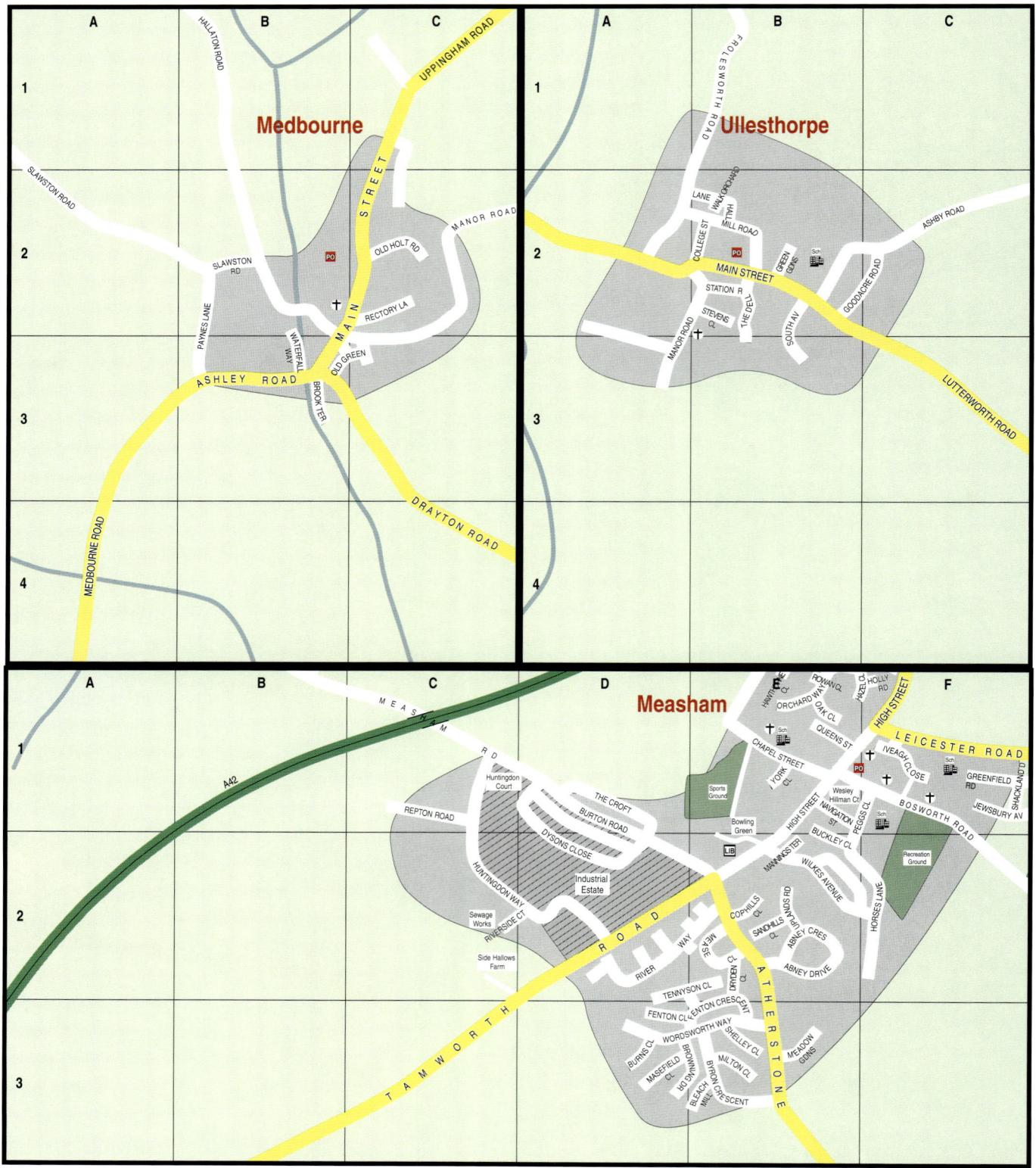

For a selection of guaranteed clocks (including 12-15 Grandfathers) and choice pieces of antique furniture

Antique Clock Specialists
Sales & Restoration

High Street, Swinford, Nr. Lutterworth, Leicestershire LE17 6BL

Tel: (01788) 860311   Mobile: 07836 505111

www.old-timers.co.uk

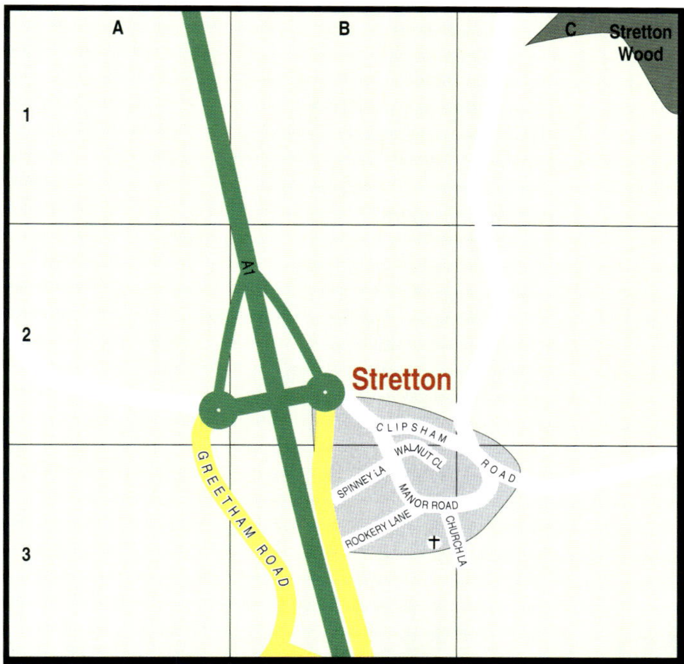

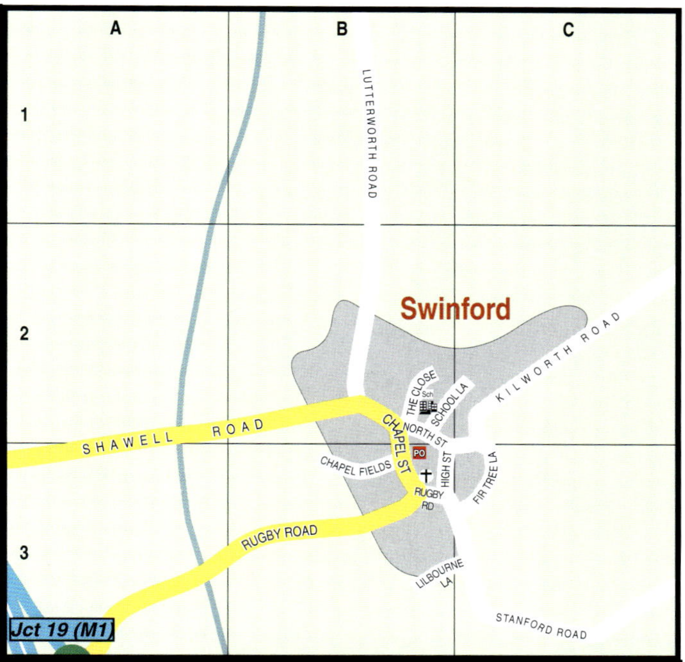

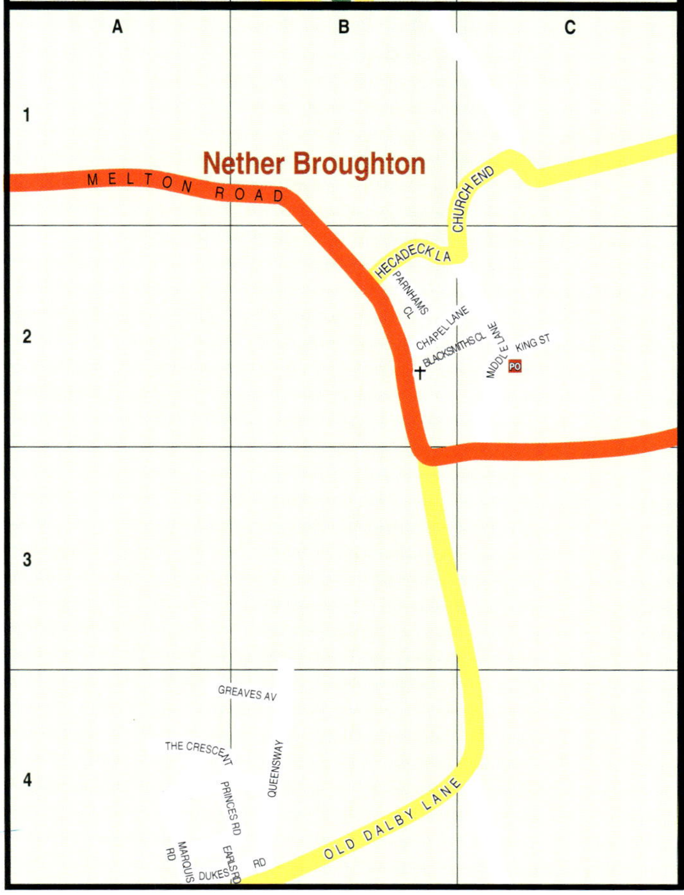

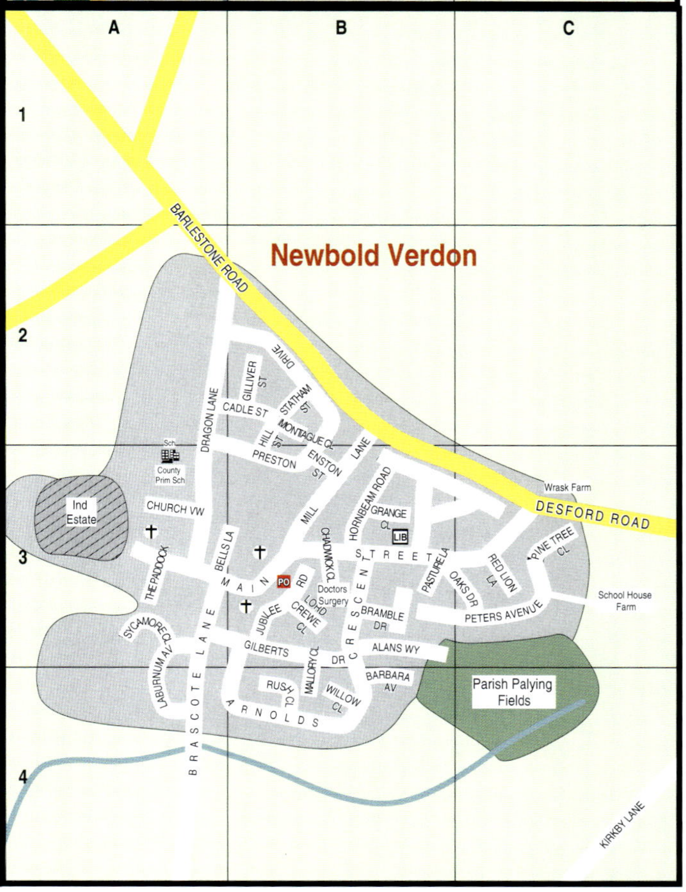

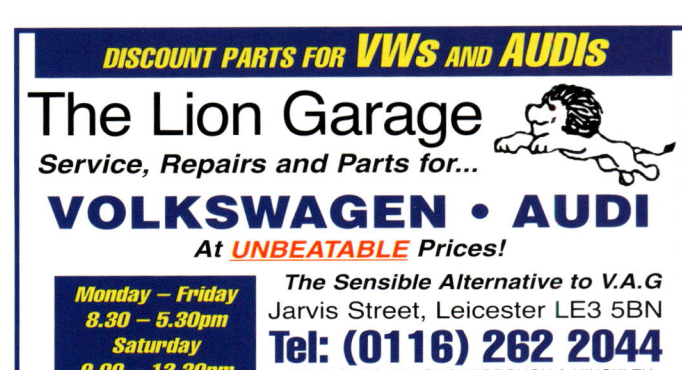

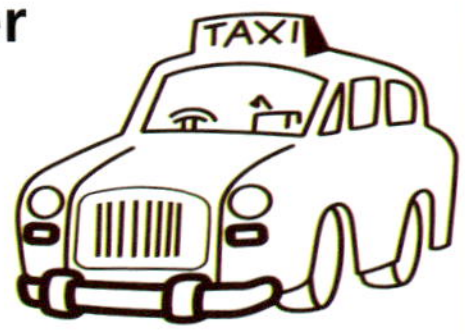

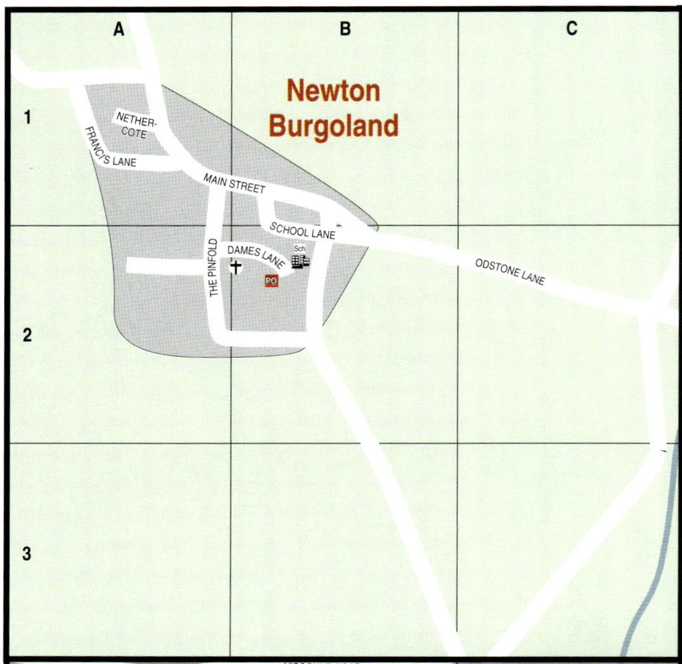
A
B
C
1
2
3
Newton Burgoland
NETHER-COTE
FRANCIS LANE
MAIN STREET
SCHOOL LANE
Sch
DAMES LANE
THE PINFOLD
PO
ODSTONE LANE

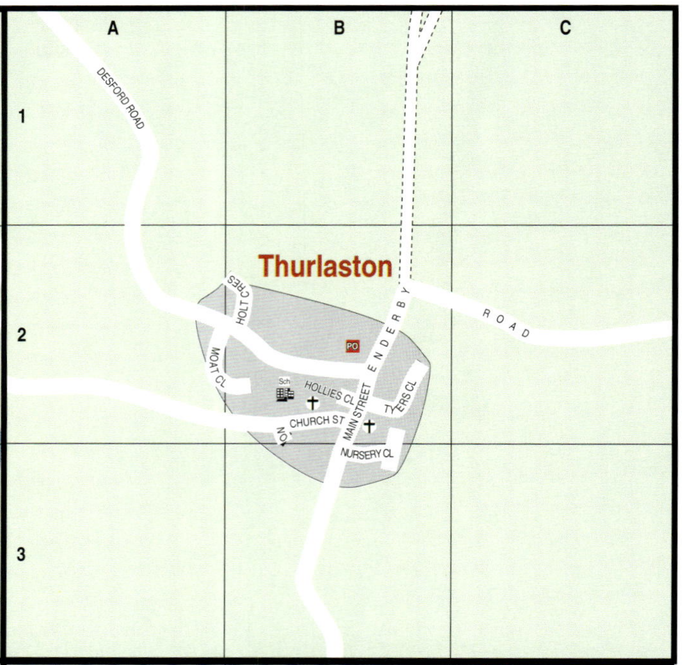
A
B
C
1
2
3
DESFORD ROAD
Thurlaston
HOLT CRES
ENDERBY
ROAD
PO
MOAT CL
Sch
HOLLIES CL
MAIN STREET
TYERS CL
CHURCH ST
NURSERY CL

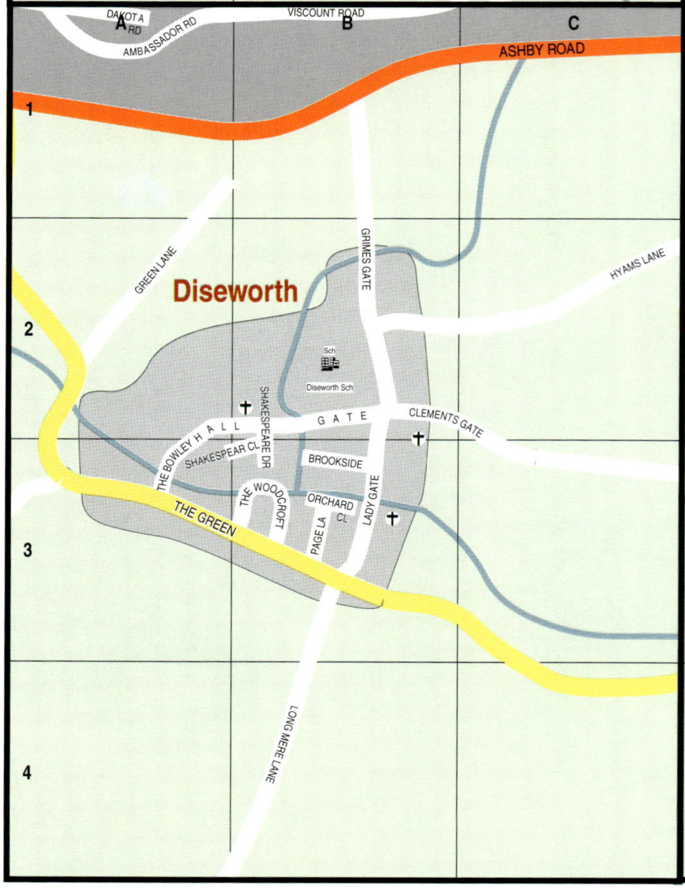
A
B
C
1
2
3
4
DAKOTA RD
AMBASSADOR RD
VISCOUNT ROAD
ASHBY ROAD
GRIMES GATE
HYAMS LANE
GREEN LANE
Diseworth
Sch
Diseworth Sch
SHAKESPEARE DR
HALL GATE
CLEMENTS GATE
THE BOWLEY
SHAKESPEAR CL
BROOKSIDE
THE WOODCROFT
ORCHARD CL
LADY GATE
PAGE LA
THE GREEN
LONG MERE LANE

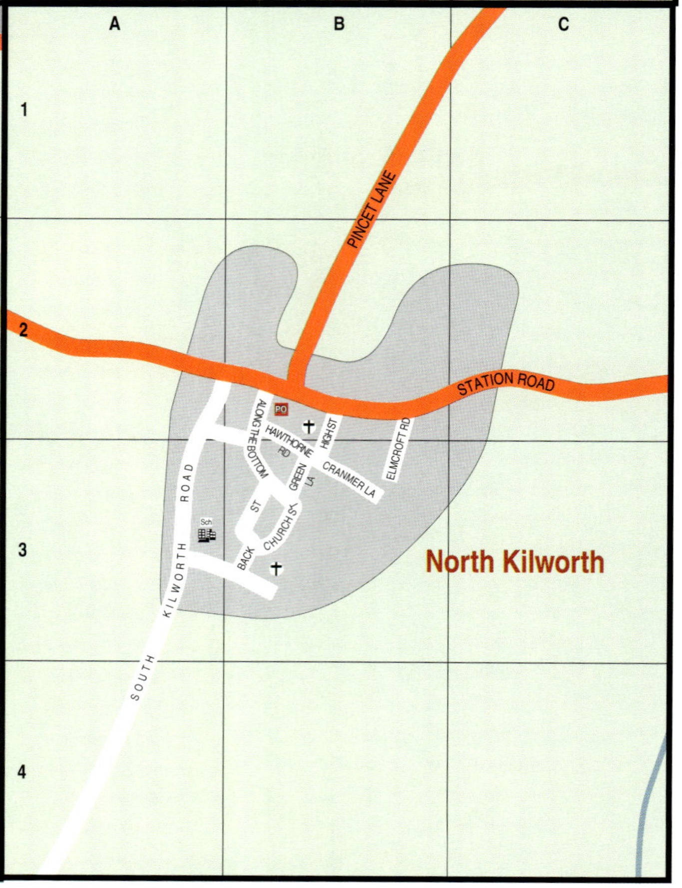
A
B
C
1
2
3
4
PINCET LANE
STATION ROAD
PO
ALONG THE BOTTOM
HAWTHORNE RD
HIGH ST
GREEN LA
CRANMER LA
ELMCROFT RD
SOUTH KILWORTH ROAD
Sch
ST
CHURCH ST
BACK
North Kilworth

ABACAB SOUND & LIGHTING

For all your Mobile DJ Equipment, Amps, Speakers, Lighting Equipment etc...
All leading makes supplied

Tel/Fax: Carl (0116) 247 7338/278 2094
Mobile: 07774 903331

QUALITY FLOORING SERVICES LTD.

THE SMALL SHOP WITH THE BIG SELECTION AND AFFORDABLE PRICES!

Looking for a New Carpet? Look no more!
Top Quality Carpets and Quality Service
EXPERT FITTING SERVICE
by our own Professional Fitters
Choose at Home Service
FREE Estimates • Insurance Quotes
Corner of Broomleys Avenue/
Bardon Road, Coalville.

Tel: 01530 810446

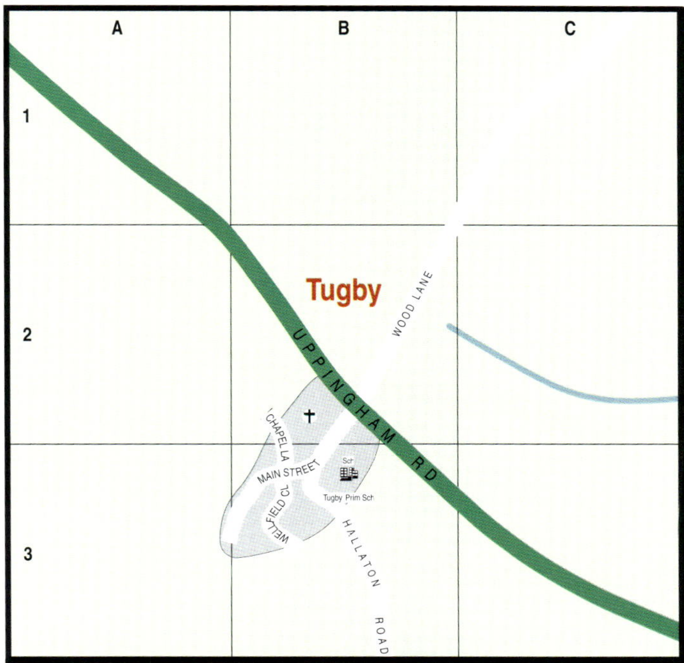

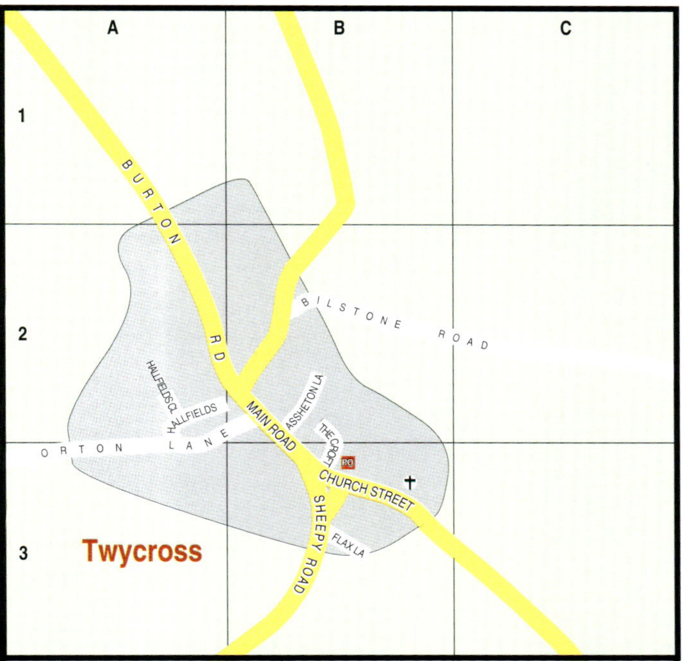

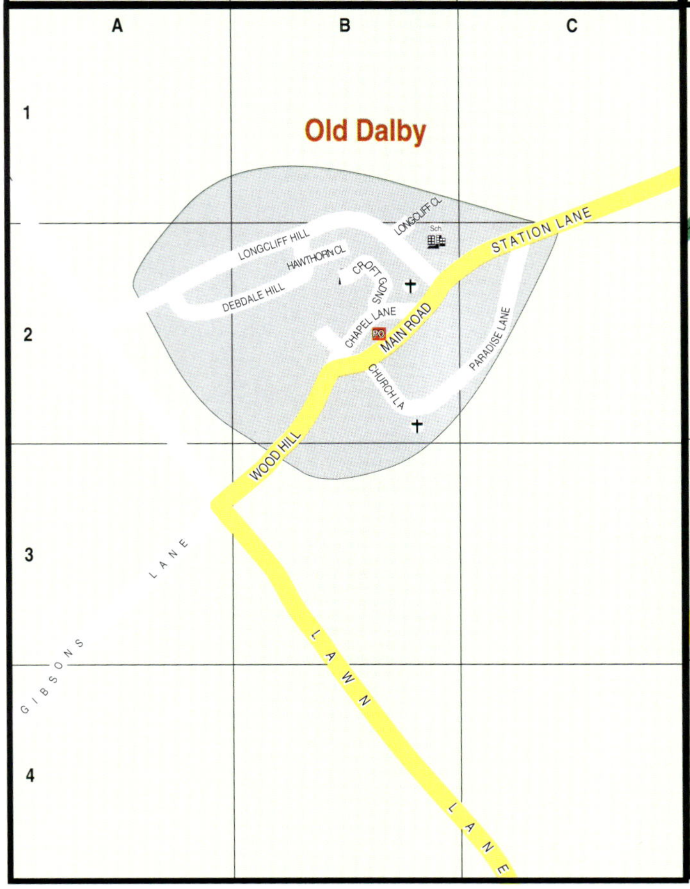

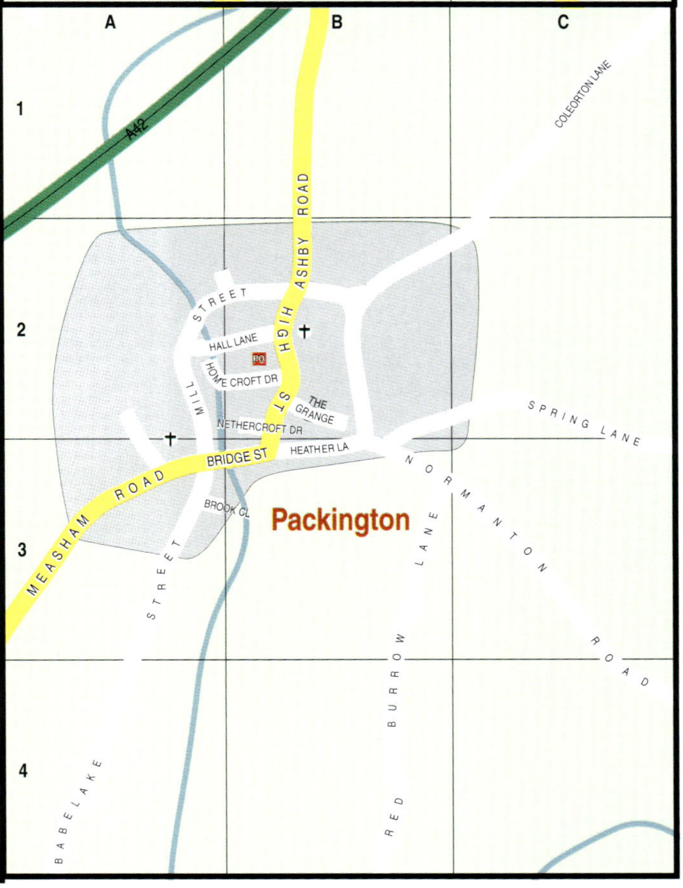

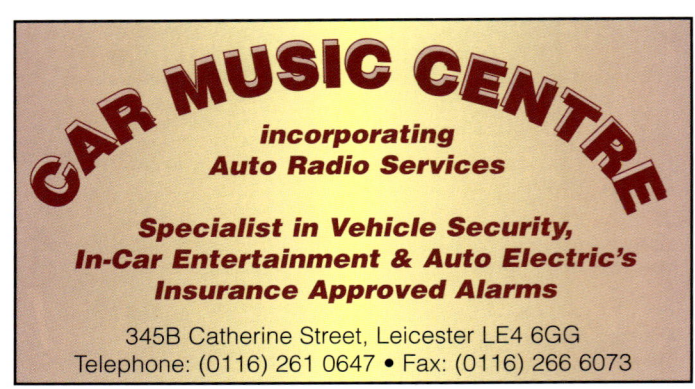

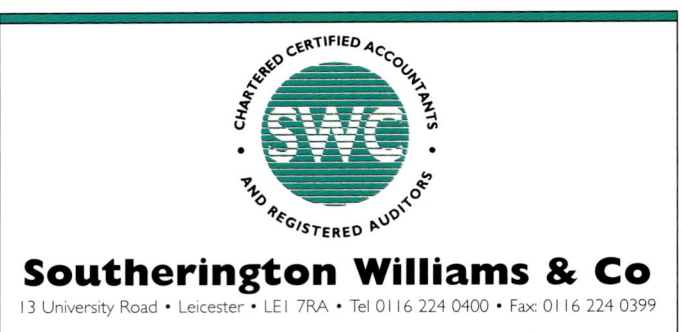

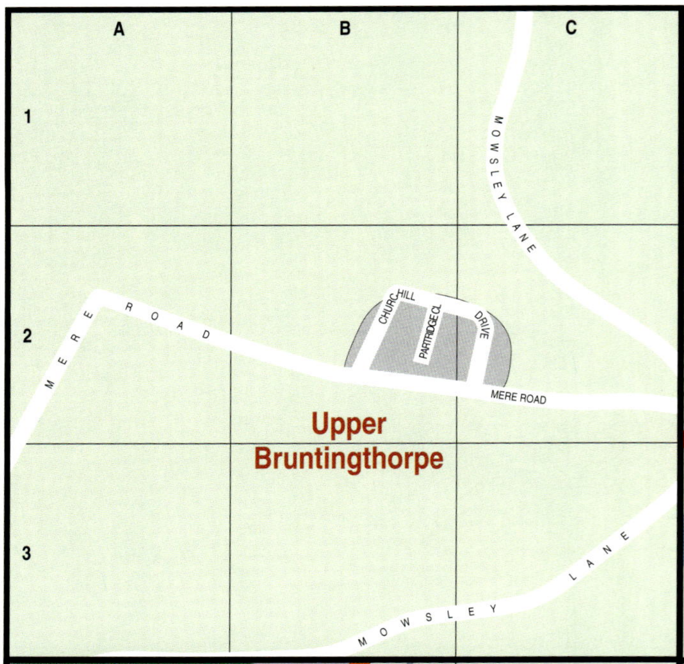
Upper Bruntingthorpe
MERE ROAD
MOWSLEY LANE
CHURCH HILL
PARTRIDGE CL
DRIVE
MOWSLEY LANE

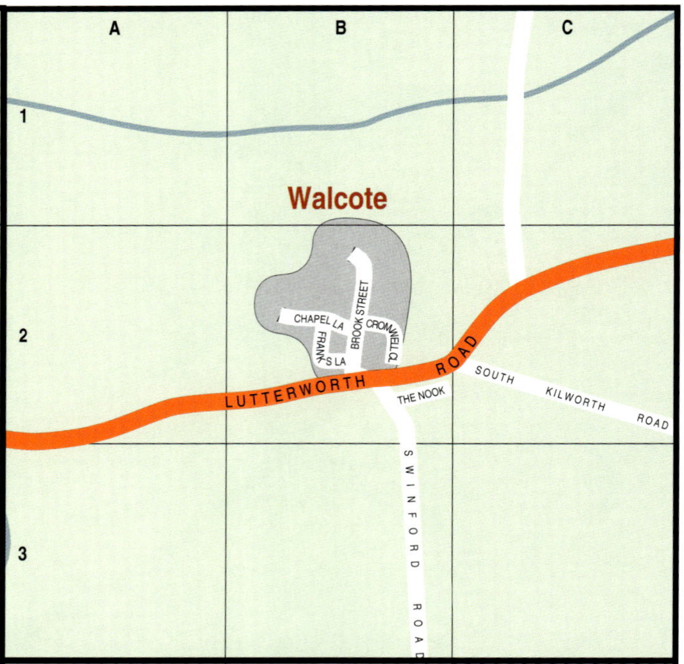
Walcote
LUTTERWORTH ROAD
SOUTH KILWORTH ROAD
SWINFORD ROAD
THE NOOK
CHAPEL LA
BROOK STREET
CROMWELL CL

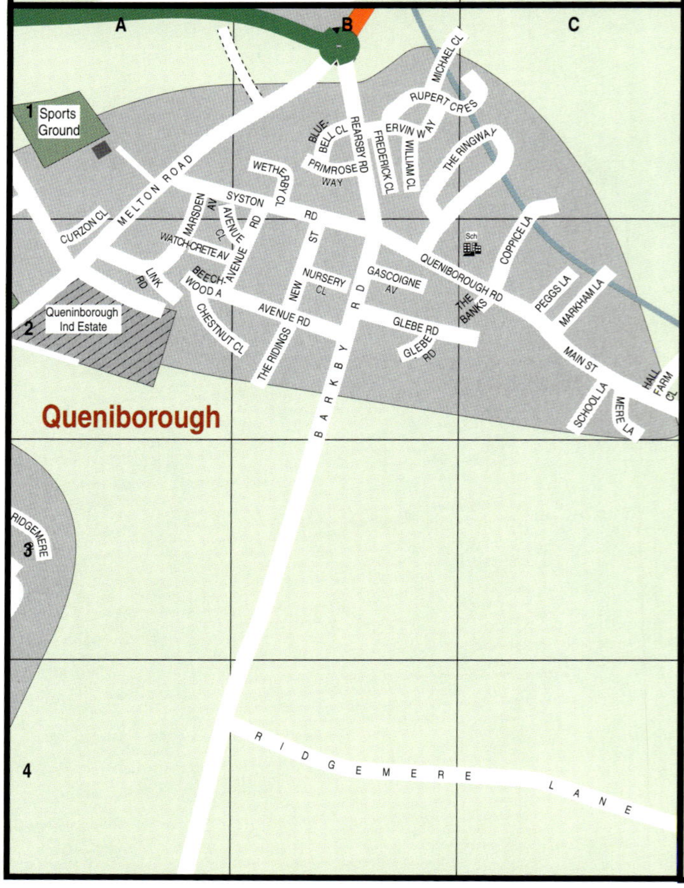
Queniborough
Sports Ground
Queniborough Ind Estate
MELTON ROAD
BARKBY RD
QUENIBOROUGH RD
SYSTON RD
THE RINGWAY
RUPERT CRES
MICHAEL CL
ERVIN WAY
WILLIAM CL
FREDERICK CL
REARSBY RD
PRIMROSE WAY
BLUE BELL CL
WETHERBY CL
CURZON CL
MARSDEN AV
WATCHCRETE AV
LINK RD
BEECHWOOD A
CHESTNUT CL
AVENUE RD
THE RIDINGS
NEW ST
NURSERY CL
GASCOIGNE AV
GLEBE RD
THE BANKS
COPPICE LA
PEGGS LA
MARKHAM LA
MAIN ST
SCHOOL LA
MERE LA
HALL FARM CL
RIDGEMERE LANE

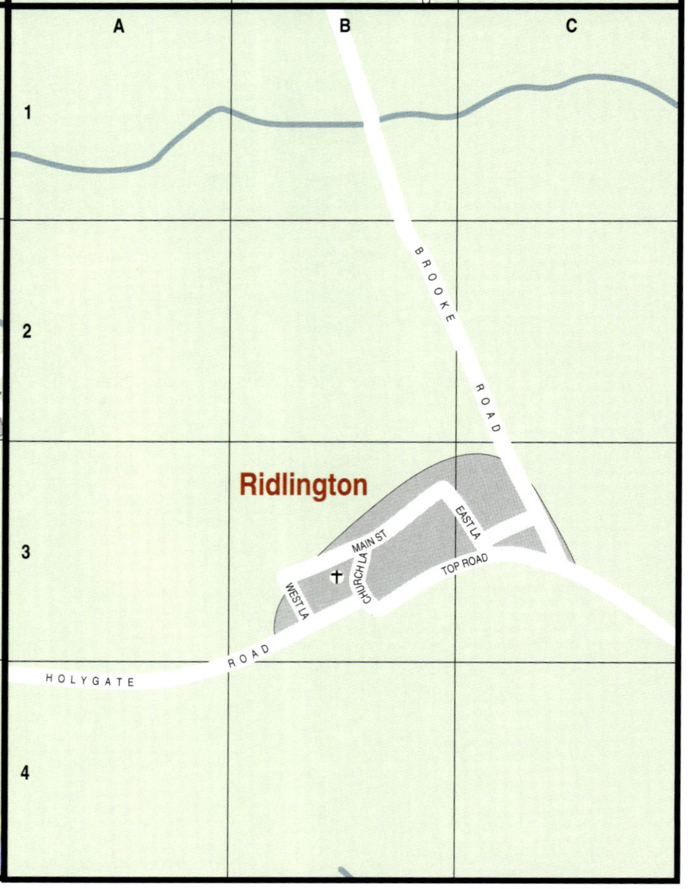
Ridlington
BROOKE ROAD
HOLYGATE ROAD
TOP ROAD
EAST LA
MAIN ST
CHURCH LA
WEST LA

LEICESTER SCRAP PROCESSORS & SUPPLIERS LTD
CASH OR ACCOUNT CUSTOMERS WELCOME
Ferrous and Non Ferrous Metal Merchants
Waste Collection Service • Manpower Services • Site Clearance
Machinery - Removal and Installation • Crane Hire
Demolition and Factory Clearance • Second-Hand Steel Stockists - R.S.J., Channel etc.

Contact: David, Jim or Frank Berry
TEL: (0116) 278 8114
TEL/FAX: (0116) 278 8380
61–70 Harrison Close, South Wigston,
Leicester LE18 4ZL

Anne of Cleves
A fine old 14th Century house, faithfully restored,
with two Bars and a Restaurant serving
our prize winning dishes.
Well kept cask conditioned ales (Camra Guide)
Large variety of wines in stock • Log fires in winter
Own large car park • Picturesque garden and patio
Children over 7 years are welcome in the Restaurant and Snug
Smoking area
We are open every lunchtime and in the evening (except Sunday evening)
12 Burton Street ~ Melton Mowbray ~ LE12 1AE
Telephone: (01664) 481336

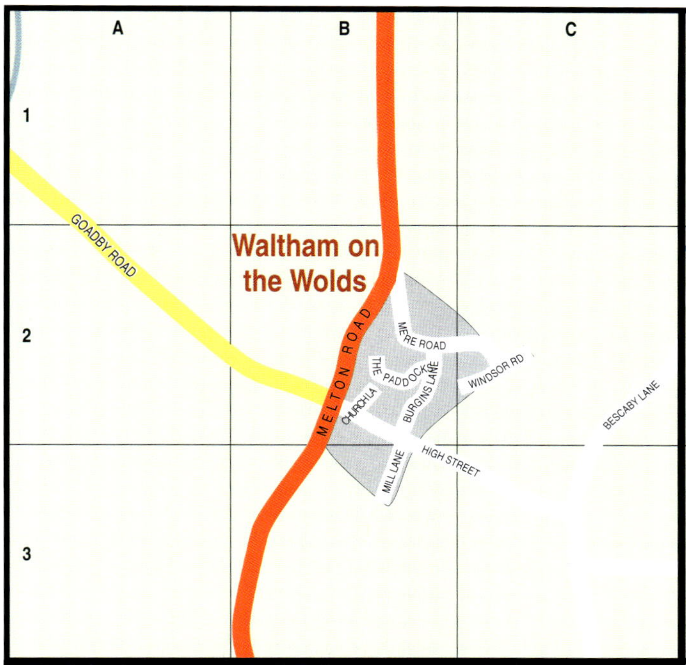

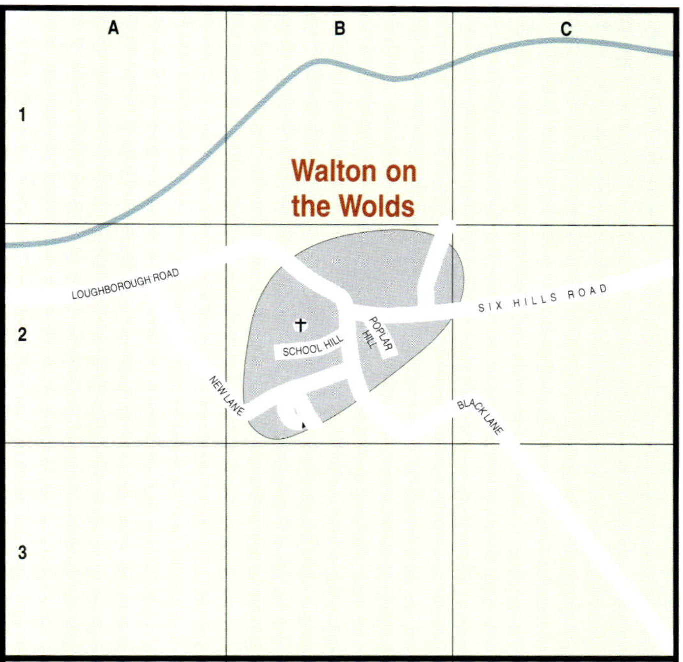

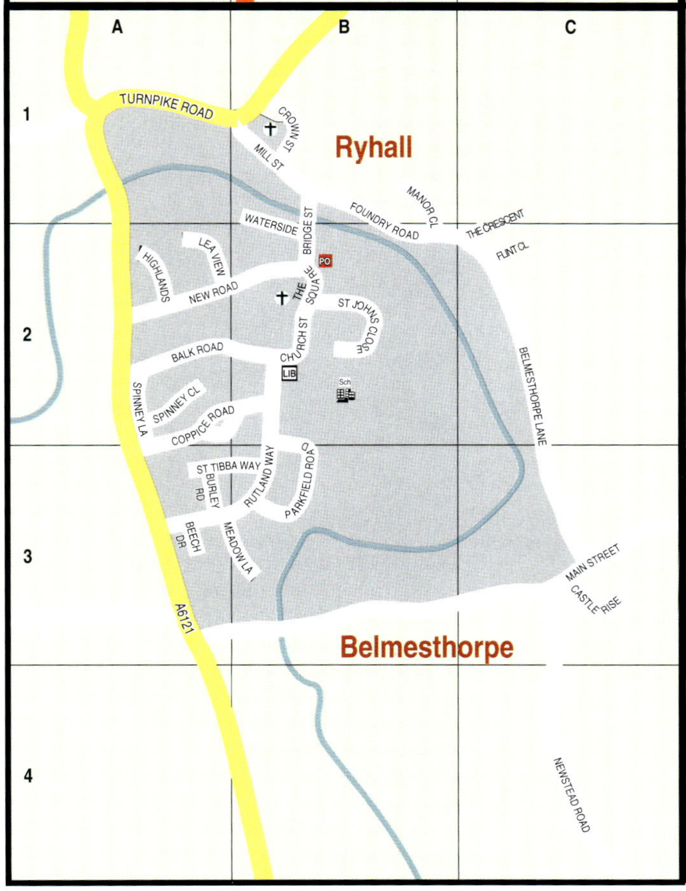

149

Waltham on the Wolds

Walton on the Wolds

Ryhall

Belmesthorpe

Seagrave

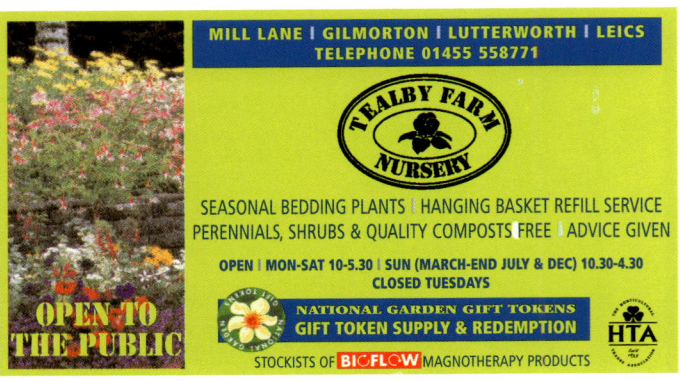

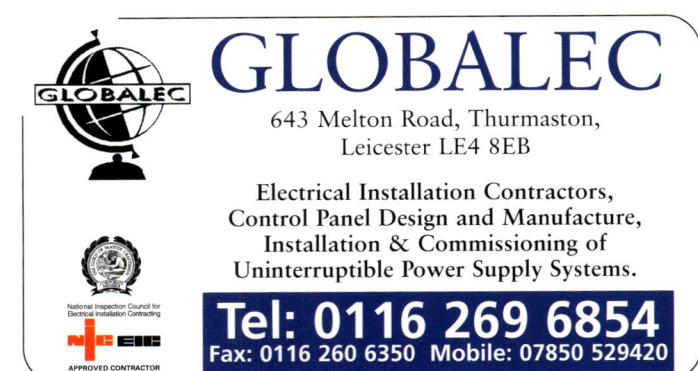

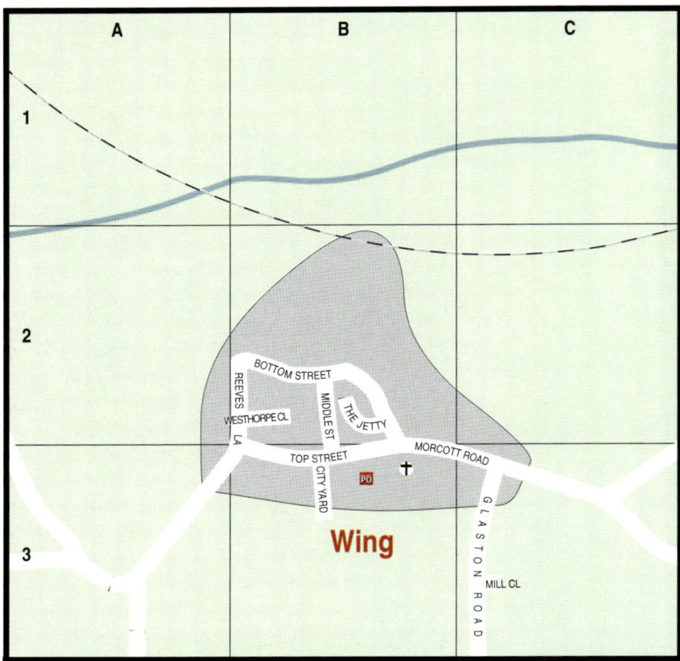
A
B
C
1
2
3
Wing
BOTTOM STREET
REEVES LA
WESTHORPE CL
MIDDLE ST
THE JETTY
TOP STREET
CITY YARD
MORCOTT ROAD
GLASTON ROAD
MILL CL
PO

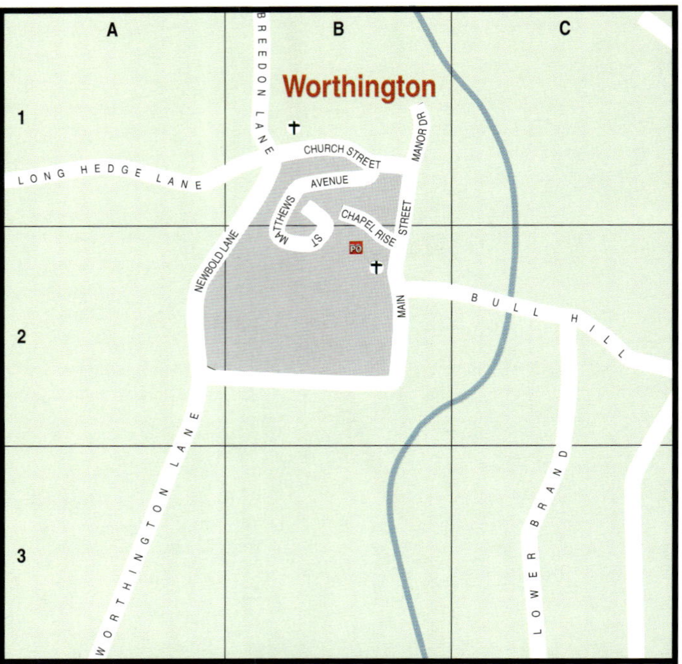
A
B
C
1
2
3
Worthington
BREEDON LANE
LONG HEDGE LANE
CHURCH STREET
MANOR DR
AVENUE
ST MATTHEWS
CHAPEL RISE
STREET
MAIN
NEWBOLD LANE
BULL HILL
WORTHINGTON LANE
LOWER BRAND
PO

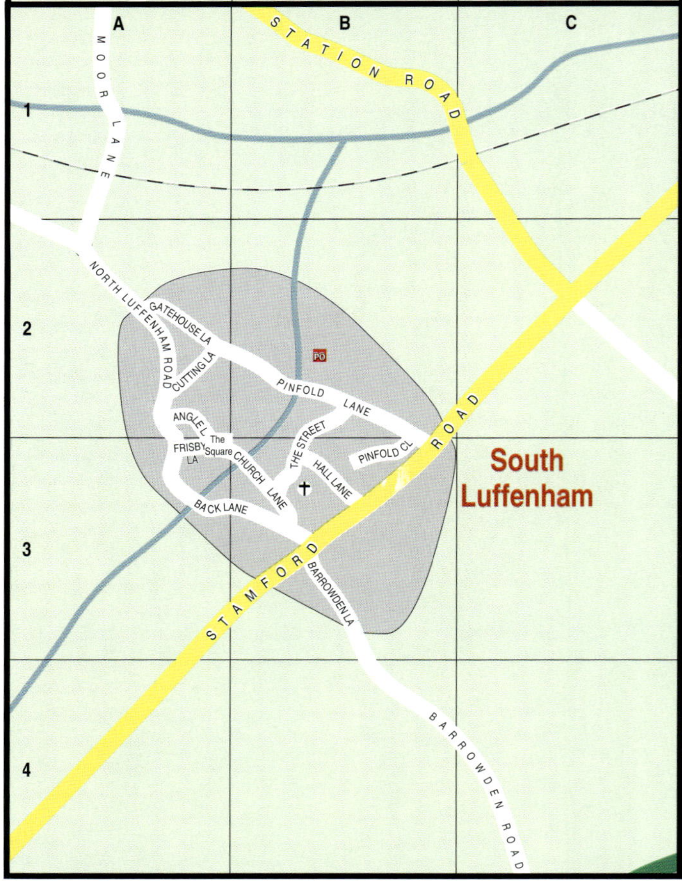
A
B
C
1
2
3
4
South Luffenham
STATION ROAD
MOOR LANE
NORTH LUFFENHAM ROAD
GATEHOUSE LA
CUTTING LA
PINFOLD LANE
ANGEL
FRISBY LA
The Square
CHURCH LANE
THE STREET
HALL LANE
PINFOLD CL
BACK LANE
ROAD
STAMFORD ROAD
BARROWDEN LA
BARROWDEN ROAD
PO

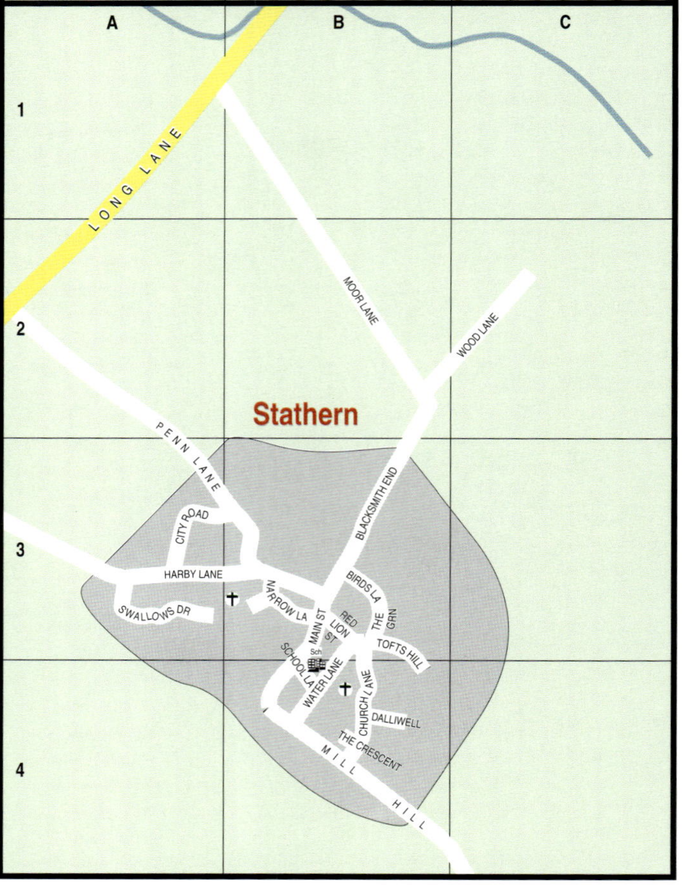
A
B
C
1
2
3
4
Stathern
LONG LANE
MOOR LANE
WOOD LANE
PENN LANE
CITY ROAD
HARBY LANE
SWALLOWS DR
NARROW LA
MAIN ST
RED LION ST
BIRDS LA
THE GRN
TOFTS HILL
BLACKSMITH END
SCHOOL LA
WATER LANE
CHURCH LANE
DALLIWELL
THE CRESCENT
MILL HILL
Sch

Maps: Tilton on the Hill, Somerby, Woodhouse Eaves, Whissendine

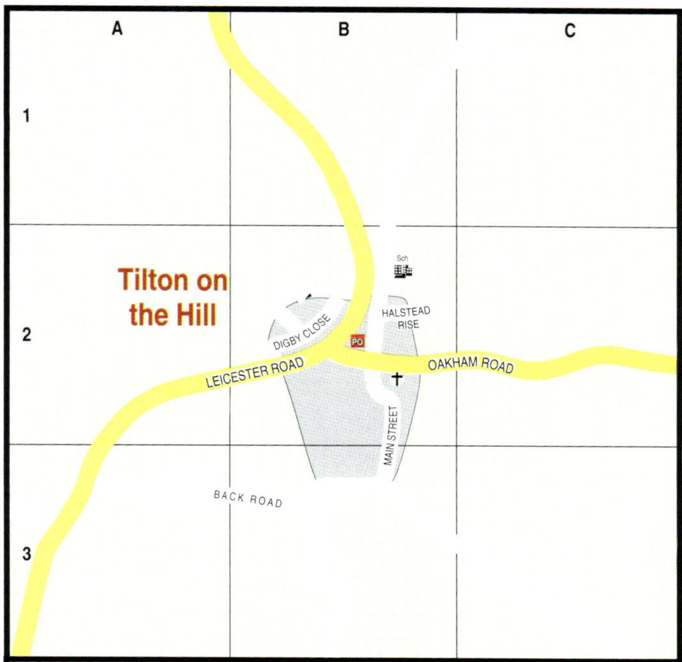

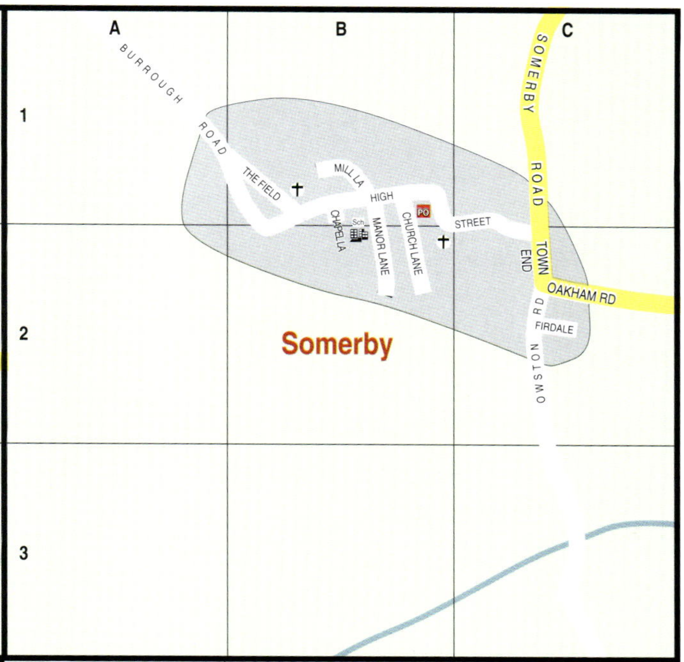

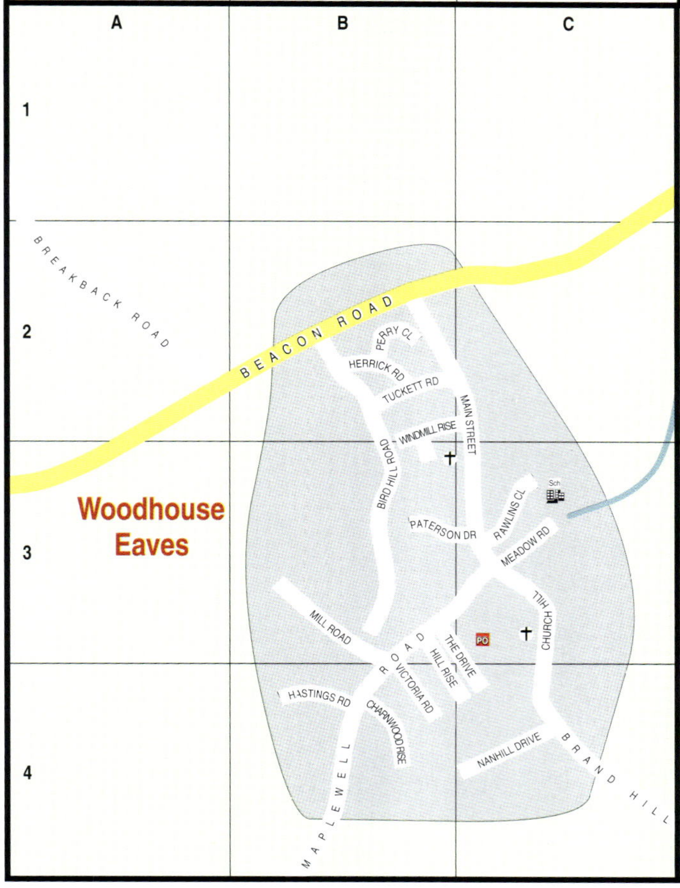

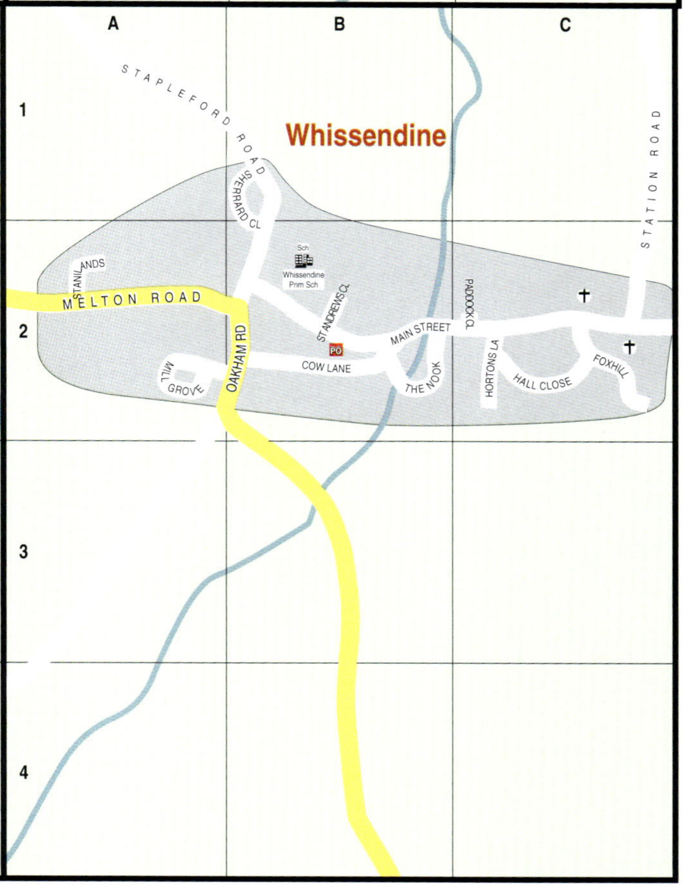

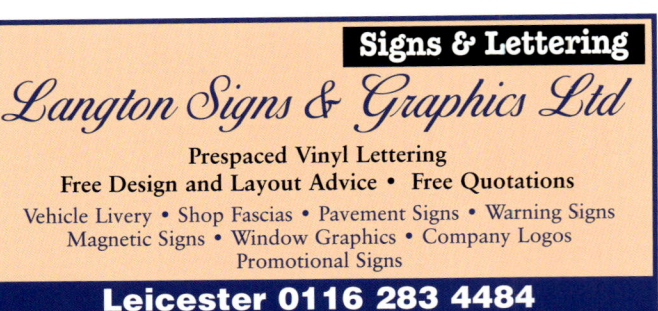

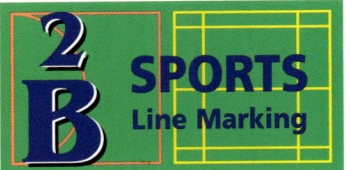

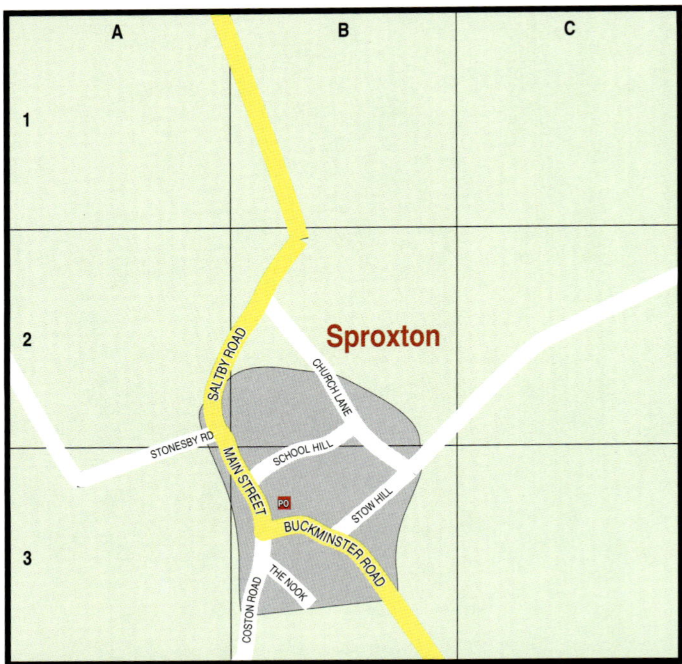
A
B
C
1
2
3
Sproxton
SALTBY ROAD
CHURCH LANE
STONESBY RD
SCHOOL HILL
MAIN STREET
PO
STOW HILL
BUCKMINSTER ROAD
COSTON ROAD
THE NOOK

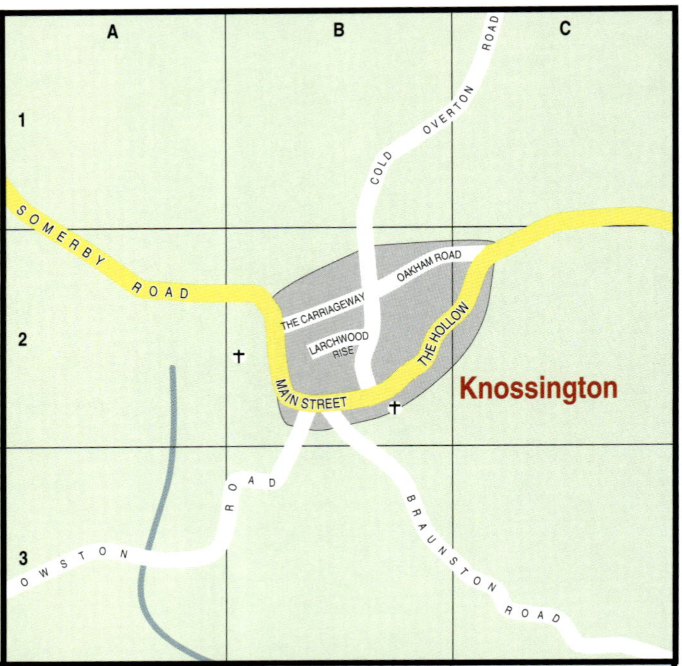
A
B
C
1
2
3
SOMERBY ROAD
COLD OVERTON ROAD
OAKHAM ROAD
THE CARRIAGEWAY
LARCHWOOD RISE
THE HOLLOW
MAIN STREET
Knossington
OWSTON ROAD
BRAUNSTON ROAD

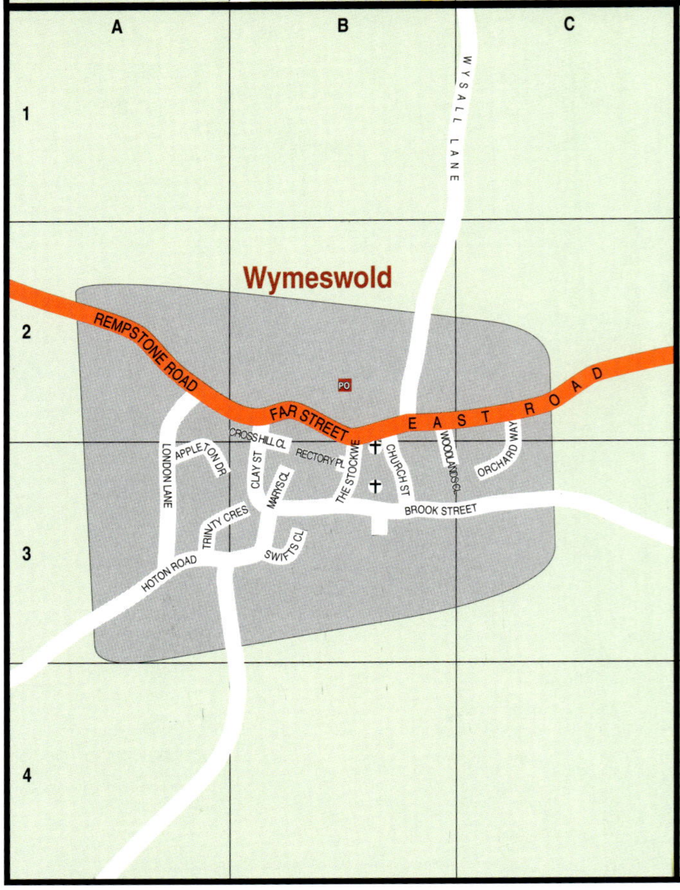
A
B
C
1
2
3
4
WYSALL LANE
Wymeswold
REMPSTONE ROAD
PO
FAR STREET
EAST ROAD
CROSS HILL CL
RECTORY PL
THE STOCKWELL
CHURCH ST
WOODLANDS CL
ORCHARD WAY
LONDON LANE
APPLETON DR
CLAY ST
MARYS CL
BROOK STREET
TRINITY CRES
SWIFTS CL
HOTON ROAD

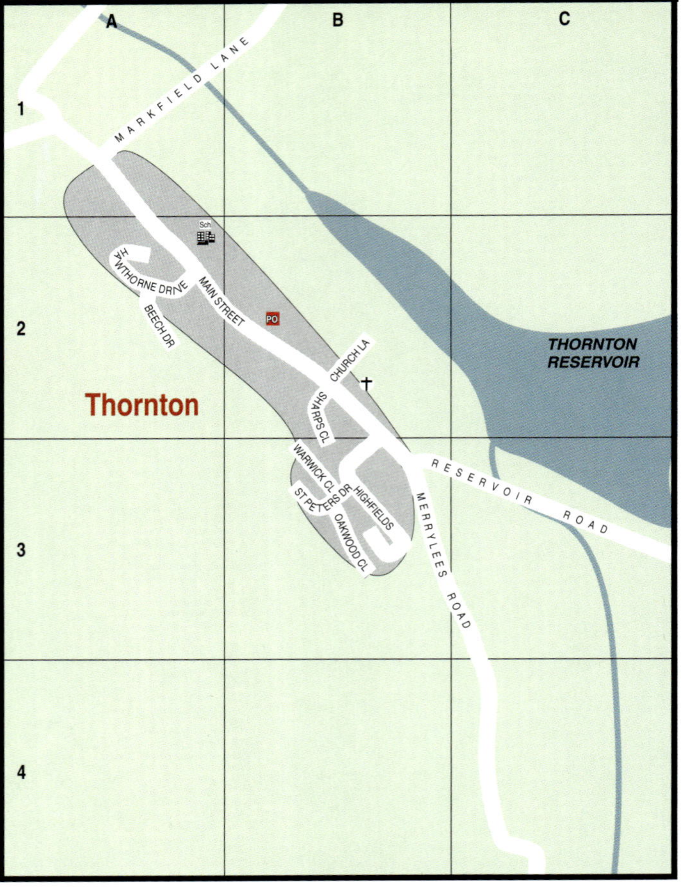
A
B
C
1
2
3
4
MARKFIELD LANE
Sch
HAWTHORNE DRIVE
BEECH DR
MAIN STREET
PO
CHURCH LA
Thornton
SHARPS CL
WARWICK CL
ST PETERS DR
HIGHFIELDS
OAKWOOD CL
MERRYLEES ROAD
RESERVOIR ROAD
THORNTON RESERVOIR

CROWFOOTS CARRIERS LTD

THE MIDLANDS LEADING EXPRESS PARCELS SERVICE IS NOW IN LANCASHIRE AND YORKSHIRE

Established 1912

VOLUME CONTRACT AT VERY COMPETITIVE RATES
- NO premium charge for express service • NO weight restrictions
- FULLY computerised distribution • IMMEDIATE communication with drivers

Mill Street Industrial Estate, Barwell, Leicester, LE9 8EY.
Tel: 01455 842911 Fax: 01455 841647 Email: phil@crowfoots.co.uk

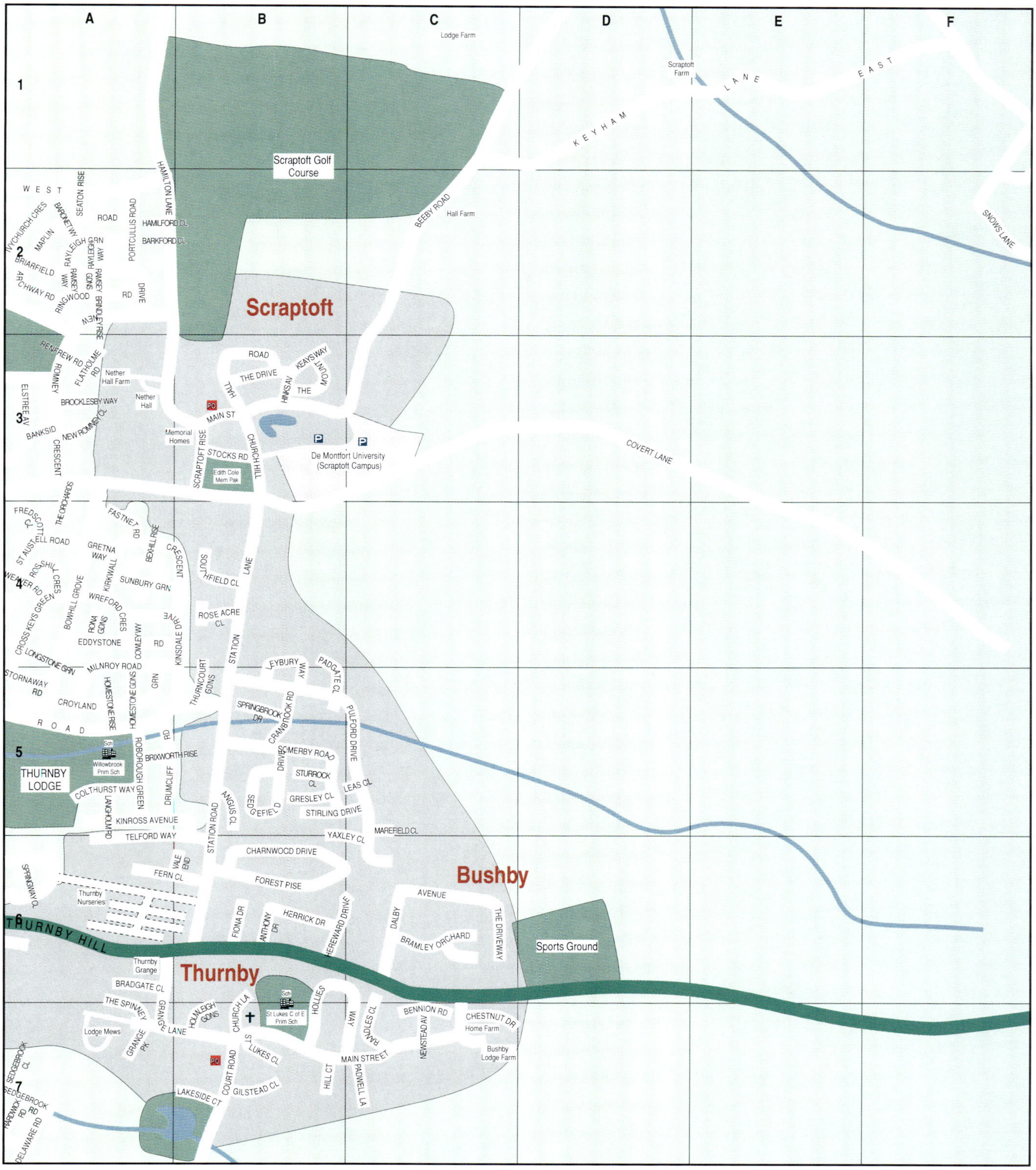

153

STREET INDEX - SECTION ONE

HOW TO USE THIS STREET INDEX:

Streets are listed alphabetically throughout this section. Against each street name there are two references; the first relates to the map number upon which the street appears (NOT the page number); the second reference relates to the grid square in which the street can be found.

For example: [ABBEY COURT ROAD 39 B6] will be found on map 39, grid square B6.

Street	Map	Grid
ABBEY COURT	39	B7
ABBEY COURT ROAD	39	B6
ABBEY GATE	43	A2
ABBEY LANE	39	B7
ABBEY MEADOWS	43	B1
ABBEY PARK ROAD	43	B1
ABBEY PARK STREET	43	C2
ABBEY RISE	39	B6
ABBEY ROAD		
Leicester	49	F3
Agar Nook	23	A1
ABBEY STREET		
Leicester	43	B3
Market Harborough	83	D2
ABBEYMEAD ROAD	39	B6
ABBOTS CLOSE	44	D2
ABBOTS ROAD	44	D2
ABBOTSFORD ROAD	44	B3
ABER ROAD	47	F1
ABERDALE ROAD	47	D5
ABINGDON ROAD	43	E6
ABNEY STREET	43	E6
ACACIA AVENUE	39	D1
ACACIA CLOSE	45	B1
ACAN WAY	49	C5
ACER CLOSE		
Leicester	38	C5
Leicester	49	C4
ACORN STREET	39	D7
ACORN WAY	52	A2
ACRES ROAD	41	C7
ACRESFORD ROAD		
Donisthorpe	20	C4
Overseal	20	B3
Netherseal	20	B5
ADCOCK ROAD	42	D3
ADDERLEY ROAD	47	D2
ADLINGTON ROAD	48	E5
AGAR STREET	43	D1
AIKMAN AVENUE	42	C2
AIKMAN CLOSE	42	C3
AINSDALE ROAD	42	D5
AINTREE CLOSE	44	F6
AINTREE CRESCENT	48	B5
AISNE ROAD	51	A1
ALAN CLOSE	39	D5
ALAN MOSS ROAD	13	A4
ALBERT ROAD	47	E2
ALBERT STREET	75	E2
ALBION STREET		
Leicester	38	A3
Leicester	43	B5
Leicester	48	C6
Leicester	51	B2
ALCESTER DRIVE	44	F6
ALDEBY CLOSE		
Leicester	46	D7
Leicester	50	A1
ALDER CLOSE	45	B1
ALDERLEIGH ROAD	51	E3
ALDERSTONE CLOSE	51	E4
ALDERTON CLOSE	39	D4
ALDGATE AVENUE	44	C1
ALEXANDER AVENUE	49	A4
ALEXANDER STREET	43	F2
ALEXANDRA ROAD	47	
ALEXANDRA STREET		
Leicester	40	A1
Leicester	49	E4
ALFRETON ROAD	47	A4
ALL SAINTS ROAD	43	A2
ALLANDALE ROAD	48	A2
ALLENWOOD ROAD	47	B4
ALLEXTON FIELD ROAD	67	
ALLEXTON GARDENS	41	F3
ALLEXTON ROAD	66	D6
ALLIANCE ROAD	41	E2
ALLINGTON DRIVE	39	D1
ALLINGTON STREET	43	D2
ALLINSON CLOSE	44	D4
ALLOWAY CLOSE	39	F5
ALMA STREET	42	E3
ALMEYS LANE	63	B5
ALMOND ROAD	43	B7
ALPORT WAY	52	A2
ALTAR STONES LANE	23	C6
ALTHORPE CLOSE	46	E6
ALTON HILL	21	E2
ALTON ROAD	47	A5
ALVASTON ROAD	46	D2
ALVECOTE ROAD	46	F6
ALYSSUM WAY	49	C3
AMADIS ROAD	38	C5
AMANDA ROAD	46	D7
AMBASSADOR ROAD	44	C4
AMBERGATE DRIVE	39	F5
AMBERLEY CLOSE	40	A3
AMBION LANE	62	A3
AMBLER CLOSE	51	F3
AMBLESIDE CLOSE	50	E1
AMBLESIDE DRIVE	50	F1
AMBLESIDE WAY	50	E1
AMBROSE CLOSE	42	D4

Street	Map	Grid
AMESBURY ROAD	51	E4
AMHURST CLOSE	42	B1
AMOS ROAD	41	F4
AMY STREET	46	D3
AMYSON ROAD	44	E4
ANCHOR LANE	11	B7
ANCHOR STREET	39	B7
ANDOVER STREET	43	D5
ANDREW ROAD	38	A2
ANDREWES CLOSE	42	F5
ANDREWES STREET	42	F5
ANDREWS LANE	76	E1
ANEFORD ROAD	44	A1
ANGELA DRIVE	44	D6
ANGLESEY ROAD	51	B1
ANKLE HILL	16	F6
ANN STREET	43	C4
ANNS WAY	48	E6
ANNWELL LANE	10	A6
ANSTEY LANE		
Leicester	37	D5
Leicester	37	C6
Leicester	38	B5
Leicester	38	D7
ANTHONY ROAD	42	F1
APOLLO CLOSE	43	D5
APOLLO COURT	43	D5
APPLEBY CLOSE	41	E4
APPLEBY HILL	33	B3
APPLEBY ROAD		
Leicester	40	C2
Snarestone	33	F1
APPLEGATE	43	A5
APPLETON AVENUE	38	F5
AQUEDUCT ROAD	11	A7
AQUITAINE CLOSE	49	C1
ARBOR ROAD	72	F1
ARBOUR ROAD	39	D7
ARCHDEACON LANE	43	B3
ARCHER CLOSE	40	A5
ARCHERS LANE	63	A2
ARDATH ROAD	43	E1
ARDEN AVENUE	46	B2
ARDERN TERRACE	46	D1
ARMADALE DRIVE	44	F2
ARMADALE GREEN	44	E2
ARMSON AVENUE	41	A5
ARNCLIFFE ROAD	44	E2
ARNDALE	52	B3
ARNESBY CRESCENT	47	B6
ARNESBY LANE	74	C4
ARNESBY ROAD	75	A4
ARNHEM STREET	43	C5
ARNOLD AVENUE	51	C3
ARRAN ROAD	39	F5
ARRETON CLOSE	47	E4
ARUM WAY	41	F4
ARUNDEL STREET	42	E5
ASCOT ROAD	39	D7
ASFORDBY ROAD		
Hoby	15	D7
Melton Mowbray	16	D5
ASFORDBY STREET	43	F4
ASH COURT	37	A7
ASH GROVE	50	D4
ASH STREET	43	E2
ASH TREE CLOSE	48	D7
ASH TREE ROAD	48	E7
ASHA MARGH	39	C7
ASHBOURNE ROAD	47	E7
ASHBOURNE STREET	43	E5
ASHBURTON ROAD	22	C5
ASHBY LANE	80	A2
ASHBY ROAD		
Ashby-De-La-Zouch	9	E5
Barwell	62	D7
Belton	11	D4
Breedon On The Hill	11	A2
Coalville	22	B3
Diseworth	4	E6
Donisthorpe	20	E3
Gilmorton	80	E1
Ibstock	22	A7
Kegworth	5	B5
Loughborough	13	A5
Markfield	23	C7
Measham	21	A4
Moira	20	E1
Normanton le Heath	21	D4
Packington	21	C2
Ravenstone	22	A4
Shepshed	12	C6
Stapleton	62	D4
Thringstone	11	D6
Twycross	33	F4
Ullesthorpe	79	F2
ASHBY ROAD CENTRAL	12	B6
ASHCLOSE AVENUE	47	E4
ASHDOWN AVENUE	42	F7
ASHDOWN ROAD	47	F4
ASHFIELD DRIVE	37	F4
ASHFIELD ROAD		
Leicester	40	D4

Street	Map	Grid
Leicester	43	F7
ASHFORD ROAD	47	C2
ASHINGTON CLOSE	42	D2
ASHLANDS ROAD	65	B3
ASHLANDS WAY	49	C3
ASHLEIGH ROAD		
Leicester	41	E2
Leicester	42	E6
ASHLEY ROAD		
Medbourne	77	D4
Middleton	78	A5
Weston by Welland	77	C5
ASHLYNS RISE	42	A5
ASHOVER ROAD	43	F6
ASHTHORPE ROAD	42	D7
ASHTON CLOSE		
Leicester	51	E3
Leicester	52	D1
ASHTREE WALK	40	E7
ASHURST CLOSE	52	A4
ASHURST ROAD	46	B3
ASHVILLE WAY	50	B7
ASHWELL ROAD		
Cottesmore	30	B4
Langham	29	B5
Whissendine	29	C5
ASHWELL STREET	43	C6
ASKRIGG WAY	52	A2
ASPLIN ROAD	47	A5
ASQUITH BOULEVARD	47	D6
ASQUITH WAY	47	D6
ASTILL DRIVE	39	B4
ASTILL LODGE ROAD	38	C3
ASTLEY CLOSE	42	D7
ASTON HILL	47	C3
ASTON LANE	72	B4
ATHERSTONE CLOSE	48	F6
ATHERSTONE ROAD		
Fenny Drayton	61	B6
Measham	20	F6
Norton Juxta Twycross	33	D3
Pinwall	60	C4
Ratcliffe Culey	60	E4
ATKINS STREET	43	B6
ATKINSON STREET	43	F4
ATLAS CLOSE	43	D5
ATTERTON ROAD	61	A5
ATTFIELD DRIVE	50	B5
ATTLEBOROUGH ROAD	70	C5
ATTINGHAM CLOSE	43	F1
AUBURN ROAD	50	D4
AUDEN CLOSE	38	D7
AUDIT HALL ROAD	58	B2
AUDLEY END	46	D2
AUGUSTA CLOSE	41	E4
AUGUSTINE ROAD	42	F5
AUSTIN RISE	44	F2
AUSTREY LANE		
No Man's Heath	33	A2
Orton-on-the-Hill	33	C6
AUSTREY ROAD	33	C2
AUSTWICK CLOSE	38	E6
AVEBURY ROAD	42	E1
AVENUE GARDENS	47	E2
AVENUE ROAD		
Leicester	47	E2
Nuneaton	70	C6
AVENUE ROAD EXTENSION	47	D2
AVERIL ROAD	44	D3
AVERY HILL	41	F6
AVOCA CLOSE	44	D4
AVON CLOSE	48	E6
AVON DRIVE	50	B5
AVON ROAD	46	A1
AVON STREET	43	D6
AVONSIDE DRIVE	44	B5
AXBRIDGE CLOSE	42	F1
AYLESHAM COURT	41	A7
AYLESTONE DRIVE	46	F6
AYLESTONE LANE		
Leicester	47	C7
Leicester	51	D1
AYLESTONE ROAD		
Leicester	43	B1
Leicester	47	A2
AYLESTONE WALK	43	B7
AYLMER ROAD	42	C6
AYSGARTH ROAD	38	E6
AYSTON ROAD		
Leicester	46	C2
Uppingham	67	E3

Street	Map	Grid
BABELAKE STREET	21	B4
BABINGDON ROW	47	C6
BABINGLEY DRIVE	38	F7
BACK LANE		
Belton In Rutland	66	F2
Harston	3	C7
Long Clawson	6	C4
Morcott	68	E3
Sileby	25	C4

Street	Map	Grid
South Luffenham	68	F2
BACK ROAD		
Barrowden	69	A3
Tilton On The Hill	54	D5
BACK STREET		
Gaulby	64	F3
Saltby	8	D7
BADDELY DRIVE	47	D7
BADEN ROAD	44	A7
BADGER CLOSE	49	C5
BADGER DRIVE	50	B7
BADGERS CLOSE	38	D6
BADGERS HOLT	48	C7
BADMINTON ROAD	39	F4
BAGGRAVE ROAD	53	E3
BAGGRAVE STREET	43	F4
BAGWORTH LANE	35	F2
BAGWORTH ROAD		
Barlestone	35	D4
Nailstone	35	C3
Newbold Verdon	35	E5
BAINBRIDGE ROAD		
Leicester	46	D2
Leicester	52	A3
BAINES LANE	41	D7
BAKERS LANE		
Redmile	2	D3
Thorpe Satchville	27	E6
BAKEWELL ROAD	47	E7
BAKEWELL STREET	43	E4
BALCOMBE AVENUE	42	D4
BALDERSTONE CLOSE	44	C4
BALDWIN AVENUE	51	C3
BALDWIN ROAD	47	D6
BALE ROAD	44	A1
BALFOUR STREET	42	F3
BALISFIRE GROVE	38	D6
BALLADINE ROAD	38	A2
BALLARDS CLOSE	38	D6
BALLATER CLOSE	44	F7
BALMORAL CLOSE	47	E4
BALMORAL DRIVE	46	B1
BAMBURY LANE	73	F2
BAMPTON CLOSE	51	F4
BANDALLS LANE	13	E4
BANKART AVENUE	48	A2
BANKS ROAD	46	F4
BANNERMAN ROAD	44	A6
BANTLAM LANE	49	D1
BARBARA AVENUE		
Leicester	41	A7
Leicester	44	D3
BARBARA CLOSE	41	E2
BARBARA ROAD	46	E2
BARCLAY STREET	42	E6
BARDOLPH STREET	43	D2
BARDON ROAD	22	E4
BARFOOT ROAD	47	B6
BARFORD CLOSE	51	E4
BARGE CLOSE	51	C3
BARKBY HOLT LANE	53	A1
BARKBY LANE	25	E7
BARKBY ROAD		
Beeby	53	B2
Leicester	40	A6
Queniborough	26	A6
Syston	25	F6
BARKBY THORPE LANE	40	D1
BARKER STREET	43	F3
BARLESTONE ROAD		
Bagworth	35	E3
Newbold Verdon	35	E6
BARLEY CLOSE	41	E2
BARLEY LEAS	53	E4
BARLEYTHORPE ROAD	56	D1
BARMOUTH AVENUE	47	C5
BARN CLOSE	52	A4
BARNARD CLOSE	43	D5
BARNES CLOSE	40	A4
BARNES HEATH ROAD	44	C5
BARNET CLOSE	52	C1
BARNFIELD CLOSE	12	B1
BARNGATE CLOSE	39	B1
BARNSDALE ROAD	38	C3
BARNSTAPLE CLOSE	51	F4
BARNSTAPLE ROAD	44	F7
BARNWELL AVENUE	39	B5
BARR LANE	70	E1
BARRATT CLOSE	47	F1
BARRINGTON ROAD	48	A2
BARROW CLOSE	52	B3
BARROW LANE	41	D1
BARROW ROAD		
Barrow Upon Soar	25	B1
Burton On The Wolds	14	A4
Cotes	13	D4
Quorn	13	E7
BARROWDEN LANE	69	A2
BARROWDEN ROAD		
Ketton	58	D7
South Luffenham	69	A2
BARRY CLOSE	41	A7
BARRY DRIVE	41	A7

~178~

BARRY ROAD 44 F1
BARSTON STREET 43 B3
BARTHOLOMEW STREET 43 E6
BARTON CLOSE 51 E3
BARTON LANE
- Congerstone 34 D5
- Nailstone 35 A4
BARTON ROAD
- Barlestone 35 C5
- Carlton 35 A6
- Leicester 42 E2
- Market Bosworth 35 A6
- Odstone 34 F3
BARWELL LANE 62 F3
BASIN BRIDGE LANE 61 E7
BASLOW ROAD 43 F6
BASSETT STREET
- Leicester 42 F3
- Leicester 51 B3
BATEMAN ROAD 42 D3
BATH LANE
- Bruntingthorpe 74 C7
- Leicester 43 A5
- Moira 20 C2
BATH STREET
- Ashby-De-La-Zouch 21 B1
- Leicester 39 C5
BATHURST ROAD 44 F6
BATTEN STREET 47 A2
BATTENBERG ROAD 42 F4
BATTERSBEE ROAD 42 A2
BATTERSBEE WAY 42 A2
BATTRAM ROAD 35 C1
BAULK ROAD 68 A4
BAXTERS CLOSE 38 D6
BAY STREET 43 B3
BAYCLIFF CLOSE 42 D2
BAYHAM CLOSE 44 D5
BAYSDALE 52 B2
BAYSWATER ROAD 50 F3
BEACON AVENUE 40 B2
BEACON CLOSE
- Leicester 37 B7
- Leicester 38 C3
BEACON COURT 41 F1
BEACON ROAD 23 F3
BEACONSFIELD ROAD 42 E6
BEADSWELL LANE 64 D6
BEAL STREET 43 D4
BEATRICE ROAD 42 E3
BEATTY AVENUE 44 A3
BEATTY ROAD 44 A3
BEAUFORT CLOSE 48 F7
BEAUFORT ROAD 46 C2
BEAUFORT WAY 48 F7
BEAUMANOR GARDENS 24 C2
BEAUMANOR ROAD 39 B6
BEAUMONT GREEN
- Coleorton 11 A7
- Leicester 37 B7
BEAUMONT LEYS LANE 38 F2
BEAUMONT LODGE ROAD 38 D3
BEAUMONT ROAD
- Leicester 43 E4
- Nuneaton 70 B5
BEAUMONT STREET 48 C5
BEAUMONT WAY 38 D5
BEAUVILLE DRIVE 38 D6
BEAVER CLOSE 50 B7
BECK CLOSE 50 C1
BECKETT ROAD 44 A2
BECKINGHAM ROAD 43 E7
BEDALE DRIVE 38 F4
BEDE STREET 42 F5
BEDFORD DRIVE 37 B7
BEDFORD ROAD 51 C1
BEDFORD STREET 43 B4
BEDFORD STREET NORTH 43 C3
BEEBY ROAD
- Barkby 53 A1
- Leicester 43 F4
- Scraptoft 53 B4
BEECH AVENUE 41 A1
BEECH CROFT ROAD 47 E2
BEECH DRIVE
- Blackfordby 9 E5
- Leicester 41 F7
BEECH ROAD
- Leicester 48 C6
- Leicester 50 D5
BEECH STREET 43 E3
BEECHCROFT AVENUE 46 C2
BEECHFIELD AVENUE 39 C2
BEECHWOOD AVENUE
- Leicester 40 A3
- Leicester 41 C6
BEECHWOOD CLOSE 44 E5
BEECHWOOD ROAD 49 D6
BEGGARS LANE 45 B4
BEGONIA CLOSE 45 B1
BELCHERS HILL 67 A7
BELER WAY 16 D7
BELFRY DRIVE 41 F5
BELGRAVE AVENUE 39 C6
BELGRAVE BOULEVARD
- Leicester 38 F4
- Leicester 39 A5
BELGRAVE GATE 43 B4
BELGRAVE ROAD 43 C1
BELL LANE
- Husbands Bosworth 82 A5
- Leicester 43 D4
- Leicester 49 E5
BELL STREET 51 F1
BELLAMY CLOSE 50 C1
BELLE VUE AVENUE 39 A7
BELLEVILLE DRIVE 48 E5
BELLFLOWER ROAD 40 D6
BELLHOLME CLOSE 39 D6
BELMONT STREET 46 F4
BELPER CLOSE
- Leicester 51 C4
- Leicester 52 C1
BELPER STREET 43 D1
BELTON CLOSE 47 B6
BELTON ROAD
- Leicester 46 C2
- Loddington 66 D1
- Loughborough 13 B4
BELTON STREET 12 B5
BELVOIR AVENUE 16 C1
BELVOIR CLOSE 48 E7
BELVOIR DRIVE 46 F5
BELVOIR DRIVE EAST 46 F5
BELVOIR ROAD
- Bottesford 1 C7
- Denton 3 D5
- Ravenstone 22 C3
- Redmile 2 E3
BELVOIR STREET 43 B5
BEMAN CLOSE 40 A4
BEMBRIDGE CLOSE 42 F2
BEMBRIDGE ROAD 42 F2
BENCROFT CLOSE 37 F3
BENDBOW 41 F7
BENDBOW RISE 42 A7
BENNETT RISE 49 A4
BENNETT WAY 51 C2
BENNETTS LANE 25 C4
BENNION ROAD 38 D3
BENSCLIFFE GARDENS 50 F1
BENSCLIFFE ROAD 23 F5
BENSKINS OVAL 38 F2
BENSON STREET 44 A5
BENTINGHOUSE ROAD 46 F7
BENTLEY ROAD 39 C1
BERESFORD DRIVE 47 F3
BERKELEY CLOSE 48 F6
BERKLEY STREET 43 A3
BERKSHIRE ROAD 46 F4
BERNERS STREET 43 D5
BERRIDGE DRIVE 48 D7
BERRIDGE LANE 39 D6
BERRIDGES LANE 82 A5
BERRINGTON CLOSE 44 A2
BERRY AVENUE 11 B1
BERRY ROAD 78 C6
BERRYCOTT LANE 14 E6
BESCABY LANE 7 E6
BEST CLOSE 51 B3
BEVAN ROAD 38 E1
BEVERIDGE LANE 22 D6
BEVERLEY AVENUE 43 D1
BEVERLEY CLOSE 40 A2
BEWCASTLE GROVE 38 F4
BEWICKE ROAD 46 D1
BIAM WAY 46 C3
BIDDLE ROAD
- Leicester 42 D3
- Leicester 49 E6
BIDDULPH AVENUE 43 E6
BIDDULPH STREET 43 E6
BIDEFORD CLOSE 51 F5
BIDEFORD ROAD 44 F7
BIDFORD CLOSE 46 A1
BIDFORD ROAD 46 A1
BIDWELL LANE 31 C2
BIG LANE 14 C6
BIGGIN HILL ROAD 44 D7
BIGGS CLOSE 50 C7
BIGNAL DRIVE 41 D6
BILBERRY CLOSE 46 C5
BILLINGTON CLOSE 39 A6
BILLINGTON ROAD 62 A7
BILSDALE ROAD 52 B2
BILSTONE ROAD 34 C5
BINGHURST GREEN 42 A3
BINGLEY ROAD 49 E6
BIRCH CLOSE 45 F1
BIRCHNALL ROAD 45 F2
BIRCHTREE ROAD 47 F7
BIRCHWOOD CLOSE 45 B1
BIRDS NEST AVENUE 42 C2
BIRKDALE AVENUE 47 F2
BIRKDALE ROAD 37 F3
BIRKENSHAW ROAD 42 C1
BIRSMORE AVENUE 39 F5
BIRSTALL ROAD 39 D4
BIRSTALL STREET 43 D3
BIRSTOW CRESCENT 38 F4
BISHOP STREET 43 B5
BISHOPDALE ROAD 38 E6
BISHOPS CLEEVE 33 B4
BISLEY STREET 42 F7
BITTESWELL ROAD 80 B4
BLABY BY PASS 50 C4
BLABY ROAD
- Leicester 49 E1
- Leicester 51 C3
BLACK LANE 14 B5
BLACKBERRY LANE 25 D3
BLACKBIRD AVENUE 43 A2
BLACKBIRD ROAD 42 F2
BLACKETT AVENUE 42 C2
BLACKFRIARS STREET 43 A4
BLACKMORE DRIVE 42 C5
BLACKSMITH END 2 B7
BLACKSPINNEY LANE 54 E3
BLACKTHORN DRIVE 38 C3
BLACKTHORN LANE 48 D4
BLACKTHORN ROAD 41 D2
BLACKWELL CLOSE 52 B3
BLAIRMORE ROAD 41 E4
BLAISE GROVE 43 F1
BLAKE COURT 49 C1
BLAKE STREET 43 B4
BLAKENHALL CLOSE 49 B5
BLAKENHALL ROAD 44 C5
BLAKESLEY ROAD 52 B1
BLAND ROAD 42 B1
BLANKLE DRIVE 47 F2
BLANKLYN AVENUE 43 F5
BLASTON HILL 77 E1
BLASTON ROAD 77 C2
BLAYDON CLOSE 42 D2
BLENHEIM CLOSE 51 B3
BLENHEIM ROAD 39 D1
BLENHEIM WAY 39 A5
BLISSETT ROAD 42 D3
BLOOMFIELD ROAD 47 B4
BLOUNT ROAD 40 B3
BLOXHAM ROAD 42 D3
BLOXOMS CLOSE 46 B5
BLUE BANKS AVENUE 50 C1
BLUE GATES ROAD 38 C4
BLUE POTS CLOSE 45 B1
BLUEBELL CLOSE 41 A4
BLUEBELL DRIVE 47 B7
BLUEBELL LANE 76 E1
BLUNDELL ROAD 44 C7
BLUNTS LANE 51 F2
BODENHAM CLOSE 51 E4
BODICOAT CLOSE 50 C7
BODMIN AVENUE 51 E4
BODNANT AVENUE 44 A7
BOLLINGTON ROAD 48 E5
BOLSOVER STREET 44 A4
BOLTON LANE 6 D2
BOLTON ROAD 42 E5
BONCHURCH STREET 42 F3
BOND LANE 24 F3
BONDGATE
- Castle Donnington 4 E4
- Nuneaton 70 C5
BONDMAN CLOSE 39 A4
BONEHAMS LANE 80 C3
BONNER CLOSE 48 F7
BONNERS LANE 43 B6
BONNEY ROAD 42 C1
BONNINGTON ROAD 47 D2
BONSALL STREET 43 E6
BONVILLE PLACE 46 D2
BOOTH CLOSE 44 D5
BOOTHORPE LANE 9 E7
BORDER DRIVE 39 A4
BORLACE STREET 42 F4
BOSTON ROAD 38 B5
BOSWELL STREET 49 C3
BOSWORTH LANE 35 D7
BOSWORTH ROAD
- Barlestone 35 C5
- Kirby Mallory 62 D2
- Market Bosworth 34 D6
- Measham 21 A6
- Sutton Cheaney 62 B2
- Theddingworth 82 B3
- Walton 81 C3
BOSWORTH STREET 42 F4
BOTCHESTON ROAD 36 C6
BOTTOM ROAD 11 B6
BOULDER LANE 47 B5
BOULTER CRESCENT 52 A1
BOULTON COURT 52a G7
BOUNDARY ROAD 46 F2
BOURNE ROAD 32 E4
BOURTON CRESCENT 48 E6
BOWBRIDGE LANE 1 B6
BOWDEN LANE 77 A4
BOWDEN ROAD 76 E5
BOWLEYS LANE 33 D1
BOWLING GREEN STREET 43 B5
BOWMANS WAY 41 D2
BOWMARS LANE 43 A3
BOYERS WALK 41 C7
BRABAZON ROAD 48 B5
BRACKEN CLOSE
- Leicester 44 D6
- Leicester 45 B1
BRACKEN HILL 37 A1
BRACKENFIELD WAY 40 C1
BRACKENTHWAITE 39 F6
BRACKLEY CLOSE 44 A1
BRADBOURNE ROAD 43 F5
BRADFIELD CLOSE 44 A5
BRADFORDS LANE 11 A7
BRADGATE AVENUE 40 B1
BRADGATE DRIVE 47 D6
BRADGATE HILL 36 E2
BRADGATE ROAD
- Cropston 24 D6
- Leicester 37 D2
BRADGATE STREET 42 F2
BRADING ROAD 42 E2
BRADLEY LANE 31 C1
BRADSHAW AVENUE 50 E1
BRADSHAW COURT 50 E1
BRADSTON ROAD 47 A6
BRAEMAR CLOSE 39 E4
BRAEMAR DRIVE 39 F5
BRAILSFORD ROAD
- Leicester 42 B5
- Leicester 47 D7
BRAMALL ROAD 44 A3
BRAMBER CLOSE 40 A3
BRAMBLE CLOSE 40 F7
BRAMBLE WAY 46 C2
BRAMBLING ROAD 43 F3
BRAMBLING WAY 48 C6
BRAMCOTE ROAD
- Leicester 46 D3
- Leicester 47 E7
BRAMLEY COURT 41 D2
BRAMLEY ROAD
- Leicester 39 D2
- Leicester 42 E4
BRAMPTON AVENUE 42 D4
BRAMPTON WAY 48 B5
BRANCASTER CLOSE 38 F7
BRAND HILL 24 B4
BRAND LANE 24 B3
BRANDON STREET 43 D2
BRANSDALE ROAD 52 B2
BRANTING HILL 37 D6
BRANTING HILL AVENUE 37 D6
BRANTING HILL GROVE 37 D6
BRASCOTE LANE 62 E1
BRAUNSTON ROAD
- Knossington 55 E2
- Oakham 56 D2
BRAUNSTONE AVENUE
- Leicester 42 D6
- Leicester 46 C1
BRAUNSTONE CLOSE 46 B2
BRAUNSTONE GATE 42 F5
BRAUNSTONE LANE
- Leicester 41 F7
- Leicester 46 D3
- Leicester 46 C2
BRAUNSTONE WAY 42 A6
BRAYBROOKE ROAD
- Leicester 44 A1
- Market Harborough 83 E3
BRAZIL STREET 43 A7
BRECON CLOSE 51 B2
BREEDON AVENUE 51 E1
BREEDON LANE
- Osgathorpe 11 C4
- Worthington 11 A4
BREEDON STREET 43 E5
BRENT KNOWLE GARDENS 44 F5
BRENTWOOD ROAD 47 C2
BRETBY ROAD 47 A5
BRETTELL ROAD 46 F7
BRETTON CLOSE 39 A6
BREWER CLOSE 40 A4
BREX RISE 41 F4
BRIAN ROAD 42 F1
BRIAR CLOSE 48 D7
BRIAR MEADS 52 D1
BRIAR ROAD 44 F3
BRIAR WALK 48 D7
BRIARGATE DRIVE 39 A1
BRICK KILN LANE 12 B6
BRICKMAN CLOSE 45 B1
BRIDEVALE ROAD 47 A6
BRIDGE CLOSE 40 B1
BRIDGE PARK ROAD 39 F2
BRIDGE ROAD 43 F4
BRIDGE STREET
- Barrow upon Soar 13 F7
- Loughborough 13 B4
BRIDGE WAY 50 B5
BRIDLE PATH ROAD 71 F7
BRIDLESPUR WAY 39 A4
BRIDPORT CLOSE 51 F3
BRIGHTON AVENUE 47 F6
BRIGHTON CLOSE 47 E6
BRIGHTON ROAD 44 A2
BRIGHTSIDE ROAD 44 A6
BRIGHTWELL DRIVE 41 D6
BRINGHURST ROAD 41 F3
BRINGTON CLOSE 52 A2
BRINSMEAD ROAD 47 D4
BRISCOE LANE 24 B2
BRISTOL AVENUE 42 F1
BRITANNIA STREET 43 C3
BRITFORD AVENUE 51 E4
BRITON STREET 42 F6
BRIXHAM DRIVE 47 C6
BROAD AVENUE 44 B4
BROAD LANE 36 B1
BROAD MEADOW 52 A3
BROAD STREET 49 D1
BROADBENT CLOSE 50 B5
BROADFORD CLOSE 39 F5
BROADGATE CLOSE 39 C1
BROADGATE ROAD 19 F5
BROADMEAD ROAD 50 C6
BROADWAY FURLONG 38 A2
BROADWAY ROAD 47 F1
BROCKENHURST DRIVE 46 A3
BROCKS HILL CLOSE 48 D7
BROCKS HILL DRIVE 48 D6
BROOK CLOSE 50 D1
BROOK CRESCENT 16 C5
BROOK HOUSE AVENUE 43 D6
BROOK LANE 65 C1
BROOK ROAD 44 F3
BROOK STREET
- Leicester 39 F2
- Leicester 49 D1
- Leicester 50 B5
- Shepshed 12 C4
- Wymeswold 14 C1
BROOKDALE ROAD 41 F5
BROOKE ROAD
- Braunstone 56 B4
- Oakham 56 D3
- Ridlington 56 C6
BROOKES AVENUE 72 F1

Street	Page	Grid
BROOKFIELD RISE	47	B5
BROOKFIELD RISE	47	C5
BROOKHOUSE STREET	43	D6
BROOKLAND ROAD	47	C2
BROOKLANDS CLOSE	50	B5
BROOKSBY CLOSE	48	C5
BROOKSBY DRIVE	48	C5
BROOKSBY STREET	47	A2
BROOKSIDE		
Barkby	53	A1
Rearsby	26	B3
BROOKSIDE DRIVE	48	E6
BROOM LEYS ROAD	22	E3
BROOM WAY	49	C3
BROOME LANE	25	F3
BROOMHILLS ROAD	49	B4
BROUGHAM STREET	43	C4
BROUGHTON CLOSE	38	A2
BROUGHTON FIELD	52	A4
BROUGHTON LANE		
Broughton Astley	73	A5
Long Clawson	6	A5
BROUGHTON ROAD		
Broughton Astley	72	F5
Cosby	73	C2
Croft	72	F1
Leicester	47	B5
Stoney Stanton	72	D2
BROUGHTON WAY	73	A3
BROWNING STREET		
Leicester	42	E6
Leicester	49	C3
BROWNS WAY	50	B7
BROXBURN CLOSE	39	F5
BROXFIELD CLOSE	52	C1
BRUCE STREET	42	F7
BRUCE WAY	50	A7
BRUCES LANE	55	D2
BRUIN STREET	43	C1
BRUINS WALK	48	C6
BRUNEL AVENUE	42	D2
BRUNSWICK STREET	43	D4
BRUNTINGTHORPE ROAD		
Bruntingthorpe	74	B7
Shearsby	74	E6
BRYNGARTH CRESCENT	44	D3
BRYONY ROAD	40	F6
BUCKFAST CLOSE		
Leicester	44	B7
Leicester	51	E3
BUCKHAVEN CLOSE	39	F5
BUCKINGHAM CLOSE	37	A7
BUCKINGHAM DRIVE	46	E6
BUCKLAND ROAD	43	F2
BUCKMINSTER ROAD		
Leicester	42	F2
Sproxton	8	D7
Stainby	19	B2
BUDE DRIVE	41	E1
BUDE ROAD	51	F3
BUFTON LANE	35	A5
BULKINGTON LANE	70	E7
BULL BRIG LANE	57	E2
BULL HEAD STREET	51	F1
BULL HILL	11	B4
BULL LANE		
Ketton	58	E6
North Witham	19	F3
BULL RING	70	B6
BULLACES LANE	84	C3
BULLER ROAD	43	C1
BULWER ROAD	47	D2
BUMBLEBEE LANE	72	B7
BUNKERS HILL	82	D2
BURBAGE COMMON ROAD	72	A1
BURBAGE ROAD	71	E3
BURDET CLOSE	46	A2
BURDETT WAY	38	F5
BURFIELD STREET	43	D2
BURGESS ROAD	47	A5
BURGESS STREET		
Leicester	43	A4
Leicester	51	F1
BURGIN ROAD	37	F4
BURLEIGH AVENUE	47	E7
BURLEY ROAD		
Cottesmore	30	B4
Langham	29	D6
Oakham	56	E1
BURLEYS FLYOVER	43	C3
BURLEYS WAY	43	B3
BURLINGTON ROAD	47	E2
BURNABY AVENUE	43	F4
BURNASTON ROAD	47	A5
BURNEL ROAD	46	D1
BURNESTON WAY	52	A2
BURNHAM CLOSE	51	F5
BURNHAM DRIVE		
Leicester	38	F7
Leicester	50	B6
BURNMOOR STREET	43	A7
BURNS STREET		
Leicester	47	C3
Leicester	49	D3
BURNSIDE ROAD	47	C5
BURROUGH END	27	E3
BURROUGH ROAD		
Somerby	28	B6
Twyford	54	D1
BURROUGHS ROAD	36	E4
BURSDON CLOSE	41	F3
BURSOM ROAD	38	D3
BURTON CLOSE	48	F7
BURTON OVERY LANE	64	F5
BURTON ROAD		
Measham	20	F6
Norton Juxta Twycross	33	E4
Overseal	20	A1
Woodville	9	C4
BURTON STREET		
Leicester	43	C4
Melton Mowbray	16	F6
BUSCOT CLOSE	43	F2
BUSHBY ROAD	43	F3
BUSHEY CLOSE	49	D4
BUSHLOE END	51	E2
BUSSETT ROAD	42	D3
BUTCHERS LANE	14	E7
BUTCOMBE ROAD	42	F1
BUTLER CLOSE	40	A5
BUTT CLOSE	52	A3
BUTT CLOSE LANE	43	B4
BUTT LANE		
Blackfordby	9	E6
Normanton on Soar	13	A1
Wymondham	18	D5
BUTTERCUP CLOSE	49	C3
BUTTERMERE STREET	43	A7
BUTTERWICK DRIVE	38	E5
BUXTON CLOSE	50	C5
BUXTON STREET	43	E4
BYFIELD DRIVE	52	A1
BYFORD ROAD	39	A7
BYRON CLOSE	49	C2
BYRON STREET	43	C4
BYWAY ROAD	48	A1
CADEMAN CLOSE	47	D4
CAIRNGORM CLOSE	47	B4
CAIRNSFORD ROAD	47	D5
CALAIS HILL	43	C5
CALAIS STREET	43	C5
CALDECOTE ROAD	46	C2
CALDECOTT CLOSE	52	B2
CALDECOTT ROAD	78	E5
CALDER ROAD	38	E6
CALEDINE ROAD	42	C2
CALGARY ROAD	43	C3
CALLAN CLOSE	49	C4
CALLANS LANE	10	C3
CALVER HEY ROAD	38	D6
CALVERTON AVENUE	47	E7
CAMBORNE CLOSE	51	E3
CAMBRIDGE ROAD		
Cosby	73	D1
Leicester	50	A7
CAMBRIDGE STREET	42	E6
CAMDEN ROAD	46	C2
CAMELLIA CLOSE	49	C3
CAMELOT WAY	49	C2
CAMERON AVENUE	39	D6
CAMFIELD RISE	46	F7
CAMPBELL AVENUE	40	A3
CAMPBELL STREET	43	C5
CAMPION CLOSE	49	C3
CAMVILLE ROAD	42	B6
CANAL LANE		
Hose	6	D2
Long Clawson	6	C4
CANAL STREET		
Leicester	40	A1
Leicester	46	E4
Leicester	51	B3
Oakthorpe	20	E4
CANK STREET	43	B4
CANNAM CLOSE	50	C7
CANNING PLACE	43	B3
CANNOCK STREET	40	C5
CANON CLOSE	48	D6
CANON STREET	43	D1
CANONS CLOSE	49	D4
CANONSLEIGH ROAD	39	A6
CANTERBURY TERRACE	42	E7
CANTRELL ROAD	41	F7
CANVEY CLOSE	52	B1
CAPERS CLOSE	49	C1
CAPESTHORNE CLOSE	44	A2
CARBERY CLOSE	48	F7
CARDIGAN DRIVE	51	B2
CARDINALS WALK	44	E2
CAREY CLOSE	51	F4
CAREYS CLOSE	43	A5
CARFAX AVENUE	48	B4
CARISBROOKE AVENUE	47	E4
CARISBROOKE GARDENS	47	E3
CARISBROOKE PARK	47	E4
CARISBROOKE ROAD	47	E3
CARL STREET	46	E5
CARLISLE STREET	42	E5
CARLTON AVENUE	49	E4
CARLTON DRIVE	47	E7
CARLTON LANE	64	D6
CARLTON ROAD		
Kibworth	75	E1
Market Bosworth	34	E7
CARLTON STREET	43	B6
CARMEN GROVE	37	A6
CARNATION CLOSE	45	B1
CARNATION STREET	39	B6
CARNOUSTIE ROAD	41	F4
CAROLINE COURT	47	A5
CAROLINE STREET	43	B3
CARPE ROAD	43	F1
CARPENTERS CLOSE	41	D3
CARROW ROAD	41	D5
CARTER CLOSE	49	C1
CARTER STREET	43	E2
CARTS LANE	43	B4
CARTWRIGHT DRIVE	48	C6
CASHMORE VIEW	38	F5
CASTELL DRIVE	37	C6
CASTERTON LANE	59	A4
CASTLE BYTHAM ROAD	31	D1
CASTLE FIELDS	38	C4
CASTLE RISE	37	B7
CASTLE STREET	43	A5
CASTLE VIEW	43	A5
CASTLE VIEW ROAD	1	D7
CASTLE YARD	43	A5
CASTLEFORD ROAD	46	A3
CASTLEGATE AVENUE	39	C1
CASTLETON ROAD	47	E7
CASWELL CLOSE	38	F5
CATERS CLOSE	37	F3
CATESBY STREET	42	F5
CATHERINE STREET	43	D2
CATHKIN CLOSE	41	F5
CATMOS STREET	56	E2
CATTHORPE ROAD	84	C3
CAULDWELL LANE	80	B2
CAUSEWAY LANE	43	B4
CAVENDISH ROAD	47	A2
CAVERSHAM ROAD	50	E1
CAWSAND ROAD	51	E3
CECIL ROAD	43	E4
CECILIA ROAD	47	D1
CEDAR AVENUE		
Leicester	39	C2
Leicester	51	F2
CEDAR CLOSE	42	A1
CEDAR COURT	37	B7
CEDAR CRESCENT	49	D5
CEDAR ROAD		
Leicester	43	E6
Leicester	50	D6
CEDARS COURT	47	E1
CEDARWOOD CLOSE	43	F1
CELADINE ROAD	40	E6
CELT STREET	42	F6
CEMETERY LANE	56	F6
CEMETERY ROAD	50	B5
CENTRAL AVENUE		
Leicester	47	E1
Leicester	51	E2
CENTRAL CLOSE	50	B4
CENTRAL ROAD		
Leicester	42	F3
Ravenstone	22	C4
CENTRE COURT	45	F4
CENTURION WAY	45	F3
CHADDERTON CLOSE	47	C4
CHADWELL ROAD	42	A3
CHAFFINCH CLOSE	38	D3
CHAINAMA CLOSE	41	E4
CHALE ROAD	39	B7
CHALVINGTON CLOSE	44	E7
CHAMPION CLOSE	44	D5
CHANCEL ROAD	38	F1
CHANCERY STREET	43	A5
CHANDOS STREET	43	E6
CHAPEL HILL	37	A6
CHAPEL LANE		
Hoby	15	C7
Leicester	47	D3
Tugby	66	A2
Walton	81	B3
Witherley	60	F6
CHAPEL STREET		
Barwell	62	E7
Belton In Rutland	66	F2
Donisthorpe	20	E5
Leicester	48	C6
Leicester	49	C1
Leicester	50	E3
Swinford	84	E3
CHAPLE LANE	16	C2
CHAPPELL CLOSE	40	A2
CHARLECOTE AVENUE	46	B2
CHARLES DRIVE	38	A2
CHARLES STREET	43	B4
CHARLES WAY	50	C7
CHARLEY ROAD	23	D3
CHARLTON CLOSE	50	C6
CHARNOR ROAD	42	A2
CHARNWOOD AVENUE		
Leicester	40	B1
Leicester	50	B4
CHARNWOOD CLOSE	41	C6
CHARNWOOD DRIVE	41	C6
CHARNWOOD ROAD		
Leicester	37	F2
Shepshed	12	B6
CHARNWOOD STREET	43	E4
CHARTER STREET	43	B3
CHARTLEY ROAD	42	E7
CHARTWELL DRIVE	51	C1
CHATER CLOSE	44	F3
CHATHAM STREET	43	B5
CHATSWORTH AVENUE	51	C3
CHATSWORTH STREET	43	E4
CHATTERIS AVENUE	44	F7
CHAUCER STREET		
Leicester	43	E7
Leicester	49	C3
CHEAPSIDE	43	B4
CHECKETTS CLOSE	39	D6
CHECKETTS ROAD	39	D6
CHECKLAND ROAD	40	A1
CHEDDAR ROAD	52	A1
CHELLASTON LANE	4	A2
CHELSEA CLOSE	50	F3
CHELTENHAM ROAD	38	F7
CHEPSTOW ROAD	43	E7
CHERITON ROAD	46	F6
CHERRY ROAD	50	D5
CHERRY STREET	51	D2
CHERRY TREE AVENUE	41	A7
CHERRY TREE CLOSE	37	F4
CHERRY TREE GROVE	49	C1
CHERRYBROOK CLOSE	38	D2
CHERRYLEAS DRIVE	42	E6
CHESHIRE DRIVE	51	C1
CHESHIRE GARDENS	46	F4
CHESHIRE ROAD	46	F4
CHESTER CLOSE	43	D3
CHESTER ROAD	50	E5
CHESTERFIELD ROAD	43	F6
CHESTNUT AVENUE		
Leicester	44	F1
Leicester	48	C5
CHESTNUT CLOSE	49	D6
CHESTNUT ROAD	41	E2
CHESTNUT WALK	37	B7
CHETTLE ROAD	42	C3
CHEVIN AVENUE	41	F5
CHEVIOT ROAD	47	B4
CHILCOMBE CLOSE	39	A6
CHILTERN GREEN	47	C5
CHISLEHURST AVENUE	46	B3
CHISWICK ROAD	47	B2
CHORLEY WOOD ROAD	44	F6
CHRISETT CLOSE	44	D4
CHRISTOPHER DRIVE	40	B5
CHRISTOW STREET	43	D3
CHURCH AVENUE	42	E5
CHURCH FARM LANE	73	F4
CHURCH GATE	43	B4
CHURCH HILL		
Cranoe	77	A1
Leicester	39	D3
Lowesby	54	C3
Swannington	11	B7
Woodhouse Eaves	24	B3
CHURCH HILL ROAD		
Cranoe	76	F1
Leicester	40	B2
CHURCH LANE		
Ashby Folville	27	A6
Cadeby	62	C1
Chilcote	20	A6
Clipsham	31	D1
Dunton Bassett	73	C6
East Norton	66	C3
Eaton	7	D2
Glaston	68	B3
Goadby	65	F5
Hoby	15	C7
Leicester	37	F3
Leicester	40	A2
Leicester	47	D4
Leicester	49	E4
Leicester	50	B4
Little Dalby	28	B3
Muston	3	A1
Osgathorpe	11	D5
Pickwell	28	C6
Preston	67	F1
Redmile	2	D3
Saxelbye	16	A4
Sewstern	19	A3
South Witham	19	E5
Stockerston	67	B6
Stoughton	64	A1
Swannington	22	C1
CHURCH NOOK	51	F1
CHURCH ROAD		
Barlestone	35	B3
Egleton	56	F3
Great Glen	64	B6
Ketton	58	E6
Kibworth	75	E3
Kirby Mallory	62	F3
Leicester	41	D1
Leicester	46	E5
Leicester	48	D1
Lyndon	57	C6
Peckleton	63	B3
CHURCH STREET		
Appleby Magna	33	D1
Belton In Rutland	66	F2
Braunstone	56	B4
Donisthorpe	20	D3
Earl Shilton	63	B5
Hinckley	71	E4
Kegworth	5	A4
Leicester	39	F3
Leicester	43	C5
Leicester	48	C6
Leicester	50	E4
Lutterworth	80	C5
North Luffenham	57	F7
North Witham	19	E3
Nuneaton	70	C5
Scalford	7	A7
South Witham	19	E5
Sweepstone	21	C7
Thurlaston	63	E4
Twycross	33	F6
Worthington	11	A4
CHURCH VIEW	49	E4
CHURCH WALK		
Bruntingthorpe	74	C7
Leicester	39	C6
CHURCHILL CLOSE	48	C6
CHURCHILL DRIVE	41	D6
CHURCHILL STREET	43	D6
CHURCHWARD AVENUE	38	F5
CIVIC WAY	9	B5
CLARE GROVE	45	F1
CLAREFIELD ROAD	42	D5
CLAREMONT STREET	39	D6
CLARENCE ROAD	49	F2

CLARENCE STREET 43 C4
CLARENDON PARK ROAD 47 D2
CLARENDON STREET 43 A6
CLARK GARDENS 50 C4
CLARKE GROVE 39 C3
CLARKE STREET 39 D6
CLARKES ROAD 51 D2
CLAWSON LANE
Hickling 6 A3
Long Clawson 6 E5
Nether Broughton 6 A5
CLAY LANE 11 B7
CLAY STREET 14 C1
CLAYBROOK AVENUE 46 C3
CLAYDON ROAD 44 A2
CLAYMILL ROAD 40 B5
CLAYTON DRIVE 40 B3
CLEMATIS CLOSE 38 C4
CLEMENT AVENUE 39 C6
CLEMENTS GATE 4 F7
CLEVEDON CRESCENT 44 A2
CLEVELAND ROAD 51 F1
CLEVELEYS AVENUE 46 C3
CLIFF ROAD 3 C4
CLIFFE HILL ROAD 23 B7
CLIFFE HOUSE MEWS 50 B4
CLIFFE LANE 23 B7
CLIFFE ROAD 39 B3
CLIFFORD STREET
Leicester 42 F4
Leicester 51 B2
CLIFFWOOD AVENUE 39 B2
CLIFTON DRIVE 51 C3
CLIFTON ROAD
Leicester 47 B3
Netherseal 20 A4
CLIPPER ROAD 40 B6
CLIPSHAM ROAD 31 B2
CLIPSTONE GARDENS 52 A2
CLOUD HILL VIEW 11 A5
CLOVELLY ROAD
Leicester 41 F1
Leicester 44 B6
CLOVER CLOSE 49 C4
CLUMBER ROAD 44 A4
CLYDE STREET 43 C4
COOPERATION STREET 49 D1
COAL BAULK 53 E3
COAL PIT LANE 79 A3
COALBOURN CLOSE 39 A4
COALES AVENUE 50 C7
COATBRIDGE AVENUE 39 F5
COATES AVENUE 42 C3
COBDEN STREET 43 D2
COKAYNE ROAD 41 F4
COLBERT DRIVE 46 C4
COLBY DRIVE 40 C3
COLBY ROAD 40 B4
COLCHESTER ROAD 44 D3
COLD OVERTON ROAD
Knossington 55 E1
Langham 29 A7
Oakham 56 D2
COLEBROOK CLOSE 44 B7
COLEFORD ROAD 40 C4
COLEMAN CLOSE 44 B3
COLEMAN ROAD 44 B3
COLEORTON LANE 21 C2
COLERIDGE DRIVE 49 C1
COLES CLOSE 39 F4
COLIN GRUNDY DRIVE 44 D1
COLINDALE AVENUE 39 C1
COLLATON ROAD 51 E2
COLLEGE FARM LANE 66 F1
COLLEGE ROAD
Leicester 50 C4
Sutton Bonington 5 E5
COLLEGE STREET
Leicester 43 D5
Nuneaton 70 C6
COLLEGE WALK 43 D6
COLLETT ROAD 38 E5
COLLIN PLACE 39 F7
COLLINGHAM ROAD 46 E1
COLLINS CLOSE 45 F1
COLNE CLOSE 48 F6
COLSTERDALE CLOSE 38 F4
COLSTERWORTH ROAD 19 D1
COLTBECK AVENUE 49 C4
COLTON STREET 43 C5
COLTSFORD ROAD 40 E6
COLUMBIA CLOSE 49 C1
COLUMBINE CLOSE 46 A1
COLUMBINE ROAD 40 D6
COLWELL ROAD 42 F2
COMBE CLOSE 42 E2
COMET CLOSE 42 D3
COMMERCIAL SQUARE 47 B1
COMPASS ROAD 44 F3
COMPTON ROAD 46 E1
CONAGLEN ROAD 46 D5
CONDUIT STREET 43 C5
CONERY LANE 45 C7
CONGERSTONE LANE 34 D4
CONINSBY CLOSE 46 D2
CONISTON AVENUE 43 A7
CONNAUGHT STREET 43 D6
CONSTABLE AVENUE 43 D2
CONSTANCE ROAD 43 F5
CONSTITUTION HILL 43 C5
CONWAY ROAD 43 F7
COODEN AVENUE 42 D6
COOKE CLOSE 45 F1
COOKS LANE 52 B5
COOMBE PLACE 48 D7
COOMBE RISE 52 E1
COOPER CLOSE
Leicester 46 E5
Leicester 49 A4
COOPER GARDENS 48 F7
COOPER STREET 43 C1
COOPERS LANE 73 C6
COPDALE ROAD 44 A5
COPELAND AVENUE 42 C1
COPELAND ROAD 39 B3
COPINGER ROAD 47 B4
COPLOW AVENUE 48 A1
COPLOW LANE 54 B6
COPSE CLOSE
Leicester 45 B2
Leicester 48 E4
COPT OAK COURT 49 C4
COPT OAK ROAD 23 B5
COPTHORNE CLOSE 41 F4
CORAH STREET 43 A5
CORAL STREET 43 C1
CORBET CLOSE 38 D6
CORBETT ROAD 45 F1
CORBY ROAD 78 C7
CORDELIA CLOSE 44 A1
CORDERY ROAD 44 D7
CORFIELD RISE 42 A7
CORK LANE 50 D1
CORK STREET 43 E5
CORKSCREW LANE 21 D1
CORNFIELD CLOSE 49 E5
CORNWALL ROAD
Leicester 42 F1
Leicester 51 C2
CORNWALL STREET 49 D1
CORNWALLIS AVENUE 38 D7
CORONATION AVENUE 51 D2
CORONATION LANE 20 D5
CORPORATION ROAD 39 B7
CORT CRESCENT 42 A6
COSBY LANE 73 D4
COSBY ROAD
Broughton Astley 73 B3
Countesthorpe 73 E1
Leicester 49 E6
COSSINGTON LANE 25 B5
COSSINGTON ROAD 25 C3
COSSINGTON STREET 43 D1
COSTON ROAD
Buckminster 18 F2
Sproxton 8 D7
COTES ROAD 13 E5
COTLEY ROAD 38 F4
COTTAGE FARM CLOSE 46 B5
COTTAGE LANE
Markfield 23 C6
Norton Juxta Twycross 33 E3
COTTAGE ROAD 52 A3
COTTAGE ROW 46 D3
COTTAGERS CLOSE 47 B6
COTTESBROOK CLOSE 51 F2
COTTESMORE AVENUE 48 F7
COTTESMORE ROAD
Ashwell 29 F4
Burley 30 A7
Cottesmore 30 D3
Exton 30 D5
Leicester 43 F3
COTTINGHAM ROAD
Corby 78 D5
Rockingham 78 D7
COTTON BRIDGE LANE 61 E1
COTTON CLOSE 39 F4
COTTON ROAD 70 C6
COULSON CLOSE 50 C6
COUNCIL ROAD 71 C2
COUNTESTHORPE ROAD
Countesthorpe 73 D2
Leicester 51 B3
COUNTRY ROAD 49 C6
COURT CLOSE 41 A5
COURT ROAD 50 D2
COURTENAY ROAD 42 E1
COVENTRY ROAD
Croft 72 F2
Hinckley 71 A3
Hinckley 71 D4
Leicester 49 D5
Lutterworth 80 A5
Market Harborough 83 C2
Nuneaton 70 C6
Sapcote 72 D4
Sharnford 72 C6
COVENTRY STREET 42 F5
COVERDALE ROAD 52 B3
COVERT CLOSE 48 E5
COVERT LANE 53 B5
COVETT WAY 42 A5
COWDALL ROAD 42 A7
COW-SLIP CLOSE 49 B4
COXS LANE 55 B3
CRABTREE CORNER 47 C6
CRABTREE ROAD 19 B1
CRACKBOTTLE ROAD 66 B4
CRADOCK ROAD 47 D1
CRAFTON STREET EAST 43 C4
CRAIG GARDENS 41 F4
CRAIGHILL ROAD 47 D3
CRANBERRY CLOSE 45 F1
CRANBOURNE GARDENS 48 D3
CRANE LEY ROAD 37 A6
CRANE STREET 43 B3
CRANESBILL ROAD 44 E1
CRANFIELD ROAD 46 F5
CRANMER CLOSE 50 C6
CRANMER STREET 42 F6
CRANOE ROAD
Cranoe 76 C2
Glooston 76 F1
CRANSTONE CRESCENT 41 E3
CRANTOCK CLOSE 44 F7
CRANWELL CLOSE 48 D1
CRAVEN STREET 43 A3
CRAVENS ROUGH 23 E6
CRAYFORD WAY 44 F1
CRAYTHORNE WAY 52 B2
CREATON COURT 52 A2
CREDITON CLOSE 51 F4
CRESSWELL CLOSE 40 C3
CRETE AVENUE 51 A2
CROFT AVENUE 46 E5
CROFT DRIVE 47 D6
CROFT HILL ROAD 63 F6
CROFT LANE 63 E6
CROFT ROAD
Cosby 73 B1
Leicester 38 E2
Nuneaton 70 A5
Thurlaston 63 E6
CROFTERS CLOSE 41 D2
CROMARTY CLOSE 39 F6
CROMFORD AVENUE 51 C3
CROMFORD STREET 43 E4
CROMPTON ROAD 16 C5
CROPSTON ROAD 38 B1
CROPTHORNE AVENUE 44 B5
CROSS BANK 78 C4
CROSS HEDGE CLOSE 38 E5
CROSS LANE 67 F1
CROSS ROAD 47 E1
CROSS ROADS 65 B4
CROSS STREET
Leicester 43 C1
Leicester 48 C4
Leicester 49 D1
Leicester 50 D4
Leicester 51 F2
CROSSLEY STREET 41 E2
CROW LANE 42 F6
CROWAN DRIVE 51 E3
CROWHILL ROAD 70 D6
CROWHURST DRIVE 46 A3
CROWN HILLS AVENUE 44 B5
CROWN HILLS RISE 44 B6
CROXTON ROAD
Beeby 53 D2
Croxton Kerral 8 C4
Queniborough 26 B6
CROYDE CLOSE 44 B6
CUFFLING CLOSE 41 F4
CUFFLING DRIVE 41 F4
CULHAM AVENUE 43 F2
CULVER ROAD 42 E2
CULWORTH DRIVE 52 A2
CUMBERLAND ROAD 51 A1
CUMBERLAND STREET 43 A4
CUMBERWELL DRIVE 49 F3
CURTEYS CLOSE 46 D2
CURTIS CLOSE 50 C5
CURZON AVENUE
Leicester 39 C3
Leicester 51 C3
CURZON ROAD 47 A4
CURZON STREET
Ibstock 22 B7
Leicester 43 D3
CUTTERS CLOSE 49 D5
CYPRUS ROAD 47 A5
CYRIL STREET 46 C3

DADLINGTON LANE 62 C5
DAG LANE 75 A7
DAKYN ROAD 44 F4
DALBY AVENUE 39 D1
DALBY DRIVE 37 B6
DALBY ROAD
Leicester 38 F2
Melton Mowbray 16 F6
DALE AVENUE 47 C7
DALE STREET 43 E5
DALKEITH ROAD 39 F5
DANBURY DRIVE 38 F7
DANE STREET 42 F5
DANEHURST AVENUE 42 D4
DANESHILL ROAD 42 E5
DANNETT STREET 42 F4
DANS LANE 63 C2
DANVERS ROAD 42 E7
DARENTH DRIVE 38 C6
DARKER STREET 43 B4
DARLEY AVENUE 51 C3
DARLEY ROAD 50 C5
DARLEY STREET 43 E5
DARLINGTON ROAD 42 D2
DART CLOSE 48 F5
DARTFORD ROAD 46 F2
DARWEN CLOSE 42 D2
DASHWOOD ROAD 43 E7
DAVENPORT AVENUE 48 B6
DAVENPORT ROAD
Leicester 44 E5
Leicester 51 F3
DAVETT CLOSE 44 D4
DAVID AVENUE 39 A4
DAVISON CLOSE 44 C4
DAWLISH CLOSE 44 F5
DAWSONS LANE 54 F1
DAWSONS ROAD 11 D5
DAY STREET 39 C6
DAYBELL CLOSE 50 B3
DE MONTFORT PLACE 43 C6
DE MONTFORT SQUARE 43 C6
DE MONTFORT STREET 43 C6
DEACON ROAD 38 F1
DEACON STREET 43 A6
DEAN ROAD 43 E1
DEANCOURT ROAD 47 D5
DEANERY CRESCENT 38 F1
DEANS LANE 23 E2
DEBDALE LANE 75 E5
DEEPDALE 44 B4
DEEPING LANE 35 B7
DENACRE AVENUE 51 C3
DENBYDALE 52 B2
DENEGATE AVENUE 39 B1
DENHAM CLOSE 41 E4
DENIS CLOSE 42 D4
DENMARK ROAD 47 A3
DENTON LANE
Denton 3 D2
Harston 3 C7
DENTON STREET 42 D5
DERBY LANE 34 B2
DERBY ROAD
Ashby-De-La-Zouch 21 B1
Aston-on-Trent 4 B1
Kegworth 5 C4
Loughborough 12 D2
Smisby 10 A5
Swadlincote 9 C5
DERSINGHAM ROAD 38 F7
DERWENT STREET 43 E5
DERWENT WALK 48 E6
DESFORD LANE
Kirby Mallory 63 A2
Kirby Muxloe 36 E6
Newton Unthank 36 D6
Peckleton 63 B2
Ratby 36 E5
DESFORD ROAD
Enderby 63 F2
Leicester 49 D4
Newbold Verdon 35 F7
Thurlaston 63 D3
DEVANA ROAD 43 F7
DEVON WAY 44 B5
DEVONIA ROAD 48 F7
DEVONSHIRE AVENUE 51 C3
DEVONSHIRE ROAD 43 A1
DEVONSHIRE STREET 43 B3
DICKENS COURT 42 C5
DICKINSON WAY 40 C2
DIDSBURY STREET 42 A6
DIGBY CLOSE 42 D6
DIGBY DRIVE 16 D7
DIGBY ROAD 57 F7
DILLON GREEN 42 A1
DILLON RISE 42 B2
DILLON ROAD 42 B2
DILLON WAY 42 B1
DIMMINGSDALE CLOSE 38 A2
DINGLE LANE 33 C2
DINGLEY AVENUE 43 E1
DINGLEY LINK 52 B1
DINGLEY ROAD 83 E1
DISEWORTH STREET 43 E5
DISRAELI STREET 46 F4
DITCHLING AVENUE 42 C4
DIXON DRIVE 43 E7
DOCTORS LANE 11 A2
DODWELLS ROAD 71 A3
DOG AND GUN LANE 50 B7
DOG LANE 4 A7
DOMINION ROAD 41 F2
DONALD CLOSE 40 B5
DONALDSON ROAD 43 C2
DONCASTER ROAD 43 D1
DONNETT CLOSE 44 D4
DONNINGTON STREET 43 E5
DONNITHORPE AVENUE 70 C6
DORCHESTER CLOSE
Leicester 50 E6
Leicester 51 F4
DORCHESTER ROAD 42 D6
DORE ROAD 43 F6
DOREST AVENUE 51 B1
DOROTHY AVENUE
Leicester 39 F3
Leicester 50 D1
DOROTHY ROAD 43 F5
DORSET AVENUE 41 E1
DORSET STREET 43 C2
DOUBLE RAIL CLOSE 51 C3
DOVE COTE 11 B1
DOVE RISE 48 E5
DOVEDALE AVENUE 50 D5
DOVEDALE ROAD
Leicester 40 A4
Leicester 48 A2
DOVER STREET 43 C5
DOWN STREET 43 D1
DOWNHAM AVENUE 39 A7
DOWNING DRIVE 44 F6
DRAGON LANE 35 E6
DRAPER STREET 43 E7
DRAYTON LANE 61 A7
DRAYTON ROAD
Drayton 77 F3
Great Easton 78 B4
Leicester 42 A3
Medbourne 77 E4
DRIFT HILL 2 D3
DRIFT SIDE 9 E7
DRINKSTONE ROAD 44 A5
DRONFIELD STREET 43 E5
DROVERS WAY 49 D5
DRUMMOND ROAD

Leicester	39	B6
Leicester	49	C1
DRURY LANE	48	B5
DRYDEN STREET	43	C3
DUDLESTON CLOSE	44	C5
DUDLEY AVENUE	44	E4
DUDLEY CLOSE	44	E3
DUFFIELD AVENUE	47	E7
DUFFIELD STREET	43	E5
DUKE STREET	43	B6
DUKES CLOSE		
Leicester	40	B2
Leicester	51	D1
DULVERTON CLOSE	51	F4
DULVERTON ROAD	42	E5
DUMBLETON AVENUE	46	E2
DUMPS ROAD	22	D1
DUNBAR ROAD	40	A7
DUNBLANE AVENUE	39	F5
DUNCAN ROAD	47	A4
DUNDEE ROAD	50	D6
DUNDONALD STREET	43	C1
DUNHOLME ROAD	44	A1
DUNIRE CLOSE	38	E6
DUNKIRK STREET	43	C5
DUNLIN ROAD	43	E3
DUNS LANE	43	A5
DUNSTALL AVENUE	41	F7
DUNSTER STREET	42	E5
DUNTON LANE	73	B7
DUNTON ROAD		
Broughton Astley	73	B5
Leire	73	B7
DUNTON STREET		
Leicester	42	F3
Leicester	51	B3
DUPONT CLOSE	41	F3
DUPONT GARDENS	41	F3
DURHAM DRIVE	47	C7
DURNFORD ROAD	51	F4
DURSTON CLOSE	44	F6
DUXBURY ROAD	44	A3
DYSART WAY	43	D3
EALING ROAD	47	B2
EARL HOWE STREET	43	E6
EARL HOWE TERRACE	42	F5
EARL RUSSELL STREET	46	E5
EARL SHILTON ROAD	63	C5
EARLE SMITH CLOSE	50	C5
EARLS CLOSE	40	B2
EARLS WAY	40	B2
EARLSWOOD ROAD	44	F6
EAST AVENUE		
Leicester	47	E1
Leicester	50	B4
EAST BOND STREET	43	B4
EAST END	6	C4
EAST LINK	46	A4
EAST NORTON ROAD	66	C6
EAST PARK ROAD	43	F6
EAST ROAD		
Leicester	39	C4
Wymeswold	14	C1
EAST STREET		
Leicester	43	C5
Leicester	48	C5
EASTBORO WAY	70	D5
EASTCOURT ROAD	47	E5
EASTERN BOULEVARD	43	A6
EASTFIELD ROAD		
Leicester	40	B1
Leicester	42	D5
EASTGATE	66	C7
EASTHORPE LANE		
Bottesford	1	E7
Muston	3	A1
EASTHORPE ROAD	1	D7
EASTLEIGH ROAD	42	F7
EASTMERE ROAD	52	B1
EASTWAY ROAD	47	F7
EASTWOOD ROAD	46	F6
EBCHESTER CLOSE	50	E1
EBCHESTER ROAD	46	E7
EDALE CLOSE	42	A7
EDEN CLOSE	48	E5
EDEN HALL CLOSE	48	F7
EDEN ROAD	48	F5
EDEN WAY	50	F2
EDENHALL CLOSE	39	F5
EDENHURST AVENUE	46	B4
EDENSOR STREET	39	E6
EDGBASTON CLOSE	38	F2
EDGCOTE COURT	44	A2
EDGEHILL ROAD	40	A7
EDITH AVENUE	46	C4
EDITH WESTON ROAD	57	F7
EDMONDTHORPE MERE	29	D1
EDMONDTHORPE ROAD	18	D6
EDMONTON ROAD	43	C3
EDWARD AVENUE	46	B3
EDWARD CLOSE	48	E6
EDWARD DRIVE	51	A3
EDWARD ROAD	47	D1
EDWARD STREET		
Albert Village	9	C6
Leicester	38	A3
Leicester	43	E3
Nuneaton	70	B5
EGERTON AVENUE	39	A7
EGGINTON STREET	43	E6
EILEEN AVENUE	39	A7
ELBOW LANE	43	A4
ELDER LANE	11	B6
ELGIN AVENUE	42	B2
ELISABETH DRIVE	40	A1
ELIZABETH CLOSE	41	D1
ELIZABETH COURT	51	F2
ELIZABETH DRIVE	48	E7
ELIZABETH GARDENS	50	B5
ELIZABETH STREET	44	A5
ELLAND ROAD	41	D5
ELLESMERE PLACE	46	D1
ELLESMERE ROAD	46	D1
ELLIOT CLOSE	52a	G7
ELLIOTT DRIVE		
Leicester	40	C3
Leicester	41	D6
ELLIOTT ROAD	38	F5
ELLIOTTS LANE	36	B1
ELLIS AVENUE	43	C1
ELLIS CLOSE	41	E2
ELLIS DRIVE	41	B7
ELLIS STREET	37	F3
ELLISON CLOSE	51	B4
ELLISTOWN TERRACE ROAD	22	D7
ELLWOOD CLOSE	44	D6
ELM CLOSE	37	B7
ELM FIELD GREEN	43	E7
ELM TREE AVENUE	41	D2
ELMCROFT AVENUE	44	E3
ELMDALE STREET	39	C7
ELMESTHORPE LANE	62	A7
ELMFIELD AVENUE		
Leicester	39	B2
Leicester	43	E7
ELMHURST CLOSE	49	C5
ELMS CLOSE	48	D6
ELMS COURT	47	F3
ELMS ROAD	47	F3
ELMSLEIGH AVENUE	47	F2
ELMSTHORPE RISE	42	C7
ELMTREE CLOSE	40	E7
ELMWOOD ROW	47	C7
ELSADENE AVENUE	39	D5
ELSHAM CLOSE	41	F5
ELSTON FIELDS	47	B5
ELSWORTH WALK	41	F4
ELWIN AVENUE	47	F7
EMBERTON CLOSE	52	B1
EMERSON CLOSE	38	C6
EMON CLOSE	50	F1
EMPINGHAM ROAD		
Exton	30	E7
Ketton	58	D6
Stamford	59	C3
EMPIRE ROAD	42	F3
ENDERBY ROAD		
Leicester	50	C4
Thurlaston	63	E4
ENDERBYS LANE	54	B4
ENGLEFIELD ROAD	44	F5
ENNERDALE CLOSE	48	F7
ENSBURY GARDENS	44	D7
EPINAL WAY	13	A5
EPPING WAY	50	F1
EPSOM ROAD	39	D7
EQUITY ROAD		
Leicester	42	F6
Leicester	49	C1
ERDYNGTON ROAD	42	B6
ERITH ROAD	47	A2
ERNEE CLOSE	41	F3
ERSKINE STREET	43	C4
ERVINGTON COURT	45	F5
ERVINS LOCK	51	C4
ESKDALE CLOSE	48	F7
ESKDALE ROAD	38	F6
ESSENDINE ROAD	32	D6
ESSEX ROAD		
Leicester	40	A7
Leicester	51	B1
ESTORIL AVENUE	52	B1
ETHEL ROAD	44	A6
ETON CLOSE	47	D3
EUSTON STREET	47	B2
EVELYN DRIVE	46	F1
EVELYN ROAD	46	A1
EVERARD WAY	46	B6
EVERETT CLOSE	40	C3
EVERY STREET	43	B5
EVESHAM ROAD	46	E1
EVINGTON CLOSE	44	A6
EVINGTON DRIVE	44	A7
EVINGTON LANE	48	C1
EVINGTON PARK ROAD	43	F7
EVINGTON ROAD	43	D6
EVINGTON STREET	43	D5
EVINGTON VALLEY ROAD	43	F7
EXETER ROAD	47	D7
EXMOOR AVENUE	43	A2
EXMOOR CLOSE	51	F3
EXTON LANE	30	B6
EXTON ROAD		
Cottesmore	30	C4
Empingham	58	A1
Leicester	44	A3
EYNSFORD CLOSE	48	B3
FAIRBOURNE ROAD	46	C2
FAIRE ROAD	41	F1
FAIRESTONE AVENUE	41	E2
FAIRFAX CLOSE	40	A7
FAIRFAX ROAD	40	A7
FAIRFIELD CRESCENT	42	A1
FAIRFIELD ROAD	48	F6
Leicester		
Market Harborough	83	D2
FAIRFIELD STREET		
Leicester	43	E5
Leicester	51	B2
FAIRFORD AVENUE	44	D7
FAIRHAVEN ROAD	38	B1
FAIRHOLME ROAD	47	D5
FAIRSTONE HILL	48	D6
FAIRVIEW AVENUE	50	B5
FALCON CLOSE	45	A1
FALCON ROAD	37	F4
FALCONER CRESCENT	42	A2
FALDO CLOSE	40	A4
FALLOWFIELD ROAD	44	F6
FALMOUTH DRIVE	51	F3
FALMOUTH ROAD	44	C6
FAR STREET	14	C1
FARLEY ROAD	47	F3
FARLEY WAY		
Leicester	41	A3
Quorn	13	D7
FARM CLOSE		
Leicester	39	D2
Leicester	47	B6
Leicester	49	E5
FARMERS CLOSE	41	D2
FARMWAY	46	A4
FARNDALE	52	B2
FARNDON ROAD	83	C3
FARNHAM STREET	43	E4
FARNWORTH CLOSE	40	A6
FARR WOOD CLOSE	37	A5
FARRIER LANE	38	D5
FARRINGDON STREET	43	E3
FAVERSHAM CLOSE	41	E4
FAYRHURST ROAD	47	A5
FEATHERBY DRIVE	50	C1
FEATHERSTONE DRIVE	50	E2
FEDERATION STREET	49	D1
FELLEY WAY	42	E2
FELSTEAD ROAD	38	F5
FENN LANES	61	B6
FENTON CLOSE	52	C1
FENWICK ROAD	52a	G7
FERMAIN CLOSE	44	F5
FERN RISE	44	E1
FERNDALE ROAD		
Leicester	40	B3
Leicester	47	D5
FERNDOWN CLOSE	41	E4
FERNHURST ROAD	46	B3
FERNIE CLOSE	48	E7
FERNIE ROAD	43	F3
FERNLEA	49	B3
FERNLEYS CLOSE	38	D6
FERRARS COURT	45	F1
FERRERS RISE	37	A6
FERRERS STREET	47	B6
FERROUS CLOSE	43	E2
FESTIVAL AVENUE	40	A3
FIELD CLOSE	49	E5
FIELD COURT ROAD	37	B6
FIELD HURST AVENUE	46	A3
FIELD LANE		
Blackfordby	9	F6
Tonge	11	C2
FIELD STREET	12	B5
FIELD VIEW	40	C2
FIELDGATE CRESCENT	39	B1
FIELDHOUSE ROAD	39	D6
FIELDING ROAD	39	B2
FILBERT STREET	43	A7
FILBERT STREET EAST	43	B7
FINCH CLOSE	42	A5
FINCH WAY	49	C5
FINESHADE AVENUE	42	E2
FINSBURY ROAD	43	E1
FINSON CLOSE	51	F1
FIR TREE CLOSE	47	E6
FIR TREE LANE	37	A5
FIRFIELD AVENUE	39	C2
FIRTREE CLOSE	42	F1
FISH PONDS CLOSE	41	D2
FISHLEY CLOSE	41	D3
FISHPOOLS	46	A4
FITZROY STREET	42	F5
FITZWILLIAM CLOSE	48	F7
FLAMBOROUGH ROAD	44	F3
FLAX ROAD	39	D7
FLAXFIELD CLOSE	37	B6
FLECKNEY ROAD		
Arnesby	74	E4
Fleckney	75	B4
Kibworth	75	D3
Kilby	74	E2
FLEETWOOD ROAD	47	C2
FLESH HOVEL LANE	13	E7
FLETCHERS CLOSE	49	D5
FLORA STREET	42	F6
FLORENCE AVENUE	51	C3
FLORENCE STREET	47	A4
FLORENCE WRAGG WAY	48	F7
FLOYD CLOSE	40	A4
FOAN HILL	22	B1
FOLVILLE RISE	46	D1
FOLVILLE STREET	27	A6
FONTWELL DRIVE	46	D6
FORBES CLOSE	41	E3
FORD CLOSE	50	E1
FOREST AVENUE		
Leicester	39	F1
Leicester	40	A1
FOREST DRIVE	41	B6
FOREST GATE	37	F3
FOREST HOUSE LANE	45	B2
FOREST LANE	11	F4
FOREST RISE		
Leicester	41	B7
Leicester	48	E5
FOREST ROAD		
Field Head	36	C1
Huncote	63	F5
Leicester	43	E2
Leicester	49	B2
Loughborough	13	A6
Quorn	24	B2
FORESTERS CLOSE	41	D2
FORGE CLOSE	41	C2
FORRYANS CLOSE	52	A3
FORTY FOOT LANE	4	A6
FOSSE CLOSE	49	F2
FOSSE LANE		
Leicester	42	E3
Thistleton	19	C6
FOSSE PARK AVENUE	46	B6
FOSSE ROAD	42	F3
FOSSE ROAD CENTRAL	42	E5
FOSSE ROAD NORTH	42	E4
FOSSE ROAD SOUTH	42	E7
FOSSE WAY	25	D7
FOSTON GATE	52	A4
FOSTON LANE	74	C2
FOSTON ROAD	74	B1
FOTHERINGHAY ROAD	78	E7
FOUNDRY LANE	43	B3
FOUNDRY SQUARE	43	C3
FOUNTAINS AVENUE	50	F1
FOWLER CLOSE	38	F5
FOX COVERT	50	B7
FOX LANE	43	B4
FOX STREET	43	C5
FOXCOVERT LANE	61	E6
FOXCROFT CLOSE	46	E3
FOXGLOVE CLOSE	49	C3
FOXGLOVE ROAD	40	E7
FOXHILL DRIVE	50	C1
FOXHOLES ROAD	41	F6
FOXHUNTER DRIVE	48	B5
FOXON STREET	42	F5
FOXON WAY	45	F2
FOXTON LOCK CLOSE	51	C4
FOXTON ROAD		
Gumley	75	E7
Lubenham	82	F1
FRAMPTON AVENUE	42	D5
FRANCHE ROAD	42	E4
FRANCIS AVENUE	46	B3
FRANCIS STREET	47	F2
FRANKLYN ROAD	46	D5
FRANKSON AVENUE	46	C2
FRASER CLOSE	43	C3
FREDERICK ROAD	43	E4
FREDERICK STREET	51	F1
FREE LANE	43	B4
FREEBOARD ROAD	46	B4
FREEHOLD ROAD	39	C4
FREEHOLD STREET	43	D3
FREEMAN ROAD	44	B3
FREEMAN ROAD NORTH	44	B3
FREEMANS HOLT	46	E4
FREEMANTLE ROAD	48	A2
FREEMENS COMMON ROAD	47	B1
FREER CLOSE		
Leicester	50	D4
Leicester	52	A4
FREESCHOOL LANE	43	A4
FRENCH ROAD	44	A3
FRENSHAM CLOSE	48	C7
FRESHWATER CLOSE	51	F5
FREWIN STREET	44	A3
FRIAR LANE	43	B5
FRIARS CAUSEWAY	43	A4
FRIDAY STREET	43	A3
FRINTON AVENUE	44	F5
FRISBY ROAD	43	F2
FRITCHLEY CLOSE	49	A5
FRITH CLOSE	41	F2
FROANES CLOSE	45	C7
FROG ISLAND	43	A3
FROLESWORTH LANE	72	D7
FROLESWORTH ROAD		
Broughton Astley	73	A4
Frolesworth	72	E7
Leicester	42	A3
Leire	73	A6
FROLESWORTH WAY	42	A4
FROME AVENUE	48	F5
FRONT STREET	39	D2
FULBECK AVENUE	44	F5
FULFORD ROAD	41	E5
FULLHURST AVENUE	46	D1
FULMAR ROAD	37	F3
FURROWS CLOSE	49	E6
GADDESBY AVENUE	42	E7
GADDESBY LANE		
Rearsby	26	B4
Rotherby	26	D1
GAINSBOROUGH ROAD	47	D2
GALAHAD CLOSE	45	C1
GALBY STREET	43	F2
GALLARDS HILL		
Leicester	41	F6
Leicester	42	A6
GALLEYWOOD DRIVE	38	F7
GALLIMORE CLOSE	42	A1
GALLOW FIELD ROAD	76	A7

GALLOWS LANE 21 A5
GALLOWTREE GATE 43 B4
GALSWORTHY COURT 42 C5
GALWAY ROAD 39 A4
GAMEL ROAD 44 D5
GANTON ROAD 41 E4
GARDEN CLOSE 48 C6
GARDEN STREET
  Leicester 40 A2
  Leicester 43 B3
  Leicester 51 B3
GARDENFIELD ROAD 40 B5
GARENDON STREET 43 D4
GARENDON WAY 37 A7
GARFIELD STREET 43 C2
GARLAND CRESCENT 42 E2
GARLAND LANE 35 E4
GARNETT CRESCENT 46 E7
GARRETT STREET 70 D6
GARSDALE 52 B2
GARTH AVENUE 39 A4
GARTREE ROAD
  Carlton Curlieu 64 F5
  Illston 65 A6
  Leicester 48 D2
  Little Stretton 64 A2
GAS LANE 51 E2
GAS STREET 43 B3
GATEWAY STREET 43 A6
GAUL STREET 42 F6
GAULBY LANE
  Gaulby 64 F1
  Leicester 48 F3
  Stoughton 64 A1
GAULBY ROAD
  Billesdon 65 A1
  Illston On The Hill 65 A4
GAWNEY LANE 81 A1
GAYHURST CLOSE
  Leicester 46 B4
  Leicester 52 B1
GAYTON AVENUE 43 E1
GAYTON HEIGHTS 45 C7
GEDDING ROAD 44 A5
GEDDINGTON CLOSE 52 A2
GEDGE WAY 47 A5
GEES LOCK CLOSE 46 D7
GELERT AVENUE 44 F4
GELSCOE LANE 11 C2
GELSMOOR ROAD 11 A6
GEORGE FOX LANE 61 B7
GEORGE STREET
  Leicester 37 F3
  Leicester 43 C3
  Leicester 49 D1
  Lutterworth 80 C5
GEORGEHAM CLOSE 51 F3
GERVAS ROAD 44 E3
GIBBET LANE
  Bilstone 34 B7
  Shawell 84 B2
GIBBONS CLOSE 43 C2
GIBSON CLOSE 51 F1
GIBSONS LANE 15 B2
GIFFORD CLOSE 44 D7
GILBERT CLOSE 40 A4
GILLIVER STREET 47 D3
GILLMAN ROAD 42 C2
GILMORTON AVENUE 46 D6
GILMORTON CLOSE 46 D6
GILMORTON LANE 73 F5
GILMORTON ROAD
  Ashby Magna 73 E7
  Lutterworth 80 D4
GILMOUR CLOSE 38 D4
GIMSON CLOSE 44 C1
GIMSON ROAD 42 D5
GIPSY LANE
  Leicester 39 F7
  Leicester 40 A1
  Leicester 44 B1
GIPSY ROAD
  Leicester 39 D7
  Nuneaton 70 C7
GLADSTONE STREET
  Leicester 38 A3
  Leicester 51 F1
GLAISDALE CLOSE 38 F6
GLAISDALE ROAD 52 A3
GLAMORGAN AVENUE 51 B2
GLASTON PARK 68 B3
GLASTON ROAD
  Bisbrooke 68 A4
  Morcott 68 D3
  Preston 67 F2
  Uppingham 67 F4
  Wing 68 B1
GLAZEBROOK ROAD 42 C2
GLAZEBROOK SQUARE 42 C2
GLEBE CLOSE
  Leicester 41 D2
  Leicester 48 A3
  Leicester 51 F1
GLEBE GARDENS 48 B3
GLEBE ROAD
  Leicester 37 A6
  Leicester 48 B3
  Melton Mowbray 16 C5
  North Luffenham 57 F7
  Wymondham 18 C6
GLEBE STREET 43 C6
GLEBELANDS ROAD 38 F1
GLEN GATE 51 B2
GLEN PARK AVENUE 37 D6
GLEN RISE 46 D7
GLEN ROAD
  Great Glen 64 A6
  Leicester 48 E6
  Leicester 52 F1
GLEN WAY 48 E7
GLENBARR AVENUE 42 F2
GLENBORNE ROAD 47 C7
GLENCOE AVENUE 39 E5
GLENDALE AVENUE 37 D6
GLENDON STREET 43 D1
GLENDOWER CLOSE 44 D4
GLENEAGLES AVENUE 39 F6
GLENFIELD CRESCENT 41 E2
GLENFIELD FRITH DRIVE 41 F1
GLENFIELD LANE 41 A2
GLENFIELD PARADE 42 F5
GLENFIELD ROAD 42 C4
GLENFRITH CLOSE 38 B6
GLENFRITH WAY 38 B7
GLENGARRY CLOSE 42 C3
GLENGARRY COURT 42 C3
GLENGARRY WAY 42 B2
GLENHILLS BOULEVARD 46 F6
GLENHILLS WAY 46 F6
GLENMORE ROAD 39 F6
GLENROTHES CLOSE 41 E5
GLENVILLE AVENUE
  Leicester 37 F7
  Leicester 50 D2
GLOSSOP STREET 43 E6
GLOUCESTER CRESCENT 51 B1
GLOVER COURT 46 E5
GOADBY HILL 65 E5
GOADBY ROAD 7 D6
GODDARDS AVENUE 38 D7
GODDARDS CLOSE 48 C6
GODFREY CLOSE 38 D3
GODWIN AVENUE 52 A2
GOLDHILL 47 C6
GOLDHILL ROAD 47 F4
GOLF COURSE LANE 41 F5
GOODING AVENUE 42 B6
GOODING AVENUE 42 C7
GOODING CLOSE 42 D7
GOODWOOD CRESCENT 44 D5
GOODWOOD ROAD 44 D5
GOPSALL ROAD 34 C5
GOPSALL STREET 43 D5
GORES LANE 83 E2
GORSE HILL 38 B4
GORSE LANE 52 F1
GORSEY LANE 20 A4
GORSTY CLOSE 38 D6
GOSCOTE HALL ROAD 39 C3
GOSLING STREET 43 A6
GOTHAM STREET 43 D6
GOUGH ROAD 44 A4
GOWER STREET 43 C3
GRABTREE ROAD 48 C2
GRACE DIEU ROAD 11 D7
GRACE ROAD 47 A3
GRAFTON DRIVE 52 B2
GRAFTON PLACE 43 B3
GRAHAM STREET 43 D4
GRAMPIAN CLOSE 47 B4
GRANARY CLOSE 41 D2
GRANBY LANE 2 A4
GRANBY PLACE 43 B5
GRANBY ROAD 46 F4
GRANBY STREET 43 C5
GRANGE AVENUE 41 D7
GRANGE CLOSE 41 D2
GRANGE DRIVE 50 E1
GRANGE LANE
  Leicester 43 B6
  Nailstone 35 B2
GRANGE ROAD
  Carlton Curlieu 64 F6
  Coalville 22 D5
  Leicester 47 F6
GRANGEWAY ROAD 47 F7
GRANITE CLOSE 45 C7
GRANTHAM ROAD
  Bottesford 1 D7
  Leicester 44 E2
GRANVILLE AVENUE 48 B4
GRANVILLE CRESCENT 47 D6
GRANVILLE ROAD
  Leicester 43 D6
  Leicester 47 E6
GRASMERE ROAD 52 B1
GRASMERE STREET 43 A6
GRASS ACRES 46 A4
GRASSINGTON CLOSE 38 E5
GRASSINGTON DRIVE 52 A3
GRAVEL STREET 43 B3
GRAY STREET 43 A6
GRAYS COURT 49 C1
GRAYSWOOD DRIVE 38 C2
GREAT ARLER ROAD 47 C3
GREAT BOWDEN ROAD 83 E2
GREAT CENTRAL STREET 43 A4
GREAT CENTRAL WAY 46 F1
GREAT DALBY ROAD 27 D5
GREAT EASTON ROAD
  Caldecott 78 D4
  Drayton 78 B4
  Great Easton 78 C4
GREAT LANE
  Frisby On The Wreake 15 F7
  Greetham 30 E2
GREAT MEADOW ROAD 38 D7
GREBE WAY 50 B7
GREEN LANE
  Ashley 77 D6
  Claybrook Parva 79 B2
  Goadby Marwood 7 C4
  Medbourne 77 C3
  Seagrave 14 D7
  Tilton on the Hill 54 C6
  Wilson 4 A7
GREEN LANE CLOSE 44 B4
GREEN LANE ROAD
  Leicester 43 F3
  Leicester 44 A4
GREEN WALK 42 A5
GREENACRE DRIVE
  Leicester 44 D5
  Leicester 48 D6
GREENBANK ROAD 44 F1
GREENCOAT ROAD 42 B3
GREENFIELDS 50 B5
GREENGATE LANE 39 B1
GREENHILL CLOSE 49 C5
GREENHILL ROAD 47 D2
GREENHITHE ROAD 47 A2
GREENLAND AVENUE 44 C2
GREENLAND DRIVE 44 C2
GREENMOOR ROAD 70 B5
GREENSIDE PLACE 47 B6
GREENWICH CLOSE 49 D4
GREENWOOD ROAD 44 B4
GREETHAM ROAD
  Greetham 30 D3
  Stretton 31 A2
GREGORY CLOSE 40 C2
GREGORYS CLOSE 45 F2
GREGSON CLOSE 39 F4
GRENDALE ROAD 50 D1
GRENDON CLOSE 52 A1
GRENFELL ROAD 48 A3
GRESLEY CLOSE 38 E5
GRETTON ROAD 67 F7
GREY CLOSE 37 B5
GREY CRESCENT 23 F7
GREY FRIARS 43 B5
GREYLAND PARK 37 B5
GREYS DRIVE 37 A7
GREYSTOKE CLOSE 39 A6
GREYSTONE AVENUE 44 D4
GRISEDALE CLOSE 43 B7
GRIZEDALE GROVE 49 C2
GROBY BY PASS 37 A5
GROBY LANE 37 A2
GROBY ROAD
  Leicester 37 F4
  Leicester 37 D6
  Leicester 42 B1
  Leicester 42 C1
  Ratby 36 F4
GROCOT ROAD 44 C7
GROSVENOR CLOSE 50 F3
GROSVENOR CRESCENT 48 B4
GROVE ROAD
  Hinckley 71 E4
  Leicester 43 E4
  Leicester 50 B6
  Leicester 50 C5
GROVE WAY 46 B6
GROVEBURY ROAD 39 B6
GUILDFORD DRIVE 47 D6
GUILDHALL LANE 43 B5
GUILFORD ROAD 48 A2
GULLET LANE 77 D6
GUMLEY ROAD
  Foxton 75 F7
  Laughton 75 C7
  Smeeton Westerby 75 D5
GUMLEY SQUARE 49 C1
GUNBY HILL 19 A3
GUNBY ROAD
  North Witham 19 E3
  Sewstern 19 B3
GUNTHORPE ROAD 41 F6
GURNALL ROAD 38 C5
GURNEY CRESCENT 49 E6
GURNEY LANE 81 B3
GUTHLAXTON STREET 43 D5
GUTHLAXTON WAY 52 A3
GUTHRIDGE CRESCENT 42 D6
GWENCOLE AVENUE 46 C3
GWENCOLE CRESCENT 46 C4
GWENDOLEN ROAD 44 A6
GWENDOLIN AVENUE 39 D1
GYNSILL LANE 38 A4
GYNSILL ROAD 37 F6

HACKETT ROAD 42 B2
HADDENHAM ROAD 46 E1
HADDON STREET 43 E4
HADES LANE 15 A1
HADRIAN ROAD
  Leicester 39 A4
  Leicester 40 A2
HALCROFT RISE 51 F3
HALF MOON CRESCENT 48 E5
HALFORD CLOSE 50 B6
HALFORD STREET 43 B5
HALIFAX DRIVE 39 A6
HALKIN STREET 43 D1
HALL CLOSE
  Cottesmore 30 C4
  Leicester 46 D7
HALL DRIVE 48 D5
HALL GATE 4 E7
HALL LANE
  Ashley 77 D6
  Bitteswell 80 B2
  Eastwell 7 B3
  Leicester 46 F4
  Walton 81 B3
HALL WALK 45 D7
HALLAM AVENUE 39 B2
HALLAM CRESCENT EAST 46 B1
HALLAMFORD ROAD 12 B4
HALLATON ROAD
  Allexton 66 F4
  Hallaton 66 E7
  Leicester 44 B2
  Medbourne 77 D2
  Tugby 66 A3
HALLATON STREET 47 A4
HALLEY CLOSE 38 C3
HALLFIELDS LANE 25 A5
HALSBURY STREET 43 F7
HALSTEAD STREET 43 F4
HALTER SLADE 52 A3
HAMBLE ROAD 48 F5
HAMBLETON ROAD 56 F3
HAMBLTON CLOSE 45 B1
HAMELIN ROAD 42 B6
HAMILTON LANE 53 A4
HAMILTON STREET 43 D6
HAMMERCLIFFE ROAD 43 E2
HAMPDEN ROAD 40 A7
HAMPSHIRE ROAD 46 F4
HAMPSTEAD CLOSE 49 D4
HAMPTON CLOSE
  Leicester 50 F3
  Leicester 52 A2
HANBURY ROAD 44 F6
HAND AVENUE 42 A6
HANDLEY STREET 47 A4
HANOVER CLOSE 44 D1
HANSEN COURT 51 D2
HARBOROUGH HILL ROAD 67 B7
HARBOROUGH ROAD
  Billesdon 65 C2
  Braybrooke 83 F4
  Glooston 76 E1
  Kibworth 76 A4
  Leicester 48 D6
  Lubenham 83 B2
  Market Harborough 76 B6
  Theddingworth 82 D3
HARBY LANE 6 D2
  Hose
  Plungar 2 A5
  Stathern 2 A7
HARCOURT ROAD 52 A3
HARCOURT WAY 46 A5
HARDIE CRESCENT 45 F1
HARDING STREET 43 A3
HARDWICK COURT 42 E6
HARDWICKE ROAD 49 B4
HARDYS AVENUE 39 E5
HAREBELL CLOSE 40 D7
HAREFIELD AVENUE 46 E3
HAREWOOD STREET 43 F3
HARLAXTON STREET 46 E1
HARLEQUIN WAY 50 B7
HAROLD STREET 47 A3
HAROLDS LANE 45 D7
HARRINGTON ROAD 52 A1
HARRINGTON STREET 43 E2
HARRINGWORTH ROAD 44 D5
HARRIS GREEN 41 E7
HARRIS ROAD 38 D6
HARRISON CLOSE
  Leicester 41 E2
  Leicester 50 C7
  Leicester 51 D3
HARRISON STREET 40 A1
HARROGATE ROAD 43 E1
HARROGATE WAY 52 A2
HARROW CLOSE 45 B2
HARROW ROAD 42 E6
HARROWDEN RISE 44 C4
HARROWGATE DRIVE 39 B1
HARSTON ROAD 3 D6
HART CLOSE 50 B6
HART ROAD 43 E4
HARTFIELD ROAD 44 F2
HARTINGTON ROAD 43 E4
HARTOPP ROAD 47 D1
HARTSHORN CLOSE 40 B3
HARVARD CLOSE 48 D5
HARVEST CLOSE 38 D5
HARVESTER CLOSE 45 B2
HARWIN ROAD 44 D6
HASSAL ROAD 42 A2
HASTINGS ROAD
  Leicester 41 A6
  Leicester 43 F2
HAT ROAD 46 A4
HATHAWAY AVENUE 46 B2
HATHERLEIGH ROAD 44 B7
HATHERN ROAD
  Loughborough 12 C1
  Shepshed 12 C3
HATTERN AVENUE 38 F5
HAUNCHWOOD ROAD 70 A5
HAVELOCK STREET 43 A6
HAVEN CLOSE 45 B1
HAVENCREST DRIVE 44 D3
HAWARDEN AVENUE 44 B3
HAWCLIFFE ROAD 24 F2
HAWKER ROAD 48 F7
HAWKESBURY ROAD 47 A4
HAWKES HILL 47 B6
HAWLEY ROAD 71 C3
HAWTHORN AVENUE 39 D1
HAWTHORN CLOSE 45 A1
HAWTHORN DRIVE 50 D5
HAWTHORN RISE 37 B6
HAWTHORNE DRIVE 44 C7
HAWTHORNE STREET 42 E3

Street	Page	Grid
HAYBARN CLOSE	49	F6
HAYDEN AVENUE	48	F7
HAYDEN CLOSE	39	A6
HAYES ROAD	52	A1
HAYFIELD CLOSE	41	D2
HAYLING CRESCENT	44	C2
HAYMARKET	43	B4
HAYNES ROAD	44	B3
HAYWOOD CLOSE	44	D6
HAZEL CLOSE		
Leicester	39	D1
Leicester	49	E6
HAZEL DRIVE	46	B5
HAZEL STREET	43	B7
HAZELBANK CLOSE	38	F7
HAZELDENE ROAD	40	F7
HAZELHEAD ROAD	37	F2
HAZELNUT CLOSE	44	D6
HAZELWOOD ROAD		
Leicester	43	F7
Leicester	51	C3
HEACHAM DRIVE	38	D6
HEADINGLEY CLOSE	38	E2
HEADLAND ROAD	44	C7
HEADLEY ROAD	46	B4
HEALEY STREET	51	B3
HEALY CLOSE	38	F5
HEANOR STREET	43	A3
HEARDS CLOSE	52	A4
HEATH AVENUE	50	A2
HEATH END ROAD	70	A6
HEATH LANE		
Blackfordby	9	F6
Smisby	10	A5
HEATH ROAD	35	F3
HEATHCOTT ROAD	47	B4
HEATHER LANE	21	E5
HEATHER ROAD	47	C3
HEATHERBROOK ROAD	38	C4
HEATHFIELD ROAD	47	F6
HEATHGATE CLOSE	39	B1
HEATHLEY CLOSE	45	B1
HEAWOOD WAY	45	F2
HEAYS CLOSE	42	A2
HEBDEN CLOSE	50	E2
HEDDINGTON CLOSE	47	C6
HEDDINGTON WAY	47	C6
HEDGEROW LANE	36	F6
HEFFORD GARDENS	38	F5
HEIGHTON CRESCENT	49	E6
HELENA CRESCENT	39	B5
HELMSLEY ROAD	47	B5
HELSTON CLOSE	51	E3
HEMINGTON HILL	4	F4
HEMINGTON LANE	5	A3
HEMINGTON ROAD	44	F7
HEMLOCK CLOSE	49	B3
HENLEY CRESCENT	46	B2
HENRAY AVENUE	50	E2
HENRY CLOSE	45	B1
HENRY ROAD	42	E4
HENRY STREET	70	C6
HENSHAW STREET	43	B6
HENSON CLOSE	39	B3
HENTON ROAD	42	E5
HERBERT AVENUE	39	D7
HERBERT CLOSE	50	C5
HERDSMANS CLOSE	49	E5
HEREFORD ROAD	46	F4
HERLE AVENUE	46	B1
HERMITAGE CLOSE	48	C6
HERMITAGE ROAD		
Leicester	39	C4
Whitwick	22	D2
HERON ROAD	43	E3
HERON WAY	49	F2
HERRICK CLOSE	49	C1
HERRICK ROAD	47	C3
HERRICK WAY	52	A3
HERRICKS AVENUE	40	B4
HERSCHELL STREET	43	E7
HESKETH AVENUE	50	E1
HESKETH CLOSE	50	E1
HEWES CLOSE	50	D1
HEWITT DRIVE	41	B6
HEXTALL ROAD	44	C7
HEYBROOK AVENUE	50	C5
HEYFORD ROAD	41	F6
HEYTHROP CLOSE	48	F7
HEYWORTH ROAD	46	E1
HICKLING LANE	6	B5
HIDCOTE ROAD	48	C7
HIGGS CLOSE	44	D5
HIGH CROSS ROAD	79	B1
HIGH STREET		
Barrow upon Soar	13	F7
Barwell	62	E7
Blackfordby	9	D6
Bottesford	1	C7
Braunstone	56	B4
Castle Donnington	4	E5
Caulby	32	E4
Cottingham	78	C6
Desford	36	B7
Duddington	69	E3
Earl Shilton	63	A6
Exton	30	E6
Fleckney	75	A3
Great Easton	78	C3
Hallaton	66	C7
Husbands Bosworth	82	A5
Ibstock	35	A1
Kegworth	5	C5
Ketton	58	E6
Kibworth	75	D3
Leicester	43	B4
Leicester	48	D1
Leicester	48	C5
Leicester	49	D1
Leicester	50	B5
Loughborough	13	B5
Market Harborough	83	D2
Measham	20	F5
Morcott	68	E3
Oakham	56	D2
Packington	21	C3
Quorn	24	E1
Ravenstone	22	C3
Somerby	28	C7
Stoke Golding	61	F6
Uppingham	67	E4
Waltham On The Wolds	7	E7
Walton	81	B2
HIGHAM LANE		
Nuneaton	70	D3
Stoke Golding	61	E7
HIGHBURY ROAD	43	E2
HIGHCLIFFE ROAD	40	C6
HIGHCROFT AVENUE	48	E7
HIGHCROFT ROAD	52	F1
HIGHCROSS STREET	43	A4
HIGHFIELD CRESCENT	47	F7
HIGHFIELD DRIVE	47	F7
HIGHFIELD END	27	A5
HIGHFIELD ROAD	37	A7
HIGHFIELD STREET		
Leicester	38	A3
Leicester	43	D6
HIGHGATE	47	C6
HIGHGATE AVENUE	39	B1
HIGHGATE DRIVE	47	D6
HIGHGATE LANE	2	B5
HIGHGROVE CRESCENT	46	E6
HIGHLAND AVENUE	45	A1
HIGHMERES ROAD	40	B6
HIGHWAY ROAD		
Leicester	40	B1
Leicester	48	A1
HILARY BEVINS CLOSE	70	D1
HILDERS ROAD	42	C4
HILDYARD ROAD	43	C1
HILL FIELD	52a	G7
HILL LANE		
Countesthorpe	73	E1
Markfield	23	C7
HILL RISE		
Leicester	39	C1
Leicester	40	B4
HILL STREET	43	C4
HILL TOP		
Castle Donnington	4	D5
Earl Shilton	63	A5
HILL VIEW	50	A1
HILL WAY	48	E7
HILLARY PLACE	46	C1
HILLBERRY CLOSE	49	C4
HILLCREST ROAD	47	E5
HILLCROFT CLOSE	40	B1
HILLCROFT ROAD	44	B5
HILLRISE AVENUE	46	C3
HILLSBOROUGH CLOSE	50	E1
HILLSBOROUGH CRESCENT	50	E2
HILLSIDE AVENUE	51	F3
HILLTOP ROAD	40	D5
HINCKLEY LANE	70	F1
HINCKLEY ROAD		
Barlestone	35	B4
Barwell	62	D7
Cadeby	62	C1
Earl Shilton	62	F6
Hinckley	71	E3
Ibstock	35	A1
Leicester	42	E5
Leicester	42	B5
Leicester	42	F5
Nailstone	35	B4
Nuneaton	70	D4
Sapcote	72	B3
Stapleton	62	D5
Stoke Golding	62	A6
Stoney Stanton	72	C2
Thurlaston	63	C3
HIND CLOSE	50	C6
HINDOOSTAN AVENUE	51	A1
HIPWELL CRESCENT	39	A6
HOBALL CLOSE	42	A2
HOBART STREET	43	D5
HOBILL CLOSE		
Leicester	45	D1
Leicester	49	A4
HOBSON ROAD	39	B6
HOBY ROAD	26	B1
HOBY STREET	42	F4
HOCKLEY FARM ROAD	41	F6
HODGSON CLOSE	42	C1
HODSON CLOSE	50	B6
HOLBROOK	52a	G7
HOLBROOK ROAD	48	A3
HOLDEN CLOSE	50	C7
HOLDEN STREET	39	C7
HOLDERNESS ROAD	38	F4
HOLGATE CLOSE	38	A2
HOLKHAM AVENUE	43	F1
HOLLAND WAY	49	D4
HOLLIERS WALK	71	D2
HOLLINGTON ROAD	43	F6
HOLLINS ROAD	42	A6
HOLLINWELL CLOSE	41	E5
HOLLOW ROAD	37	F2
HOLLOWTREE ROAD	40	E7
HOLLY GROVE	50	D4
HOLLY LANE	60	C5
HOLLY TREE AVENUE	39	C1
HOLLYBROOK CLOSE	40	C3
HOLLYBUSH CLOSE	44	F3
HOLLYTREE CLOSE	13	F2
HOLMDEN AVENUE	51	D1
HOLME DRIVE	48	D4
HOLMES CLOSE	37	A6
HOLMEWOOD DRIVE	41	B5
HOLMFIELD AVENUE	47	F1
HOLMFIELD AVENUE EAST	41	E7
HOLMFIELD AVENUE WEST	41	E7
HOLMFIELD CLOSE	15	C7
HOLMFIELD ROAD	47	F1
HOLMWOOD DRIVE	42	A1
HOLT DRIVE	41	B6
HOLT LANE	73	D4
HOLT ROAD		
Leicester	39	C3
Medbourne	77	F2
HOLTS CLOSE	46	D7
HOLYGATE ROAD	67	C1
HOLYOAKE STREET	49	D2
HOLYWELL ROAD		
Clipsham	31	D2
Leicester	46	E5
HOME CLOSE	50	D4
HOME FARM CLOSE	38	E6
HOMEMEAD AVENUE	38	F7
HOMER DRIVE	49	C4
HOMESTEAD DRIVE	51	F3
HOMEWAY ROAD	44	A7
HONEYBOURNE CLOSE	48	C7
HONEYCOMB CLOSE	49	C4
HONEYSUCKLE ROAD	40	E7
HONITON CLOSE	51	E3
HOPEFIELD ROAD	46	E1
HOPPNER CLOSE	24	F7
HOPWOOD CLOSE	38	D6
HOPYARD CLOSE	46	D7
HORNBEAM CLOSE	49	C4
HORNDEAN AVENUE	51	F1
HORNINGHOLD LANE	66	E7
HORNINGHOLD ROAD	66	D7
HORSE HILL	65	F5
HORSEFAIR STREET	43	B5
HORSEWELL LANE	51	F3
HORSTON ROAD	44	A7
HOSE LANE		
Hose	6	E1
Long Clawson	6	D4
HOSKINS CLOSE	52	A4
HOSPITAL CLOSE	44	C6
HOSPITAL LANE	50	F6
Leicester		
Swannington	11	B7
HOTEL STREET		
Leicester	43	B5
Ravenstone	22	C3
HOTOFT ROAD	44	D2
HOTON ROAD	14	B1
HOUGH HILL	22	B2
HOUGHTON LANE	64	B1
HOUGHTON STREET	43	F3
HOULDITCH ROAD	47	D3
HOWARD ROAD		
Leicester	47	C2
Leicester	50	D1
HOWDEN ROAD	46	E7
HOWDON ROAD	52	D1
HOYLAKE CLOSE	48	A1
HUBBARD CLOSE	50	C7
HUDSON CLOSE	42	C2
HUGGETT CLOSE	40	A5
HUGHENDEN DRIVE	47	A1
HUMBER CLOSE	44	D1
HUMBERSIDE DRIVE	44	C2
HUMBERSTONE DRIVE	44	C2
HUMBERSTONE GATE	43	B4
HUMBERSTONE LANE	40	B3
HUMBERSTONE ROAD	43	D3
HUMBLE LANE	25	D4
HUMPHRIES CLOSE	44	C5
HUNCOTE ROAD		
Croft	63	E7
Leicester	49	B5
Stoney Stanton	72	D1
HUNGARTON BOULEVARD	44	E1
HUNGARTON LANE	53	C3
HUNGARTON ROAD	54	A4
HUNGARY LANE	5	F6
HUNTER BOULEVARD	79	F5
HUNTER ROAD	43	C1
HUNTERS RISE	16	B7
HUNTERS WAY		
Leicester	45	B1
Leicester	48	F6
HUNTINGDON ROAD	40	A7
HUNTS LANE		
Desford	36	A7
Netherseal	20	A4
HUNTSMAN WAY	39	F6
HUNTSMANS WAY	40	A6
HURSLEY CLOSE	48	E6
HURST RISE	44	C5
HUTCHINSON STREET	43	D5
HYDE CLOSE		
Leicester	49	D4
Leicester	52	E1
HYDE LODGE ROAD	55	A3
HYLION ROAD	47	C5
IBBETSON AVENUE	41	E3
IBSLEY WAY	50	F1
IBSTOCK ROAD		
Ellistown	22	C6
Nailstone	35	B2
Ravenstone	22	A4
ICKWORTH CLOSE	44	A2
IFFLEY CLOSE	44	C4
ILIFFE AVENUE	48	B6
ILIFFE ROAD	44	A1
ILLINGWORTH ROAD	44	D4
ILLSTON LANE	65	B4
ILLSTON ROAD	65	C4
ILMINGTON CLOSE	41	E1
IMPERIAL AVENUE	42	D7
INFIRMARY CLOSE	43	B6
INFIRMARY ROAD	43	B6
INFIRMARY SQUARE	43	B6
INGARSBY DRIVE	44	E7
INGARSBY LANE	53	E5
INGARSBY ROAD	53	D4
INGLE STREET	42	D3
INGLEBY ROAD	51	E1
INGOLD AVENUE	38	F6
INGRAMS WAY	52	A4
INVERGARY CLOSE	39	F4
IONA CLOSE	38	D6
IPSWICH CLOSE	38	C3
IRETON AVENUE	40	B7
IRETON ROAD	44	A1
IRIS AVENUE		
Leicester	39	D1
Leicester	50	D1
IRLAM STREET	51	B4
IRMINGTON GARDENS	44	E4
IRONWORKS ROAD	43	E2
ISIS CLOSE	48	F5
ISLINGTON STREET	47	B1
IVANHOE CLOSE	41	E3
IVANHOE ROAD	51	B2
IVANHOE STREET	42	E3
IVESHEAD LANE	12	B7
IVY ROAD	42	F7
IVYDALE ROAD	40	B3
JACKLIN DRIVE	39	F4
JACKSON STREET	39	D6
JACOB CLOSE	49	C1
JACQUES CLOSE	49	C1
JAMES GAVIN WAY	52a	G6
JAMES STREET		
Leicester	37	F2
Leicester	50	C4
JARRETT CLOSE	49	C1
JARROM STREET	43	A6
JARVIS STREET	43	A4
JASMINE CLOSE	40	D6
JASMINE COURT		
Leicester	49	C3
Leicester	51	B2
JEAN DRIVE	42	F1
JEFFCOATS LANE	11	B7
JELLICOE ROAD	44	A4
JENNETT CLOSE	44	E4
JENNYS LANE	22	A4
JEREMY CLOSE	39	D7
JERMYN STREET	39	D7
JERSEY ROAD	39	A4
JESSONS CLOSE	39	F6
JESSOP CLOSE	42	C2
JOHN STREET	49	D1
JOHNSON CLOSE	50	C5
JOHNSON ROAD	39	B2
JOHNSON STREET	43	A3
JOLLY FARMERS LANE	12	B7
JONATHAN CLOSE	37	C6
JORDAN CLOSE	41	E2
JOWETT CLOSE	42	C1
JOYCE ROAD	42	D2
JUBILEE CRESCENT	49	E5
JUBILEE DRIVE	41	E3
JUDITH DRIVE	44	D6
JULIAN ROAD	50	E2
JUNCTION ROAD		
Leicester	43	C3
Leicester	51	F1
JUNE AVENUE	40	C4
JUNIPER CLOSE	45	B1
JUNO CLOSE	41	E3
JUNOR STREET	43	A4
JUPITER CLOSE	43	D4
KAMLOOPS CRESCENT	43	C3
KASHMIR ROAD	43	D3
KATE STREET	42	F5
KAY ROAD	42	B2
KEATS CLOSE	49	C1
KEBLE ROAD	47	C2
KEDLESTON AVENUE	39	C4
KEDLESTON ROAD	43	F6
KEENAN CLOSE	46	D6
KEGWORTH AVENUE	44	B5
KEGWORTH LANE	5	C7
KEGWORTH ROAD	5	D3
KEIGHTLEY ROAD	42	B2
KELBROOK CLOSE	38	E5
KELMARSH AVENUE	52	B2
KELSO GREEN	50	F1
KELVON CLOSE	41	F1
KEMP ROAD	42	B1

KEMPSON ROAD 47 A3
KENDAL ROAD 39 F6
KENDRICK DRIVE 48 D6
KENILWORTH DRIVE 48 B6
KENILWORTH ROAD 51 B2
KENNEDY WAY 45 D1
KENNEL LANE 60 E6
KENNETH GAMBLE COURT 47 D7
KENNY CLOSE 50 B6
KENSINGTON CLOSE
  Leicester 51 A3
  Leicester 52 E1
KENSINGTON DRIVE 47 F6
KENSINGTON STREET 43 C1
KENT CRESCENT 51 B1
KENT DRIVE 48 E6
KENT STREET 43 D4
KENTON AVENUE 51 E3
KENWOOD ROAD 47 E4
KEPSTON CLOSE 46 F7
KERRIAL ROAD 42 A3
KERRYSDALE AVENUE 39 F7
KESTREL CLOSE
  Leicester 43 E3
  Leicester 45 A1
KESWICK CLOSE 39 D1
KESWICK ROAD 50 C5
KETTERING ROAD
  Market Harborough 83 D2
  Stamford 59 C5
KETTON ROAD
  Ketton 58 F7
  North Luffenham 58 A7
KEVERN CLOSE 51 F3
KEW DRIVE
  Leicester 47 D6
  Leicester 52 E1
KEYHAM CLOSE 44 D1
KEYHAM LANE
  Keyham 53 C3
  Leicester 44 D1
KEYHAM LANE EAST 53 C4
KEYHAM LANE WEST 44 F1
KEYTHORPE STREET 43 E4
KIBWORTH ROAD
  Carlton Curlieu 65 A6
  Saddington 75 C3
  Tur Langton 76 A2
KIELDER CLOSE 49 B2
KILBURN AVENUE 48 B5
KILBY AVENUE 39 C4
KILBY DRIVE 52 A3
KILBY ROAD 74 F3
KILN AVENUE 40 B3
KILVERSTONE AVENUE 44 F7
KILWARDBY STREET 21 B1
KILWORTH DRIVE 44 A6
KILWORTH ROAD
  Husbands Bosworth 81 F6
  North Kilworth 81 B4
  Swinford 84 F3
KIMBERLEY ROAD 43 E7
KIMCOTE ROAD 81 B3
KINCAPLE ROAD 39 F5
KINCHLEY LANE 24 E3
KINCRAIG ROAD 39 F5
KINDER CLOSE 50 C7
KING EDWARD AVENUE 49 E4
KING EDWARD ROAD 44 B3
KING RICHARDS ROAD 42 F5
KING STREET
  Leicester 40 F2
  Leicester 43 B5
  Leicester 48 D6
  Leicester 49 D1
  Leicester 50 B5
  Scalford 7 A7
  Seagrave 14 D7
  Sileby 25 C2
KING WILLIAMS WAY 38 A2
KINGCUP CLOSE 45 B1
KINGFISHER AVENUE 43 E3
KINGFISHER CLOSE 45 A1
KINGS DRIVE
  Leicester 51 F1
  Leicester 41 C7
KINGS LOCK CLOSE 46 D7
KINGS NEWTON STREET 43 E5
KINGS WALK
  Leicester 41 C7
  Leicester 45 C1
KINGS WAY 37 B7
KINGSBRIDGE CLOSE 49 C4
KINGSBRIDGE CRESCENT 38 D2
KINGSBURY AVENUE 44 F6
KINGSCLIFFE CRESCENT 44 F6
KINGSGATE AVENUE 39 B1
KINGSLEY CLOSE 49 C3
KINGSLEY STREET 47 C2
KINGSMEAD CLOSE 47 E5
KINGSMEAD ROAD 47 E4
KINGSTHORPE AVENUE 78 E7
KINGSTHORPE CLOSE 39 B6
KINGSTON AVENUE 47 E6
KINGSTON ROAD 43 F7
KINGSTONE LANE 5 D4
KINGSWAY 46 B3
KINGSWAY NORTH 46 A1
KINGSWAY ROAD 48 A1
KINGSWOOD AVENUE 42 D5
KINLEY ROAD 39 A5
KINTYRE DRIVE 39 E5
KIPLIN DRIVE 49 C2
KIPLING GROVE 38 D6
KIRBY LANE
  Leicester 41 B3
  Leicester 41 B7
KIRBY ROAD 42 E5
KIRK LANE 49 E1
KIRKBY LANE
  Newbold Verdon 35 F7
  Peckleton 63 A3
KIRKBY ROAD
  Barwell 62 E6
  Desford 36 B7
KIRKDALE ROAD 51 B2
KIRKHILL 12 C5
KIRKLAND ROAD 46 B3
KIRKSTONE CLOSE 41 F1
KIRLOE AVENUE 41 C7
KITCHENER ROAD
  Leicester 38 A2
  Leicester 44 A4
KLONDYKE LANE 27 D5
KNIGHT CLOSE 40 B2
KNIGHTON CHURCH ROAD 47 F4
KNIGHTON DRIVE 47 F2
KNIGHTON FIELDS ROAD EAST 47 C3
KNIGHTON FIELDS ROAD WEST 47 B3
KNIGHTON GRANGE ROAD 48 A3
KNIGHTON JUNCTION LANE 47 C2
KNIGHTON LANE 47 A3
KNIGHTON LANE EAST 47 B3
KNIGHTON PARK ROAD 47 E1
KNIGHTON RISE 48 A2
KNIGHTON ROAD 47 E3
KNIGHTON STREET 43 B6
KNIGHTS ROAD 38 E3
KNIGHTSBRIDGE DRIVE 50 F3
KNIPTON LANE 3 B7
KNOB HILL ROAD 66 F6
KNOLLGATE CLOSE 39 A1
KNOSSINGTON ROAD
  Braunstone 56 B4
  Owston 55 C2
  Somerby 55 C1
KNOWLES ROAD 42 A3
KREFELD WAY 38 C6

LABURNUM ROAD 44 E2
LADYSMITH ROAD 51 A1
LAG LANE 17 B5
LAITHWAITE CLOSE 38 D3
LAMBERT ROAD 46 E1
LAMBORNE ROAD 47 C5
LAMBOURNE ROAD 39 D1
LAMEN ROAD 42 B1
LAMPORT CLOSE 52 B2
LANCASHIRE STREET 39 E6
LANCASTER COURT 37 A7
LANCASTER ROAD
  Hinckley 71 C3
  Leicester 43 C7
LANCASTER STREET 44 A4
LANCASTER WAY 51 A3
LANCING AVENUE 42 C4
LANDCROFT LANE 5 E6
LANDSCAPE DRIVE 44 E6
LANDSEER ROAD 47 D2
LANDYKE LANE 6 D7
LANE CLOSE 41 E2
LANESBOROUGH ROAD 39 D5
LANGDALE ROAD 40 B2
LANGHAM DRIVE 49 D4
LANGHAM LANE 29 F7
LANGHAM ROAD
  Ashwell 29 E4
  Leicester 40 B6
LANGLEY AVENUE 39 B6
LANGLEY CLOSE 49 A4
LANGTON ROAD
  Foxton 76 B6
  Great Bowden 76 E7
  Hallaton 77 A1
  Kibworth 75 E2
  Leicester 51 F3
LANGTON STREET 43 B4
LANKS LANE 19 D7
LANSDOWNE GROVE 51 C3
LANSDOWNE ROAD 47 A3
LAPWING CLOSE 38 D3
LAPWING COURT 49 C5
LARCH GROVE 41 E7
LARCH STREET 43 F3
LARCHWOOD AVENUE 37 B7
LARCHWOOD CLOSE 47 C4
LARK CLOSE 45 B1
LARKSPUR CLOSE 40 D6
LASTINGHAM CLOSE 47 C5
LATIMER CLOSE 50 C6
LATIMER STREET
  Leicester 38 A3
  Leicester 42 F5
LAUGHTON LANE 82 B1
LAUGHTON ROAD 82 E1
LAUNCESTON ROAD 51 E4
LAUNDE ROAD
  Leicester 48 E5
  Tilton on the Hill 55 B5
LAUNDON CLOSE 37 B7
LAUNDON WAY
  Leicester 37 B7
  Leicester 50 C7
LAUNDRY LANE 39 D6
LAUREL CLOSE 42 A2
LAUREL DRIVE 52 F1
LAUREL ROAD
  Leicester 43 E6
  Leicester 50 D4
LAURESTON DRIVE 47 F1
LAVENDER CLOSE 50 D4
LAVENDER ROAD 42 E7
LAVERSTOCK ROAD 51 E4
LAW STREET 43 C1
LAWFORD ROAD 46 F7
LAWN AVENUE 39 D2
LAWN LANE 15 D1
LAWRENCE CLOSE 24 F7
LAWYERS LANE 48 C6
LAXFORD CLOSE 38 E7
LAXTON CLOSE
  Leicester 39 D1
  Leicester 52 B2
LAYTON ROAD 44 A3
LEA CLOSE 40 A2
LEA LANE 23 D6
LEAKE LANE 13 C1
LEAMINGTON DRIVE 50 D6
LEATHERMILL LANE 70 A1
LEDBURY CLOSE 48 F7
LEDBURY GREEN 38 F4
LEDWELL DRIVE 41 E1
LEE STREET 43 C4
LEESIDE 36 A4
LEESON STREET 47 A4
LEESTHORPE ROAD 28 C4
LEGION WAY 45 F3
LEICESTER LANE
  Desford 63 D1
  Great Bowden 76 C7
  Leicester 45 E7
  Swithland 24 C5
LEICESTER ROAD
  Barwell 62 F7
  Belton-in-Rutland 67 A3
  Billesdon 65 B1
  Broughton Astley 72 F2
  Coalville 22 E2
  Field Head 36 D1
  Fleckney 75 A2
  Frisby On The Wreake 16 B7
  Hinckley 71 D2
  Husbands Bosworth 81 F5
  Ibstock 22 B6
  Kibworth 75 D1
  Leicester 37 B6
  Leicester 37 F7
  Leicester 38 A3
  Leicester 38 F1
  Leicester 47 E7
  Leicester 48 B5
  Leicester 49 E4
  Leicester 50 D1
  Leicester 51 B6
  Leicester 51 F1
  Loughborough 13 C5
  Lutterworth 80 C3
  Market Harborough 83 C1
  Markfield 23 D7
  Melton Mowbray 16 E6
  Mountsorrel 25 A3
  Mowsley 82 A1
  Nuneaton 70 C4
  Quorn 24 E1
  Ravenstone 22 B4
  Sapcote 72 D3
  Sharnford 72 C5
  Shepshed 12 C6
  South Croxton 54 B1
  Thurcaston 24 F7
  Tilton On The Hill 54 D5
  Uppingham 67 D3
LEICESTER STREET
  Leicester 43 F4
  Melton Mowbray 16 F5
LEIRE LANE
  Broughton Astley 73 A5
  Dunton Bassett 73 C6
  Leire 73 A7
LEIRE ROAD 72 F6
LEIRE STREET 39 D7
LEMA CLOSE 40 A4
LEOPOLD ROAD 47 C2
LEOPOLD STREET 51 B2
LETCHWORTH ROAD 42 C4
LETHBRIDGE CLOSE 43 C3
LEVERET DRIVE 50 B6
LEVERIC ROAD 44 A2
LEWETT CLOSE 38 F5
LEWIS CLOSE 38 D7
LEWISHER ROAD 40 B6
LEXHAM STREET 39 D7
LEYCROFT ROAD 38 E4
LEYLAND ROAD
  Leicester 46 B4
  Nuneaton 70 D6
LEYS CLOSE 48 E5
LEYS DRIVE 48 D7
LEYSIDE CLOSE 38 D6
LIBERTY ROAD 41 F3
LICHFIELD DRIVE 50 D6
LICHFIELD STREET 43 B3
LIDSTER CLOSE 44 D2
LILAC AVENUE 44 E1
LIMBER CRESCENT 42 A7
LIMBY HALL LANE 22 A1
LIME AVENUE 37 A7
LIME GROVE 50 D4
LIME GROVE CLOSE 38 E5
LIME KILNS 52 A4
LIME TREE AVENUE 39 C1
LIME TREE ROAD 49 F2
LIMEHURST ROAD 44 F1
LINCOLN DRIVE
  Leicester 50 D6
  Leicester 51 B2
LINCOLN STREET 43 D5
LINDEN DRIVE 44 C7
LINDEN LANE 41 B6
LINDEN STREET 44 A5
LINDFIELD ROAD 42 C3
LINDRICK DRIVE 48 A1
LINDRIDGE LANE 36 B6
LINDSAY ROAD 46 E2
LINFORD CLOSE 52 A1
LINFORD STREET 39 C6
LINK ROAD
  Leicester 37 F2
  Leicester 48 A4
LINKWAY GARDENS 42 E5
LINNETT CLOSE 49 C5
LINNEY ROAD 38 E6
LINTON STREET 43 E6
LINWOOD LANE 47 B5
LIPTON ROAD 38 C3
LIT BARLEY CLOSE 38 D6
LITELMEDE 44 A3
LITTLE AVENUE 39 D6
LITTLE CASTERTON ROAD 59 B1
LITTLE DALE 52 A3
LITTLE END 74 C7
LITTLE GLEN ROAD 50 F3
LITTLE HOLME STREET 42 F5
LITTLE JOHN STREET 42 F2
LITTLE LUNNON 73 C6
LITTLE MASONS CLOSE 45 F2
LITTLE MEER CLOSE 45 F2
LITTLE SHAW LANE 23 B6
LITTLE WOOD CLOSE 38 E5
LITTLEGARTH 47 B7
LITTLEJOHN ROAD 47 A7
LITTLEMORE CLOSE 44 B4
LITTLEWORTH LANE 66 F2
LIVINGSTONE STREET 42 E5
LOBBS WOOD CLOSE 44 D2
LOBELIA CLOSE 49 B4
LOCKE AVENUE 39 F4
LOCKERBIE AVENUE 39 E5
LOCKHOUSE CLOSE 46 D7
LOCKINGTON ROAD 4 F3
LODDINGTON LANE
  Allexton 66 E2
  East Norton 66 C3
LODDINGTON ROAD 54 E5
LODGE CLOSE 40 B3
LODGE FARM ROAD 44 E4
LODGE ROAD 20 A3
LODGEWOOD AVENUE 39 B2
LOGAN AVENUE 46 E5
LOMBARDY RISE 43 E3
LOMOND CRESCENT 38 E7
LONDON ROAD
  Coalville 22 D3
  Great Glen 64 A5
  Hinckley 71 D3
  Kegworth 5 D6
  Leicester 43 D6
  Leicester 47 F2
  Leicester 48 D6
  Markfield 36 C1
  Uppingham 67 E4
LONDON STREET 43 F4
LONG HEDGE LANE 11 A4
LONG LANE
  Kegworth 5 C3
  Leicester 43 A4
  Owston 55 B3
  Redmile 2 E4
  Stathern 2 B6
LONG MEADOW 52 A4
LONG MERE LANE 11 F1
LONG STREET
  Belton 11 E4
  Leicester 51 F2
  Stoney Stanton 72 D2
LONGCLIFFE ROAD 43 F3
LONGFELLOW ROAD 47 C3
LONGFORD CLOSE 51 E3
LONGHADE FURLONG 38 B1
LONGHEDGE LANE 1 A4
LONGHURST CLOSE 40 A4
LONGLEAT CLOSE 43 F2
LONSDALE ROAD 40 A3
LONSDALE STREET 43 E6
LORD BYRON STREET 47 C3
LORNE ROAD 47 C2
LORRAINE ROAD 47 A4
LORRIMER ROAD 47 A3
LOSEBY LANE 43 B5
LOTHAIR ROAD 47 A2
LOUGHBOROUGH ROAD
  Asfordby 16 A5
  Burton On The Wolds 13 E4
  Cotes 13 E3
  Hoton 13 F1
  Leicester 39 C2
  Leicester 39 C6
  Loughborough 12 E3
  Mountsorrel 25 A4
  Quorn 13 C7
  Thringstone 11 A7
  Walton Le Wolds 14 A5
  Whitwick 22 E1
LOUISE AVENUE 37 B7
LOUNT ROAD 35 B5
LOVELACE CLOSE 61 B3
LOVES LANE 58 B1
LOW WOODS LANE 11 E5

LOWCROFT DRIVE 48 E7
LOWER BRAND 11 B5
LOWER PACKINGTON ROAD 21 C2
LOWESBY LANE 54 C3
LOWICK DRIVE 52 B2
LOWLAND AVENUE 45 C1
LOXLEY ROAD 41 E1
LUBBESTHORPE BRIDLE ROAD 46 A2
LUBBESTHORPE ROAD 46 A5
LUBBESTHORPE WAY
Leicester 45 F2
Leicester 46 A1
Leicester 46 A6
LUBENHAM HILL 83 C2
LUDGATE CLOSE 39 A1
LUDLOW CLOSE 48 E7
LUFFENHAM ROAD
Barrowden 69 A3
Ketton 58 C7
Lyndon 57 D6
LULLINGTON ROAD 20 A3
LULWORTH CLOSE
Leicester 44 C6
Leicester 51 F5
LUNSFORD ROAD 43 F2
LUTHER STREET 42 F5
LUTTERWORTH ROAD
Arnesby 74 C5
Bitteswell 80 B4
Dunton Bassett 73 D6
Gilmorton 80 D3
Hinckley 71 E5
Leicester 46 E6
Leicester 50 C7
Magna Park 79 C7
North Kilworth 80 F3
Nuneaton 70 D6
Shawell 84 C1
Swinford 84 E1
Ullesthorpe 79 F2
Walcote 81 A6
Whetstone 73 D2
LOWER BROWN STREET 43 B5
LOWER HILL STREET 43 B4
LOWER LEE STREET 43 B4
LOWER MOOR ROAD 11 A6
LOWER WILLOW STREET 43 C3
LYCHGATE LANE 71 F4
LYDALL ROAD 47 A7
LYDDINGTON ROAD 78 F2
LYDFORD ROAD 40 A7
LYLE CLOSE 40 A4
LYME ROAD 43 E7
LYMINGTON ROAD 44 F2
LYNCOTE ROAD 46 D3
LYNDALE CLOSE 40 A3
LYNDALE ROAD 46 B3
LYNDON DRIVE 48 B4
LYNDON ROAD
Manton 57 A6
North Luffenham 57 E7
LYNGATE AVENUE 39 C1
LYNHOLME ROAD 47 D5
LYNMOUTH CLOSE 41 E3
LYNMOUTH DRIVE 47 D6
LYNMOUTH ROAD 44 F2
LYON CLOSE 47 C7
LYTHAM ROAD 47 D2
LYTTON ROAD 47 D1

MABLOWE FIELD 52 A4
MACAULAY STREET 47 B3
MACDONALD ROAD 43 C1
MACKENZIE WAY 43 C3
MADELINE ROAD 38 E3
MADRAS ROAD 43 D4
MAGNA ROAD 51 C3
MAGNOLIA CLOSE
Leicester 45 B1
Leicester 46 E6
MAGNUS ROAD 39 E7
MAIDENWELL AVENUE 40 E7
MAIDSTONE ROAD 43 D5
MAIDWELL CLOSE 52 B2
MAIN ROAD
Ab Kettleby 16 C1
Austrey 33 B4
Bilstone 34 C5
Bisbrooke 68 B3
Claybrooke Magna 79 D1
Collyweston 69 F1
Cotesbach 80 B7
Oakham 56 D1
Old Dalby 15 D1
Ratcliffe Culey 60 E4
Redmile 2 D3
Sheepby Magna 60 E2
Stainby 19 C2
Twycross 33 F5
Upton 61 C4
Wycomb 7 B7
MAIN STREET
Albert Village 9 C6
Asfordby 16 A5
Ashby Parva 80 A1
Ashley 77 D6
Bagworth 35 E2
Barlestone 35 C5
Barsby 26 F5
Barton In The Beans 34 F4
Beeby 53 C2
Belton In Rutland 66 F2
Bisbrooke 68 A4
Blackfordby 9 F6
Botcheston 36 C6
Branston 7 E2
Breedon On The Hill 11 A2
Bruntingthorpe 74 C7
Burrough on the Hill 27 F7
Cadeby 62 C1
Caldecott 78 E3
Clipsham 31 D1
Cold Newton 54 B4
Cold Overton 28 F7
Congerstone 34 C5
Cossington 25 C4
Cottesmore 30 C4
Croxton Kerral 8 B2
Dadlington 62 A5
Desford 36 B7
Drayton 78 B4
Dunton Bassett 73 C6
East Langton 76 C4
Eaton 7 D2
Empingham 58 B2
Fleckney 75 A3
Foxton 75 F7
Frisby On The Wreake 15 F7
Frolesworth 72 E6
Gaddesby 26 E5
Gilmorton 80 F2
Glaby 64 F2
Goadby Marwood 7 C5
Glooston 76 E1
Great Bowden 83 D1
Great Dalby 27 E3
Great Glen 64 B6
Greetham 30 E3
Grimston 15 E3
Gumley 75 E6
Gunby 19 D3
Harby 6 E1
Heather 21 F7
Hemington 4 F3
Higham on the Hill 70 E1
Hoby 15 D7
Holwell 16 E1
Houghton On The Hill 53 D7
Huncote 63 F6
Hungarton 53 F3
Illston On The Hill 65 A4
Keyham 53 D4
Kibworth 75 E2
Kilby 74 E1
Kirby Bellars 16 B6
Kirby Mallory 62 F3
Knossington 55 E2
Laughton 75 C7
Leicester 40 E1
Leicester 41 D1
Leicester 41 A4
Leicester 44 D2
Leicester 44 D7
Leicester 46 B1
Leire 73 A6
Lockington 5 A3
Loddington 66 C1
Long Whatton 12 B1
Lubenham 83 A2
Lyddington 67 F6
Market Overton 30 B1
Medbourne 77 E3
Middleton 78 B7
Mowsley 75 A7
Nailstone 35 B3
Netherseal 20 A4
Newbold Verdon 35 E7
Newton Burgoland 34 C1
Normanton Le Heath 21 D5
Normanton on Soar 12 F1
Norton Juxta Twycross 33 E3
Oakthorpe 20 E4
Orton On The Hill 33 C6
Osgathorpe 11 C5
Overseal 20 B2
Owston 55 B3
Queniborough 26 A5
Peatling Magna 74 B4
Peatling Parva 74 A7
Peckleton 63 B2
Preston 67 F1
Ragdale 15 C5
Ratby 36 F5
Ratcliffe on the Wreake 25 F3
Redmile 2 D3
Rotherby 26 D1
Ryhall 32 E7
Saddington 75 B5
Saltby 8 D5
Saxelbye 16 A3
Seaton 68 C5
Sewstern 19 A3
Shackerstone 34 D4
Shangton 65 B7
Shawell 84 C2
Shenton 61 E3
Skeffington 65 E1
Smeeton Westerby 75 D4
Snarestone 34 A1
South Croxton 26 E7
Sproxton 8 D7
Stanford on Soar 13 C2
Stanton under Bardon 23 A7
Stapleton 62 D5
Stathern 2 B7
Stonesby 8 A7
Sutton Bonington 5 E6
Sutton Cheney 62 B3
Swannington 22 B1
Swepston 21 C7
Swithland 24 D5
Theddingworth 82 C4
Thistleton 19 D7
Thornton 36 A3
Thorpe Satchville 27 D6
Thurlaston 63 E4
Tilton On The Hill 54 E5
Tugby 66 A2
Tur Langton 76 B2
Ullesthorpe 79 E2
Wakerley 69 B4
Whissendine 29 B3
Willoughby Waterleys 73 F4
Wilson 4 A7
Woodhouse Eaves 24 B3
Worthington 11 A4
Wymondham 18 C6
Zouch 12 E1
MALABAR ROAD 43 D3
MALHAM CLOSE 38 E6
MALHAM WAY 48 F6
MALLARD AVENUE 37 A6
MALLARD WAY 45 A1
MALLORY PLACE 44 A2
MALLOW CLOSE 40 E6
MALTON DRIVE 48 E5
MALVERN ROAD 47 F1
MANDERVELL ROAD 48 B6
MANITOBA ROAD 43 C3
MANN CLOSE 45 F1
MANNERS ROAD 47 A4
MANOR CLOSE 48 D3
MANOR COURT ROAD 70 B5
MANOR DRIVE 38 C4
MANOR FARM LANE 32 E4
MANOR FARM WAY 41 E3
MANOR GARDENS 41 E2
MANOR LANE
Barleythorpe 56 C1
Glaston 68 B3
Peckleton 63 A3
MANOR ROAD
Bottesford 1 D7
Desford 36 B7
Leicester 39 F3
Leicester 48 C3
Medbourne 77 E3
MANOR ROAD EXTENSION 48 D4
MANOR STREET 51 D2
MANSFIELD STREET 43 B4
MANSTON CLOSE 40 C4
MANTLE LANE 22 C2
MANTLE ROAD 42 F4
MANTON ROAD 57 E5
MAPLE AVENUE
Leicester 41 E7
Leicester 50 D5
MAPLE ROAD 39 F3
MAPLE TREE WALK 49 E5
MAPLETON ROAD 51 E1
MAPLEWELL DRIVE 38 C3
MARBLE STREET 43 B5
MAREFIELD LANE
Burrough on the Hill 54 D1
Lowesby 54 C2
Tilton On The Hill 54 E4
MARFITT STREET 39 E7
MARGARET ANNE ROAD 48 D7
MARGARET CLOSE 40 A1
MARGARET CRESCENT 51 D1
MARGARET ROAD 44 A5
MARIGOLD WAY 49 B4
MARINA DRIVE 37 C6
MARJORIE STREET 43 C1
MARKET PLACE
Leicester 43 B5
Mountsorrel 25 A2
Whitwick 22 D1
MARKET PLACE APPROACH 43 B5
MARKET STREET
Ashby-De-La-Zouch 21 B1
Leicester 43 B5
Lutterworth 80 C5
MARKFIELD LANE
Botcheston 36 C4
Markfield 23 D7
Thornton 36 A2
MARKFIELD ROAD
Leicester 37 A5
Ratby 36 E4
MARKLAND 46 E7
MARLBOROUGH STREET 43 B5
MARLOW ROAD 46 F1
MAROMME SQUARE 51 F1
MARQUIS STREET 43 B6
MARRIOTT ROAD 47 A5
MARSDEN LANE 46 E5
MARSH CLOSE 40 A4
MARSHALL STREET 42 F3
MARSTON CLOSE 52 C1
MARSTON DRIVE 37 B6
MARSTON LANE 70 D7
MARSTON ROAD 40 A7
MARSTOWN AVENUE 51 B2
MARTIN AVENUE
Leicester 41 B7
Leicester 48 E6
MARTIN CLOSE 43 D2
MARTIN STREET 43 E2
MARTINDALE CLOSE 43 A7
MARTINSHAW LANE 37 A6
MARTIVAL 44 A2
MARVIN CLOSE 42 D4
MARWELL CLOSE 39 B5
MARWOOD ROAD 38 F5
MARY LANE 7 F6
MARY ROAD 42 D2
MARYDENE COURT 44 E7
MARYDENE DRIVE 44 E7
MASEFIELD AVENUE 49 C2
MASONS CLOSE 49 D5
MATLOCK AVENUE 51 C3
MATLOCK STREET 43 E4
MATTS CLOSE 46 F6
MAURA CLOSE 50 C7
MAVIS AVENUE 46 F1
MAWBY CLOSE 50 C7
MAY TREE LANE 24 B2
MAYFIELD DRIVE 47 F6
MAYFIELD ROAD 43 E7
MAYFLOWER ROAD 44 A7
MAYNARD ROAD 43 D4
MAYNS LANE 64 D6
MAYTREE CLOSE 41 A7
MAYTREE DRIVE 45 A1
MCVICKER CLOSE 44 C4
MEADHURST ROAD 42 C5
MEADOW COURT 49 C3
MEADOW COURT ROAD 37 B6
MEADOW GARDENS 47 C5
MEADOW LANE
Agar Nook 22 E3
Leicester 39 E1
MEADOW VIEW 48 D6
MEADOW WAY
Leicester 37 B6
Leicester 52 B2
MEADOWCOURT ROAD 48 B4
MEADOWCROFT CLOSE 41 D3
MEADOWS EDGE 49 C2
MEADOWS LANE 6 C1
MEADOWSWEET ROAD 44 E1
MEADVALE ROAD 47 E4
MEADWAY 42 C4
MEADWELL ROAD 41 F6
MEASHAM ROAD
Acresford 20 C5
Appleby Magna 20 D7
Ashby-de-la-Zouch 21 A3
Donisthorpe 20 D3
Moira 20 D2
Oakthorpe 20 E4
Packington 21 B4
MEDBOURNE ROAD
Drayton 78 A5
Hallaton 66 D7
Slawston 77 C2
MEDHURST CLOSE 50 C7
MEDINA ROAD 42 F2
MEDWAY STREET 43 E6
MELBOURNE LANE 11 A1
MELBOURNE ROAD
Leicester 43 D4
Ravenstone 22 A5
MELBOURNE STREET 43 E5
MELCROFT AVENUE 42 D5
MELFORD STREET 44 B3
MELLAND PLACE 47 A6
MELLIER CLOSE 49 C2
MELLOR ROAD 42 C5
MELROSE STREET 43 D1
MELTON AVENUE 39 E4
MELTON LANE 27 F5
MELTON ROAD
Asfordby Hill 16 C5
Langham 29 C6
Leicester 39 F4
Leicester 40 A1
Long Clawson 6 B5
Lowesby 54 C2
Rearsby 26 B3
Shangton 65 B6
Syston 25 D7
Tilton on the Hill 54 D6
Tur Langton 76 C4
Waltham On The Wolds 7 E7
Wymondham 18 C6
MELTON SPINNEY ROAD 17 A2
MELTON STREET 43 C3
MEMORY LANE 43 B2
MENDIP AVENUE 42 F1
MENSA CLOSE 43 E5
MENZIES ROAD 39 A7
MERCIA DRIVE 48 B5
MERCURY CLOSE 43 D5
MERE CLOSE 43 E3
MERE LANE 52 F2
MERE ROAD
Illston 65 C4
Leicester 43 E5
Leicester 52 B1
Little Stretton 64 C3
Tur Langton 76 A1
Upper Bruntingthorpe 81 D1
MEREDITH ROAD 46 E2
MEREVALE LANE 60 A6
MEREWORTH CLOSE 43 F2
MERIDIAN EAST 45 F3
MERIDIAN NORTH 45 F4
MERIDIAN SOUTH 45 F5
MERIDIAN WAY 45 F2
MERIDIAN WEST 45 F4
MERLIN CLOSE 45 C1
MERRYLEES ROAD
Newbold Verdon 35 E5
Thornton 36 B4
MERTHULL ROAD 44 F4
MERTON AVENUE 42 E5

MERVYN ROAD 43 F6
METHUEN AVENUE 40 A1
MEYNELL CLOSE 48 E7
MEYNELL ROAD 43 F3
MICHAEL RAMSEY COURT 50 E1
MICKLETON DRIVE 44 D7
MIDDLE ROAD 11 B6
MIDDLE STREET 8 B2
MIDDLESEX ROAD 46 F4
MIDDLETON CLOSE 52 B1
MIDDLETON ROAD
Ashley 77 E5
Great Easton 78 C5
MIDDLETON STREET 46 E4
MIDHURST AVENUE 46 B3
MIDLAND STREET 43 C4
MIDLAND ROAD 70 A4
MIDLANDS ROAD 22 C5
MIDWAY ROAD 47 F1
MILBY DRIVE 70 D3
MILFORD CLOSE 49 D4
MILFORD ROAD 47 D3
MILL CLOSE 51 B4
MILL HILL
Laughton 82 C2
Leicester 45 C7
Stathern 7 B1
MILL HILL CLOSE 50 C4
MILL HILL LANE 43 D6
MILL LANE
Belton 11 E3
Earl Shilton 63 B6
Gilmorton 80 F1
Heather 21 F7
Leicester 39 F1
Leicester 43 A6
Leicester 50 F4
Leicester 51 A4
Leicester 49 E2
Long Whatton 12 C1
Sheepby Magna 60 F2
Shenton 61 E4
South Witham 19 D6
MILL ROAD
Cottingham 78 D5
Rearsby 26 A3
Thurcaston 24 E6
MILL STREET
Barwell 62 E7
Duddington 69 E3
Leicester 43 B6
Oakham 56 E2
MILLBROOK CLOSE 39 B6
MILLER CLOSE 40 A4
MILLERS CLOSE 41 D2
MILLERSDALE AVENUE 44 F5
MILLFIELD CLOSE 37 F4
MILLFIELD CRESCENT 46 B5
MILLFIELD STREET 9 E6
MILLIGAN ROAD 47 A4
MILLSTONE LANE 43 B5
MILLWOOD CLOSE 39 A4
MILTON CLOSE 52 A2
MILTON CRESCENT 38 D6
MILTON GARDENS 48 C6
MILTON STREET 49 C3
MILVERTON AVENUE 42 F1
MILVERTON CLOSE 47 E7
MILVERTON DRIVE 47 E7
MINEHEAD STREET 42 D5
MINSTER CRESCENT 42 F1
MIRA DRIVE 70 C1
MITCHELL ROAD 49 C1
MOAT ROAD 43 F5
MOAT STREET 51 F2
MODBURY AVENUE 39 A4
MOIRA ROAD 21 B1
MOIRA STREET 43 D1
MOLES LANE 68 C5
MONAR CLOSE 39 F5
MONARCH CLOSE 39 E1
MONCKTON CLOSE 43 C3
MONICA ROAD 46 B4
MONMOUTH DRIVE 50 E2
MONSELL DRIVE 46 E6
MONTAGUE ROAD 47 D1
MONTREAL ROAD 43 C3
MONTROSE ROAD 46 F5
MONTROSE ROAD SOUTH 46 F6
MOON CLOSE 43 D5
MOOR HILL 66 C5
MOOR LANE
East Norton 66 C3
Normanton on Soar 12 F1
South Luffenham 68 F1
South Witham 19 C5
Stathern 2 B6
Tonge 11 B1
MOORBARNS LANE 80 B6
MOORES CLOSE 51 A2
MOORES LANE 49 D1
MOORES ROAD 39 D7
MOORFIELDS 44 F2
MOORGATE AVENUE 39 B1
MOORGATE STREET 43 C2
MORBAN ROAD 46 D5
MORCOTE ROAD 42 A6
MORCOTT ROAD
Barrowden 68 F3
Glaston 68 C3
Wing 68 B1
MORLAND AVENUE 48 A3
MORLEDGE STREET 43 C4
MORLEY LANE 12 B7
MORLEY ROAD 43 E4
MORNINGTON STREET 43 F3
MORPETH AVENUE 38 F4
MORPETH CLOSE 48 F7
MORRIS COURT 74 C7
MORRIS ROAD 47 C2
MORTIMER PLACE 46 D2
MORTIMER ROAD 49 C5
MORTIMER WAY 46 D2
MORTOFT ROAD 39 D6
MOSSDALE CLOSE 43 A6
MOSSDALE ROAD 46 A3
MOSSE WAY 48 E5
MOSSGATE 42 D3
MOSTYN STREET 42 D5
MOTTISFORD ROAD 39 B5
MOUNT AVENUE 43 F4
MOUNT PLEASANT 52 F1
MOUNT ROAD
Leicester 43 E4
Leicester 48 D6
MOUNTAIN ROAD 40 C5
MOUNTCASTLE ROAD 46 E1
MOUNTSORREL LANE
Rothley 25 A4
Sileby 25 B2
MOWSLEY END 51 F2
MOWSLEY LANE 81 C2
MOWSLEY ROAD
Saddington 75 B6
Theddingworth 82 B3
MUIRFIELD CLOSE 41 E4
MULBERRY AVENUE 41 E4
MUNDELLA STREET 43 E7
MUNNINGS CLOSE 43 D2
MUNTJACK ROAD 50 B6
MURIEL ROAD 42 E5
MURRAY STREET 43 D4
MURRAYFIELD ROAD 41 E5
MUSEUM SQUARE 43 C6
MUSGROVE CLOSE 42 F5
MUSHROOM LANE 9 C7
MUSSON ROAD 42 A3
MUSTON LANE 1 D7
MYRTLE ROAD 43 E6
MYTHE LANE 60 E5

NAGLE GROVE 39 F4
NAILSTONE ROAD 35 A4
NAMUR ROAD 51 A1
NANSEN ROAD 44 A6
NARBOROUGH ROAD
Cosby 73 C1
Leicester 46 D2
NARBOROUGH ROAD NORTH 42 F5
NARBOROUGH ROAD SOUTH 46 A6
NARROW BOAT CLOSE 51 C4
NARROW LANE
Hathern 12 E2
Leicester 46 E5
Wymeswold 14 D1
NASEBY CLOSE 52 A2
NASEBY ROAD 40 A7
NAVIGATION STREET 43 B3
NEAL AVENUE 46 A1
NEDHAM STREET 43 D4
NEEDHAM AVENUE 50 C1
NEEDHAM CLOSE 52a G7
NEEDLEGATE 43 A3
NEEDWOOD WAY 49 B2
NELOT WAY 44 D5
NELSON STREET 43 C6
NENE DRIVE 48 E6
NEPTUNE CLOSE 43 E5
NESTON GARDENS 47 C5
NESTON ROAD 47 B5
NETHER END 26 E5
NETHER HALL ROAD 44 E1
NETHERFIELD LANE 5 A2
NETHERFIELD ROAD 38 A2
NETHERFIELD WAY 45 F2
NETHERHALL LANE 39 D3
NETHERSEAL ROAD 20 A5
NETTON CLOSE 51 E4
NEVANTHON ROAD 42 D5
NEVILLE ROAD 42 D4
NEVILLHOLT ROAD 78 A4
NEW BOND STREET 43 B4
NEW BRIDGE ROAD 50 D2
NEW BRIDGE STREET 43 B7
NEW FIELDS AVENUE 46 C1
NEW FIELDS SQUARE 46 D2
NEW FOREST CLOSE 51 F4
NEW HENRY STREET 43 A3
NEW INN LANE 65 B5
NEW KING STREET 13 C5
NEW PARK CRESCENT 42 D2
NEW PARK ROAD 47 A3
NEW PARK STREET 42 F5
NEW PARKS BOULEVARD
Leicester 41 F5
Leicester 42 A3
NEW PARKS WAY
Leicester 41 F5
Leicester 42 A4
NEW PINGLE STREET 43 A3
NEW ROAD
Appleby Magna 33 D1
Belton In Rutland 66 F3
Coleorton 11 B7
Illston On The Hill 65 A4
Kibworth 75 E3
Leicester 43 B3
Stoney Stanton 72 C2
Stretton 19 E7
NEW STREET
Leicester 43 B5
Leicester 48 D5
Leicester 50 D4
Measham 20 F5
NEW STAR ROAD 40 C5
NEW WALK 43 C6
NEW WAY ROAD 47 F1
NEWARK ROAD 40 A2
NEWARK WALK 42 F5
NEWARKE CLOSE 43 A6
NEWARKE STREET 43 B5
NEWBOLD LANE 11 A4
NEWBOLD ROAD
Barlestone 35 D5
Desford 36 B7
Kirby Mallory 62 F1
Owston 55 A2
NEWBURY CLOSE 51 E3
NEWBY CLOSE 50 B3
NEWBY GARDENS 48 F7
NEWCOMBE ROAD 46 D1
NEWGATE END 51 F2
NEWHAVEN ROAD 44 F7
NEWINGTON STREET 39 D7
NEWLYN PARADE 44 F1
NEWMARKET STREET 47 D3
NEWPOOL BANK 52a G7
NEWPORT PLACE 43 C5
NEWPORT STREET 42 E3
NEWQUAY DRIVE 41 E1
NEWSTEAD AVENUE
Leicester 42 E1
Leicester 47 E7
NEWSTEAD ROAD
Belmesthorpe 59 E1
Leicester 47 E3
NEWTON DRIVE 39 E1
NEWTON LANE
Austrey 33 A3
Great Glen 64 B6
Leicester 52 B3
NEWTON ROAD 34 E2
NEWTOWN LINFORD LANE 37 A4
NEWTOWN ROAD 70 C4
NEWTOWN STREET 43 B6
NICHOLS STREET 43 C4
NICKLAUS ROAD 40 A4
NIDDERDALE ROAD 52 B2
NO MANS HEATH ROAD 20 A6
NOB HILL 33 E4
NOBLE STREET 42 F4
NOEL STREET 42 F7
NOOK STREET 42 D3
NORBURY AVENUE 43 E1
NORFOLK ROAD 51 B1
NORFOLK STREET 42 F5
NORMAN COURT 48 F7
NORMAN ROAD 40 A1
NORMAN STREET 42 F6
NORMAN WAY 16 F5
NORMANDY CLOSE 41 E3
NORMANTON LANE
Bottesford 1 C6
Heather 21 E6
Normanton le Heath 21 D5
Stanford on Soar 13 B2
NORMANTON ROAD
Edith Weston 57 F5
Leicester 43 F6
Packington 21 C3
NORRIS CLOSE 38 C6
NORTH AVENUE 47 E1
NORTH BRIDGE PLACE 42 F3
NORTH DRIVE 44 C2
NORTH END CLOSE 47 B5
NORTH KILWORTH ROAD 81 C7
NORTH LUFFENHAM ROAD
Morcott 68 E2
South Luffenham 68 F1
NORTH STREET
Asfordby 16 B5
Leicester 48 C5
Leicester 51 F1
Quorn 13 F7
Rothley 25 A5
Whitwick 22 D1
NORTH STREET EAST 67 E4
NORTH STREET WEST 67 E4
NORTH WITHAM ROAD 19 E4
NORTHAMPTON ROAD 83 D3
NORTHAMPTON STREET 43 C5
NORTHCOTE ROAD 47 E3
NORTHDENE ROAD 47 C6
NORTHDOWN DRIVE 40 A3
NORTHERN PERIMETER ROAD 71 B1
NORTHFIELD AVENUE
Leicester 39 D1
Leicester 47 D7
NORTHFIELD ROAD
Hinckley 71 C3
Leicester 44 A1
Leicester 50 D3
NORTHFOLD ROAD 47 E5
NORTHGATE 43 A3
NORTHGATE STREET 43 A3
NORTHUMBERLAND AVENUE
Leicester 39 E7
Nuneaton 70 A5
NORTHUMBERLAND ROAD 51 B1
NORTHUMBERLAND STREET 43 A3
NORTON HILL 33 C4
NORTON LANE 33 C6
NORTON STREET 43 B5
NORWICH ROAD 38 F6
NORWOOD ROAD 44 A7
NOSELEY ROAD 65 B4
NOTTINGHAM ROAD
Barrow upon Soar 13 F7
Bottesford 1 A7
Coleorton 11 B6
Kegworth 5 C5
Leicester 43 F4
Loughborough 13 C4
NUGENT STREET 42 F4
NUNEATON LANE 70 D2
NURSERY CLOSE 39 F3
NURSERY HOLLOW 50 C1
NURSERY LANE 16 C1
NURSERY ROAD 44 F3
NUTFIELD ROAD 42 E7
NUTHALL GROVE 46 D7
NUTTS LANE 71 B4

OADBY HILL DRIVE 48 B5
OADBY ROAD 52 A1
OAK CRESCENT 45 E1
OAK POOL GARDENS 50 F1
OAK ROAD 49 E6
OAK STREET 43 E3
OAKCROFT AVENUE 41 A4
OAKDALE CLOSE 41 E4
OAKDENE ROAD 47 C5
OAKENSHAW CLOSE 39 A4
OAKFIELD AVENUE
Leicester 37 F7
Leicester 39 B2
OAKFIELD CRESCENT 50 E5
OAKFIELD ROAD 43 E7
OAKHAM ROAD
Ashwell 29 E4
Braunstone 56 B3
Exton 30 D7
Greetham 30 E3
Langham 29 C7
Little Dalby 28 C3
Oakham 29 F7
Preston 56 F7
Somerby 28 C7
Tilton On The Hill 54 E5
Whissendine 29 A3
OAKLAND AVENUE 39 E4
OAKLAND ROAD 47 C2
OAKLEIGH AVENUE 51 A3
OAKLEY DRIVE 12 C2
OAKLEY ROAD 43 F3
OAKMEADOW 41 D3
OAKMEADOW WAY 37 A7
OAKS COURT 49 C4
OAKS DRIVE 50 E5
OAKS ROAD 64 C6
OAKS WAY 48 B3
OAKSIDE CLOSE 44 E5
OAKSIDE CRESCENT 44 E5
OAKTHORPE AVENUE 42 D6
OAKTREE CLOSE
Leicester 37 A6
Leicester 40 E7
OAKWOOD AVENUE 47 F7
OAKWOOD CLOSE 45 B1
OBAN STREET 42 E3
OCCUPATION LANE 9 C6
OCCUPATION ROAD
Albert Village 9 B7
Middleton 78 B5
OCEAN CLOSE 44 E3
OCEAN ROAD 44 E3
ODAM CLOSE 46 B1
ODSTONE LANE 34 D2
ODSTONE ROAD 34 F3
OFFRANVILLE CLOSE 40 B3
OGWEN CLOSE 44 F4
OKEHAMPTON AVENUE 44 B7
OLD CHURCH STREET 46 E4
OLD FORGE ROAD
Ashby Magna 73 E6
Fenny Drayton 61 B6
OLD GATE ROAD 15 A6
OLD GREAT NORTH ROAD 59 B3
OLD HALL CLOSE
Leicester 37 B6
Leicester 40 A1
OLD MILL LANE 43 A3
OLD MILTON STREET 43 C3
OLD PARSONAGE LANE 13 F2
OLD SCHOOL CLOSE 81 B3
OLIVER ROAD 39 F7
OLIVER STREET 47 A3
OLPHIN STREET 43 C2
OLYMPIC CLOSE 41 F2
ONTARIO CLOSE 43 C3
ORANGE STREET
Leicester 51 B3
Uppingham 67 E4
ORCHARD AVENUE 50 D1
ORCHARD CLOSE 48 C7
ORCHARD GARDENS 40 C3
ORCHARD ROAD 39 E2
ORCHARDS DRIVE 51 D2
ORCHARDSON AVENUE 43 D2
ORCHID CLOSE
Leicester 40 E6
Leicester 49 C3
ORME CLOSE 38 C6
ORMEN GREEN 41 F4
ORONSAY ROAD 38 E6
ORPINE ROAD 40 D6
ORSON DRIVE 51 D1

ORSON STREET 43 F5
ORSTON LANE 1 B6
ORTON HILL 33 D5
ORTON LANE
Norton Juxta Twycross 33 D4
Orton on the Hill 33 C6
Sheepy Magna 60 E1
Twycross 33 E6
ORTON ROAD
Leicester 39 B6
Warton 33 B7
ORWELL DRIVE 38 C5
OSBASTON LANE 35 C6
OSBORNE ROAD 43 F5
OSMASTON ROAD 43 F6
OSPREY ROAD 38 C3
OSWIN ROAD 42 A5
OTTAWA ROAD 43 C3
OTTER WAY 50 B7
OUT WOODS LANE 11 A7
OUTWOOD CLOSE 41 F5
OVERDALE AVENUE 37 D6
OVERDALE CLOSE 37 D7
OVERDALE ROAD
Leicester 40 B3
Leicester 47 D5
OVERFIELD CLOSE 49 C5
OVERING CLOSE 39 C6
OVERPARK AVENUE 42 B6
OVERSEAL ROAD 42 A2
OVERTON ROAD
Ibstock 35 A1
Leicester 43 F3
OWEN CLOSE 40 A4
OWSTON DRIVE 51 D1
OWSTON ROAD
Knossington 55 D2
Somerby 55 C1
OWSTON WOOD ROAD 55 D3
OXENDON STREET 43 D5
OXFORD DRIVE 51 B1
OXFORD ROAD 47 D1
OXON WAY 44 C4
OXTED RISE 52 C1

PACKER AVENUE 41 D6
PACKHORSE ROAD 50 F1
PACKWOOD ROAD 39 A6
PADDOCK CLOSE 48 B5
PADDOCK LANE 77 F3
PADDOCK STREET 51 F2
PADDYS LANE 15 A2
PADSTOW ROAD 40 A6
PAGET AVENUE 39 D1
PAGET ROAD 42 F4
PAGET STREET 46 E5
PAIGLE ROAD 46 F5
PAINTER STREET 43 C2
PAISLEY CLOSE 46 F7
PALFREYMAN LANE 52a G7
PALLETT DRIVE 70 D3
PALMER STREET 39 C6
PALMERS LANE 65 F4
PALMERSTON BOULEVARD 47 E5
PALMERSTON WAY 47 E5
PALSEY ROAD 46 F7
PAMELA PLACE 39 A5
PANKHURST ROAD 38 D3
PAPER MILL CLOSE 37 F3
PARAMORE CLOSE 50 C7
PARES STREET 43 B3
PARK AVENUE 47 A3
PARK CRESCENT 48 E7
PARK DRIVE
Leicester 41 E2
Leicester 41 E7
PARK HILL 26 E4
PARK HILL AVENUE 46 F4
PARK HILL DRIVE 46 F4
PARK HILL LANE 25 F1
PARK LANE
Castle Donnington 4 C4
Sutton Bonington 5 E7
Walton 81 B2
PARK RISE 42 A5
PARK ROAD
Cosby 73 C1
Hinckley 71 D3
Leicester 37 F3
Leicester 39 B3
Leicester 49 D5
Leicester 50 D4
Leicester 51 B4
Lowesby 54 B3
PARK STREET 43 B5
PARK VALE ROAD 43 E5
PARK VIEW 42 A4
PARKDALE ROAD 40 B3
PARKHILL 46 F3
PARKHOUSE CLOSE 39 C4
PARKLAND DRIVE 48 C5
PARKSIDE 37 B5
PARKSIDE CLOSE 38 C2
PARKSTONE ROAD 44 F2
PARLOUR CLOSE 51 E2
PARRY STREET 43 E3
PARSONS DRIVE 50 C1
PARTRIDGE ROAD 40 B3
PASTURE LANE
Gaddesby 26 F4
Hathern 12 E2
Hose 6 E4
Knipton 3 A7
Leicester 43 A3
Sutton Bonington 5 E7
PATE ROAD 16 D7
PATERSON CLOSE 38 D3
PATON STREET 42 F6
PATTERDALE ROAD 40 A2
PAUDY LANE 15 A4
PAUL DRIVE 40 B5
PAULINE AVENUE 39 D5
PAWLEY CLOSE 50 C6
PAWLEY GARDENS 46 F7
PAWLEY GREEN 46 F7
PAYNE STREET 39 D6
PAYNES LANE 77 D3
PEACE HILL 65 F5
PEACOCK DRIVE 50 B7
PEACOCK LANE 43 A5
PEAKDALE 52 B3
PEAKE ROAD 43 F1
PEARTREE CLOSE
Leicester 37 F4
Leicester 41 D3
PEATLING ROAD
Ashby Magna 73 F6
Countesthorpe 74 A2
PEBBLES WAY 39 F6
PECKLETON COMMON 63 B2
PECKLETON LANE
Desford 63 B1
Peckleton 63 D2
PECKLETON ROAD 62 F3
PEDLARS CLOSE 38 D6
PEEWIT CLOSE 50 C1
PEGASUS CLOSE 43 D5
PELDON CLOSE 38 F7
PELHAM STREET
Leicester 43 B6
Leicester 48 C5
PELHAM WAY 43 B6
PEMBROKE AVENUE 51 B2
PEMBROKE STREET 43 E3
PEN CLOSE 47 A7
PENDENE ROAD 47 E2
PENDLEBURY DRIVE 47 D4
PENDRAGON WAY 45 C1
PENHALE ROAD 46 B3
PENN LANE
Claybrooke Parva 79 B3
Stathern 2 A7
PENNANT CLOSE 41 F3
PENNEY CLOSE 51 E1
PENNINE CLOSE 48 F6
PENNY LONG LANE 41 B7
PENRITH ROAD 39 E7
PENRYN DRIVE 51 F3
PENSILVA CLOSE 51 E3
PENTRIDGE CLOSE 51 E4
PENZANCE AVENUE 51 F3
PEPPERCORN CLOSE 38 F6
PERCIVAL STREET 43 F3
PERCY ROAD 47 A4
PERCY STREET 46 D3
PEREGRINE RISE 38 C3
PERKINS LANE 15 E2
PERKYN ROAD 44 F4
PERSEVERANCE ROAD 39 C4
PERTH AVENUE 42 C3
PETERBOROUGH ROAD 68 F3
PETERS CLOSE 11 B1
PETERS DRIVE 44 D3
PETUNIA CLOSE 45 B1
PETWORTH DRIVE 42 E4
PEVENSEY AVENUE 44 F7
PEVEREL ROAD 46 C1
PEVERIL ROAD 73 E6
PHILIP DRIVE 51 A3
PHILLIPS CRESCENT 38 D3
PHIPPS CLOSE 50 C6
PHOENIX CLOSE 42 D3
PICCAVER RISE 41 F4
PICKERING CLOSE 43 F1
PICKWELL CLOSE 42 A2
PIERS ROAD 41 E1
PILKINGTON ROAD 42 A7
PILTON ROAD 68 D1
PIMPERNEL CLOSE 49 C3
PINCET LANE 81 E5
PINDAR ROAD 42 C2
PINE ROAD 41 E2
PINE TREE AVENUE
Leicester 37 B7
Leicester 44 C2
PINE TREE CLOSE 48 D7
PINE TREE GROVE 45 A1
PINEWOOD AVENUE 40 A3
PINEWOOD CLOSE 38 C4
PINFOLD 46 B4
PINFOLD LANE 57 F7
PINFOLD ROAD 39 F3
PINGLE LANE 63 D7
PINGLE STREET 43 A3
PINWALL LANE 60 D3
PIPE LANE 33 C7
PIPER CLOSE
Leicester 42 C3
Long Whatton 12 C2
PIPER DRIVE 12 C2
PIPER WAY 42 C3
PIT LANE 58 E5
PITCHENS CLOSE 38 B4
PITS AVENUE 46 A4
PITTON CLOSE 51 E4
PLANTATION AVENUE 46 E5
PLATTS LANE 25 C4
PLAYER CLOSE 39 F4
PLEASANT CLOSE 45 B1
PLOUGH CLOSE 45 B2
PLOVER CRESCENT 38 D3
PLOWMAN CLOSE 41 E1
PLUNGAR LANE 2 B4
PLUTO CLOSE 43 D5
PLYMOUTH DRIVE 44 B6
PLYMSTOCK CLOSE 42 D4
POACHERS CLOSE 41 D2
POACHERS PLACE 48 F7
POCHINS BRIDGE ROAD 51 C4
POCHINS CLOSE 51 E3
POCKLINGTONS WALK 43 B5
POLARIS CLOSE 43 D5
POLLARD ROAD 42 A6
POLLY BOTTS LANE 23 E6
POMEROY DRIVE 48 B6
POOL ROAD 42 E4
POPE CRESCENT 49 C1
POPE STREET 47 C3
POPLAR AVENUE 39 C1
POPLAR ROAD 49 D6
POPLARS CLOSE 37 A6
POPPY CLOSE 47 B7
PORLOCK STREET 42 D5
PORTGATE 52 A3
PORTISHEAD ROAD 44 A2
PORTLAND ROAD
Leicester 41 A5
Leicester 47 E2
PORTLOC DRIVE 51 F4
PORTMAN STREET 39 D7
PORTMORE CLOSE 38 E7
PORTSDOWN ROAD 47 F5
PORTSMOUTH ROAD 43 D1
POST OFFICE LANE
Leicester 52 F5
Lyndon 57 C6
Redmile 2 D3
POTTERTON ROAD 38 F5
POULTNEY LANE 81 A3
POWYS AVENUE 48 A2
POWYS GARDENS 48 A2
POYNINGS AVENUE 42 C4
PREBEND STREET 43 D6
PRESTON RISE 44 E1
PRESTON ROAD 68 A1
PRESTONS LANE 22 A1
PRESTWOLD LANE 13 F3
PRESTWOLD ROAD 43 F2
PRETORIA ROAD 22 B7
PRICE WAY 40 C2
PRIESTLEY ROAD 42 C5
PRIMROSE CLOSE 49 C4
PRIMROSE HILL 48 C5
PRIMROSE WAY 41 A4
PRINCE ALBERT DRIVE 41 E3
PRINCE DRIVE 48 E6
PRINCES CLOSE 38 A3
PRINCESS AVENUE 48 E7
PRINCESS ROAD EAST 43 C6
PRINCESS ROAD WEST 43 C6
PRINCESS STREET 49 E4
PRIORY CRESCENT 42 A5
PRIORY LANE 23 D5
PRIORY WALK 41 C6
PROGRESS WAY 40 C6
PROSPECT HILL 43 F4
PROSPECT ROAD 43 F4
PULLMAN ROAD 51 D2
PURBECK CLOSE 51 F4
PURCELL ROAD 43 C2
PURLEY ROAD 43 E1
PUTNEY ROAD 47 B1
PYMM LEY CLOSE 37 B6
PYMM LEY LANE 37 B6
PYTCHLEY CLOSE 39 A4

QUARRY BERRY LANE 33 A1
QUARRY LANE
Leicester 45 C7
Snarestone 21 B7
QUEBEC ROAD 43 C4
QUEEN ELIZABETH ROAD 70 A4
QUEEN STREET
Leicester 40 F2
Leicester 43 C4
Leicester 48 D6
QUEENS DRIVE
Leicester 41 C7
Leicester 49 F2
Leicester 51 D2
QUEENS PARK WAY 50 F2
QUEENS ROAD
Leicester 47 D1
Leicester 50 D5
Loughborough 13 C5
Nuneaton 70 B5
QUEENSFERRY PARADE 50 F1
QUEENSGATE DRIVE 39 B1
QUEENSMEAD CLOSE 37 A7
QUENBY STREET 43 F3
QUENIBOROUGH ROAD
Leicester 43 E1
Queniborough 26 A5
Syston 25 F7
QUINEY WAY 48 E5
QUINTON RISE 48 C6
QUORN AVENUE 48 F7
QUORN ROAD 43 F3
QUORNDON RISE 37 A7

RADCOT LAWNS 50 F1
RADFORD DRIVE 41 E7
RADIANT ROAD 44 E3
RADNOR COURT 49 B2
RADNOR ROAD 51 C1
RAEBURN ROAD 47 D2
RAGDALE ROAD
Hoby 15 C6
Leicester 43 F1
RAILWAY STREET 51 B4
RAINE WAY 52 F1
RAINSFORD CRESCENT 39 A6
RAMSBURY ROAD 47 D6
RAMSDEAN AVENUE 51 E1
RANCLIFFE CRESCENT 42 C6
RANNOCH CLOSE 38 E6
RANTON WAY 42 E2
RATBY LANE
Leicester 41 B4
Markfield 36 D1
RATBY MEADOW LANE 50 A1
RATBY ROAD 37 A6
RATCLIFFE COURT 47 F3
RATCLIFFE HOUSE LANE 60 F4
RATCLIFFE LANE
Ratcliffe on Soar 5 C2
Sheepby Magna 60 E3
RATCLIFFE ROAD
Leicester 47 E3
Loughborough 13 C4
Ratcliffe Culey 60 D5
Sileby 25 D2
Thrussington 26 A2
RATCLIFFE STREET 39 D7
RAVEN ROAD 42 A7
RAVENHURST ROAD 46 B3
RAVENSBRIDGE DRIVE 43 A2
RAVENSTHORPE ROAD 52 A2
RAVENSTONE ROAD
Heather 21 F6
Ibstock 22 A6
RAW DYKES ROAD 47 A1
RAWDON ROAD 20 D1
RAWLINGS COURT 52a G7
RAWSON STREET
Leicester 43 C6
Leicester 49 D1
RAYMOND ROAD 42 E7
RAYNER ROAD 40 B5
REARSBY LANE 26 D4
REARSBY ROAD
Leicester 43 E1
Queniborough 26 A5
Thrussington 26 B2
RECTORY GARDENS 48 D1
RECTORY LANE
Appleby Magna 20 D7
Bottesford 1 C6
Market Bosworth 35 A7
Stretton en le Field 20 C6
RED BURROW LANE 21 C4
RED HILL 39 C4
RED HILL AVENUE 49 D4
RED HILL CLOSE 40 A1
RED HILL LANE 40 B1
RED HILL WAY
Leicester 38 F4
Leicester 39 B5
RED HOUSE CLOSE 46 E7
RED HOUSE GARDENS 46 E7
RED HOUSE RISE 46 E7
RED HOUSE ROAD 46 E7
RED LODGE ROAD 54 E4
REDCAR ROAD 43 E1
REDMARLE ROAD 42 C7
REDMILE LANE 2 C3
REDPATH CLOSE 43 D2
REDRUTH AVENUE 51 E3
REES GROVE 39 F4
REETH CLOSE 38 E6
REEVES CLOSE 50 B7
REGENCY CLOSE 50 F3
REGENT CLOSE 51 D1
REGENT ROAD
Hoby 15 C7
Leicester 43 B6
REGENT STREET
Hinckley 71 C2
Leicester 43 C6
Leicester 48 C4
Leicester 49 E4
REGENTS WALK 41 C7
REMPSTONE ROAD
Coleorton 11 A6
Hoton 13 F2
Wymeswold 14 B1
RENDELL ROAD 43 D1
RENISHAW DRIVE 48 A1
REPINGTON ROW 47 B6
REPTON ROAD 47 D7
REPTON STREET 42 F3
RESERVOIR ROAD
Cropston 24 D6
Thornton 36 B3
REYNOLDS PLACE 46 C1
RIBBLE AVENUE 48 F5
RICHARD CLOSE 41 E7
RICHARD III ROAD 43 A5
RICHMOND AVENUE 47 A3
RICHMOND CLOSE 47 A3
RICHMOND DRIVE 51 A3
RICHMOND ROAD
Leicester 47 A3
Ravenstone 22 B6

RICHMOND STREET 43 A5
RICHMOND WAY 52 E1
RIDDINGTON ROAD
Leicester 46 B4
Leicester 49 E6
RIDGE WAY 52 D1
RIDGEWAY 49 E6
RIDGEWAY DRIVE 40 B3
RIDGWAY ROAD 47 F3
RIDLEY CLOSE 50 C6
RIDLEY STREET 42 F6
RIDLINGTON ROAD 67 E1
RING ROAD
Leicester 47 F5
Leicester 48 A4
RINGERS SPINNEY 48 C3
RINGWOOD CLOSE 51 E3
RIPON DRIVE 50 D6
RIPON STREET 43 E7
RISTON CLOSE 52 D1
RIVERS STREET 42 F4
RIVERSDALE CLOSE 39 D2
RIVERSIDE DRIVE 46 E4
RIVERSIDE WAY 49 E5
RIVETS MEADOW CLOSE 45 F2
ROBERT HALL STREET 39 B6
ROBERTS ROAD 43 C1
ROBERTSBRIDGE AVENUE 39 A6
ROBIN CLOSE 47 A4
ROBINSON ROAD 44 A3
ROBOTHAM CLOSE 49 A5
ROCHE CLOSE 46 E7
ROCKBRIDGE ROAD 48 F7
ROCKINGHAM CLOSE
Leicester 44 D4
Leicester 50 D6
ROCKINGHAM ROAD
Caldecott 78 E4
Cottingham 78 C6
Market Harborough 83 E2
ROCKLEY ROAD 42 E1
ROEBUCK CLOSE 50 B7
ROECLIFFE ROAD 24 B6
ROEHAMPTON DRIVE 47 D6
ROGERSTONE ROAD 44 F6
ROGUES LANE
Cottesmore 30 C3
Hinckley 62 B7
ROLLESTON ROAD
Billesdon 65 C1
Leicester 51 D1
ROLLESTON STREET 43 F4
ROMAN HILL 52 A4
ROMAN ROAD 39 C4
ROMAN STREET 42 F6
ROMWAY AVENUE 48 A1
ROMWAY ROAD 48 A1
ROOKERY 37 B6
ROOKERY LANE
Leicester 37 B6
Leicester 39 F3
ROSAMUND AVENUE 46 C3
ROSE CRESCENT 45 B1
ROSE FARM CLOSE 42 B6
ROSE STREET 39 B7
ROSE TREE AVENUE 39 C1
ROSEBARN WAY 44 F1
ROSEBERRY STREET 43 F4
ROSEBERY AVENUE 16 B5
ROSEBERY ROAD 38 A2
ROSEDALE AVENUE 39 F7
ROSEDALE ROAD 52 B2
ROSEDENE AVENUE 40 A3
ROSEDENE CLOSE 41 B6
ROSEMEAD DRIVE 48 C7
ROSENEATH AVENUE 40 A6
ROSEWAY 39 F6
ROSLYN STREET 43 E6
ROSS WALK
Leicester 39 C1
Leicester 43 C1
ROSSETT DRIVE 38 F7
ROSSETTI ROAD 49 C1
ROTHERBY AVENUE 43 F1
ROTHERBY LANE 15 E7
ROTHERBY ROAD 26 E3
ROTHLEY ROAD 25 A3
ROTHLEY STREET 43 C1
ROUGHTON STREET 39 D7
ROUNDHAY ROAD 46 E1
ROUNDHILL ROAD 44 A7
ROWAN STREET 42 E3
ROWANBERRY AVENUE 41 E4
ROWDEN LANE 76 F5
ROWLANSON CLOSE 24 F7
ROWLATTS HILL ROAD 44 C4
ROWLEY FIELDS AVENUE 46 D2
ROWSLEY AVENUE 43 F6
ROWSLEY STREET 43 E7
ROY CLOSE 49 E4
ROYAL EAST STREET 43 B3
ROYAL KENT STREET 43 A3
ROYAL ROAD 39 D7
ROYANNE RINGWAY 70 B5
ROYDENE AVENUE 42 E1
ROYDENE CRESCENT 38 E7
ROYSTON CLOSE 50 F2
RUBY STREET 42 E3
RUDING ROAD 42 F6
RUDING STREET 43 A4
RUFFORD STREET 44 A4
RUGBY ROAD
Cotesbach 80 B7
Hinckley 71 C3
Lutterworth 80 C5
South Kilworth 85 A2
Swinford 84 E3
RUGBY STREET 42 F3
RUMSEY DRIVE 50 C4
RUNCORN CLOSE 50 F1
RUNCORN ROAD 50 F1
RUNNEYMEDE GARDENS 41 F3
RUSHEY CLOSE 39 E5
RUSHFORD CLOSE 43 F1
RUSHFORD DRIVE 43 F1
RUSHLEY LANE 24 E3
RUSHMERE WALK 45 C1
RUSHTON DRIVE 46 D7
RUSKINGTON DRIVE 47 F6
RUTHERFORD ROAD 38 C5
RUTLAND AVENUE
Leicester 47 A2
Leicester 51 D1
RUTLAND CLOSE 41 C7
RUTLAND DRIVE 40 A2
RUTLAND STREET 43 C5
RYCROFT ROAD 4 F3
RYDAL STREET 43 A6
RYDE AVENUE 47 F4
RYDER ROAD 41 E4
RYE CLOSE 47 A7
RYEGATE CRESCENT 39 B1
RYHALL ROAD 59 D2

SACHEVEREL ROAD 41 F4
SACHEVERELL WAY 41 A1
SACKVILLE GARDENS 47 E3
SADDINGTON ROAD
Fleckney 75 B3
Mowsley 75 A7
Shearsby 74 F5
Smeeton Westerby 75 D4
SADDLERS CLOSE 41 D2
SAFFRON HILL ROAD 47 B3
SAFFRON LANE 47 B4
SAFFRON ROAD 51 A2
SAFFRON WAY 47 A5
ST ALBANS ROAD 43 D6
ST ANDREWS DRIVE 48 B2
ST ANDREWS ROAD 47 A4
ST ANNES DRIVE 46 F4
ST AUGUSTINE ROAD 43 A5
ST BARNABAS ROAD 44 A3
ST BERNARD STREET 39 D7
ST BERNARDS AVENUE 39 D6
ST DAVIDS CLOSE
Leicester 41 B7
Leicester 48 B2
ST DENYS ROAD 44 D7
ST DUNSTAN ROAD 42 E4
ST GEORGE STREET 43 C5
ST GEORGES HILL 11 B7
ST GEORGES WAY 43 C4
ST HELENS CLOSE 42 F1
ST HELENS DRIVE 42 F1
ST IVES ROAD
Leicester 40 A7
Leicester 51 F3
ST JAMES CLOSE 52 E1
ST JAMES ROAD 43 E7
ST JAMES STREET 43 C4
ST JAMES TERRACE 43 E7
ST JOHN STREET 43 B3
ST JOHNS 50 A1
ST JOHNS ROAD
Asfordby Hill 16 C5
Leicester 47 E1
ST LEONARDS ROAD 47 D1
ST MARGARETS STREET 43 B3
ST MARGARETS WAY 43 A2
ST MARKS STREET 43 C3
ST MARTINS 43 B5
ST MARYS AVENUE
Leicester 41 E7
Leicester 44 E2
ST MARYS COURT 41 E7
ST MARYS ROAD
Leicester 47 D1
Market Harborough 83 D2
ST MATTHEWS WAY 43 C3
ST MELLION CLOSE 38 D2
ST MICHAELS AVENUE 39 E6
ST NICHOLAS CIRCLE 43 A5
ST NICHOLAS PARK DRIVE 70 D3
ST NICHOLAS PLACE 43 A4
ST OSWALDS ROAD 42 B2
ST PAULS CLOSE 48 F5
ST PAULS ROAD 42 E4
ST PETERS CLOSE 41 D2
ST PETERS DRIVE 50 C4
ST PETERS LANE 43 B4
ST PETERS ROAD 43 E6
ST PHILIPS ROAD 43 F7
ST SAVIOURS HILL 43 E4
ST STEPHENS ROAD 43 E6
ST SWITHINS ROAD 44 F5
ST THOMAS ROAD 51 B3
ST WOLSTANS CLOSE 52 A1
SAINTBURY ROAD 37 F7
SALCOMBE CLOSE 51 E3
SALCOMBE DRIVE 41 E1
SALISBURY AVENUE 43 D6
SALISBURY ROAD 43 D6
SALKELD ROAD 50 E2
SALT STREET 33 B2
SALTASH CLOSE 51 E3
SALTBY ROAD
Croxton Kerral 8 B2
Sproxton 8 D7
SALTCOATES AVENUE 39 E5
SALTERSFORD ROAD 44 B3
SALTERSGATE DRIVE 39 C1
SALTS CLOSE 49 D2
SAMSON ROAD 42 D3
SAMUEL STREET 43 D4
SAND PIT LANE 6 C4
SANDACRE STREET 43 B4
SANDERSON CLOSE 50 C6
SANDFIELD CLOSE
Leicester 40 A4
Leicester 44 C4
SANDGATE AVENUE 39 B1
SANDHILL DRIVE 49 F2
SANDHILLS AVENUE 40 D6
SANDHURST CLOSE 42 D4
SANDHURST ROAD 42 D3
SANDHURST STREET 48 C5
SANDIACRE DRIVE 40 B2
SANDOWN ROAD
Leicester 41 E1
Leicester 47 F1
Leicester 47 F7
SANDPIPER CLOSE 43 E3
SANDRINGHAM AVENUE 39 D6
SANDRINGHAM ROAD 51 A3
SANDY LANE 16 F6
SANDY RISE 48 B7
SANVEY CLOSE 46 E5
SANVEY GATE 43 A3
SANVEY LANE 46 E5
SAPCOTE ROAD
Hinckley 71 E3
Stoney Stanton 72 D2
SAUNDERSON ROAD 38 F5
SAVERSNAKE ROAD 42 E1
SAVILLE ROAD 50 E6
SAVILLE STREET 44 A4
SAWDAY STREET 43 A7
SAWGATE ROAD 17 C7
SAWLEY STREET 43 F7
SAXBY ROAD 17 A5
SAXBY STREET 43 D6
SAXELBY ROAD 16 A5
SAXELBYE LANE 15 E3
SAXON DALE 50 E2
SAXON STREET 42 F6
SAXONDALE ROAD 52 A4
SCALFORD ROAD
Eastwell 7 B3
Melton Mowbray 16 F3
SCALPAY CLOSE 38 D6
SCARBOROUGH ROAD 39 E7
SCHOOL CLOSE 9 C7
SCHOOL HOUSE CLOSE 37 F4
SCHOOL LANE
Coleorton 11 B6
Cranoe 77 A1
Gaulby 64 F3
Leicester 39 C3
Leicester 40 F1
Leicester 48 D1
Leicester 49 D5
Newbould 11 A6
Normanton Le Heath 21 E5
Sewstern 19 A2
Thistleton 19 D6
Woodhouse 24 B2
SCHOOL STREET 20 E4
SCHOOLGATE 47 B6
SCOBOROUGH ROAD 82 E3
SCOTLAND ROAD 83 E3
SCOTSWOOD CRESCENT 50 F1
SCOTT STREET 47 C3
SCRAPTOFT LANE
Beeby 53 C3
Leicester 44 D3
SCRAPTOFT MEWS 44 C3
SCUDAMORE ROAD 41 D5
SEAFORD ROAD 46 F6
SEAGRAVE DRIVE 48 B5
SEAGRAVE ROAD
Sileby 25 D1
Thrussington 26 A1
SEATON ROAD
Barrowden 68 F4
Bisbrooke 68 A4
Glaston 68 B3
Leicester 51 E2
SEDDONS CLOSE 38 F5
SEDGEBROOK ROAD 3 B3
SEGRAVE ROAD 46 D1
SEINE LANE 45 B7
SELBURY DRIVE 48 B6
SELBY AVENUE 44 F1
SELKIRK ROAD 39 F6
SEVERN ROAD 48 F5
SEVERN STREET 43 D6
SEWSTERN ROAD 19 C3
SEXTANT ROAD 44 E3
SEYMOUR ROAD 47 D1
SEYMOUR STREET 43 D5
SEYMOUR WAY 41 B7
SHACKERDALE ROAD 47 D6
SHACKERSTONE ROAD 34 C4
SHACKLETON STREET 43 C3
SHADY LANE 48 D1
SHAEFFER COURT 38 E7
SHAFTESBURY AVENUE 39 D7
SHAFTESBURY ROAD 42 F6
SHAKESPEARE CLOSE 46 A2
SHAKESPEARE DRIVE 46 B2
SHAKESPEARE STREET 47 B2
SHANGTON ROAD 76 B2
SHANKLIN AVENUE 47 F4
SHANKLIN DRIVE 47 F4
SHANKLIN GARDENS 47 F4
SHANTI MARGH 39 E6
SHARDLOW ROAD
Aston-on-Trent 4 B2
Leicester 51 E1
SHARMON CRESCENT 41 F4
SHARNFORD ROAD
Sapcote 72 D3
Sharnford 72 A4
SHARPLAND 46 E6
SHARPLEY DRIVE 38 C3
SHARPLY HILL 23 F7
SHAW LANE 23 A6
SHAW WOOD CLOSE 37 A5
SHAWELL ROAD
Cotesbach 80 C7
Swinford 84 D3
SHEARER CLOSE 40 A5
SHEARSBY COURT 51 F2
SHEARSBY ROAD 75 A5
SHEENE ROAD 38 C5
SHEEPY ROAD
Atherstone 60 C5
Sheepy Magna 60 D3
Sibson 61 A3
Twycross 33 F6
SHEFFIELD STREET 42 F7
SHELFORD LANE 33 F3
SHELLASTON ROAD 51 E1
SHELLEY ROAD 49 C2
SHELLEY STREET 47 C3
SHELTHORPE ROAD 13 B6
SHENLEY ROAD 48 B7
SHENTON AVENUE 51 E1
SHENTON CLOSE
Leicester 40 C3
Leicester 50 B5
SHENTON LANE
Shenton 61 F3
Sibson 61 C3
Upton 61 D4
SHEPHERDS CLOSE 41 A7
SHEPSHED ROAD 12 D3
SHERARD ROAD 43 E4
SHERARD WAY 45 F2
SHERBORNE AVENUE 51 F4
SHERFORD CLOSE 51 E2
SHERIDAN CLOSE 49 C1
SHERIDAN STREET 47 B3
SHERINGHAM ROAD 38 F7
SHERLOYD CLOSE 40 B5
SHERRARD STREET 16 F5
SHERWOOD STREET 44 A4
SHETLAND ROAD 43 E1
SHETLAND WAY 78 F6
SHIELD CRESCENT 50 E2
SHILTON ROAD
Barwell 62 E7
Kirby Mallory 62 F3
SHIPLEY ROAD 43 F6
SHIPSTON HILL 48 C7
SHIPTON CLOSE 52 B2
SHIRE CLOSE 42 A5
SHIRES LANE 43 A4
SHIRLEY AVENUE 47 F3
SHIRLEY ROAD 47 F3
SHIRLEY STREET 39 C7
SHOBY LANE 15 E3
SHORT HILL 4 A7
SHORT STREET 43 B4
SHORTHEATH ROAD 20 D2
SHORTRIDGE LANE 49 D1
SHOTTENS CLOSE 38 D7
SHOTTERY AVENUE 46 B2
SHREWSBURY AVENUE 47 C5
SHROPSHIRE ROAD 46 F4
SHUTTLEWORTH LANE 73 C3
SIBBERTOFT ROAD 82 B7
SIBSON LANE 61 D3
SIBSON ROAD
Leicester 39 C2
Sheepy Magna 60 F2
Sibson 61 A4
SIBTON LANE 48 C7
SICKLEHOLM DRIVE 48 A1
SIDMOUTH AVENUE 44 C6
SIDNEY ROAD 47 F4
SIDWELL STREET 44 A5
SILBURY ROAD 42 E1
SILEBY ROAD
Barrow upon Soar 25 A1
Mountsorrel 25 A2
SILSDEN RISE 50 F1
SILVER STREET
Leicester 43 B4
Whitwick 22 D2
SILVERDALE DRIVE 40 B3
SILVERSTONE DRIVE 39 F4
SILVERTON ROAD 48 E5
SILVERWOOD CLOSE 44 E4
SIMMINS CRESCENT 46 F7
SIMONS CLOSE 52 A4
SISKIN HILL 48 C7
SITWELL WALK 48 A1
SIX HILLS LANE 15 C3
SIX HILLS ROAD
Ragdale 15 B4
Walton Le Wolds 14 B5
SKAMPTON ROAD 44 D5
SKEFFINGTON GLEBE ROAD 54 E6
SKEFFINGTON WOOD ROAD 54 F7
SKEG HILL ROAD 54 B4

SKELTON DRIVE	47	C5
SKETCHLEY CLOSE	44	F4
SKETCHLEY LANE	71	C4
SKILLINGTON ROAD	19	C1
SKIPWORTH STREET	43	E6
SLACKEY LANE	20	C2
SLADE LANE	4	A7
SLATE BROOK CLOSE	37	C6
SLATE CLOSE	41	D2
SLATE STREET	43	D5
SLATER STREET	43	A3
SLAWSTON ROAD		
Medbourne	77	C3
Slawston	77	B2
Welham	77	A4
SLOANE CLOSE	49	C1
SLUDGE HALL HILL	54	C5
SMEDMORE ROAD	43	F2
SMEETON ROAD	75	E3
SMISBY ROAD	10	B6
SMITH AVENUE	40	B3
SMITH DORRIEN ROAD	44	A3
SMITHY LANE		
Hinckley	71	F2
Long Whatton	12	B2
SMOCKINGTON LANE	71	E7
SMORE SLADE HILLS	52a	G7
SNARESTONE ROAD		
Appleby Magna	33	E1
Newton Burgoland	34	C1
SNARROWS ROAD	11	D5
SNOW HILL	42	E1
SNOWDENS END	52	A3
SNOWDROP CLOSE	49	B4
SNOWS LANE	53	C4
SOAR LANE		
Leicester	43	A4
Sutton Bonington	5	E6
SOAR ROAD	40	A1
SOAR VALLEY WAY	46	C6
SOMERBY DRIVE	48	E6
SOMERBY ROAD		
Burrough on the Hill	28	A6
Knossington	55	D1
Owston	55	C2
Somerby	28	C7
SOMERFIELD WAY	45	B2
SOMERS ROAD	44	E4
SOMERSET AVENUE	38	F7
SOMERSET DRIVE	41	D3
SOMERVILLE ROAD	46	E2
SONNING WAY	50	E2
SORREL ROAD	40	E7
SORREL WAY	49	B3
SOUTH ALBION STREET	43	C5
SOUTH AVENUE		
Leicester	41	D7
Leicester	51	E2
SOUTH CROXTON ROAD		
Queniborough	26	E6
South Croxton	54	A1
SOUTH DRIVE	44	C2
SOUTH KILWORTH ROAD		
North Kilworth	81	D6
Walcote	80	F6
SOUTH KINGSMEAD ROAD	47	E5
SOUTH KNIGHTON ROAD	47	F4
SOUTH STREET		
Asfordby Hill	16	C5
Barrow upon Soar	13	F7
Blackfordby	9	E6
Leicester	48	C5
SOUTHAMPTON STREET	43	C4
SOUTHDOWN DRIVE	40	A4
SOUTHDOWN ROAD	43	F4
SOUTHERNHAY AVENUE	47	E2
SOUTHERNHAY CLOSE	47	E2
SOUTHERNHAY ROAD	47	E2
SOUTHEY CLOSE		
Leicester	43	D2
Leicester	49	C2
SOUTHFIELD CLOSE	50	C1
SOUTHFIELD ROAD	71	D3
SOUTHFIELDS AVENUE	48	B5
SOUTHFIELDS DRIVE	47	B6
SOUTHGATES	43	A5
SOUTHLAND ROAD	47	F5
SOUTHMEADS CLOSE	48	C4
SOUTHMEADS ROAD	48	D3
SOUTHVIEW DRIVE	48	B1
SOUTHWAY	50	D6
SPA LANE		
Hinckley	71	D2
Leicester	52	A2
SPALDING STREET	44	A4
SPARKENHOE STREET	43	D5
SPEEDWELL CLOSE	49	C3
SPEEDWELL DRIVE	40	D6
SPEERS ROAD	42	A2
SPENCEFIELD DRIVE	44	D7
SPENCEFIELD LANE	44	E7
SPENCER AVENUE	40	A2
SPENCER STREET		
Leicester	43	F3
Leicester	48	C4
SPENDLOW GARDENS	47	A7
SPENDLOW GREEN	47	A7
SPINNEY CLOSE	37	A7
SPINNEY HALT	50	B5
SPINNEY HILL ROAD	43	E3
SPINNEY RISE	39	C2
SPINNEYSIDE	37	A6
SPONNE RISE	47	B7
SPORTS ROAD	41	F2
SPRING CLOSE	46	F6
SPRING COTTAGE ROAD	20	C1
SPRING FIELD CLOSE	41	D3
SPRING LANE		
Glaston	68	B3
Leicester	51	F1
Long Whatton	12	C2
Packington	21	C3
Thornborough	22	C2
SPRINGFIELD ROAD	47	E1
SPRINGFIELD STREET	83	D2
SPRINGWELL LANE	73	D1
SPROXTON ROAD	18	F2
SQUIRREL CLOSE	49	C5
SQUIRREL LANE	11	A1
STABLE CLOSE	49	E5
STADIUM PLACE	39	A7
STADON ROAD	37	F3
STAFFORD DRIVE	51	B2
STAFFORD LEYS	41	B7
STAFFORD STREET	39	E6
STAINBY ROAD	19	A2
Buckminster	19	A2
Gunby	19	D2
STAINDALE	52	B2
STAINMORE AVENUE	49	C2
STAMFORD CLOSE	41	E1
STAMFORD DRIVE	37	B7
STAMFORD LANE	13	B2
STAMFORD ROAD		
Carlby	32	F3
Duddington	69	E3
Easton on the Hill	59	B7
Empingham	58	C3
Essendine	32	E5
Ketton	58	F5
Leicester	41	B6
Normanton on Soar	13	A2
Oakham	56	F2
Sewstern	19	B3
South Luffenham	69	A1
STAMFORD STREET		
Leicester	41	D2
Leicester	43	B5
STANBRIG	52	A4
STANCLIFF ROAD	40	B4
STANDARD HILL	22	B4
STANFELL ROAD	47	D3
STANFORD ROAD	84	F3
STANHOPE ROAD	52	A3
STANHOPE STREET	43	F5
STANLEY DRIVE	44	C2
STANLEY ROAD	43	E7
STANTON LANE		
Croft	63	E7
Sapcote	72	B3
Stanton under Bardon	23	B6
Thornton	36	A2
STANTON ROAD		
Asfordby Hill	16	C5
Elmesthorpe	63	A6
Sapcote	72	C3
STANTON ROW	47	B5
STAPLEFORD ROAD		
Leicester	38	F5
Whissendine	29	A2
STAPLEHURST AVENUE	46	A3
STAPLETON LANE		
Barwell	62	D6
Dadlington	62	B5
Kirby Mallory	62	E3
STATHERN ROAD	7	B2
STATION CLOSE	41	A6
STATION DRIVE		
Moira	20	D2
Leicester	41	A6
STATION HILL		
Swannington	22	B2
Twyford	54	D1
STATION LANE		
Asfordby	16	A6
Old Dalby	15	E1
STATION ROAD		
Ashby-De-La-Zouch	21	B1
Bagworth	35	E1
Bottesford	1	C6
Broughton Astley	73	B4
Castle Donnington	4	E3
Coalville	22	C5
Croft	72	F1
Cropston	24	D5
Desford	36	C7
Essendine	32	E5
Great Bowden	83	E1
Great Easton	78	D4
Great Glen	64	B7
Hemington	4	F3
Higham on the Hill	70	D1
Hinckley	71	C3
Husbands Bosworth	81	F6
Kegworth	5	D4
Ketton	58	E6
Leicester	39	B4
Leicester	41	A6
Leicester	41	E1
Leicester	49	E5
Leicester	51	D2
North Kilworth	81	D6
North Luffenham	69	A1
Oakham	56	D1
Ratby	36	F5
Rearsby	26	B3
South Luffenham	69	A1
Stoke Golding	61	F6
Waltham on the Wolds	7	D4
Whissendine	29	B2
Wing	57	A7
STATION STREET		
Leicester	43	C5
Leicester	50	B4
Leicester	51	C2
STAVELEY CLOSE	52	A2
STAVELEY ROAD	43	F6
STEADFOLD LANE	58	F4
STEBBINGS ROAD	46	F6
STEELE CLOSE	44	C5
STEEPLE CLOSE	48	A7
STEINS LANE	44	D2
STEMBOROUGH LANE	73	A6
STENSON ROAD	42	C1
STEPHENSON CLOSE	37	A6
STEPHENSON COURT	37	E7
STEPHENSON DRIVE	42	E3
STEPHENSON WAY		
Coalville	22	B2
Leicester	37	A6
STEVENSTONE CLOSE	43	F6
STEWART AVENUE	49	C2
STEYNING CRESCENT	41	F1
STOKE ALBANY ROAD	77	D6
STOCKERSTON ROAD		
Allexton	67	A3
Uppingham	67	C5
STOCKERSTONE LANE	78	B1
STOCKING LANE	11	C3
STOCKLAND ROAD	47	A7
STOCKTON ROAD	44	A1
STOCKWELL ROAD	47	F4
STOKE LANE		
Stoke Golding	62	A6
Wykin	71	A1
STOKE ROAD		
Lyddington	67	F6
Stoke Golding	62	A7
Upton	61	C5
STOKES DRIVE	42	D2
STOKESBY RISE	50	E2
STONE CLOSE	38	C3
STONEBRIDGE STREET	43	F4
STONEHAVEN ROAD	39	F5
STONEHILL AVENUE	39	C1
STONEHURST ROAD	46	B3
STONELEIGH WAY	42	E2
STONESBY AVENUE	47	A6
STONESBY ROAD		
Saltby	8	C5
Sproxton	8	D7
Waltham On The Wolds	7	F7
STONEY HOLLOW	80	C5
STONEY LANE		
Appleby Magna	33	D1
Coleorton	11	A7
Stanton under Bardon	23	B7
STONEYGATE AVENUE	47	E2
STONEYGATE ROAD	47	F1
STONEYWELL ROAD	38	B4
STONTON ROAD	76	C3
STORDON LANE	11	B6
STOREY STREET	42	F3
STOUGHTON AVENUE	47	F2
STOUGHTON CLOSE	48	D5
STOUGHTON DRIVE	48	B1
STOUGHTON DRIVE NORTH	43	F7
STOUGHTON DRIVE SOUTH	48	B2
STOUGHTON LANE	48	E2
STOUGHTON ROAD		
Leicester	48	C5
Leicester	48	A2
Leicester	48	D4
Thurnby	53	A7
STOUGHTON STREET	43	D5
STOUGHTON STREET SOUTH	43	D5
STOUR CLOSE	48	F5
STOW HILL	8	D7
STRANCLIFFE LANE	13	F6
STRASBOURG DRIVE	38	E6
STRATFORD ROAD	46	B2
STRATHAVEN ROAD	39	F4
STRATHMORE AVENUE	39	F7
STRENSALL ROAD	50	F1
STRETTON LANE	64	C2
STRETTON ROAD		
Clipsham	31	C1
Great Glen	64	B5
Leicester	42	E5
STROUD ROAD	43	F3
STRUDWICK WAY	50	C3
STUART CRESCENT	76	A7
STUART ROAD	50	E1
STUART STREET	42	E6
STUBBS ROAD	43	D2
STURDEE CLOSE	46	F7
STURDEE GREEN	46	E7
STURDEE ROAD	46	E7
STYGATE LANE	28	D5
STYON ROAD	42	B1
SUDELEY AVENUE	39	A7
SUFFOLK CLOSE	51	C1
SUFFOLK STREET	44	A5
SULGRAVE ROAD	43	F3
SUMMERLEA ROAD	44	F4
SUN WAY	41	F7
SUNDEW ROAD	40	E7
SUNNINGDALE ROAD	41	D6
SUNNY SIDE	48	E7
SUNNYCROFT ROAD	42	C5
SUNNYFIELD CLOSE	44	E5
SURREY STREET	43	D1
SUSAN AVENUE	44	D6
SUSSEX ROAD	51	B1
SUSSEX STREET	43	D4
SUTHERINGTON WAY	38	A2
SUTHERLAND STREET	43	E6
SUTTON AVENUE	39	E7
SUTTON CLOSE	52	D1
SUTTON LANE		
Cadeby	62	C2
Dadlington	62	A5
Market Bosworth	62	A1
SUTTON PLACE	39	E7
SUTTON ROAD		
Great Bowden	76	E7
Leicester	47	C3
Weston by Welland	77	B5
SWAIN STREET	43	C5
SWAINSON ROAD	44	A1
SWALE CLOSE	48	F5
SWALLOW CLOSE	45	B2
SWALLOWDALE DRIVE	38	D3
SWAN STREET		
Leicester	43	A3
Seagrave	14	D7
Sileby	25	C2
SWANNINGTON ROAD		
Leicester	42	E3
Ravenstone	22	A3
SWANNYMOTE ROAD	11	E7
SWANSCOMBE ROAD	46	F2
SWEETBRIAR ROAD	42	E7
SWEETHILL	20	E1
SWEPSTONE ROAD		
Heather	21	E7
Swepstone	21	A6
SWINFORD AVENUE	50	F2
SWINFORD ROAD		
Lutterworth	80	D6
Shawell	84	C2
Walcote	80	E6
SWINSTEAD ROAD	44	F6
SWITHLAND AVENUE	43	A1
SWITHLAND LANE	24	E5
SWITHLAND ROAD	24	D6
SWORD CLOSE	41	E3
SYBIL ROAD	46	D2
SYCAMORE CLOSE	48	B2
SYCAMORE DRIVE	37	B7
SYCAMORE GROVE	37	B6
SYCAMORE ROAD	39	C1
SYCAMORE STREET	50	D4
SYCAMORE WAY	49	E5
SYKEFIELD AVENUE	42	E6
SYLVAN AVENUE	43	F4
SYLVAN STREET	42	E3
SYLVAN WAY	41	D6
SYSTON ROAD		
Cossington	25	B4
South Croxton	26	D7
SYSTON STREET	43	C2
SYSTON STREET EAST	43	D3
SYWELL DRIVE	52	B2
TADCASTER AVENUE	50	F1
TAILBY AVENUE	44	A2
TALBOT LANE		
Leicester	43	A5
Thringstone	11	C7
TALBOT STREET		
Leicester	39	C6
Whitwick	22	D1
TAMAR ROAD		
Leicester	40	A7
Leicester	48	F6
TAMERTON ROAD	47	A6
TAMWORTH ROAD		
Ashby-De-La-Zouch	21	B1
Measham	20	D7
TANSLEY AVENUE	51	C3
TARBAT ROAD	44	F3
TATLOW ROAD	41	F4
TAUNTON CLOSE	51	E3
TAUNTON ROAD	42	D6
TAURUS CLOSE	43	D5
TAVISTOCK DRIVE	44	B7
TAYLOR ROAD	43	C3
TAYLORS BRIDGE ROAD	51	C3
TEAL CLOSE	45	B1
TEASEL CLOSE	49	C3
TEDWORTH GREEN	38	F4
TEESDALE CLOSE	43	A7
TEIGH ROAD		
Ashwell	29	E3
Market Overton	29	F1
TEIGNMOUTH CLOSE	44	B7
TEMPEST ROAD	39	B3
TEMPLE ROAD	44	A5
TENDRING DRIVE	52	B1
TENNIS COURT DRIVE	44	C2
TENNYSON STREET		
Leicester	43	E6
Leicester	49	C3
TETUAN ROAD	42	E4
TEWKESBURY STREET	42	F4
THACKERAY STREET	47	B2
THAMES STREET	43	B3
THATCHER CLOSE	38	D5
THE APPROACH	44	B6
THE AVENUE		
Goadby	65	D4
Leicester	41	D1
Leicester	47	E1
Leicester	50	C4
Medbourne	77	F3
THE BALK	41	E1
THE BARROON	4	E4
THE BRIANWAY	44	B3
THE BRIDLE	46	D7
THE BROADWAY	48	C3

THE BURROWS .49 C4
THE BUTTS .8 D5
THE CEDARS .47 D4
THE CHASE .46 B4
THE CIRCLE .44 B5
THE CLOSE
Albert Village .9 C7
Leicester .37 F2
Leicester .49 C2
THE COMMON
Barwell .62 E7
Leicester .44 C7
THE COPPICE
Leicester .40 C2
Leicester .49 C4
THE CRESCENT
Leicester .47 E7
Leicester .50 D5
Melton Mowbray .16 F5
THE CRESTWAY .50 C4
THE CROFT .41 A5
THE CROFTERS .44 C3
THE CROSS .49 D1
THE CROSSWAY
Leicester .46 C3
Leicester .47 B5
THE CROSSWAYS .39 D2
THE DICKEN .50 B5
THE DRIFT
Buckminster .19 A1
Essendine .32 C5
Harston .3 D7
Sewstern .19 B4
THE DRIVE .39 C3
THE ELMS .50 D4
THE FAIRWAY
Leicester .41 B5
Leicester .47 B5
Leicester .48 C3
Leicester .50 C5
THE FORD .50 E3
THE GLADE .46 B4
THE GREEN
Coalville .22 C5
Dadlington .62 A6
Diseworth .4 E7
Long Whatton .12 C1
Lyndon .57 C6
Mountsorrel .25 A3
Orton on the Hill .33 C7
Thrussington .26 A2
THE GREENWAY .39 C7
THE HASTINGS .45 F1
THE HILL .78 B7
THE HOLLOW
Bagworth .35 F2
Knossington .55 E2
Leicester .48 D1
Normanton Le Heath .21 D5
THE LANGHILL .44 B4
THE LITTLEFARE .45 F1
THE LITTLEWAY .44 B4
THE LONG SHOOT .70 E4
THE MALTINGS .4 E1
THE MEADOWS .49 F5
THE MEADS .42 A5
THE MEADWAY .39 C1
THE MILL LANE .41 C2
THE MORWOODS .48 D6
THE MOUNT .73 C6
THE NEWARKE .43 A5
THE NEWRY .47 B6
THE NOOK
Leicester .49 D1
Leicester .50 B5
THE OASIS .41 D2
THE ORCHARD .37 A6
THE OSIERS .46 B4
THE OVAL
Leicester .43 C6
Leicester .48 B7
THE PADDOCKS .49 F5
THE PARADE .48 C5
THE PARK .35 B7
THE PARKWAY .44 D3
THE PASTURES .49 C4
THE POPLARS .46 C4
THE POPPINS .38 D3
THE PORTWEY .44 B2
THE RETREAT .44 B5
THE RIDGE WAY .42 B3
THE RIDGEWAY .24 F5
THE RIDING .38 D3
THE RIDINGS .24 F4
THE RISE .49 D2
THE ROUNDWAY .40 B4
THE ROWLANDS .22 A1
THE SANDS .6 C4
THE SHRUBBERY .9 E6
THE SLADE GREENS .46 E7
THE SQUARE
Leicester .41 D1
Leicester .49 E6
Leicester .52 F6
Sutton Cheney .62 B3
THE STREET .65 E5
THE TENTAS .11 B6
THE TOFTS .51 F3
THE WAYNE WAY
Leicester .39 C2
Leicester .44 B4
THE WISP .55 F4
THE WOODLANDS .48 B7
THE WOOLROOMS .11 A7
THE YEWS .48 D5
THEDDINGWORTH ROAD
Husbands Bosworth .82 B5
Lubenham .82 E3
Mowsley .82 A1
THIMBLE HALL ROAD .54 C1
THIRLMERE ROAD .52 A1
THIRLMERE STREET .43 A7
THISTLE CLOSE .49 C4
THISTLETON LANE .19 E6
THISTLETON ROAD .30 B1
THOMASSON ROAD .44 D4
THOMSON CLOSE .39 F3
THORESBY STREET .44 A4
THORN STREET .9 D6
THORNBOROUGH CLOSE .49 B5
THORNBOROUGH ROAD .22 C2
THORNBY GARDENS .52 A2
THORNDALE ROAD .40 B2
THORNHILLS .49 C2
THORNHILLS GROVE .49 C2
THORNHOLME CLOSE .38 E5
THORNTON DRIVE .49 E4
THORNTON LANE
Bagworth .35 F3
Markfield .36 C2
Stanton under Bardon .36 A1
THORNVILLE CLOSE .44 A1
THORPE DRIVE .47 F7
THORPE END .16 F5
THORPE FIELD DRIVE .40 B1
THORPE LANE .40 F1
THORPE LANGTON ROAD
East Langton .76 C4
Welham .76 F4
THORPE ROAD
Lyddington .67 F7
Melton Mowbray .17 A5
THORPE SATCHVILLE ROAD
Great Dalby .27 D4
Twyford .27 D7
THORPE STREET .42 F5
THORPEWELL .44 B4
THREADGOLD CLOSE .38 D3
THREE GATES ROAD .65 C5
THRUSSINGTON ROAD .25 F2
THURCASTON LANE .24 E6
THURCASTON ROAD .39 B5
THURCROFT CLOSE .50 F1
THURLASTON LANE
Earl Shilton .63 B5
Thurlaston .63 F4
THURLBY ROAD .43 F3
THURLINGTON ROAD .42 C7
THURLOW CLOSE .48 F7
THURLOW ROAD .47 C2
THURMASTON BOULEVARD .40 B6
THURMASTON LANE .40 C6
THURNBY HILL .53 A6
THURNBY LANE .64 A1
THURNCOURT CLOSE .44 E3
THURNCOURT ROAD .44 F3
THURNVIEW ROAD .44 E7
TICHBORNE STREET .43 D6
TICKOW LANE .12 A6
TIGERS CLOSE .51 A2
TIGERS ROAD .51 A2
TILFORD CRESCENT .50 F2
TILLEY CLOSE .45 F2
TILLING ROAD .38 E5
TILTON DRIVE .52 C1
TILTON LANE .54 A6
TIMBER HILL .19 B2
TIMBER STREET .51 B3
TIMBERWOOD DRIVE .37 A7
TINSEL LANE .61 C2
TINWELL ROAD .59 A4
TITHE STREET .44 B4
TIVERTON AVENUE .39 E7
TIVERTON CLOSE
Leicester .48 E6
Leicester .49 C4
TOLCARNE ROAD .44 E2
TOLCHARD CLOSE .44 C5
TOLL BAR .30 C4
TOLLEMACHE AVENUE .39 A7
TOLLER ROAD .47 E2
TOLTON ROAD .38 F5
TOLWELL ROAD .38 E4
TOM PAINE CLOSE .45 F1
TOMKINSON ROAD .70 A5
TOMLIN ROAD .44 A1
TONGE LANE .11 B1
TOP CLOSE .45 F2
TOP ROAD
Ridlington .67 D1
Thringstone .11 B6
TOP STREET
Exton .30 E6
Wing .68 B1
TORCROSS CLOSE .42 A2
TORONTO CLOSE .43 D3
TORRIDON CLOSE .38 F6
TORRINGTON CLOSE .51 F4
TOTLAND ROAD .42 E2
TOURNAMENT ROAD .41 F3
TOVEY CRESCENT .46 F7
TOWER STREET .43 B6
TOWERS CLOSE .41 A6
TOWERS DRIVE .41 A6
TOWLE ROAD .42 A1
TOWN HALL SQUARE .43 B5
TOWN STREET .64 D6
TOWNSEND CLOSE .39 F4
TOWNSEND DRIVE .70 D5
TOWNSEND ROAD .49 D1
TOWPATH LINK .51 C4
TRAFALGAR WAY .50 F3
TRAFFORD ROAD .44 B3
TRANTER PLACE .39 F7
TREASURE CLOSE .41 E3
TREATY ROAD .41 F3
TREDINGTON ROAD .41 F1
TREETOPS CLOSE .44 D3
TREFOIL CLOSE .40 E7
TREMAINE DRIVE .51 E3
TRENANT ROAD .47 B7
TRENT AVENUE .38 F2
TRENT CLOSE .48 F6
TRESCOE RISE .42 A5
TRESSELL WAY .45 F1
TREVANTH ROAD .40 B6
TREVINO DRIVE .40 A4
TREVOSE GARDENS .44 F3
TRIGO CLOSE .38 C5
TRINITY LANE .71 C3
TRINITY ROAD
Leicester .50 A2
Leicester .50 B4
TRIUMPH ROAD .41 F3
TROON WAY .40 A5
TRUEWAY ROAD .48 A1
TRURO DRIVE .51 F3
TUDOR CLOSE .42 F5
TUDOR DRIVE .48 D5
TUDOR GROVE .41 B1
TUDOR ROAD .42 F3
TUGBY ROAD .65 F4
TUNSTALL CRESCENT .44 A2
TURNBULL DRIVE .46 B3
TURNBURY WAY .48 A1
TURNER RISE .48 D7
TURNER ROAD .44 B3
TURNPIKE ROAD .32 D6
TUROLOUGH ROAD .11 D7
TURVEY LANE .12 C2
TURVILLE CLOSE .52 A4
TURVILLE ROAD .42 D7
TUSKAR ROAD .44 F3
TUXFORD ROAD .40 C6
TWICKENHAM ROAD
TWYCROSS LANE
Bilstone .34 B5
Orton on the Hill .33 D6
TWYCROSS ROAD
Sheepby Magna .60 E2
Sibson .61 B3
TWYCROSS STREET .43 E5
TWYFORD ROAD
Burrough on the Hill .27 E7
Lowesby .54 D2
Twyford .27 D6
TYES END .38 C6
TYNDALE STREET .42 F5
TYNEDALE CLOSE .48 F6
TYRINGHAM ROAD .52 A2
TYRRELL STREET .42 F4
TYSOE HILL .41 F1
TYTHORN DRIVE .47 C6

UFFINGTON ROAD .59 E3
ULLESTHORPE ROAD
Ashby Parva .80 A1
Bitteswell .80 A3
Gilmorton .80 D2
ULLSWATER DRIVE .48 F7
ULLSWATER STREET .43 A6
ULVERSCROFT DRIVE .37 B7
ULVERSCROFT LANE .23 F6
ULVERSCROFT ROAD .43 E2
UNA AVENUE .46 C3
UNICORN STREET .40 A1
UNITY ROAD .41 E2
UNIVERSITY ROAD .43 C7
UPLANDS ROAD
Leicester .47 B6
Leicester .48 E5
UPPER BOND STREET .71 C2
UPPER CHARNWOOD STREET .43 D4
UPPER GEORGE STREET .43 C3
UPPER HALL CLOSE .44 F2
UPPER HALL GREEN .44 F2
UPPER NEW WALK .43 D6
UPPER TICHBORNE STREET .43 D6
UPPERTON RISE .42 E6
UPPERTON ROAD .42 E6
UPPINGHAM CLOSE .44 E5
UPPINGHAM ROAD
Billesdon .65 C1
Caldecott .78 E2
Corby .78 E7
East Norton .66 C3
Houghton On The Hill .53 C7
Leicester .44 C3
Medbourne .77 F2
Oakham .56 E2
Preston .67 F1
Stockerston .67 B5
Tugby .66 A2
UPTON DRIVE .52 B2
UPTON LANE
Sibson .61 C3
Upton .61 B5
UTAH CLOSE .41 E3
UTTOXETER CLOSE .39 F4
UXBRIDGE ROAD .39 E5

VALE CLOSE .44 E3
VALENCE ROAD .42 D6
VALENTINE DRIVE .48 B5
VALENTINE ROAD .44 F5
VALIANT CLOSE .41 F3
VALLEY DRIVE .45 F1
VALLEY ROAD .16 B5
VALLEY VIEW .11 A5
VANCOUVER ROAD .43 C3
VANDYKE ROAD .48 D7
VAUGHAN ROAD .47 A4
VAUGHAN STREET .42 F4
VAUGHAN WAY .43 A4
VENTNOR ROAD .47 F4
VENTOR STREET .43 F5
VERDALE AVENUE .40 C4
VERNON ROAD .47 A4
VERNON STREET .42 F4
VERNONS LANE .70 A5
VESTRY STREET .43 C4
VETCH CLOSE .49 B4
VIAN WAY .78 E7
VICARAGE CLOSE
Leicester .41 A3
Newbold .11 A5
VICARAGE LANE
Leicester .39 C6
Leicester .40 F1
Leicester .44 D2
Leicester .50 B3
VICARAGE STREET .70 C5
VICTOR ROAD .41 F2
VICTORIA AVENUE .43 D6
VICTORIA DRIVE .37 B7
VICTORIA GARDENS .43 E7
VICTORIA PARK ROAD .47 D1
VICTORIA PASSAGE .43 D6
VICTORIA ROAD
Ellistown .22 E7
Leicester .39 D6
Leicester .44 A1
Leicester .50 B4
VICTORIA STREET
Leicester .40 A1
Leicester .49 E4
Leicester .51 F1
VICTORS CLOSE .46 E7
VIKING ROAD .47 C7
VILLAGE STREET .3 B5
VINCENT CLOSE .42 C4
VINE STREET .43 A4
VINE TREE TERRACE .13 F2
VOSTOCK CLOSE .43 D5
VULCAN ROAD .43 D4

WADE STREET .39 B6
WAKEFIELD PLACE .39 E7
WAKELEY CLOSE .49 C5
WAKERLEY ROAD
Barrowden .69 B4
Leicester .44 B7
WAKES ROAD .51 F1
WALCOTE ROAD
Leicester .40 B7
South Kilworth .81 B7
WALDALE DRIVE .47 F1
WALDRON DRIVE .48 E6
WALE ROAD .50 B5
WALKER ROAD
Leicester .39 B3
Leicester .40 B3
WALLINGFORD ROAD .39 B7
WALNUT AVENUE .39 B2
WALNUT CLOSE .48 C6
WALNUT GROVE .46 D7
WALNUT STREET .43 A7
WALNUT WAY .50 D6
WALPOLE COURT .42 C5
WALSGRAVE AVENUE .44 F5
WALSHE ROAD .44 D4
WALSINGHAM CRESCENT .41 D7
WALTHAM AVENUE .46 C1
WALTHAM LANE
Eaton .7 D3
Harby .6 E1
Long Clawson .6 D4
WALTHAM ROAD
Branston .7 F3
Eastwell .7 A3
WALTON CLOSE .41 B6
WALTON HILL .4 C6
WALTON LANE .13 F5
WALTON STREET .42 F7
WAND STREET .43 C1
WANLIP AVENUE .39 D2
WANLIP LANE .39 D1
WANLIP ROAD .25 D6
WANLIP STREET .43 C3
WANSBECK GARDENS .44 E2
WANSTEAD ROAD .41 C5
WAR MEMORIAL APPROACH .43 D7
WARD CLOSE .46 E4
WARDENS WALK .41 E7
WARDS CLOSE .52 A4
WAREHAM ROAD .50 D6
WARING CLOSE .42 A1
WARMSLEY AVENUE .47 E7
WARNER CLOSE .50 C7
WARREN AVENUE .40 C4
WARREN CLOSE .44 D2
WARREN DRIVE .40 C4
WARREN HILL .24 A5

Street	Page	Grid
WARREN LANE		
Kegworth	5	B1
Leicester	45	A1
Thringstone	11	D7
WARREN ROAD	49	F3
WARREN STREET	42	F4
WARREN VIEW	40	C4
WARRINGTON DRIVE	37	A7
WARTON LANE		
Austrey	33	B4
Orton-on-the-Hill	33	C6
WARWICK ROAD		
Kibworth	75	D2
Leicester	49	F6
Leicester	50	B6
Leicester	51	D1
WARWICK STREET	42	F4
WASH LANE	22	A3
WASHBROOK LANE	64	D5
WASHDYKE LANE	16	B7
WASHDYKE ROAD	55	F3
WASHSTONES LANE	15	E7
WASTE LANE	60	A5
WATER LANE		
Frisby On The Wreake	15	
South Witham	19	
Stainby	19	
WATERFORD CLOSE	44	
WATERGATE LANE	46	A4
WATERLOO CRESCENT	48	A7
WATERLOO SPINNEY LANE	24	B2
WATERLOO WAY	43	C6
WATERMEAD WAY	39	D4
WATERSIDE ROAD	40	C5
WATERY GATE LANE	63	C6
WATLING STREET		
Hinckley	70	F3
Leicester	43	B3
WATSON ROAD	39	C6
WATTS CLOSE	38	F5
WAVENEY RISE	48	
WAVERLEY ROAD		
Leicester	50	E6
Leicester	51	B2
WAVERTREE DRIVE	39	D5
WAYSIDE DRIVE		
Leicester	40	A2
Leicester	48	E6
WEBB CLOSE	45	D1
WEBSTER ROAD	42	A6
WEDDINGTON LANE	70	B2
WEDDINGTON ROAD	70	C3
WEIR ROAD	75	B5
WELBECK AVENUE	39	E6
WELBECK CLOSE	50	E6
WELBY LANE	16	C4
WELBY ROAD	16	C5
WELCOMBE AVENUE	46	B2
WELDON ROAD	47	F7
WELFORD COURT	47	D4
WELFORD PLACE	43	B5
WELFORD ROAD		
Arnesby	74	D4
Husbands Bosworth	82	A7
Leicester	47	C2
Leicester	50	D4
Leicester	51	F3
Sibbertoft	82	D7
South Kilworth	85	E3
WELHAM LANE	77	A2
WELHAM ROAD		
Great Bowden	76	F7
Slawston	77	B3
Thorpe Langton	76	A4
Welham	77	C2
WELL LANE	16	A4
WELL SPRING HILL	52	A4
WELLAND AVENUE	76	A7
WELLAND PARK ROAD	83	C2
WELLAND STREET	43	D6
WELLAND VALE ROAD	44	F6
WELLES STREET	43	A4
WELLESBOURNE DRIVE	41	F1
WELLFIELD CLOSE	66	A3
WELLGATE AVENUE	39	C1
WELLHOUSE CLOSE	51	E4
WELLINGER WAY	42	A6
WELLINGTON PARKWAY	79	F5
WELLINGTON STREET	43	B5
WELLSBOROUGH ROAD		
Sheepy Magna	61	A1
Wellsborough	61	D5
WEMBLEY ROAD	41	F3
WENDYS CLOSE	44	C5
WENLOCK WAY	40	E2
WENSLEY RISE	50	B3
WENSLEYDALE ROAD	52	C2
WENT ROAD	39	F6
WENTBRIDGE ROAD	39	E4
WENTWORTH ROAD	42	B6
WESLEY STREET	39	A5
WESSEX DRIVE	42	
WEST AVENUE		
Leicester	47	D1
Leicester	47	E1
Leicester	51	D1
WEST DRIVE	44	C2
WEST END		
Long Clawson	6	B4
Long Whatton	12	C3
WEST FIELD ROAD	71	F5
WEST HOLME STREET	42	F6
WEST LANE	22	A3
WEST LANGTON ROAD	76	D2
WEST ROAD	56	

Street	Page	Grid
WEST SIDE	16	C5
WEST STREET		
Clipsham	31	C1
Leicester	41	E1
Leicester	43	C6
Leicester	49	D2
Leicester	50	C4
WEST STREET OPEN	42	F6
WEST VIEW AVENUE	50	D1
WEST WALK	43	C6
WESTBOURNE STREET	43	C2
WESTBURY ROAD	47	E6
WESTCOTES DRIVE	42	C2
WESTDALE AVENUE	50	A3
WESTDOWN DRIVE	40	C4
WESTERBY CLOSE	47	E7
WESTERDALE ROAD	52	B2
WESTERN BOULEVARD	43	A6
WESTERN DRIVE	50	D5
WESTERN PARK ROAD	42	C5
WESTERN ROAD	42	F7
WESTERNHAY ROAD	47	E2
WESTFIELD AVENUE	47	D7
WESTFIELD LANE	24	F5
WESTFIELD ROAD	42	C4
WESTGATE AVENUE	39	B1
WESTGATE ROAD	47	D4
WESTHILL ROAD	42	C4
WESTLEIGH AVENUE	42	E7
WESTLEIGH ROAD		
Leicester	42	E7
Leicester	51	A2
WESTMEATH AVENUE	44	D4
WESTMINSTER DRIVE	50	C5
WESTMINSTER ROAD	48	A2
WESTMORLAND AVENUE		
Leicester	39	E7
Leicester	51	B2
WESTON CLOSE	52a	G7
WESTON ROAD		
Aston-on-Trent	4	A3
Welham	77	A4
WESTOVER	45	F1
WESTHORPE	77	D6
WETHERBY ROAD	39	F5
WEXFORD CLOSE	48	F7
WEYMOUTH CLOSE	51	F4
WEYMOUTH STREET	43	D2
WHARF LANE	62	B4
WHARF STREET		
Leicester	40	A1
Leicester	43	C4
WHARF STREET NORTH	43	C3
WHARF WAY	50	D2
WHATBOROUGH ROAD	55	B3
WHATTON ROAD		
Hathern	12	D2
Kegworth	5	C6
WHEAT STREET	43	C4
WHEATFIELD CLOSE	41	E3
WHEATLAND CLOSE	48	F6
WHEATLAND ROAD	38	F4
WHEATLEY ROAD	38	F5
WHEATLEYS ROAD	39	F2
WHEELDALE	52	B2
WHEELDALE CLOSE	38	F6
WHILES LANE	39	D2
WHINCHAT ROAD	43	E4
WHISSENDINE ROAD		
Ashwell	29	D4
Little Dalby	28	C2
WHITCROFTS LANE	23	C5
WHITE HORSE LANE	39	D3
WHITE HOUSE CLOSE	37	A6
WHITEACRES	50	A7
WHITEBEAM CLOSE	49	C4
WHITEFIELD ROAD	39	B6
WHITEHALL ROAD	44	E6
WHITEHEAD CRESCENT	51	E1
WHITEHILL ROAD	22	D6
WHITEOAKS ROAD	52	E1
WHITESAND CLOSE	41	F1
WHITESTONE ROAD	70	E7
WHITLEY CLOSE	42	D2
WHITMAN CLOSE	41	F4
WHITTENEY DRIVE NORTH	46	F7
WHITTENEY DRIVE SOUTH	46	F7
WHITTIER ROAD	47	B3
WHITTLE CLOSE	50	B6
WHITWELL ROAD	57	F2
WHITWELL ROW	47	A6
WHITWICK MOOR	11	C7
WHITWICK ROAD	23	B5
WHITWICK WAY	42	E2
WICKHAM ROAD	48	C4
WICKLOW DRIVE	44	E2
WIGLEY ROAD	44	E2
WIGSTON LANE	46	F5
WIGSTON ROAD		
Leicester	48	C6
Leicester	50	E4
WILBERFORCE ROAD	42	F6
WILLESLEY LANE		
Ashby-De-La-Zouch	21	A2
Moira	20	E2
WILLIAM NADIN WAY	9	A5
WILLIAM PARDON COURT	51	E1
WILLIAM STREET		
Leicester	43	D4
Leicester	49	D5
WILLIAMS CLOSE	49	E6
WILLOUGHBY GARDENS	41	C7
WILLOUGHBY ROAD		
Ashby Magna	73	E5
Countesthorpe	73	F1

Street	Page	Grid
Morcott	68	E2
WILLOW BROOK CLOSE	37	E7
WILLOW BROOK ROAD		
Corby	78	F7
Leicester	43	F3
WILLOW CLOSE	49	E6
WILLOW COURT	43	D5
WILLOW DRIVE	41	A1
WILLOW PARK DRIVE	51	E1
WILLOW PLACE	51	F2
WILLOW ROAD	50	D5
WILLOWTREE CLOSE	40	E7
WILMINGTON COURT	48	B3
WILMINGTON ROAD	42	E7
WILMORE CRESCENT	41	A3
WILNE STREET	43	B2
WILNICOTT ROAD	46	B2
WILSFORD CLOSE	51	E4
WILSON CLOSE	45	F1
WILSON ROAD	51	A3
WILSON STREET	43	E4
WILTON CLOSE	48	E6
WILTON ROAD	16	F5
WILTON STREET	43	C3
WILTSHIRE ROAD		
Leicester	38	F7
Leicester	51	D1
WIMBLEDON STREET	43	C4
WIMBORNE CLOSE	51	E3
WIMBORNE ROAD	47	F5
WINCHENDON CLOSE	44	A2
WINCHESTER AVENUE		
Leicester	42	E7
Leicester	50	C3
WINCHESTER ROAD	50	E7
WINDERMERE ROAD	52	B1
WINDERMERE STREET	43	A6
WINDERS WAY	46	F6
WINDLEY ROAD	47	B5
WINDMILL AVENUE	39	D1
WINDMILL BANK	52	A3
WINDMILL CLOSE	40	B1
WINDMILL RISE	37	A5
WINDRUSH DRIVE	48	F6
WINDSOR AVENUE		
Leicester	37	A7
Leicester	39	D7
Leicester	51	A3
WINDSOR CLOSE	52	E1
WINDSOR STREET	71	F6
WINFORCE CRESCENT	41	F6
WING ROAD		
Glaston	68	B3
Manton	57	A7
Morcott	68	D2
WINGFIELD STREET	39	D7
WINIFRED STREET	43	A6
WINSLOW DRIVE	48	A7
WINSLOW GREEN	44	C7
WINSTANLEY DRIVE	42	A1
WINSTER DRIVE	40	B5
WINTERBURN GARDENS	50	D3
WINTERFIELD CLOSE	41	F5
WINTERSDALE ROAD	44	B1
WINTERTON CLOSE	40	E1
WINTON AVENUE	46	A6
WIRE LANE	78	
WISTOW ROAD		
Kibworth	75	A1
Leicester	52	A3
Newton Harcourt	52	F5
WITHAM ROAD		
Gunby	19	D3
Thistleton	19	A6
WITHCOTE AVENUE	44	C4
WITHENS CLOSE	42	C3
WITHERDELL	38	C6
WITHERLEY ROAD	60	E6
WITHERS WAY	45	F1
WOBURN CLOSE		
Leicester	46	E7
Leicester	52	A2
WOKINGHAM AVENUE	50	F2
WOLLATON CLOSE	41	F4
WOLSEY CLOSE		
Leicester	37	B7
Leicester	45	B1
WOLSEY STREET	43	A2
WOLVERTON ROAD	46	E1
WOLVEY ROAD	71	D5
WOOD END	42	C3
WOOD GATE	13	B5
WOOD HILL		
Leicester	43	F4
Old Dalby	15	D1
WOOD LANE		
Barkstone	2	D5
Braunstone	56	B4
Higham on the Hill	70	D1
Norton Juxta Twycross	33	F4
Quorn	24	F2
Stathern	2	B7
Tugby	66	B1
WOOD MARKET	80	C5
WOOD ROAD	35	C2
WOOD STREET		
Ashby-De-La-Zouch	21	C1
Earl Shilton	63	A6
Leicester	43	B3
WOODBANK	50	D2
WOODBANK ROAD	47	E5
WOODBOROUGH ROAD	44	D6
WOODBOY STREET	43	C3
WOODBRIDGE ROAD	39	D6
WOODBY LANE	80	A4

Street	Page	Grid
WOODCOTE ROAD	46	B4
WOODCROFT AVENUE	47	C5
WOODFIELD CLOSE	49	D4
WOODFIELD ROAD	48	D4
WOODFORD LANE	60	F7
WOODGATE		
Leicester	42	F3
Rothley	25	A5
WOODGATE DRIVE	39	B1
WOODGON ROAD	37	F2
WOODGREEN ROAD	43	F1
WOODHALL CLOSE	41	F5
WOODHOUSE LANE	23	E7
WOODHOUSE ROAD		
Leicester	49	C4
Quorn	24	D1
WOODLAND AVENUE		
Leicester	47	E2
Leicester	49	D3
WOODLAND DRIVE	41	F7
WOODLAND ROAD	43	F3
WOODLANDS LANE	41	A4
WOODNEWTON DRIVE	44	F5
WOODPECKER CLOSE	45	A1
WOODS CLOSE	48	F4
WOODSHAWE RISE	46	A1
WOODSIDE CLOSE		
Leicester	43	F1
Leicester	49	B4
WOODSIDE ROAD	52	F1
WOODSTOCK CLOSE	39	A5
WOODSTOCK ROAD	39	A5
WOODVILLE GARDENS	47	E6
WOODVILLE ROAD	42	D5
WOODWAY LANE	79	C2
WOOLDALE CLOSE	38	A2
WOOLSTHORPE LANE		
Harston	3	B2
Muston	3	B6
WOOTTON CLOSE	50	F6
WOOTTON RISE	46	F6
WORCESTER AVENUE	39	E1
WORCESTER DRIVE	51	B2
WORCESTER ROAD	46	F4
WORDSWORTH CRESCENT	49	C3
WORDSWORTH ROAD	47	C3
WORRALL CLOSE	41	F6
WORRALL ROAD	41	F6
WORSLEY WAY	50	C6
WORTHINGTON LANE		
Breedon On The Hill	11	A2
Worthington	11	A5
WREAKE ROAD	40	A1
WREN CLOSE	47	A4
WRIGHT LANE	48	F7
WROXALL WAY	42	E2
WYATT CLOSE	41	E6
WYCHWOOD ROAD	50	C7
WYCOMB LANE	7	B5
WYCOMBE ROAD	44	B2
WYE DEAN DRIVE	51	F2
WYKEHAM CLOSE	50	E6
WYKIN LANE	62	A7
WYKIN ROAD	71	A1
WYLAM CLOSE	42	C2
WYMAR CLOSE	38	E6
WYMESWOLD LANE	14	B2
WYMESWOLD ROAD	14	A2
WYNDALE ROAD	47	D4
WYNDHAM CLOSE	48	E3
WYNFIELD ROAD	42	D5
WYNGATE DRIVE	42	D6
WYNTHORPE RISE	42	D6
WYNTON CLOSE	50	E6
WYVERN AVENUE	39	F7
WYVILLE ROW	46	C2
YARDLEY DRIVE	47	D6
YARMOUTH STREET	43	B3
YARROW CLOSE	44	E1
YARWELL DRIVE	52	A2
YELVERTON AVENUE	44	E7
YEOMAN LANE	43	C4
YEOMAN STREET	43	C4
YEW CLOSE	45	B2
YEW TREE DRIVE	41	E1
YORK CLOSE	51	A3
YORK ROAD	43	B5
YORK STREET	43	C5
ZION HILL	11	B7
ZOUCH ROAD	12	D2

STREET INDEX - SECTION TWO

HOW TO USE THIS STREET INDEX:
In this section streets are listed alphabetically under the town or village in which they appear. Against each street name there are two references; the first relates to the map number upon which the street appears (NOT the page number); the second reference relates to the grid square in which the street can be found. (See example at start of section one, page 178)

Agar Nook
See Coalville & Agar Nook

Appleby Magna
Street	Map	Grid
ATHERSTONE ROAD	117	A4
BOTTS LANE	117	C4
BOWLEYS LANE	117	A3
CHURCH STREET	117	C3
DIDCOTT WAY	117	C4
DUCK LAKE	117	C3
HILLSIDE	117	C3
MAWBYS LANE	117	C3
MOORE CLOSE	117	C3
NEW ROAD	117	A4
OLD END	117	C2
PARKFIELD CRESCENT	117	C2
RECTORY LANE	117	C2
ST MICHAELS DRIVE	117	C3
SNARESTONE ROAD	117	C3
STONEY LANE	117	C3
TAMWORTH ROAD	117	B1
TOP STREET	117	C4
WREN CLOSE	117	C4

Arnesby
Street	Map	Grid
CHESTNUT LANE	117	A2
CHURCH LANE	117	B2
LUTTERWORTH ROAD	117	A2
MILL HILL ROAD	117	B2
OAK LANE	117	B2
ROBERT HALL ROAD	117	B2
ST PETERS ROAD	117	B2
SOUTH CLOSE	117	A2
THE BANK	117	A2
WELFORD ROAD	117	B1

Asfordby
Street	Map	Grid
ALL SAINTS CLOSE	123	B2
ANTILL CLOSE	123	B2
ASFORDBY PLACE	123	B3
BRADGATE LANE	123	B2
BROOK LANE	123	B3
BURNABY PLACE	123	B2
CHADWELL CLOSE	123	A3
CHARNWOOD AVENUE	123	B2
CHURCH LANE	123	B2
DALGLIESH WAY	123	B3
DEBDALE PLACE	123	A3
GLENDON CLOSE	123	A3
HALL DRIVE	123	A3
HAZLEWOOD CRESCENT	123	A2
JUBILEE AVENUE	123	C2
KLONDYKE WAY	123	A2
LOUGHBOROUGH ROAD	123	A2
MAIN STREET	123	B2
MILL LANE	123	B3
NEW STREET	123	B2
PRINCE CHARLES STREET	123	B2
PUMP LANE	123	B3
REGENCY ROAD	123	B2
SARSON CLOSE	123	C2
SAXELBY ROAD	123	A2
SOUTH VIEW	123	A3
STATION LANE	123	B3
THE GROVE	123	A2
TOWNEND CLOSE	123	A2
WESTERN ROAD	123	B2
WHITLOCK WAY	123	B2
WOODHOUSE ROAD	123	B2
WREAKE CRESCENT	123	A3

Asfordby Hill
See Melton Mowbray

Ashby-de-la-Zouch
Street	Map	Grid
ABBEY CLOSE	86	B5
ABBEY DRIVE	86	B4
ABBOTSFORD ROAD	86	F6
ALTON WAY	86	E6
ANCHOR CLOSE	86	E6
ANNWELL LANE	86	A2
ASTLEY CLOSE	86	F4
ATKINSON ROAD	86	B4
BAKER AVENUE	86	B7
BATH STREET	86	D5
BEAUMONT AVENUE	86	B6
BEECH WAY	86	F5
BELVOIR DRIVE	86	D6
BENENDEN WAY	86	C4
BERWICK ROAD	86	F6
BOWER CRESCENT	86	B6
BRENDON WAY	86	E6
BRISTOL AVENUE	86	C7
BRITTANY AVENUE	86	C4
BROOK STREET	86	D5
BURTON ROAD	86	C4
CAMBRIAN WAY	86	D6
CANTERBURY DRIVE	86	C4
CASTLE WAY	86	C7
CEDAR CLOSE	86	F5
CHELTENHAM DRIVE	86	C4
CHILTERN RISE	86	E6
CHURCHILL CLOSE	86	C5
CLIFTON AVENUE	86	C3
CLIFTON DRIVE	86	C4
COLEORTON LANE	86	C1
CONISTON GARDENS	86	E6
COTSWOLD WAY	86	E6
CROMWELL CLOSE	86	F4
DENSTONE CLOSE	86	C3
DERBY ROAD	86	D4
DERWENT GARDENS	86	E6
DONINGTON DRIVE	86	C6
DOWNSIDE DRIVE	86	C4
DUNBAR WAY	86	F6
DYSON CLOSE	86	C4
ELFORD STREET	86	D5
ELM AVENUE	86	F4
ENNERDALE GARDENS	86	F6
ETON CLOSE	86	C3
FAIRFAX CLOSE	86	F4
FEATHERBED LANE	86	F4
FERRERS CLOSE	86	B6
GLENALMOND CLOSE	86	C4
GRANGE CLOSE	86	C6
HACKETT CLOSE	86	C5
HALEBURY AVENUE	86	C6
HARROW CLOSE	86	C3
HASTINGS WAY	86	E6
HIGHFIELDS CLOSE	86	C5
HIGHGATE	86	C3
HILL STREET	86	C5
HOLYWELL AVENUE	86	C4
HUNTINGDON ROAD	86	B6
INGLE DRIVE	86	B4
IVANHOE DRIVE	86	B4
KELSO CLOSE	86	F5
KENILWORTH DRIVE	86	E6
KILWARDBY STREET	86	C5
KING GEORGE AVENUE	86	C4
KNIGHTS CLOSE	86	C4
LEICESTER ROAD	86	F6
LEITH CLOSE	86	F6
LOCKSLEY CLOSE	86	C4
LOCKTON CLOSE	86	E4
LODGE CLOSE	86	C6
LOIRE CLOSE	86	C4
LOUDOUN WAY	86	B6
LOWER CHURCH STREET	86	D5
LOWER PACKINGTON ROAD	86	D6
MALVERN CRESCENT	86	C4
MARKET STREET	86	D5
MARLBOROUGH WAY	86	C4
MEASHAM ROAD	86	C7
MELROSE CLOSE	86	F6
MENDIP CLOSE	86	D6
MILL BANK	86	D5
MILL LANE	86	D5
MILLFIELD CLOSE	86	C3
MOIRA ROAD	86	C5
MONEYHILL	86	D3
MUSSON DRIVE	86	F4
NASEBY DRIVE	86	F4
NORTH STREET	86	D5
NORTHFIELDS	86	D3
NOTTINGHAM ROAD	86	F4
OAKHAM GROVE	86	C4
OUNDLE CLOSE	86	C3
PACKINGTON NOOK LANE	86	A1
PARIS CLOSE	86	C4
PARK CLOSE	86	C7
PARK ROAD	86	D4
PAULYN WAY	86	C6
PENNINE WAY	86	E6
PENTLAND ROAD	86	F5
PINE CLOSE	86	F4
PITHIVIERS CLOSE	86	C6
PRESTOP DRIVE	86	B4
PRIOR PARK ROAD	86	E6
PRIORFIELDS	86	E6
RANGE ROAD	86	F5
RATCLIFF CLOSE	86	C5
RENNES CLOSE	86	C5
REPTON CLOSE	86	C4
RIDGWAY ROAD	86	C7
ROCKINGHAM CLOSE	86	E6
ROEDEAN CLOSE	86	C4
ROSSAL DRIVE	86	C4
ROTHERWOOD DRIVE	86	C4
ROUEN WAY	86	C4
ROWENA DRIVE	86	C4
RUGBY CLOSE	86	C3
RYDALE GARDENS	86	E7
ST MICHAELS CLOSE	86	E6
SAXON WAY	86	C4
SCOTTS CLOSE	86	C4
SHELLBROOK CLOSE	86	A5
SHERBOURNE DRIVE	86	C4
SMEDLEY CLOSE	86	B6
SMISBY ROAD	86	C3
SOUTH STREET	86	D5
STALEY AVENUE	86	C6
STATION ROAD	86	D6
STOWE CLOSE	86	C4
STUART WAY	86	D6
SYCAMORE DRIVE	86	F4
TAMWORTH ROAD	86	C7
THE GABLES	86	E7
THE GREEN	86	D5
TOULOUSE PLACE	86	C4
TOWER GARDENS	86	C5
TRINITY CLOSE	86	C5
TRINITY COURT	86	C5
TUDOR CLOSE	86	D6
TUTBURY CLOSE	86	E6
ULLESWATER CRESCENT	86	E6
UNION PASS	86	D5
UPPER PACKINGTON ROAD	86	E6
UPPINGHAM DRIVE	86	C4
UPPER CHURCH ROAD	86	E5
WARWICK WAY	86	E6
WELLS ROAD	86	B7
WESTERN CLOSE	86	D6
WESTFIELDS AVENUE	86	B4
WESTFIELDS TERRACE	86	B4
WESTMINSTER WAY	86	C3
WILFRED GARDENS	86	C6
WILFRED PLACE	86	C6
WILLESLEY CLOSE	86	B7
WILLESLEY GARDENS	86	B7
WILLESLEY LANE	86	C7
WILLOWBROOK CLOSE	86	D3
WINCHESTER WAY	86	C4
WINDERMERE AVENUE	86	F6
WINDMILL CLOSE	86	E6
WINDSOR ROAD	86	D6
WOOD STREET	86	D5
WOODCOCK WAY	86	E4
WOODSIDE	86	C6
WREKIN CLOSE	86	E7

Ashwell
Street	Map	Grid
BRAESIDE	123	B2
BROOK DENE	123	B2
CHURCH CLOSE	123	B2
COTTESMORE ROAD	123	C2
CROFT LANE	123	B2
OAKHAM ROAD	123	A2
WATER LANE	123	B3

Barkstone le Vale
Street	Map	Grid
FISHPOND LANE	127	B3
JERICHO LANE	127	A2
MIDDLE STREET	127	B3
PLUNGAR LANE	127	A3
REDMILE LANE	127	B3
RUTLAND SQUARE	127	B3
TOWN END	127	B3
WOOD LANE	127	B3

Barlestone & Nailstone
Street	Map	Grid
AVONDALE ROAD	87	C6
BAGWORTH ROAD	87	D1
BARLESTONE ROAD	87	F3
BARTON LANE	87	A2
BARTON ROAD	87	B5
BOSWORTH ROAD	87	B6
BROOKSIDE	87	D6
CHAPEL STREET	87	C7
CHURCH ROAD (Nail)	87	B2
CHURCH ROAD (Barl)	87	D5
COPE DALE CLOSE	87	C5
CROFTERS VALE PARK	87	E5
CUNNERY CLOSE	87	C5
CURTIS WAY	87	B5
DEACON AVENUE	87	C5
FERRERS CROFT	87	D6
GARLAND LANE	87	F3
GRANGE LANE	87	C1
GREGORY CLOSE	87	C5
GREGORY ROAD	87	C5
HINCKLEY ROAD	87	A2
IBSTOCK ROAD	87	A1
LOUNT ROAD	87	B5
MAIN STREET (Nail)	87	B2
MAIN STREET (Barl)	87	D5
MALTHOUSE CLOSE	87	B2
MANOR ROAD	87	C5
MEADOW ROAD	87	D6
NEW STREET	87	D5
NEWBOLD ROAD	87	F6
OCCUPATION ROAD	87	B2
ORCHARD CLOSE	87	D5
RECTORY LANE	87	B2
RUSHEY CLOSE	87	D6
ST GILES CLOSE	87	D5
SMITHY CLOSE	87	D6
SPINNEY DRIVE	87	D6
THE GLEBE	87	C6
THE PINGLE	87	D5
VEROS LANE	87	B2
WASHPIT LANE	87	B2
WESTFIELDS	87	D5
WOOD ROAD	87	C1

Barrow upon Soar
See Quorn

Barrowden
Street	Map	Grid
BACK ROAD	125	B2
CHAPEL LANE	125	B2
CHURCH LANE	125	B3
CIDER CLOSE	125	B2
CROWN LANE	125	B2
CUCKOO CLOSE	125	A2
KINGS LANE	125	B2
LUFFENHAM ROAD	125	B1
MAIN STREET	125	B2
MILL LANE	125	C3
MORCOTT ROAD	125	A2
PETERBOROUGH ROAD	125	B1
REDLAND CLOSE	125	B2
SCHOOL LANE	125	B3
SEATON ROAD	125	A3
TIPPINGS LANE	125	B2
WAKERLEY ROAD	125	B2
WHEEL LANE	125	B2

Barwell & Stapleton
Street	Map	Grid
ADCOTE CLOSE	112	D6
ADRIAN DRIVE	112	D5
AMBLESIDE	112	F5
ANGUS ROAD	112	D6
APPLE TREE CLOSE	112	F3
ARTHUR STREET	112	E5
ASHBY ROAD	112	C2
ASHLEIGH GARDENS	112	F4
AYRSHIRE CLOSE	112	D6
BANK TERRACE	112	D6
BARDON ROAD	112	E4
BEALES CLOSE	112	B2
BELLE VUE ROAD	112	F5
BLACKBURN ROAD	112	D6
BOSTON WAY	112	C6
BRADGATE ROAD	112	E4
BROCKEY CLOSE	112	E5
BYRON CLOSE	112	E4
CHAPEL STREET (Stap)	112	C3
CHAPEL STREET (Bar)	112	D6
CHARLESTON CRESCENT	112	D6
CHARNWOOD ROAD	112	F4
CHERRY TREE DRIVE	112	E4
CHESTERFIELD WAY	112	F5
CHURCH CLOSE	112	D6
CHURCH LANE (Stap)	112	B3
CHURCH LANE (Bar)	112	D6
CRABTREE ROAD	112	C7
CROFT CLOSE	112	E6
CUMBERLAND WAY	112	D5
DADLINGTON LANE	112	C2
DAWSONS LANE	112	F6
DOCTOR COOKES CLOSE	112	D6
DOVECOTE WAY	112	E6
EAST GREEN	112	D6
ELWELL AVENUE	112	F4
FAIRACRE ROAD	112	D5
FARM ROAD	112	F4
FIRTREE CLOSE	112	F4
FOREST VIEW ROAD	112	F5
FRISBY ROAD	112	E5
FRISWELL LANE	112	D5
GALLOWAY CLOSE	112	C5
GEORGE STREET	112	E5
GLYN CLOSE	112	D5
GOOSE LANE	112	D6
GREEN LANE	112	B2
GREENHILL DRIVE	112	E5
HASTINGS DRIVE	112	F5
HAWTHORNE WAY	112	E6
HAZEL WAY	112	D5
HEREFORD CLOSE	112	C5
HIGH STREET	112	D6
HILL STREET	112	E6
HINCKLEY ROAD (Stap)	112	C3
HINCKLEY ROAD (Bar)	112	C7
HOLLY LANE	112	F5
HOWARD CLOSE	112	D5
JERSEY WAY	112	D6
KERRY CLOSE	112	E5
KING STREET	112	E5
KINGSFIELD ROAD	112	E5
KIRKBY ROAD	112	F1

~193~

LEICESTER ROAD 112 F7
LINCOLN ROAD 112 D6
MAIN STREET 112 C3
MALLORY STREET 112 F4
MANOR CRESCENT 112 C2
MARYLAND CLOSE 112 C6
MASEFIELD CLOSE 112 F4
MAYFIELD WAY 112 F5
MEADOW ROAD 112 F5
MILL STREET 112 C7
MOAT WAY 112 C7
MOORE ROAD 112 F5
MOUNT AVENUE 112 F5
MYRTLE CLOSE 112 D5
NEWLANDS ROAD 112 E5
NORTHERN PERIMETER ROAD 112 F7
NOTLEY CLOSE 112 F4
NOTLEY MANOR DRIVE 112 F4
OXFORD STREET 112 E5
PEAR TREE CLOSE 112 F3
PECKLETON GREEN 112 F4
PENNY LANE 112 D5
POWERS ROAD 112 C7
QUEEN STREET 112 E6
QUEENSWAY 112 F5
RED HALL DRIVE 112 E5
RED HALL ROAD 112 F5
REGENT STREET 112 E5
ROGUES LANE 112 A6
SAFFRON CLOSE 112 F4
ST MARTINS 112 C2
ST MARYS AVENUE 112 C7
ST MARYS COURT 112 D6
SCHOOL LANE 112 C2
SHENTON ROAD 112 E5
SHILTON ROAD 112 F5
SHREWSBURY CLOSE 112 D5
STAFFORD STREET 112 D5
STANLEY STREET 112 D6
STAPLETON LANE 112 C4
THE BARRACKS 112 D6
THE CLOSE 112 E5
THE COMMON 112 F7
THE DRIVE 112 F4
TOWNEND ROAD 112 D5
WASHINGTON CLOSE 112 D6
WATERFALL WAY 112 C7
WATERS END 112 D7
WENSLEYDALE AVENUE 112 D7
WENSLEYDALE CLOSE 112 D7
WIGHTMAN ROAD 112 F5
WILLOW TREE CLOSE 112 E4
WILLOWDENE WAY 112 E6
WORCESTER CLOSE 112 D5
YEW TREE CLOSE 112 F3

Belton
CHURCH STREET 127 C2
DE VERDUN AVENUE 127 B3
FOREST LANE 127 C4
HAVEN CLOSE 127 B2
LONG STREET 127 B3
LOW WOODS LANE 127 A4
MILL LANE 127 B1
PRESENTS LANE 127 B2
SADLERS WELLS 127 B2
SANDHILLS CLOSE 127 B2
SCHOOL LANE 127 B2
THE TOFT 127 B2
THOMPSON AVENUE 127 B2
TYLERS ROAD 127 B2
VICARAGE LANE 127 B2

Belton in Rutland & Allexton
BACK LANE 124 A2
BUTTRESS CLOSE 124 B2
CHAPEL STREET 124 B2
CHURCH STREET 124 B2
COLLEGE FARM LANE 124 A1
HALLATON ROAD 124 B4
LITTLEWORTH LANE 124 B2
LODDINGTON LANE 124 B2
MAIN STREET 124 A2
NETHER STREET 124 B2
NEW ROAD 124 A2
TOKYES CLOSE 124 B2

Billesdon
BROOK LANE 114 C3
CHURCH STREET 114 C3
COPLOW LANE 114 B2
GALBY ROAD 114 C4
GLEBE CLOSE 114 C4
HIGH ACRES 114 C2
KNIGHTS CLOSE 114 B3
LEICESTER ROAD 114 A3
LONG LANE 114 B2
ROLLESTON ROAD 114 C4
THE POPLARS 114 C3
UPPINGHAM ROAD 114 C3
VICARAGE CLOSE 114 C4
WEST LANE 114 B3

Bisbrooke
BAULK ROAD 125 A2
CHURCH LANE 125 B2
GLASTON ROAD 125 C1
MAIN STREET 125 A3
SEATON ROAD 125 F4
THE INHAMS 125 A2
TOP LANE 125 A2
WALNUT CLOSE 125 A3

Bitteswell
See Lutterworth & Bitteswell

Blackfordby
ASHBY LANE 128 C4
ASHBY ROAD 128 C1
BEECH DRIVE 128 A1
BOOTHORPE LANE 128 A1
BRIAR CLOSE 128 B4
BUTT LANE 128 A3
CHURCH CLOSE 128 B3
DRIFT SIDE 128 B1
ELSTEAD LANE 128 B3
FENTON AVENUE 128 B3
FIELD LANE 128 C2
HALL CLOSE 128 C4
HEATH LANE 128 C3
HIGH STREET 128 A2
MAIN STREET 128 C3
MILLFIELD STREET 128 A1
NORTH CLOSE 128 B4
PARKERS CLOSE 128 B3
SANDTOP CLOSE 128 B4
SANDTOP LANE 128 C4
SOUTH CLOSE 128 B4
SOUTH STREET 128 A3
STRAWBERRY LANE 128 C3
THE SHRUBBERY 128 A2
THORNTOP CLOSE 128 B4
VICARAGE CLOSE 128 C4
WELL LANE 128 B3

Bottesford
ALBERT STREET 123 B3
ASH GROVE 123 A2
BARKESTONE LANE 123 B4
BEACON WAY 123 C2
BECKINGTHORPE DRIVE 123 D2
BELVOIR AVENUE 123 B4
BELVOIR ROAD 123 C3
BOWBRIDGE GARDENS 123 B2
BOWBRIDGE LANE 123 B2
CASTLE CLOSE 123 E3
CASTLE VIEW ROAD 123 D3
CHAPEL STREET 123 C2
CHESTNUT CLOSE 123 D2
CHURCH STREET 123 C2
CHURCH VIEW 123 B2
COX DRIVE 123 B2
DAYBELL CLOSE 123 C2
DEVON LANE 123 C2
EASTHORPE LANE 123 F4
EASTHORPE ROAD 123 D3
EASTHORPE VIEW 123 D3
FARMHOUSE CLOSE 123 B2
FLEMING AVENUE 123 D2
GRANBY DRIVE 123 B3
GRANTHAM ROAD 123 D2
GREEN LANE 123 D3
HIGH STREET 123 C3
KEEL DRIVE 123 C3
LAUREL WAY 123 A3
LIME GROVE 123 B3
LONGHEDGE LANE 123 A3
MANOR ROAD 123 D3
MUSTON LANE 123 D4
NORMANTON LANE 123 C2
NORTH CRESCENT 123 C3
NOTTINGHAM ROAD 123 A3
ORSTON LANE 123 A2
PINFOLD CLOSE 123 B2
PINFOLD LANE 123 B3
QUEEN STREET 123 C2
RECTORY LANE 123 C2
RIVERSIDE CLOSE 123 B2
RIVERSIDE WALK 123 B2
RUTLAND LANE 123 D3
ST MARYS CLOSE 123 C2
SCHOOL VIEW 123 B3
SILVERWOOD ROAD 123 B3
SOUTH CRESCENT 123 B3
STATION ROAD 123 D2
THE PADDOCKS 123 C3
THE SQUARE 123 B2
TOLL BAR AVENUE 123 B2
VAUGHAN AVENUE 123 D2
WALFORD CLOSE 123 B3
WALNUT ROAD 123 B3
WEST END CLOSE 123 B2
WINTERBECK CLOSE 123 B2
WYGGESTON AVENUE 123 C2
WYGGESTON ROAD 123 C2

Braunston in Rutland
BROOKE ROAD 126 B2
CEDAR STREET 126 B2
CHURCH STREET 126 B3
HIGH STREET 126 B2
KNOSSINGTON ROAD 126 A2
LAMMAS CLOSE 126 C2
OAKHAM ROAD 126 C1
RATTS LANE 126 B2
THE WISP 126 A2
WOOD LANE 126 B3

Breedon on the Hill
ASHBY ROAD 128 A4
BERRY AVENUE 128 C2
BURNEY LANE 128 A4
CROSS STREET 128 B2
DOCTORS LANE 128 B2
HASTINGS CLOSE 128 A3
HILLSIDE COURT 128 B3
HOLLOW ROAD 128 A2
MAIN STREET 128 B2
MELBOURNE LANE 128 A2
NOTTINGHAM ROAD 128 A4
RECTORY CLOSE 128 B3
SQUIRREL LANE 128 A2
STOCKING LANE 128 C4
STUDFARM CLOSE 128 B3
THE CRESCENT 128 A3
THE DELPH 128 A2
THE DOVECOTE 128 B3
THE GREEN 128 A3
TONGE LANE 128 C2
WORTHINGTON LANE 128 B3

Broughton Astley
ALAND GARDENS 88 E4
AMBER GATE CLOSE 88 F4
AMSDEN RISE 88 C3
BALDWIN RISE 88 B3
BENFORD CLOSE 88 D6
BERFORD CLOSE 88 D5
BEVERLEY DRIVE 88 C3
BLENHEIM CRESCENT 88 C3
BODYCOTE CLOSE 88 D5
BRAMLEY CLOSE 88 C3
BROOKLANDS CLOSE 88 D3
BROUGHTON LANE 88 C7
BROUGHTON ROAD 88 A7
BROUGHTON WAY 88 D3
BURNSIDE ROAD 88 D6
BUSHNELL CLOSE 88 E6
BYRE CRESCENT 88 D5
CHANDLER WAY 88 F5
CHESTNUT CLOSE 88 E5
CHURCH CLOSE 88 D4
CONDOR CLOSE 88 D3
COOKES DRIVE 88 C3
CORONATION AVENUE 88 C3
COSBY ROAD 88 E3
COTTAGE LANE 88 F4
COTTON CLOSE 88 D5
COVENTRY ROAD 88 C3
CROFT WAY 88 F5
CROMFORD WAY 88 F4
CROWFOOT WAY 88 D6
DARWIN CLOSE 88 D5
DENISTON CLOSE 88 B3
DERBY CLOSE 88 F5
DEVITT WAY 88 E5
DUNTON ROAD 88 F7
EAGLE CLOSE 88 C3
ESTLEY ROAD 88 C3
FALCON CLOSE 88 C3
FARLEIGH CLOSE 88 C3
FROLESWORTH ROAD 88 C5
GLEBE ROAD 88 C4
GORHAM RISE 88 B3
GOSHAWK CLOSE 88 C3
GRANGE ROAD 88 C3
GRANTHAM AVENUE 88 B2
GREEN ROAD 88 C3
HALL FARM CRESCENT 88 E6
HALLBROOK ROAD 88 D6
HARRIER CLOSE 88 C3
HARRIS CLOSE 88 E5
HARVEST WAY 88 D6
HAWK CLOSE 88 C3
HOBBY CLOSE 88 C3
HOLBECK DRIVE 88 F4
JOHNSON CLOSE 88 F5
JUBILEE ROAD 88 C3
KENILWORTH CLOSE 88 C2
KESTREL CLOSE 88 C3
KILN CLOSE 88 E5
KIRTLEY WAY 88 E4
KITE CLOSE 88 C2
KNIGHTON CLOSE 88 E6
LEA CLOSE 88 E5
LEICESTER ROAD 88 C3
LEIRE LANE 88 C6
LICHFIELD AVENUE 88 C3
MAIN STREET 88 C3
MALLING AVENUE 88 C3
MANOR FARM CLOSE 88 D4
MANTON CLOSE 88 F4
MELTON DRIVE 88 C2
MERLIN CLOSE 88 C3
MERTON CLOSE 88 C3
MILLBROOK DRIVE 88 D5
MILLERS GRANGE 88 D5
MONTAGUE ROAD 88 D3
NEW INN CLOSE 88 F5
NEWTON WAY 88 D6
OLD MILL ROAD 88 D5
OLD RECTORY CLOSE 88 C4
ORCHARD ROAD 88 C3
OSPREY CLOSE 88 C3
PEREGRINE ROAD 88 D3
PICKERING ROAD 88 D6
POPPLE CLOSE 88 E5
RICHARDSONS CLOSE 88 E5
ST MARYS CLOSE 88 C4
SCHOOL CRESCENT 88 C3
SITCH CLOSE 88 E5
SIX ACRES 88 C4
STANIER ROAD 88 E4
STATION ROAD 88 D4
STATION ROAD 88 E5
STEMBOROUGH LANE 88 E7
STILES CLOSE 88 D5
STREAMSIDE CLOSE 88 D5
SWANNINGTON ROAD 88 E4
TALBOTT CLOSE 88 E6
THE AVENUE 88 C3
THE FIELDWAY 88 D5
THE MEADOW 88 E5
THE PASTURES 88 D5
THORNEYCROFT CLOSE 88 F6
THORNTON CLOSE 88 E6
TOWNSEND CLOSE 88 F5
TRENT CLOSE 88 E4
UPPINGHAM DRIVE 88 B2
WALNUT CLOSE 88 D4
WARWICK ROAD 88 C2
WHINHAM AVENUE 88 B3
WHITBY CLOSE 88 C2
WHITE CLOSE 88 E4
WILLOWBROOK CLOSE 88 D3
WILLSMER CLOSE 88 E5
WYVERN CLOSE 88 E5

Burton Lazars
BARNARD CLOSE 126 B2
CHURCH LEA 126 A3
CROSS LANE 126 B2
DOG LANE 126 B2
HOLLOW LANE 126 B2
LIME STREET 126 A3
MELTON ROAD 126 A2
NEW ROAD 126 A3
PEPPERS LANE 126 A2
SAWGATE ROAD 126 C2
THE CLOSE 126 A3

Burton on the Wolds
BRICKWOOD PLACE 129 A2
BROOK STREET 129 B2
HALL DRIVE 129 B2
HUNTINGDON CLOSE 129 B2
LOUGHBOROUGH ROAD 129 A2
MELTON ROAD 129 C2
MUNDY CLOSE 129 A2
ST ANDREWS CLOSE 129 B2
ST LEONARDS CLOSE 129 B2
ST MARYS CLOSE 129 B2
ST PHILIPS ROAD 129 B2
SEALS CLOSE 129 C2
SEYMOUR ROAD 129 A2
SOMERSET CLOSE 129 A2
SOWTERS LANE 129 B2
SPRINGFIELD CLOSE 129 A2
THE WILLOWS 129 B3
TOWLES FIELDS 129 A3

Burton Ovary
See Great Glen & Burton Ovary

Bushby
See Scraptoft

Caldecott
CHURCH CLOSE 129 B2
CHURCH LANE 129 B2
GREAT EASTON ROAD 129 B3
LYDDINGTON ROAD 129 C1
MAIN STREET 129 B2
MILL LANE 129 B2
ROCKINGHAM ROAD 129 B3
UPPINGHAM ROAD 129 B1
WELLAND CLOSE 129 C2

Castle Donington
AMBASSADOR ROAD 89 B1
ANSON ROAD 89 D7
APIARY GATE 89 D4
ASTON AVENUE 89 C5
BACK LANE 89 C1
BAKEWELL DRIVE 89 C5
BARN CLOSE 89 D4
BENTLEY ROAD 89 B3
BONDGATE 89 C4
BOROUGH STREET 89 C4
BOSWORTH ROAD 89 B4
CAMPION HILL 89 B3
CARRS CLOSE 89 C4
CASTLE HILL 89 D4
CAVENDISH CLOSE 89 C5
CEDAR ROAD 89 D5
CHARNWOOD AVENUE 89 E4
CHERIBOUGH ROAD 89 C4
CHURCH LANE 89 D4
CLAPGUN STREET 89 D4
COOKS AVENUE 89 C4
CORDWELL CLOSE 89 B4
CRABTREE CLOSE 89 C5
DARSWAY 89 B3
DELVEN LANE 89 C4
DISEWORTH ROAD 89 C5
EASTWAY 89 D4
EATON ROAD 89 D4
FERRERS CLOSE 89 C4
FOSBROOK DRIVE 89 B3
FOX ROAD 89 B4
GARDEN CRESCENT 89 E4
GASNEY AVENUE 89 D2
GRANGE DRIVE 89 C4
HALL FARM CLOSE 89 C4
HALLAM FIELDS 89 D4
HARCOURT PLACE 89 D3
HARVEY ROAD 89 D5
HASTING STREET 89 D4

HAULTON DRIVE .89 C3
HAWTHORN ROAD .89 D2
HAZELRIGG CLOSE .89 B3
HEMINGTON HILL .89 E3
HIGH STREET .89 C4
HILL TOP .89 C5
HUNTINGDON DRIVE .89 C3
KIRKLAND CLOSE .89 C4
LOCKINGTON ROAD .89 F2
LOTHIAN PLACE .89 C4
LOUDOUN PLACE .89 C3
MAIN STREET .89 F3
MEADOW CRESCENT .89 D5
MINTON ROAD .89 B3
MOIRA DALE .89 E4
MONTEITH PLACE .89 D4
MOUNT PLEASANT .89 D4
NEWBOLD DRIVE .89 D2
ORCHARD AVENUE .89 C4
ORLY AVENUE .89 C5
PADDOCK CLOSE .89 B4
PARK AVENUE .89 B4
PARK LANE .89 B4
PEARTREE CLOSE .89 C4
QUEENSWAY .89 B3
RAWDON CLOSE .89 C3
ROBY LEA .89 B3
ROUTH AVENUE .89 D5
RYCROFT ROAD .89 F1
ST ANNES LANE .89 D4
ST EDWARDS ROAD .89 C5
SALTER CLOSE .89 B3
SCHOOL LANE .89 C4
SELINA CLOSE .89 C3
SHIELDS CRESCENT .89 B4
SHIRLEY CLOSE .89 C3
SHORT LANE .89 B3
SPITTAL HILL .89 B3
STARKIE AVENUE .89 B4
STATION ROAD .89 D3
STATION ROAD .89 E1
STAUNTON CLOSE .89 C3
STONEHILL .89 C5
STUDBROOK CLOSE .89 B4
SYCAMORE ROAD .89 D2
TANYARD CLOSE .89 D3
THE BARROON .89 E3
THE BIGGIN .89 D4
THE GREEN .89 B4
THE MOAT .89 D4
THE SPINNEY .89 C3
THE SPITTAL .89 C3
TIPNALL ROAD .89 C4
TOWLES PASTURES .89 C4
TRENT LANE .89 D2
VANGUARD ROAD .89 D7
VICTORIA STREET .89 D2
WALTON HILL .89 B3
WILLOW ROAD .89 D2
WINDMILL CLOSE .89 D5

Claybrooke Magna

BACK LANE .139 B2
BELL STREET .139 B2
FOSSEWAY GARDENS .139 B2
FROLESWORTH LANE .139 C1
GREWCOCK CLOSE .139 B2
HIGH CROSS ROAD .139 A2
HOLLY TREE WALK .139 B2
MAIN ROAD .139 B2
MANOR ROAD .139 A1
ROMAN CLOSE .139 B2
WESTERN DRIVE .139 B3
WOODLAND AVENUE .139 B2
WOODWAY LANE .139 B4

Coalville & Agar Nook

ABBOTTS OAK DRIVE .111 E2
AGAR NOOK LANE .111 F2
ALBERT ROAD .111 F2
ASH TREE ROAD .110 D4
ASHBURTON ROAD .110 D4
ASHBY ROAD .110 A3
ASHLAND DRIVE .110 B1
ASPEN CLOSE .110 B1
ATLAS ROAD .110 F1
AVENUE ROAD .110 F3
BAKER STREET .110 E1
BAKEWELL STREET .111 A2
BARDON CLOSE .111 C4
BARDON ROAD .111 C4
BEACON CRESCENT .111 E3
BEDALE CLOSE .110 E3
BEECH AVENUE .110 A3
BEECH ROAD .111 C3
BELGRAVE CLOSE .111 E2
BELMONT DRIVE .110 C1
BELTON CLOSE .111 E2
BELVOIR ROAD .110 F3
BERRISFORD STREET .110 F3
BERRY CLOSE .110 C1
BERRYHILL LANE .110 D5
BLACKBROOK DRIVE .111 D3
BLACKWOOD .111 E2
BOTTS WAY .111 C3
BRACKEN CLOSE .110 E5
BRADGATE DRIVE .111 D4
BRAMBLES ROAD .110 E5
BREACH ROAD .110 F4
BRIDGE ROAD .110 F3
BROAD STREET .110 F3
BROOM LEYS AVENUE .111 B3
BROOM LEYS ROAD .111 B2
BROUGHTON STREET .110 F3
CAMBRIDGE STREET .111 A2
CAMELFORD ROAD .110 E4
CANNOCK CLOSE .110 F7
CASTLE ROCK DRIVE .111 E1
CAVENDISH CRESCENT .110 E4
CENTRAL ROAD .110 F4
CHANNING WAY .110 F1
CHAPEL CLOSE .110 B2
CHARLES STREET .110 C1
CHARNBOROUGH ROAD .111 D3
CHARNWOOD STREET .111 A2
CHESTNUT GROVE .111 D3
CHURCH LANE .110 A3
CLAREMONT DRIVE .110 B1
CLARKE ROAD .111 E3
COALVILLE LANE .110 B2
COPPICE CLOSE .110 B1
COPSE CLOSE .110 E4
CRESCENT ROAD .110 E4
CRESWELL DRIVE .110 A3
CROMORE CLOSE .111 E2
CROPSTON DRIVE .111 E3
CURLEW WAY .111 C3
DAUPHINE CLOSE .111 F2
DEGENS WAY .110 D4
DENNIS STREET .110 F5
DEVANA AVENUE .111 B3
DEVERON CLOSE .111 E2
DOVE ROAD .111 C4
DROME CLOSE .111 F2
DUNBAR ROAD .111 E3
DURRIS CLOSE .111 E2
EAST LANE .111 F7
EXMOOR CLOSE .110 E7
FAIRFIELD ROAD .110 E4
FARM LANE .110 D6
FLORET CLOSE .110 C2
FORDICE CLOSE .110 E4
FOREST ROAD .111 F3
FOSBROOKE CLOSE .110 A3
FRANKS ROAD .111 E7
FREASON FIELDS .110 D4
FULTON DRIVE .110 C1
GARDEN ROAD .111 A1
GARENDON ROAD .111 E3
GARFIELD ROAD .110 E4
GILLAMORE DRIVE .111 C1
GLEN WAY .111 B4
GOLIATH ROAD .110 F1
GORSE ROAD .110 E5
GRANGE ROAD .111 D5
GRASMERE .111 E1
GREENFIELDS DRIVE .111 C2
GREENHILL ROAD .111 E2
GUTTERIDGE STREET .110 E3
HALL GATE .111 E3
HAMILTON ROAD .111 E3
HASLYN WALK .111 D3
HAWLEY CLOSE .111 A5
HAWTHORN CLOSE .111 A2
HEATHER LANE .110 A4
HECTOR ROAD .110 F1
HEDGE ROAD .110 E4
HELMSDALE CLOSE .111 F3
HERON WAY .111 B3
HIGH STREET .110 F2
HIGHFIELD STREET .110 D4
HOLLY BANK .110 F5
HOLTS LANE .110 D5
HOSPITAL LANE .110 A3
HOTEL STREET .110 F2
IBSTOCK ROAD .110 B4
JACKS WALK .110 D4
JACKSON STREET .110 E3
JACQUEMART CLOSE .111 F2
JAMES STREET .110 E3
JENNYS LANE .110 A3
KANE CLOSE .110 E2
KENDAL ROAD .110 F7
KENMORE CRESCENT .111 F3
KING STREET .110 F3
KIRKHILL CLOSE .111 E2
KIRTON ROAD .111 F3
LANCASTER CLOSE .111 F1
LAUNCESTON DRIVE .110 E4
LEICESTER ROAD .110 B3
LINFORD CRESCENT .111 D2
LINKS CLOSE .110 F5
LONDON ROAD .111 F2
LONG LANE .111 A1
LONGCLIFF ROAD .111 D3
MAIN STREET .110 A3
MAMMOTH STREET .110 F2
MANOR ROAD .110 D5
MAPLEWELL .111 D3
MARGARET STREET .110 E2
MARKET STREET .110 E2
MARSDEN CLOSE .110 B1
MEADOW VIEW .110 E6
MELBOURNE ROAD .110 B7
MELBOURNE STREET .110 F2
MICKLEDEN GREEN .111 C1
MIDLANDS ROAD .110 F7
MILL DAM .110 F5
MILL POND .110 F5
MUSCOVEY ROAD .111 C3
NELSON FIELDS .111 C1
NENE WAY .111 C4
NEVILLE DRIVE .111 C1
NEW STREET .110 D4
NEW STREET .110 F3
NORTH AVENUE .110 F4
NORTHFIELD DRIVE .111 E3
OAK CLOSE .111 C3
OAKHAM DRIVE .111 E2
OAKTREE ROAD .110 D4
OLD STATION CLOSE .110 F2
ORCHARD CLOSE .110 B1
OWEN STREET .110 E2
OXFORD STREET .111 A2
PARK ROAD .110 F2
PEGGS GRANGE .110 F5
PELDAR PLACE .111 E3
PERRAN AVENUE .111 C1
PIPER LANE .110 A3
POLLARD WAY .110 C1
PRINCE STREET .110 F3
QUEEN STREET .110 F3
QUELCH CLOSE .110 F5
QUORN CRESCENT .111 D3
RAVENSLEA .110 A3
RAVENSTONE ROAD .110 D1
RICHMOND ROAD .110 E1
ROBIN ROAD .111 B3
ROCHDALE CRESCENT .111 F2
ROMANS CRESCENT .111 F2
ROWAN AVENUE .111 D3
ST DAVIDS COURT .111 E2
ST DAVIDS CRESCENT .111 E2
ST FAITHS CLOSE .110 E3
ST IVES .111 D3
ST JOHNS CLOSE .110 F5
ST MARYS AVENUE .110 D4
ST MARYS LANE .110 B4
ST MICHAELS DRIVE .110 A3
ST SAVIOURS ROAD .110 E3
SCOTLANDS DRIVE .110 F3
SCOTLANDS ROAD .110 F3
SEAGRAVE CLOSE .111 E2
SHARPLEY AVENUE .111 C1
SHAW LANE .111 F7
SHERWOOD CLOSE .110 F7
SMITH CRESCENT .111 E3
SNIBSTON DRIVE .110 C2
SNIPE CLOSE .110 D4
SOUTH LANE .111 E7
STAINSDALE GREEN .111 C1
STAMFORD DRIVE .111 F1
STANDARD HILL .110 D4
STATION ROAD .110 E6
STENSON ROAD .111 A2
STONEHAVEN CLOSE .111 F3
STRATHMORE CLOSE .111 E3
STRETTON DRIVE .111 E2
SWAN WAY .111 B3
SWITHLAND ROAD .111 E3
SYCAMORE ROAD .111 C3
TARA STREET .111 E7
TAVISTOCK CLOSE .110 E4
TEAL CLOSE .111 B3
THE GREEN .110 E6
THE LIMES .110 B1
THIRLMERE .111 E2
THORNTON CLOSE .111 E2
THORNTREE CLOSE .110 B1
TORRINGTON AVENUE .111 C1
TOTNES CLOSE .110 E4
TOWNSEND LANE .110 D6
TWEENTOWN .110 E6
TWYFORD CLOSE .111 E2
VAUGHAN STREET .110 E3
VERCOR CLOSE .111 F2
VERDON CRESCENT .111 D2
VICTORIA ROAD .111 F2
VULCAN WAY .110 F1
WAINWRIGHT ROAD .110 F5
WALKER ROAD .111 E7
WASH LANE .110 B2
WATERWORKS ROAD .111 C4
WELLAND CLOSE .111 C3
WENTWORTH ROAD .110 E3
WESTERN AVENUE .110 C1
WHETSTONE DRIVE .111 A2
WHITWICK ROAD .110 F2
WILLN CLOSE .111 D3
WILLOW GREEN .111 E1
WINDSOR CLOSE .111 D2
WOLSEY ROAD .110 E1
WOODHOUSE ROAD .111 D3
WOODS CLOSE .110 E5
WORTLEY CLOSE .111 A2
WYATT ROAD .111 A2
WYGGESTON ROAD .110 F3
YORK PLACE .111 F2
ZETLAND CLOSE .110 E3

Cosby & Whetstone

ANDREW AVENUE .90 C4
ARMSTON ROAD .90 C5
ARNOLD CLOSE .90 C6
ASH TREE ROAD .90 C5
ASHOVER CLOSE .90 C4
ASHVILLE WAY .90 D3
ATTFIELD DRIVE .90 E1
AVON DRIVE .90 E1
BADGER DRIVE .90 E3
BEAVER CLOSE .90 E3
BEECHWOOD ROAD .90 A2
BELL LANE .90 B1
BIDDLE ROAD .90 B1
BIGGS CLOSE .90 F3
BINGLEY ROAD .90 A2
BLABY BY PASS .90 F2
BODICOAT CLOSE .90 E3
BRADBURY CLOSE .90 C5
BRIDGE WAY .90 E1
BRIERFIELD ROAD .90 C7
BROADBENT CLOSE .90 E1
BROADMEAD ROAD .90 F1
BROOK STREET .90 E1
BROOKLANDS CLOSE .90 E1
BROOKLANDS ROAD .90 C4
BROUGHTON ROAD .90 B6
BROWNS WAY .90 E3
BRUCE WAY .90 D3
BURLEY CLOSE .90 C5
BURNHAM DRIVE .90 F2
BUXTON CLOSE .90 F1
CAMBRIAN CLOSE .90 C6
CAMBRIDGE ROAD .90 D3
CANNAM CLOSE .90 F3
CEDAR CRESCENT .90 A1
CEMETERY ROAD .90 E1
CHAPEL LANE .90 C7
CHARLES WAY .90 F3
CHARLTON CLOSE .90 F2
CHEER CLOSE .90 E4
CHESTNUT CLOSE .90 A2
CHILTERN AVENUE .90 D5
COALES AVENUE .90 F3
CORNFIELD CLOSE .90 B1
COSBY ROAD .90 B3
COTSWOLD AVENUE .90 D5
COULSON CLOSE .90 F2
COVENTRY ROAD .90 A1
CRANMER CLOSE .90 F2
CROFT ROAD .90 A5
CROMFORD ROAD .90 C4
CURTIS CLOSE .90 F1
CUTTERS CLOSE .90 A1
DARLEY ROAD .90 F1
DESFORD ROAD .90 A1
DOG AND GUN LANE .90 F4
DROVERS WAY .90 A1
EARLE SMITH CLOSE .90 F1
EIDER CLOSE .90 E4
ELIZABETH GARDENS .90 E1
ELM TREE ROAD .90 B6
EMPEROR WAY .90 E4
FAIRVIEW AVENUE .90 E1
FARM CLOSE .90 B1
FIELD CLOSE .90 B1
FLAMINGO DRIVE .90 E4
FLETCHERS CLOSE .90 A1
FORRESTER CLOSE .90 D5
FOX COVERT .90 E3
FURROWS CLOSE .90 B1
GIMSON AVENUE .90 C5
GREBE WAY .90 E3
GREENFIELDS .90 E1
GREYLAG WAY .90 E4
GROVE ROAD .90 F1
GURNEY CRESCENT .90 B2
HALFORD CLOSE .90 E2
HARLAND CLOSE .90 C5
HARLEQUIN WAY .90 E4
HARRISON CLOSE .90 F3
HART CLOSE .90 E2
HAYBARN CLOSE .90 C1
HAZEL CLOSE .90 B2
HEIGHTON CRESCENT .90 B2
HERBERT CLOSE .90 F1
HERDSMANS CLOSE .90 B1
HEYBROOK AVENUE .90 F1
HIGH STREET .90 E1
HILL VIEW DRIVE .90 C5
HIND CLOSE .90 F2
HODSON CLOSE .90 F2
HOLDEN CLOSE .90 F3
HUBBARD CLOSE .90 F3
HUMES CLOSE .90 E4
JAMESWAY .90 C4
JOHNSON CLOSE .90 F1
JUBILEE CRESCENT .90 B1
KENNY CLOSE .90 F2
KINDER CLOSE .90 F3
KING EDWARD AVENUE .90 A1
KING STREET .90 E1
KINGSFIELD ROAD .90 B6
LADY LEYS .90 C5
LATIMER CLOSE .90 F2
LAUNDON WAY .90 F3
LEICESTER ROAD .90 B1
LEVERET DRIVE .90 E2
LINLEY GREEN .90 C5
LUTTERWORTH ROAD .90 F7
MAIN STREET .90 C5
MALVERN CRESCENT .90 C5
MANDARIN WAY .90 E4
MANOR ROAD .90 C4
MAPLE TREE WALK .90 B1
MASONS CLOSE .90 A1
MAURA CLOSE .90 E3
MAWBY CLOSE .90 F3
MEDHURST CLOSE .90 F3
MONAL CLOSE .90 E4
MOUNT ROAD .90 C5
MUNTJACK ROAD .90 E2
NARBOROUGH ROAD .90 C5
OAK ROAD .90 A2

OTTER WAY 90 E3
PARAMORE CLOSE 90 E3
PARK CLOSE 90 C6
PARK ROAD 90 A1
PARK ROAD 90 C5
PAWLEY CLOSE 90 F2
PEACOCK DRIVE 90 E3
PHIPPS CLOSE 90 F2
PINTAIL CLOSE 90 E4
POPLAR ROAD 90 A2
PORTLAND STREET 90 C5
QUEENS ROAD 90 F1
REEVES CLOSE 90 E3
RICHMOND CLOSE 90 B6
RIDDINGTON ROAD 90 B2
RIDGEWAY 90 B2
RIDLEY CLOSE 90 F2
RIVERSIDE WAY 90 B1
ROEBUCK CLOSE 90 E3
SANDERSON CLOSE 90 F1
SEVERN CLOSE 90 C5
SHELLDUCK CLOSE 90 E4
SHENTON CLOSE 90 E1
SPRINGWELL LANE 90 E5
STABLE CLOSE 90 B1
STATION ROAD 90 B1
STEADMAN AVENUE 90 D5
STEVENSON GARDENS 90 C4
SYCAMORE WAY 90 A1
THE BANKS 90 C6
THE DICKEN 90 E1
THE FAIRWAY 90 F1
THE GRANGE 90 A1
THE MEADOWS 90 C1
THE NOOK 90 E1
THE PADDOCKS 90 B1
TUDOR DRIVE 90 C7
WALE ROAD 90 E1
WALNUT LEYS 90 C6
WARNER CLOSE 90 F3
WARWICK ROAD 90 D2
WAVERTREE CLOSE 90 C4
WHITE BARN DRIVE 90 C5
WHITEACRES 90 D3
WHITTLE CLOSE 90 E2
WILLIAM STREET 90 A1
WILLIAMS CLOSE 90 A1
WILLOW CLOSE 90 B2
WINTERBURN GARDENS 90 E1
WOOTTON CLOSE 90 E2
WORSLEY WAY 90 F2
WYCHWOOD ROAD 90 F3

Cottesmore

ASHWELL ROAD 126 B4
AUSTHORP GROVE 126 B4
BEAUFORT ROAD 126 D1
BEDALE STREET 126 E1
BLANKNEY ROAD 126 E1
BURGHLEY CIRCLE 126 F1
BURLEY ROAD 126 B4
CLATTERPOT LANE 126 C3
COTLEY CRESCENT 126 E1
COTSWOLD STREET 126 E1
COTTESMORE ROAD 126 E1
CRESSWELL DRIVE 126 C3
DEBDALE 126 C3
DEVON WALK 126 D1
FITZWILLIAM WALK 126 E1
GARTH STREET 126 E1
HALL CLOSE 126 D3
HAMBLEDON CRESCENT 126 F1
HEATH DRIVE 126 D3
LEDBURY WALK 126 E1
LONG MEADOW WAY 126 D2
MAIN STREET 126 C3
MILL LANE 126 C3
NETHER CLOSE 126 D3
OAKLEY ROAD 126 E1
PERCY ROAD 126 E1
ROGUES LANE 126 D2
SHEEPDYKE 126 C3
SOMERSET ROAD 126 E1
THE LEAS 126 C3
THE PASTURES 126 D3
TIVERTON ROAD 126 E1
TOLLBAR 126 D3
WENTON CLOSE 126 B4
WESTLAND ROAD 126 D3
WHADDON CHASE 126 E1
WOODLAND ROAD 126 E1

Countesthorpe

ALMOND CLOSE 125 D2
ARCHERY CLOSE 125 E2
ARRAN WAY 125 E3
ASPEN DRIVE 125 D2
BARNLEY CLOSE 125 D2
BASSETT AVENUE 125 D3
BEECHINGS CLOSE 125 C3
BENSKYN CLOSE 125 C2
BLADEN CLOSE 125 C2
BORROWCUP CLOSE 125 B2
BROADFIELD WAY 125 C2
BROOK COURT 125 E2
BROOMLEYS 125 C2
BUCKINGHAM ROAD 125 E2
BUTE WAY 125 E3
CENTRAL STREET 125 E2
CHERRYTREE CLOSE 125 D2
CHRISTOPHER CLOSE 125 D3
CHURCH STREET 125 E2
COSBY ROAD 125 B3
COUNTESTHORPE ROAD 125 A3
DALE ACRE 125 E2
EDGELEY ROAD 125 E2
FAIRISLE WAY 125 E3
FIR TREE AVENUE 125 D2
FOSTON ROAD 125 F2
GILLAM BUTTS 125 D3
GLEBE DRIVE 125 D3
GREEN LANE 125 E2
GWENDOLINE DRIVE 125 D2
HALLCROFT AVENUE 125 D3
HAZELBANK ROAD 125 F2
HEATHER WAY 125 E3
HILL LANE 125 A3
HOLYROOD DRIVE 125 C2
IONA WAY 125 E3
JUDITH DRIVE 125 E2
KIRKFIELD ROAD 125 F2
LADBROKE GROVE 125 E2
LARCHWOOD 125 D2
LAUREL DRIVE 125 D2
LEICESTER ROAD 125 E1
LEOPOLD CLOSE 125 D2
LEWIS WAY 125 E3
LEYSLAND AVENUE 125 B2
LINDEN AVENUE 125 C2
LINDEN FARM DRIVE 125 D2
LUDLAM CLOSE 125 C2
MAIN STREET 125 E2
MAPLE AVENUE 125 E2
MARSTON CRESCENT 125 D3
MAURICE DRIVE 125 C3
MENNECY CLOSE 125 C3
MULL WAY 125 E3
NEW STREET 125 E2
OLD FIELD CLOSE 125 B2
ORCHARD LANE 125 E3
ORKNEY WAY 125 F3
PADDOCK CLOSE 125 D2
PEATLING ROAD 125 E3
PENFOLD DRIVE 125 C2
PINEWOOD CLOSE 125 D2
POPLAR AVENUE 125 D2
REEDPOOL CLOSE 125 E2
REGENT ROAD 125 E2
ROSEBANK ROAD 125 E2
SCALBOROUGH CLOSE 125 C2
SCOTLAND WAY 125 E2
SHETLAND WAY 125 E2
SKYE WAY 125 E3
SPINNEY AVENUE 125 E2
SPRINGWELL DRIVE 125 D2
STANYON CLOSE 125 E2
STATION ROAD 125 E3
STONECROFT 125 B3
STROMA WAY 125 E3
SUNBURY RISE 125 B2
TEBBS CLOSE 125 B2
THE CHESTNUTS 125 D2
THE DALES 125 B2
THE DRIVE 125 B2
THE ELMS 125 D2
THE HAWTHORNS 125 D2
THE LEYS 125 B3
THE PLANTATION 125 D2
THE ROWANS 125 D2
THE VINERIES 125 C3
THE WOODLANDS 125 C2
TOPHALL DRIVE 125 D3
WALNUT WAY 125 D2
WATERLOO CRESCENT 125 C3
WESTFIELD AVENUE 125 C2
WHEATLANDS DRIVE 125 C2
WIGSTON STREET 125 E2
WILLOUGHBY ROAD 125 B3
WILLOW DRIVE 125 E2
WINCHESTER ROAD 125 B1

Croft

ARBOR ROAD 139 B2
ASH ROAD 139 C3
BALA ROAD 139 C2
BROOKES AVENUE 139 B3
BROUGHTON ROAD 139 B3
CONISTON WAY 139 C2
DOVECOTE LANE 139 B1
HILL STREET 139 B1
HOLLIERS WAY 139 B2
HUNCOTE ROAD 139 B2
KENDALLS AVENUE 139 B2
LEICESTER ROAD 139 C2
MARSTON ROAD 139 A1
PETERSFIELD 139 B2
POCHIN STREET 139 C2
SALISBURY AVENUE 139 B2
SCHOOL CLOSE 139 B3
SOPERS ROAD 139 B3
SPARKENHOE 139 B3
STATION ROAD 139 B2
WINDERMERE DRIVE 139 C2
WINSTON AVENUE 139 C2

Croxton Kerral

CHAPEL LANE 130 A2
CHURCH LANE 130 B2
CROXTON ROAD 130 B3
HIGHFIELD CRESCENT 130 B2
MAIN STREET 130 A2
MIDDLE STREET 130 A2
MILLS LANE 130 B2
SALTBY ROAD 130 B2
SCHOOL LANE 130 A2
SHIRES ORCHARD 130 B2
THE NOOK 130 A2
THORPES LANE 130 B2
TOP ROAD 130 B2

Desford

BAMBROOK CLOSE 129 D3
BEAUFORT CLOSE 129 C4
BEDFORD CLOSE 129 C3
BEECH WAY 129 C3
BELVOIR CLOSE 129 C3
BOTCHESTON ROAD 129 F1
BURLEY CLOSE 129 C3
CAMBRIDGE DRIVE 129 B3
CHAPEL LANE 129 C2
CHURCH LANE 129 C2
COTTAGE LANE 129 C2
DESFORD LANE 129 B4
ESSEX CLOSE 129 C3
FULLER CLOSE 129 D2
GLOUCESTER CLOSE 129 C4
GRACE ROAD 129 D3
GRANGE COURT 129 C2
HAMBLE CLOSE 129 C3
HAYES END 129 C3
HAZEL STREET 129 B3
HIGH STREET 129 D3
HOLMFIELD ROAD 129 C3
HUNTS LANE 129 B2
KIRKBY ROAD 129 C3
LANCASTER CLOSE 129 C3
LEICESTER LANE 129 E3
LINDRIDGE LANE 129 C1
LITTLE LANE 129 C2
LYNWOOD CLOSE 129 C3
MAIN STREET 129 C2
MANOR GARDENS 129 C3
MANOR ROAD 129 C3
MAPLE WAY 129 B3
NEWBOLD ROAD 129 C2
NORFOLK ROAD 129 C4
OAK ROAD 129 C3
OXFORD ROAD 129 B3
PARKSTONE ROAD 129 C3
PECKLETON LANE 129 C3
RICHMOND CLOSE 129 C4
RINGWOOD CLOSE 129 C3
ST MARTINS DRIVE 129 C3
SALISBURY CLOSE 129 C3
STATION ROAD 129 D2
STEWARDS COURT 129 C3
SUFFOLK WAY 129 C4
THE GROVE 129 B3
WARWICK CLOSE 129 B3
WILLOW STREET 129 C3

Diseworth

ASHBY ROAD 146 C1
BROOKSIDE 146 B3
CLEMENTS GATE 146 C2
GREEN LANE 146 A1
GRIMES GATE 146 B1
HALL GATE 146 B2
HYAMS LANE 146 C2
LADY GATE 146 B2
LONG HOLDEN 146 C3
LONG MERE LANE 146 B3
ORCHARD CLOSE 146 B3
PAGE LANE 146 B3
SHAKESPEARE CLOSE 146 B3
SHAKESPEARE DRIVE 146 B2
THE GREEN 146 B3
THE WOODCROFT 146 B3

Donisthorpe, Moira & Oakthorpe

ACRESFORD ROAD 118 A5
ASHBY ROAD (Don) 118 C4
ASHBY ROAD (Moira) 118 B1
BARKLAM CLOSE 118 A4
BLACKTHORN WAY 118 E7
CANAL STREET 118 C6
CHAPEL STREET 118 A4
CHURCH STREET 118 B5
CORONATION LANE 118 C6
DONISTHORPE LANE 118 A2
FURNACE LANE 118 B2
GREENSIDE CLOSE 118 A4
HALL LANE 118 B5
HILL STREET 118 A4
IVY CLOSE 118 A4
LIME AVENUE 118 E7
MAIN STREET 118 C6
MEASHAM ROAD 118 B2
NEW STREET (Don) 118 A4
NEW STREET (Oak) 118 C6
PARK ROAD 118 A3
POPLAR AVENUE 118 A3
POPLAR DRIVE 118 E7
RAMSCLIFF AVENUE 118 B5
SCHOOL STREET 118 C6
SEALS ROAD 118 A4
SHORTHEATH ROAD 118 B1
SILVER STREET 118 C6
STATION DRIVE 118 B1
STRETTON VIEW 118 B7
TALBOT PLACE 118 B5
WILLESLEY WOOD SIDE 118 E2

Dunton Bassett

See Leire & Dunton Bassett

Earl Shilton & Elmesthorpe

ALEXANDER AVENUE 113 C4
ALMEYS LANE 113 D3
ALMOND WAY 113 B6
ASH ROAD 113 A5
ASTLEY ROAD 113 C5
AVENUE NORTH 113 D3
AVENUE SOUTH 113 D3
BALMORAL ROAD 113 A5
BILLINGTON ROAD 113 B7
BIRCH CLOSE 113 A6
BORROWDALE CLOSE 113 C5
BOSWORTH GREEN 113 D3
BREACH LANE 113 C5
BYRON STREET 113 B5
CANDLE LANE 113 C4
CARRS DRIVE 113 C4
CARRS ROAD 113 C4
CEDAR ROAD 113 A5
CHAPEL STREET 113 D3
CHURCH STREET 113 D3
CONISTON CLOSE 113 C4
CORONATION ROAD 113 A5
COTTAGE GARDENS 113 C4
DERWENT CLOSE 113 C5
DOCTORS FIELDS 113 A5
EARL STREET 113 D3
EAST EQUITY ROAD 113 C5
EDINBURGH ROAD 113 A5
ELMDALE ROAD 113 A5
ELMESTHORPE LANE 113 A6
EQUITY ROAD 113 C5
FIELD WAY 113 A5
FRANK BOOTON CLOSE 113 E4
GARTREE CRESCENT 113 A4
GREEN LANE 113 C3
HARRISON CLOSE 113 C4
HEATH LANE 113 B4
HIGH STREET 113 C4
HIGH TOR EAST 113 B3
HIGH TOR WEST 113 B3
HIGHFIELD STREET 113 A5
HILL TOP 113 C3
HINCKLEY ROAD 113 A5
HOLLYDENE CRESCENT 113 A5
HURST ROAD 113 B5
IVYDENE CLOSE 113 C4
JAMES STREET 113 B5
KEATS CLOSE 113 C3
KEATS LANE 113 C3
KING RICHARDS HILL 113 E3
KINGS WALK 113 B4
KNIGHTS LINK 113 E3
LABURNUM DRIVE 113 A5
LAND SOCIETY LANE 113 B4
LEIGHTON CRESCENT 113 C7
LIME GROVE 113 B5
LOVELACE CRESCENT 113 C7
LUCAS WAY 113 B5
LYNDENE CLOSE 113 C5
MAPLE WAY 113 B6
MAUGHAN STREET 113 C3
MEADOW COURT ROAD 113 C5
MELTON STREET 113 B5
METCALFE STREET 113 B5
MILL LANE 113 D3
MONA STREET 113 B5
MONTGOMERY ROAD 113 D4
MOUNTFIELD ROAD 113 B4
NEW STREET 113 B5
NOCK VERGES 113 D3
NORTHLEIGH WAY 113 C5
NORTON ROAD 113 F5
NURSERY GARDENS 113 A5
OAKDALE ROAD 113 A5
OAKS WAY 113 B4
OXFORD STREET 113 C4
PARK ROAD 113 C3
PEGGS CLOSE 113 C4
PROSPECT WAY 113 B4
ROMAN CLOSE 113 D3
RONALD TOON ROAD 113 D4
ROSSENDALE ROAD 113 A5
SANDRINGHAM AVENUE 113 A5
STANTON ROAD 113 B5
STATION ROAD 113 B5
STONEYCROFT ROAD 113 A5
THE CLOISTERS 113 B4
THE CRESCENT 113 A7
THE GRANGE 113 B5
THE LEECROFTS 113 C5
THE POPLARS 113 D3
THE ROUNDHILLS 113 C7
THURLASTON LANE 113 D3
TOWER ROAD 113 C4
ULLSWATER CLOSE 113 C5
VICARAGE STREET 113 C4
WATERY GATE LANE 113 F3
WEAVER ROAD 113 C4
WEST STREET 113 C4
WILEMANS CLOSE 113 B6
WILF BROWN CLOSE 113 D3
WILKINSON LANE 113 B6
WINDERMERE CLOSE 113 C4
WOOD STREET 113 B4

East Goscote

ARCHERS GREEN 119 B7
BACK LANE 119 D2
BADGERS CORNER 119 B6
BLEAKMOOR CLOSE 119 E3
BRACKEN DALE 119 C6

BROOK HOUSE CLOSE 119 D5
BROOK STREET 119 E5
BROOKSIDE 119 D4
BROOME AVENUE 119 C6
BROOME LANE 119 B5
BROOMFIELD 119 C7
CHESTNUT WAY 119 C7
CHURCH LANE (Thrus) 119 D2
CHURCH LANE (Rears) 119 E4
CHURCH LANE (Ratcl) 119 A4
CHURCH LEYS AVENUE 119 E4
COOPERS NOOK 119 B7
COUNTRYMANS WAY 119 C6
FARRIERS WAY 119 B7
FERNELEY RISE 119 D2
FLETCHERS WAY 119 B7
FOX HOLLOW 119 C6
FOXGLOVE CLOSE 119 C6
FREEMANS WAY 119 C6
GLEBELAND CLOSE 119 D1
GRANGE AVENUE 119 D6
GREENSWARD 119 C6
HARVEST CORNER 119 C7
HOBY ROAD 119 F1
HUNTSMANS DALE 119 C6
KEEPERS CROFT 119 C7
LING DALE 119 C6
LONG FURROW 119 B7
MAIN STREET 119 A4
MELTON ROAD 119 F4
MILL ROAD 119 D5
NEW AVENUE 119 D5
OLD GATE ROAD 119 D1
PLOUGHMANS LEA 119 C7
RATCLIFFE ROAD 119 B3
REARSBY ROAD 119 D2
REGENT STREET 119 D2
SADDLERS CLOSE 119 B7
SEAGRAVE ROAD 119 C1
SQUIRES RIDE 119 B6
SQUIRRELS CORNER 119 C6
STATION ROAD 119 E4
THATCHERS CORNER 119 B7
THE CHASE 119 B6
THE GREEN 119 D2
THE HEADLAND 119 C6
THE MEADOWS 119 C6
THE WARREN 119 B7
THE WOLDS 119 C6
THRUSSINGTON ROAD 119 B3
TINKERS DELL 119 B7
WATERGATE 119 C7
WAYFARER DRIVE 119 C6
WESTFIELD CLOSE 119 D6
WOODMANS CHASE 119 B7
WREAKE DRIVE 119 E3
YEOMANS DALE 119 C7

Eaton & Branston
CHAPEL STREET 124 B2
CHURCH LANE 124 B2
LINGS CLOSE 124 A2
MAIN STREET (Eat) 124 B2
MAIN STREET (Bran) 124 D2
VICARAGE LANE 124 B2
WALTHAM LANE 124 A3

Edith Weston
CHILTERN DRIVE 127 D2
CHURCH LANE 127 C2
CONISTON ROAD 127 B2
CRUMMOCK AVENUE 127 B2
DERWENT AVENUE 127 B2
GIBBET LANE 127 B1
KING EDWARDS WAY 127 C2
MANTON ROAD 127 C2
MENDIP ROAD 127 D2
NORMANTON ROAD 127 D1
PENNINE DRIVE 127 E2
RECTORY LANE 127 C2
SEVERN CRESCENT 127 E2
ST MARYS CLOSE 127 C1
ULLSWATER AVENUE 127 A2
WELL CLOSE 127 C2
WELLAND ROAD 127 E2
WESTON ROAD 127 C2
WINDERMERE ROAD 127 B2

Egleton
CHURCH ROAD 96 B2
MAIN STREET 96 B2
MEADOW WAY 96 B2
ORCHARD CLOSE 96 B2

Empingham
AUDIT HALL ROAD 135 B3
BAYLEYS CLOSE 135 B2
BECKWORTH GROVE 135 B2
CHURCH STREET 135 B2
CROCKET LANE 135 B2
EXTON ROAD 135 A1
GUNNEL LANE 135 C2
LOVES LANE 135 B1
MAIN STREET 135 C2
MILL LANE 135 C2
NURSERY CLOSE 135 B2
SCHOOL LANE 135 C2
STAMFORD ROAD 135 C4
WHITWELL ROAD 135 A2
WILLOUGHBY DRIVE 135 B2

Exton
BLACKSMITHS LANE 140 B2
CAMPDEN CLOSE 140 B2
EMPINGHAM ROAD 140 B2
GARDEN ROAD 140 C2
HIGH STREET 140 B2
MALTINGS YARD 140 B2
NEW FIELD ROAD 140 B2
OAKHAM ROAD 140 A2
PUDDING BAG LANE 140 B2
STAMFORD ROAD 140 B2
TOP STREET 140 B2
VICARS CLOSE 140 B2
WEST END 140 A2

Fenny Drayton
ATHERSTONE ROAD 131 B1
CHURCH LANE 131 B1
DRAYTON CLOSE 131 A2
DRAYTON LANE 131 B2
FOXS COVERT 131 B2
GEORGE FOX LANE 131 B2
HUNTERS LANE 131 B2
OLD FORGE ROAD 131 B1
QUAKER CLOSE 131 B2
ROOKERY CLOSE 131 B1

Fleckney & Saddington
AINSDALE 93 D4
ALBERT STREET 93 C3
ARNESBY ROAD 93 B4
BAKEHOUSE LANE 93 E7
BARFOOT CLOSE 93 B2
BATCHELOR ROAD 93 C3
BRATMYR 93 C2
BROOKSIDE 93 D3
BYRON CLOSE 93 D4
CHURCH LANE 93 C4
CHURCHILL WAY 93 D4
COBWELLS CLOSE 93 D4
COLEMAN ROAD 93 B3
CONEYGREY 93 B2
CROSSLEYS 93 C4
DRIBDALE 93 D4
EDWARD ROAD 93 C4
ELIZABETH CLOSE 93 C5
ELIZABETH ROAD 93 C4
FLECKNEY ROAD 93 D5
FORGE CLOSE 93 C3
GLADSTONE STREET 93 C4
HASTINGS CLOSE 93 D5
HENSMAN CLOSE 93 D5
HEYCOCK CLOSE 93 D5
HIGH STREET 93 C4
HIGHFIELD STREET 93 C3
HOBROOK ROAD 93 D4
KERTLEY 93 C3
KIBWORTH ROAD (Flec) 93 D4
KIBWORTH ROAD (Sadd) 93 F5
KILBY ROAD 93 A3
LANGDALE 93 C3
LEICESTER ROAD 93 C3
LODGE ROAD 93 C5
LONGGREY 93 B2
LOVELACE WAY 93 D4
MAIN STREET (Flec) 93 C4
MAIN STREET (Sadd) 93 E7
MANOR ROAD 93 D4
MARLBOROUGH DRIVE 93 D5
MARMION CLOSE 93 D5
MOSSWITHY 93 C5
MOWSLEY ROAD 93 E7
ORCHARD STREET 93 C4
PARK STREET 93 C3
PELLS CLOSE 93 C3
PENCLOSE ROAD 93 C3
PRIEST MEADOW 93 C4
ROWLEY CLOSE 93 C5
SADDINGTON ROAD 93 D4
SAWBROOK 93 D4
SCHOOL STREET 93 C4
SHEARSBY ROAD 93 E7
SHORT CLOSE 93 D4
SHOULBARD 93 B3
STENOR CLOSE 93 B3
STORES LANE 93 C4
THE MEER 93 D5
THE WRANGLANDS 93 D4
VICTORIA STREET 93 C4
WEIR ROAD 93 E7
WENTWORTH ROAD 93 D4
WESTERN AVENUE 93 D4
WOLSEY CLOSE 93 C3
WOLSEY LANE 93 C4

Foxton
FOXTON ROAD 140 A4
GALLOW FIELD ROAD 140 B4
GUMLEY ROAD 140 A4
LANGTON ROAD 140 C2
MAIN STREET 140 B2
MIDDLE STREET 140 B2
NORTH LANE 140 B2
PARK CLOSE 140 B2
STUART CRESCENT 140 C3
SWEDISH CLOSE 140 B2
SWINGBRIDGE STREET 140 B2
VICARAGE DRIVE 140 B2

Frisby on the Wreake
ASH WAY 131 B2
CHURCH LANE 131 B2
GADDESBY LANE 131 C3
GREAT LANE 131 B2
HALL ORCHARD LANE 131 B2
HOBY ROAD 131 A2
HOLLOW LANE 131 B2
LEICESTER ROAD 131 C2
MAIN STREET 131 B2
MILL LANE 131 B2
OAK WAY 131 B2
ROTHERBY LANE 131 A2
WASHSTONES LANE 131 A2
WATER LANE 131 A2
WELL FIELD LANE 131 B2

Gaddesby
ASHBY ROAD 132 C3
BARROW CRESCENT 132 B1
CHAPEL LANE 132 B2
CHURCH LANE 132 B2
CROSS STREET 132 B2
MAIN STREET 132 B2
NETHER END 132 C3
PARK HILL 132 B1
PASKE AVENUE 132 C1
PASTURE LANE 132 C1
REARSBY LANE 132 B2
ROTHERBY ROAD 132 B1

Gilmorton
ASHBY ROAD 141 B2
BURDETT CLOSE 141 B2
CHURCH DRIVE 141 B3
CHURCH LANE 141 B2
GAWNEY LANE 141 C2
GILMORTON ROAD 141 A1
HOME FARM CLOSE 141 B2
LUTTERWORTH ROAD 141 B4
LYNMOUTH DRIVE 141 B3
LYNTON CLOSE 141 B3
MACKANESS CLOSE 141 B3
MAIN STREET 141 B2
MILL LANE 141 C2
ORCHARD CLOSE 141 B3
PORLOCK DRIVE 141 B3
SPINNEY CLOSE 141 B3
TEALBY CLOSE 141 B3
TURVILLE ROAD 141 B2
ULLESTHORPE ROAD 141 A3

Great Bowden
See Market Harborough

Great Easton
BANBURY LANE 141 B3
BARNSDALE CLOSE 141 B3
BROADGATE 141 B2
BROOK LANE 141 B3
CHURCH BANK 141 B2
CLARKES DALE 141 B3
CROSS BANK 141 B3
DEEPDALE 141 B2
DRAYTON ROAD 141 A3
GREAT EASTON ROAD 141 B3
HIGH STREET 141 B2
LOUNTS CRESCENT 141 B2
MIDDLETON ROAD 141 A4
MOULDS LANE 141 B2
MUSK CLOSE 141 B2
PITCHERS LANE 141 B2
ST ANDREWS CLOSE 141 B2
STATION ROAD 141 C3
STOCKERSTON LANE 141 A1

Great Glen & Burton Ovary
ASHBY RISE 130 C2
BACK LANE 130 F2
BAILEYS LANE 130 F2
BARNFIELD CLOSE 130 B2
BEADSWELL LANE 130 F2
BEECHFIELD CLOSE 130 B2
BELL LANE 130 F3
BINDLEY LANE 130 B2
BRIDGEWATER DRIVE 130 B2
CARLTON LANE 130 F3
CHERRY GROVE 130 C2
CHURCH ROAD 130 B3
COVERSIDE ROAD 130 C2
CROMWELL ROAD 130 B3
EDGEHILL CLOSE 130 B3
ELMS LANE 130 F2
FERNIE DENE 130 C2
FIELDWAY CRESCENT 130 B2
FORDVIEW CLOSE 130 A2
GARFIELD PARK 130 C1
GRANGE CLOSE 130 B2
HALFORD CLOSE 130 B3
HALL GARDENS 130 C3
HERON CLOSE 130 B2
HEWETT CLOSE 130 A3
HIGH STREET 130 A2
HIGHER GREEN 130 B3
HILLTOP AVENUE 130 C2
KINGFISHER CLOSE 130 B2
LONDON ROAD 130 C4
MAIN STREET (GG) 130 B3
MAIN STREET (BO) 130 F2
MAYNS LANE 130 F3
MEADOW HILL 130 A2
MOUNT VIEW 130 C2
NASEBY WAY 130 B3
OAKFIELD CLOSE 130 B2
OAKS ROAD 130 D3
ORCHARD LANE 130 B4
PEMBURY CLOSE 130 C2
RIVERSIDE CLOSE 130 B1
RUPERT WAY 130 B3
ST CUTHBERTS AVENUE 130 B2
ST THOMAS'S ROAD 130 C2
SCOTLAND LANE 130 F2
SENCE CRESCENT 130 A3
SPINNEY VIEW 130 C2
STACKLEY ROAD 130 B2
STONEHILL DRIVE 130 C2
STRETTON ROAD 130 B1
THE CHASE 130 C2
THE GLEBELANDS 130 A3
THE GRAVEL 130 F3
THE MERE 130 A2
THE NOOK 130 B3
TOWN STREET 130 F3
WASHBROOK LANE 130 F2
WOODBURY RISE 130 C2
WYCH ELM CLOSE 130 C2

Greetham
BRIDGE LANE 132 C1
BULLFIELD CLOSE 132 B1
CHURCH LANE 132 B1
GREAT LANE 132 B1
GREETHAM ROAD 132 A2
KIRKS CLOSE 132 B2
LITTLE LANE 132 B1
MAIN STREET 132 B2
OAKHAM ROAD 132 A2
POND LANE 132 B1
SHEPHERDS LANE 132 B1
STRETTON ROAD 132 C1
WHEATSHEAF LANE 132 C2

Hallaton
ALLEXTON ROAD 133 C1
CHURCHGATE 133 B2
EAST NORTON ROAD 133 C1
EASTGATE 133 B3
GOADBY ROAD 133 B2
HARE PIE VIEW 133 C3
HIGH STREET 133 B2
HOG LANE 133 B2
HORN LANE 133 B2
HORNINGHOLD ROAD 133 C2
HUNTS LANE 133 B2
LANGTON ROAD 133 A3
MEDBOURNE ROAD 133 C3
NORTH END 133 B2
TUGWELL LANE 133 B2

Harby
BOYERS ORCHARD 133 B2
BURDEN LANE 133 B2
BURTON CLOSE 133 A2
COLSTON LANE 133 A2
DICKMANS LANE 133 B3
GAS WALK 133 B2
GREEN LANE 133 B3
HOSE LANE 133 B3
LANGAR LANE 133 A1
MAIN STREET 133 A2
NETHER STREET 133 A2
PINFOLD LANE 133 B2
PINFOLD PLACE 133 C2
SCHOOL LANE 133 A2
STATHERN ROAD 133 B3
WALNUT PADDOCK 133 B2
WALTHAM LANE 133 B3
WATSONS LANE 133 B3

Hathern
See Loughborough

Heather
BELCHER CLOSE 135 B2
BLACKETT DRIVE 135 B2
COTSMORE CLOSE 135 C2
HOLYOAKE CRESCENT 135 C2
HOLYOAKE DRIVE 135 C2
MAIN STREET 135 C2
MANOR ROAD 135 B2
MILL LANE 135 C2
NEWTON ROAD 135 C2
NORMANTON LANE 135 C1
PISCA LANE 135 B2
ST JOHNS CLOSE 135 C2
STATION TERRACE 135 C2
SWEPSTONE ROAD 135 C2
THE ROOKERY 135 B2

Hinckley
ABBOTTS GREEN 96 D1
ALAN BRAY CLOSE 94 B5
ALBERT ROAD 95 B4
ALDIN WAY 94 F2
ALDRIDGE ROAD 95 B7
ALESWORTH DRIVE 96 D2
ALEXANDER GARDENS 95 A3
ALFRETON CLOSE 96 D1
ALMA ROAD 95 B4
APPLEBEE ROAD 95 A7
ARGENTSMEAD 95 B5
ARMADALE CLOSE 94 E4
ARMOUR CLOSE 96 C1
ARRAN WAY 94 F4
ASHBURTON CLOSE 95 E6
ASHFORD ROAD 94 F6
ASTER CLOSE 95 C7

ASTER WAY 95 B1
ASTON LANE 95 E7
ATKINS WAY 95 D6
AULTON CRESCENT 94 F4
AULTON WAY 94 F4
AZALEA CLOSE 96 C1
AZALEA DRIVE 95 C1
BAINES LANE 95 B4
BALFOUR CLOSE 95 C6
BALLIOL ROAD 95 D7
BANKY MEADOW 95 E6
BARDSEY CLOSE 94 F4
BARLESTON DRIVE 94 E4
BARLEYFIELD 95 A2
BARRIE ROAD 95 B2
BARWELL LANE 95 D1
BASIN BRIDGE LANE 94 B2
BATTLEDOWN CLOSE 94 F3
BEARSDON CRESCENT 95 F4
BEATTIE CLOSE 95 B2
BEAUFORT CLOSE 96 C2
BEAUMONT AVENUE 94 F6
BEDALE AVENUE 95 D2
BEDFORD CLOSE 95 C2
BEECHWOOD AVENUE 96 C3
BENBOW CLOSE 95 B2
BERYL AVENUE 94 E3
BLAKE CLOSE 95 B1
BLENHEIM CLOSE 95 D1
BODMIN CLOSE 95 C1
BOSWORTH CLOSE 94 E5
BOWLING GREEN ROAD 95 C4
BOWMAN GREEN 95 D7
BOYSLADE ROAD 96 D1
BRADGATE ROAD 95 D3
BRAMCOTE CLOSE 95 D2
BRAME ROAD 95 A3
BRASCOTE ROAD 94 D5
BRECHIN CLOSE 94 E5
BRENFIELD DRIVE 94 F5
BRIAR CLOSE 95 D7
BRIARMEAD 96 C2
BRICK KILN STREET 95 A5
BRIDGE ROAD 95 B6
BRINDLEY ROAD 94 C5
BRITANNIA ROAD 96 E1
BROADSWORD WAY 96 B2
BROCKHURST AVENUE 96 C2
BRODICK CLOSE 94 D5
BRODICK ROAD 94 D5
BROOKDALE 94 F5
BROOKFIELD ROAD 95 A6
BROOKSIDE 95 D6
BROSDALE DRIVE 94 E4
BROWNING DRIVE 95 A5
BRUNEL ROAD 95 B5
BUCKINGHAM CLOSE 95 D1
BULLFURLONG LANE 96 D1
BURBAGE COMMON ROAD 95 F2
BURBAGE ROAD 95 D5
BURLEIGH ROAD 95 A3
BURNS WAY 95 A4
BUTE CLOSE 95 A4
BUTT LANE CLOSE 95 D4
CALDON CLOSE 94 F5
CAMBOURNE ROAD 95 E7
CAMPTON CLOSE 95 D6
CANNING STREET 95 A4
CARPENTERS CLOSE 96 D1
CASTLE COURT 95 B6
CASTLE STREET 95 B5
CASTLEMAINE DRIVE 95 C2
CHARLES STREET 95 B4
CHARNWOOD CLOSE 95 C4
CHARNWOOD ROAD 95 B4
CHATSWORTH CLOSE 95 D7
CHESSHER STREET 95 B4
CHURCH CLOSE 96 E1
CHURCH WALK 95 B5
CHURCH STREET 95 E1
CLARENCE ROAD 95 C5
CLARENDON ROAD 95 A6
CLEVELAND ROAD 95 A5
CLIFTON WAY 94 F4
CLIVESWAY 95 A4
CLOVERFIELD 95 F2
COLDSTREAM CLOSE 94 E5
COLEY CLOSE 95 B6
COLLEGE LANE 95 C5
COLTS CLOSE 96 B2
COPPICE CLOSE 95 D2
CORAL CLOSE 96 D1
CORNFIELD 95 A1
CORNWALL WAY 95 C1
COTES ROAD 96 D1
COTMAN DRIVE 94 F2
COUNCIL ROAD 95 B5
COVENTRY ROAD 95 F5
COVENTRY ROAD 96 E1
COWPER ROAD 95 B7
CRAMMOND CLOSE 94 F5
CROMARTY DRIVE 94 D4
CROSSWAYS 96 D1
CROWNHILL ROAD 96 C2
CUMBRAE DRIVE 94 F4
DAHLIA CLOSE 95 C7
DALE END CLOSE 94 D6
DAMSON COURT 94 F6
DARES WALK 95 B4
DARLEY ROAD 95 C7
DART CLOSE 94 E5
DARWIN CLOSE 95 C2
DAVENPORT TERRACE 95 C5
DE LA BERE CRESCENT 95 F1
DE MONTFORT ROAD 95 D4
DEAN COURT 95 C3
DEAN ROAD 95 C3
DERBY ROAD 95 B4
DEVERON WAY 94 F4
DODWELLS ROAD 94 C5
DORCHESTER ROAD 95 F6
DRAKE WAY 95 B1
DRUID STREET 95 B4
DUNBLANE WAY 94 E4
DUPORT ROAD 95 D6
EAST CLOSE 95 B6
EASTWOODS ROAD 95 D3
EDENDALE DRIVE 95 C2
EDWARD STREET 95 A2
ELIZABETH ROAD 95 B2
ELM TREE DRIVE 95 D5
EMBLETON CLOSE 94 F5
ERSKINE CLOSE 94 E4
ESKDALE ROAD 94 E5
FACTORY ROAD 95 B4
FALCONERS GREEN 95 D7
FALMOUTH DRIVE 95 C1
FAR LASH 95 D6
FARADAY ROAD 95 C6
FARM ROAD 95 C7
FARNEWAY 94 F4
FEATHERSTON ROAD 95 B6
FERNESS CLOSE 94 F3
FERNESS ROAD 94 F3
FIELD CLOSE 95 D2
FLAMVILLE ROAD 96 F1
FLEMING ROAD 94 C6
FLETCHER ROAD 95 C6
FOREST ROAD 95 D5
FORRESTERS CLOSE 95 D7
FORRESTERS ROAD 95 E6
FORRYAN ROAD 95 D6
FREDERICK AVENUE 94 F3
FREEMANS LANE 96 E1
FRIARY CLOSE 95 C4
FRITH WAY 94 E2
FROBISHER CLOSE 95 B1
GAINSBOROUGH AVENUE 94 E2
GARDEN ROAD 95 B4
GEORGE STREET 95 B5
GLADSTONE CLOSE 95 C2
GLADSTONE TERRACE 95 C5
GLEBE ROAD 95 D5
GLEN BANK 95 C4
GLENBARR CLOSE 94 E5
GLENBARR DRIVE 94 E5
GOOSEHILLS ROAD 96 C1
GOPSALL ROAD 95 B4
GOSFORD DRIVE 94 E4
GOWRIE CLOSE 94 F3
GRANBY CLOSE 95 A6
GRANBY ROAD 95 A6
GRANGE DRIVE 96 C1
GRANVILLE GARDENS 95 A5
GRANVILLE ROAD 95 A5
GREENMOOR ROAD 95 B1
GROSVENOR CRESCENT 95 D7
GROVE PARK 95 E7
GROVE ROAD 95 E1
GWENDOLINE AVENUE 94 E2
HALBERD CLOSE 96 B1
HALL ROAD 95 B1
HAMILTON CLOSE 94 E3
HANGMANS LANE 95 C2
HANSOM ROAD 95 D3
HARDY CLOSE 95 B1
HARROWBROOK ROAD 94 C6
HARWOOD DRIVE 95 D1
HAWKINS CLOSE 95 B1
HAWLEY ROAD 95 A6
HAWTHORN CRESCENT 96 C1
HAYS LANE 94 F6
HENRY STREET 94 E2
HERALD WAY 96 C2
HERFORD WAY 95 D6
HIGHAM WAY 95 C6
HIGHFIELDS ROAD 95 C4
HILL STREET 95 B5
HILL RISE 95 D6
HILLSIDE ROAD 95 A7
HINCKLEY LANE 94 C2
HINCKLEY ROAD 95 E6
HOGARTH CLOSE 94 E2
HOGARTH DRIVE 94 E2
HOLLIERS WALK 95 B4
HOLLY CLOSE 96 C1
HOLLYCROFT 95 B4
HOLLYCROFT CRESCENT 95 A4
HOLT ROAD 95 B6
HORSEPOOL 96 E1
HURST ROAD 96 B6
HYACINTH WAY 96 C1
ILMINSTER CLOSE 95 F6
IRIS CLOSE 96 C1
ISLAND CLOSE 95 D3
JACKNELL ROAD 94 B5
JARVIS CLOSE 95 B1
JEFFERIES CLOSE 95 B3
JELLICOE WAY 95 B2
JOHN NICHOLS STREET 94 F6
JOHN STREET 95 B4
JOHNS CLOSE 96 B1
KENMORE DRIVE 94 F3
KENT DRIVE 95 D1
KESTREL CLOSE 95 D7
KILBY GREEN 95 D7
KILMARE CLOSE 94 D4
KING GEORGES WAY 94 F6
KING RICHARD ROAD 95 A3
KING STREET 95 B4
KINGSTON DRIVE 95 C1
KINROSS WAY 94 D4
KINTYRE CLOSE 94 F4
KIRFIELD DRIVE 95 D2
KNAPTON DRIVE 94 E2
KNIGHTS CLOSE 96 B2
LAMFORD CLOSE 94 F4
LANCASTER ROAD 95 B5
LANCE CLOSE 96 B1
LANDSEER DRIVE 94 F2
LANESIDE DRIVE 95 D2
LANGDALE ROAD 94 D5
LAWNSWOOD 94 E5
LAWTON CLOSE 94 D5
LEICESTER ROAD 95 F2
LEVEN CLOSE 94 F5
LIBRARY CLOSE 96 E1
LINDEN ROAD 95 A4
LINWOOD CLOSE 94 F4
LISMORE DRIVE 95 F4
LOBELIA CLOSE 96 C1
LOCHMORE CLOSE 94 E5
LOCHMORE DRIVE 94 E5
LOCHMORE WAY 94 E5
LODGE CLOSE 96 E1
LOMOND CLOSE 94 F5
LONDON ROAD 95 C5
LOVE LANE 95 E7
LOVETTS CLOSE 94 D5
LUCAS ROAD 95 C7
LUNDY CLOSE 94 F4
LUPIN CLOSE 95 B1
LUTTERWORTH ROAD 96 F1
LYCHGATE CLOSE 96 E1
LYCHGATE LANE 96 F1
LYNDHURST CLOSE 95 F6
LYNEHAM CLOSE 94 E4
MAGEE CLOSE 95 A2
MAIZEFIELD 95 A2
MANOR CLOSE 96 B1
MANOR PLACE 95 B4
MANOR STREET 95 A4
MANOR WAY 96 B1
MANSION STREET 95 A5
MAPLE CLOSE 96 D1
MARCHANT ROAD 95 A5
MARIGOLD DRIVE 96 C1
MARLBOROUGH CLOSE 95 F6
MASON COURT 94 F5
MEADOW DRIVE 95 F6
MELROSE CLOSE 94 F5
MEREVALE AVENUE 95 A6
MEREVALE CLOSE 95 A6
MERRIFIELD GARDENS 96 C1
MIDDLEFIELD CLOSE 95 B3
MIDDLEFIELD COURT 95 B3
MIDDLEFIELD LANE 95 B2
MIDDLEFIELD PLACE 95 B2
MILL HILL ROAD 95 A5
MILL VIEW 95 C4
MILLERS GREEN 95 D7
MILTON CLOSE 95 A5
MORAY CLOSE 94 E5
MORLAND DRIVE 94 F2
MOUNT ROAD 95 B5
NELSON DRIVE 95 B1
NETHERLEY ROAD 95 B2
NEW BUILDINGS 95 B5
NEW ROAD 95 E7
NEW STREET 95 B4
NEWQUAY CLOSE 95 C1
NEWSTEAD AVENUE 96 C2
NEWTON ROAD 94 C6
NORFOLK CLOSE 96 C2
NORTH CLOSE 95 C7
NORTHERN PERIMETER ROAD 94 F2
NORTHFIELD ROAD 95 A6
NORWOOD CLOSE 95 C2
NUFFIELD ROAD 94 C6
OAK CLOSE 96 C1
OBAN ROAD 94 E6
ODSTONE DRIVE 94 D5
ORCHARD CLOSE 96 E1
ORCHARD STREET 95 B5
ORKNEY CLOSE 95 F4
OSBASTON CLOSE 95 D2
OUTLANDS DRIVE 94 E3
PALMER ROAD 94 F3
PARK ROAD 95 D5
PARSONS LANE 95 D5
PENNANT ROAD 96 B1
PENTLAND CLOSE 94 F4
PENZANCE CLOSE 95 C1
PIKE CLOSE 96 B1
PORTLAND DRIVE 95 D1
PRESTON ROAD 94 F3
PRIESTHILLS ROAD 95 B5
PRIMROSE DRIVE 95 C1
PRINCESS ROAD 95 C5
PRIORY WALK 95 C5
PYEHARPS ROAD 96 C1
QUEENS ROAD 95 C5
RADMORE ROAD 95 B2
RALEIGH CLOSE 95 B1
RAMSEY CLOSE 94 F4
RANNOCH CLOSE 94 F5
RATCLIFFE ROAD 95 D7
REEVES ROAD 95 D7
REGENT STREET 95 B5
RIBBLESDALE AVENUE 95 D2
RICHMOND ROAD 95 A2
RIDDON DRIVE 94 F5
ROBINSON WAY 96 D1
RODNEY CLOSE 95 B1
ROMNEY CLOSE 94 E2
ROSEMARY WAY 94 F6
ROSEWOOD CLOSE 95 D7
ROSTON DRIVE 94 F4
ROYAL COURT 95 B6
RUFFORD CLOSE 96 B3
RUGBY ROAD 95 A6
RUTLAND AVENUE 95 A6
RYDAL CLOSE 94 D6
ST CATHERINES 95 D6
ST GEORGES AVENUE 95 A5
ST JAMES CLOSE 96 B1
ST MARTINS 95 C7
ST MARYS ROAD 95 B5
SALEM ROAD 96 E1
SALISBURY ROAD 95 F6
SAPCOTE ROAD 95 F6
SAVILLE CLOSE 95 C2
SCHOOL CLOSE 95 E7
SEAFORTH DRIVE 94 F4
SEATON CLOSE 95 F6
SEVERN AVENUE 94 F5
SHAKESPEARE DRIVE 95 A4
SHARPLESS ROAD 95 D6
SHELLEY GARDENS 95 C2
SHERBORNE ROAD 95 F6
SISLEY WAY 94 F2
SKETCHLEY LANE 96 D1
SKETCHLEY MANOR LANE 96 B1
SKETCHLEY MEADOWS 96 A1
SKETCHLEY OLD VILLAGE 96 A1
SOAR WAY 94 E5
SOUTHFIELD ROAD 95 B6
SPA CLOSE 95 C4
SPA LANE 95 C4
SPENCER STREET 95 B4
SPINNEY ROAD 95 A1
SPRINGFIELD ROAD 95 B6
STANLEY ROAD 95 A4
STATION ROAD 95 B6
STEPHENSON ROAD 94 C6
STIRLING AVENUE 94 E4
STOCKWELL HEAD 95 B4
STOKE LANE 94 D1
STOKE ROAD 94 F2
STONEYGATE DRIVE 94 D2
STRATHMORE ROAD 94 F6
STRETTON CLOSE 95 A7
STRUTT ROAD 96 E1
SUNNYDALE CRESCENT 94 E6
SUNNYDALE ROAD 94 D6
SUNNYHILL SOUTH 95 D6
SUNNYSIDE 95 B2
SURREY CLOSE 96 C2
SUTTON CLOSE 95 D2
SWAINS GREEN 95 D7
SWINBURNE ROAD 95 F4
SYCAMORE CLOSE 96 C1
TAME WAY 94 E5
TEIGN BANK CLOSE 95 B3
TEIGN BANK ROAD 95 A2
TENNYSON ROAD 95 F4
THE BOROUGH 95 B5
THE COPPICE 95 D5
THE FAIRWAY 95 D6
THE GROVE 95 A5
THE HORSEFAIR 95 B5
THE LAWNS 95 C5
THE MEADOWS 95 E6
THE MEADWAY 95 D6
THE NARROWS 95 B5
THE RIDGEWAY 95 C7
THE RILLS 95 C3
THIRLMERE ROAD 94 E5
THORNFIELD WAY 95 C5
THORNYCROFT ROAD 95 C5
THREE POTS ROAD 96 C2
TILTON ROAD 95 C7
TORRIDON WAY 94 F4
TRAFFORD ROAD 95 D4
TRENT ROAD 94 F5
TREVOR ROAD 95 D4
TRINITY LANE 95 A4
TRINITY VICARAGE ROAD 95 A5
TRURO CLOSE 95 C1
TUDOR ROAD 95 A2
TURNER DRIVE 94 E2
TWEEDSIDE CLOSE 95 D1
TWYCROSS ROAD 95 D1
UPPER BOND STREET 95 B4
VENTURE COURT 94 C5
VICTORIA ROAD 96 D1
VICTORIA STREET 95 B4
VILIA CLOSE 96 D2
WALCOTE CLOSE 94 D5
WALNEY CLOSE 94 F4
WARWICK GARDENS 95 C2
WATERLOO ROAD 95 B5
WATLING CLOSE 96 A2
WATLING DRIVE 96 A1

WATLING STREET 94 B6
WAVENEY CLOSE 94 F5
WELBECK AVENUE 96 B2
WELL LANE 95 B4
WELWYN ROAD 95 D4
WENDOVER DRIVE 95 C2
WENSUM CLOSE 94 F5
WENTWORTH CLOSE 95 C2
WEST CLOSE 95 B6
WESTFIELD ROAD 95 A6
WESTMINSTER DRIVE 96 D2
WESTON CLOSE 94 F4
WESTRAY DRIVE 95 F4
WHEATFIELD WAY 95 A2
WHITTLE ROAD 94 C6
WILLIAM ILIFFE STREET 94 F6
WILLOW CLOSE 96 D1
WILLOWBANK ROAD 95 A6
WINCHESTER DRIVE 95 F6
WINDRUSH DRIVE 94 F5
WINDSOR COURT 96 E1
WINDSOR STREET 96 E1
WOBURN CLOSE 95 C2
WOLVEY ROAD 96 C2
WOOD STREET 95 B4
WOOD STREET CLOSE 95 C4
WOODBANK 95 E6
WOODFIELD ROAD 95 A1
WOODGATE ROAD 95 D5
WOODLAND AVENUE 95 E6
WOODLAND ROAD 95 D4
WORKHOUSE LANE 96 F2
WYE CLOSE 94 E5
WYKIN HOUSE FARM 94 C2
WYKIN ROAD 94 D2
YORK ROAD 95 A2
ZEALAND CLOSE 95 D2

Hose
BOLTON LANE 134 B2
CANAL LANE 134 B1
CHURCH CLOSE 134 B2
DAIRY LANE 134 B2
HARBY LANE 134 B1
HOSE LANE 134 B2
MEADOWS LANE 134 A1
MIDDLE STREET 134 B2
PASTURE LANE 134 C3
THE GREEN 134 B2

Houghton on the Hill
CHAPEL CLOSE 142 B2
DEANE GATE DRIVE 142 B2
ELIZABETH CLOSE 142 B2
FIELD CLOSE 142 C2
FIRS CLOSE 142 C2
FIRS ROAD 142 C2
FORSELLS END 142 B2
FREER CLOSE 142 B3
HOME CLOSE ROAD 142 C2
INGARSBY CLOSE 142 C2
INGARSBY LANE 142 C2
LINWAL AVENUE 142 B2
MAIN STREET 142 C2
NORTH WAY 142 B2
ST CATHARINES WAY 142 B2
SCHOOL LANE 142 B3
SCOTLAND LANE 142 B2
STRETTON LANE 142 A4
THE RISE 142 B2
THOMAS CLOSE 142 B2
UPPINGHAM ROAD 142 C2
WEIR LANE 142 C2
WINCKLEY CLOSE 142 B2

Huncote
BENNETT RISE 130 C2
BROOK STREET 130 B3
CAREY ROAD 130 B3
CHANTRY CLOSE 130 B3
CHENEY END 130 B3
COMPTON DRIVE 130 B2
COOPER CLOSE 130 C2
CRITCHLOW ROAD 130 B2
CROFT HILL ROAD 130 A3
DENMAN LANE 130 B2
DUNCAN AVENUE 130 B3
EUNICE AVENUE 130 B2
FRITCHLEY CLOSE 130 C3
HOBILL CLOSE 130 C2
LANGLEY CLOSE 130 C2
LODGE CLOSE 130 B2
MAIN STREET 130 B3
MILL VIEW 130 A3
NARBOROUGH ROAD 130 B3
RATCLIFFE DRIVE 130 B3
ROBOTHAM CLOSE 130 C3
ST JAMES CLOSE 130 B3
SCHOOL LANE 130 B3
SPORTS FIELD LANE 130 B2
THE GREEN 130 B3

Hungarton
BAGGRAVE ROAD 134 C1
BARLEY LEAS 134 C2
CHURCH LANE 134 C2
COAL BAULK 134 B2
MAIN STREET 134 C1

Husbands Bosworth
BELL LANE 142 B2
BERRIDGES LANE 142 B2
BUTT LANE 142 B3
CHURCH LANE 142 B3
CHURCH STREET 142 B3
GREEN LANE 142 B3
HIGH STREET 142 C3
HIGHCROFT 142 B2
HILLCREST LANE 142 B3
HONEYPOT LANE 142 C3
HUNTERS CLOSE 142 B2
KILWORTH ROAD 142 B3
LAMMAS CLOSE 142 B3
LEICESTER ROAD 142 A1
MOWSLEY ROAD 142 B2
SCHOOL LANE 142 B3
THEDDINGWORTH ROAD 142 C2
WELFORD ROAD 142 B3
WELLS CLOSE 142 B3

Ibstock
ALBERT STREET 131 C1
ARGYLE STREET 131 C2
ASHBY ROAD 131 C2
ASHDALE 131 B3
BEECH WAY 131 B2
BERNARD CLOSE 131 C3
BROOKSIDE CRESCENT 131 D2
CEDAR DRIVE 131 B2
CENTRAL AVENUE 131 C2
CHAPEL STREET 131 C2
CHESTNUT CLOSE 131 B3
CHRISTOPHER CLOSE 131 D1
CHURCH VIEW 131 B4
COPSON STREET 131 D3
COSTELLO CLOSE 131 C1
CURZON STREET 131 D3
DEEPDALE CLOSE 131 C2
DOUGLAS DRIVE 131 D3
EAST WALK 131 C3
ELIZABETH AVENUE 131 C2
ELM CLOSE 131 B2
FAIRFIELD 131 C3
FERNDALE 131 B3
GAMBLE CLOSE 131 C1
GLADSTONE STREET 131 C3
GLEN AVENUE 131 D4
GRANGE ROAD 131 C3
HALL STREET 131 B4
HAREATTS CLOSE 131 C3
HAWTHORNE DRIVE 131 B4
HEATHERDALE 131 B3
HIGH STREET 131 C3
HINCKLEY ROAD 131 B4
JACQUES ROAD 131 C1
LAUD CLOSE 131 B3
LEGION DRIVE 131 C4
LEICESTER ROAD 131 F1
LINDEN CLOSE 131 B2
MAPLE DRIVE 131 C2
MEADOW WALK 131 D2
MELBOURNE ROAD 131 C1
OAK DRIVE 131 B3
ORCHARD STREET 131 D3
OVERTON ROAD 131 C4
PAGGETT ROAD 131 C1
PARKDALE 131 B2
PENISTONE STREET 131 C2
PRETORIA ROAD 131 F3
RAVENSTONE ROAD 131 C1
REDLANDS ESTATE 131 D1
ROWAN DRIVE 131 B3
ST DENYS CRESCENT 131 B3
SLAYBARNS WAY 131 C2
SPRING ROAD 131 D2
SPRINGFIELD CLOSE 131 C2
STATION ROAD 131 B3
SUNNYSIDE 131 B4
SWIFTS CLOSE 131 C2
SYCAMORE CLOSE 131 B2
THE HASTINGS 131 C2
THORNDALE 131 B3
THORNHAM GROVE 131 C2
VALLEY ROAD 131 C3
VICTORIA ROAD 131 D1
WEST WALK 131 C3
WILLOW WAY 131 B3
WINCHESTER COURT 131 C1

Illston
ASHLANDS ROAD 136 C1
GAULBY ROAD 136 B1
ILLSTON LANE 136 C2
MAIN STREET 136 B2
NEW ROAD 136 A1

Kegworth
ASHBY ROAD 132 C3
BEDFORD CLOSE 132 E4
BOROUGH STREET 132 E3
BORROWELL 132 E2
BRIDGE FIELDS 132 F3
BROADHILL ROAD 132 D3
BULSTODE PLACE 132 D3
BURLEY RISE 132 E3
CHURCH LANE 132 A1
CHURCH STREET 132 B1
CITRUS GROVE 132 D2
DERBY ROAD 132 E3
DRAGWELL 132 E3
FOXHILLS 132 D4
FREDERICK AVENUE 132 D3
GERRARD CRESCENT 132 E4
HEAFIELD DRIVE 132 E3
HIGH STREET 132 E3
HILLSIDE 132 E4
KIRBY DRIVE 132 D4
KIRK AVENUE 132 E3
LANGLEY DRIVE 132 D3
LONDON ROAD 132 E3
LONG LANE 132 E1
MAIN STREET 132 A1
MILL LANE 132 E2
MOORE AVENUE 132 E2
NEW BRICKYARD LANE 132 E4
NEW STREET 132 E2
NINE ACRES 132 D3
NORMAN COURT 132 E3
NOTTINGHAM ROAD 132 E2
OLDERSHAW AVENUE 132 D3
OSIERS 132 F3
PACKINGTON HILL 132 D3
PEPPERS DRIVE 132 C3
PLEASANT PLACE 132 E3
PLUMMER LANE 132 D3
QUEENS ROAD 132 E2
ROBERTS CLOSE 132 E4
ROPEWALK 132 D3
ST ANDREWS RISE 132 D3
SHEPHERD WALK 132 D4
SIBSON DRIVE 132 C3
SIDE LEY 132 E2
SPRINGFIELD 132 D3
STAFFORDS ACRE 132 D3
STATION ROAD 132 E2
STONEHILLS 132 D3
SUTHERS ROAD 132 D3
SUTTON ROAD 132 D4
THE CROFT 132 E3
THOMAS ROAD 132 D4
WALTON CLOSE 132 E3
WEST BANK MEWS 132 D3
WHATTON ROAD 132 E3
WINDMILL WAY 132 C3
WYVELLE CRESCENT 132 D2

Ketton
AVELAND ROAD 133 C3
BARROWDEN ROAD 133 D4
BARTLES HOLLOW 133 C3
BRAITHEWAITE CLOSE 133 C3
BULL LANE 133 D3
BURNHAMS ROAD 133 C3
CAPENDALE CLOSE 133 C2
CHAPEL LANE 133 D3
CHURCH ROAD 133 D3
EDMUNDS DRIVE 133 D3
EMPINGHAM ROAD 133 A1
GRENEHAMS CLOSE 133 C3
HIGH STREET 133 C3
HUNTS LANE 133 C2
KELTHORPE CLOSE 133 D4
KETCO AVENUE 133 E1
KETTON ROAD 133 E4
LUFFENHAM ROAD 133 C4
MANOR GREEN 133 C2
NORTHWICK ROAD 133 C3
PARK ROAD 133 C4
PIT LANE 133 C1
REDMILES LANE 133 D3
SAND FURROWS 133 C3
SHARPES PLAIN 133 C2
SPENCERS ROAD 133 C3
SPINNEY ROAD 133 C3
STAMFORD ROAD 133 E1
STATION ROAD 133 D3
SULTHORPE ROAD 133 C3
THE GREEN 133 D3
TIMBERGATE ROAD 133 C3
WHEATLANDS CLOSE 133 C2
WINSTON CLOSE 133 C3
WYTCHLEY ROAD 133 B3

Kibworth & Smeeton Westerby
ALBERT STREET 97 C1
BEAKER CLOSE 97 B5
BEAUCHAMP ROAD 97 B3
BEECH TREE CLOSE 97 C1
BIRDIE CLOSE 97 D3
BLACKSMITHS LANE 97 B5
BRAYMISH CLOSE 97 D3
BROOKFIELD WAY 97 D3
BULLER STREET 97 B3
CEDAR CLOSE 97 B3
CHURCH CLOSE 97 C2
CHURCH ROAD 97 C2
DEBDALE LANE 97 B5
DISRAELI CLOSE 97 B3
DOVER STREET 97 B3
FAIRWAY 97 D3
FLECKNEY ROAD 97 A3
GAINSBOROUGH ROAD 97 C2
GLADSTONE STREET 97 B3
GRANARY CLOSE 97 C4
GREENWAY 97 D3
GUMLEY ROAD 97 B6
HALFORD ROAD 97 B3
HALL CLOSE 97 C2
HARBOROUGH ROAD 97 E3
HARCOURT ROAD 97 B3
HIGH STREET 97 B3
HILLCREST AVENUE 97 C2
HOME CLOSE 97 C4
IMPERIAL ROAD 97 B3
KIBWORTH ROAD 97 E2
KIMBERLEY STREET 97 B3
LANGTON ROAD 97 E2
LARKSWOOD 97 D3
LEICESTER ROAD 97 B1
LINKS ROAD 97 D3
LODGE CLOSE 97 B1
MAIN STREET (Kib) 97 C1
MAIN STREET (SW) 97 B5
MARRIOTT DRIVE 97 E3
MARSH AVENUE 97 D2
MARSH DRIVE 97 C2
MEADOWBROOK ROAD 97 B3
MELBOURNE CLOSE 97 B3
MERTON WAY 97 C2
MILESTONE CLOSE 97 E3
MILL CLOSE 97 B4
MILL LANE 97 B4
MORRISON COURT 97 C3
NEW ROAD 97 E3
OAKTREE CLOSE 97 D2
PAGET COURT 97 C3
PEEL CLOSE 97 B3
PIT HILL 97 B5
PLAMERSTONE CLOSE 97 B3
PROSPECT ROAD 97 B3
RECTORY LANE 97 C2
ROCHESTER CLOSE 97 B1
ROOKERY CLOSE 97 D3
ROSEBERY AVENUE 97 B3
SADDINGTON ROAD 97 A5
ST WILFRIDS CLOSE 97 C2
SCHOOL ROAD 97 C3
SCHOOL WALK 97 C3
SMEETON ROAD 97 C4
SOUTH WAY 97 D3
SPRINGFIELD CLOSE 97 D4
SPRINGFIELD CRESCENT 97 C4
SPRINGFIELD LANE 97 B5
STATION HOLLOW 97 C3
STUART STREET 97 C3
THE DRIVE 97 D3
THE LEA 97 C2
THE LEYS 97 C2
THE PADDOCK 97 D4
THE TITHINGS 97 C2
WEIR ROAD 97 C4
WESTERBY LANE 97 B5
WHITE STREET 97 B3
WINDMILL GARDENS 97 C2
WISTOW ROAD 97 A1

Kirby Mallory & Peckleton
ARCHERS LANE 128 D1
BARWELL LANE 128 B2
BOSWORTH ROAD 128 A2
BROOK LANE 128 D1
CHURCH ROAD (KM) 128 B2
CHURCH ROAD (Peck) 128 E1
DESFORD LANE 128 E1
ELMS DRIVE 128 E1
HILL CLOSE 128 E1
KIRKBY LANE 128 D1
MAIN STREET (KM) 128 A2
MAIN STREET (Peck) 128 D1
MANOR LANE 128 D1
PECKLETON COMMON 128 E1
PECKLETON ROAD 128 B2
SHILTON ROAD 128 B2

Kirby Muxloe
See Ratby

Knipton
CHURCH HILL 136 B2
FINNS LANE 136 B2
KNIPTON LANE 136 C1
KNIPTON ROAD 136 B3
NURSERY LANE 136 C2
PASTURE LANE 136 C2
THE OLD HILL 136 C2

Knossington
BRAUNSTON ROAD 152 C3
COLD OVERTON ROAD 152 C1
LARCHWOOD RISE 152 B2
MAIN STREET 152 B2
OAKHAM ROAD 152 C2
OWSTON ROAD 152 B2
SOMERBY ROAD 152 A1
THE CARRIAGEWAY 152 B2
THE HOLLOW 152 C2

Langham
ASHWELL ROAD 122 C2
BRIDGE STREET 122 B2
BURLEY ROAD 122 B2
CHURCH STREET 122 B2
COLD OVERTON ROAD 122 B3
FAIRFIELD CLOSE 122 B2
HAREWOOD CLOSE 122 C2
JUBILEE DRIVE 122 B2
LOWTHER CLOSE 122 B2
MANOR LANE 122 B2
MELTON ROAD 122 B2
OAKHAM ROAD 122 B3
ORCHARD ROAD 122 B2
RANKSBOROUGH DRIVE 122 A2
SHARRADS WAY 122 C2
SQUIRES CLOSE 122 B2

THE RANGE 122 B2
THE ROOKERY 122 B2
WELL STREET 122 B2
WESTONS LANE 122 B2

Leire & Dunton Bassett

ANDREWS CLOSE 135 B1
BACK LANE 135 B2
BENNETTS HILL 135 F1
CHAPEL CLOSE 135 F1
CHURCH CLOSE 135 F2
CHURCH LANE 135 F2
COOPERS LANE 135 F1
DUNTON LANE 135 D3
DUNTON ROAD 135 D3
ELWELLS AVENUE 135 F1
FROLESWORTH ROAD 135 B3
LEIRE LANE 135 E2
LITTLE LANE 135 B3
LITTLE LUNNON 135 E2
LOVES LANE 135 E2
MAIN STREET (Leire) 135 B2
MAIN STREET (DB) 135 F1
OAK AVENUE 135 A3
RALPHS CLOSE 135 F1
ST MARGARETS DRIVE 135 A3
ST PETERS CLOSE 135 B2
STATION LANE 135 A2
THE MOUNT 135 E1
WAKES CLOSE 135 F1
WALES ORCHARD 135 A2
WHITE HOUSE CLOSE 135 A1

Long Clawson

BACK LANE 134 C3
BARKERS FIELD 134 C3
BROUGHTON LANE 134 B4
CANAL LANE 134 D1
CHURCH LANE 134 C3
CLAXTON RISE 134 C3
CORONATION AVENUE 134 B4
EAST END 134 D3
HICKLING LANE 134 B3
HOLLYTREE LANE 134 C3
HOSE LANE 134 E2
KINGS ROAD 134 C3
MELTON ROAD 134 B4
MILL LANE 134 D4
SAND PIT LANE 134 C3
SCHOOL LANE 134 C3
THE SANDS 134 C3
WALTHAM LANE 134 D3
WATER LANE 134 E2
WEST END 134 C3

Loughborough

ABBERTON WAY 108 C3
ACER CLOSE 109 C6
AFTON CLOSE 108 D2
ALAN MOSS ROAD 107 B7
ALAN MOSS ROAD 109 A1
ALBANY STREET 107 B7
ALBERT PLACE 109 D2
ALBERT PROMENADE 109 E2
ALBERT STREET 109 D2
ALFRED STREET 107 D7
ALLSOPPS LANE 107 F6
ALSTON DRIVE 107 A6
ALTHORPE DRIVE 106 E1
ALTHORPE DRIVE 108 E1
AMBLESIDE CLOSE 108 F5
AMIS CLOSE 106 E7
ANCHOR CLOSE 106 C4
ANCHOR LANE 106 C3
ANGEL YARD 109 D1
ANGUS DRIVE 109 A1
ARCHER CLOSE 106 D6
ARMITAGE CLOSE 109 C1
ARTHUR STREET 109 C1
ASH GROVE 106 C3
ASHBY CRESCENT 108 F2
ASHBY ROAD 106 A2
ASHBY ROAD 109 D1
ASHDOWN CLOSE 106 E7
ASHLEIGH DRIVE 109 A3
ASPEN AVENUE 109 C6
ATHERSTONE ROAD 109 B6
AUMBERRY GAP 109 D1
AVON VALE ROAD 109 E4
BADGER COURT 108 F5
BAGLEY CLOSE 106 E6
BAILEY CLOSE 108 F5
BAINBRIDGE ROAD 109 E4
BAKEWELL ROAD 107 B5
BAMPTON STREET 109 D2
BARDEN CLOSE 108 D2
BARRACK ROW 107 E7
BARRETT DRIVE 106 F6
BARROW STREET 109 D2
BARSBY DRIVE 107 A6
BAXTER GATE 109 D1
BEACON AVENUE 109 C4
BEACON DRIVE 109 C4
BEACON ROAD 109 B5
BEACON ROAD 109 C3
BEAUFORT AVENUE 109 C5
BEAUMONT ROAD 109 D4
BEDFORD SQUARE 109 D2
BEDFORD STREET 109 D2
BEE HIVE LANE 109 D2
BEECHES ROAD 109 F2
BELMONT WAY 108 C3
BELTON ROAD 107 D6
BELTON ROAD WEST 107 A5
BELVOIR DRIVE 109 B5
BENSCLIFFE DRIVE 109 A3
BERKELEY ROAD 108 F5
BIGGIN STREET 109 D1
BISHOP MEADOW ROAD 107 B5
BISHOP STREET 107 E7
BLACKBROOK COURT 107 B6
BLACKBROOK ROAD 108 E2
BLACKHAM ROAD 109 C4
BLAKE DRIVE 107 A7
BLENHEIM CLOSE 106 E1
BLITHFIELD AVENUE 108 E2
BLUEBELL DRIVE 109 B4
BOND CLOSE 109 E4
BOTTLEACRE LANE 107 D6
BOWLER COURT 109 E1
BOYER STREET 109 E1
BRADDON ROAD 106 E5
BRADGATE ROAD 109 A5
BRAMCOTE ROAD 109 B6
BRIDGE STREET 107 D1
BRIDGE STREET 109 C1
BRISCO AVENUE 107 B6
BROAD STREET 109 C1
BROADWAY 109 D5
BROOK LANE 108 F5
BROOK LANE 109 A5
BROOKFIELD AVENUE 109 B4
BROOKSIDE ROAD 109 A5
BROOM AVENUE 109 C6
BROUGHTON CLOSE 108 E1
BROWNING ROAD 108 F1
BROWNS LANE 109 C2
BUCKHORN SQUARE 109 E1
BUCKINGHAM DRIVE 106 E7
BURBAGE CLOSE 107 A6
BURDER STREET 107 D6
BURFIELD AVENUE 109 C2
BURLEIGH ROAD 109 C1
BURTON STREET 109 D2
BURTON WALKS 109 D2
BUTTERLEY DRIVE 108 D3
BUTTHOLE LANE 106 A7
BYLAND WAY 106 D7
BYRON STREET 107 A7
CABIN LEAS 107 D6
CALDWELL STREET 109 C1
CAMBRIDGE STREET 107 D7
CANNING WAY 106 E5
CARILLON CLOSE 109 D1
CARRINGTON STREET 107 B7
CARTLAND DRIVE 106 F6
CARTWRIGHT STREET 107 E7
CASTLEDINE STREET 109 D3
CATTLE MARKET 109 D2
CEDAR ROAD 109 E4
CHAINBRIDGE CLOSE 107 C7
CHAPMAN STREET 109 D1
CHARLES STREET 107 D7
CHARLEY DRIVE 109 A3
CHARNWOOD ROAD 109 D3
CHARTERIS CLOSE 106 F6
CHATSWORTH ROAD 106 F7
CHELKER WAY 108 E2
CHERRY CLOSE 109 C6
CHESTER CLOSE 109 B2
CHESTNUT STREET 109 C1
CHICHESTER CLOSE 108 E5
CHISWICK DRIVE 108 E1
CHRISTIE DRIVE 106 F6
CHURCH GATE 109 D1
CHURCH STREET 106 C3
CHURCHLANDS 107 D6
CLAWSON CLOSE 106 F6
CLEEVE MOUNT 108 E1
CLEVELAND ROAD 109 B6
CLIFF AVENUE 107 B6
CLIFFORD ROAD 107 B7
CLOWBRIDGE DRIVE 108 E2
COBDEN STREET 109 E1
COLGROVE ROAD 109 C3
COMPTON CLOSE 108 E5
CONISTON CRESCENT 108 F4
CONWAY CLOSE 106 E7
COOKSON PLACE 106 E6
COOPER COURT 109 F3
CORDELL ROAD 106 F6
COTES YARD 107 E7
COTHELSTONE AVENUE 106 E7
COTSWOLD CLOSE 109 A2
COTTESMORE DRIVE 109 B5
COTTON WAY 107 A5
COWDRAY CLOSE 109 C4
CRADOCK STREET 109 D1
CRAVEN CLOSE 109 B6
CRICKET LANE 108 F5
CROOME CLOSE 109 E4
CROPSTON AVENUE 108 D3
CROSS HILL LANE 109 B5
CROSS STREET 107 E7
CROSSWOOD CLOSE 108 E2
CUMBERLAND ROAD 109 B1
CURZON STREET 109 C1
DE LISLE COURT 108 D2
DE MONTFORT CLOSE 106 E7
DEAD LANE 109 D1
DEANE STREET 107 A7
DEANSIDE DRIVE 107 A6
DEER ACRE 107 D6
DEIGHTON WAY 106 E6
DERBY ROAD 106 B1
DERBY ROAD 107 F5
DERWENT DRIVE 108 F4
DEVONSHIRE LANE 109 D2
DEVONSHIRE SQUARE 109 D2
DOVECOTE STREET 106 C3
DOYLE CLOSE 106 F6
DUKE STREET 107 D1
DULVERTON CLOSE 108 F5
DUNCAN WAY 106 E6
DUNHOLME AVENUE 108 D1
DUNSMORE CLOSE 108 F5
DURHAM ROAD 107 A6
DURRELL CLOSE 106 E6
EASBY CLOSE 106 D7
EDELIN ROAD 109 D4
EDEN CLOSE 106 E6
EDWARD STREET 107 C7
EGGINGTON COURT 109 A3
ELIOT CLOSE 106 D6
ELLABY ROAD 106 F6
ELMS GROVE 109 E2
EMPRESS ROAD 109 F1
EPINAL WAY 107 A7
EPINAL WAY 109 A2
EXMOOR CLOSE 108 F5
EYE BROOK CLOSE 108 D3
FACTORY STREET 109 D2
FAIRMEADOWS WAY 109 B6
FAIRMOUNT DRIVE 109 A3
FALCON STREET 107 E7
FALKNER COURT 109 A3
FARNDALE DRIVE 109 B5
FARNHAM ROAD 109 D4
FEARON STREET 109 B1
FENNEL STREET 109 D1
FESTIVAL DRIVE 107 C6
FINSBURY AVENUE 109 E2
FLEMING CLOSE 106 F6
FOREST COURT 109 C2
FOREST ROAD 109 C2
FORGE CLOSE 106 C3
FORSYTH CLOSE 106 D6
FOX COVERT 107 D6
FOXCOTE DRIVE 108 C3
FRANCIS DRIVE 106 E5
FREDERICK STREET 109 C1
FREEHOLD STREET 109 E1
GALLICO CLOSE 106 F6
GARDNER CLOSE 106 E6
GARENDON AVENUE 106 C4
GARENDON GREEN 109 A1
GARENDON ROAD 109 A1
GARTON ROAD 109 D2
GAVIN DRIVE 106 F6
GEORGE STREET 109 B1
GEORGE YARD 109 D1
GISBOROUGH WAY 106 C7
GLADSTONE AVENUE 107 D7
GLADSTONE STREET 106 C3
GLADSTONE STREET 107 D7
GLEBE STREET 107 E7
GOLDEN SQUARE 106 C3
GOLDING CLOSE 106 E6
GORDON ROAD 107 D6
GRACEDIEU ROAD 108 E2
GRAFTON ROAD 107 A6
GRAHAM RISE 106 F6
GRANBY STREET 109 D2
GRANGE STREET 107 C7
GRANVILLE STREET 109 C1
GRASMERE ROAD 109 B6
GRASSHOLME DRIVE 108 C2
GRAY STREET 109 D2
GREAT CENTRAL ROAD 109 F2
GREEN HILL 106 C3
GREENCLOSE LANE 109 C1
GREGORY STREET 109 D2
GRIGGS ROAD 109 D5
GROVE ROAD 109 A2
GUILDFORD WAY 108 E5
HAILEY AVENUE 106 E7
HAMBLEDON CRESCENT 109 B5
HANFORD WAY 107 E7
HANOVER COURT 106 F7
HARDWICK DRIVE 108 E1
HARLECH CLOSE 107 A7
HASTINGS STREET 109 C1
HATHERN ROAD 106 A2
HAVELOCK STREET 107 B1
HAWTHORNE AVENUE 106 C3
HAYDON ROAD 109 A1
HAYWARD AVENUE 109 E3
HAZEL ROAD 109 C6
HEATHCOTE STREET 109 C1
HERBERT STREET 107 D7
HERMITAGE ROAD 108 E2
HERRICK ROAD 109 D4
HERRIOT WAY 106 F6
HICKLING COURT 109 B1
HIGH MEADOW 106 C3
HIGH STREET 109 D1
HILL TOP ROAD 109 B5
HODSON COURT 109 D3
HOLBEIN CLOSE 109 E1
HOLLYTREE CLOSE 109 C6
HOLMFIELD AVENUE 107 B6
HOLT DRIVE 109 B4
HOLYWELL DRIVE 109 A3
HOLYWELL WAY 108 E4
HOSPITAL WAY 109 A1
HOWARD CLOSE 106 E7
HOWARD STREET 107 D7
HOWDEN CLOSE 108 D2
HOWE ROAD 109 D4
HUDSON STREET 107 E7
HUME STREET 109 D1
HUNTINGTON COURT 107 C1
HURSTWOOD ROAD 108 D2
HUSTON COURT 109 C2
IRWIN AVENUE 106 E6
JAMES AVENUE 106 E6
JAPONICA CLOSE 109 C6
JASMINE CLOSE 109 C6
JETCOTT AVENUE 109 C6
JOHN PHILLIPS CLOSE 109 A1
JOHN PHILLIPS COURT 109 A1
JOHNS LEE CLOSE 109 B4
JUBILEE DRIVE 107 C7
JUDGES STREET 109 F2
JUNIPER WAY 109 C6
KEATS WAY 106 F7
KENILWORTH AVENUE 106 E1
KENSINGTON AVENUE 106 E7
KERNAN DRIVE 107 B5
KESWICK AVENUE 108 F4
KING EDWARD ROAD 109 E2
KING GEORGE AVENUE 109 F2
KING GEORGE ROAD 109 F2
KINGFISHER WAY 109 C3
KINGS AVENUE 107 B6
KINGSWOOD AVENUE 106 C6
KINROSS CRESCENT 106 F7
KIRKSTONE DRIVE 108 E4
KNIGHTTHORPE COURT 108 F1
KNIGHTTHORPE ROAD 106 F7
KNIGHTTHORPE ROAD 107 B7
KNIPTON DRIVE 108 D2
LABURNUM CLOSE 106 C3
LADYBOWER ROAD 108 D2
LAMPORT CLOSE 106 E1
LANESBOROUGH COURT 109 D3
LANESHAW AVENUE 108 D2
LANGDALE AVENUE 108 F4
LANSDOWNE DRIVE 109 D4
LAUREL ROAD 109 C6
LAWRENCE WAY 106 E5
LECKHAMPTON ROAD 106 E1
LECONFIELD ROAD 108 E5
LEDBURY ROAD 109 B6
LEICESTER ROAD 109 D2
LEIGHTON AVENUE 108 D2
LEMONTREE LANE 109 C6
LEMYNGTON STREET 109 D1
LEOPOLD STREET 107 C1
LESLIE CLOSE 106 F5
LEWIS ROAD 107 A7
LILAC CLOSE 109 C6
LILLESHALL WAY 106 D7
LIME AVENUE 109 E2
LIMEHURST AVENUE 107 D1
LINDEN ROAD 107 C7
LINDISFARNE DRIVE 106 C7
LINFORD ROAD 109 A5
LING AVENUE 109 E5
LING ROAD 109 D4
LINGDALE CLOSE 109 D4
LISLE STREET 107 C7
LITTLE MOOR LANE 107 F1
LONGCLIFFE GARDENS 108 C6
LORRIMER WAY 106 E7
LOUGHBOROUGH ROAD 106 C3
LOWER CAMBRIDGE STREET 107 D7
LOWER GLADSTONE STREET 107 D7
LOWER GREEN 108 F5
LOWESWATER DRIVE 108 E4
LOWTHER WAY 109 E4
LUDLOW CLOSE 108 E5
LYALL CLOSE 106 F5
MACLEAN AVENUE 106 E6
MAGNOLIA AVENUE 109 D6
MAIN STREET 106 C1
MANOR DRIVE 109 D5
MANOR ROAD 109 D6
MAPLE ROAD 109 D5
MAPLE ROAD NORTH 109 D5
MAPLE ROAD SOUTH 109 D6
MARDALE WAY 108 F5
MARKET PLACE 109 D1
MARKET STREET 109 D1
MARTINDALE CLOSE 109 A4
MAXWELL DRIVE 106 E7
MAYFIELD DRIVE 109 D3
MAYO CLOSE 109 B6
MEADOW AVENUE 107 D6
MEADOW LANE 107 D5
MELBREAK AVENUE 109 A5
MELVILLE CLOSE 106 D6
MESSENGER CLOSE 107 A5
MIDDLE AVENUE 107 B6
MIDDLETON PLACE 109 D3
MILDENHALL ROAD 108 E1
MILL LANE 107 E7
MILL LANE 109 C1
MILLS YARD 109 D2
MILTON STREET 107 A6
MITCHELL DRIVE 106 E6
MOAT ROAD 109 A5
MODEL FARM CLOSE 109 A5
MOIRA STREET 109 D2

MONARCH WAY 107 C5
MONSARRAT WAY 106 F6
MONTAGUE DRIVE 108 D5
MOOR LANE 109 D1
MORLEY STREET 107 E7
MORRIS CLOSE 109 E1
MORTIMER WAY 106 D6
MOUNT GRACE ROAD 106 D6
MOUNTFIELDS DRIVE 109 A3
MURDOCH RISE 106 F6
NANPANTAN ROAD 108 C6
NARROW LANE 106 C3
NASEBY DRIVE 108 C3
NAVIGATION WAY 107 C7
NAYLOR AVENUE 109 F3
NEW ASHBY ROAD 108 E3
NEW ASHBY ROAD 109 A2
NEW KING STREET 109 E2
NEW STREET 109 D2
NEW WALKS 109 E3
NEWBON CLOSE 109 A2
NEWTON CLOSE 106 F6
NICOLSON ROAD 108 E5
NIGHTINGALE AVENUE 106 C3
NORMANTON LANE 107 C2
NORTH ROAD 107 D6
NOTTINGHAM ROAD 107 E7
NURSERY END 108 F5
NUTKIN CLOSE 109 C3
OAKHAM CLOSE 107 A6
OAKHURST COURT 108 E1
OAKLANDS AVENUE 109 B3
OAKLEY DRIVE 109 B4
OAKWOOD DRIVE 108 D4
OLD ASHBY ROAD 108 E2
OLD WAY 106 C3
OLIVER ROAD 109 D3
ORWELL CLOSE 106 F6
OSBORNE ROAD 106 E6
OSTERLEY CLOSE 108 E1
OUTWOODS AVENUE 109 B4
OUTWOODS DRIVE 109 B4
OUTWOODS ROAD 109 B5
OXBURGH CLOSE 106 E7
OXFORD STREET 107 C1
OXLEY GUTTER 106 C7
PACK HORSE LANE 109 D2
PACKE STREET 109 C1
PAGET STREET 107 C7
PALMER AVENUE 107 B7
PANTAIN ROAD 109 B4
PARK AVENUE 109 D4
PARK COURT 109 D3
PARK ROAD 109 C5
PARK STREET 109 D2
PARKLANDS DRIVE 109 C5
PASTURE LANE 106 E1
PATTERDALE DRIVE 108 E4
PEEL DRIVE 109 E1
PERRY GROVE 109 E4
PETWORTH DRIVE 106 E7
PEVENSEY ROAD 107 A6
PINE CLOSE 109 D6
PINFOLD GARDENS 109 E1
PINFOLD GATE 109 D1
PINFOLD JETTY 109 D1
PIPER CLOSE 109 B4
PITSFORD DRIVE 108 C3
PLEASANT CLOSE 109 C1
PLUMTREE CLOSE 107 B6
POPLAR ROAD 109 D6
PRESTBURY ROAD 108 D1
PRINCE WILLIAM ROAD 107 C6
PRINCESS STREET 109 D2
PRIORY ROAD 109 A5
PULTENEY AVENUE 109 D5
PULTENEY ROAD 109 D5
PYTCHLEY DRIVE 109 B6
QUEENS ROAD 107 E7
QUORN CLOSE 109 E4
RADMOOR ROAD 109 C1
RAILWAY TERRACE 107 E7
RATCLIFFE ROAD 107 D6
RAVENSTHORPE DRIVE 108 D2
RAYMOND AVENUE 106 F6
RAYNHAM DRIVE 106 E7
RECTORY PLACE 107 D1
RECTORY ROAD 107 D7
REDMIRES CLOSE 108 D2
REDWOOD ROAD 109 D6
REGENT COURT 107 C7
REGENT STREET 109 C1
RENDELL STREET 107 D7
RIVINGTON DRIVE 108 E3
ROCKINGHAM ROAD 107 A6
RONALD WEST COURT 108 F4
ROSEBERY STREET 109 B1
ROSEHILL 108 E1
ROUNDHILL WAY 108 D2
ROWAN AVENUE 106 C2
ROWBANK WAY 108 D2
ROYAL WAY 107 C6
ROYDALE CLOSE 107 A6
ROYLAND ROAD 109 D2
RUDYARD CLOSE 108 E3
RUFFORD CLOSE 106 D7
RUPERT BROOKE ROAD 108 F1
RUSSELL STREET 109 E1
RYDAL AVENUE 108 E4
ST MARYS CLOSE 109 C1
ST OLAVES CLOSE 106 D7
ST PETERS AVENUE 106 C3
SALISBURY STREET 109 E1
SANDALWOOD ROAD 109 A4
SANDRINGHAM DRIVE 106 F7
SCHOFIELD ROAD 108 E2
SCHOOL STREET 109 D1
SELBOURNE COURT 109 E1
SELBOURNE STREET 109 E1
SETON CLOSE 106 E5
SEWARD STREET 109 B2
SEYMOUR CLOSE 106 E7
SHAKESPEARE STREET 109 D1
SHARPLEY ROAD 108 E2
SHELDON CLOSE 106 D6
SHELTHORPE AVENUE 109 E4
SHELTHORPE ROAD 109 E3
SHEPSHED ROAD 106 A4
SILVERTON ROAD 109 B5
SIR ROBERT MARTIN COURT 106 F7
SKEVINGTON AVENUE 109 A2
SNELLS NOOK LANE 108 C6
SOARBANK WAY 107 A5
SOUTH STREET 109 D2
SOUTHDOWN ROAD 109 C6
SOUTHFIELD ROAD 109 D2
SPARROW HILL 109 D1
SPRINGFIELD CLOSE 109 A5
SPRUCE AVENUE 109 B6
SQUIRREL WAY 109 C3
STANFORD HILL 107 D6
STANLEY STREET 109 D3
STATION AVENUE 107 B7
STATION STREET 109 B2
STAVELEY COURT 107 D7
STEEPLE ROW 109 D1
STEWART DRIVE 106 E6
STIRLING AVENUE 106 F7
STONEBOW CLOSE 106 D6
STONEBOW WALK 106 C6
STORER ROAD 109 B1
SULLIVANS WAY 107 B5
SUMMERPOOL ROAD 107 B5
SUNNYHILL ROAD 109 B4
SWALLOW WALK 106 C3
SWINGBRIDGE ROAD 107 B5
SWITHLAND CLOSE 106 E7
SYCAMORE WAY 109 C6
SYWELL AVENUE 108 D2
TANNERS LANE 106 C3
TATMARSH 107 D7
TENNYSON ROAD 106 F7
THE CONERIES 109 D1
THE FARTHINGS 106 C3
THE GREEN 106 C3
THE GROVE 109 B1
THE HOLT 109 B3
THE OSIERS 109 C6
THE WIDON 109 A5
THIRLMERE DRIVE 108 F5
THOMAS STREET 109 F2
THORNY CLOSE 107 A6
THORPE ACRE ROAD 106 F7
THORPE HILL 108 E2
TIVERTON ROAD 109 B6
TOWN HALL PASSAGE 109 D2
TRELISSICK CLOSE 106 D7
TRINITY STREET 107 E2
TRUE LOVERS WALK 109 C1
TUCKERS CLOSE 109 E3
TUCKERS ROAD 109 E2
TURNER AVENUE 109 C3
TYLER AVENUE 107 B7
TYNEDALE ROAD 108 E5
ULVERSCROFT ROAD 109 A5
UNION STREET 109 C1
UNIVERSITY ROAD 108 E3
UNIVERSITY ROAD 109 A2
UPPER GREEN 108 F5
VAL WILSON COURT 108 D3
VALLEY ROAD 109 A5
VICTORIA STREET 109 D2
WAIN DRIVE 106 E5
WALLACE ROAD 109 C3
WALNUT ROAD 109 D5
WARDS END 109 D2
WARNER PLACE 109 E1
WARNER'S LANE 109 D1
WARWICK WAY 107 A6
WATERSIDE CLOSE 107 D7
WEAVER CLOSE 109 E4
WELDON ROAD 107 A5
WELLINGTON STREET 109 D2
WESLEY CLOSE (Hath) 106 C3
WESLEY CLOSE (Lough) 106 D6
WESTFIELD DRIVE 109 B2
WESTMORLAND AVENUE 108 F4
WHADDON DRIVE 109 E4
WHARNCLIFFE ROAD 109 E2
WHATTON ROAD 106 A2
WHEATLANDS DRIVE 109 E4
WHITBY CLOSE 106 D6
WHITEGATE 107 E7
WHITEHOUSE AVENUE 109 E3
WIDE LANE 106 C3
WIDE STREET 106 C3
WILLIAM STREET 109 C2
WILLOW ROAD 109 D5
WILMINGTON COURT 109 E3
WILSTONE CLOSE 108 E2
WILTON AVENUE 109 E4
WINDLEDEN ROAD 108 D2
WINDMILL ROAD 109 F2
WINDSOR ROAD 106 F7
WINTERBURN WAY 108 D2
WOBURN CLOSE 106 E1
WOLLATON AVENUE 106 E1
WOLSEY WAY 109 E1
WOOD GATE 109 D2
WOODBROOK ROAD 109 A5
WOODGATE DRIVE 109 B3
WOODHOUSE LANE 108 C6
WOODLANDS DRIVE 109 C4
WOODTHORPE AVENUE 109 D4
WOODTHORPE ROAD 109 E4
WORDSWORTH ROAD 108 F1
WORTLEY COURT 109 D1
WYNDHAM ROAD 106 E6
WYTHBURN CLOSE 108 F4
YORK ROAD 109 C1
ZOUCH ROAD 106 C1

Lubenham

ACORN CLOSE 122 B2
CHURCH WALK 122 C2
HARBOROUGH ROAD 122 C2
MAIN STREET 122 C2
OLD HALL LANE 122 C2
PAGET ROAD 122 B2
RUSHES LANE 122 C2
SCHOOL LANE 122 C2
THE GREEN 122 C2
THEDDINGWORTH ROAD 122 A3
TOWER COURT 122 C2
WESTGATE LANE 122 C2
WESTLAND CLOSE 122 B2

Lutterworth & Bitteswell

ACACIA AVENUE 98 C3
ALDER CRESCENT 98 C4
ALEXANDER DRIVE 98 C5
ALMOND WAY 98 B4
ASHBY LANE 98 C2
ASHLEIGH DRIVE 98 C4
ASPEN WAY 98 C3
ATTLEE CLOSE 98 C5
AVERY CLOSE 98 D5
BAKER STREET 98 D5
BANK STREET 98 D5
BEECH AVENUE 98 C4
BELL STREET 98 E5
BILTON WAY 98 E2
BITTESWELL ROAD 98 C3
BLACKTHORN CLOSE 98 B3
BOUNDARY ROAD 98 E4
BROOKFIELD WAY 98 C3
BYRON CLOSE 98 D2
CANADA FIELDS 98 D3
CARLSON GARDENS 98 E4
CEDAR AVENUE 98 C4
CENTRAL AVENUE 98 E3
CHAPEL STREET 98 D4
CHERRYTREE AVENUE 98 C5
CHESHIRE CLOSE 98 C5
CHESTNUT AVENUE 98 B4
CHURCH CLOSE 98 D5
CHURCH GATE 98 D5
CHURCH STREET 98 D5
CHURCHILL CLOSE 98 B5
CONIFER CLOSE 98 C4
COUNCIL STREET 98 E3
COVENTRY ROAD 98 D5
CRESCENT ROAD 98 D3
CUNNINGHAM DRIVE 98 C5
DE VERDON ROAD 98 B5
DEACON CLOSE 98 B2
DENBIGH PLACE 98 D2
DUNLEY WAY 98 D2
DYSON CLOSE 98 D3
ELIZABETHAN WAY 98 E3
ELM AVENUE 98 C4
ELMHIRST ROAD 98 C5
FARINGDON AVENUE 98 E4
FEILDINGWAY 98 D3
FERRERS ROAD 98 C5
FIRTREE AVENUE 98 C5
GEORGE STREET 98 E4
GIBSON WAY 98 C5
GILMORTON ROAD 98 F2
GLADSTONE STREET 98 E4
GOSCOTE DRIVE 98 D4
GREENACRES DRIVE 98 C3
GUTHLAXTON AVENUE 98 D4
HAZEL DRIVE 98 C4
HAZELAND COURT 98 D4
HOLLY DRIVE 98 C3
HOLMFIELD CLOSE 98 C4
HUNTERS DRIVE 98 C5
JUNIPER CLOSE 98 C3
KINGS WAY 98 C5
LABURNUM AVENUE 98 C4
LARCH DRIVE 98 C4
LEICESTER ROAD 98 E1
LEYTON CLOSE 98 E5
LINDEN DRIVE 98 C4
LUTTERWORTH ROAD 98 D2
MACAULAY ROAD 98 C3
MAGNOLIA DRIVE 98 C3
MAINO CRESCENT 98 C5
MANOR ROAD 98 C2
MAPLE DRIVE 98 C4
MARKET STREET 98 D5
MARYLEBONE DRIVE 98 E4
MERITON ROAD 98 C5
MILL GROVE 98 D5
MISTERTON WAY 98 D5
MONTGOMERY CLOSE 98 B6
MOORBARNS LANE 98 C5
MOUNTBATTEN WAY 98 C5
MULBERRY CLOSE 98 C3
NEW STREET 98 D3
OAKBERRY ROAD 98 E2
OAKFIELD AVENUE 98 C4
ORANGE HILL 98 E5
ORCHARD ROAD 98 D5
PALMER DRIVE 98 D5
PEAR TREE CLOSE 98 B4
PINE CLOSE 98 C3
POPLAR AVENUE 98 C4
RAMSEY CLOSE 98 E4
REGENT STREET 98 D5
RIVERSIDE ROAD 98 D5
ROWAN DRIVE 98 C4
RUGBY ROAD 98 D5
RYDER WAY 98 C5
ST JOHNS CLOSE 98 C5
ST MARYS ROAD 98 D5
SHELLEY DRIVE 98 D2
SHERRIER WAY 98 D2
SPENCER ROAD 98 D3
SPRING CLOSE 98 D5
SPRUCE WAY 98 C3
STATION ROAD 98 D5
STONEY HOLLOW 98 D5
SWIFT WAY 98 D2
SYCAMORE DRIVE 98 C4
TEDDER CLOSE 98 B5
TENNYSON ROAD 98 D3
THE HAWTHORNS 98 C4
THE NOOK 98 C2
ULLESTHORPE ROAD 98 C2
VALLEY LANE 98 C2
WALKER COURT 98 E4
WHITTLE ROAD 98 C5
WICLIFWAY 98 E3
WILLOW TREE CRESCENT 98 B4
WOODBINE CRESCENT 98 D5
WOODLEA AVENUE 98 B3
WOODMARKET 98 D5
WOODWAY ROAD 98 C5
YEW TREE CLOSE 98 B4

Lyddington

BLUECOAT LANE 143 B2
CHURCH LANE 143 B3
GRETTON ROAD 143 B4
MAIN STREET 143 B2
STOKE ROAD 143 A2
THE GREEN 143 B2
THORPE ROAD 143 C3
WINDMILL WAY 143 B3

Magna Park

COVENTRY ROAD 143 B3
HUNTER BOULEVARD 143 B1
SHACKELTON WAY 143 C3
VULCAN WAY 143 B1
WELLINGTON PARKWAY 143 C1

Manton

CEMETERY LANE 137 A1
CHATER CLOSE 137 B2
CHURCH LANE 137 B2
LYNDON ROAD 137 C2
PRIORY ROAD 137 B2
ST MARYS ROAD 137 B2
SOUTH VIEW CLOSE 137 B2
STOCKS HILL 137 B2
WING ROAD 137 B3

Market Bosworth

AMBION RISE 136 C3
BACK LANE 136 D3
BARTON ROAD 136 E3
BECKETT AVENUE 136 E3
BOSWORTH ROAD 136 A1
CARLTON ROAD 136 A2
CEDAR DRIVE 136 E3
CHESTNUT CLOSE 136 E4
CHURCH STREET 136 E3
CHURCH WALK 136 E3
GODSONS HILL 136 C3
HAVEN ROAD 136 D4
HEATH ROAD 136 C3
HILLSIDE 136 C3
LANCASTER AVENUE 136 D4
MOORLAND CLOSE 136 E3
NORTHUMBERLAND AVENUE 136 D4
PARK STREET 136 E3
PRIORY ROAD 136 C3
RECTORY LANE 136 E3
REDMOOR CLOSE 136 C3
ST CATHERINES AVENUE 136 D3
ST PETERS CLOSE 136 C3
SHENTON LANE 136 E3
SOUTHFIELD WAY 136 D3
SPINNEY HARCOURT 136 D2
SPINNEY HILL 136 D3
SPRINGFIELD AVENUE 136 C3
STANLEY ROAD 136 D4
STATION ROAD 136 D3
STCAMORE WAY 136 F3
SUTTON LANE 136 E3
THE PARK 136 E3

TUDOR CLOSE 136 D4
WARWICK LANE 136 D3
WELLSBOROUGH ROAD 136 A3
WESTHAVEN COURT 136 D3
WESTON DRIVE 136 D3
YORK CLOSE 136 D4

Market Harborough

ABBEY STREET 99 C4
ADAM & EVE STREET 99 C4
ALBERT ROAD 99 D4
ALVINGTON WAY 99 B2
ARDEN CLOSE 99 E2
ARDEN WAY 99 E2
ARGYLE PARK 99 C7
ASHFIELD ROAD 99 C4
ASTLEY CLOSE 99 B6
AURIGA STREET 99 D5
AUSTINS CLOSE 99 B4
BALFOUR GARDENS 99 B6
BAMBURGH CLOSE 99 F4
BANKFIELD DRIVE 99 E2
BARNARD GARDENS 99 B7
BATES CLOSE 99 C2
BATH STREET 99 C6
BELLFIELDS LANE 99 E4
BELLFIELDS STREET 99 E5
BERRY CLOSE 99 E2
BIRCH TREE GARDENS 99 D3
BISHOP CLOSE 99 C7
BLENHEIM WAY 99 C2
BOWDEN LANE 99 C3
BOWDEN RIDGE 99 E2
BRAYBROOKE ROAD 99 F6
BROOKFIELD ROAD 99 A4
BROOKLANDS GARDENS 99 C4
BURGHLEY CLOSE 99 F4
BURNMILL ROAD 99 C3
BUTLER GARDENS 99 A6
CAXTON STREET 99 D6
CHARLES STREET 99 B4
CHATER CLOSE 99 E1
CHATSWORTH DRIVE 99 F4
CHILTERN CLOSE 99 C2
CHURCH SQUARE 99 C4
CHURCH STREET 99 C4
CLAREMONT DRIVE 99 E4
CLARENCE STREET 99 D4
CLARKE STREET 99 B4
CLIPSTON STREET 99 D6
CONNAUGHT ROAD 99 D4
COVENTRY ROAD 99 B4
CRESCENT CLOSE 99 D3
CROMWELL CRESCENT 99 B6
CROSBY ROAD 99 D6
CROSS STREET 99 D5
DALLISON CLOSE 99 C7
DE LISLE CLOSE 99 B6
DINGLEY ROAD 99 F2
DINGLEY TERRACE 99 E4
DODDRIDGE ROAD 99 C4
DOUGLASS DRIVE 99 D3
DUNSLADE CLOSE 99 F5
DUNSLADE ROAD 99 E5
EAST STREET 99 B4
EDINBURGH CLOSE 99 D3
EDWARD ROAD 99 B3
ELM DRIVE 99 B5
ESSEX GARDENS 99 B6
FAIRFAX ROAD 99 C6
FAIRFIELD ROAD 99 B3
FAIRWAY 99 B3
FARNDON ROAD 99 B4
FERNIE ROAD 99 E4
FIELDHEAD CLOSE 99 A4
FIR TREE WALK 99 C3
FLEETWOOD GARDENS 99 B6
GARDINER STREET 99 B4
GERRARD GARDENS 99 B7
GLADSTONE STREET 99 D5
GLEBE ROAD 99 E5
GORES LANE 99 E4
GOWARD STREET 99 C4
GRANVILLE STREET 99 C5
GREAT BOWDEN ROAD 99 E2
GREEN LANE 99 C6
GRENVILLE GARDENS 99 B6
GUNNSBROOK CLOSE 99 E1
HAGLEY CLOSE 99 F4
HAMMOND WAY 99 C3
HARCOURT STREET 99 B4
HARRISON CLOSE 99 B7
HARROD DRIVE 99 E4
HEARTH STREET 99 B4
HEYGATE STREET 99 C3
HIGH STREET 99 C4
HIGHCROSS STREET 99 B4
HIGHFIELD STREET 99 B4
HILL GARDENS 99 A4
HILLCREST AVENUE 99 B3
HILLSIDE ROAD 99 D3
HOLLY CLOSE 99 C3
HOPTON FIELDS 99 B7
HORSE SHOE LANE 99 E1
HORSEFAIR CLOSE 99 B3
HOWARD WAY 99 B6
HUNTINGDON GARDENS 99 B6
IRETON ROAD 99 B6
JACKSON CLOSE 99 C7
JERWOOD WAY 99 D5
JUBILEE GARDENS 99 D3
KETTERING ROAD 99 E4
KINGS HEAD PLACE 99 C4
KNIGHTS END ROAD 99 F2
KNOLL STREET 99 B4
LANGTON ROAD 99 E1
LATHKILL STREET 99 D6
LATIMER CRESCENT 99 D5
LAUNDE PARK 99 E5
LEICESTER LANE 99 D1
LEICESTER ROAD 99 A1
LENTHALL SQUARE 99 C6
LINCOLN COURT 99 D2
LINDSEY GARDENS 99 B7
LOGAN COURT 99 B3
LOGAN CRESCENT 99 B3
LOGAN STREET 99 B4
LUBENHAM HILL 99 A4
MADELINE CLOSE 99 E2
MAIN STREET 99 E1
MANOR ROAD 99 E1
MANOR WALK 99 C4
MARLBOROUGH WAY 99 C2
MAURICE ROAD 99 B7
MEADOW STREET 99 C3
MEDWAY CLOSE 99 E4
MIDDLEDALE ROAD 99 F4
MILL HILL ROAD 99 C4
MONTROSE CLOSE 99 B6
MORLEY STREET 99 B4
NASEBY CLOSE 99 C6
NELSON STREET 99 B4
NEWCOMBE STREET 99 C5
NITHSDALE AVENUE 99 C5
NITHSDALE CRESCENT 99 D5
NORBURY CLOSE 99 B4
NORTH BANK 99 C4
NORTHAMPTON ROAD 99 C4
NUNNELEY WAY 99 D3
OAK CLOSE 99 D3
ORCHARD STREET 99 C3
OVERDALE CLOSE 99 E4
OVERFIELD AVENUE 99 D2
PARK DRIVE 99 B3
PATRICK STREET 99 C5
PEAR TREE GARDENS 99 B5
PERKINS CLOSE 99 D3
POCHIN DRIVE 99 C2
POST OFFICE LANE 99 D4
PRIDE PLACE 99 B5
QUEEN STREET 99 E5
RAINSBOROUGH CLOSE 99 B6
RAINSBOROUGH GARDENS 99 B7
RECTORY LANE 99 E4
RIDGEWAY WEST 99 C2
RITCHIE PARK 99 C7
RIVERSIDE 99 F3
ROCHESTER GARDENS 99 B6
ROCKINGHAM ROAD 99 F4
ROLLESTON CLOSE 99 E4
ROMAN WAY 99 C4
ROOKWELL DRIVE 99 E6
ROSEMOOR CLOSE 99 F4
ROWAN AVENUE 99 C6
RUGBY CLOSE 99 B5
RUPERT ROAD 99 B6
RUSSETT CLOSE 99 D2
ST MARYS ROAD 99 E4
ST NICHOLAS CLOSE 99 D5
ST NICHOLAS WAY 99 E5
SCHOOL LANE 99 C4
SCOTLAND ROAD 99 E5
SCOTT CLOSE 99 C2
SELBY CLOSE 99 C7
SHERRARD ROAD 99 D3
SHREWSBURY AVENUE 99 F5
SHROPSHIRE CLOSE 99 C3
SHROPSHIRE PLACE 99 C3
SKIPPON CLOSE 99 B5
SMYTH CLOSE 99 C2
SPENCER STREET 99 B4
SPINNEY CLOSE 99 A4
SPRINGFIELD STREET 99 D4
STABLEGATE WAY 99 E4
STAMFORD CLOSE 99 C5
STANWAY CLOSE 99 E4
STATION ROAD 99 E2
STEVENS STREET 99 B4
STUART ROAD 99 B6
TALBOT YARD 99 C4
THE BROADWAY 99 C3
THE CRESCENT 99 D3
THE HEADLANDS 99 E3
THE HEIGHTS 99 F5
THE OVAL 99 C3
THE PASTURES 99 A4
THE RIDGEWAY 99 E2
THE WOODLANDS 99 A3
THORNBOROUGH CLOSE 99 E5
VALLEY WAY 99 F3
VAUGHAN CLOSE 99 C7
VICTORIA AVENUE 99 B3
WALCOT ROAD 99 C4
WARTNABY STREET 99 B4
WARWICK CLOSE 99 D2
WATERFIELD PLACE 99 C2
WATSON AVENUE 99 A6
WELLAND PARK ROAD 99 B5
WESTERN AVENUE 99 B6
WESTFIELD CLOSE 99 A4
WILLOW CRESCENT 99 B5
WILLSON CLOSE 99 E4
WORCESTER DRIVE 99 C2
YORK STREET 99 D4
DUNSLADE GROVE 99 F5
NORTHLEIGH GROVE 99 B3
SOUTHLEIGH GROVE 99 B3

Market Overton

BERRYBUSHES 137 B2
BOWLING GREEN LANE 137 B2
CHURCH LANE 137 A1
CORDLE WAY 137 B2
KINGS CLOSE 137 B2
MAIN STREET 137 C2
PINFOLD LANE 137 C2
TEIGH ROAD 137 A2
THE FINCHES 137 C2
THE LIMES 137 C2
THISTLETON ROAD 137 C1

Markfield

ALTAR STONES LANE 100 A3
ASHBY ROAD 100 B3
AVERY DRIVE 100 B4
BEACON CLOSE 100 C4
BEECH CLOSE 100 C5
BIRCH CLOSE 100 C7
BIRCHFIELD AVENUE 100 B5
BRACKEN WAY 100 C4
BRADGATE HILL 100 E6
BRADGATE ROAD 100 C4
CHAMBERS CLOSE 100 D5
CHARNWOOD DRIVE 100 D5
CHESTNUT WALK 100 C7
CHITTERMAN WAY 100 C4
CHURCH DRIVE 100 B5
COTTAGE LANE 100 B2
COUNTRYMAN WAY 100 D5
CRAVENS ROUGH 100 F1
CROFTWAY 100 B5
DABEY CLOSE 100 B5
DANDEES CLOSE 100 C4
FOREST ROAD 100 B5
HILL LANE 100 B4
HILL LANE CLOSE 100 B3
HILLSIDE 100 B4
HUNTSMANS CLOSE 100 C5
JACQUELINE ROAD 100 E5
JANES WAY 100 C5
LAUNDE ROAD 100 D5
LEA LANE 100 C1
LEICESTER ROAD 100 D5
LILLINGSTONE CLOSE 100 C4
LINFORD CRESCENT 100 C4
LINK RISE 100 D5
LONDON ROAD 100 B5
MAIN STREET 100 B4
MARKFIELD LANE 100 E5
MAYFLOWER CLOSE 100 B5
MEADOW LANE 100 C4
MILL HILL LANE 100 B4
NEVILLE DRIVE 100 B5
OAKFIELD AVENUE 100 B5
PARK AVENUE 100 B4
PINEWOOD DRIVE 100 C7
POLLY BOTTS LANE 100 E1
POPLAR AVENUE 100 B5
PRIORY LANE 100 C1
QUEEN STREET 100 B5
RATBY LANE 100 C6
RECTORY ROAD 100 C4
ROECLIFF CLOSE 100 C4
ST MICHAELS CLOSE 100 B4
SWITHLAND CLOSE 100 C5
THE BLOSSOMS 100 C7
THE CHASE 100 C5
THE COPPICE 100 C5
THE GREEN 100 B5
THE HAWTHORNS 100 C5
THE PADDOCK 100 C4
THE RUSHES 100 C4
ULVERS CROFT 100 C4
ULVERSCROFT LANE 100 F1
UPLAND CLOSE 100 B4
UPLAND DRIVE 100 B4
WALNUT CLOSE 100 B5
WARREN CLOSE 100 C5
WESLEY WAY 100 D5
WHITCROFT CLOSE 100 C5
WHITCROFTS LANE 100 C1
WHITWICK ROAD 100 B2
WOODHOUSE CLOSE 100 C4
WOODLAND CLOSE 100 C5

Measham

ABNEY CRESCENT 144 E2
ABNEY DRIVE 144 E2
ATHERSTONE ROAD 144 E2
BLEACH MILL 144 E3
BOSWORTH ROAD 144 F2
BROWNING DRIVE 144 E3
BUCKLEY CLOSE 144 E2
BURNS CLOSE 144 D3
BURTON ROAD 144 E2
BYRON CRESCENT 144 E3
CHAPEL STREET 144 E1
COPHILLS CLOSE 144 E2
DRYDEN CLOSE 144 E2
DYSONS CLOSE 144 D1
FENTON CLOSE 144 E3
FENTON CRESCENT 144 E2
GREENFIELD ROAD 144 F1
HAZEL CLOSE 144 E1
HIGH STREET 144 E2
HOLLY ROAD 144 F1
HORSES LANE 144 E2
HUNTINGDON WAY 144 C1
IVEAGH CLOSE 144 F1
MANNINGS TERRACE 144 E2
MASEFIELD CLOSE 144 E3
MEADOW GARDENS 144 E3
MEASE CLOSE 144 E2
MEASHAM ROAD 144 C1
MILTON CLOSE 144 E3
NAVIGATION STREET 144 E1
OAK CLOSE 144 E1
ORCHARD WAY 144 E7
PEGGS CLOSE 144 E2
QUEENS STREET 144 E1
REPTON ROAD 144 C1
RIVER WAY 144 E2
RIVERSIDE COURT 144 D2
ROWAN CLOSE 144 E1
SANDHILLS CLOSE 144 E2
SHACKLAND DRIVE 144 F1
SHELLEY CLOSE 144 E3
TAMWORTH ROAD 144 E2
TENNYSON CLOSE 144 E2
THE CROFT 144 D1
UPLANDS ROAD 144 E2
WILKES AVENUE 144 E2
WILLOW CLOSE 144 E7
WORDSWORTH WAY 144 E3
YORK CLOSE 144 E1

Medbourne

ASHLEY ROAD 144 B3
DRAYTON ROAD 144 B3
HALLATON ROAD 144 B2
MAIN STREET 144 B2
MANOR ROAD 144 B2
MEDBOURNE ROAD 144 A4
OLD GREEN 144 B3
OLD HOLT ROAD 144 C2
PAYNES LANE 144 B3
RECTORY LANE 144 C2
SLAWSTON ROAD 144 B2
UPPINGHAM ROAD 144 C1
WATERFALL WAY 144 B3

Melton Mowbray

ABINGDON ROAD 120 E4
ACRES RISE 121 C5
ALBERT STREET 122 E1
ALGERNON ROAD 121 B6
ALVASTON ROAD 120 E4
ANKLE HILL 121 D1
ARDEN DRIVE 120 E5
ASFORDBY ROAD 120 E6
ASH GROVE 120 F4
ASHTON CLOSE 122 D1
AVON ROAD 122 C1
BALDOCKS LANE 121 E1
BALMORAL ROAD 121 A4
BANBURY DRIVE 122 E2
BARKER CRESCENT 122 D2
BARNGATE CLOSE 121 B4
BAYSWATER ROAD 121 B5
BEACONSFIELD ROAD 120 E4
BEAUMONT GARDENS 121 B4
BEECHWOOD AVENUE 121 C4
BELER WAY 122 A2
BELVOIR STREET 121 C5
BENTLEY STREET 121 A6
BICKLEY AVENUE 121 B5
BIRCH CLOSE 120 F4
BISHOP STREET 121 B6
BLAKENEY CRESCENT 122 D2
BLENHEIM WAY 120 F4
BLYTH AVENUE 120 C1
BOWLEY AVENUE 121 C4
BRAMPTON ROAD 120 E3
BRANSTON CRESCENT 121 C7
BRENTINGBY CLOSE 122 E1
BREWARD WAY 121 B3
BRIDEWELL OLD 121 B3
BRIGHTSIDE AVENUE 120 E5
BROCKLEHURST ROAD 121 C4
BROOK CRESCENT 120 A5
BROOK LANE 121 B7
BROOK STREET 121 B6
BROOKFIELD STREET 120 F4
BROWNLOW CRESCENT 122 D2
BURNS CLOSE 120 F3
BURTON ROAD 121 E1
BURTON STREET 121 A6
BYRON WAY 120 F4
CAMBRIDGE AVENUE 122 E2
CANTERBURY DRIVE 120 E3
CARNEGIE CRESCENT 121 C4
CEDAR DRIVE 120 F5
CHADWELL CLOSE 121 C7
CHALFONT CLOSE 122 E2
CHALMONDLEY DRIVE 121 B3
CHAPEL STREET 121 A6
CHARLOTTE STREET 121 A6
CHARNWOOD DRIVE 120 E5
CHESTNUT WAY 122 D1
CHETWYND DRIVE 120 D6
CHURCH STREET 121 A6
CHURCHILL CLOSE 121 A4
CLARK DRIVE 121 B3
CLUMBER STREET 120 F5

COLLEGE AVENUE 122 E2
COLLINGWOOD CRESCENT 120 D6
CONISTON ROAD 120 E3
CONVENT CLOSE 120 F7
CONWAY DRIVE 121 A4
COPLEY CLOSE 121 C5
CORNWALL PLACE 122 D3
COTSWOLD CLOSE 122 E2
COTTESMORE AVENUE 120 F6
CRANMERE ROAD 121 B4
CRAVEN STREET 122 E1
CROMPTON ROAD 120 A6
CROMWELL ROAD 122 E1
CROSSFIELD DRIVE 121 D5
DALBY ROAD 121 C3
DE MONTFORT 121 A4
DELAMARE ROAD 121 B3
DENTON RISE 121 B7
DERWENT DRIVE 122 C1
DICKENS DRIVE 120 F3
DIEPPE WAY 120 F4
DIGBY DRIVE 122 A2
DOCTORS LANE 121 C4
DORIAN RISE 120 F7
DOROTHY AVENUE 120 E5
DORSET DRIVE 122 E2
DOUGLAS JANE CLOSE 120 E5
DOVEDALE CLOSE 122 C1
DRIVE DALBY ROAD 122 D1
DRUMMOND WALK 120 F4
DUKE STREET 121 C5
DULVERTON ROAD 120 E4
EAGLES DRIVE 122 C2
EAST AVENUE 120 E5
EAST SIDE CROFT 121 B3
EASTFIELD AVENUE 121 A5
EDENDALE ROAD 122 C2
EGERTON ROAD 121 B6
EGERTON VIEW 120 F6
ELGIN DRIVE 121 A5
ELMHURST AVENUE 120 E4
ELMS ROAD 121 A6
EPPING DRIVE 121 A4
EVEREST DRIVE 120 E4
EWDEN RISE 122 C1
FAIRFIELD CLOSE 121 B4
FALDO DRIVE 121 A3
FERNELEY CRESCENT 121 C4
FERNIE AVENUE 120 F6
FIELD CLOSE 122 E1
FIRWOOD ROAD 121 C4
FOREST CLOSE 121 A4
FRAMLAND DRIVE 121 A3
FREEBY CLOSE 121 C7
FRESHNEY CLOSE 122 C1
GALSWORTHY CRESCENT 120 F3
GARDEN LANE 120 E4
GARTHORPE DRIVE 121 C7
GARTREE COURT 122 D1
GARTREE DRIVE 122 E1
GEORGE STREET 121 B6
GILPIN CLOSE 122 B1
GLADSTONE AVENUE 120 E4
GLEBE ROAD 120 A6
GLOUCESTER AVENUE 122 E2
GLOUCESTER CRESCENT 122 E2
GOLDSPINK CLOSE 122 D2
GOODRICHE STREET 121 B6
GRANBY ROAD 121 B3
GRANGE DRIVE 121 E1
GRANTWOOD ROAD 121 C4
GRANVILLE ROAD 120 E4
GREAVES AVENUE 120 E5
GREEN BANK 121 C6
GREENSLADE 121 B6
GUADALOUPE AVENUE 122 F1
HADFIELD DRIVE 121 A5
HAMILTON DRIVE 122 D1
HARLECH WAY 121 A4
HARTLAND DRIVE 122 D1
HARTOPP ROAD 122 D2
HAWTHORN DRIVE 121 A5
HIGH STREET 121 A6
HIGHFIELD AVENUE 120 E4
HILLSIDE AVENUE 120 E4
HORSE FIELD VIEW 120 E5
HUDSON ROAD 121 C6
HUMBER DRIVE 122 C1
HUNT DRIVE 121 C4
HUNTERS ROAD 121 E1
IRWELL CLOSE 122 C1
JAMES LAMBERT DRIVE 120 E4
JARVIS DRIVE 120 E5
JOHNSON CLOSE 121 A5
JUBILEE STREET 121 A6
KAPELLE CLOSE 121 C4
KEATS CLOSE 120 F3
KENNET WAY 122 B1
KESTREL DRIVE 122 C2
KING STREET 121 A6
KINGS ROAD 121 B6
KIPLING DRIVE 120 F4
KIRBY LANE 122 E3
KIRTON DRIVE 120 E3
LAG LANE 121 E6
LAKE TERRACE 120 E7
LAMBERT CLOSE 121 A3
LAYCOCK AVENUE 121 B5
LEICESTER ROAD 120 F6
LEICESTER ROAD 122 B1
LEICESTER STREET 121 A6
LILAC WAY 121 F4
LIMES AVENUE 121 B5
LINCOLN DRIVE 122 E2
LINNET CLOSE 122 C2
LODDON CLOSE 122 C1
LONGATE ROAD 121 A3
LONGFIELD ROAD 121 B3
LONGWILL AVENUE 121 B5
LOWESBY CLOSE 121 C7
LOXLEY DRIVE 122 C1
LUDLOW DRIVE 121 A4
LYLE CLOSE 121 A3
LYNTON ROAD 120 E3
MANNERS DRIVE 121 B3
MANOR CLOSE 121 C4
MAPLE CLOSE 121 F4
MARKET PLACE 121 A6
MARTEG CLOSE 122 C1
MAYFIELD STREET 120 E4
MEADOW WAY 122 E1
MEDWAY DRIVE 122 C1
MELBOURNE DRIVE 120 E6
MELBRAY DRIVE 120 F3
MELBRAY DRIVE 121 A3
MELTON SPINNEY ROAD 121 D2
MEYNELL CLOSE 122 D2
MILDMAY CLOSE 121 B3
MILL LANE 121 B7
MILL STREET 121 A6
MILTON CLOSE 120 F4
MORLEY CLOSE 120 E5
MORTIMER ROAD 121 A5
NEEDHAM CLOSE 121 A5
NEW STREET 121 A6
NEWBURY AVENUE 120 E4
NEWPORT AVENUE 121 A5
NORFOLK DRIVE 122 E2
NORMAN WAY 121 B6
NORTH STREET 121 A6
NORTHFIELD CLOSE 121 A5
NOTTINGHAM ROAD 120 E2
NOTTINGHAM STREET 121 A6
OAK ROAD 121 B6
OWEN CRESCENT 121 B5
OWEN DRIVE 121 B5
OXFORD DRIVE 122 E2
PADDOCK CLOSE 122 E1
PALL MALL 121 C4
PALMERSTON ROAD 120 E3
PARK AVENUE 120 F6
PARK LANE 121 A6
PARK ROAD 121 A6
PATE ROAD 122 A2
PETERSFIELD ROAD 120 E5
POCHIN CLOSE 120 F7
POLLARD CLOSE 121 C4
PRINCESS DRIVE 122 D3
QUEENSWAY 122 D2
QUORN AVENUE 120 F6
REDBROOK CRESCENT 122 C1
REDWOOD AVENUE 121 B5
REGENT PLACE 121 B6
REGENT STREET 121 B6
RIBBLE WAY 122 C1
RICHMOND DRIVE 122 E2
ROBIN CRESCENT 122 C2
ROCKINGHAM DRIVE 120 E5
ROSEBERY AVENUE 121 B6
ROSS CLOSE 121 C4
RUDBECK AVENUE 120 E5
RUTLAND STREET 121 B6
SAGE CROSS STREET 121 A6
ST BARTHOLEMEWS WAY 120 D3
ST JOHNS COURT 121 B6
ST JOHNS DRIVE 121 A4
ST JOHNS ROAD 120 B6
ST MARYS WAY 121 A6
SALISBURY AVENUE 121 B6
SANDY LANE 122 E3
SAPCOTE DRIVE 121 E1
SAXBY ROAD 121 B6
SCALFORD ROAD 121 A3
SEVERN HILL 122 C2
SHELLEY AVENUE 120 F4
SHERRARD STREET 121 B6
SHERWOOD DRIVE 120 E5
SNOW HILL 121 B5
SOAR CLOSE 122 C1
SOHO STREET 121 A6
SOLWAY CLOSE 122 C1
SOMERSET CLOSE 122 E2
SOUTH STREET 120 B6
SPINNEY CLOSE 121 C4
SPRINGFIELD STREET 120 F5
STAFFORD AVENUE 121 B6
STANLEY STREET 121 B6
STANTON ROAD 120 B6
STAVELEY ROAD 120 E5
STIRLING ROAD 120 F5
SUSSEX AVENUE 122 E2
SWALE CLOSE 122 C1
SWALLOWDALE ROAD 122 C2
SWAN CLOSE 122 C2
SWIFT CLOSE 122 C2
SYCAMORE CLOSE 120 F4
SYSONBY GRANGE LANE 120 D6
SYSONBY STREET 120 E5
TAMAR ROAD 120 C2
TENNIS AVENUE 122 D1
TENNYSON WAY 121 F3
THAMES DRIVE 122 C1
THE CRESCENT 121 F5
THE UPLANDS 120 F7
THORPE END 121 B6
THORPE ROAD 121 B6
THRUSH CLOSE 122 C2
TORRANCE DRIVE 121 A3
TRENT BANK 122 B1
TUDOR HILL 122 D3
TWEED DRIVE 122 C1
VALLEY ROAD 122 C2
VICTORIA STREET 122 E1
WAVERLEY COURT 122 E1
WEAVER GREEN 120 F5
WELBY LANE 120 D4
WELBY ROAD 120 B6
WELLAND RISE 122 D1
WELLINGTON WAY 120 E4
WEST AVENUE 120 E5
WEST SIDE 120 A5
WESTMINSTER CLOSE 120 E3
WHITELAKE CLOSE 122 C1
WICKLOW AVENUE 122 E1
WILLCOX DRIVE 122 F1
WILLOUGHBY CLOSE 121 B7
WILLOW DRIVE 121 B5
WILTON ROAD 121 A6
WILTON TERRACE 121 A6
WINCHESTER DRIVE 120 E2
WINDSOR STREET 121 A6
WINSTER CRESCENT 122 C1
WITHAM CLOSE 122 C1
WOODCOCK DRIVE 122 C2
WOODLAND AVENUE 122 E1
WORCESTER DRIVE 122 E2
WREN CLOSE 122 C2
WYCLIFFE AVENUE 121 A5
WYCOMBE GROVE 121 C7
WYFORDBY CLOSE 122 F1
WYMONDHAM WAY 121 B3
WYNDHAM AVENUE 122 D1
YEW TREE CRESCENT 121 A4

Moira

See Donisthorpe, Moira & Oakthorpe

Morcott

BACK LANE 138 B2
CHURCH LANE 138 B2
GLASTON ROAD 138 B3
HIGH STREET 138 B2
MOUNT PLEASANT ROAD 138 C2
PINGLE LANE 138 C2
SCHOOL LANE 138 B2
STAMFORD ROAD 138 C3
STATION ROAD 138 C2
WILLOUGHBY ROAD 138 B2
WING ROAD 138 A1

Mountsorrel & Rothley

ANTHONY STREET 101 E6
ARUNDEL CLOSE 101 B4
ASH GROVE 101 D3
BABINGTON ROAD 101 D6
BADGERS BANK 101 D5
BALMORAL ROAD 101 C3
BARLEY WAY 101 D5
BARNARD WAY 101 C3
BARONS WAY 101 D1
BEAUMARIS ROAD 101 B4
BEECHES AVENUE 101 D2
BELVOIR CLOSE 101 C4
BLAIR CLOSE 101 B4
BOND LANE 101 C1
BOUNDARY ROAD 101 C3
BRAEMAR CLOSE 101 C4
BREECH HEDGE 101 C5
BROWNHILL CRESCENT 101 B7
BULLRUSH CLOSE 101 E3
CAERNARVON CLOSE 101 C4
CARISBROOKE ROAD 101 B4
CASTLE ROAD 101 C3
CELANDINE CLOSE 101 E2
CHURCH HILL ROAD 101 C3
CHURCH STREET 101 E6
CLOUD LEA 101 D4
CLOVER LANE 101 E3
CONWAY ROAD 101 C3
COSSINGTON LANE 101 F5
CROMWELL ROAD 101 C4
CROSS HEDGE 101 D5
CROSS LANE 101 D4
CROWN LANE 101 C1
DANVERS ROAD 101 D3
DUNSTER ROAD 101 C3
EDINBURGH WAY 101 C3
ELM CLOSE 101 D3
FAIR MEAD 101 D4
FARNHAM CLOSE 101 E5
FIELD CRESCENTT 101 C5
FLAXLAND 101 D5
FORT ROAD 101 C3
FOWKE STREET 101 E6
FURROW CLOSE 101 D5
GARLAND 101 D5
GIPSY LANE 101 B5
GLAMIS CLOSE 101 B4
GLEBE CLOSE 101 C3
GRANGE LANE 101 C4
GRANGEFIELDS DRIVE 101 E5
GREENWAY CLOSE 101 E6
HALLFIELDS LANE 101 E7
HALSTEAD ROAD 101 C3
HAWTHORN ROAD 101 D3
HERON CLOSE 101 E2
HIGHFIELDS ROAD 101 C3
HOMEFIELD LANE 101 F5
HORNECROFT 101 E6
HOWE LANE 101 D6
JOHNS AVENUE 101 D4
KESTREL LANE 101 E2
KINGFISHER ROAD 101 E3
KIRBY CLOSE 101 C4
KNIGHTS CRESCENT 101 D6
LAUREL CLOSE 101 D3
LEICESTER ROAD 101 D2
LINDEN GROVE 101 D3
LINKFIELD AVENUE 101 E3
LINKFIELD ROAD 101 E3
LONG FURLONG 101 D4
LOUGHBOROUGH ROAD 101 E3
MACAULAY ROAD 101 D6
MAITLAND 101 D3
MALLARD ROAD 101 E2
MARIGOLD LANE 101 E2
MARKET PLACE 101 D1
MARL FIELDS 101 E3
MARSH ROAD 101 E3
MARTIN AVENUE 101 C3
MEADOW ROAD 101 C5
MERE CLOSE 101 D4
MONTSOREAU WAY 101 C4
MOUNTSORREL LANE 101 D4
NORTH STREET 101 D7
ORCHARD VIEW 101 D4
OTTER LANE 101 E2
PADDOCK CLOSE 101 C7
PARTRIDGE CLOSE 101 E2
PLAIN GATE 101 B5
PLOUGH CLOSE 101 C4
POTT ACRE 101 E3
RENNING END 101 D4
ROCHESTER CLOSE 101 B4
ROCKHILL DRIVE 101 D4
ROCKINGHAM ROAD 101 B4
ROSSLYN AVENUE 101 B4
ROTHLEY ROAD 101 D3
ROWE LEYES FURLONG 101 E3
ROWENA COURT 101 D4
RUSHLEY LANE 101 A3
SCHOOL STREET 101 E6
SHEEPCOTE 101 D5
SILEBY ROAD 101 D1
SPEEDWELL ROAD 101 E3
STATION ROAD 101 A7
STIRLING CLOSE 101 B4
STRACHAN CLOSE 101 E3
SWALLOW CLOSE 101 E2
SWITHLAND LANE 101 B4
TEMPLAR WAY 101 C6
THE GREEN 101 D2
THE HOMESTEAD 101 C1
THE NAVINS 101 C1
THE OSIERS 101 B3
THE RIDGEWAY 101 B6
THE RIDINGS 101 B5
THE RISE 101 F6
THE ROMANS 101 C3
TOWN GREEN STREET 101 D7
WALKERS LANE 101 D7
WALTON WAY 101 C3
WATLING STREET 101 D1
WAUGHS DRIVE 101 C4
WELLSIC LANE 101 D7
WEST CROSS LANE 101 B5
WESTFIELD LANE 101 C7
WILLOW GROVE 101 B3
WINDMILL CLOSE 101 C1
WINDMILL END 101 D5
WINDSOR CLOSE 101 C4
WOODFIELD ROAD 101 C6
WOODGATE 101 C6
YORK CLOSE 101 C4

Nailstone

See Barlestone & Nailstone

Nether Broughton

BLACKSMITHS CLOSE 145 B2
CHAPEL LANE 145 B2
CHURCH END 145 C1
CLAWSON LANE 145 C1
DUKES ROAD 145 B4
EARLS ROAD 145 B4
GREAVES AVENUE 145 B4
KING STREET 145 C2
MARQUIS ROAD 145 A4
MIDDLE LANE 145 C3
NOTTINGHAM ROAD 145 B3
OLD DALBY LANE 145 B4
PARNHAMS CLOSE 145 B2
PRINCES ROAD 145 B4
QUEENSWAY 145 B4
THE CRESCENT 145 B4

New Swannington

See Whitwick

Newbold Verdon

ALANS WAY 145 B3
ARNOLDS CRESCENT 145 B3
BARBARA AVENUE 145 B4
BARLESTONE ROAD 145 F6

BELLS LANE 145 B3
BRAMBLE DRIVE 145 B3
BRASCOTE LANE 145 A3
CADLE STREET 145 B2
CHADWICK CLOSE 145 B3
CHURCH VIEW 145 A3
DESFORD ROAD 145 C3
DRAGON LANE 145 B2
ENSTON STREET 145 B3
GILBERTS DRIVE 145 B3
GILLIVER STREET 145 B2
GRANGE CLOSE 145 B3
HILL STREET 145 B2
HORNBEAM ROAD 145 B3
JUBILEE ROAD 145 B3
LABURNUM AVENUE 145 A3
LORD CREWE CLOSE 145 B3
MAIN STREET 145 C3
MALLORY CLOSE 145 B3
MILL LANE 145 B2
MONTAGUE CLOSE 145 B2
OAKS DRIVE 145 C3
PASTURE LANE 145 B3
PETERS AVENUE 145 C3
PINE TREE CLOSE 145 C3
PRESTON DRIVE 145 B2
RED LION LANE 145 C3
RUSH CLOSE 145 B4
STATHAM STREET 145 B2
SYCAMORE CLOSE 145 A3
THE PADDOCK 145 A3
WILLOW CLOSE 145 B4

Newton Burgoland
DAMES LANE 146 B2
FRANCIS LANE 146 A1
MAIN STREET 146 B1
NETHERCOTE 146 A1
ODSTONE LANE 146 C2
SCHOOL LANE 146 B1
SNARESTONE ROAD 146 A1
THE PINFOLD 146 A1

Norris Hill
ASHBY ROAD 138 A3
ASHFIELD DRIVE 138 B2
BLACKFORDBY LANE 138 B1
CEDAR GROVE 138 B2
CHERRY TREE COURT 138 B2
CHESTNUT CLOSE 138 B3
CORONATION AVENUE 138 B2
DEVON CLOSE 138 C2
DORSET DRIVE 138 C2
ELM GROVE 138 B2
HAZEL GROVE 138 B2
HOLLY CLOSE 138 C2
KOPPE CLOSE 138 B2
NORRIS HILL 138 B2
ROWAN CLOSE 138 B2
SWEET HILL 138 A3
SYCAMORE DRIVE 138 B2
TANDY AVENUE 138 B2
WILLOW CLOSE 138 B2
WOODLANDS WAY 138 B2

North Kilworth
ALONG THE BOTTOM 146 B2
BACK STREET 146 B3
CHURCH STREET 146 B3
CRANMER LANE 146 B3
ELMCROFT ROAD 146 B2
GREEN LANE 146 B3
HAWTHORNE ROAD 146 B2
HIGH STREET 146 B2
NORTH KILWORTH ROAD 146 A4
PINCET LANE 146 B2
SOUTH KILWORTH ROAD 146 B2
STATION ROAD 146 C2

North Luffenham
ANCASTER WAY 139 C3
BUTT LANE 139 C2
CHAPEL LANE 139 C3
CHURCH STREET 139 C3
DEWEYS CLOSE 139 C3
DIGBY ROAD 139 C3
EDITHWESTON ROAD 139 C2
GLEBE ROAD 139 B3
JOHNSON CLOSE 139 C3
KETTON ROAD 139 C3
KINGS ROAD 139 C3
LYNDON ROAD 139 B3
MOOR LANE 139 C3
NEWMANS CLOSE 139 C3
NORTH LUFFENHAM ROAD 139 B3
OVAL CLOSE 139 C2
PINFOLD LANE 139 B2
ROSE CLOSE 139 C3
STATION ROAD 139 C3
SWANN CLOSE 139 C2
SYCAMORE ROAD 139 C3

Norton Juxta Twycross
BURTON ROAD 139 A3
CHAPEL LANE 139 B2
COCK LANE 139 B2
COTTAGE LANE 139 B1
MAIN STREET 139 B2
NOB HILL 139 B2
ORTON HILL 139 A3
ORTON LANE 139 A2

SHELFORD LANE 139 C1

Oakham
ALEXANDER CRESCENT 102 C5
ALPINE CLOSE 102 C4
ASHFIELD 102 E2
ASHWELL ROAD 102 E3
AVON CLOSE 102 D5
BALMORAL ROAD 102 C5
BANFF CLOSE 102 F4
BARLEYTHORPE ROAD 102 D3
BARLOW ROAD 102 D4
BEECH ROAD 102 F3
BOWLING GREEN CLOSE 102 E5
BRAUNSTON ROAD 102 B5
BROOKE ROAD 102 E5
BROWNING ROAD 102 C4
BUCKINGHAM ROAD 102 C5
BULL LANE 102 E4
BULLFINCH CLOSE 102 E3
BURLEY ROAD 102 E3
CALDER CLOSE 102 C5
CALGARY CRESCENT 102 F4
CAMROSE CLOSE 102 F4
CATMOS STREET 102 E5
CATMOSE PARK ROAD 102 F5
CHAFFINCH CLOSE 102 F2
CHATER ROAD 102 D5
CHESTNUT ROAD 102 E3
CHEVIOT CLOSE 102 C4
CHILTERN CLOSE 102 B4
CHURCH PASS 102 E3
CHURCH STREET 102 E3
CHURCHILL ROAD 102 C5
CLARESHOLM CRESCENT 102 F4
COLD OVERTON ROAD 102 A4
CRICKET LAWNS 102 E5
CROWN STREET 102 E4
DEANS STREET 102 E4
DEE CLOSE 102 C6
DERWENT DRIVE 102 D4
DIGBY DRIVE 102 C4
DON CLOSE 102 C6
DOVE CLOSE 102 C5
EDMONTON WAY 102 F4
ELM CLOSE 102 F3
FAIR VIEW 102 F4
FERRERS CLOSE 102 B3
FINCH AVENUE 102 B4
FINKEY STREET 102 D4
FORTH CLOSE 102 C6
FOXFIELD WAY 102 E2
GAOL STREET 102 D4
GLEBE WAY 102 B5
GLEN DRIVE 102 D5
GRAMPIAN WAY 102 B4
GREENFIELD ROAD 102 E2
HAMBLETON ROAD 102 B2
HANBURY CLOSE 102 B5
HARRINGTON WAY 102 C5
HERON ROAD 102 E2
HIGH STREET 102 E4
HILL ROAD 102 C3
HOLYROOD CLOSE 102 D4
HUDSON CLOSE 102 B4
IRWELL CLOSE 102 C5
JASPER ROAD 102 F4
JAY CLOSE 102 F2
JOHN STREET 102 D4
KENNEDY CLOSE 102 C4
KESTREL ROAD 102 E2
KILBURN ROAD 102 D3
KINGFISHER CLOSE 102 F3
KINGS ROAD 102 C4
LADYWELL 102 F3
LETHBRIDGE CLOSE 102 F4
LIMEFIELD 102 E2
LODGE GARDENS 102 E4
LONG ROW 102 D4
LONSDALE WAY 102 B4
MAIN ROAD 102 B2
MANOR LANE 102 A3
MARKET PLACE 102 E4
MARKET STREET 102 E4
MARTIN CLOSE 102 F2
MAYFIELD 102 E2
MEADOWFIELD 102 E2
MENDIP ROAD 102 B4
MILL STREET 102 E5
MOUNTBATTEN ROAD 102 B5
NENE CRESCENT 102 D5
NEW STREET 102 D4
NIGHTINGALE WAY 102 F2
NOEL AVENUE 102 C5
NORTHGATE STREET 102 E4
OAKFIELD 102 E2
OAKHAM RELIEF ROAD 102 E2
PARK LANE 102 D3
PARKFIELD ROAD 102 C3
PARTRIDGE WAY 102 F2
PASTURE LANE 102 B2
PENN STREET 102 E5
PETERBOROUGH AVENUE 102 E3
PILLINGS ROAD 102 D3
PLOVER CLOSE 102 E2
PRINCESS AVENUE 102 C4
QUEENS ROAD 102 E3
REDLAND ROAD 102 B3
REDWING CLOSE 102 F3
ROBIN CLOSE 102 F2
RYEFIELD 102 E2
ST ALBANS CLOSE 102 E4
ST ANNES CLOSE 102 D4
ST PETERS CLOSE 102 E4
SANDRINGHAM CLOSE 102 C5
SCHOOL ROAD 102 E3
SEVERN CLOSE 102 C5
SHANNON WAY 102 C6
SNOWDON AVENUE 102 C4
SOUTH STREET 102 D4
SPEY DRIVE 102 C6
SPRINGFIELD WAY 102 E2
STAMFORD ROAD 102 E4
STATION APPROACH 102 D3
STATION ROAD 102 E3
SUMMERFIELD 102 E2
SUNNYFIELD 102 E2
TAY CLOSE 102 C6
TEES CLOSE 102 D5
THE DELL 102 E5
THE VALE 102 E5
TRENT ROAD 102 C6
TYNE ROAD 102 D5
UPPINGHAM ROAD 102 E6
VICARAGE ROAD 102 E3
WARN CRESCENT 102 B5
WELLAND WAY 102 C6
WEST ROAD 102 C4
WESTFIELD AVENUE 102 C4
WESTGATE STREET 102 D4
WILLOW CRESCENT 102 F3
WINDSOR DRIVE 102 C5
WITHAM AVENUE 102 C5
WOODLAND VIEW 102 E3
WREN CLOSE 102 E2

Oakthorpe
See Donisthorpe, Moira & Oakthorpe

Old Dalby
CHAPEL LANE 147 B2
CHURCH LANE 147 B2
CROFT GARDENS 147 B2
DEBDALE HILL 147 B2
GIBSONS LANE 147 A3
HAWTHORN CLOSE 147 B2
LAWN LANE 147 B3
LONGCLIFF CLOSE 147 B1
LONGCLIFF HILL 147 B1
MAIN ROAD 147 C2
NOTTINGHAM LANE 147 A1
PARADISE LANE 147 C2
STATION LANE 147 C1
WOOD HILL 147 B2

Packington
ASHBY ROAD 147 B1
BABELAKE STREET 147 A3
BROOK CLOSE 147 A3
HALL LANE 147 B2
HIGH STREET 147 B2
HOME CROFT DRIVE 147 A2
MEASHAM ROAD 147 A3
MILL STREET 147 B2
NETHERCROFT DRIVE 147 B2
NORMANTON ROAD 147 C3
SPRING LANE 147 C2
THE GRANGE 147 B2

Plungar
CHAPEL STREET 140 B1
CHURCH LANE 140 B1
FROG LANE 140 B2
GRANBY LANE 140 B1
HARBY LANE 140 A3
HIGHGATE LANE 140 B2
POST OFFICE LANE 140 B2

Queniborough
AVENUE CLOSE 148 B2
AVENUE ROAD 148 B2
BARKBY ROAD 148 B2
BEECHWOOD AVENUE 148 A2
BELVOIR DRIVE 148 A3
BLUEBELL CLOSE 148 B1
CHESTNUT CLOSE 148 B2
COPPICE LANE 148 C1
CURZON CLOSE 148 A1
ERVIN WAY 148 B1
FREDERICK CLOSE 148 B1
GASCOIGNE AVENUE 148 B2
GLEBE ROAD 148 B2
LINK ROAD 148 A2
MAIN STREET 148 C2
MARKHAM LANE 148 C2
MARSDEN AVENUE 148 A1
MELTON ROAD 148 A1
MERE LANE 148 C2
MICHAEL CLOSE 148 C1
MOWBRAY DRIVE 148 A3
NEW STREET 148 B1
NEW ZEALAND LANE 148 A1
NURSERY CLOSE 148 B2
PEGGS LANE 148 C2
PRIMROSE WAY 148 B1
QUENIBOROUGH ROAD 148 C2
REARSBY ROAD 148 B1
RIDGEMERE CLOSE 148 A3
RIDGEMERE LANE 148 C4
RUPERT CRESCENT 148 C1
SCHOOL LANE 148 C2
SYSTON ROAD 148 B1
THE BANKS 148 C2
THE RIDINGS 148 B2
THE RINGWAY 148 C1
WATCHCRETE AVENUE 148 B2
WETHERBY CLOSE 148 B1
WILLIAM CLOSE 148 B1

Quorn
ALEXANDER ROAD 116 C4
ALLEN AVENUE 116 B4
ASH CLOSE 116 F2
AVON ROAD 116 F5
BABINGTON ROAD 117 A3
BARROW ROAD 117 A3
BARROW ROAD 116 D4
BARROWCLIFFE CLOSE 116 E3
BAYLISS CLOSE 116 B4
BEACON AVENUE 116 A6
BEARDSLEY ROAD 116 B4
BEAUMONT ROAD 116 F3
BEVERIDGE STREET 116 F3
BIRCH AVENUE 116 F3
BRANSTON AVENUE 117 A3
BREACHFIELD ROAD 117 F4
BREADCROFT LANE 116 F3
BRIDGE STREET 116 E4
BROOKSIDE CLOSE 116 F3
BROWN AVENUE 116 C4
BRYAN CLOSE 116 F3
BUDDON LANE 116 A6
BUTTERMERE WAY 116 E2
CASTLEDINE AVENUE 116 C4
CASTLEDINE STREET 116 B5
CATHERINES CLOSE 116 D5
CAVE ROAD 117 A3
CHAVENEY ROAD 116 A6
CHERWELL ROAD 116 F4
CHESTNUT CLOSE 116 A6
CHURCH LANE (Barr) 116 F3
CHURCH LANE (Q) 116 B5
CHURCH STREET 116 F3
CONDON ROAD 117 A4
CONISTON ROAD 116 F3
COTES ROAD 116 D1
CRADOCK DRIVE 116 A6
CRAMPS CLOSE 116 E4
CROSSLEY CLOSE 116 E4
DEEMING DRIVE 116 B4
DERWENT ROAD 116 F3
DEXTERS CLOSE 116 C4
DISRAELI STREET 116 C5
DOWER HOUSE GARDENS 116 C5
ELLIS CLOSE 117 A3
ELLIS CLOSE 116 B4
ELMS DRIVE 116 B6
ELMS GROVE 116 F2
ENNERDALE ROAD 116 F3
FARLEY WAY 116 A4
FARNHAM STREET 116 B5
FISHPOOL WAY 117 A3
FLESH HOVEL LANE 116 C3
FOREST ROAD 116 A6
FREEHOLD STREET 116 D5
FREEMAN WAY 116 B4
GAMBLE WAY 116 A4
GILES CLOSE 116 D7
GRASMERE CLOSE 116 F3
GREBE CLOSE 117 A3
GROVE LANE 116 F4
HALL LEYS 116 C6
HARRINGTON CLOSE 116 C5
HAYHILL 117 C6
HERON ROAD 117 A3
HIGH STREET (Barr) 116 F4
HIGH STREET (Q) 116 B5
HIGHFIELDS 116 F3
HOLBOURNE CLOSE 116 E4
HUNTSMANS CLOSE 116 D4
HUSTON CLOSE 117 B6
ILIFFES CLOSE 117 A3
KERCEY ROAD 116 B4
KINGFISHER CLOSE 117 A3
LEICESTER ROAD 116 E7
LODGE CLOSE 116 F4
LONG CLOSE 116 B4
LOUGHBOROUGH ROAD 116 A4
LOWESWATER CLOSE 116 F3
MALLARD ROAD 117 A3
MANSFIELD STREET 116 C5
MARTIN AVENUE 116 F4
MEADOW CLOSE 117 A3
MEETING STREET 116 C6
MELTON ROAD 117 B3
MEYNELL ROAD 116 D4
MILL LANE 116 F4
MILLS ARMSTON ROAD 116 C6
MORGANS ORCHARD 116 F3
NEW STREET 116 F4
NEWTON CLOSE 117 A3
NORTH STREET 116 F3
NORTHAGE CLOSE 116 D7
NOTTINGHAM ROAD 117 A2
NOTTINGHAM ROAD 116 F3
NURSERY LANE 116 C5
PADDOCK CLOSE 116 C6
PARKERS FIELDS 116 C4
PEPPER DRIVE 116 B4
POULTENEY DRIVE 116 A5
PROCTORS PARK ROAD 116 E4
REVELL CLOSE 116 D4
RIBBLE DRIVE 116 F4

RIVER VIEW 117 B5
RUMSEY CLOSE 116 A5
RUPERT LANEW CLOSE 116 B4
RUSS CLOSE 116 B4
SANDERS ROAD 116 B5
SARSON STREET 116 B5
SCHOOL LANE 116 C6
SELVESTER DRIVE 116 D6
SHIRREFFS CLOSE 117 A3
SHOOTING CLOSE LANE 116 F4
SILEBY ROAD 117 F4
SILVER BIRCHS 116 B5
SOAR ROAD 116 D5
SOUTH STREET 116 E4
SPINNEY DRIVE 116 B6
STATION ROAD 116 C6
STIRLING CLOSE 116 B4
STOOP LANE 116 C5
STRANCLIFFE LANE 116 E2
SUTTON CLOSE 116 B5
SWAN CLOSE 117 A3
SWINFIELD ROAD 116 C5
THE BANKS 117 A3
THE BANKS 116 D6
THE COPPICE 116 D7
THE DEEPWAY 116 A6
THE MILLS 116 C6
THE PASTURES 117 A5
THE RETREAT 116 F3
THE ROOKERY 116 E3
THE SANDHILLS 116 A5
THIRLMERE ROAD 116 F3
THOMPSON CLOSE 116 B5
TOLLER ROAD 116 A6
TURNER CLOSE 116 B4
ULLSWATER AVENUE 116 F2
UNITT ROAD 116 D7
VICTORIA STREET 116 C5
WARNER STREET 116 F4
WARWICK AVENUE 116 A5
WELLAND ROAD 116 F5
WHALL CLOSE 116 C6
WHITE STREET 116 B5
WILLOW ROAD 116 F2
WILLOWCROFT 116 A6
WINDERMERE ROAD 116 F3
WINDSOR CLOSE 116 C5
WOOD LANE 116 B1
WOODHOUSE ROAD 116 A6
WOODSIDE 116 F3
WOODWARD AVENUE 116 A5
WRIGHTS CLOSE 116 B5
WYCLIFFE AVENUE 116 F3
WYVERNHOE DRIVE 116 A6

Ratby
ARMSON AVENUE 91 E6
ASH CLOSE 91 B2
ASH COURT 91 E1
BARNS CLOSE 91 C6
BARONS CLOSE 91 C6
BARWELL ROAD 91 D6
BEACON CLOSE 91 F1
BEAUMONT GREEN 91 F1
BEDFORD DRIVE 91 F1
BEECH AVENUE 91 E2
BELL CLOSE 91 C3
BERRYS LANE 91 C3
BEVINGTON CLOSE 91 B2
BLUEBELL CLOSE 91 E5
BRADGATE DRIVE 91 B2
BUCKINGHAM CLOSE 91 E1
BURROUGHS ROAD 91 C3
CALVERTON CLOSE 91 C3
CARDINAL CLOSE 91 C3
CASTLE ROAD 91 D6
CASTLE RISE 91 F1
CEDAR COURT 91 F1
CENTURIAN COURT 91 D4
CHAPEL LANE 91 C3
CHARNWOOD 91 B2
CHESTNUT WALK 91 F1
CHURCH LANE 91 C3
CHURCH ROAD 91 D6
COTTAGE CLOSE 91 C2
COURT CLOSE 91 E6
CUFFLIN CLOSE 91 D3
DANE HILL 91 C3
DESFORD LANE 91 A5
DESFORD ROAD 91 E5
ELM CLOSE 91 F1
FARLEY WAY 91 E4
FERNDALE DRIVE 91 C3
FOREST DRIVE 91 E7
FOX LANE 91 D5
GARENDON WAY 91 E1
GILLBANK DRIVE 91 C3
GLENFIELD LANE 91 E4
GRANGE CLOSE 91 D3
GREYS DRIVE 91 E1
GROBY ROAD 91 D1
GULLET LANE 91 C6
HASTINGS ROAD 91 E7
HEATHBROOK DRIVE 91 D3
HEDGEROW LANE 91 D5
HEWITT DRIVE 91 F7
HIGHFIELD ROAD 91 E1
HOLMEWOOD DRIVE 91 F7
HOLT DRIVE 91 F7
INGLE DRIVE 91 C3
JORDAN COURT 91 D3
JOURNEYMANS GREEN 91 D3
KINGS WAY 91 F1
LADYSMITH ROAD 91 D5
LANCASTER COURT 91 E1
LAUNDON CLOSE 91 F1
LAUNDON WAY 91 E2
LEE RISE 91 D3
LIME AVENUE 91 E2
LIME GROVE 91 D6
LINDEN LANE 91 F7
LINKS ROAD 91 C6
LOUISE AVENUE 91 F1
MAIN STREET (Ratby) 91 C3
MAIN STREET (KM) 91 E6
MARKFIELD ROAD 91 A1
MARTIN SQUARE 91 D3
MEADOW CLOSE 91 D3
MILL DRIVE 91 D4
NICHOLAS DRIVE 91 C3
NOOK CLOSE 91 C3
OAKCROFT AVENUE 91 E6
OAKMEADOW WAY 91 E1
OVERFIELD CLOSE 91 C3
PARKFIELD CLOSE 91 D3
PARK ROAD 91 D4
PINE TREE AVENUE 91 F1
PORTLAND ROAD 91 E7
PRETORIA ROAD 91 D6
PRIMROSE WAY 91 E5
PRINCESS DRIVE 91 D7
PYMMLEY LANE 91 F1
QUEENSMEAD CLOSE 91 E1
QUORNDON RISE 91 E1
RATBY ROAD 91 E1
ROSEDENE CLOSE 91 F7
SACHEVERELL WAY 91 E2
SAXONS RISE 91 C2
SPINNEYSIDE 91 E1
SPRING CLOSE 91 D3
SPRINGFIELD 91 E1
STAMFORD DRIVE 91 F1
STAMFORD ROAD 91 E7
STAMFORD STREET 91 B2
STATION CLOSE 91 E7
STATION DRIVE 91 E7
STATION ROAD (Ratby) 91 C3
STATION ROAD (KM) 91 E7
SYCAMORE DRIVE 91 F1
TAVENER DRIVE 91 E3
THE CROFT 91 E6
THE FAIRWAY 91 F7
THE HUNTINGS 91 C6
THE KEEP 91 E6
THE POPLARS 91 B1
TIMBERWOOD DRIVE 91 E1
TOWERS CLOSE 91 E7
TOWERS DRIVE 91 E7
TUDOR GROVE 91 E2
TYLER ROAD 91 D4
ULVERSCROFT DRIVE 91 F1
VICARAGE CLOSE 91 E4
VICTORIA DRIVE 91 F1
WALTON CLOSE 91 F7
WARRINGTON DRIVE 91 E2
WENTWORTH GREEN 91 E7
WESLEY CLOSE 91 C3
WHITTINGTON DRIVE 91 C2
WILLOW DRIVE 91 E2
WILSHERE CLOSE 91 D6
WINDMILL CLOSE 91 D4
WINDSOR AVENUE 91 E1
WOLSEY CLOSE 91 F1
WOLSEY DRIVE 91 B2
WOODLANDS LANE 91 E5
WOODLEY ROAD 91 C3

Ravenstone
See Coalville & Agar Nook

Rearsby
See East Goscote

Ridlington
BROOKE ROAD 148 C2
CHURCH LANE 148 B3
EAST LANE 148 C3
HOLYGATE ROAD 148 B3
MAIN STREET 148 B3
TOP ROAD 148 C3
WEST LANE 148 B3

Rothley
See Mountsorrel & Rothley

Ryhall
BALK ROAD 149 B2
BEECH DRIVE 149 A3
BELMESTHORPE LANE 149 C2
BRIDGE STREET 149 B1
BURLEY ROAD 149 A3
CASTLE RISE 149 C3
CHURCH STREET 149 B2
COPPICE ROAD 149 B2
CROWN STREET 149 B1
ESSENDINE ROAD 149 B1
FLINT CLOSE 149 C2
FOUNDRY ROAD 149 B1
HIGHLANDS 149 A2
LEA VIEW 149 A2
MAIN STREET 149 C3
MANOR CLOSE 149 B1
MEADOW LANE 149 B3
MILL STREET 149 B1
NEW ROAD 149 B2
NEWSTEAD ROAD 149 C3
PARKFIELD ROAD 149 B2
RUTLAND WAY 149 B2
ST JOHNS CLOSE 149 B2
ST TIBBA WAY 149 B3
SPINNEY CLOSE 149 A2
SPINNEY LANE 149 A2
THE CRESCENT 149 C1
THE SQUARE 149 B2
TURNPIKE ROAD 149 B1
WATERSIDE 149 B1

Saddington
See Fleckney & Saddington

Sapcote
See Stoney Stanton & Sapcote

Scalford
CHURCH STREET 140 B2
KING STREET 140 B2
KINGS CLOSE 140 B2
MELTON ROAD 140 B2
NEW STREET 140 B2
SANDY LANE 140 B2
SCHOOL LANE 140 B2
SOUTH STREET 140 B2
THORPE SIDE 140 C2

Scraptoft
ANGUS CLOSE 153 B5
ANTHONY DRIVE 153 B6
ARCHWAY ROAD 153 A2
BANKSIDE 153 A3
BARKFORD CLOSE 153 A2
BARONET WAY 153 A2
BEEBY ROAD 153 C2
BENNION ROAD 153 C7
BEXHILL RISE 153 A4
BOWHILL GROVE 153 A4
BRADGATE CLOSE 153 A6
BRAMLEY ORCHARD 153 C6
BRIARFIELD DRIVE 153 A2
BRINDLEY RISE 153 A2
BRIXWORTH RISE 153 A5
BROCKLESBY WAY 153 A3
CHARNWOOD DRIVE 153 B6
CHESTNUT DRIVE 153 C7
CHURCH HILL 153 B3
CHURCH LANE 153 B7
COLTHURST WAY 153 A5
COURT ROAD 153 B7
COVERT LANE 153 D3
COWLEY WAY 153 A4
CRANBROOK ROAD 153 B5
CROSS KEYS GREEN 153 A4
CROYLAND GREEN 153 A5
DALBY AVENUE 153 C6
DELAWARE ROAD 153 A7
DRUMCLIFF ROAD 153 A5
EDDYSTONE ROAD 153 A4
ELSTREE AVENUE 153 A3
FASTNET ROAD 153 A4
FERN CLOSE 153 A6
FIONA DRIVE 153 B6
FLATHOLME ROAD 153 A3
FOREST RISE 153 B6
FREDSCOTT CLOSE 153 A4
GILSTEAD CLOSE 153 B7
GRANGE LANE 153 A7
GRANGE PARK 153 A7
GRESLEY CLOSE 153 B5
GRETNA WAY 153 A4
HALL ROAD 153 B3
HAMILFORD CLOSE 153 A2
HAMILTON LANE 153 A2
HARDWICK ROAD 153 A7
HEREWARD DRIVE 153 B6
HERRICK DRIVE 153 B6
HILL COURT 153 B7
HINKS AVENUE 153 B3
HOLLIES WAY 153 B7
HOLMLEIGH GARDENS 153 B7
HOMESTONE GARDENS 153 A5
HOMESTONE RISE 153 A5
IVYCHURCH CRESCENT 153 A2
KEAYS WAY 153 B3
KEYHAM LANE EAST 153 D1
KINROSS AVENUE 153 A5
KINSDALE DRIVE 153 A4
KIRKWALL CRESCENT 153 A4
LAKESIDE COURT 153 B7
LANGHOLM ROAD 153 A5
LEAS CLOSE 153 C5
LEYBURY WAY 153 B5
LONGSTONE GREEN 153 A4
MAIN STREET (Scraptoft) 153 B3
MAIN STREET (Thurnby) 153 C7
MAPLIN ROAD 153 A2
MAREFIELD CLOSE 153 C5
MILNROY ROAD 153 A4
NEW ROMNEY CLOSE 153 A3
NEW ROMNEY CRESCENT 153 A3
NEWSTEAD AVENUE 153 C7
PADGATE CLOSE 153 B5
PADWELL LANE 153 C7
PORTCULLIS ROAD 153 A2
PULFORD DRIVE 153 C5
RAMSEY GARDENS 153 A2
RAMSEY WAY 153 A2
RANDLES CLOSE 153 C7
RAYLEIGH GREEN 153 A2
RAYLEIGH WAY 153 A2
RENFREW ROAD 153 A3
RINGWOOD ROAD 153 A2
ROBOROUGH GREEN 153 A5
RONA GARDENS 153 A4
ROSE ACRE CLOSE 153 B4
ROSSHILL CRESCENT 153 A4
ST AUSTELL ROAD 153 A4
ST LUKES CLOSE 153 B7
SCRAPTOFT RISE 153 B3
SEATON RISE 153 A2
SEDGEBROOK CLOSE 153 A7
SEDGEBROOK ROAD 153 A7
SEDGEFIELD DRIVE 153 B5
SNOWS LANE 153 F2
SOMERBY ROAD 153 B5
SOUTHFIELD CLOSE 153 B4
SPRINGBROOK DRIVE 153 B5
SPRINGWAY CLOSE 153 A6
STATION LANE 153 B4
STATION ROAD 153 B5
STIRLING DRIVE 153 B5
STOCKS ROAD 153 B3
STORNAWAY ROAD 153 A5
STURROCK CLOSE 153 B5
SUNBURY GREEN 153 A4
TELFORD WAY 153 A6
THE DRIVE 153 B3
THE DRIVEWAY 153 C6
THE MOUNT 153 B3
THE ORCHARDS 153 A3
THE SPINNEY 153 A7
THURNBY HILL 153 A6
THURNCOURT GARDENS 153 B5
VALE END 153 B6
WEAVER ROAD 153 A4
WREFORD CRESCENT 153 A4
YAXLEY CLOSE 153 B6

Seagrave
BERRYCOTT LANE 149 C1
BIG LANE 149 A3
BUTCHERS LANE 149 C4
CHURCH STREET 149 B3
GREEN LANE 149 B2
GREEN LANE CLOSE 149 B3
KING STREET 149 C3
MUCKLE GATE LANE 149 B2
PARK HILL LANE 149 C4
POND STREET 149 B3
SEAGRAVE ROAD 149 A4
SWAN STREET 149 B3
THE ORCHARD 149 B3
WATER LANE 149 B3

Seaton
BAINES LANE 141 B2
CHURCH LANE 141 B2
DRURYS LANE 141 B2
MAIN STREET 141 C2
MOLES LANE 141 B2
THOMPSONS LANE 141 B2

Sharnford
ASTON LANE 141 A1
BROOKFIELD 141 B1
BUCKINGHAMS WAY 141 A1
CHAPEL LANE 141 B2
CHAPEL STREET 141 B2
COVENTRY ROAD 141 B2
FOSSE CLOSE 141 B2
FOX HOLLIES 141 A2
HALLS CRESCENT 141 B1
HENSON WAY 141 B1
HOLYOAK DRIVE 141 A1
LEES HIGH 141 A2
LEICESTER ROAD 141 C1
MILL LANE 141 B1
PARK VIEW 141 B1
ST HELENS CLOSE 141 B2
SCHOOL LANE 141 B2
SHARNBROOK GARDENS 141 B2

Shawell
BULLACES LANE 142 B2
CATTHORPE ROAD 142 C2
GIBBET LANE 142 B1
MAIN STREET 142 B2
SWINFORD ROAD 142 C2

Shearsby
BACK LANE 142 B1
BRUNTINGTHORPE ROAD 142 B2
CHURCH LANE 142 A1
FENNY LANE 142 A2
MAIN STREET 142 A2
MILL LANE 142 A2
THE BANK 142 A2
THE SQUARE 142 A2
WELFORD ROAD 142 B2

Sheepy Magna
ASH CROFT 143 B1
BROOKSIDE PLACE 143 B1
CHURCH CROFT 143 B2
CHURCH LANE 143 B2
HIGHFIELD CLOSE 143 B1

Street	Page	Grid
MAIN ROAD	143	B2
MEADOW CLOSE	143	B2
MILL LANE	143	C2
OAKFIELD WAY	143	B1
RIVERSIDE CLOSE	143	B1
SIBSON ROAD	143	C2
TWYCROSS ROAD	143	B1
WELLSBOROUGH ROAD	143	C1

Shepshed

Street	Page	Grid
ANSON ROAD	103	B4
ARBURY DALE	103	E5
ARUNDEL GROVE	103	C5
ASHBY ROAD	103	F6
ASHBY ROAD	103	B6
ASHBY ROAD CENTRAL	103	C6
BALMORAL AVENUE	103	C5
BANBURY DRIVE	103	B4
BEAUMARIS CRESCENT	103	C5
BELTON STREET	103	D3
BELVOIR WAY	103	C5
BLACKBROOK CLOSE	103	C4
BLACKSMITHS AVENUE	103	E2
BOUNDARY WAY	103	E2
BRENDON CLOSE	103	E6
BRICK KILN LANE	103	C7
BRIDGE STREET	103	E3
BROOK STREET	103	E3
BROOKSIDE CLOSE	103	C5
CAERNARVON CLOSE	103	C5
CAMBRIDGE STREET	103	D5
CENTRAL AVENUE	103	D4
CHAPEL STREET	103	E3
CHARNWOOD ROAD	103	D3
CHATSWORTH CLOSE	103	B4
CHESTNUT CLOSE	103	E4
CHEVIOT DRIVE	103	F4
CHILTERN AVENUE	103	F4
CHURCH GATE	103	E3
CHURCH SIDE	103	E3
CHURCH STREET	103	E3
COACHMANS COURT	103	E2
CONWAY DRIVE	103	C5
COOMBE CLOSE	103	E5
COTTON CROFT	103	D5
COUNTRYMANS WAY	103	E3
CUMBRIAN WAY	103	F4
DANVERS LANE	103	E3
DEACON CLOSE	103	E4
DOMONT CLOSE	103	D4
DOVECOTE	103	E3
FACTORY STREET	103	D3
FAIRWAY ROAD	103	F4
FIELD AVENUE	103	D1
FIELD STREET	103	D3
FOREST STREET	103	E3
FORMAN ROAD	103	D3
FREEHOLD STREET	103	E3
GARENDON CLOSE	103	E4
GARENDON ROAD	103	D3
GELDERS HALL ROAD	103	C6
GLENFIELDS	103	D4
GLENMORE AVENUE	103	C3
GRANGE LANE	103	C4
GRANGE ROAD	103	C4
GRIFFIN CLOSE	103	C3
HALL CROFT	103	D3
HALLAMFORD ROAD	103	D3
HARRINGTON ROAD	103	E4
HATHERN ROAD	103	F1
HIGHFIELD DRIVE	103	E2
HOLT RISE	103	E6
HOMEWAY CLOSE	103	E4
INGLEBERRY ROAD	103	F7
IVESHEAD LANE	103	C7
IVESHEAD ROAD	103	C7
JOLLY FARMERS LANE	103	C7
KINGS ROAD	103	D5
KIRKHILL	103	E3
LACEY COURT	103	D4
LAMBERT AVENUE	103	D4
LANSDOWNE AVENUE	103	E2
LANSDOWNE ROAD	103	E2
LEICESTER ROAD	103	E4
LINLEY AVENUE	103	E5
LITTLE HAW LANE	103	C4
LONGCLIFFE ROAD	103	C4
LOUGHBOROUGH ROAD	103	E3
MALVERN AVENUE	103	E5
MANOR GARDENS	103	D3
McCARTHY ROAD	103	C3
MENDIP CLOSE	103	F4
MILL CLOSE	103	E2
MOORFIELD PLACE	103	D3
MORLEY LANE	103	C6
MOSCOW LANE	103	C6
NELSON CLOSE	103	F3
NEVILLE CLOSE	103	C3
NEW WALK	103	D3
NEWARK CLOSE	103	B4
NEWLANDS AVENUE	103	E5
NOOK CLOSE	103	E5
NORTHWOOD DRIVE	103	E2
NORWICH CLOSE	103	C5
NURSERY ROAD	103	E1
OAKLEY AVENUE	103	D3
OAKLEY CLOSE	103	D2
OAKLEY ROAD	103	D3
OLD STATION CLOSE	103	D6
OXFORD STREET	103	D5
OXLEY CLOSE	103	C4
PARK AVENUE	103	E5
PARK CLOSE	103	D3
PARK RISE	103	D3
PATERSON PLACE	103	E2
PEARTREE AVENUE	103	F4
PENNINE CLOSE	103	F5
PENRITH AVENUE	103	B5
PENTLAND AVENUE	103	F4
PICK STREET	103	D3
PIPER CLOSE	103	E2
PLOUGHMANS DRIVE	103	E2
POLDEN CLOSE	103	E5
PORLOCK CLOSE	103	E5
PUDDING BAG LANE	103	C7
PURBECK AVENUE	103	F4
PURLEY RISE	103	E5
QUANTOCK RISE	103	F5
QUEEN STREET	103	E3
RADNOR DRIVE	103	D2
RING FENCE ROAD	103	D5
RINGWOOD ROAD	103	E2
ROCKINGHAM CLOSE	103	C5
ROMWAY CLOSE	103	E4
ST BERNARDS CLOSE	103	C4
ST BOTOLPH ROAD	103	D4
ST JAMES ROAD	103	D4
ST WINEFRIDE ROAD	103	D4
SANDRINGHAM RISE	103	C4
SHEPHERDS CLOSE	103	E2
SMITHY WAY	103	E3
SNOWDON CLOSE	103	E5
SPRING CLOSE	103	E4
SPRING LANE	103	D5
SPRINGFIELD ROAD	103	D4
SULLINGTON ROAD	103	D4
TAMWORTH CLOSE	103	B5
TEMPLE CLOSE	103	E6
TETBURY DRIVE	103	B4
THE INLEYS	103	F4
THE LANENT	103	E3
THE MEADOWS	103	D4
THORPE ROAD	103	C4
TICKOW LANE	103	C3
TRUEWAY DRIVE	103	E4
TYLER COURT	103	E1
WELL YARD CLOSE	103	E4
WESTOBY CLOSE	103	F3
WICKLOW CLOSE	103	F5
WIGHTMAN CLOSE	103	D4
WINDSOR DRIVE	103	C5
WOOD CLOSE	103	F4
WOODLANDS DRIVE	103	E2
WOODMANS WAY	103	E2
WORTLEY CLOSE	103	E1

Sileby

Street	Page	Grid
AINSWORTH DRIVE	104	D4
ALBERT AVENUE	104	C3
ALBION ROAD	104	B4
AVENUE ROAD	104	C4
BACK LANE	104	B4
BARNARDS DRIVE	104	D3
BARRADALE AVENUE	104	B3
BARROW ROAD	104	A4
BENNETTS LANE	104	C7
BLACKBERRY LANE	104	D7
BROOK STREET	104	B4
BRUSHFIELD AVENUE	104	C3
CAUBY CLOSE	104	D4
CEMETERY ROAD	104	C4
CHADDERSLEY PARK	104	A4
CHALFONT DRIVE	104	C6
CHARLES STREET	104	B5
COLLINGWOOD DRIVE	104	C3
COSSINGTON ROAD	104	B4
DICKENS CLOSE	104	C3
FINSBURY AVENUE	104	D4
FLAXLAND CRESCENT	104	B5
FOREST DRIVE	104	B3
GIBSON ROAD	104	C3
GREEDON RISE	104	C2
HANOVER DRIVE	104	C3
HAYBROOKE ROAD	104	C3
HEATHCOTE DRIVE	104	C3
HICKLING DRIVE	104	C3
HIGHBRIDGE	104	B4
HIGHGATE ROAD	104	C4
HOMEFIELD ROAD	104	C2
HUDSON ROAD	104	B3
HUMBLE LANE	104	F6
JUBILEE AVENUE	104	C2
KENDAL ROAD	104	C4
KILBOURNE CLOSE	104	B5
KING STREET	104	B4
LANES CLOSE	104	C3
LITTLE CHURCH LANE	104	B4
MAIN STREET	104	C7
MANOR DRIVE	104	B4
MARSHALL AVENUE	104	C3
MILNER CLOSE	104	B5
MOLYNEUX DRIVE	104	C6
MORETON DALE	104	C3
MOUNTSORREL LANE	104	A4
NEWBOLD CLOSE	104	C3
PARK ROAD	104	B3
PARSONS DRIVE	104	D3
PEASHILL CLOSE	104	D4
PHOENIX DRIVE	104	C5
POCHIN WAY	104	C3
PRESTON CLOSE	104	B5
PRYOR ROAD	104	C3
QUAKER ROAD	104	B6
RATCLIFFE ROAD	104	D4
ST GREGORYS DRIVE	104	D4
ST MARYS ROAD	104	B3
SHERRARD DRIVE	104	C5
SPRINGFIELD ROAD	104	C3
STANAGE ROAD	104	D3
STAVELEY CLOSE	104	C5
STORER CLOSE	104	C4
SWAN STREET	104	C4
THE BANKS	104	B4
THE BANKS CLOSE	104	C4
WALLACE DRIVE	104	C6
WARDS CRESCENT	104	C4
WELDON CLOSE	104	C3
WELLBROOK AVENUE	104	C4
WRIGHTS ACRE	104	A3

Skeffington

Street	Page	Grid
HUNTERS AVENUE	143	C2
MAIN STREET	143	B2
SKEFFINGTON GLEBE ROAD	143	A1
UPPINGHAM ROAD	143	B2
WOOD LANE	143	B3

Smeeton Westerby
See Kibworth & Smeeton Westerby

Somerby

Street	Page	Grid
BURROUGH ROAD	151	B1
CHAPEL LANE	151	B1
CHURCH LANE	151	B1
FIRDALE	151	C2
HIGH STREET	151	C1
MANOR LANE	151	B1
MILL LANE	151	B1
OAKHAM ROAD	151	C2
OWSTON ROAD	151	C2
SOMERBY ROAD	151	C1
THE FIELD	151	B1

South Luffenham

Street	Page	Grid
ANGLE LANE	150	A2
BACK LANE	150	B3
BARROWDEN LANE	150	B3
BARROWDEN ROAD	150	C4
CHURCH LANE	150	B3
CUTTING LANE	150	A2
FRISBY LANE	150	A3
GATEHOUSE LANE	150	A2
HALL LANE	150	B3
NORTH LUFFENHAM ROAD	150	A2
PILTON ROAD	150	A1
PINFOLD CLOSE	150	B2
PINFOLD LANE	150	B2
STAMFORD ROAD	150	C1
THE STREET	150	B2

Sproxton

Street	Page	Grid
BUCKMINSTER ROAD	152	B3
CHURCH LANE	152	B2
COSTON ROAD	152	B3
MAIN STREET	152	A2
SALTBY ROAD	152	B2
SCHOOL HILL	152	B2
STONESBY ROAD	152	A2
STOW HILL	152	C2
THE NOOK	152	B3

Stapleton
See Barwell & Stapleton

Stathern

Street	Page	Grid
BIRDS LANE	150	B3
BLACKSMITH END	150	B3
CHURCH LANE	150	B3
CITY ROAD	150	A3
DALLIWELL	150	B4
HARBY LANE	150	A3
LONG LANE	150	A1
MAIN STREET	150	B3
MILL HILL	150	C4
MOOR LANE	150	B1
NARROW LANE	150	B3
PENN LANE	150	A3
RED LION STREET	150	B3
SCHOOL LANE	150	B3
SWALLOWS DRIVE	150	A3
THE CRESCENT	150	B4
THE GREEN	150	B3
TOFTS HILL	150	B3
WATER LANE	150	B3
WOOD LANE	150	C3

Stoke Golding

Street	Page	Grid
ANDREW CLOSE	137	C2
ARNOLD ROAD	137	D3
BASIN BRIDGE LANE	137	B4
BENNET CLOSE	137	C2
CHURCH CLOSE	137	C2
CHURCH WALKS	137	C2
GREENHILL ROAD	137	C2
GREENWOOD ROAD	137	D2
HALL DRIVE	137	D2
HIGH STREET	137	C2
HIGHAM LANE	137	B2
HINCKLEY ROAD	137	E1
IVY CLOSE	137	C2
MAIN STREET	137	E1
PINE CLOSE	137	D2
ROSEWAY	137	D2
ST MARGARET ROAD	137	D2
SHENTON CLOSE	137	D2
SHERWOOD ROAD	137	D2
STAPLETON LANE	137	F1
STATION ROAD	137	B2
STOKE LANE	137	E1
STOKE ROAD	137	E2
STONELEY ROAD	137	D3
THORNFIELD AVENUE	137	D2
TITHE CLOSE	137	C3
WHITEMOORS CLOSE	137	D2
WHITEMOORS ROAD	137	D2
WYKIN LANE	137	C2

Stoney Stanton & Sapcote

Street	Page	Grid
ALL SAINTS CLOSE	105	C6
BASSETT LANE	105	C5
BATH CLOSE	105	C5
BROUGHTON ROAD	105	F4
BROWNS CLOSE	105	D6
BUCKWELL ROAD	105	C6
CADLES CLOSE	105	C2
CALVERT CRESCENT	105	D6
CAREY HILL ROAD	105	C3
CASTLE CLOSE	105	C6
CHURCH STREET (Sap)	105	C6
CLINT HILL DRIVE	105	D2
COOKS LANE	105	C6
DISNEY CLOSE	105	C3
DOUDNEY CLOSE	105	C4
DOVECOTE CLOSE	105	C6
FARNDON DRIVE	105	C4
FISHER CLOSE	105	B3
FLETCHER ROAD	105	C5
FREWEN DRIVE	105	C5
GEORGE MARIOTT CLOSE	105	B4
GRACE ROAD	105	D6
HARECROFT CRESCENT	105	D5
HINCKLEY ROAD (SS)	105	C4
HINCKLEY ROAD (Sap)	105	C6
HOWE CLOSE	105	C4
HUNCOTE ROAD	105	C2
JOHN BOLD AVENUE	105	D2
JOHNSON RISE	105	D4
KIRBY CLOSE	105	C6
KNIGHTS CLOSE	105	C5
LANES HILL GROVE	105	D4
LEE CLOSE	105	C2
LEICESTER ROAD	105	F6
LIVESEY DRIVE	105	C6
LOUND ROAD	105	C5
MANOR BROOK CLOSE	105	D2
MANOR ROAD	105	C5
MARTIN CLOSE	105	C3
MAYS FARM DRIVE	105	C2
MEADOW CLOSE	105	C2
METCALF CLOSE	105	C3
MIDDLETON CLOSE	105	D3
MILL CLOSE	105	D5
MORLEY ROAD	105	D6
MORTIBOYS WAY	105	C3
CHURCH STREET (SS)	105	C3
HIGHFIELD STREET	105	C2
JAMES STREET	105	C2
LONG STREET	105	D2
NEW ROAD	105	C3
NEW WALK	105	C6
NOCK VERGES	105	C3
PARK ROAD	105	C6
PENFOLD CLOSE	105	C5
PETERS CLOSE	105	B3
POUGHER CLOSE	105	C6
RICHARDSON CLOSE	105	C4
RILEY CLOSE	105	C4
ROBERTSON CLOSE	105	B2
SAPCOTE ROAD	105	C5
SHADRACK CLOSE	105	C4
SHARNFORD ROAD	105	D6
SMITHY FARM DRIVE	105	C3
SOUTH DRIVE	105	D4
SPA DRIVE	105	C5
STANTON LANE	105	B4
STANTON ROAD	105	C5
STEVENS CLOSE	105	D3
TANSEY CRESCENT	105	C3
TAYLORS CLOSE	105	C3
THE FLEET	105	D2
THE ORCHARD	105	D3
THE OVAL	105	D3
TOWNSEND ROAD	105	C4
TUCKEY CLOSE	105	C5
UNDERWOOD CRESCENT	105	D5
UNDERWOOD DRIVE	105	C4
WEBBS WAY	105	C4
WESLEY CLOSE	105	D6

Stretton

Street	Page	Grid
CHURCH LANE	145	C3
CLIPSHAM ROAD	145	C2
GREETHAM ROAD	145	B3
HOOBY LANE	145	A2
MANOR ROAD	145	C3
ROOKERY LANE	145	B3
SPINNEY LANE	145	B3
WALNUT CLOSE	145	B2

Swinford

Street	Page	Grid
CHAPEL FIELDS	145	B3
CHAPEL STREET	145	B2
FIR TREE LANE	145	C2
KILWORTH ROAD	145	C2